The Neville Chamberlain
Diary Letters

Undated portrait of Neville Chamberlain, probably late 1920s. Labelled by his wife: 'Very good, almost my favourite.' (Photography taken by H.J. Whitlock & Sons, London; courtesy of Birmingham University Library.)

The Neville Chamberlain
Diary Letters

VOLUME TWO

The Reform Years, 1921–27

edited by

ROBERT SELF

Ashgate

Aldershot • Burlington USA • Singapore • Sydney

Published by
Ashgate Publishing Limited
Gower House, Croft Road
Aldershot
Hants GU11 3HR
England

Ashgate Publishing Company
131 Main Street
Burlington
Vermont 05401–5600
USA

Ashgate website: http://www.ashgate.com

ISBN 1 84014 692 3

British Library Cataloguing-in-Publication Data
Chamberlain, Neville, 1869–1940
  The Neville Chamberlain diary letters
  Vol. 2: The reform years, 1921–27
  1. Chamberlain, Neville, 1869–1940 — Diaries   2. Chamberlain, Neville, 1869–1940 — Correspondence   3. Politicians — Great Britain — Biography   4. Great Britain — Politics and government — 1901–1936
  I. Title   II. Self, Robert C., 1953–
  941'.083'092

Library of Congress Cataloging-in-Publication Data
Chamberlain, Neville, 1869–1940.
  [Correspondence. Selections]
  The Neville Chamberlain diary letters / edited by Robert Self.
    p. cm. Includes bibliographical references. (v. 2 : alk. paper)
  Contents: v. 2. The reform years, 1921–27
  1. Chamberlain, Neville, 1869–1940—Correspondence.   2. Great Britain—Politics and government—20th century.   3. Prime ministers—Great Britain—Correspondence.   I. Self, Robert C., 1953–   II. Title.

DA585.C5 Z48 2000
941.083'092—dc21   00–026601

This volume is printed on acid free paper.

Typeset by Manton Typesetters, Louth, Lincolnshire, UK.
Printed in Great Britain by T.J. International, Padstow, Cornwall.

Contents

Acknowledgements

A large number of debts are incurred during the preparation of a study of this sort. First and most obvious, I owe an immense debt of gratitude to the generosity of the University of Birmingham for granting its kind permission to reproduce so extensively the letters of Neville Chamberlain to his sisters and to quote from other Chamberlain family correspondence in their care. Thanks are due to Miss Christine Penney and the Special Collection staff of the Heslop Room at Birmingham University Library who cheerfully provided so much valuable assistance during this research. By the same token, the editor is indebted to the owners, custodians and archivists of the other collections of private papers and diaries used in the preparation of the text. For access and permission to quote from material in privately owned collections I am grateful to Viscount Addison, the Earl of Derby, John Grigg, Captain J. Headlam and the Durham Record Office, the Syndics of Cambridge University Library, the Warden and Fellows of New College Oxford, the Clerk of Records of the House of Lords acting on behalf of the Beaverbrook Foundation Trust, the Marquess of Salisbury, Mrs A. Stacey and the Trustees of the Bridgeman family archive, Mrs R.M. Stafford, the Masters and Fellows of Churchill College, Cambridge and the Conservative Party. I have also consulted archive collections held by a number of other libraries and institutions, namely the Birmingham Central Library, Department of Western Manuscripts of the Bodleian Library, British Library, British Library of Political and Economic Science, Durham Record Office, the House of Lords Record Office, Liverpool City Central Library, the Public Records Office, the Rhodes House Library, Oxford and Sheffield University Library. My thanks are due to the keepers, librarians and curators of these institutions and their staff. Every effort has been made to trace the copyright holders of unpublished documents from which quotations have been made. To anyone whose copyright I have unwittingly infringed I offer my sincere apologies. Considerable thanks are also due to the Arts & Humanities Research Board for an award under the Research Leave Scheme which permitted me to devote an entire academic year to the preparation of these volumes in 1999–2000.

Debts of a more personal kind also exist. I am particularly deeply indebted to Dr Stuart Ball for all the practical and scholarly assistance he has so freely given during the course of this project. By the same token, Professors John Ramsden, Iwan Morgan, Peter Mandler and Brian Harrison all provided valuable advice or assistance on various aspects of this work. Alec McAulay of Ashgate Publishing has provided unstinting enthusiasm and support from the outset and without his great vision and encouragement this project may never have come to fruition. At the other end of the publishing process, Ruth Peters has also lent patient and very helpful support throughout. Thanks are also due to Helen Dalton, Dan Herbert, Christine Smart and their colleagues at the London Guildhall University Library who have been unfailing in their cheerful assistance during the research for these volumes. Finally, there is the vast debt of gratitude I owe to Katie – for all she has contributed to this project and for just being there.

Editor's Note

Although the general approach to the task of editing these letters is thoroughly discussed in the introduction to the first volume, the reader should note that where sentences and paragraphs have been removed these have all been marked by the use of suspension dots. In every other respect the letters themselves have been reproduced in their original form. Although Neville Chamberlain's punctuation and use of capital letters is erratic and inconsistent and his spelling of surnames is idiosyncratic, his abbreviations and original spellings have been retained throughout. Editorial insertions have been made in some places for the sake of clarity, but these are always denoted by a square bracket. Only the style of dating has been standardised in the interests of consistency. Chamberlain almost always closed his letters with 'Your affecte. brother, Neville Chamberlain'. These words have been omitted to avoid needless repetition.

List of Abbreviations

AEU	Amalgamated Engineering Union
AG	Attorney-General
AMC	Association of Municipal Corporations
ASE	Amalgamated Society of Engineers
BDP	Birmingham Daily Post
BL	Andrew Bonar Law
BSA	Birmingham Small Arms Company
BUA/BCUA	Birmingham Conservative and Unionist Association
B/T	Board of Trade
Bart	Baronet
CC	County Council
CCR	Committee of Civil Research
C/E	Chancellor of Exchequer
C-in-C	Commander-in-Chief
CL	Coalition Liberal
CPRE	Council for the Preservation of Rural England
DC	District Council
DM	Daily Mail
EMC	Elliott's Metal Company
EPD	Excess Profits Duty
FBI	Federation of British Industry
FE	F.E. Smith, Lord Birkenhead
FTU	Fair Trade Union for Safeguarding British Work and Wages
GCMG	Knight Grand Cross of the Order of St Michael and St George
GHK	George Hamilton Kenrick
ILP	Independent Labour Party
KG	Knight of the Order of the Garter
LA	Local Authority
LCC	London County Council
LGB	Local Government Board
LMRS	London Municipal Reform Society
LSA	Leo Amery
LlG	David Lloyd George
M & CW	Mother and Child Welfare
MD	Mental Deficiency [Bill]

MFGB	Miners' Federation of Great Britain
MH	Ministry of Health
MOH	Medical Officer of Health
MP	Morning Post
MU	Midland Union (of Conservative and Unionist Associations)
NFU	National Farmers Union
NUA	National Unionist Association
NUCUA	National Union of Conservative & Unionist Associations
NUR	National Union of Railwaymen
OD	Outdoor relief, Poor Law
PLP	Parliamentary Labour Party
PMG	Post-Master General
PO	Post Office
PPS	Parliamentary Private Secretary
PS	Private Secretary
PUS	Public Utility Society
R&V	Rating and Valuation [Bill]
RAMC	Royal Army Medical Corps
RDC	Rural District Council
RHS	Royal Horticultural Society
RIC	Royal Irish Constabulary
RM	Ramsay MacDonald
RR	Rent Restrictions [Bill]
SB	Stanley Baldwin
TM	Their Majesties
WO	War Office

Other personal nicknames

All Highest	Curzon
Bal	Balcarres
Bobby	Eyres-Monsell
Bosky	Griffith-Boscawen
Jix/Jicks	Joynson-Hicks
Linkie	Lord Hugh Cecil
The Goat	Lloyd George
Top	Viscount Wolmer
Wee Frees	Independent (Asquithian) Liberal Party
Worthy	Workington-Evans

1

Introduction
Neville Chamberlain, 1921–1927:
The Reform Years

I

The fall of the Lloyd George Coalition on 19 October 1922 marked a decisive watershed in Neville Chamberlain's political career. Like so many Conservative leaders between the wars, Chamberlain was a beneficiary of the unique situation created by the Carlton Club revolt. When the bulk of the party's most experienced leadership went into the political wilderness rather than submit to the wishes of rebellious subordinates, Bonar Law was forced 'to depend upon the under-secretaries and bottle-washers of the late Government' to form his administration.[1] Yet although Neville Chamberlain had undoubtedly established a strong claim to ministerial preferment within the ranks of this so-called 'Second Eleven', few could have predicted the meteoric rise that these developments made possible. Appointed as Postmaster-General outside the Cabinet in October 1922, within ten months Chamberlain had risen, via the Ministry of Health, to become Chancellor of the Exchequer and one of Baldwin's closest ministerial confidants. Thereafter, he remained at the pinnacle of national and Conservative politics until his death in 1940. Moreover, beyond its direct implications for Chamberlain's political career, October 1922 marked an equally significant personal watershed. With Austen stranded in the wilderness and his own rapidly rising prominence on the Conservative front bench, Neville Chamberlain swiftly moved out of the shadow of his older half-brother. Perhaps for the first time in his life, Neville Chamberlain was now his own man, standing on terms of equality with his more fortunate and privileged sibling.

During the last two years of the Lloyd George Coalition such an outcome had appeared extremely unlikely. At the end of 1920 Chamberlain had gloomily resigned himself to the life of a useful but unfulfilled backbencher with a reputation for sound opinions and the sort of persuasive power that could influence backbench sentiment and lead debate. Valuable work was also achieved in his many committees during 1921–22, particularly with regard to canals and 'unhealthy areas' where he advanced many of the ideas developed privately

---

[1] Cuthbert Headlam Diary, 24 October 1922, Headlam MSS D/He/18 fol. 297 (Durham Record Office).

1

since his mayoralty about the need for municipal 'reconditioning' of slum properties as an important interim measure before eventual clearance.[2] Yet for all the
constructive work and political kudos to be obtained from such labours, Chamberlain was also forced to recognise that too much time and effort were devoted
to far less rewarding tasks such as his chairmanship of a wearisome Joint
Committee of Lords and Commons on water tolls for London and an equally
arduous but ultimately frustrating Royal Commission on the Government of
London.

The depth of Chamberlain's gloom about his personal position during 1921–
22 was intensified by two factors. First, his half-brother's emergence as leader
of the Unionist party in March 1921 raised a variety of difficulties. In part, these
stemmed from a rapidly growing awareness that Austen had fallen under the
mesmeric spell of the Welsh Wizard, whose plans to turn the Coalition into a
new party under his leadership were likely to split the Conservatives and place
the two brothers on opposite sides. Yet beyond fundamental strategic dilemmas
of this sort, Austen's emergence as Conservative leader also had unwelcome
implications for Neville's ability to maintain his own independent position and
influence at a day-to-day level. Such constraints became apparent almost immediately when he felt obliged to decline the chairmanship of the backbench
Unionist Reconstruction Committee because he 'could not agree to head a revolt
against Austen & a revolt might be wanted'.[3] Secondly, these political frustrations were compounded by deepening financial anxieties. Already living off his
capital after only two years as an MP, as the severity of the post-war slump
increased during 1921 the returns from his various business interests in the
Birmingham Small Arms Company (BSA) and Elliotts correspondingly collapsed. Only Hoskins proved 'a little gold mine' with its bulging order book and
record dividends, although even here Chamberlain correctly predicted that this
would not last much longer.[4] As a result of these combined trials, he lamented in
his review of 1921 that it had been 'a very trying year' and sometimes he wished
he were out of politics altogether.[5]

Yet ironically, at the moment Chamberlain was penning these melancholy
reflections, the fortunes of both Lloyd George and the Coalition suffered a major
blow from which they never recovered. Flushed with success over the Irish
Treaty, Lloyd George decided that the Coalition should snatch another election
victory in order to bring about by stealth the merger which could not be achieved

---

[2] Unhealthy Areas Committee: Second and Final Report, April 1921, NC8/6/2. For the development of these ideas see Robert Self (ed.), *Neville Chamberlain Diary Letters, Volume I, The Making
of a Politician, 1915–20* (Aldershot, 2000), pp. 317–8, 324, 353.

[3] N. Chamberlain to Hilda, 31 July 1921. Also 'Mr Chamberlain's Work in Parliament', n.d.,
NC5/10/39.

[4] N. Chamberlain to Hilda, 15 January, 12 February 1921 and to Ida, 19 March 1921.

[5] Neville Chamberlain Diary, 31 December 1921, NC2/20.

by direct calls for 'fusion'. Chamberlain's half-brother was alone among the Coalition leadership in opposing the idea of an election in January 1922. Unable to prevent it directly, Austen Chamberlain's decision to sound party opinion on the question represented a subtle means of winning the argument indirectly, by enabling latent Conservative hostility to make itself apparent. Speaking as the effective leader of Midland Unionism, Neville Chamberlain's response to these soundings echoed the almost unanimous opposition of those consulted towards the idea of an early election, arguing that the government would be severely handicapped by the fact that Ireland, Second Chamber reform and economies were unsettled, while unemployment remained a major source of vulnerability at a time when 'the Coalition has no friends to speak of'. Against this background, he pessimistically predicted that 'if an Election were held now, half the seats ... might be swept away'. He was equally sceptical about the prospects for 'fusion' between the two wings of the Coalition as 'there [were] a number of Unionists who would not agree to give up the old name and scrap the old machine and enter a new combination under a new name, and with Lloyd George accepted as Leader of their party'. Conceding that he might himself be among the rebels, Chamberlain thus emphasised privately that his own preference was to dissolve the Coalition and go to the country as an independent party.[6] At Austen's request, to strengthen his hand in the Cabinet battle, Neville reiterated these objections to the Midland Union Executive on 9 January which then passed a resolution endorsing the view that no election should be held before the government tackled Lords reform and the reduction of national expenditure.[7]

Although plans for an early election were abandoned, the tensions it unleashed established the tone of mounting crisis which characterised the Coalition's final months. After the failure of the election kite in January 1922, Chamberlain derived malicious comfort from the belief that 'whatever line Ll.G. takes ... the mischief is done and that the Coalition wont be the same again'.[8] Beneath the surface, Chamberlain's own response to these developments reflected an increasing Unionist resentment towards both the Prime Minister's underhand manoeuvres to bounce them into an unwanted election and the disproportionate influence of his Coalition Liberal allies. At the Midland Union in January, Chamberlain had taken the opportunity to warn publicly that 'some of the Liberal members of the Coalition should be made to realise the weight the Unionist Party was carrying ... The Unionists had put

---

[6] N. Chamberlain to A. Chamberlain and memorandum, 29 December 1921, Austen Chamberlain MSS AC32/2/13–14 (Birmingham University Library). The latter is also in Lloyd George MSS F/7/5/1 (House of Lords Record Office, Hist. Coll. 192).

[7] Midland Union Executive: Minutes, 9 January 1922 (Conservative Party Archive, Bodleian Library, Oxford).

[8] N. Chamberlain to Hilda, 14 January 1922.

loyalty to their Country first and unless that was recognised they would refuse to be dragged at the tail of the Liberal Wing of the Party'.[9] When these tensions culminated in a divisive battle over tariff protection for fabric gloves in the summer, it confirmed Chamberlain's frustration with the limitations of Coalition and stiffened his determination 'to adopt a very firm attitude' towards these nominal allies should the matter come to a crisis.[10] Yet, although regularly confessing that he 'should like to be rid of the Goat', he still gloomily anticipated 'the little Welshman' would remain in control for some time given doubts about Diehard influence, the surprising strength of pro-Coalition Unionist sentiment and the assumption that his own party could not win an overall majority without Lloyd George.[11] Moreover, even optimistic thoughts about the apparent decline of the Coalition aroused ambivalent feelings, for, although he loathed Lloyd George and the Coalition, he was reluctant to participate actively in a rebellion against his own half-brother as its joint leader. Torn between a desire to end the Coalition and fraternal loyalty, therefore, Chamberlain remained silent to avoid providing ammunition for critics of the government. Symptomatic of the depth of his political frustrations and growing financial worries during 1922 was the fact that during the autumn his doctor diagnosed Chamberlain's feeling of extreme tiredness over the past few months as a stress-related 'condition arising from excessive mental strain'.[12]

Given the complications of his position, it was perhaps fortunate that Chamberlain was absent on a tour of Canada during the final crisis of the Coalition. He was still in Ottawa when the news came that Conservative MPs had voted decisively to end the Coalition and that Lloyd George and most of the Unionist leadership (including his own half-brother) had resigned rather than submit to the rebels. Although naturally sorry for Austen, Neville Chamberlain's principal initial impulse was to offer 'profound thanks to Providence for delivering us from the Goat'.[13] Second thoughts then appeared briefly to intensify the acute personal dilemma with which he had grappled since the spring of 1920 based on his need to choose between either loyalty to Austen (and the hated Lloyd George) or to his own career with the bulk of the Conservative party. Yet if much doubt really existed in his mind, it was swiftly dispelled. Two days out from New York he had already excluded the possibility of going out of politics because of his half-brother's difficulties on the grounds that 'the more I thought of it the more it became clear to me that with no fundamental difference of policy but only of personalities I could not see myself following Ll.G. and that if

---

[9] Midland Union Executive: Minutes, 9 January 1922.

[10] Birmingham Conservative and Unionist Association: Minutes, 14 July 1922, vol. II, pp. 213–14, (Birmingham Central Library). Hereafter BCUA.

[11] N. Chamberlain to Hilda, 14 January 1922 and to Ida, 4 and 18 March 1922.

[12] Neville Chamberlain Diary, 4 September 1922, NC2/20.

[13] N. Chamberlain to Hilda, 24 October 1922.

Austen were out of the question I would have no hesitation in remaining with the Unionists & even, if I were asked, joining the new Govt'.[14]

On 30 October, the morning after his arrival in England, Amery informed Chamberlain that Law wished him to become Postmaster-General.[15] His uncharacteristically acrimonious meeting with his overwrought half-brother later in the day was a considerable trial for both men as they sought to exert moral blackmail to achieve their own tactical goals. Austen 'took the idea very badly evidently feeling that if [Neville] accepted it would be the last drop of bitterness in the cup',[16] and such was Neville's distress at the thought of a permanent breach in their relations that when Amery met him later in the day he believed him capable of refusing Law's offer.[17] When the brothers met over dinner, Neville again assured Austen that his acceptance would not put them in opposite camps, but would rather serve 'as a link between him and the new Govt, making relations easier & facilitating his acceptance as one of the leaders if not the leader in the event of B.L.'s being unable to carry on'. When Austen bitterly refused to be convinced, however, Neville angrily played his emotional ace by threatening to refuse office in deference to Austen's feelings, but making it clear that if he did so he would withdraw from politics altogether. Confronted explicitly with such a heavy personal responsibility, Austen withdrew his objection and urged his half-brother to accept.[18]

Law's motives for including Neville Chamberlain in his government are open to question, but they could not have been entirely without thought of its impact upon both Austen's attitude and the cohesion of his following.[19] In accepting Law's invitation, Neville had himself stressed that his presence in the Government 'may help to heal the wounds left by recent differences in the party'.[20] Nevertheless, Maurice Cowling overstates the cynicism of Law's motivation in asserting that Chamberlain was 'used as a disposable pawn until given his chance … to take the Ministry of Health'.[21] The far more likely explanation for Chamberlain's inclusion was Law's urgent need to fill portfolios with men of proven ability at a time when most of the party's experienced talent refused to join his government. Thus,

---

[14] Neville Chamberlain Diary, 22 October 1922; N. Chamberlain to Hilda, 24 October 1922.

[15] L.S. Amery to Bonar Law, 31 October 1922, Law MSS 108/1/28 (House of Lords Record Office, Hist. Coll. 191).

[16] N. Chamberlain to Hilda, 31 October 1922.

[17] Amery Diary, misdated 25 October 1922, John Barnes and David Nicholson (eds), *The Leo Amery Diaries, Volume I, 1869–1929* (London, 1980), p. 309.

[18] Neville Chamberlain Diary, 19 November 1922 and 'The Unionist Government under Bonar Law', NC2/20–21.

[19] For calculations of this sort see Amery Diary, 19 October 1922, I, p. 300; Amery to Bonar Law, 31 October 1922, Law MSS 108/1/28.

[20] N. Chamberlain to Bonar Law, 31 October 1922, Law MSS 109/2/11a.

[21] Maurice Cowling, *The Impact of Labour 1920–1924: The Beginning of Modern British Politics*, (Cambridge, 1971), p. 296.

although Law hoped that 'it will not be long before we are all in the same boat again', he was almost certainly sincere when he assured Chamberlain that it was 'a real pleasure to have you in the Government and in saying this I am not thinking of the political advantage of your having joined us'.[22]

In the general election which followed, Chamberlain was confident of a comfortable majority in Ladywood, given his organisational reforms in the constituency since 1918 and the high morale of his party workers. To provide volunteer helpers at election times, a Junior Unionist Club opened in September 1921 and a Unionist Worker's League was launched four months later.[23] Similarly, Annie had assiduously cultivated this poor, largely working-class constituency since her husband's election in 1918 through her promotion of the Women's Unionist Association and the opening of four constituency Women's Clubs. In the Chamberlain archives two leather-bound volumes detail all of her social work visits to constituents between October 1919 and November 1922, accompanied by notes of their appearance, domestic circumstances and the remedial assistance provided, along with reminders for future reference about any flowers or Christmas cards subsequently despatched or received.[24] With characteristic zeal, she threw herself wholeheartedly into the election campaign during November 1922, touring Ladywood on her bicycle in a hat with a large orange plume 'talking encouraging scolding cajoling charming and converting the multitude' with house visits, street-corner meetings and mass rallies.[25] As one local party official remarked, 'There wasn't a dog-hanging … that they didn't attend'.[26] Yet, despite all these efforts, the electoral climate had become distinctly more hostile in Birmingham as the severity of economic slump and unemployment increased.[27] Given the nature and vulnerability of Chamberlain's constituency, Ladywood became one of the main battlegrounds in an election characterised by 'systematic door to door misrepresentation about Unionist candidates, flagrant exploitation of the miseries of the unemployed, organised rowdyism … and a great deal of literature which would not have commended itself to George Washington'.[28] In the event, while Chamberlain attributed Unionist victory in all

---

[22] Bonar Law to N. Chamberlain, 1 November 1922, NC7/11/15/10. Also N. Chamberlain to Ida, 22 November 1930, NC18/1/718.

[23] Ladywood Divisional Unionist Association: Annual Report 1922–23, April 1923, p. 28 (Birmingham Central Library); N. Chamberlain to Ida, 18 September 1921 and to Hilda, 29 January 1922.

[24] Ladywood Minute Books 2–3, NC5/11/1–2.

[25] N. Chamberlain to Ida, 11 November 1922.

[26] Austen Chamberlain to Ida, 18 November 1922, AC5/1/250; R.C. Self (ed.), *The Austen Chamberlain Diary Letters: The Correspondence of Sir Austen Chamberlain with his Sisters Hilda and Ida, 1916–1937* (Cambridge, 1995), p. 200.

[27] BCUA Central Committee: Minutes, 2 December 1921, II, pp. 100–103; Ladywood Divisional Unionist Association: Annual Report, 1921–22, n.d., p. 16.

[28] BCUA Central Committee: Minutes, 13 April 1923, III, p. 33.

twelve Birmingham seats largely to his efforts at strengthening the party's organisation throughout the city, Ladywood produced the second smallest majority on an increased turnout.

II

As a member of Law's government, Chamberlain swiftly established a formidable reputation as a minister of imagination and outstanding administrative competence with a talent for parliamentary debate. Although well equipped to have stepped directly into the Ministry of Health as some supporters suggested, after his disastrous experience at National Service in 1917, Chamberlain was grateful for the 'comfortable obscurity' of the Post Office in order to serve a proper ministerial apprenticeship before advancing to more prominent positions.[29] The direct departmental policy responsibilities of the Postmaster-General were relatively modest. Although on 18 January 1923 Chamberlain had the distinction of granting the first broadcasting licence to the newly-established British Broadcasting Company, he was less sympathetic to its request to broadcast the King's Speech in January 1923, on the grounds that it may be used as a precedent for broadcasting Commons debates – 'a prospect which makes one shudder' – and was 'entirely unhelpful' when John Reith, the BBC's first managing director, pressed him to uphold his own licensing system in order to prevent amateur 'experimenters' rebroadcasting BBC output and disturbing its transmissions.[30] A more important departmental victory was achieved over plans to build a chain of wireless stations across the empire, when Chamberlain carried his proposal for a government monopoly through Cabinet against the scepticism of the Prime Minister and the initial preferences of the Chancellor. After Chamberlain's detailed and persuasive exposition of the case to Cabinet, Curzon decisively intervened to conclude 'Capital cost small, commercial prospects good, object excellent, decision immediate and affirmative'.[31]

Although the Post Office offered the opportunity for a sound apprenticeship in the arts of ministerial leadership, it was scarcely the place to earn a great reputation. Yet from the outset, Chamberlain rapidly acquired broader opportunities to demonstrate his abilities. Perhaps because of the kindred spirit which develops between men of similar character and temperament,[32] a warm mutual

---

[29] N. Chamberlain to Hilda, 27 January and 11 March 1923.

[30] N. Chamberlain to Bonar Law, n.d., Law MSS 113/3/3; Reith Diary, 5 February 1923, J.C.W. Reith, *Into the Wind*, (London, 1949), p. 90; Asa Briggs, *A History of Broadcasting in the United Kingdom, Volume I, The Birth of Broadcasting* (London, 1961), pp. 148–50.

[31] Neville Chamberlain Diary, 28 February 1923, NC2/21; CAB 13(23)1, 28 February 1923, CAB 23/45 (Public Record Office).

[32] Thomas Jones, *A Diary with Letters 1931–1950* (London, 1954), p. xxviii.

regard soon developed between Law and Chamberlain. Given Chamberlain's 'affectionate feeling for him' since his National Service days, it was no mere conventional expression of deference when he accepted office with the assurance that he would serve 'with real pleasure for ... I have long felt a special personal regard for you'.[33] For his own part, Law evidently had considerable confidence in Chamberlain's judgement, and he had been keen to sound his opinions over a variety of issues such as the government's response to the politically embarrassing demands of unemployed marchers who wished to meet the Prime Minister and the dubious wisdom of the Health Minister's plans for housing. Law also entrusted Chamberlain with the politically-sensitive responsibility of winding up the debate on the Safeguarding of Industries Act in difficult circumstances in January, and appointed him to both the Cabinet's Home Affairs Committee and that dealing with housing, before elevating him to succeed as Minister of Health in March.[34] It was indicative of Law's increasing respect for his judgement that when he resigned as Prime Minister, Chamberlain's name was the first to be considered when asked for someone to advise the King about a successor, before Law eventually suggested Lord Salisbury.[35] Perhaps Beaverbrook was even telling the truth some years later when he told Chamberlain that Bonar Law believed that with a little more parliamentary experience he would have been the right man to have succeeded him in May 1923.[36]

Given his proven expertise on housing, Chamberlain was certainly the obvious candidate to succeed the unfortunate Griffith-Boscawen as Minister of Health after his humiliating failure to be re-elected at the Mitcham by-election in March 1923. Yet the sheer scale of the political and administrative challenge posed by housing policy was truly formidable, given the existence of two fundamental and interlocking problems. First, during the war the pressure of unfulfilled demand had created a deficit which reached an estimated 805,000 units by 1921, excluding the replacement need for insanitary and unfit dwellings.[37] Second, such shortages were compounded by the effects of the Increase of Rent and Mortgage Interest (War Restrictions) Act in 1915 which had fixed all rents on houses with a rateable value not exceeding £35 in London, £30 in Scotland and £26 elsewhere at the level prevailing at the outbreak of war or their first wartime letting. Although this measure achieved its wartime political objective, the problem was that these restrictions trapped later governments in a vicious spiral which militated against any easy resolution of the housing problem. Thus, on the

---

[33] N. Chamberlain to Ida, 19 March 1921 and to Hilda, 13 March 1920; N. Chamberlain to Bonar Law, 31 October 1922, Law MSS 109/2/11a.

[34] N. Chamberlain to Hilda, 13 and 27 January 1923.

[35] Robert Blake, *The Unknown Prime Minister: The Life and Times of Andrew Bonar Law, 1858–1923* (London, 1955), p. 518.

[36] Neville Chamberlain Diary, 23 November 1930, NC2/22.

[37] Marion Bowley, *Housing and the State, 1919–1944* (London, 1945), pp. 10–13, 262.

one hand, it was politically impossible to repeal rent restrictions both because tenants regarded controlled rents as a 'fair' level and because the acute shortage of houses would immediately produce a potentially catastrophic increase in rents. Yet on the other hand, insofar as the existence of rent controls removed all prospect of a reasonable profit, they acted as a major disincentive to speculative builders and investors who may otherwise have entered the market to satisfy the demand for low cost working-class housing for rent. Little wonder that soon after becoming Minister of Health Chamberlain had compared housing to 'a skein of wool inextricably entangled so that they could not find the end to begin unwinding'.[38] It is indicative of the bleak legacy which Chamberlain inherited that although some 252,000 houses had been built between 1919 and March 1923 when he became minister, the total outstanding deficit of 822,000 houses was greater than at the Armistice.[39] Against a background of chronic policy failure and potentially disastrous electoral discontent, Chamberlain was thus scarcely exaggerating when he claimed that 'it seems my fate to be given the most dangerous and responsible position in the front line and probably the fate of the Govt will depend upon poor me'.[40]

From its commencement, the Cabinet Committee considering housing policy had been far more strongly influenced by Chamberlain's perceptions of problems and responses than by those of the nominal Minister of Health. While Griffith-Boscawen initially opposed the reintroduction of a subsidy for new houses, the committee (and later the Cabinet) accepted Chamberlain's view both that a new subsidy was unavoidable and that it should take the form of a fixed financial liability for the State over a set period.[41] The Housing Bill which Chamberlain introduced into the Commons on 11 April was a financially far more conservative measure than its 1919 predecessor and clearly reflected Chamberlain's belief that the housing shortage was an essentially temporary problem. Although the government revived Addison's principle of subsidised house building, the novelty of the 1923 Act was derived from its central objective to 'get rid of the unlimited liability of the State for all losses exceeding the produce of a 1d rate on housing schemes … carried out by Local Authorities' with which Addison had saddled the Coalition.[42] The Treasury subsidy was thus set at £6 per house per annum for twenty years without requiring any accompanying rate subsidy and applied to houses built before October 1925, whether by local authorities or private enterprise and whether for rent or sale. As the capital value of the

---

[38] D. Walker-Smith, *Neville Chamberlain: Man of Peace* (London, n.d.), p. 138.

[39] Bowley, *Housing and the State*, pp. 24–25, 33.

[40] N. Chamberlain to Hilda, 11 March 1923.

[41] CP 8(23) 'Interim Report on Housing Policy', 8 January 1923, CAB 24/158 and CAB 3(23)2, 26 January 1923, CAB 23/45.

[42] CP 110(23) 'The Housing Bill' and CP 133(23), 'Home Affairs Committee: The Housing Bill', 19 and 28 February 1923, CAB 24/158–59.

subsidy at a 5 per cent interest rate was £75, to encourage private enterprise this could be given to the builder as a lump sum. Although the new subsidy was available on dwellings built within specified parameters of size and amenity, in practice the severity of these limitations led critics like John Wheatley to condemn Chamberlain's houses as squalid 'rabbit hutches' with rooms smaller than the desk on which the bill had been drafted.[43] In his own defence, however, Chamberlain replied that he had concentrated the subsidy on the cheapest housing to meet the greatest needs within the community.

Although the 1923 Housing Act represented an important legislative landmark by establishing the principle of fixed annual subsidies as the dominant method of central government support for house building for the next forty years, it is important not to exaggerate its novelty – particularly as the underlying idea was first proposed by Sir Alfred Mond, Addison's successor at the Ministry of Health, although the Coalition fell before he could introduce it. Yet, on the other hand, the 1923 Housing Act did embody some eminently Conservative principles – albeit reflecting a significantly modified view of the solution since Chamberlain's commitment to a far more generous scheme of State funding and ownership under local authority management, that he had advocated during the 1918 general election and the housing debates of 1919–20.[44] First, the emphasis was now upon the restoration of the position of private enterprise as the principal source of working-class housing. Second, the Act equally resolutely closed the door to Addison's fundamental objective of making public housing a species of social service to be met principally by local authority provision. To this end, Section 1 specified that local authorities were permitted to build only if they could convince the minister that this would be preferable or because private enterprise would not meet an unfulfilled need. Third, the Act was designed to promote Chamberlain's well-established commitment to owner-occupation, and by 1925 he was rejoicing that it was already 'building up a whole new class of good citizens'.[45] As such, it did much to give substance to the Conservative notion of a 'property-owning democracy'; a concept and a term first coined by Noel Skelton in 1923 and popularised by Anthony Eden after 1945. Fourth, by limiting the liability of the State to a fixed subsidy, local financial responsibility was restored in a manner which conformed with Chamberlain's more general preference for devolving responsibility down to those best able to assess their own needs and conditions.

More vexatious and intractable problems arose over the future of the rent controls introduced in 1915 and subsequently extended in 1919 and 1920. Al-

---

[43] Ian Wood, *John Wheatley* (Manchester, 1990), pp. 99–102. *Parliamentary Debates: House of Commons Debates*, Fifth Series (hereafter *H.C. Debs*, 5s) 163 col. 325–32, 24 April 1923.

[44] For his earlier ideas see 'To the Electors of Ladywood 1918', NC5/10/79; Self (ed.), *Neville Chamberlain Diary Letters*, I, pp. 83–84, 297, 301, 307.

[45] N. Chamberlain to Hilda, 17 October 1925.

though immediate decontrol was never a realistic option, under pressure for a clear statement of policy at a time when rent restrictions were central to the outcome of three ministerial by-elections, the Cabinet agreed in February 1923 that all controls should come to an end in June 1925.[46] In contrast, Chamberlain's initial preference was for a gradual relaxation of restrictions over a five- or possibly ten-year period, in the belief that this offered some degree of certainty about the future while progressively reducing the scope and impact of controls until they were finally abolished.[47] Dissatisfied with a policy formulated in panic to win by-elections, Chamberlain had thus stipulated that he would accept the Ministry of Health only if Bonar Law agreed to give him a free hand to reconsider this aspect of policy.[48] In the event, although initially 'floundering' over rent restrictions, Chamberlain built largely on the recommendations of the Onslow Committee to forge an 'equitable compromise' between the interests of the landlord seeking free-market rents and tenants anxious to avoid exploitation and hardship.[49] The Rent and Mortgage Interest Restrictions Bill, approved by the Cabinet on 20 May and introduced in the Commons the same day, extended the 1920 Act in the first instance until mid-1925 with certain modifications. Thus, while decontrol was permitted where owners gained vacant possession, Clause 4 specified that landlords who neglected their own property would not be eligible for permitted rent increases under the earlier Acts until the Sanitary Authority certified that the property was in reasonable repair – a principle which Chamberlain had championed in his maiden speech during the passage of the 1919 Rent Restrictions Act. Although during the Second Reading debate Chamberlain declared that he expected a further extension of five years before a complete return to free-market rents, the persistence of the housing problem obliged the Conservatives to extend the Act in 1925, 1927 and then each successive year until the entire scheme was revised in 1933.

As his diary letters during this period testify, Chamberlain's brief term at the Ministry of Health was one of frenetic activity and remarkable legislative success. The sense of crisis, failure and despondency which had blighted the government's early months had been dispelled by the summer recess and it was widely believed to be more firmly established than at any time since coming into power – a fact for which Chamberlain rightly believed he could claim much of the personal credit.[50] Ultimately, it was a perverse indication of this success that

---

[46] CAB 12(23)1, 24 February 1923, CAB 23/45.

[47] N. Chamberlain to Ida, 18 February 1923.

[48] Neville Chamberlain Diary, 9 March 1923, NC2/21.

[49] N. Chamberlain to Ida, 17 March 1923. For the Onslow Committee's recommendations see Cmd. 1803, Committee on Rent Restrictions Act, 9 February 1923.

[50] N. Chamberlain to Ida, 9 June 1923; Sanders Diary 29 April and 9 June 1923 (Bodleian Library, Oxford); John Ramsden (ed.), *Real Old Tory Politics: The Political Diaries of Sir Robert Sanders, Lord Bayford, 1910–1935* (London, 1984), pp. 204, 205–6.

during the recess in August Chamberlain was unceremoniously plucked from a job he loved to become Chancellor of the Exchequer. Although by any standard this represented a remarkably rapid promotion, it was also a profoundly unwelcome personal development. Press speculation about his appointment to the Exchequer in May had prompted him to decide that he would not accept such an offer because 'it is an office which I should particularly dislike, quite apart from my objection to be continually pulled up by the roots. I never could understand finance, and moreover I should hate a place whose main function was to put spokes in other people's wheels'.[51] When the Liberal McKenna finally declined to accept the Exchequer in mid-August, however, Baldwin immediately offered it to Chamberlain.

'What a day!' Chamberlain replied to Baldwin's request by return of post. 'Two salmon this morning, and the offer of the Exchequer this afternoon!'. While thanking him for 'the greatest compliment I ever received in my life', however, he firmly declined with the protest that 'I do not feel that I have any gifts for finance which I have never been able to understand, and I fear that as Chancellor I should not fulfil your expectations'.[52] Yet despite this very definite tone, as anticipated, Baldwin persisted in a telegram which acknowledged Chamberlain's reasons but stressed that his own were 'overwhelming'.[53] Rather than risk the discourtesy of a further refusal by telegram, Chamberlain reluctantly gave up the last two days of his fishing holiday to meet Baldwin at Downing Street on the morning of 24 August. After dismissing the alternative candidates with 'considerable frankness', Baldwin put the decisive argument that he had felt the need to discuss affairs with a close colleague whose judgement he trusted, just as he had previously discussed them with Bonar Law, and that from this perspective there was no other satisfactory alternative.[54] In reality, Chamberlain's meteoric rise from the backbenches to Chancellor and second place in the government in little more than nine months was undoubtedly assisted by the fortuitous circumstances created by the Carlton Club revolt. Yet this fact should not obscure the importance of Chamberlain's personal merit and achievement in winning this promotion. Countering protests about his desire to remain at Health, Baldwin had pointed out that Chamberlain had brought this predicament upon himself through this proven skill over recent months. Like many others, Curzon's congratulations upon a 'splendid and entirely deserved promotion' were also accompanied by the observation that during his short ministerial career Chamberlain had demonstrated 'qualities and abilities which would be a source of

---

[51] N. Chamberlain to Ida, 26 May 1923. See also N. Chamberlain to Mary Carnegie, 8 September 1923, NC1/20/1/125 and Diary, 17 September 1923, NC2/21.

[52] Baldwin to N. Chamberlain, 14 August and reply on 16 August 1923, NC7/11/16/3–4.

[53] Baldwin to N. Chamberlain telegram, n.d., NC7/11/16/5.

[54] N. Chamberlain to Hilda, 26 August 1923; Neville Chamberlain Diary, 17 September 1923, NC2/21.

strength to any Government and indeed raise you by a natural process to the highest responsibilities'.[55]

<h2 style="text-align:center">III</h2>

Chamberlain's brief first period at the Treasury between August 1923 and January 1924 was remarkable only for its lack of any significant departmental achievement. Excluding Iain Macleod, whose tenure of the office was cut short by his sudden death after less than a month, Chamberlain's was the shortest Chancellorship since Sir Robert Peel in 1834–35, and he was one of only four Chancellors not to introduce a Budget. Yet despite the paucity of departmental initiatives, Chamberlain played a significant, if sometimes misunderstood, role in Baldwin's ill-fated decision to resurrect tariff reform in October 1923. Standing amid the ruins of Bonar Law's majority after the December 1923 election, stunned observers inevitably searched for scapegoats for the disaster which had befallen them. Curzon and the Earl of Crawford believed the 'evil geniuses' were 'the whipper snappers in the Cabinet, Amery, Lloyd-Greame, and I believe N. Chamberlain'.[56] George Younger in a 'graphic ac[count]' for Herbert Gladstone made 'Davison [sic] the real villain of the piece with Neville Chamberlain as a leading actor, Amery and others chipping in'.[57] Given his past antipathy it was not surprising that Auckland Geddes also named Neville Chamberlain as the principal instigator and Lord Derby subsequently concurred.[58] In retrospect, it is easy to understand why suspicion fell on Chamberlain and the other leading Cabinet tariff reformers with whom Baldwin had closeted himself in the fortnight leading up to his declaration to the party conference at Plymouth on 25 October. In the case of Amery, and to a lesser degree Lloyd-Greame, there was some substance in the allegation. In contrast, however, Chamberlain represented a consistent brake upon Baldwin's ill-considered ambitions for an early election and he played a curiously indirect role in the disaster which befell the party.

Contrary to David Dilks's supposition that 'it is scarcely conceivable that Baldwin would have pressed Neville Chamberlain so hard to take the Treasury without some thought of the consequences for tariff reform',[59] there is no

---

[55] Curzon to N. Chamberlain, 27 August 1923, NC8/7/18.

[56] Curzon to his wife, 18 November 1923, Marchioness Curzon, *Reminiscences* (London, 1955), p.191; Crawford Diary, 8 December 1923 and 8 January 1924, John Vincent (ed.), *The Crawford Papers: The Journals of David Lindsay, twenty-seventh Earl of Crawford and tenth Earl of Balcarres during the years 1892–1940* (Manchester, 1984), pp. 488, 490.

[57] Herbert Gladstone to Donald Maclean, 12 January 1924, Gladstone MSS 46474/64 (British Library, Add. MSS).

[58] Derby Diary, 14 November 1924 (Liverpool City Central Library).

[59] David Dilks, *Neville Chamberlain: Volume I, Pioneering and Reform 1869–1929* (Cambridge, 1984), p. 339.

evidence to confirm either that Baldwin had decided on such a policy departure at this juncture or that Chamberlain's fiscal predilections were a factor in his appointment. Like the free-trade McKenna, Chamberlain's principal claim to the Treasury rested upon his proven competence and the public confidence this was likely to inspire in the absence of any other credible alternative. Although Amery had certainly 'rubbed in a bit of protection à propos of Neville's appointment' on a long walk with Baldwin at Aix-les-Bains in late August,[60] in reality Baldwin only gradually came to recognise that tariff reform offered personal and political salvation. Indeed, he probably did not embrace it privately until quite suddenly on 6 or 7 October when he crystallised his thoughts in some notes on unemployment. Moreover, this development was not part of a long-gestating strategy towards which Chamberlain's appointment was a crucial step, but rather it arose in direct response to Baldwin's inconclusive meeting with the French Prime Minister on 19 September, which finally shattered his dreams of a swift and glorious settlement of the European economic dislocation that he considered essential to any hopes for the restoration of British trade and employment.[61]

Chamberlain was not directly involved in the evolution of Baldwin's thinking until after he had privately decided to resurrect tariff reform. On the night of 5 October Chamberlain had 'lots of interesting talks' with Baldwin and was 'much encouraged' to find him 'very seriously considering the party policy and disposed to go a long way in the direction of new duties with preferences designed to help the Dominions to develop Empire cotton, sugar and tobacco'; a policy departure which Chamberlain 'warmly welcomed' as the 'salvation of the country & incidentally of the party'. At this stage, however, both men agreed that Bonar Law's 1922 election pledge against any radical fiscal change without a further mandate precluded food taxes but not a gradual extension of the McKenna duties on manufactured goods.[62] This meeting was significant because Chamberlain was given to understand that Baldwin wanted to 'go in for a few extra duties in Novr but to lead up by an education campaign to a more thorough going policy by the time we were ready for an election'. Yet, less than two days after this conversation, Baldwin informed Stanley Jackson, the Party Chairman, that 'he thought it might be necessary to go in for general protection wh. wd. necessitate an early appeal to the country' and enquired about his preparedness for a November election. When Jackson informed Neville Chamberlain of these developments on 10 October, he thus found him more than a little surprised because Baldwin 'had not intended to go nearly as fast' the previous week.[63] It is

---

[60] Amery Diary, 30 August 1923, I, p.344.

[61] See R.C. Self, *Tories and Tariffs: The Conservative Party and the Politics of Tariff Reform, 1922–1932* (New York and London, 1986), pp. 79–110.

[62] N. Chamberlain to Hilda, 6 October 1923.

[63] Neville Chamberlain Diary, 10 October 1923, NC2/21.

possible that Baldwin had pursued a characteristically circumlocutory method of sounding Chamberlain about his plans on 5 October and Chamberlain, already thinking in terms of an extended education campaign, simply misunderstood Baldwin's intentions. Yet, the fact remains that Chamberlain learned of these developments indirectly some two days after Baldwin had confided in Amery and Jackson: a curious oversight in view of the fact that Baldwin lived next door to Chamberlain, knew him to be an ardent tariff reformer and had less than two months before assured him that his judgement made him the only man to whom he felt he could entrust the Treasury. Nevertheless, having finally learned of the plan, Chamberlain became one of the 'inner circle' concerting strategy, although perhaps less intimately involved with Baldwin than either Amery or even Lloyd-Greame.[64]

Although enthusiastic about tariff protection, from the outset Chamberlain consistently urged the need to avoid any declaration at the party conference which would provoke speculation about an early election before either an education campaign could be conducted or the details of the policy were agreed. Baldwin's Plymouth speech had been consciously designed with this objective in mind. As Baldwin told Churchill shortly before the speech and Sir William Bull immediately after it, he was simply putting out a 'feeler'.[65] Moreover, if the eyewitness testimony of the 'inner circle' is to be believed, Baldwin succeeded in relation to his own supporters.[66] Yet, ironically, the free-trade parties almost immediately interpreted the Plymouth speech as a breach of Bonar Law's pledge and thus the prelude to an election campaign.[67] Moreover, despite David Dilks's claim to the contrary, in many ways it was Neville Chamberlain's speech to a simultaneous overflow meeting in Plymouth to 'dot the i's on Tariff Reform' which fuelled most speculation about an early election.[68] In an otherwise cautious speech, Chamberlain's declaration that an adequate response to unemployment next winter would require the government to be released from Bonar Law's pledge, unwittingly negated the effect of Baldwin's careful personal declaration and contributed significantly to the revival of tariff reform as an immediate focus for inter-party controversy. Even *The Times*, which had been remarkably authoritative in its pronouncements throughout, interpreted Neville Chamberlain's speech to imply 'a definite decision on the part of the Cabinet to go to the country on the question of

---

[64] Amery Diary, 14 October and 10 November 1923, I, pp. 349, 355.

[65] A. Chamberlain to Lord Lee, 14 December 1923, AC35/3/18.

[66] 'Memorandum on October 1923', Worthington-Evans MSS c.894/61, (Bodleian Library, Oxford); Amery Diary, 25 October 1923; N. Chamberlain to Ida, and his diary, both dated 26 October 1923. See also Steel-Maitland to A. Glazebrook, 27 October 1923, Steel-Maitland MSS GD193/185/A (Scottish Record Office); Headlam Diary, 26 October 1923, Headlam MSS D/He/19 fol. 299.

[67] Robert Self, 'Baldwin's Blunder: A Rejoinder to Smart on 1923', *Twentieth Century British History*, 7.1 (1996), pp. 148–49.

[68] Dilks, *Neville Chamberlain*, pp. 346–47; Neville Chamberlain Diary, 26 October 1923.

Tariff Reform'.[69] Thereafter, it swiftly became apparent that the government was losing the initiative. Convinced that the policy could only be saved by snatching victory before the free trade parties could mobilise fully, on 11 November it was decided to hold an election in early December.

In Ladywood, Chamberlain's appeal was deliberately contrived to be reminiscent of his father's pre-war tariff campaign, with its slogans about 'keeping British work for British workers' and the need to 'Make the Foreigner Pay'.[70] In contrast, Chamberlain's left-wing Labour opponent preferred to fight the election on the class war and the adverse effects of the Rent Restrictions Act on Ladywood's working-class voters: a campaign of 'malicious and unfair propaganda' and organised Labour rowdyism worse than that witnessed in any other Birmingham constituency except Deritend.[71] As a result, on the eve of the poll Chamberlain confessed that his agent had 'got the wind up badly', although he personally remained confident of victory.[72] In the event, despite strengthened local organisation and Annie 'working like 40 beavers', Chamberlain held the seat with a reduced majority of only 1554. Although Birmingham remained true to its Chamberlainite protectionist heritage by returning Conservatives for all twelve seats for the third time in succession, in the country as a whole the Conservatives remained the largest party but they were denied both their overall majority and their mandate for fiscal change.

IV

Although defeat came as an unwelcome surprise and a painful personal blow, Chamberlain did not subscribe to general fears about the prospect of a minority Labour government supported by Liberal votes in the lobbies. On the contrary, despite widespread intriguing to exclude Labour with a variety of impracticable plans for anti-socialist coalition until well into the New Year, Chamberlain positively favoured the idea of a minority Labour government on the grounds that 'they would be too weak to do much harm but not too weak to get discredited'.[73] Convinced that nothing would more effectively undermine the electoral appeal and credibility of its propaganda on unemployment than a prophylactic dose of Labour government, he thus confidently reassured the faint-hearted that 'The country has asked for it and now it must see what it tastes like'.[74] Yet while

---

[69] *The Times*, 27 October 1923. See also Derby Diary, 14 November 1923 reporting Geddes.

[70] Chamberlain Election Address and handbill, December 1923, NC5/12/24–25.

[71] BCUA: Report of Management Committee, 15 February 1924, III, pp. 155–58.

[72] N. Chamberlain to Baldwin, 3 December 1923, NC7/11/16/5A.

[73] Neville Chamberlain Diary, 9 December 1923.

[74] N. Chamberlain to P.J. Hannon, 11 December 1923, Hannon MSS 17/1, (House of Lords Record Office, Hist. Coll. 189); BCUA: Minutes, Special Meeting of Management Committee, 21 December 1923, vol. III, pp. 113–16.

in many respects a prudent judgement, the loss of power and the transition to Opposition brought with it some distinctly adverse consequences for Neville Chamberlain.

First, during 1924 his relationship with Baldwin became significantly more remote and by June Chamberlain was noting that 'I see a good deal less of him than I did & he doesn't seem so much in need of council as when he was in office'.[75] Secondly, in the immediate aftermath of defeat Chamberlain was compelled to make some unpalatable doctrinal and personal compromises with regard to the position of tariff reform, after his soundings of party opinion led him to the reluctant conclusion that they did not want 'to be tied up to putting it in the foreground having got a bad scare at the last election'.[76] As a result, Chamberlain was compelled to accept the abandonment of the general tariff and the prospect of a more limited commitment to the piecemeal protection of individual industries: a policy enunciated formally by Baldwin at the party meeting at the Hotel Cecil on 11 February. Finally, Chamberlain suffered a further rebuff in March when he sought to defend the party's doctrinal integrity against what he saw as a recrudescence of the corrupting coalitionism defeated in October 1922. Thus, although he had single-handedly engineered the party's reunion with his half-brother and his Tory coalitionist followers in early February, he was adamantly opposed to Austen's strategy of assisting sympathetic Liberals to 'repeat the history of Liberal-Unionism' by offering some form of alliance with the Conservative party.[77] This divergence over strategy culminated in a leadership crisis in March, over Churchill's decision to stand in the Westminster Abbey by-election as an 'Independent Anti-Socialist' against an official Conservative candidate in one of the safest Tory seats in Britain. From Neville Chamberlain's perspective, Churchill was an electoral liability whose return to the Conservative fold threatened to 'drive the Labour moderates into the arms of the extremists' while simultaneously driving 'a wedge under the Protection door which would fasten it up hermetically and finally he would begin inevitably to intrigue for the leadership'.[78] His inability to uphold this view, however, compelled him briefly to recognise the limitations on his own influence upon Baldwin and the collective leadership and he experienced a similar sensation in June when confronted by Shadow Cabinet concerns about his membership of the propagandist Fair Trade Union.

Yet despite these disappointments and rebuffs, Chamberlain emerged from this period in Opposition during 1924 stronger than he had gone into it. His tact and assiduous preparation had finally reunited Baldwin and Austen Chamberlain

---

[75] N. Chamberlain to Hilda, 18 May and to Ida, 7 June 1924.

[76] N. Chamberlain to Hilda, 24 January 1924.

[77] A. Chamberlain to Hoare, 28 January 1924, Templewood MSS V/1 (Cambridge University Library); see also A. Chamberlain to Hilda, 24 January 1924, AC5/1/304.

[78] N. Chamberlain to Hilda, 22 March 1924.

at a carefully stage-managed private dinner on 5 February which resulted in the return of the Chamberlainite ex-ministers to the Shadow Cabinet in an atmosphere of 'marked affability' two days later.[79] In the Commons, Chamberlain used this period to consolidate his rising stature as a parliamentary leader and tactician of formidable talents. In practice, this often simply meant outright attack on the Labour government to the delight of Conservative backbenchers. On 2 April he launched a ferocious attack during the debate on the capital levy, denouncing it as 'the biggest electoral bribe that has ever been offered'. At the same time, Wheatley's bill to prevent evictions where these were due to unemployment was subjected to brutal sarcasm when Chamberlain claimed the principle that 'My need is greater than thine' could be applied, not just to housing, but to the claims of the unemployed worker to the produce of the baker, butcher, grocer and even to Wheatley's own coat.[80] At the end of May Chamberlain further heartened his own backbenchers by attacking the Finance Bill for the 'narrow pedantry that adheres to doctrinaire opinion divorced from reality'.[81] 'He spoke of my "superabundance of spite & spleen" and my "vitriolic rhetoric" till I felt quite above myself', Chamberlain cheerfully recorded of Snowden's remarks after the debate.[82] In contrast, Chamberlain's response to Wheatley's Housing (Financial Provisions) Bill was rather more complex. Chamberlain was contemptuous of Wheatley's intelligence, ministerial competence and the underlying objectives of his legislation – particularly its increased subsidy level and restored emphasis on council housing as a social service. As a result, his forensic critique of the bill on 4 June was hailed by *The Times* as 'a deadly analysis of his proposals, and a skilful interrogation by one who knew the subject from the first to last letter of the alphabet'.[83] Yet rather than alienate public opinion by negative parliamentary criticism and obstructionism on a crucial national issue, Chamberlain believed the only safe course was to kill the Wheatley bill with kindness. Convinced that it was 'fundamentally rotten and the sooner it fails the better', he thus posed as a reasonable critic in the hopes of highlighting the bill's defects while refusing to improve it through amendments or constructive dialogue with the minister.[84]

Alongside his success in demolishing the Labour government's programme, Chamberlain simultaneously played a more constructive role in outlining the 'New Conservatism' which emerged during 1924 to fill the void left by the suspension of tariff reform. Pressure for a restatement of the party's programme –

---

[79] See Neville Chamberlain Diary, 6 February 1924 and Austen Chamberlain memorandum, 7 February 1924, AC35/4/5; A. Chamberlain to Ida, 9 February 1924, AC5/1/307.

[80] *H.C. Debs*, 5s, 171 col. 2302 and 2207, 2 April and 31 March 1924.

[81] *H.C. Debs*, 5s, 174 col. 247–59, 27 May 1924.

[82] N. Chamberlain to Hilda, 1 June 1924.

[83] *The Times*, 5 June 1924.

[84] N. Chamberlain to Hilda, 1 and 28 June, 12 July 1924.

particularly on social policy – was already apparent when the Conservatives retired into Opposition.[85] To satisfy these demands a Leaders' Conference met for the first time on 2 April to 'decide larger questions of policy', while a parallel Standing Conference of ex-ministers from the Commons organised subcommittees on the Cabinet Committee model, assisted by an innovative small Policy Secretariat under Lancelot Storr.[86] The statement of *Aims and Principles* which emerged from this structure was in gestation for only two months and largely reflected Chamberlain's dominance and social reforming preoccupations. Having discussed the preliminary drafts prepared first by Hoare, Wood and Amery and then by Curzon, Chamberlain rejected both as unsatisfactory and produced his own draft offering an 'authoritative statement of the attitude of the Unionist Party towards the main political questions of the day'.[87] At the Leaders' Conference on 1 May this was accepted after 'the usual somewhat desultory discussion'.[88]

Chamberlain's draft was as comprehensive as it was deliberately unspectacular. Abroad, it committed the party to strengthen and develop the empire, to work towards gradual Indian self-government, to protect Irish Loyalists and to defend British interests in Egypt and the Sudan. Beyond this, there were declarations in favour of honouring the post-war treaties, support for the League of Nations and a vague suggestion of arms limitation, although again only insofar as was compatible with British interests. At home, there were references to co-partnership in industry, abolition of the political levy, greater assistance for agriculture, housing, pensions, temperance without compulsion and the cause of ex-servicemen and Lords Reform.[89] In short, therefore, *Aims and Principles* provided a statement of good intentions appropriated as the exclusive preserve of Conservatism. Yet although Chamberlain was pleased with the public response to *Aims and Principles*, many others considered that there 'never was a more colourless document'.[90] The veteran tariff reformer W.A.S. Hewins thought it 'deplorable' and symptomatic of the party's decline into 'a sort of amiable dotage'. Two weeks later he proclaimed that it had 'fallen quite flat'.[91] From the other end of the fiscal spectrum, Lord Robert Cecil was equally pessimistic when he declared, 'I hope it pleases someone but I really don't know who'.[92] Yet in drafting

---

[85] Neville Chamberlain Diary, 6 February 1924.

[86] For the structure and membership see Lancelot Storr to Lord Robert Cecil, 5 April 1924, Cecil MSS 51085/124 (British Library, Add. MSS). Also Worthington-Evans MSS c.894/125–205.

[87] L.C.3(24), Chamberlain memorandum, Worthington-Evans MSS c.895/5–8.

[88] N. Chamberlain to Ida, 4 May 1924. For the discussion see L.C.4(24), 1 May 1924, Cecil MSS 51075/135 and Amery Diary, 1 May 1924.

[89] *Gleanings and Memoranda*, July 1924, pp. 11–15.

[90] Sir Edward Grigg to Sir Abe Bailey, 10 July 1924, Altrincham MSS (Bodleian Library, Oxford).

[91] Hewins Diary, 20 June and 3 July 1924 (reproduced by the kind permission of the University Librarian, University of Sheffield).

[92] Lord Robert Cecil to Lord Salisbury, 17 May 1924, Salisbury MSS 109/50 (Hatfield House).

Aims and Principles Neville Chamberlain had not intended to excite political histrionics. At the Hotel Cecil in February the general tariff had been abandoned as the central plank in the Conservative platform in favour of something less disruptive: *Aims and Principles* spelled out Chamberlain's vision of this alternative foundation for popular Conservatism in terms of political stability and social reform. With its publication the age of modified 'tranquillity' had dawned, with Baldwin as its articulator and living expression and Neville Chamberlain as its principal architect.

Despite these plans for a return to government, throughout 1924 the narrowness of his majority and the vigour of Labour campaigning in Ladywood had ensured that Chamberlain remained anxious about the outcome of the next election. Yet, although the electoral battle in the constituency was fiercely contested and characterised by an even greater degree of organised rowdyism than in previous elections, he found the campaign less exhausting than in 1923. After disappointing indications earlier in the day, however, the Chamberlains attended the count prepared 'to face the worst with calmness', in the knowledge that they had Edgbaston to fall back on should they be defeated. In the event, after five recounts Chamberlain was finally declared the victor by seventy-seven votes, amidst scenes of exceptional rowdiness stirred up by Mosley. Confident that next time the seat would be lost, Chamberlain accepted the Edgbaston invitation when it was formally offered in July 1926. At the 1929 general election Ladywood was lost to Labour by eleven votes. In the wake of their electoral landslide in October 1924, however, Chamberlain rejoiced at a relatively lucrative ministerial salary which he dearly needed to dispel increasing financial worries,[93] and the opportunity to achieve worthwhile reforms. Although aware that his friends wanted him to accept the Treasury and that Baldwin would feel obliged to offer it to him, Chamberlain was determined that he should return to Health in the belief that he 'might be a great Minister of Health but ... not likely to be more than a second rate Chancellor'.[94] Convinced that 'unless we leave our mark as social reformers the country will take it out of us hereafter',[95] he immediately settled down to plan a four-year programme of comprehensive reform going well beyond housing to embrace local government finance, Poor Law, pensions, health insurance and the reorganisation of the medical services.

---

[93] N. Chamberlain to John St Loe Strachey, 20 September 1924, Strachey MSS 5/4/7/4 (House of Lords Record Office, Hist. Coll. 196); N. Chamberlain to Hilda, 14 February 1925.

[94] N. Chamberlain to Ida, 26 October 1924 and Amery Diary, 1–3 November 1924, I, pp. 389–90.

[95] N. Chamberlain to Ida, 1 November 1924.

V

Soon after the Conservative's 1924 election landslide Beaverbrook noted that 'Britain has at last attained Bonar Law's ideal of tranquillity – under Baldwin. As long as the Conservative Government do nothing, they can go on for a very long time'.[96] Yet the idea that 'tranquillity' could be equated with legislative inertia had no part in Chamberlain's vision. By 19 November Chamberlain had presented his provisional programme to the Cabinet, outlining twenty-five measures covering everything from reform of pensions, housing, rent restrictions, rating, the Poor Law and local government to legislation dealing with milk hygiene, the control of therapeutic substances, smoke abatement, the regulation of maternity homes and the registration of births, marriages and deaths.[97] By the time the second Baldwin government left office in 1929 no fewer than twenty-one of these proposals had been passed. On these legislative foundations Chamberlain built his reputation as 'the most effective social reformer of the interwar years'.[98]

Perhaps the most popular of Neville Chamberlain's social reforms was introduced during his first parliamentary session in the shape of the Widows', Orphans' and Old Age Contributory Pensions Act of 1925. Against a background of mounting pressure for some form of unified social insurance scheme, an interdepartmental committee under Sir Henry Betterton had concluded in December 1923 that the gaps in existing public welfare provision could only be filled by a comprehensive rebuilding of the entire benefits system. On these lines, both Liberals and Conservatives included the proposal in their manifestos for the December 1923 election and in the following month Beveridge's famous pamphlet, *Insurance for All and Everything*, proposed a contributory flat-rate national insurance stamp to cover a unified system embracing not merely sickness and unemployment but old age, industrial accidents and the support of widows and orphans.[99] Although Chamberlain appears to have given little thought to the issue when at the Ministry of Health, before leaving office the government had established a review of the coordination of welfare services by a semi-official committee of seven senior civil servants under Sir John Anderson. In July 1924 their report dismissed Beveridge's ideas of 'all-in' insurance, but proposed a less ambitious scheme of compulsory contributory pensions to cover widows, orphans and old age to which the State would be the principal contribu-

---

[96] Beaverbrook to R.L. Borden, 28 January 1925, Beaverbrook MSS C/51 (House of Lords Record Office, Hist. Coll. 184).

[97] CP 499(24) 'Provisional Programme of Legislation', 19 November 1924, CAB 24/168.

[98] A.J.P. Taylor, *English History, 1914–1945* (London: Pelican, 1975), p.303; Bentley B. Gilbert, *British Social Policy 1914–1939* (London: Batsford, 1970), p. 195; R. Blake, *The Conservative Party from Peel to Thatcher* (London, 1975), p. 228.

[99] José Harris, *William Beveridge: A Biography* (Oxford, 1977), pp. 313, 349–51.

tor.[100] At the same time, Chamberlain had already come to similar conclusions before establishing his own party subcommittee to consider the details.[101] Although the actuarial provisions still remained unresolved, in their 1924 manifesto the Conservatives thus argued that the only method of overcoming existing problems with the means test, the discouragement of thrift and the inadequacy of the existing level of pensions was to introduce a contributory scheme integrating pensions for old age, widows and orphans 'as a right, for which payment has been made, instead of as a dole or a charity'.[102]

Although Chamberlain had initially scheduled pension reform for 1926, at Churchill's instigation the measure was moved forward to 1925 on the grounds that it was 'a fence to jump at a gallop'.[103] In part, this was because it appeared to be a popular measure with the working class, capable of balancing the planned income tax cuts for the middle class in Churchill's first Budget. Yet pensions also satisfied Churchill's desire for the government to leave behind it a number of 'big landmarks': a priority which required it to 'concentrate on a few great issues in the social sphere ... rather than fritter away our resources on a variety of services which, though possibly good in themselves, were not of vital national importance'.[104] Known only to Baldwin, within two weeks of returning to office Chamberlain and Churchill had begun work on the scheme. At the heart of the plan presented to the Cabinet for the first time in April, was a compulsory contributory scheme encompassing all those already covered by health insurance, offering old age pensions of 10s (50p) per week to insured men and their wives between sixty-five and seventy before they passed into the 1908 non-contributory scheme; widows also received 10s per week plus 5s (25p) for their eldest child and 3s (15p) for each subsequent child under fourteen. Orphans of insured men were to receive 7s 6d (37½p) for the eldest child under fourteen and 6s (30p) for each additional orphan. These pensions for widows and orphans came into force on 1 January 1926, but to spare the Treasury further cost, regular contributors were scheduled to receive the other benefits two years later.[105] By 'rounding off the great insurance plan of 1911', Chamberlain declared that the Bill completed what he called 'the circle of security for the worker'.[106]

---

[100] Committee on Insurance and other Social Services: Second Interim Report, appended to CP 204(25), 18 April 1925, CAB 24/173.

[101] N. Chamberlain to Hilda, 22 March and 12 July 1924.

[102] *Gleanings and Memoranda*, November 1924, p. 505; N. Chamberlain Election Address 1924, NC18/1/457a.

[103] Martin Gilbert, *Winston S. Churchill, Volume V, 1922–1939* (London, 1976), pp. 77–78.

[104] CAB 64(24)6, 26 November and CAB 65(24)5, 3 December 1924, CAB 23/49. Also Jones Diary, 28 November 1924, Keith Middlemas (ed.), *Thomas Jones: Whitehall Diary*, 2 vols (London, 1969), I, p.307.

[105] CP 204(25) 'Improved Old Age Pensions and Pensions for Widowed Mothers', 18 April 1925, CAB 24/173.

[106] *H.C. Debs*, 5s, 184 col. 92, 18 May 1925.

Although pensions encountered opposition both in the Commons and from vested interests outside it, Chamberlain experienced far more difficulty with his other major measure of 1925 designed to reform the system of rating and valuation. The Conservatives had planned to reform the machinery of rating and valuation while leaving the principles unchanged in 1923, but the government had fallen before it had time to act. By March 1925, however, Chamberlain was pressing the Cabinet for immediate action to introduce essentially the same Rating and Valuation Bill given the length and complexity of its over seventy clauses and seven or eight schedules.[107] Part 1 of the Bill proposed the abolition of parochial rating in order to reduce the number of rating authorities from 12,844 to 648 in rural districts and from 2,550 to 1,148 in urban areas. In future, rating was to be concentrated in the larger local authorities as the 'real living bodies of today', while consolidating up to twenty charges in some rural districts into a single 'general rate' for all local purposes. Part 2 sought to simplify the process of assessment and to introduce uniformity of practice, without which it would be 'impossible to formulate any practicable scheme for the settlement of the vexed question of the relations between national and local taxation'.[108] By 29 April the Cabinet had approved the Bill and its passage given the 'desirability of passing it during the present session of Parliament as an indispensable preliminary to the reform of the Poor Law and other portions of the Government's social reform policy'.[109]

While Chamberlain was convinced that 'when it has time to work the Party will point to it as one of the great reforms of which it can be proud',[110] he always anticipated stiff opposition. Such fears were fully justified – particularly given the obstruction of Churchill, and the repeated faint-heartedness of the whips who regularly employed their almost unlimited 'powers of passive resistance' to delay a measure they believed to be unpopular with core supporters in the country. After a series of crises in May, efforts to force the bill's complete withdrawal were only prevented when Chamberlain stood firm with Baldwin's resolute support. Thereafter, although Chamberlain drew on all his formidable gifts to overwhelm opposition during its Second Reading in May, the Bill made 'very heavy weather in Committee' until a meeting with anxious MPs in July persuaded him to make significant concessions. By October, however, alarm at the bill's unpopularity with government backbenchers and the voters again prompted the Cabinet to reaffirm 'that there was no question of dropping so important a measure which has already reached an advanced stage', but that

---

[107] CP 189(25) 'Rating and Valuation', 31 March 1925, CAB 24/172 and CAB 19(25)10; 1 April 1925, CAB 23/49.

[108] CP 193(25) and CP 209(25) 'Home Affairs Committee: Rating and Valuation', 2 and 22 April 1925, CAB 24/172–73. Also *H.C. Debs*, 5s, 183 col. 1873–92, 13 May 1925.

[109] CAB 23(25)7, 29 April 1925, CAB 23/50.

[110] N. Chamberlain to Baldwin, 30 August 1925, Baldwin MSS 43/51 (Cambridge University Library).

further concessions would facilitate its passage through the remaining stages.[111] In particular, to appease the backbench Agricultural Committee it was agreed that farm buildings should also receive the 75 per cent rating rebate scheduled for machinery and that both should be left to a free vote in order to maximise support. After a final address to a mass meeting of Conservative backbenchers in late November, Chamberlain steadied nerves sufficiently for the bill to complete its passage in December.[112]

Rather less satisfactory progress was made with regard to efforts to solve the housing shortage. By offering his subsidy over two years in the 1923 Housing Act, Chamberlain had acknowledged that it was essentially an interim measure, designed to prevent the situation getting any worse while the government developed new methods of stimulating private enterprise to bridge the gap between construction costs and an economic rent that lower-paid tenants could afford.[113] Anxious to avoid any unnecessary interference with private enterprise, Chamberlain was reluctant to intervene directly to tackle the problems of labour and material shortages which had driven up building costs since the Armistice. Yet, on the other hand, such logic did not preclude the promotion of alternative materials and techniques to reduce construction costs. Ultimately, this quest led Chamberlain into a frustrating campaign to encourage the widespread acceptance of prefabricated timber-framed steel-clad houses mass-produced in factories and assembled on-site by unemployed unskilled labour working for engineering rates of pay.

The principal exponent of this concept was Lord Weir, a self-confident, aggressively anti-union Glasgow industrialist and technocratic problem-solver. The success of Weir's steamship engineering business had been founded upon the principles of standardisation in production and payment by results and he hoped to apply the same practices to the housing problem. By building cheap prefabricated steel houses with standardised fittings, Weir believed he could simultaneously solve the housing shortage, reduce expenditure on unemployment relief and undermine the stranglehold of the National Federation of Building Trades Operatives in order to force down building costs and wage rates in an exploitative sheltered trade.[114] Contrary to claims that Churchill was the enthusiastic driving force behind the Conservative government's entanglement with steel houses while Chamberlain remained cautious,[115] within two weeks of becoming

---

[111] CAB 50(25)6, 23 October 1925, CAB 23/51.

[112] CAB 54(25)2, 25 November 1925, CAB 23/51; N. Chamberlain to Ida, 22 November 1925.

[113] N. Chamberlain to Ida, 17 March 1923; *H.C. Debs*, 5s, 163 col. 303–22, 24 April 1923.

[114] W.J. Reader, *Architect of Air Power: The Life of the First Viscount Weir of Eastwood 1877–1959* (London, 1968), pp. 117–26, and Reader, *The Weir Group: A Centenary History* (London, 1971), pp. 98–102.

[115] Reader, *Architect*, p. 120. Also Paul Addison, 'Churchill and Social Reform', in Robert Blake and Wm. Roger Louis, *Churchill* (Oxford, 1996), p. 67.

Minister of Health in 1923 Chamberlain began discussions with Weir on his proposals, and after examining a demonstration model in July 1924 he was even more convinced that it offered a viable solution given an estimated price of £300 for a non-parlour house.[116] The Conservative manifesto in October 1924 thus emphasised that sufficient new houses for the poorer classes could only be achieved by the employment of these new methods of construction.

In practice, this implied a direct commitment to ensure the success of Weir's scheme given the unrealistically higher cost of the other models available.[117] Yet, unfortunately for the government, there were two major problems with such a commitment. First, Chamberlain recognised that the novelty of the method and materials would inevitably ensure that local authorities would not place the necessary bulk orders before extensive and protracted trials were completed. To overcome this problem, one of his first actions on returning to office was to subsidise various demonstration models in order to popularise the concept with local authorities. Second, and more immediately damaging, Weir had an established reputation as an aggressive class warrior and there was little doubt that his direct challenge to the craft unions owed as much to political motives as to an entrepreneurial desire to generate profits.[118] As a result, Weir's plans inevitably provoked the determined opposition of the building unions, who contended that the 'fair wages clause' in Wheatley's Housing Act demanded that Weir's men should be paid the rates prevailing in the building trade rather than in engineering. To make this demand effective, in December 1924 the union withdrew its labour from Glasgow Corporation in order to halt the erection of twenty experimental Weir houses at Drumoyne using unemployed men.[119]

While this politically explosive threat remained unresolved, the government recognised that other councils would not place orders. Yet despite the pessimism of his Permanent Secretary, and the increasing timidity of local authorities such as Leeds and Sheffield, Chamberlain refused to accept defeat. In late February he decided 'to risk everything on a Court of Enquiry', in the confident expectation that it would recommend a modification to the 'fair wages clause' in such a way as to absolve the government from 'reasonable suspicion that we are making an attack upon trade union standards'.[120] Yet while the enquiry did find in favour of Weir, by the end of the year the position in Scotland remained deadlocked, despite Chamberlain's proposal for an additional subsidy of £40 per unit for the first 4000 steel houses erected in Scotland, and then the government's direct intervention to construct them independently of the local authorities through the Scottish National

---

[116] N. Chamberlain to Ida, 19 July 1924.
[117] CP 49(25) 'Weir Houses', 28 January 1925, CAB 24/171.
[118] Reader, *Weir Group*, p. 100; Reader, *Architect*, p. 119.
[119] *The Times*, 19 December 1924.
[120] N. Chamberlain to Hilda, 21 February 1925; CP 132(25) 'Weir Houses', 3 March 1925, CAB 24/172.

Housing Company.[121] Ultimately, it was a measure of Chamberlain's initiative, determination and ascendancy, that although these developments were technically outside the remit of his department, his lack of confidence in the Scottish Office ensured that he became the principal force in shaping policy during 1925 on the grounds that it was 'too important to be allowed to go wrong'.[122] By early 1926, however, Weir had lost interest in the project[123] and Chamberlain also swiftly became less enthusiastic, given the very satisfactory progress of building south of the border and the relatively high cost of Weir houses. Indeed, in July 1926 he proposed a reduction in the house building subsidies from £6 to £4 for twenty years under the Chamberlain Act and from £9 to £7 10s for forty years (£11 in rural areas) under Wheatley's Act.[124] As building costs continued to fall, in 1928 a further cut was announced in the Wheatley subsidy along with the total abolition of its 1923 counterpart on all houses completed after September 1929.

Despite this frustration over steel houses, Chamberlain's first full year at the Ministry of Health was one of remarkable achievement. Beside contributory pensions and rating reform, bills were passed to regulate the manufacture and distribution of proprietary medicines and therapeutic substances, along with important consolidation Acts for Housing, Public Health and Town Planning. On this basis, after only six months in office Chamberlain was talking of 'the Golden Age at the Ministry' and confiding to his sisters the hope that although he was never likely to become a favourite of the Press like his father or Churchill, 'if I have 4 or 5 years of office I may leave behind as ... great a reputation as Minister of Health as Father did as Colonial Secretary'.[125] Plans for 1926 included eight bills, of which perhaps the most important was the Housing (Rural Workers) Bill which provided Exchequer grants to cover half the total cost of local authority loans to those owners engaged in improvements to rural housing, in return for controls over future rent levels.[126] Although to Chamberlain's intense frustration these new powers generated relatively little response from the local authorities, they represented a minor victory for his commitment to the concept of subsidised property 'reconditioning', over those like Churchill who preferred to demolish and build new and better houses.[127] In 1927 more worthwhile legislation was added with regard to the registration and supervision of nursing homes and a humane reform of the definition of 'mental deficiency' to assist the treatment and care of those suffering from 'sleepy sickness'.

---

[121] CP 466(25) 'Scottish Housing Conference', 9 November 1925, CAB 24/175; CAB 52(25)8, 11 November 1925 and CAB 60(25)1, 18 December 1925, CAB 23/51.

[122] N. Chamberlain to Hilda, 14 November 1925.

[123] Reader, *Architect*, p.125.

[124] CP 290(26) 'Housing, Reconsideration of Subsidy', 27 July and CP 357(26) 'Housing Subsidies', 21 October 1926, CAB 24/180–81.

[125] N. Chamberlain to Ida, 23 May 1925.

[126] CAB 48(26)10, 28 July 1927, CAB 23/53.

[127] Jones Diary, 29 January 1926, II, pp. 5–6.

Yet despite the scope of all this useful activity, the middle period of Chamberlain's term at the Ministry of Health did not live up to the confident constructive optimism of 1925. In part this change in tone can be attributed to the shadow cast by the General Strike in May and the devastating effects of the coal stoppage which continued until the end of the year. Government responses to these events inevitably cast Chamberlain in a essentially negative role as the upholder of harsh regulations on outdoor relief scales over Boards of Guardians inclined to be more generous and humane. Equally inevitably, this posture provoked ferocious Labour condemnation for policies alleged to have increased infant mortality and contributed to the near-starvation of entire mining communities – particularly as Chamberlain made little effort to disguise his contempt for the 'sentimental sob-stuff' uttered by Labour MPs or his disbelief in the existence of any abnormal hardship.[128] Yet partisan tensions of this sort were already evident after his leading role in the passage of the deeply unpopular Economy (Miscellaneous Provisions) Bill in March-April 1926, which included a wide range of cuts in public expenditure. Moreover, while the substance of the bill ensured that he was 'cursed and abused for a thief, a cad and a bully', his tough-minded tactics in dealing with concerted Labour obstructionism aroused still more violent denunciations and hostility.[129] Perhaps significantly, during this period Chamberlain's tone and manner were undoubtedly sharpened by deep personal alarm and depression, caused by his wife's slide into something approaching a nervous breakdown in March and then the painful protracted separation during her recovery.[130] Beyond his aggressive conduct during the Economy Bill and the coal dispute, however, the bitterness of Labour attacks was also intensified by Chamberlain's determination to deal effectively with what he saw as the pervasive abuse and corruption of the Poor Law. Although in the longer term these efforts resulted in his greatest administrative achievement in the Local Government Act of 1929, during 1926–27 the subject of Poor Law reform was dominated by a largely negative battle for control over the 'extravagance' of Boards of Guardians, while simultaneously attempting to persuade more timorous Cabinet colleagues of the need for more radical restructuring.

VI

Bentley B. Gilbert had rightly argued that Poor Law reform was one of the oldest and most complex questions of social politics and one 'easier to deplore than to discuss intelligently, let alone to try and solve'. After the failure of

---

[128] N. Chamberlain to Hilda, 13 June and 20 June 1926.

[129] N. Chamberlain to Hilda, 18 April 1926. Also Hugh Dalton, *Call Back Yesterday: Memoirs 1887–1931* (London, 1953), pp. 160–61. *Annual Register, 1926*, pp. 40–41.

[130] N. Chamberlain to Ida, 13 and 27 March 1926.

Addison's effort at reform, the matter was effectively allowed to lapse until Neville Chamberlain emerged determined to act where all others lacked the knowledge, the enthusiasm and the political courage to reform effectively. Yet it is often alleged that the principal difference between Chamberlain and his reforming antecedents, such as Addison, Morant, the Webbs and the Maclean Committee, was that while these all hoped to resolve the inadequacy of Poor Law provision by making it part of a general administrative structure dealing with all forms of social and economic need, Chamberlain's approach to reform was motivated by a far narrower bureaucratic desire simply to improve functional efficiency: 'Chamberlain cared less about the effect of the Poor Law on economic society than that it functioned badly, that it was a broken piece of administrative apparatus. The writers of the MacLean [sic] Report saw relief from the bottom, from the "consumer's" point of view. Chamberlain looked at it from the top down'.[131] On this basis, Chamberlain's achievements at the Ministry of Health are too often dismissed as simple matters of 'administrative rationalisation'.[132]

While such distinctions of motivation and perspective did exist, they have far more validity with regard to Chamberlain's determination to curb the 'extravagant' expenditure and 'lax' administration of some Poor Law Unions than they do when applied to his broader vision of reform for the entire structure of Poor Law and health provision. Without doubt, Chamberlain's bureaucratic cast of mind was offended by the wasteful overlap and untidy confusion of administrative boundaries and responsibilities, at a time when no fewer than seven public authorities might provide financial assistance in the home, six supplied various forms of medical treatment and five supported the able-bodied unemployed.[133] It is equally undeniable that Chamberlain's unrivalled knowledge of local government meant that he dwelt at length upon the institutional obstacles and bureaucratic details in a manner in which Churchill's febrile imagination unencumbered by any practical understanding never did. Yet it was precisely this direct personal grasp and experience which enabled Chamberlain to see, as few others did, both the need for unified local authority services and the importance of a programme of interlocking stages of reform to achieve this ultimate objective. As his private secretary later recalled, from the outset Chamberlain 'saw the whole thing as none of us in the Ministry saw it, as just part of a single great problem'.[134] From this perspective, reform of rating and valuation in 1925 was an essential prerequisite for any progressive change in the system of central government grants to local authorities. In their turn, such reforms were a neces-

---

[131] Bentley B. Gilbert, *British Social Policy*, pp. 204, 210–12

[132] Clive Unsworth, *The Politics of Mental Health Legislation*, (Oxford, 1987), pp. 236–37.

[133] Dilks, *Neville Chamberlain*, p.493.

[134] Sir Douglas Veale interview with Professor Brian Harrison, 14 January 1969, Interview I, c.608/01, F4381, (British Library, National Sound Archive); Dilks, *Neville Chamberlain*, p. 413.

sary prelude to the eventual abolition of the Poor Law, the fundamental restructuring of central–local relations and the emergence of a properly organised and efficient health service. Similarly, his efforts 'to tighten the reins and bring ... the Guardians back to their proper functions' were less an indication of Chamberlain's narrow bureaucratic inhumanity than a realistic recognition of the fact that sustained post-war unemployment had exposed fundamental gaps in existing provision for the able-bodied unemployed. Effectively abandoned by the Ministry of Health in 1921, Chamberlain deprecated the fact that by forcing these men onto Poor Law relief the government had demoralised both the guardians and the recipients of their relief, as it ended 'in pushing them down in the scale, instead of pulling them up to something better'. Against this background, Chamberlain's efforts to control expenditure on outdoor relief stemmed less from a mean-spirited, soulless concern about the primacy of punitive regulations than a more radical recognition that the national and international causes of unemployment implied the need to accept State responsibility for unemployment relief as a national charge, rather than permitting it to remain an inequitable burden on local authorities dispensed by corrupted institutions.[135]

The roots of Chamberlain's battle for control over outdoor relief can be traced back to the 'Revolt of Poplar' in the autumn of 1921.[136] Although the practice of granting outdoor relief to able-bodied men was scarcely new, when Poplar Borough Council refused to levy rates for the Metropolitan Asylums Board, the Metropolitan Police and the London County Council (LCC) in order to cover its own abnormally high outdoor relief costs, thirty councillors were imprisoned. In the event, both the LCC and the government backed away from confrontation by releasing the councillors after an apology, before Mond hurriedly passed the Local Authorities (Financial Provisions) Act in November 1921, which increased the Metropolitan Common Poor Fund contribution for indoor relief and took over the entire cost of outdoor relief, thereby ensuring that the wealthier parts of London heavily subsidised those poorer Unions with highest levels of unemployment and pauperism.

From Chamberlain's perspective, the 'extravagance' and 'lax' administration of Poplarist Boards of Guardians, in blatant defiance of Poor Law principles and central government direction, offended his cardinal Benthamite belief that 'local government can only be kept efficient and vigorous if it is made to exercise responsibility, and if necessary, suffer the consequences of its own mistakes'.[137]

---

[135] Jones Diary, 2 December 1927, II, pp. 118–20.

[136] For 'Poplarism' and its origins see Sidney and Beatrice Webb, *English Poor Law History: Part II The Last Hundred Years* (London, 1929), pp. 896–900; P.A. Ryan, '"Poplarism" 1894–1930', in Pat Thane (ed.), *The Origins of British Social Policy* (London, 1978), pp. 56–83; Noreen Branson, *Poplarism, 1919–1925: George Lansbury and the Councillors' Revolt*, (London, 1979).

[137] CP 266(23), 'The Question of an Exchequer Grant for Necessitous Areas', 6 June 1923, CAB 24/160.

Equally important, the cynical exploitation of their powers by Labour-controlled Boards of Guardians to win elections added a further political outrage to administrative delinquency in circumstances in which Chamberlain, like many others, feared the ignorance and capricious gullibility of a new mass electorate prepared to bankrupt national and local government to obtain generous benefits for which they were not obliged to pay: concerns given substance by the fact that the Representation of the People Act of 1918 had removed the disqualifications of paupers in respect of Guardians' election as well as for municipal and parliamentary contests. In this context, he thus considered the willingness of the Poplar guardians to pay generous scales of relief to their constituents at the expense of wealthy ratepayers in other areas of London to be the high road to political corruption of the very worst sort.[138]

Before leaving office in 1923 the Conservatives had already decided to obtain powers to replace defaulting Boards of Guardians with ministry nominees.[139] After returning to office in 1924, the problem was soon brought into sharp focus by the predicament of the West Ham guardians, who by 31 March 1925 had accumulated a debt of £1,975,000 and were expending £500,000–£600,000 per annum more than they raised from rates in the Union.[140] When West Ham applied for another advance of £350,000 in June 1925, the Ministry of Health refused to sanction any further loans unless accompanied by new restrictions on outdoor relief. When the guardians refused, the Cabinet agreed that they had no alternative but to intervene without statutory authority and then subsequently pass indemnifying legislation.[141] Yet Chamberlain's longer-term response to the underlying problem was to prepare a 'Guardian Coercion Bill'. In February 1926 he gave the Cabinet a gloomy analysis of the situation in Poplar, West Ham and half a dozen other London Unions, as well as in Durham and South Wales, where the guardians 'adopted a definite policy of transforming Poor Law administration into a system of providing maintenance in lieu of work' on an automatic (and sometimes illegal) basis. As current controls over guardians were 'limited and unsatisfactory', Chamberlain proposed legislation to disqualify recipients of poor relief (other than medical) from voting in Board of Guardian elections, to disqualify guardians who refused to obey restraining injunctions from service and to provide for the replacement of defaulting guardians with Ministry nominees.[142] Although Conservative

---

[138] See HA 20(26), 'Guardians (Default) Bill', 24 June 1926, CAB 26/8. For the issue generally see Alan Deacon and Eric Briggs, 'Local Democracy and Central Policy: The Issue of Pauper Votes in the 1920s', *Policy and Politics*, 2 (1974), pp. 353, 355, 358–64.

[139] CAB 49(23)1, 22 October 1923, CAB 23/46.

[140] Webb, *English Poor Law*, II, pp. 926–29. See also MH 68/81–85 for departmental papers on West Ham.

[141] CP 379(25) 'West Ham', 3 August 1925, CAB 24/174 and CAB 43(25)7, 5 August 1925, CAB 23/50.

[142] CP 50(26) 'The Position and Powers of Boards of Guardians Bill', 9 February 1926, CAB 24/178.

backbench opposition to the likely disenfranchisement of ex-servicemen encouraged the abandonment of the first proposal, when West Ham requested a further loan in July 1926 the Cabinet decided to strike and the Board of Guardians (Default) Act received Royal Assent on 15 July 1926.[143] The West Ham guardians were superseded by Chamberlain's commissioners on 20 July and outdoor relief lists and payments were cut dramatically. Six weeks later the guardians in Chester-le-Street (Durham) were also superseded, according to the Webbs 'not so much because of their bankruptcy, or even of the excessive amount of the Out-Relief, as because of their recalcitrancy in defying the Orders of the Ministry'. In February 1927 the bankrupt guardians of Bedwellty were also displaced.[144] In addition to the imposition of direct control in these three cases, the ministry instituted an intrusive but highly effective Campaign of Inspection of Outdoor Relief in other Unions during 1927–28. Inspectors reviewed the routine administration and operation of guardians by attending meetings, scrutinising relief applications, visiting paupers' homes and urging the use of relief-in-kind along with workhouse and labour tests for suspected malingerers. Although these measures further reduced both scales of relief and the numbers of those relieved in the most insolvent Unions, the Webbs denounced such practices as the replacement of local self-government with 'local dictatorship': a view echoed by modern historians of social policy.[145] Yet while critics denounced Chamberlain's callous inhumanity, from the ministerial perspective such actions were nothing more than a long overdue reassertion of elementary financial discipline to restore the probity of a corrupted and irresponsible local institution.

While Chamberlain believed that the imposition of direct control had been forced upon him, more constructive Poor Law reform had been a prominent feature of the four-year programme outlined in November 1924. This measure was justified on four main grounds. First, the overlap in the health functions of the Poor Law and the local authorities caused administrative confusion and retarded 'real advance in the direction of a properly organised Health Service'. Second, the anticipated conclusions of the Royal Commission on National Health Insurance required the creation of a single unified health authority of an appropriate size in each area. Third, the gradual decrease in the number of recipients of Poor Law relief due to extended unemployment and pension benefits also indicated the opportunity for reform. Finally, at a pragmatic level, Chamberlain warned that unless reform was undertaken in 1926 the need to renew the Local Authorities (Emergency Provisions) Acts, which centralised the cost of outdoor relief in London, 'would revive in an acute form the problem of London government'.[146] At the heart of his plan was the desire to implement the Maclean report

---

[143] CAB 40(26)1, 42(26)7 and 43(26)13 dated 16, 23 and 30 June 1926, CAB 23/53.

[144] Webb, *English Poor Law*, II, pp. 926–934.

[145] Ibid., pp. 929, 934–45; Gilbert, *British Social Policy*, p. 222.

[146] CP 499(24), 'Provisional Programme of Legislation', 19 November 1924.

of January 1918 which proposed the abolition of Boards of Guardians and the break up of the entire system of parochial relief by devolving all of its existing functions and institutions to the appropriate subcommittees of the county and county borough councils.[147] By March 1925 Chamberlain had concluded that such reform should be 'rather a gradual process than a drastic uprooting of present arrangements'.[148] Two months later, the Cabinet agreed that in the first instance the 'Break Up of the Poor Law' should be restricted to the transference of administrative powers in order to provide a unified basis for future reform,[149] and in September an outline scheme had been prepared with the objective of coordinating and improving health and public assistance provision, decentralising the responsibility currently falling on the Ministry of Health and simplifying its financial relationship with the major local authorities.[150] On the explicit understanding that they were not being committed to any particular scheme of Poor Law reform, the Cabinet thus authorised negotiations with the local authorities in October 1925.[151]

Chamberlain's problem was that his own more limited two-stage plan of advance almost immediately became entangled in Churchill's far more grandiose vision of Poor Law reform as part of a wholesale restructuring of rating and local government finance. From the outset, the differences in style and habits of mind between the two men had become apparent.[152] For a man who devoted vast amounts of time, thought and energy to allow for every practical objection before announcing his plans, there was something profoundly unsettling about Churchill's brainstorms and flights of imagination, which lacked any sustained consideration and might easily be cast aside the following day. Worse still, it was painfully apparent that not only did Churchill envy Chamberlain's ability to achieve 'the glory of doing something spectacular' at Health, but that as Chancellor he was determined to make the Treasury 'an active instrument of Government social policy instead of a passive concomitant or even, as it sometimes was, an active opponent'.[153] Churchill's quest for the political limelight became evident immediately over pensions. By October 1925 he clearly also wanted to hijack Chamberlain's plans for Poor Law reform and turn them to his own purposes.

In November 1926 Chamberlain informed the Cabinet that, as consultation with the various local authorities was now complete, he sought authority to

---

[147] CP 219(25), 'A Scheme of Poor Law Reform', 4 April 1925, CAB 24/173.

[148] N. Chamberlain to Ida, 14 March 1925.

[149] CAB 25(25)1, 13 May 1925, CAB 23/50.

[150] CP 410(25), 'Poor Law Reform', 25 September 1925, CAB 24/175.

[151] CAB 50(25)9, 23 October 1925, CAB 23/51.

[152] N. Chamberlain to Hilda, 24 November 1924. Also N. Chamberlain to Baldwin, 30 August 1925, Baldwin MSS 43/49–50.

[153] Neville Chamberlain Diary, 26 November and 1 December 1924; Jones Diary, 28 November 1924, I, p. 307; P.J. Grigg, *Prejudice and Judgement* (London, 1948), p. 174

introduce a bill in the next Session.[154] By this stage, however, Churchill was prepared to support the proposal only if it was accompanied by 'the adoption of a complete scheme of block grants for local services' to replace the traditional system of assigned revenue and percentage grants: a bold approach which offered the Treasury the advantage of being able to forecast and plan precisely for the full range of local services over a fixed period.[155] Although clearly a major obstacle, Chamberlain was heartened by the belief that the 'not unsatisfactory reception' given to his own more limited proposals contrasted favourably with the 'rather chilly atmosphere' created by Churchill's grander scheme[156] – particularly as he pointed out that to proceed on these lines necessitated the establishment of a satisfactory block grant formula and Percy, Guinness, Gilmour and Joynson-Hicks expressed their respective concerns about the problems and implications for education, agriculture, Scotland and the police. As electoral concerns were also uppermost in most minds after their poor performance in the municipal elections earlier in the month, the Cabinet deferred decision for a fortnight to enable Sir George Barstow's committee on block grants to devise a comprehensive scheme.[157] After 'a full discussion' of Chamberlain's proposals at two further meetings on 16–17 December, the Cabinet finally agreed to the preparation of a bill embracing the comprehensive block grant scheme, and authorised negotiations with local authorities while work continued on the block grant formula.[158] The decision was then postponed until the New Year.

In the event, party opposition rapidly mounted towards any measure of controversial reform. At Cabinet on 2 February the subject occupied most of the meeting before it was agreed to include a general statement on Poor Law reform in the King's Speech, but only on the understanding that it 'must be regarded as associated with the adoption of a system of block grants' and that if an acceptable formula could not be devised then Poor Law reform should be completely re-examined.[159] To make matters worse, when the Chief Whip omitted the measure from the parliamentary timetable for the coming session, an unenthusiastic Cabinet cheerfully agreed to postpone it until November. With little support in the Cabinet, the whips' office, the backbenches or in the country, Chamberlain had no option but to accept the delay, in the certain knowledge that in the meanwhile 'all the critics & the diehards and the fainthearts will croak in chorus' to kill the bill.[160] Moreover, in contrast to the Prime Minister's support-

---

[154] CP 389(26) 'Poor Law Reform', 18 November 1926, CAB 24/182. For these consultative talks see MH 57.

[155] CP 395 'Poor Law Reform and Block Grants', November 1926, CAB 24/182.

[156] N. Chamberlain to Hilda, 27 November 1926.

[157] CAB 60(26)7, 24 November 1926, CAB 23/53.

[158] CAB 66(26)5 and CAB 67(26)3, 16–17 December 1926, CAB 23/53.

[159] CAB 5(27)5, 2 February 1927, CAB 23/54.

[160] N. Chamberlain to Hilda, 5 February and 19 March and to Ida, 26 March 1927; Neville Chamberlain Diary, 4 March 1927; Sanders Diary, 13 March 1927.

ive stance over pensions and rating, at a meeting with Baldwin, the Party Chairman and Chief Whip, in early March, Chamberlain found that Baldwin had 'got very cold feet again and the other two are assiduously laying ice packs to his extremities'.[161]

The position was complicated still further in June when Churchill unveiled a new and still more grandiose scheme of rate relief. On 7 June Churchill sent a six-page summary to Chamberlain arguing that a reduction in rates would help 'every class, all parts of the country, every town, every Constituency' while establishing 'a sound relation between national and local finance, with proper incentive to economy and real responsibility for the local bodies'. In reply, Chamberlain cautiously warned that to spend the £30 million proposed 'would provoke quite as much criticism as approval', but undeterred, the Chancellor argued that this was 'fundamental' to the scheme's merits.[162] Not for the first time, Chamberlain privately lamented that 'Winston has gone off the deep end and is in full cry after a new and I fear fantastic plan … He has a fertile mind but I do wish he were steadier. I fear in pursuing these imaginative flights he will lose interest in really practical proposals'.[163] Thereafter, despite Churchill's persistent efforts to persuade Chamberlain to cooperate in a bolder scheme to achieve their mutual objectives,[164] their differences of outlook, objective and ambition were to dog the progress of both men's plans throughout the remainder of 1927. By mid-December, however, Churchill's plan for de-rating was complete and he was ready to resume the offensive against Chamberlain scepticism.[165] From Chamberlain's perspective, the plan was 'unwise immoral and dangerous', but while Churchill held the government's purse strings he had no choice but to humour him. Trapped between a Chancellor seeking to go much further than he believed either practicable or desirable and the collective opposition to any controversial reform from the guardians, local authorities, Cabinet, party managers and backbenchers, Chamberlain ended the year convinced that his own plans for Poor Law reform would be deferred until after the next general election and so deny him the crowning achievement of five years of solid reform.[166]

---

[161] N. Chamberlain to Hilda, 5 March 1927.

[162] Churchill to N. Chamberlain, 7 June and reply 10 June 1927, Gilbert, *Churchill*, V, pp. 241–42 and *Companion* V.I, pp. 1006–11.

[163] Neville Chamberlain Diary, 16 June 1927. Also N. Chamberlain to Hilda, 24 July, 30 October and 12 November 1927.

[164] Churchill to N. Chamberlain, 18 October 1927, NC7/9/12.

[165] Churchill to Baldwin, 17 December 1927, Gilbert, *Churchill*, V, p. 254; Churchill to N. Chamberlain, 17 December 1927, NC7/9/14.

[166] N. Chamberlain to Hilda, 11 December 1927. Also Sanders Diary, 23 December 1927.

2

1921

'To Speculate on Austen's Position': Backbench Frustrations and Disappointments

1 January 1921
Westbourne, Edgbaston

My dear Hilda,

I can hear the rain sousing down outside but I suppose it cant go on raining always so I wish you a very Happy New Year. We did enjoy having you and Ida here for Christmas. Writing is very well and has the advantage of making a sort of diary but it is good to meet occasionally and say some of the things which one is too lazy to write. Besides as you say in your letter to Annie we are interested in one another's doings and like to hear about them at first hand.

… Miss P[arkes][1] has been kept busy doing my report on Living in on Canal Boats which I have completed today to my great content, as Mr Pepys says. Tomorrow I must begin working at the draft of the Slum report & on Wed. & Thurs. I must be in London for Canals. Still I hope to be rid of 3 committees before long.

I see my protégé Holcroft[2] *is* among the new baronets today so there is one obligation worked off and the field is free for the next naughty trick. I wonder if Mr Calthorpe has spotted him!

I hear from Hall that he thinks Hoskins has done very well this year. If only it wasn't for A's[3] beastly E.P.D. we might do very well too but as it is I suppose he will grab most of it. But perhaps there may be "something for me, Mr Weller" too.

I have just finished Dizzy. It is certainly an extraordinarily interesting life & I feel I ought now to read Morley's Gladstone. But I don't look forward to it!

…

---

[1] Secretary to the Chamberlains from June 1919 but 'not congenial' to either and she left in April 1921 after 'words' were regularly exchanged.

[2] George Henry Holcroft (1856–1951). JP for Warwickshire and Staffordshire. Created Bart 1921.

[3] (Joseph) Austen Chamberlain (1863–1937). Liberal Unionist MP for Worcestershire East 1892–1914 (a Conservative from 1906) and Birmingham West 1914–37. Civil Lord of Admiralty 1895–1900; Financial Secretary to Treasury 1902; Postmaster-General 1902–3; Chancellor of Exchequer 1903–5 and 1919–21; Secretary of State for India 1915–17; Minister without Portfolio in War Cabinet 1918–19; Lord Privy Seal and Leader of Conservative Party 1921–22; Foreign Secretary 1924–29; First Lord of Admiralty 1931. Created KG 1925.

8 January 1921
Westbourne

My dear Ida,

… I offer my sympathy in respect of the Housing Problem. It really will be interesting to see what does happen eventually, but meanwhile the position here is significant. The Finance Committee have declared that they can find no more money and any further extensions of the Housing programme have been stopped amid the usual general execration of the Government. I darent say in public what I feel "A good job too!" but I hope it may all help towards an appreciation of my little plans for the improvement of Slum Property. I am engaged in drafting our Final Report … I don't suppose anything will come of it.

…

I had quite interesting meetings in London (all Canals) but it ended in my undertaking to draft another interim Report. I don't feel that I can give it to anyone else to do & of course it has got to be done sometime but it seems like goodbye to any hopes of finishing my memoir of Norman[4] this recess. However there it is; it keeps me very busy with all the other things I have to do but it prevents time from hanging heavy on my hands! The first night I spent alone in London bored me stiff so the second I decided to pass at some place of entertainment. I didn't feel like a "high brow" play in my solitude and the alleged farces generally make me tired so I went to the Coliseum and enjoyed myself right ealong [sic]. There was a performing sea lion and marvellous acrobats, Madame Karsavina[5] in Nursery Rhymes and finally Grock[6] "the famous French clown". Oh dear how I cried! The tears streamed down my cheeks and my sides fairly ached. I haven't seen anything so funny for a long time.

I went down to Hoskins on Friday and was there for several hours. I went all round the works and talked to a number of the men especially the older hands. It was pleasant to be received with such welcoming smiles and to find every one apparently so glad to see me. Things seem to be going very well there. Not only are they still as busy as bees but they have 9 months full work still on the books and as prices of materials are rapidly falling they are making money as rapidly. If only that beastly Ch. of the Exch. wasn't going to grab so much of it …

---

[4] Norman Chamberlain (1884–1917). See Appendix I: The Chamberlain household and family.

[5] Tamara (Platonovna) Karsavina (1885–1978). Russian ballet dancer. Prima ballerina, Mariinsky Theatre 1902–9; an original member of Diaghilev Ballets Russes 1909–18. Married English diplomat and moved to London in 1918. Vice-President, Royal Academy of Dancing until 1955.

[6] Charles Adrien Wettach (1880–1959). Swiss clown and mime known as Grock – particularly famous for clowning with violin and piano.

15 January 1921
Westbourne

My dear Hilda,

...

... Evidently the wind is up at the Ministry about Housing as I see it is now being put about that after all we dont need anything like the number of houses we thought and consequently we needn't bother to raise all that money! No wonder people scoff. I have finished my report & sent it to the Secretary to be circulated. I think its an interesting document though I don't expect anything to come of it. My first report (on living-in on Canal Boats) which was drafted in accordance with the unanimous decisions of the Comee has already provoked protests & disagreements from 3 out of the six members of the Committee! It remains to be seen whether I can shepherd them back into the fold but I dont much care as their objections cancel one another out.

Annie and I visited two Womens Club parties on Tuesday night. They were both packed in spite of most inclement weather and the women were thoroughly enjoying themselves. We listened to some vulgar songs (loudly applauded) and said "a few words" but I avoided making "speeches" as on Thursday I had a public meeting for the whole constituency. It went off with great éclat. The room was crowded and 3 recently victorious councillors occupied the platform besides ourselves. Having more time then usual I had taken greater pains with my speech than I generally am able to do and so it was above the average. They were very enthusiastic and assured me that it would make no difference to them how I voted. They would know it was all right. I dont think "Anti-waste" would go down here in an election though of course there is plenty of grousing going on. Dover[7] was a great disappointment for I believe that Polson[8] to be a bad lot but I doubt the Govt being seriously disturbed. It would be different if the victory had been won by a member of an organised party but you can't make a party out of a programme that is all "anti", and neither Liberal nor Labour can make anything satisfactory out of it.

I attended a meeting of the [Birmingham Municipal] Bank Committee and found that deposits amounted to £1,250,000. In the 2nd week of Jan they had the record in deposits which is rather remarkable with so much unemployment about. ...

I have been at B.S.A today & things look pretty gloomy there. Our dividend this year will have to be cut down to ⅓ of what it was last and when I asked the managing director, usually a great optimist, what he thought of next year he

---

[7] Dover by-election, 12 January 1921. Rothermere's Anti-Waste League defeated the official Unionist by 3130 votes by attacking waste and high taxes.

[8] Thomas Andrew Polson (1865–1946). Personal Assistant to Rothermere at Air Ministry 1917–18; Independent Anti-Waste MP for Dover 1921–22. Chairman of Beaverbrook's United Empire Party 1930. Director, British Motor Trade Corporation. Knighted 1919.

declared that he saw no possibility of making profits in any of our companies! Lovely, isn't it. And having just made up my a/cs for last year I find as I expected that I am living on my capital already & that I am likely to be much worse off this year with increased taxation & diminished income.

...

23 January 1921
Westbourne

My dear Ida,

...

... I suspect that our beloved P.M.[9] has been intriguing away while A was at sea and making arrangements for the reversion of the Chancellorship. No doubt you saw the Times article on Monday. I thought it was written with very deadly skill in the first part. The description of A. as a civil servant rather than a politician was not a caricature and the analysis of his weaknesses and in particular his want of originality and constructional power was merciless. Sufficient was said on the other side to give an air of impartiality and yet the general impression was damaging. If the writer had stopped there he would have been able to congratulate himself on a very successful attempt at assassination. But when he proceeded to indicate what a "real statesman" would have done as S. of S. for India & as C. of E. he showed his hand too carelessly, and laid himself open to attack. Moreover he very seriously weakened the power of his opening. But it was a nasty underhand attempt and I was told on Monday by a friend that from information in his possession he believed it to be contrived with the knowledge if not at the instigation of Downing St. He promised on a more favourable opportunity to give me the information: till then I preserve an open mind.

...

30 January 1921
Westbourne

My dear Hilda,

...

We too have heard from Austen & Ivy of the success of their holiday and apparently we may find Ivy still at Westbourne when we get down there. Annie is annoyed at the rather casual way in which they acknowledge our hospitality

---

[9] David Lloyd George (1863–1945). Liberal MP for Caernarvon Boroughs 1890–1945. President, Board of Trade 1906–8; Chancellor of Exchequer 1908–15; Minister of Munitions 1915–16, Secretary for War 1916; Prime Minister 1916–22. Created Earl Lloyd-George of Dwyfor 1945.

and is I believe sending word that Dorothy is to take the end of the table and carve while A. & I. sit on the high chairs!

Personally I don't much believe in A's retirement for I think his successes in the House rather "bucked" him. I thought possibly W. Long[10] might have hung on till after the Budget & that A. might then have had the Admiralty which I believe he would like. But apparently that has been bestowed on the donor of Chequers.[11] Of course *if* it were true as the Times declares that Ll.G. means to have a dissolution after the Budget that wd be followed by a reconstruction of the Cabinet in wh. A. might find a new place. But I don't much believe in the Gen. Election story & if untrue then I don't believe Ll.G. will ask him to budge. But I shouldn't be surprised if Eric Geddes[12] went and A. Neal[13] became the Transport Secretary of a Transport Department of the Bd. of Trade. I don't really see how that Ministry can go on much longer; all its raison d'être is being gradually taken away from it.

…

5 February 1921
Fortfield Hotel, Sidmouth

My dear Ida,

To think that at this very moment our pure souled P.M. is receiving the freedom of Birmingham. I can scarce restrain a tear. But I will do so …

…

Your housing difficulties show I think the effect of changed conditions and changed attitudes at the Ministry of Health. It is my belief that they have got thoroughly frightened and that they are not sorry when an opportunity presents itself of delaying progress to seize it [sic]. The Building trades operatives have

---

[10] Walter Hume Long (1854–1924). Conservative MP for Wiltshire North 1880–85, Devizes 1885–92, Liverpool, West Derby 1893–1900, Bristol South 1900–1906, County Dublin South 1906–10, Strand 1910–18, St George's Westminster 1918–21. Parliamentary Secretary to LGB 1886–92. President, Board of Agriculture 1895–1900; President, LGB 1900–1905 and 1915–16; Chief Secretary for Ireland 1905; Colonial Secretary 1916–19; First Lord of Admiralty 1919–21. Created Viscount 1921.

[11] Arthur Hamilton Lee (1868–1947). Soldier and Conservative MP for Fareham 1900–1918. Civil Lord of Admiralty 1903–5; Parliamentary Secretary, Ministry of Munitions 1915–16; Parliamentary Military Secretary to War Minister 1916; Director-General of Food Production 1917; Minister of Agriculture 1919–21; First Lord of Admiralty 1921–22. Created Baron Lee of Fareham 1918 and Viscount 1922.

[12] Eric Campbell Geddes (1875–1937). Unionist MP for Cambridge 1917–22. First Lord of Admiralty 1917–19; Minister without Portfolio 1919; Minister of Transport 1919–21. Chairman, FBI 1923–24 and of Dunlop and Imperial Airway. Chairman of Committee on National Expenditure 1921. Knighted 1916.

[13] Arthur Neal (1862–1933). Member, Sheffield City Council 1903–21. Coalition Liberal MP for Sheffield Hillsborough 1918–22. Parliamentary Secretary, Ministry of Transport 1919–22.

now got a good answer to the demand to admit fresh hands and as a matter of fact in Birmingham the labour shortage has so far ceased to be acute that the Council has given up all attempts to check "luxury" building ...

...

So Austen has thought it wise to announce the end of E.P.D. I am very glad he has. It was quite obvious that it must go, if only for the reason that E.P. have disappeared and can no longer produce revenue, but the uncertainty was hampering to trade and its removal will give more confidence to manufacturers and assist in the revival of trade which I believe we shall see before very long. I see that the Times has another vicious & spiteful article today. Its ridiculous story about an impending election has been pricked so it endeavours to take its revenge by declaring that if only the Ch. of the E. wd really attend to economy it wd be possible to reduce income tax. Judging by my own feelings it is defeating its own ends for such manifest unfairness inclines me to defend where otherwise I might be disposed to criticise.

...

12 February 1921
Westbourne

My dear Hilda,

...

... I went up to town on Tuesday night in order to attend a Canal Committee next day. I have got my interim Report agreed upon recommending some work on the Trent to be undertaken at once as an unemployed relief scheme. I feel by no means confident that it will go through but it is probably the only bit of canal development that has any chance of success at the moment and if it did get sanctioned I think it would help the general cause a good deal hereafter.

... I am going this afternoon to walk with Platten in order to hear the latest news about Elliotts before leaving for London. They are feeling the slump in some departments but on the whole are fairly well off for work and going ahead all the time with new developments.

At B.S.A where I spent an afternoon this week I believe we are at present losing money on every single thing we make and after discharging 2000 hands we can only employ the remainder 4 days a week. There is absolutely no sign of any improvement there but though we have not sufficient reserves to enable us to pay dividends when we don't earn them yet I believe we shall make money there again before the year is out and then I hope we shall have the sense to build up our resources. As for Hoskins it continues its marvellous career and still sees 8 months work ahead of it. It is an oasis in a desert of unemployment and with great pride Hall had a photo taken last Saturday of the whole street blocked with carts and lorries being despatched with goods to the station ...

...

26 February 1921
Westbourne

My dear Ida,

... Yesterday I came down by the early train in order to attend a B.S.A. board and thereby missed the debate on Mond's[14] estimates in which the Govt were so nearly defeated.

Further developments in the Tudor[15]–Crozier[16] case don't seem to be very favourable to Greenwood[17] and rather tend to confirm the impression that he wasn't telling us the whole truth before.[18] And the battle with the cadets also gives a bad impression as to the success of his methods. Altogether Govt stock seems to me rather low just now. I see from the Post that H.G[reenwood] has answered my question & says that Black & Tans are just new recruits to the permanent force of the R.I.C. whilst the "cadets" or "Auxiliary Service" are officers temporarily enlisted to assist them. From this it would seem that the latter could be got rid of but not the former – at least not so easily.

Last night I, in company with some 6 or 7 others, was initiated into the mystery of the "Buffaloes". A more childish performance I never beheld; it was just like the children's make believes. ... In fact it appeared to me that the Lodge meeting while indulging in a good deal of high falutin sentiment was really only an opportunity for many drinks.

Today Annie insisted on taking me to the Lickey Hills. It certainly was a lovely day. ... The Corporation now own 450 acres at the Lickey and certainly it is a wonderful provision for a great town. It remains to be seen what they will do with it but I confess I fear that as soon as a tramway is laid its beauty will be spoiled unless a large staff is employed to collect bottles and papers and to prevent damage to trees and flowers. Town dwellers are so ignorant of the country & so untamed that their first instinct is to tear up anything that attracts their attention.

---

[14] Alfred Moritz Mond (1868–1930). Liberal MP for Chester 1906–10, Swansea 1910–23 and Camarthen 1924–28 (Conservative from 1926). First Commissioner of Works 1916–21; Minister of Health 1921–22. Created Bart 1910 and Baron Melchett 1928.

[15] Major-General Sir (Henry) Hugh Tudor (1871–1965). Entered Army 1890. Commander, 9th Division Artillery 1916–18 and 9th Division 1918. Chief of Royal Irish Constabulary 1920–21. Inspector-General of Prisons and G-O-C Palestine 1922–25. Knighted 1923.

[16] Brigadier-General Frank Percy Crozier (1879–1937). Commander 119th Infantry Brigade 1916; 3rd Battalion Welsh Regiment 1919; G-O-C 40th Division 1919; Lithuanian Army 1919–20; Commandant, Auxiliary Division, Royal Irish Constabulary 1920–21.

[17] (Thomas) Hamar Greenwood (1870–1948). Liberal MP for York 1906–10, Sunderland 1910–22 and Conservative MP for Walthamstow East 1924–29. Under-Secretary, Home Affairs 1919; Secretary for Overseas Trade 1919–20; Chief Secretary for Ireland 1920–22. Created Bart 1915, Baron Greenwood 1929 and Viscount 1937.

[18] On 19 February 1921 Crozier resigned as head of the notorious 'Auxis' in protest at their undisciplined reprisals, drunkenness and insubordination.

I wish I could attend a public dinner just once without having to make a speech! ... [T]he light & airy after dinner speech only comes to me with long and painful toil!

...

6 March 1921
Westbourne

My dear Ida,

...

Yes, alas! Dudley is in the area of the Midland Union and our people are very depressed at the defeat.[19] I am very sorry myself and now I hear Labour has won Kirkaldy [sic] from the C.L. so we have lost 2 very quickly after our one gain. I expect to have some sort of official report on Dudley but meanwhile the general view seems to be that the defeat is due primarily to the persistent and scurrilous attacks of the Daily Express which represented to the women that Boscawen[20] was trying to keep up the price of meat and bread. Seeing that Beaverbrook[21] who owns the Express is B.L.'s[22] greatest friend I do not quite follow the proceedings!

I had a very strenuous week. The railway estimates came on Monday and I got called at the very last just before Geddes replied. Of course one doesn't get reported in the press under such circumstance but I had no reason to be dissatisfied with the attention given me either by the House or the Minister who returned a very sympathetic reply. I am told by the way that little Neal has had a preliminary meeting with Nottingham and that things look promising.

On Tuesday I had my final meeting of the Living-in on Canal boats committee. We sat all morning & lunched in the room on (1) a plate of cold beef and

---

[19] Dudley by-election, 3 March 1921. The defeat of Griffith-Boscawen, the new Minister of Agriculture, was widely attributed to Beaverbrook's *Daily Express* campaign to end the embargo on Canadian cattle.

[20] Arthur Sackville Trevor Griffith-Boscawen (1865–1946). Conservative MP for Tunbridge 1892–1906, Dudley 1910–21, Taunton 1921–22. Parliamentary Secretary, Ministry of Pensions 1916–19 and to Ministry of Agriculture 1919–21; Minister of Agriculture 1921–22; Minister of Health 1922–23 but resigned after his defeat in Mitcham by-election, March 1923. Knighted 1911.

[21] (William) Maxwell Aitken (1879–1964). Conservative MP for Ashton-under-Lyne 1910–16. Chancellor, Duchy of Lancaster and Minister of Information 1918–19; Minister of Aircraft Production 1940–41; Minister of State 1941; Minister of Supply 1941–42; Minister of War Production 1942; Lord Privy Seal 1943–45. Knighted 1911. Created Bart 1916 and Baron Beaverbrook 1917. Acquired *Daily Express* 1918 and later *Evening Standard*.

[22] Andrew Bonar Law (1858–1923). Conservative MP for Glasgow Blackfriars 1900–1906, Camberwell 1906–10, Bootle 1911–18, Glasgow Central 1918–23. Parliamentary Secretary, Board of Trade 1902–5; Colonial Secretary 1915–16; Chancellor of Exchequer 1916–19; member of War Cabinet 1916–19; Lord Privy Seal 1919–21; Prime Minister 1922–23. Leader of Conservative Party 1911–21 and 1922–23.

ham with plain boiled potatoes (2) cold stewed figs and rice and (3) a bit of mousetrap & bread. This is the stereotyped lunch at the M/Health and it has the merit of being soon over. We finished fairly early in the afternoon with a unanimous Report though the most tiresome member of the Comee insists on making an addition to it. Still I have much reason to congratulate myself on my success and I have reason to know that the principal official at the Ministry is very pleased with the Report which he says is crisp & practical & will be very helpful.

That evening I dined with the Warwickshire Folk in London ... I got away early on pretext of going to the House but didn't go because I didn't want to vote on the Irish debate. I knew the Govt wd have the best of the argument but felt very "jubous" as to the correctness of their facts or at any rate of the impression conveyed by their recital of the facts.

On Wednesday I had to go to the M/H again for Unhealthy Areas and there I once more partook of their odious lunch in order to get on with our work on my draft of the final report. We made good progress but unfortunately I had to break off in order to put some questions to Addison.[23] They were perilously late on the paper but just came in time to be called the very last of all. After that I sat all afternoon and evening in the House on Lords Amendts to Unemployed Insurance Bill and was appointed a member of the committee "to draw up reasons why the Commons disagree with certain of the Lords Amendmts". This meant a meeting behind the Speakers Chair to consider draft reasons submitted by the Parl[iamentar]y Draughtsman to which I instantly objected. So my draft was put in instead & their Lordships on consideration of the reasons decided not to insist on their amendments. So the Royal Assent was given & the old woman got home that night. In other words the unemployed got their money at the end of the week.

Thursday at 10.30 found me once more on Unhealthy Areas which kept us sitting (with a brief interval for the ham & figs) till 4 and I hope that one or at most two more sittings may enable me to bring that Comee also to a close. But as I had to go to Westminster Guildhall on Friday at 10.30 to attend a meeting of the Assocn of Local War Pensions Comees of which I am President you will realise that during this week at any rate I have not had much leisure.

...

---

[23] Christopher Addison (1869–1951). Liberal MP for Shoreditch 1910–22 and Labour MP for Swindon 1929–31 and 1934–35. Parliamentary Secretary, Board of Education 1914–15 and Ministry of Munitions 1915–16; Minister of Munitions, 1916–17; Minister of Reconstruction 1917–19; President, LGB 1919; Minister of Health 1919–21; Minister without Portfolio 1921; Parliamentary Secretary, Ministry of Agriculture 1929–30; Minister of Agriculture 1930–31; Dominion Secretary 1945–47; Commonwealth Secretary 1947; Lord Privy Seal, 1947–51; Paymaster-General 1948–49; Lord President of Council 1951. Created Baron Addison 1937 and Viscount 1945.

12 March 1921
Westbourne

My dear Hilda,

...

Here the event of the week has been Annie's Conference and Mass Meeting in connection with her West Midlands Area Committee. We had been very doubtful about Horne's[24] coming since he had thrown over the Chamber of Commerce through ill-health and I had been informed that he was really on the verge of a breakdown. However on Monday I met him at the Constitutional Club lunch and asked him whether we might count on him. He answered Oh yes certainly, in the gayest manner and I dismissed all anxiety from my mind. Would you believe that that evening he telegraphed to Annie that he couldn't come. I believe he had a good excuse but this is the 3rd time that he has failed us in Birmingham at the last moment in the last few months and I must say I did feel aggrieved. However I succeeded in getting Sir Robert Sanders[25] who was very good natured about coming and made a very good speech though of course he could not carry the same weight as a Cabinet Minister. He and I went down only in time for the mass meeting but as soon as I arrived I learned from Mr Pratt the Central Office Agent that Annie had been a model Chairman at the Conference which had been splendidly attended and that everyone had been delighted with the debates. When we got to the Mid. Institute we found it packed. Annie made an admirable speech which as usual drew tears from the audience and the whole thing went off with great éclat. A. ... deserved her success which was due not only to her powers of getting to the heart of her audience in her speech but to the immense amount of work she had put in beforehand in getting the organisation complete in every detail. The women managed the whole thing themselves and Miss Parkes is crowing loudly over the discomfiture of the men who according to her were full of gloomy prophecies and vainly hoping all through for some failure which never came.

I had a little success myself on Monday when I dined with the Unionist Club which consists mostly of Unionist M.P.'s & dines every Monday during the session. On this occasion we sat down about 40 in number with Carson[26] in the

---

[24] Robert Stevenson Horne (1871–1940). Conservative MP for Glasgow Hillhead 1918–37. Minister of Labour 1919–20; President, Board of Trade 1920–21; Chancellor of Exchequer 1921–22. Knighted 1918. Created Viscount Horne of Slamannan 1937.

[25] Robert Arthur Sanders (1867–1940). Conservative MP for Bridgwater 1910–23 and Somerset (Wells) 1924–29. Whip 1911–21; Deputy Conservative Chairman 1918–22. Under-Secretary for War 1921–22; Minister of Agriculture 1922–24. Created Bart 1920 and Baron Bayford 1929.

[26] Edward Carson (1854–1935). Unionist MP for Dublin University 1892–1918 and Belfast (Duncairn) 1918–21. Leader of Irish Unionist Party 1910–21. Irish Solicitor-General 1892; Solicitor-General 1900–1905; Attorney-General 1915; First Lord of Admiralty 1916–17; Minister without Portfolio 1917–18. Knighted 1900. Created judicial life peer 1921.

chair. After dinner Pike Pease[27] came round & asked me to propose a vote of thanks to Carson after he had spoken. I was quite unprepared and paralysed with fear but apparently succeeded in saying the right things in the right way as I had many compliments paid me not only by those present but afterwards by others who had heard about it …

The luncheon that day at the Constitl. Club was fairly accurately described in the Times which however did not convey the impression left on those present. Wilson-Fox[28] carried off the honours of the day in his speech of criticism which was frank and outspoken but not rude or discourteous. The cheers that greeted his allusion to the M/Health as an unpopular ministry were loud & prolonged and I had not realised the depth of feeling about Addison which was indeed the most remarkable feature of the whole affair. I did not think that Bonar Law was at his best in his reply which was somewhat feeble & wanting in fire [?] and directness but I daresay it served the purpose of bringing home to members the danger of voting too freely against the Govt. No doubt some members deliberately do this to get popularity with their constituents but it is not so brave as they try to make out. In fact it is rather the reverse as they leave others to bear the unpopularity that ought to be shared by the side & this was the best point Bonar made.

I am very pleased to say that I have at last got a promise from the Calthorpes to give the piece of land for a recreation ground in Ladywood that I have been after now for 2 years nearly. They are going to do it very nicely writing me a letter to connect the gift with Father's[29] name & my representation of the constituency. It is very much wanted as there is no playground near & incidentally it may keep the Ladywood children from playing in my garden!

Yesterday I presided for 4 hours at a conference here on the drink question organised by the Temperance Legislation League which advocates State purchase & control. I have been in favour of it myself but I believe it has now receded from the sphere of practical politics & I suggested a return to Father's idea of municipalisation which would be an experiment on a smaller scale & would throw much needed light on the results which might be expected from the larger scheme. In the course of the discussion a lady told a story which tickled us very much. During the Local option campaign in Glasgow the Prohibitionists

---

[27] Herbert Pike Pease (1867–1949). Liberal Unionist (later Conservative) MP for Darlington 1898– January 1910 and December 1910–23. Unionist Whip 1906–10 and 1911–15; Assistant Postmaster-General 1915–22. Ecclesiastical Commissioner 1923–49; Church Estates Commissioner 1926–48; President, Church Army 1917–49. Created Baron Daryngton 1923.

[28] Henry Wilson-Fox (1863–1921). Public Prosecutor, Rhodesia 1894; Manager of British South African Company from 1897 (Director from 1913). Unionist MP for Tamworth 1917–21.

[29] Joseph Chamberlain (1836–1914). Lord Mayor of Birmingham, 1874–76. Liberal MP for Birmingham 1876–85 and Birmingham West, 1886–1914 (Liberal Unionist from 1886). President, Board of Trade, 1880–85; President, LGB, 1886; Colonial Secretary, 1895–1903.

put up posters declaring that "The 4 corners of Hell are sodden with drink!". The Glasgow students wrote underneath "Oh Death where is thy sting?"

...

19 March 1921
Westbourne

My dear Ida,

...

I left London on Thursday ... to address the annual meeting of the Citizen's Society here having only just looked into the House for my letters. On my way up to the Club for dinner I met Hubbard[30] of the Post who told me about Bonar. It was a complete surprise to me and indeed I do not think anyone had an inkling of it except the Cabinet. I feel very sorry for him. I have always had an affectionate feeling for him since my National Service days when he was such a contrast to Ll.G. and though he no doubt feels it a relief to be free from responsibility it must be terribly depressing to reflect that his career is over. I doubt his ever doing any active political work again. They always say there is no reason why recovery should not be made in these cases but it seldom seems to come.

Naturally I began at once like you to speculate on Austen's position. I am rather disgruntled at the idea of a whole series of changes. Austen leaving the Exchequer, Horne bundled out of the Board of Trade especially when he has just had to go to the South of France to avoid a nervous breakdown. I would much prefer to see Ll.G. take the leadership of the House himself leaving it in commission when he had to be away & [?] A.C. made leader of the Unionist Party but otherwise things remaining as they are. But Hannon[31] who is a born wire puller and who is pulling them hard on Austen's behalf now tells me that an intrigue is going on to make F.E.[32] leader, inspired by F.E. himself and backed by Walter Long. The meeting on Monday consists only of Unionist M.P.'s and can only settle the leadership in the House, leaving the larger question of the party to be settled later and allowing the intriguers to work up their forces in the interval. I have no doubt that the Monday meeting will be unanimous but I think A. wd be justified in saying that he would not accept unless he had the party

---

[30] George William Hubbard (1870–1939). Journalist and editor, *Birmingham Daily Mail*, 1903–6 and *Birmingham Daily Post*, 1906–33.

[31] Patrick Joseph Henry Hannon (1874–1963). Conservative MP for Birmingham Moseley 1921–50. Vice-President, Tariff Reform League 1910–14; General Secretary, Navy League 1911–18; Director, British Commonwealth Union 1918–28; Secretary, Empire Industries Association 1925–50; President, Industrial Transport Association 1927–37. Knighted 1936.

[32] Frederick Edwin Smith (1872–1930). Conservative MP for Liverpool Walton 1906–18 and Liverpool West Derby 1918–19. Solicitor-General 1915; Attorney-General 1915–19; Lord Chancellor 1919–22; Secretary for India 1924–28. Knighted 1915. Created Bart 1918, Baron Birkenhead 1919, Viscount 1921 and Earl of Birkenhead 1922.

leadership too – in which case he would force the issue. But I doubt his taking that course and I must say I think the F.E. intrigue will fail.

As for his relations with Ll.G. I don't think the latter will take the liberties with him that he did with Bonar but they will get on all right for some time at any rate. The break up of the Coalition which the Times so joyfully predicts will not come off but on the other hand Ll.G.'s position seems to me to be definitely weakened and he will I think inevitably be forced more to the Right in order to peg out a claim to the ultimate leadership of a new party, growing out of the Coalition. One thing that strikes me at this crisis is the dearth of Unionist Ministers in the Cabinet. I can't help thinking that by degrees Ll.G. will have to bring in more.

If A. does give up the Chancellorship and take the leadership of the House I am inclined to think he will do very well. He is popular and respected though I think members are sometimes a little bothered by his sudden checks of speech. He is certainly no orator; I always feel his appeals to the emotions a little forced; but for a carefully reasoned statement he has few equals and he convinces by his own sincerity & fairness. I should think he can have 11 Downing St if he wants it but the evidence we received at the Comee on Minister's remuneration was general to the effect that these houses cost more than they save.

There is one other possibility which has not been mentioned. I do not think it very likely but it is not outside the bounds even of probability. Ll.G. might temporarily retire for a rest and A. might become P.M.! But Birkenhead wd doubtless fight hard for such a prize.

I cannot help feeling that the change does not improve my own position in the House. I don't much mind; my political ambitions being of a very limited character, but there is no doubt that it is a handicap to have a near relation in high places & the nearer he is to the highest place the greater the handicap.

My engagements down here have been fortunately timed in one respect; that they have saved me from some long sittings in the House. ... I expect the same thing will happen next week ...

I had a very successful meeting of my Unhealthy Areas Comee on Wednesday. I had spent a lot of time going through the report redrafting and adding to it and the Committee simply opened its mouth and swallowed everything at a gulp. It only now remains to get it fair copied & signed and then that is done with. I am contemplating a dinner to the Comee at the House with Annie as hostess to finish up.

...

By the time you get this or just after you will have been flabbergasted by Hoskins' behaviour. 50% free of tax is equivalent to 71% less tax at its present rate! It *is* a little gold mine isn't it, but it is perhaps well to warn you that I reckon we have had the time of our lives since the war and though it is not over yet there are signs that it wont last much longer and then we shall probably have a lean period. This year however I have divided up to the hilt feeling that all the shareholders really needed it to keep them out of the Workhouse. For myself it will enable me to buy that French Cabinet that I have been after so long with a clear conscience …

…

10 April 1921
Westbourne

My dear Hilda,

…

I expect Annie told you pretty well what I was doing up to the time when she left. Since then this strike issue has come to a crisis and it is very difficult to foretell the issue.[33] I never thought the miners would go out, nor did I think they would refuse to accept the conference to consider the pumpmen. That I was wrong both times shows I think that the men are not led by their nominal leaders but by more extreme malcontents who keep in the background so far as the public is concerned and this is what makes it so difficult to forecast anything. It seemed obvious that the Labour party in the House were very unhappy about the whole situation and I think they have done what they could to bring about a change for the better. But the fact is they are not authorised to speak for the miners and so their suggestions when accepted by the Govt are turned down by the mining delegates. I can't help thinking that something will happen between now & Tuesday to stop the Triple Alliance from executing their threat but I trust it will not be any giving way by the Govt on essential points like the safety of the mines. …The Times ran up a tree yesterday as it invariably does whenever it sees a tiger coming, but the Govt will not, I think, mistake the Times for popular opinion. Much will depend on the railwaymen. They have set a splendid example in Liverpool and I am hoping it will be followed here in Birmingham where most of the men dont want to come out. Last night I had my annual divisional meeting. The room – the largest school we have got – was packed, men standing up against the wall all round and many were turned back at the door because there was no more room. There are many railwaymen in the division and I had determined to make an appeal to them. But just before I got up I had a tip from one of them that they were divided, with a majority against coming out, but that I carried great weight with them and that the moderate ones would welcome a lead from me. This encouraged me to take a stronger line even than I had thought would be advisable. I told them with such small acts of impressiveness as I possess that it meant civil war. I suggested that it was unfair to them that such a momentous decision should be taken without consulting them & that they

---

[33] A national coal strike cum lockout began on 1 April 1921, the day after government control and subsidy ended. Within a week the prospect of a general strike loomed.

should be obliged to choose between a break with their Union or action which must cause untold hardship & suffering to their own class. I begged them to consider not only the miners but their own wives & children & those of their neighbours and finally I suggested that they should demand a ballot and if they couldn't get it they should refuse to come out. The appeal was loudly cheered & my friend said it was "tophole & just what they wanted". No doubt they will talk about it among themselves and I hope the press will give it good prominence. I spoke on Friday in the Duddeston division and the Post gave me the place of honour on its front (leader) page, unkindly dismissing Hannon, who also spoke and at greater length than I, with 2 brief lines. It must make him furious but is very good for him for I see signs of the necessity of his being made to realise that he can't do anything here without me. I think he does realise it at bottom but has cherished hopes that it wouldn't prevent his running the show *his* way.

...

I have been asked by Whitley[34] to be Chairman of a Joint Committee of Lords & Commons on 4 Bills dealing with London water. He says I am the only man with the required qualities & experience & that my name wd command general confidence. What are you to say – or do – !

17 April 1921
Westbourne

My dear Ida,

...

Well, we ought all to be very grateful to the miners for having extricated us from the very difficult position in which we found ourselves. The Press of course has had an absolutely glorious time and has made the very most of the many "dramatic moments". In particular the action of the private M.P.s is hailed as having "saved the nation", partly because the press is grateful to them for the "drama" they provided, & partly because some of them like to represent that private members succeeded where the Govt failed.[35]

In a sense it is true that the bust up of the Triple Alliance is due to the private members action. But the action was entirely unpremeditated and if the Miners

---

[34] John Henry Whitley (1866–1935). Liberal MP for Halifax 1900–1928. Junior Lord of Treasury and Liberal Whip 1907–10; Deputy Chairman, Ways and Means 1910–11; Deputy Speaker and Chairman, Ways and Means 1911–21; Speaker of House of Commons 1921–28. Chairman of Committee on Relations of Employers and Employed 1917–18; Chairman, Royal Commission on Labour in India 1929–31; Chairman of BBC 1930–35.

[35] On 14 April 1921 at a meeting of Coalition MPs, the MFGB Secretary conceded the idea of a temporary settlement but the miners' executive rejected it next day, 'Black Friday'. With the NUR refusal to lend support, the Triple Alliance collapsed, along with any threat of a general strike. The miners' strike dragged on until 1 July.

Executive had backed Hodges[36] the result would have been another postponement of trouble, possibly to a moment when we should have been in a far less advantageous position to meet it. And further it must be said that the Triple Alliance leaders were desperately anxious to find a way out because they knew in advance that they were beat. It is not so certain therefore that a fight would have meant disaster for the nation and it is quite arguable that it would have been short, sharp and decisive. I only feel moved to say all this because I resent the way in which some of the Press are exploiting the whole incident for their private ends. To read the Times for instance you would suppose that 200 private members got together and said "We have been deprived by an autocratic Government of all opportunity of discussing a crisis in which the life of the nation is involved. Yet we are ourselves responsible for what may happen. Let us then take things into our own hands, call the owners and miners before us and see if we cannot ourselves effect a settlement". Nothing could be further from the truth. There was general agreement in the Coalition that discussion in the House during these delicate negotiations was unwise, and I believe Kenworthy[37] was about the only man who thought otherwise. But the coal-owners themselves asked to be allowed to come and talk to members and many of us went in the hope of getting a better understanding of what the proposals were. We did so and, as usual, the owners made the very worst of their case. In fact the impression made was most unfavourable, partly because it appeared after long cross-examination that in some cases at any rate men would be reduced from 14/9 per day to 7/9 per day (of 7¾ hrs) so that the miners who talked of a 50% cut and a "bob an hour", & who had been derided in the House were about right after all, and partly from a general appearance of not knowing their own case. We were frequently told "Oh I could get that for you but I can't say now; I'm sorry I haven't got that" etc. It was generally agreed that the owners had done themselves much harm and when towards the end Walter Elliott[38] [sic] suggested that we should hear Hodges, some of us felt that "put the lid on" the case against the men. I went home to dinner, not intending to return but rather full of a question I had put to Evan Williams[39] and as to which several members had

---

[36] Frank Hodges (1887–1947). General Secretary, MFGB 1918–24; Member, Royal Commission on Coal Mines 1919. Labour MP for Lichfield 1923–24. Civil Lord of Admiralty 1924. Secretary, International Miners' Federation 1925–27; member, Central Electricity Board 1927–47.

[37] Joseph Montague Kenworthy (1886–1953). Entered Navy 1903; Admiralty War Staff 1917; Assistant Chief of Staff, Gibraltar 1918. MP for Hull Central 1919–31 (Liberal until November 1926 then Labour). Labour Chief Whip in Lords 1938–42. Succeeded as 10th Baron Strabolgi 1934.

[38] Walter Elliot Elliot (1888–1958). Conservative MP for Lanark 1918–23, Glasgow Kelvingrove 1924–45, 1950–58, Scottish Universities 1946–50. Parliamentary Secretary of Health for Scotland 1923–24, 1924–26; Under-Secretary for Scotland 1926–29; Financial Secretary to Treasury 1931–32; Minister of Agriculture 1932–36; Scottish Secretary 1936–38; Minister of Health 1938–40.

[39] Evan Williams (1871–1959). Coal owner. Chairman, Monmouth and South Wales Coalowners Association 1913; President, Mining Association of GB 1919–44 and National Board for Coal

spoken to me with approval. But when I told Annie she felt so strongly that my presence in the House was essential for the salvation of the country that I went back and late that night telegraphed to Pratt in Worcester that I must cancel my engagement to speak in Malvern on Friday. Indeed I felt after the second meeting that the Govt might require all the support they could command should they wish to oppose the suggestion of the temporary settlement.

Hodges is quite young – in the early thirties, I should say. He speaks slowly and quietly in a voice which is entirely free from any trace of "accent" or vulgarity. I believe he is a Ruskin College product. His manner is very winning and persuasive but towards the end of the meeting I moved close up to the table to see him better & thought I detected a sly look about the eyes. He spoke for ¾ hour and then was heckled for about an hour. My impression was not that he was unwittingly driven into making a concession as many young members thought, but that he had arranged it beforehand with J.H. Thomas[40] (who was with him) and possibly with Inskip[41] who asked the first question and straightaway got an answer that led directly to the new proposal. It was cleverly worked so that it seemed to be elicited bit by bit, but I believe it was thought out beforehand. I thought it a dangerous precedent for the House by a casual meeting at short notice to barge in upon negotiations and to go some way at any rate (some would have liked to go further) towards committing itself to approval of a new proposition without having heard what the Govt might have to say about it. However when the Executive refused to back up Hodges next morning (because they dare not face their own people) private members perhaps realised that they had not been quite so clever as they thought, and anyway I hope the Press won't encourage them to think they have set up a useful precedent in forming a Court of Appeal when everything possible has been extracted from Downing St! W. Elliott [sic] is a clever young man but he is very raw and crude & he takes himself far more seriously than other people do.

Perhaps you would like to hear my suggestion. I don't think that in their present mood either side would accept it but all the same I cant help always trying to find a way out of or round a difficulty & I dont at present see the answer.

Mining 1921–25; President, National Confederation of Employers Organisations 1925–26; Chairman, Joint Standing Consultative Committee for Coal Mining 1926–44 and of Central Council under Coal Mines Act 1930–38. Created Bart 1935.

[40] James Henry Thomas (1874–1949). President, NUR 1910 and General Secretary, 1918–24, 1925–31. Labour MP for Derby 1910–36 (from 1931 as National Labour). Colonial Secretary, 1924, 1935–36; Lord Privy Seal 1929–30; Dominion Secretary 1930–35.

[41] Thomas Walker Hobart Inskip (1876–1947). Conservative MP for Bristol Central 1918–29, Fareham 1931–39. Solicitor-General 1922–24, 1924–28, 1931–32; Attorney-General 1928–29, 1932–36; Minister for Coordination of Defence 1936–39; Dominion Secretary 1939, 1940; Lord Chancellor 1939–40; Lord Chief Justice 1940–46. Knighted 1922. Created Viscount Caldecote 1939.

Hodges proposal in its latest form was that there shd be a levy of -/- per ton on all coal raised. This should form a fund out of which poor districts were to be assisted on some plan which has never been clearly explained but which evidently means that the amount of assistance is to vary with the loss on working. Obviously this is open to all the objections which apply to the National Pool. The good mines will not work harder to put more money into the pockets of the bad. The bad will not bother to work at all but will ride comfortably on the backs of the good. My suggestion is briefly: Let a National Board of owners & miners grade or rate all mines according to workability. For the sake of argument let us suppose there are 3 grades (1) Rich mines (2) mines that did pay but dont under present conditions (3) mines that can never under any reasonable supposition pay again. Of these (2) alone is to receive a subsidy out of the levy which as in Hodges proposal is to be made on all coal raised. The subsidy is of a fixed amount per ton & for a period of 5 years when re-rating will take place.

From the men's point of view this is a national settlement. It preserves most of the poorer mines from extinction for the present and if it doesn't equalise wages it at all events tones down the differences.

From the point of view of owners and public, there is no interference with efficiency because the amount of the levy is fixed. It is therefore like a tax & becomes a charge on the industry. So too the assistance given is fixed. The harder the bad mine works the more it will put into its own pocket, and although it may get re-rated at the end of 5 years that will only be if it has become profitable in itself. In this way mines might be saved from destruction which cannot pay at the moment but could pay again when times become normal and so the nations resources would be conserved.

It seems to me quite a feasible idea. What do you say?

...

23 April 1921
Westbourne

My dear Hilda,

... I dont wonder you feel in a fog about the miners. So does everyone and I suppose thats the reason why everyone does not hesitate to express his opinion. I have not sent my scheme to the Times because it is only a sort of skeleton and it would probably be fallen upon by all the combatants and devoured – if they thought it worthy of notice. But I still think it a good one – if the mining people would look at it with an open mind. I understand that there are hardly any pits which would have permanently to be closed by being put in my 3rd category but anyhow that would have to be decided by the rating committee which would consist of owners and miners. I found an opportunity one day of imparting my ideas to Austen & he seemed rather impressed by them & said he thought Ll.G. had too hastily labelled levy "pool" and dismissed it. You never know; he may have since then passed on what I said. He is rather disposed to listen to my notions with attention – when they dont concern his own particular business!

Last Tuesday I came back here (spending 4 hours on the journey) for the purpose of presiding at a Primrose Day Concert in my constituency. My railway friend assured me that my appeal had had a tremendous effect upon the waverers. They would take from me what they wouldn't from Austen much less from Lowe,[42] because they knew I was sympathetic with Labour, and in making a vote of thanks he declared that I was a statesman, and a model employer, and a true representative of labour, winding up with the emphatic declaration that I might change my convictions as much as I liked but they would never desert me. It was an odd remark that has now been made at several of my meetings but I am sure that his discourse though extravagant was sincere and he has a good deal of influence in his ward. The room was packed out as usual.

On the way from London I found myself with an hour to spare at Rugby so I walked through the town and into the close and up to my old house. It was just 35 years since I had been there. ... I didn't want to send Frank there! ...

The next morning I had another meeting of my Living-in on Canal boats Comee. I had thought it was all finished but a difficulty had arisen over a method of annual licensing which we had proposed. I had a brilliant idea for solving it which turned out to be workable and acceptable to everyone but I had to call the Comee together to hear the case and give their sanction. So I took the opportunity of making a fresh appeal to my two dissentients, or rather the two who had insisted on adding a "note" to the report. I offered to include a passage from the note in the Report itself and gradually drove them into a corner where they surrendered. So now *that* report is unanimous. Next Friday, by the way, my old Children of Unmarried Parents Bill comes up in the name of Capt. Bowyer.[43] There were two Bills in front of it and I didn't think it had much chance of being reached but one of the Bills has now been withdrawn and I shall make a great effort to get the other closed up in time to get our second reading. I have got the Home Office squared already.

I have had a letter from Hall to say that after paying our dividends and his gratuity and the bonus to staff & workpeople (£1500) he has still got £15,000 at the Bank and £100,000 of orders on his books ...

---

[42] Francis William Lowe (1852–1929). Conservative MP for Edgbaston 1898–1929. President, Birmingham Conservative Association 1892–1918 when became Joint President of Birmingham Unionist Association; Chairman of Midland Union and the National Union; member, Council of National Unionist Association. Knighted 1905. Created Bart 1918.

[43] George Edward Bowyer (1886–1948). Conservative MP for Buckingham 1918–37. PPS to President of Board of Trade 1921–24; Conservative Whip 1925–35; Comptroller of Household 1935; Junior Lord of Treasury 1927–29; Parliamentary Secretary, Ministry of Agriculture 1939–1940; Conservative Whip in Lords 1945–47. President, Urban District Councils Association 1923–25 and from 1929. Vice-Chairman, Conservative Party Organisation 1930–35. Knighted 1929. Created Bart 1933 and Baron Denham 1937.

...

Annie has got a new cook, who seemed – on paper – to be a treasure. Alas! She has every virtue & accomplishment save one, but that is important. She does not know how to cook! Isn't it a bore? ...

30 April 1921
35 Egerton Crescent, SW3

My dear Ida,

...

Annie has had a busy time this week with Area Committees and Conferences while I've had a more idle one ... I was able to get to the flower show both days ...

...

Austen's speech at the Hotel Cecil was excellent and has pleased everybody very much. I was dining at the same place last night ... and Salisbury[44] who proposed H.M. Ministers in a very critical spirit made an exception for A. & said it was a most statesmanlike speech.

...

Alas! The Bastardy Bill was not reached yesterday before 5. Even so I think the House wd have given it a second reading only that beast Banbury[45] "objected" and it could not be taken. I cant imagine what his objection was but he obstructs everything on general principles. I took a leading part in opposing a private members Bill entitled "a Bill to prevent increase in rates" but by no means calculated to bring about that desirable object. My speech to my knowledge converted several members and various people expressed the opinion that after my criticisms it was dead. Nevertheless enough men came in for the division who had not heard the debate but who went by the title to carry the 2nd reading. However it wont get much further. I expect I shall be on the Committee and by the time I have cut out all I want there will be nothing left.

...

---

[44] James Edward Hubert Gascoyne-Cecil (1861–1947). Conservative MP for Darwen 1885–92, Rochester 1893–1903. Under-Secretary, Foreign Affairs 1900–1903; Lord Privy Seal 1903–5 and 1924–29; President, Board of Trade 1905; Chancellor, Duchy of Lancaster 1922–23; Lord President of Council 1922–24. Conservative leader in Lords 1925–31. Styled Viscount Cranborne 1868–1903, succeeded as 4th Marquess of Salisbury 1903.

[45] Frederick George Banbury (1850–1936). Conservative MP for Peckham 1892–1906 and City of London 1906–24. Chairman, Estimates Committee and Select Committee on National Expenditure 1920. Created Baron Banbury of Southam, 1924.

8 May 1921
Westbourne

My dear Hilda,

…

Annie and I dined with the Flannerys[46] at the House on Thursday & with the Sam Hoares[47] on Friday. At the latter we met the Speaker & Mrs W[hitley] & he confided to Annie all his ideas on how he was going to carry out his duties. He is very wisely going to strike out a line of his own. Lowther[48] was in the opinion of many too tolerant of hares and brazenfaces. W. does not mean to allow Jack Jones[49] and Kenworthy to monopolise all the time and he is determined not to make a joke for 6 months! He is going to have *small*, not large, parties and has got a scheme for tea on the terrace to which members & their wives wd be invited. A. thinks there will be a stampede when the forms of Mrs & Miss Wh. are seen issuing from the door of the Speakers house casting their eyes round for suitable victims of their "tea"!

I hear Austens speech to the young Coalitionists[50] in the House on Wednesday was again a great success. Ernest Wild[51] apologised for not having asked me. He had fully intended to but forgot somehow he said, but if I had gone I couldn't have seen you. Anyhow I was glad A. had pleased the Coalition Libs & the young Unionists who were rather dissatisfied with Bonar. I gather from the report in the Times that he spoke on the Coalition and the desirability of letting it pass naturally into a fusion.

---

[46] James Fortescue Flannery (1851–1943). Consulting marine engineer; Admiralty Assessor to Dockyard Committee 1895. Unionist MP for Shipley 1895–1906 and Maldon 1910–22. Director, Barclay's Bank. Created Bart 1904.

[47] Samuel John Gurney Hoare (1880–1959). Conservative MP for Chelsea 1910–44. Secretary for Air 1922–24, 1924–29, 1940. Secretary for India 1931–35; Foreign Secretary 1935; First Lord of Admiralty 1936–37; Home Secretary 1937–39; Lord Privy Seal 1939–40. Ambassador in Madrid 1940–44. Conservative Party Treasurer 1930–31. Succeeded as Bart 1915. Created Viscount Templewood 1944.

[38] James William Lowther (1855–1949). Unionist MP for Rutland 1883–85 and Penrith 1886–1921. Under-Secretary, Foreign Affairs 1891–92. Deputy Speaker and Chairman, Committee of Ways and Means, 1895–1905; Speaker 1905–21. Chairman, Speaker's Conference on Electoral Reform, 1916–17; Boundary Commission 1917, Federal Devolution Committee 1919. Created Viscount Ullswater 1921. Chairman, Review Committee on Political Honours, 1923–24 and Agricultural Wages Board 1930–40.

[49] John Joseph Jones (1873–1941). Building labourer and organiser for National Union of General and Municipal Workers. Member, West Ham Council 1904 and Board of Guardians 1908–11. Elected for West Ham, Silvertown in 1918 for the National Socialist Party in opposition to an official Labour candidate but sat as a Labour MP until retirement in 1940.

[50] On 5 May 1921 Austen Chamberlain told the New Members Coalition Group he could 'foresee no end to the necessity of Coalition' and urged the need for cooperation but stressed the need for gradual fusion as 'parties grow rather than are made'.

[51] Ernest Edward Wild (1869–1934). Coalition Unionist MP for West Ham, Upton 1918–22. Recorder, City of London 1922–34. Knighted 1918.

... This morning it is pouring steadily so I haven't yet had a chance of looking at the garden. But from the train yesterday & the car as I went to Kenilworth last night I saw that the country was looking its loveliest. I never saw the trees more perfect in their foliage and the hedges are still full of cowslips red campion & stitchwort while the fields are yellow with buttercups. I hadn't realised the year had got so far.

14 May 1921
Westbourne

My dear Ida,

... Such information as I can get seems to show that the unions are still very determined, being convinced that the only offers before them mean starvation wages. On the other hand the railwaymen evidently dont mean to come out and I fancy the atmosphere must be getting more favourable to a renewal of negotiations with a more serious desire to achieve a settlement. Meanwhile life grows more difficult. It took me 4 hours to get to London last Monday and 3 to get down on Thursday. Our weekly ration of coke has been reduced to 3 cwt which is not worth sending a motor & two men with and we aren't allowed to accumulate several weeks and take it in one load. So we are struggling on without. I am able to dispense with heat in the cool house altogether and we have cut down baths to one a week and cook on an oil stove!

I have got a lovely show of Crispums and hybrids of different kinds, far more in proportion than we used to get at Highbury ... The garden is in perfection for the time of year with huge masses of aubrietia and alyssum and German iris. The big Japanese pink double cherry at the corner of the terrace has surpassed itself this year and the apple blossom has been gorgeous. But the great feature is the mass of dark wall flowers in the big border by the peach house with dark red Darwin tulips growing through it. ... The May tulips too are in full beauty above the South border and altogether Annie thinks there never was a nicer garden anywhere. ...

The garden is full of birds young and old. Cuckoos are crying all day, young thrushes are fed on the lawn, the two tit boxes have 8 eggs apiece "blue" in one and "great" in the other, and today while sitting talking on a bench I detected a willow wren building and found the nest at the bottom of the ha-ha. It is a pleasant time of year to be at home and I welcome the week's recess which I feel I need for I am rather weary of the session.

I had my first meeting of the joint committee on Tuesday and got it over in time to go on to another committee on the Police Pensions Bill on which I had a number of amendments. On Wednesday I had canals and alas! the result was that I must draft another report next week as the Railway Bill has brought up the whole question of transport and I feel that now is the psychological moment to bring canals before the public and the House. In fact when the report has been sent in I think I must summon a meeting of M.P.'s and address them on a subject of which they always feel painfully ignorant.

We had 3 days debate on the Ways & Means Resolutions. I felt I ought to speak but didn't because I hadn't had time to prepare anything and after the first day the thing developed into pure obstruction. Squiff[52] made his best speech on it; no doubt he feels at home on Free Trade & he was certainly very amusing in picking the resolutions to pieces, particularly in his quotation from Hamlet which he delivered with great art & which sent the House into fits of laughter. I thought it a pity Austen didn't reply at once[.] Lloyd Greame[53] did very well but has hardly acquired sufficient experience to deal faithfully with such an old Parliamentary hand as Squiff. I didn't "stick" the all night sitting. I had a splitting headache that night and a Committee next morning followed by a long train journey and a "banquet" in the evening. So about 1 o clock I marched resolutely through Mr Towyn Jones[54] who timidly enquired whether I was coming back and when I said "No" found nothing more to say in reply than "Oh". So I departed and slept off my headache and next evening addressed American & Canadian Dry Goods Merchants and listened resignedly to their very tiresome speeches in return.

Last night we had our delayed Unionist annual meeting without either Austen or the Ld Chancellor. Sir F. Lowe presided and managed to take up over 20 minutes in talking without producing one single idea. But they received him with cheers on account of his good looks.

Sunday. Yesterday morning I had to go and preside at an interview between Birmingham M.P.'s and ex-service men. The M.P.'s were Hannon, myself and – after a time – Jephcott![55] The ex-service men began by being rather wild but being judiciously handled they soon saw that many of their proposals were impossible and after a 2 hours interview we parted on the best of terms. I invited Hannon to lunch and the beggar stayed till after tea, depriving us of the opportu-

---

[52] Henry Herbert Asquith (1852–1928). Liberal MP for Fife East 1886–1918 and Paisley 1920–24. Home Secretary 1892–95; Chancellor of Exchequer 1905–8; Prime Minister 1908–16; Secretary for War 1914. Leader of Liberal Party 1908–26. Created KG and Earl of Oxford and Asquith 1925.

[53] Philip Cunliffe-Lister (1884–1972). Changed his surname from Lloyd-Greame in 1924. Conservative MP for Hendon 1918–35. Parliamentary Secretary, Board of Trade 1920–21; Secretary, Overseas Trade Department 1921–22; President, Board of Trade 1922–24, 1924–29 and 1931; Colonial Secretary 1931–35; Air Secretary 1935–38; Minister Resident, West Africa 1942–44; Minister of Civil Aviation 1944–45; Chancellor, Duchy of Lancaster and Minister of Materials 1951–52; Commonwealth Secretary 1952–55. Knighted 1920. Created Viscount Swinton 1935 and Earl of Swinton 1955.

[54] Josiah Towyn Jones (1858–1925). Liberal MP for Llanelly 1912–22. Junior Lord of Treasury 1916–22. Congregational Minister from 1880 and Chairman of Welsh Congregationalist Union 1919–20.

[55] Alfred Roger Jephcott (1853–1932). Member, Birmingham School Board 1890–95 and City Council 1895–1912; Alderman 1912–32. Conservative MP for Birmingham Yardley 1918–29.

nity we had meant to take of working in the garden. Among other pieces of gossip he informed us that the new American Ambassador[56] spend a good part of his time in getting drunk (in that land of drought). If that is really true it's a mistake to send him here for it's sure to be found out and then there will be a scandal and great rejoicings among the anti prohibitionists.

P.S. Banbury has been caught napping and the Bastardy Bill is through its second reading!

17 May 1921
Westbourne

My dear Hilda,

I must send you a few lines on the occasion of your birthday. Your life was never more busy & useful and never entered into the lives of more people than now. So guard it carefully and dont run the machine too hard. Its really an awful mistake to get into that frame of mind when you cant settle down to enjoy your leisure. I feel some danger of it myself. If I am not actively working at *something*, tho' it be only weeding the garden an uneasy sensation creeps into my mind and I become restless.

In such glorious weather as this one ought to be able to sit in the garden in a long chair with a book of poetry or essays or something semi-serious for hours together. But *I* cant; tho' I can spend any amount of time in the orchid houses.

There must have been 1000 people in the Botanic Gardens yesterday and one did feel glad that they could take that form of enjoyment since the coal strike denied them the more distant form of holiday. It looks as though the atmosphere was becoming more favourable to a resumption. It's all very well to say "If the miner is starved into submission he will only go back with the fixed determination to break out again as soon as he can". But in practice that is not what happens. On the contrary he gets his bellyful to use a vulgar expression and decides that he wont try it again unless he is sure that he can win on his head.
...

[P.S.] I hope you had a nice time at Twitt's Ghyll. I see A. is getting abused over M.P.'s Income tax &c. & I dont wonder. I cant think what possessed him to do it. No coalition M.P. has a word to say for it.

---

[56] George Brinton McClellan Harvey (1864–1928). Editor and proprietor *North American Review* 1899–1926, *Harper's Weekly* 1901–13 and *Harvey's Weekly* from 1918. Tried to be a President-maker with Woodrow Wilson 1909–12 and Warren G. Harding 1920, the latter appointing him US Ambassador in London 1921–24.

28 May 1921
Westbourne

My dear Ida,

...

This afternoon A & I went to Elliotts Sports on their new recreation ground. It was a great affair; about 2000 people were present and there were many events some open to all comers and some only to the amalgamated firms while Elliotts band discoursed very creditable music. It is very satisfactory to see how the "welfare" side has developed. It is all managed by a committee with representatives of the men upon it and they have got cricket & football teams tennis courts & a bowling green rifle teams and a fishing club so all tastes are catered for. There were excellent prizes and a challenge cup for the largest number of points which was won by Elliotts.

Things seem to be moving towards a settlement of the strike but slowly. I think it much better that it should go slowly & with you I trust that the little Welshman wont be too anxious to save the men's faces. Of course the Times is as disloyal as ever; the men's leaders naturally keep up the bluff but they cant last much longer.

31 May 1921
Westbourne

My dear Hilda,

...

The strike drags on but evidently the miners front is disintegrating and the leaders feel that they cant hold their men much longer and are looking out for a soft place to fall on. We are getting desperately hard up here as they keep on cutting off gas and electricity for more and more hours in the day. We have managed so far with a combination of oil & gas cookers and an electric motor at night but we miss our hot baths painfully. All the same I would rather go dirty than see the Govt surrender for victory is not far off. So far all my works have managed to keep going and Platten tells me that he has successfully installed oil burners at Elliotts. The clearness of the atmosphere has been a joy. I have never seen the view from our terrace so beautifully fresh and green and I envy our children or children's children who will always live in an atmosphere like this.

The indefatigable Annie has succeeded in getting another cook who looks at present like being a success. She is very young, only 24, and is accordingly ready and anxious to learn. Moreover though her dishes have something to be desired in appearance and finish they *taste* right and after all that is the really important thing.

Annie herself has been spending a good deal of time in the constituency among her women. A fourth club is now in process of starting and the enthusiasm is fully maintained in those which began the movement. Other constituencies have been fired by the idea and are trying to get their own clubs and altogether it has been a remarkable success. "Mrs Chamberlain's husband" can afford to smile at abusive (anonymous) letters solemnly warning him that Ladywood is being thoroughly canvassed and that he will be visited with the wrath to come on account of the "Chamberlain – Churchill[57] conspiracy" to "make the House of Commons into a club for Chamberlains & Churchills" – apparently by means of the exemption of M.P.'s salaries from income tax! As I said before I think the proposal ill-timed and badly conceived but I confess I am almost converted to it by the outcry which is prompted by the meanest motives – jealousy at someone else's good fortune. Its the same motive that always picks out officials salaries for criticism but leaves wage advances alone.

What do you think of these figures for the Municipal Bank in April.

Deposits	£115,193	(record)
Withdrawals	66,354	
Nett increase in deposits	£48,838	

New accounts opened 2,161. Accounts closed 1,039. Total number of houses purchased by advances borrowed from Bank 1069. Amount lent £294,503. Amount repaid to date £46,010. *Isn't* it marvellous?

> 4 June 1921
> Westbourne

My dear Hilda,

...

The great event in the House this week was the division on members expenses. The House had already got nervy & short tempered over 2 late sittings and it was seriously disturbed as to what it should do. I was quite clear; it seemed to me impossible to vote for the Govt proposals when we were telling everyone that "however desirable a thing might be in itself" we must reject it if it involved new expenditure. On the other hand third class fares involved humiliation or discomfort or both without escaping the odium. So I voted against 3rd

---

[57] Winston Leonard Spencer Churchill (1874–1965). Conservative MP for Oldham 1900–1904 (as a Liberal 1904–6). Liberal MP for Manchester NW 1906–8 and Dundee 1908–22. Conservative MP for Epping 1924–45 and Woodford 1945–64. Under-Secretary for Colonies 1905–8; President, Board of Trade 1908–10; Home Secretary 1910–11; First Lord of Admiralty 1911–15 and 1939–40; Chancellor, Duchy of Lancaster 1915; Minister of Munitions 1917–19; Secretary for War and Air 1919–21; Colonial Secretary 1921–22; Chancellor of Exchequer 1924–29; Prime Minister 1940–45 and 1951–55. Minister of Defence 1940–45 and 1951–52. Created KG 1953.

class fares and against any fares at all and I am very glad we carried the negative in both cases.

I had Grant Robertson[58] to lunch last Sunday to discuss the Trade Union classes at the University. The man who has acted as tutor and who has been very successful has got another post and the present industrial difficulties hamper the Unions in sending students. However I found Ashton (the Tutor) very confident that the scheme had been a success and, what was encouraging, much more successful in the second session than the first. The T.U's didn't send quite the right type at first, but they have learnt their mistake and the last lot made excellent use of their time. So after our conversation the Principal said he should advise the Council to go on with the scheme. I find that 2 other Universities have been making enquiries about it with a view to starting on the same lines and I should [be] very vexed if the Birm. Univy gave up my idea and another one took it up and made it go.

Sunday. The Principal writes that the Council have agreed to go on.

…

On Thursday I had (very unwillingly) to go and *breakfast* at Derby House to meet the P.M. I do think breakfasting out is a barbarous practice. You dont see your paper you cant answer your letters everything is thrown out of gear. We had a quick breakfast and then Derby[59] announced that the P.M. wanted to talk about licensing. So a somewhat rambling and discursive conversation followed in the course of which the P.M. developed an interesting study of feminine psychology. They had voted for us he said in 1918 and we mustn't lose their vote. They didn't pass resolutions or make much noise but they felt keenly on subjects like this and if we only listened to the men we might go to an election thinking we had the country with us and wake to find that the women had swung over against us and that we had sustained a great disaster. And once having gone they would not come back for women in politics were more constant than men. I thought the little beast showed his usual astuteness in all this.

…

I have refused another committee – to advise the Postmaster General if you please. No thank you. Besides I'm fed up with Comees.

Sunday Post has arrived bringing me 30 letters but none from you. What has gone wrong?

…

---

[58] Charles Grant Robertson (1869–1948). Historian and academic adminstrator. Fellow, All Souls 1893–98 and domestic bursar 1897–1920; Tutor in Modern History, Exeter College, Oxford 1895–99 and Magdalen 1905–20. Principal, Birmingham University 1920–27 and Vice-Chancellor 1927–38. Knighted 1928.

[59] Edward George Villiers Stanley (1865–1948). Conservative MP for South-East Lancashire 1892–1906. Financial Secretary to War Office 1900–1903; Postmaster-General (in Cabinet) 1903–5; Under-Secretary for War 1916; Secretary for War 1916–18 and 1922–24; Ambassador to Paris 1918–20. Succeeded as 17th Earl of Derby in 1908.

11 June 1921
Westbourne

My dear Ida,

The post is as you say a scandal but on this occasion your letter arrived at breakfast time this morning. I was under the impression that my letters never arrived till Tuesday though always posted here at 6 o'clock on Sunday. I understand that there is now to be a collection late on Sunday night and I imagine that Tuesday therefore will be the day when you will receive this.

I voted with the Govt on the postal increases on Thursday, but I did so reluctantly not feeling any confidence that they were the best way (bar the Sunday delivery) of making both ends meet. But I felt first that Kellaway[60] ought to have a chance to show what he could do after so recently succeeding such an incompetent as Illingworth[61] and secondly that the Govt after losing 2 byes[62] was not in a condition when a defeat could be safely administered. But I really dont know that I can bring myself to vote for Addison's salary. I see the Times says the Govt means to make it a vote of confidence and to have a General Election if it goes against them. But the Times is not nowadays a safe guide and I have heard nothing of the kind from other sources. If it were so I think it would be putting a very severe strain on the fidelity of Unionists to the Coalition. No one can pretend that Addison is efficient in any capacity or that he is necessary to the Cabinet to preside over their committees. Really he ought to jump overboard in order to save the boat.

Willie Bridgeman[63] tells me that he thinks the miners are going to settle this time and I think so myself. But one thing has become manifest during this strike and that is that neither miners nor other working men are so thriftless as has been imagined, and represented by T.U. leaders. I am told that the miners have now got through their paper and are paying for their purchases in gold – their pre-war savings. I don't know whether this is true or whether it is a fact as I am informed that the Halford Cycle Co have sold more bicycles to miners during the strike than ever before. But I know that our BSA agent at Nottingham came

---

[60] Frederick George Kellaway (1870–1933). Liberal MP for Bedford 1910–22. Parliamentary (later Financial) Secretary, Ministry of Munitions 1916–20; Parliamentary Secretary, Department of Overseas Trade and additional Under-Secretary, Foreign Office 1920–21; Postmaster-General 1921–22. One of the founders of British Broadcasting Company and Chairman, Marconi Company 1924–33.

[61] Albert Holden Illingworth (1865–1942). Liberal MP for Heywood Lancashire 1915–21. Postmaster-General 1916–21. Joined the Conservatives, 1930. Created Baron 1921.

[62] On 7 June 1921 the Coalition Unionists lost Westminster, St George's to an Independent Anti-Waste candidate and next day a Coalition Liberal lost Heywood and Radcliffe to Labour.

[63] William Clive Bridgeman (1864–1935). Conservative MP for Oswestry 1906–29. Unionist Whip 1911; Junior Lord of Treasury 1915–16; Parliamentary Secretary, Ministry of Labour 1916–19 and to Board of Trade 1919; Secretary for Mines 1920–22; Home Secretary 1922–24; First Lord of Admiralty 1924–29. Created Viscount Bridgeman 1929.

in the other day with orders for a number of motor cycles and being asked by the sales manager who was buying them replied "Oh, the miners". For men who have been 10 weeks on strike to be buying £100 & £200 bicycles is a rather remarkable phenomenon.

…

I had a message on Monday that Austen wanted urgently to see me so I went round to his room. It appeared that the Govt wanted a chairman for that Conference of members to try and hammer out an agreed scheme of licensing and the Attorney General ("backed by the P.M." said the diplomatic Austen) was of opinion that *the* man for the job was the unhappy maid of all work who now addresses you these few lines. However on this occasion I was able to reply that the next morning I was starting on my joint committee of Lords & Commons which seemed likely to be three weeks about its work and A. with several "damns" was obliged to admit that he could not get over that stile. Afterwards the A.G. himself came to me in the lobby and in his most solemn manner adjured me to take on his little job but he too was defeated on the joint committee. I recommended Inskip but as he is a practising barrister he may decline. They want a strong hand as Lady Astor[64] is to be one of the members!

I had three days on my Water Bills with 12 large and solemn counsel droning away. My committee is not a very strong one being especially weak in Lords. Indeed one afternoon I noticed they were all asleep but one, having I supposed lunched too well! It is tiring work for the chairman as you have to keep your attention on the strain the whole time. I don't see much light at present but hope it may come.

One evening I neglected my duties and went with Annie to a "crush" at Lady St. Helier's[65] to meet the American Ambassador & Mrs Harvey. All sorts of scandals are current about them. He is said to have been drunk for weeks before he came over and to be comparable in status to H. Bottomley![66] while she is declared to have lived apart from him for many years. He is certainly not prepossessing in face having a leery smile and wearing huge spectacles which conceal his eyes and give him a peculiarly sly expression. She is a little short stout woman apparently very shy and totally destitute of charm. But we met many pleasant people and enjoyed our evening.

…

---

[64] Nancy Witcher Astor (1879–1964). Conservative MP for Plymouth Sutton 1919–45. First woman MP to take her seat, and wife of Waldorf Astor.

[65] Lady Mary St Helier (1859–1931). Alderman, LCC. Active Society hostess. Close friend of Joseph Chamberlain from the 1880s when married to Francis Jeune.

[66] Horatio William Bottomley (1860–1933). Journalist and proprietor. Liberal MP for South Hackney 1906–11 when the local Liberal Association withdrew their support. Resigned due to bankruptcy 1912. Re-elected 1918 as an Independent but expelled from Commons on 1 August 1922 having been charged with fraudulent conversion. Sentenced to seven years and released from prison 1927.

Frank has suddenly developed an intense enthusiasm for entomology and desires to catch every moth & caterpillar he sees "for my collection". "My collection" at present consists of two ancient white admirals and two broken specimens of Bahamian butterflies but in his imagination it is swelling every day and I foresee great demands upon me for assistance & advice. Dorothy who always has her own schemes and ideas is bored stiff by "my collection" but has become crazy about her music and besieges us with requests to listen to her performances on the piano.

...

18 June 1921
Westbourne

My dear Hilda,

...

I am fairly puzzled by the miners. Willie Bridgeman said they were certainly going back, Hickman,[67] a coal owner was equally positive in the same sense. Vernon Hartshorn[68] thought they would be "easily" under the ⅔ majority. Evidently nobody has fathomed their mental processes and feeling quite at sea about the considerations that have weighed with them I dont myself venture to prophesy what the next step will be. I should rather expect that a good number will go to work on Monday. Anyhow, that efforts will be made, (I hope unsuccessfully) to collar the 10 millions without the conditions attached to it, and that the Executive will be very disheartened and inclined to chuck the whole thing [sic].

I can quite appreciate the effect on your farmers and labourers of the dropping of the Agriculture Act proposals.[69] I suppose it is the first fruits of the Anti Waste campaign which is running a merry course just now and I have no doubt we shall see other "cuts" with like consequences until the inevitable reaction comes. I imagine that the Cabinet have really got frightened, not to say panicky, about the reduction in revenue which must be truly alarming and that they feel compelled to do what must be exceedingly distasteful to them lest worse should befall. A. was very furious with Godfrey L-L.[70] I believe over his Anti Waste

---

[67] Thomas Edgecumbe Hickman (1859–1930). Soldier 1881–1918. Unionist MP for Wolverhampton South 1910–22. Director Haunchwood Collieries.

[68] Vernon Hartshorn (1872–1931). President, South Wales Miners' Federation; member, National Executive of MFGB 1911–24; member, Coal Controller's Advisory Committee and Coal Trade Organisation Committee. Labour MP for Ogmore, 1918–31. Postmaster-General 1924; Lord Privy Seal 1930–31.

[69] Faced by a liability of £40,000,000 for the coming harvest, Part I of the Agriculture Act guaranteeing cereal prices and fixing labourer's wages was repealed.

[70] Godfrey Lampson Tennyson Locker Lampson (1875–1946). Conservative MP for Salisbury 1910–18 and Wood Green 1918–35. PPS to Home Secretary 1916–18 and to Assistant Foreign

memorial[71] and gave him the rough side of his tongue; but whether that really mends matters I rather doubt. M.P.'s are frightened themselves where they are not very sure of their constituencies and they are getting so restive that I shouldn't be surprised to see a bad kick-over one of these days. The feeling about Addison is so strong that I went to see A. about it, but I found him pretty well posted there and though I suppose I mustn't write exactly what he told me I came away with some hopes that Addison would either jump or be thrown overboard. I don't suppose you saw the interview he gave the Evening Standard in which he said he was not going to be driven out of office by a small number of Unionists who had nothing against him personally but who were making an opportunity to get rid of a Liberal from the Coalition. It is so far as I know a totally unfounded imputation and it has made Unionists very angry. He *is* a fool.

Winston's speech on Mesopotamia was a brilliant performance. Members wives are once more allowed into the gallery and I had a ticket so Annie was able to hear him. He kept the House amused and interested for 90 minutes interspersing argument and policy with anecdote and description and exercising great art in delivery. His speeches as Tay Pay[72] remarked to me are worth ten of Ll. G.'s he takes so much more trouble over them. But he showed his defects the next day when he gave an address at a dinner in the House given to the Dominion Premiers and the Indian representatives. He clean forgot about India and talked about "our race" "English speaking peoples" and the "four great Dominions" so that I could not help asking myself What does Mr Sastri[73] think of all this. Towards the end of the speech someone handed up a card on which "India" was written and Winston then produced an eloquent passage about the day when India would take her place on equal terms with the Dominions. But it was too late and when later on Sastri rose he administered in perfect English and with perfect taste one of the most scathing rebukes I ever heard. W. must have cussed a bit. He never mentioned Father's name but Massey[74] did & I noticed that the next day when W. had to speak again he delivered a great eulogy of him. I never

---

Secretary 1918. Represented First Commissioner of Works in Commons 1924–25; Under Secretary, Home Office 1923–24 and 1924–25 and for Foreign Office 1925–29.

[71] This added £15 million to old age pension charges. To Austen Chamberlain's fury fourteen signatories voted in favour and 80–90 abstained while Locker-Lampson was absent.

[72] Thomas Power O'Connor (1848–1929). Known as 'T.P.'. Author, journalist and politician. Editor of the *Star*, *Sun* and *Sunday Sun*, *T.P.'s Weekly*, *T.P.'s Journal* and *Cassell's Weekly*. President, United Irish League of GB from 1883; President, Trade Board of Film Censors, 1916. Nationalist MP for Galway Borough 1880–85 and Liverpool, Scotland Division 1885–1929. Father of the House of Commons 1918–29.

[73] Srinivasi Sastri (1869–1946). Indian delegate, Imperial Conference 1921. President, National Liberal Federation of India 1922. Agent of Indian Government in South Africa 1927–29.

[74] William Ferguson Massey (1856–1925). New Zealand politician and Prime Minister 1912–25. Attended Imperial War Cabinet and Conference 1917 and 1918 and Imperial Conference 1921 and 1923.

quite know whether most to admire his great gifts or to be alarmed at his impulsiveness and hasty judgement.

Yes I am rather sorry too about licensing. I might have failed to get agreement, but it is the sort of job for which I am temperamentally suited as was recognised by the A.G. and also by Johnnie Baird[75] who was regretting the other day that I hadn't taken it on. The Joint Committee is interesting as an experience but it is the sort of job from which you cannot possibly get any kudos although it is hard work. Hardly any one knows of its existence except those concerned. It is part of the procedure on Private Bills. In this case the Metrop. Water Board which supplies London with water is promoting a Bill to give it power to increase its charges both for trade supplies and to domestic consumers, & this Bill having passed its second reading has been referred to a Joint Committee of Lords & Commons instead of to 2 separate Committees. With it are 2 other Bills promoted by the Thames Conservancy & the Lea Conservancy to enable them to charge more to the Metrop. Water Board which gets its water mostly from those 2 rivers. I have 3 Commoners Lindsay[76] an Irishman, Farquharson[77] a Scot (& my word he is a fussy one) and Rose[78] a Labour man who seems completely bewildered by the whole thing & can only repeat over & over again that its all wasting his time. Then there are Lords Cowley[79] Bathurst,[80] Strafford[81] & Sandwich[82] of whom only the last seems to me to be any good at all. We sit from 11 to 4 with ¾ hr for lunch. There are 12 counsel representing various local authorities L.C.C. Chamb of Commerce &c besides the promoters and witnesses are examined & cross examined & re-examined just as in a court of law. One afternoon I noticed all the committee except one were asleep and it is dull work sometimes especially if you allow your attention to flag which of course as

---

[75] John Lawrence Baird (1874–1941). Diplomatic service 1896–1908. Conservative MP for Rugby 1910–22 and Ayr Burghs 1922–25. PPS to Bonar Law 1911–16; Under-Secretary for Air 1916–19 and Home Office 1919–22; Minister of Transport and First Commissioner of Works 1922–24. Governor-General, Australia 1925–30; Chairman, Conservative Party 1931–36. Succeeded as Bart 1920. Created Baron Stonehaven 1925 and Viscount Stonehaven 1938.

[76] William Arthur Lindsay (1866–1936). Unionist MP for South Belfast 1917–18 and Belfast Cromac 1918–22.

[77] Alexander Charles Farquharson (1864–1951). 'Medical man' serving RAMC and Deputy Assistant Director of Medical Services, Northern Command 1916–18. Coalition Liberal MP for Leeds North 1918–22.

[78] Frank Herbert Rose (1857–1928). Operative engineer and journalist. Labour MP for Aberdeen North 1918–28 often acting as an Independent Labour MP in defiance of the official whip.

[79] Christian Arthur Wellesley (1890–1962). Member of theatrical profession. Succeeded as 4th Earl of Cowley 1919.

[80] Seymour Henry Bathurst (1864–1943). Unionist. Succeeded as 7th Earl of Bathurst 1892.

[81] Edmund Henry Byng (1862–1951). Civil engineer 1881–87; member, London Stock Exchange 1889–1919; Almoner, St Barts Hospital 1919–46. Succeeded as Earl of Strafford 1918.

[82] George Charles Montagu (1874–1962). Private Secretary to President, Board of Agriculture 1898–1900 and L.G.B. 1900–1903. Conservative MP for South Huntingdonshire 1900–1906. Trustee, Tate Gallery 1934–41. Succeeded as 9th Earl of Sandwich 1916.

Chairman I cant do. I have made pretty good progress and guided my committee towards a decision and on Thursday I had an inspiration and told counsel to go and agree on a scheme on certain lines if they could & then come back again next Wednesday! I hope to get an agreed scheme then & after that there shouldn't be much more to do on the main bill while agreement has the further advantage that it stifles all criticism of the committee's decision!

But I don't think I shall take on another job like this; it has shut me out of committees on public bills as well as the licensing. I have managed this last week to get in 2 short speeches in the House, but both were made at a late hour and were therefore unreported.

...

I have sold my Bahamas property (seven thousand acres of worthless land) for £200 to the sons of Mr, now Sir James, Sands![83] I have been trying to get a bid for a long time for the place brought me in nothing and in my absence I felt squatters were likely to take possession of any fertile parts of it. Moreover I dont approve of absentee landlordism on principle. So I accepted the first offer they made and am now completing the sale. I have used most of the first instalment to buy another French Cabinet for our London house ...

25 June 1921
Westbourne

My dear Ida,

This has been a real scorcher. The first day on which I have been hot, to call hot. When one goes to the House at 11 and doesn't emerge till any time between 11.30 and 5 am one doesn't get much idea of what is going on outside. But the garden is getting a rather pitiful sight ...

On Monday I presided at the Unionist Club dinner ... I addressed the multitude, which was in fact the best gathering they have had this year, on the subject of the municipal bank and they seemed very interested. I thought it was really more informing than platitudes on a political subject.

It has been a rather lurid week politically speaking. Of course I had heard from A. what Ll.G. was going to say about Addison so it was no surprise.[84] But Ll.G. appeared in a new guise. For the first time he had a cold critical and rather hostile House to address and he did not seem to be able to find spring enough in himself

---

[83] James Patrick Sands (1859–1925). Member, Bermuda Assembly 1889–1916; Leader, Bermuda Government 1909–16; President, Legislative Council 1916–23; Member, Executive Council 1901–23. Knighted 1917.

[84] Debate on Addison's salary, 23 June 1921. Pressure from the Northcliffe press and 180 Unionist MPs forced Lloyd George to make this an issue of confidence. After a tepid defence of Addison's 'unfortunate interest' in public health and housing, he requested a ministerial salary of only £2500 – below that proposed by his critics.

to pull away from it. On the contrary he was depressed and laboured and failed to seize the prevailing spirit. All through the first part of the speech while he was skirmishing round with pictures of an overworked cabinet people kept saying "What has all this got to do with old Addison"? When he went on to say they must have an odd man to relieve them the chorus murmured "But not Addison". And when at last after many feints he came to the point and said Addison was to go at the end of the session a voice behind me said "Cuttin' the cackle and comin' to the 'osses" and others ironically cried "Saved!" And there was more laughter than cheers. Still the House's good humour was restored for the moment & if he had just said what a good father & husband Addison was all would have been well. But he must needs go on to declare that Addison had saved hundreds of millions in munitions during the War and that made men angry again. They shouted "Fantastic it wasn't Addison" and they perceived that Ll.G. was just bidding for the Labour vote. And finally his shot at Northcliffe missed the target because men thought he was aiming at alleged profiteers generally. The speech was voted a failure though the crisis was over and for long after the P.M. sat with his head in his hands looking as though he were done. But *I* wasn't sorry for him!

I had to sit up all Tuesday night because I wanted to speak against an amendment of "Josh" Wedgwoods,[85] and it didn't come on till about 3.30 a.m. It was lost without a division "Thanks to you" said Josh. "If you hadn't barged in we should have got it". But when I remarked that his philanthropy (it was to exempt capital expenditure on welfare work from income tax) was entirely misplaced he thoughtfully remarked "I believe you're right". I got to bed just after 5 and slept peacefully till 9.15 when I arose and went into my Committee.

Oh that Committee! Never again! It goes on and on and every time I think I am getting to a decision up jumps another counsel and raises a fresh point. I see at least one & possibly 2 more weeks of it and it has kept me away from a heap of other things.

I sympathise with your feelings about housing though I can see that if Mond publicly announced his policy of "concentration on urban housing" he would probably raise the very d—l of a row. I believe he thinks the subsidy plan the one to be encouraged and as I think so too I am going to give him a copy of a criticism that has been published down here of our Housing Committee's proceedings. It is a lamentable tale of errors. Wrong sites, wrong layouts sewers put down and taken up. Fireplaces left out & put in afterwards at vast expense, incorrect plans, tram fares paid when no trams were used etc etc and I fear it is substantially true.

---

[85] Josiah Clement Wedgwood (1872–1943). Naval architect 1894–1900. Served South African War 1900–1901 and Resident Magistrate, Transvaal 1902–4; Flanders and Gallipoli 1914–15; attached General Smuts Staff in East Africa 1916; Assistant Director, Trench Warfare Department 1917. Liberal MP (Labour from May 1919) for Newcastle-under-Lyme 1906–42 when created Baron Wedgwood. Vice-Chairman, PLP 1922–24; Chancellor, Duchy of Lancaster 1924.

It looks today as if the miners were coming back. Hodges speech at the Labour Conference produced in me the same impression as when I see a dog turning round & round. I conclude he's going to lie down! The fact is they are done and have got to come in or their men would come in without them. But I do trust the Govt won't give them the 10 millions. I don't mind a part of it, but to give the whole would be disastrous. I guess it will take a good many weeks before we get much coal again.

Annie and I have had a nice restful day with two meetings apiece. ... One of mine was to open Elliotts new pavilion on our recreation ground. It is a splendid place with a dancing hall and dressing rooms & the men are delighted with it. Afterwards the chairman of the shop stewards (supposed to have been a "horrible sinner" and extremist once) addressed the assembly and expressed his gratitude to the Board in the warmest terms not only for this but for all they had done in recent years. In fact the joint committees which administered the war benefits and the recreation fund and the unemployment scheme (all my ideas of which I am rather proud) and now old age pensions has quite revolutionised the feeling and I am told that if the engineers go out our men will probably break away and stop in, which as you know is a pretty strong thing for workmen to do.

...

3 July 1921
Westbourne

My dear Hilda,

...

The industrial outlook has certainly cleared considerably during the week and though there are still many pessimists I am inclined to think that we shall now see a partial revival of trade and a consequent diminution of unemployment. Ll.G. put the case as well as he could for the miners subsidy by saying that the old offer was wiped out and this was a new one based on a different principle with a limit of 10 millions. But the new wine tastes devilish like the old and though everyone saw that it was useless to protest yet I found a good many who made a very wry face over it.

I have been trying to collect opinions about the future of Coalition. I find a number of men think it impossible that it can survive another election though they generally dont know how it is to be broken up. A few see no reason why Unionists shouldn't just say they are going on their own, but those who have more experience of politics see that that is impossible as of course the C.L.'s wouldn't accept it. On the other hand fusion is equally impossible and so several have come by a process of exhaustion to an idea which had also occurred to me viz that Ll.G. might say he wanted a rest and that he should temporarily retire from office if not from politics. If he chose to do that another might accept it but the difficulty I see is how to dispose of Winston, Hewart,[86] Fisher[87] and the other C.L.'s who couldn't be asked to join a purely Unionist Govt and who wouldn't be willing to stand aside. It may be that Ll.G. will decide to stake everything upon a new party of which he should be the head, under a new name. I expect he would rope in A. & a good many Unionists but I think that if any considerable number of M.P.'s broke away and especially if they had a leader of any gifts the "machine" would go with them in many parts of the country. Anyway developments seem probable in the near future. G. Younger[88] told me he thought it was pretty nearly time for him to go to the P.M. and ask him where he stood & what he meant to do about it. "He knows I dont care a damn for him", he remarked!

I went to a very interesting dinner to Carson on Tuesday. There were only three speeches, the P.M. Carson & Hewart. The first two very good & the A.G. inimitable. He really is a wonderful little man. I know he had had hardly any time for preparation, yet his speech fairly sparkled with epigrams.

The week was dull in the House. The Key Industries bill provokes much simulated wrath over the "gag" from the opposition & Squiff had the audacity to lecture the House on its bad attendance (he is *never* there himself) but it produces nothing new in the way of argument. The Bastardy Bill got through committee at last & if Banbury looks the other way we shall get it passed. My Water Committee still goes on ...

...

9 July 1921
Westbourne

My dear Ida,

...

I forget if I told you that I had a long talk with Mond in his room one day about housing. It was refreshing to hear his comments on the Addisonian policy and its results. Of course financial straits are at the bottom of his curtailment of the subsidy policy for which I am sorry, but he quite agreed that the only thing to do with the municipal houses would be to write off about half their cost. He stated that already tenders were half what they were last year in some cases. As

---

[86] Gordon Hewart (1870–1943). Liberal MP for Leicester 1913–22. Solicitor-General 1916–19; Attorney-General 1919–22; Lord Chief Justice 1922–40. Knighted 1916. Created Baron Hewart 1922 and Viscount 1940.

[87] Herbert Albert Laurens Fisher (1865–1940). Liberal MP for Sheffield Hallam 1916–18 and English Universities 1918–26. President, Board of Education 1916–22. Warden, New College, Oxford 1925–40.

[88] George Younger (1851–1929). Conservative MP for Ayr Burghs 1906–22. President, National Union of Conservative Associations in Scotland 1904; Chairman, Unionist Party Organisation 1917–23; Treasurer, Unionist Party 1923–29. Created Bart 1911 and Viscount Younger of Leckie 1923.

regards slums he said he had always held the general views expressed in my report and he had been urging them on the L.C.C. which, of course, didn't like them. They want heroic measures still at someone else's expense!

…

I have nearly finished my blessed committee on Water Bills; in fact I expect to complete on Tuesday and as I have not been put on the Railways Bill I hope to get a bit of a "let up". It really has been very trying this last week with continual late sittings and early committees. Meanwhile I have at last got a letter out of Eric Geddes on my Canal Report after expressing myself with great frankness to little Neal. G. has agreed to publish the report & says he is with us "in principle" but cannot find any money, local or imperial, for starting a Trust for the Trent or anywhere else. This is not unreasonable but I shall return to the charge for the money is really wanted for the Trent for the present and the Trust could be set up next session if the Dept. wd set about it now. …

Annie and I got down yesterday – a very warm journey. I went to a management committee of the B. Unionist Ass. and found a cheque for £500 awaiting me there – an agreeable surprise. I *do* think we are splendid in Birmingham in the way we are running our political organisation and the enthusiasm we arouse. I consider that the mainspring of it all is Annie, and a long way after her I come. The rest come a very long way after that! Seriously I dont know what Birm. wd do without us. We had our agent & divis[iona]l sec up this morning for a 2 hour talk about fresh activities in the way of clubs &c. They declared, & gave instances, that the working men attached special importance to my words beyond any other M.P.'s because I knew something about business & moved about among my constituents. I believe I have a number of special supporters among Railwaymen.

…

16 July 1921
Westbourne

My dear Hilda,

…

It certainly has been a trying week in London and sleep at night has been difficult owing to the heat. The costumes in the House have been very weird. … I finished up my Joint Committee on Tuesday to my very great joy and am now free of Committees except one on War Pensions next Tuesday when I have got a number of amendments to move. Yesterday to keep my hand in I made an impromptu speech on Police Pensions. The whole House was trying to make the Govt give extra pensions to people who had no legal right to them and I thought it was time to give some support to the Govt in resisting the demand. I was amused to find afterwards that several members who had been silent came up and said that I was *so* right and that my speech was a "douche of cool sense" & so on. Anyhow we defeated the proposal by 100 to 68.

The sensation of the week was Addisons resignation. As you say, he was a cunning little thing to get his attack in early, before his resignation had been submitted to the King which was I believe unconstitutional. He made it clear that he meant to attack the Govt on general grounds as well as housing but the P.M.'s reply was a home [?] thrust and the opinion of members seemed to be that he could not do the Govt much harm or the oppn much good. I had a long talk one day this week with Sir Malcolm Fraser[89] about the Coalition & the political situation. He is evidently worried about the Anti Waste people and thinks they will carry the women but I don't agree with him if the latter are well organised. At any rate I don't think they will be stampeded here. From what Fraser said I judged that he thought F.E. wd make a bid some time for the leadership of the Unionist Party. He is certainly very ambitious as well as clever but he is distrusted in the country. I hear that he has become a teetotaller. It was time. By the way I got £500 out of Fraser for the Midland Union!

I don't think there is any likelihood of an autumn session though if the Irish manage to settle their affairs legislation will be needed which has not been allowed for in the time table. But even so I fancy we should sit into September rather than have an autumn session.

I certainly hope so as my plans are all made on that assumption ...

...

23 July 1921
Westbourne

My dear Ida,

I really do feel rather exhausted this week end and Annie is the same. To sit up in the hot weather night after night till 12[,] 1 and 2 in the morning when you have to attend a committee at 11 takes it out of you and I have a good many hours of sleep to make up. I got home about 7 last night after a very hot journey and Annie arrived soon after me having journeyed to Wolverhampton to address a meeting in the Cannock division. She says it is no effort to her but the audience wept as usual and she was about done up. Neither of us could eat much and so today by way of a rest we had about 60 young people from the constituency to tea in order to discuss the starting of a Young Unionists Club. It all went off very well except the young people. They were invited to "go off" at 5.30 but it was 7.30 before the last of them departed.

The housing debate on Thursday prevented my attending the garden party at Buckingham Palace ... I wanted to speak but with my usual bad luck when

---

[89] (John) Malcolm Fraser (1878–1949). Formerly editor of the *Standard* and *Daily Express*. In the Conservative reorganisation of 1911 Fraser became head of the Press Bureau at Central Office before becoming Principal Agent, 1920–23. Vice-Chairman, Conservative Party, 1937–38. Also Deputy Director of Airship Production at the Admiralty, 1918–19. Knighted 1919; created Bart 1921.

housing is on I couldn't get in till after the P.M. & that happened to be just at 8 o'clock. So I spoke to an empty House which was a pity as I really had something to say about slums and agricultural housing. The personal squabble between Addison and the P.M. was sordid and undignified and though the P.M. had the best of it in a house which was unfavourable to the Addisonian policy his jibes were in the worst possible taste. I saw him cock his ears when I said A. was not the first who had suffered from the exuberant expressions of a "warm & feeling heart" (Squiff's sarcastic phrase) but he hurried off to Austen's dinner & declared I had made a most valuable contribution to the debate! (he hadn't heard a word of it except the above observation!)

I have no doubt that the Mond policy is right so far as local authorities are concerned. I am not so sure about the subsidy but a good many well informed people tell me that it is having the effect of keeping up prices and I am disposed to think there is something in it. As regards rural housing I suppose no one will pay any attention to what I said but I still believe that my plan or a modification of it would work and that it will be necessary to give a subvention in some form if new houses are to be built in the villages. I was curious that Mond said nothing about my committee when speaking of slums but Sir Aubrey Simmonds[90] [sic] an official of the Health Ministry who gave an interview to the press a few days ago stated that the Government had "practically adopted" our policy.

I have had a very busy week with many subjects going on at once. I got my talk with Eric Geddes on Tuesday and although as usual he was impatient to get it over and go back to his Railways as soon as possible I got him to promise that his Ministry should draft out a Bill at once and that the Trent people should be called in to discuss it in the autumn. He informed me in confidence that he was not going to join Leverhulme[91] and that though he would cease to be a Minister in August he would remain for some months in close touch with Downing Street (!) carrying out a job the Govt had asked him to do and coaching his successor. So he wd be on the spot and wd see these Trent people with me. This was really much more than I had ventured to hope for and I was quite elated at having made a little further progress. I have since heard that he has given the officials instructions to get on with the Bill (and between ourselves I have told them what to put in it!)

I spoke last week on the Safeguarding of Industries Bill, attacking a new clause which Baldwin[92] had brought in & which provided that if after two years

---

[90] Aubrey Vere Symonds (1874–1931). Second Secretary, Ministry of Health, 1919–25; Permanent Secretary, Board of Education, 1925–31. Knighted 1916.

[91] William Hesketh Lever (1851–1925). Industrialist and philanthropist. Pioneer of manufacturing soap from vegetable oil and founder of Port Sunlight in 1888, combining production of Sunlight soap with model housing for workers. Merged with Dutch counterpart to form Unilever. Created Bart 1911, Baron Leverhulme of Bolton-le-Moors 1917 and Viscount Leverhulme of the Western Isles 1922.

[92] Stanley Baldwin (1867–1947). Conservative MP for Bewdley 1908–37. Joint Financial Secretary to Treasury 1917–21; President, Board of Trade 1921–22; Chancellor of Exchequer 1922–23;

a key industry was found not to be doing any good i.e. if it was insufficiently protected, the 33⅓ duty on foreign imports should be – – dropped ! I found afterwards that Addison was responsible for this precious provision. Anyhow other people attacked it too and it was incontinently thrown overboard by the Govt.

...

31 July 1921
Westbourne

My dear Hilda,

...

What are we to say of Lord Northcliffe?[93] (Did you read Punch's delightful account of the departure of Ld Thanet in the "Megalomania"?) Knowing the astounding habits of the American reporter I am ready to believe the apologia of the Times & to suppose that the actual conversation was invented by him. But it is equally obvious that he *was* only dramatising the real intention of N's communication and that the latter is out to make every bit of mischief he can between this country, U.S.A. and the Dominions. It is really alarming to think what he can do when he goes on to Canada & Australia. Talking of which, if you come across a book called "the British Commonwealth of Nations" by Duncan Hall, I recommend your reading it. It puts the Dominion point of view very well and brings out clearly how far we have drifted away from Lionel Curtis[94] & Imperial Federation & how the Imperial Conference has taken its place.

I was presented with a most artistic key on Monday (the second in the last few months) and we had quite an interesting function, opening the first branch Bank we have built ourselves. It may interest you to know that we are now collecting water rents which are payable at our branches and indeed there is talk of collecting rates in the same way since there is likely to be a great extension of direct rate paying by the tenants in the future, the increased rents having put a great number of houses out of the compound. At the Council House we have

---

Prime Minister 1923–24, 1924–29, 1935–37; Lord President of the Council 1931–35. Created KG and Earl Baldwin of Bewdley 1937.

[93] Alfred Charles William Harmsworth (1865–1922). Founder of Amalgamated Press 1881 and proprietor of *Answers*, *Daily Mail*, *Daily Mirror*, *Evening News*. Proprietor of *The Times* 1908–22. Chairman, British War Mission to USA 1917; Director of Propaganda in Enemy Countries 1918. Created Viscount Northcliffe 1905.

[94] Lionel George Curtis (1872–1955). Member of Milner's 'Kindergarten', administrator, historian and writer on imperial affairs. Served South African War 1899–1902; Town Clerk, Johannesburg 1902–3; Assistant Colonial Secretary, Transvaal 1903–9; founder and Editor of *Round Table* 1909; Fellow of All Souls and Professor of Colonial History at Oxford 1912; Attended Paris Peace Conference and Secretary to British delegation at Irish Conference, 1921; Colonial Office adviser on Ireland 1921–24.

pushed the Water Dept out of the great offices they have long occupied & taken over a number of their staff! The Bank reminds me that Hiley[95] who gave me so much help when I was Ld Mayor now wants to stand for Parlt & he will probably be adopted next week for the Duddeston Divn for which Hallas[96] now sits. Hallas is the man (also associated with the Bank) who started as a N.D.L.P.[97] & then ratted to Labour where he finds himself extremely uncomfortable!

I have been getting very active in the House lately. I made 2 speeches in the small hours of Tuesday morning on the Police Pensions Bill and another on Wednesday on the Railways Bill but the latter was cut short because the Speaker ruled my new clause out of order. This was vexing because I had been to him the day before & also just before I spoke & he said he had carefully considered it & concluded it was in order! He is not quite sure of himself yet. I daresay you saw that the Reconstruction Committee asked me to act as Chairman till the end of the session. I agreed to do so to bridge over the gap & I rather expect they wd like me to take it permanently. But there is the difficulty that I could not agree to head a revolt against Austen & a revolt might be wanted. There's where the handicap is always coming in.

Dorothy is still at Twitts Ghyll where she seems to be very happy and I am sure keeps them all lively. She writes capital letters. Frank is also perfectly happy. He talks & thinks mostly of butterflies and this morning was thrown into a transport of excitement by the appearance of a humming bird hawk in the garden. I sympathise, though it no longer gives me the thrill & the intense longing for its possession!

7 August 1921
35 Egerton Crescent, SW3

My dear Ida,

…

7.30 pm. We have just brought Dorothy back from Twitts Ghyll. … Of course all gardens are looking miserable just now and Austen's is certainly no exception but after making every allowance I still feel that it is not & never would be the garden for me. He himself is getting very tired. He has been up late 3 nights

---

[95] Ernest Varvill Hiley (1868–1949). Solicitor 1891–94; Deputy Town Clerk, Birmingham 1894–1902; Town Clerk, Leicester 1902–8; Town Clerk, Birmingham 1908–16; Deputy Director-General of National Service 1917; Director, Metropolitan Carriage Wagon & Finance Co. 1917–21; Chairman, Glover & Main. Conservative MP for Birmingham, Duddeston 1922–23. Member, Royal Commission on Lunacy and Mental Disorder 1924–26 and on Transport 1928. Knighted 1918.

[96] Eldred Hallas (1870–1926). Trade union secretary and Birmingham City Councillor 1911–18. MP for Birmingham, Duddeston 1918–22 elected for the pro-Coalition National Democratic Party with Conservative support but took the Labour whip from October 1919.

[97] National Democratic and Labour Party. Successor to British Workers' League, representing 'patriotic labour'. An electoral pact with the Conservatives enabled it to win ten seats in 1918.

running this week and has looked like a corpse. I myself sat up over the licensing bill and got home just before sunrise. The next night also I was up fairly late but on Thursday I kicked and went home at midnight.

I made rather a successful speech by the way on the Min. of Labour vote but the papers did not even mention my name as having spoken. A good number of M.P.'s however came and said how much they had been interested & what a lot they had learned. I didn't tell them that I had mugged it all up in the library the day before! Earlier in the week my Metropolitan Water Bill was taken after 11. There were a number of amendments down, but I had mugged up the evidence again and bowled them all out without any trouble, much to the admiration of Sir Keith Fraser[98] who was sitting next me and who can't understand why I don't move across to the Treasury bench. I should perhaps mention that he is generally considered to be half-witted!

On Tuesday I presided for the first time as Chairman at the Reconstruction Committee. I addressed them at some length on Second Chamber Reform and we had an excellent meeting over 60 members being present which is a great many more than we have been having. My speech appears to have given great satisfaction and many members expressed their regret afterwards that it had not been taken down as they considered it gave them a remarkably complete survey of the whole situation which they would have been glad to keep by them. Another case of mugging up! The meeting was in the end adjourned and I shall be in the chair again next Tuesday, but of course on such a delicate subject it is necessary to keep everything out of the press. The Govt haven't made any plan of their own yet and the moment anyone begins to look into the difficulties he at once takes a different view from anyone else. If only we could persuade the country to keep the House of Lords merely eliminating the backwoodsmen, I believe that would be far the simplest and most satisfactory way out.

I think there is no doubt that Mond wants to cut out as many rural houses as possible to concentrate on the crowded areas, where as he truly says the problem is more urgent because the effect on health and physique is more marked. I cannot help agreeing with him but I should all the same like to see a policy laid down for dealing with houses in agricultural districts. I tackled him on the subject one day pointing out that the agr. labourer never had and never would pay an economic rent & that he had therefore either to abandon any idea of rehousing him or face a subsidy in some form. He said he saw no way out!

...

---

[98] Keith Alexander Fraser (1867–1935). Army career 1888–1903. Conservative MP for Harborough 1918–23. Succeeded as Bart 1898.

21 August 1921
Georgeham Rectory, Braunton

My dear Ida,

... I had an exciting week because when I got to the House on Monday I found Leslie Wilson[99] had heard my prayer and starred the Ch. of Unmd Parents Bill and moreover that it was coming on that night. It then appeared that the only chance of getting it through was to square the opposition as Austen had pledged himself not to take contentious business after 11. So there was much coming and going, conference and negotiation and finally I got everyone squared without as I thought doing any serious injury to the bill. About 12.30 on Tuesday morning we got the 3rd reading and I began to shout with a loud voice. However in the next 3 days I perceived that I had been premature. The acceptance of opposition amendments in the Commons had played the deuce with the drafting and moreover made it possible that in certain cases the title and the property might be divided. So there were more conferences & discussions with Schuster[100] the Ld Chancellors Sec. Ld Onslow[101] who was to take the Bill, Ld Muir MacKenzie[102] who agreed to take it when the Govt thought they had better not be mixed up with it & once more I thought the position was saved. But the Archbishop of Canterbury[103] wouldn't have it and then Crewe[104] professed that the debate on

---

[99] Leslie Orme Wilson (1876–1955). Conservative MP for Reading 1913–22, Portsmouth South 1922–23. Assistant Secretary to War Cabinet 1918; Parliamentary Secretary to Minister of Shipping 1919–21; Parliamentary Secretary to Treasury and Chief Conservative Whip 1921–23; Governor of Bombay 1923–28 and of Queensland 1932–46.

[100] Claud Schuster (1869–1956). Civil Servant. Secretary, London Government Act Commission 1899–1902; Legal Assistant, Board of Education 1903 and Legal Adviser 1907; Principal Assistant Secretary 1911; Legal Assistant on National Insurance 1911–15; Clerk of the Crown and Permanent Secretary in Lord Chancellor's Office 1915–44; Head of Legal Branch, Allied Control Commission, Austria 1944–46. Knighted 1913. Created Baron Schuster 1944.

[101] Richard William Alan Onslow (1876–1945). Diplomatic service 1891–1909; Assistant Private Secretary to Lord Grey 1909; Private Secretary to Permanent Under-Secretary, Foreign Office 1911–13; Assistant Clerk, Foreign Office 1913–14; British War Mission, Paris 1918–19; Lord-in-Waiting 1919–20; Civil Lord of Admiralty 1920–21; Parliamentary Secretary, Agriculture and Health 1921–23 and Education 1923–24; Under-Secretary for War 1924–28; Paymaster General 1928–29. Known as Viscount Cranley from 1876. Succeeded as 5th Earl of Onslow 1911.

[102] Kenneth Augustus Muir-Mackenzie (1845–1930). Barrister. Member, Standing Committee for Revision of Statute Law; Permanent Principal Secretary to Lord Chancellor and Clerk of Crown in Chancery 1880–1915. Lord-in-Waiting 1924. Knighted 1911. Created Baron Muir-Mackenzie 1915.

[103] Randall Thomas Davidson (1848–1930). Chaplain to Queen Victoria; Dean of Windsor; Bishop of Rochester 1891–95; Winchester 1895–1903; Canterbury 1903–28. Created Baron Davidson of Lambeth 1928.

[104] Robert Offley Ashburton Crewe-Milnes (1858–1945). Lord President of Council 1905–8 and 1915–16; Colonial Secretary 1908–10; Lord Privy Seal, 1908–11 and 1912–15; Secretary of State for India 1910–11 and 1911–15; President, Board of Education 1916; Ambassador to Paris 1922–28; Secretary of War, 1931. Succeeded as 2nd Baron Houghton 1885. Created KG 1908, Earl of Crewe 1895 and Marquess of Crewe 1911.

second reading should be adjourned. The Ld Chancellor, who was keen to get the bill, accepted and I suppose if there were an autumn session it might go through. My own impression however is that we shall have to start all over again, but I have very little doubt that sooner or later we shall succeed, because we are learning more about the difficulties each time & how to overcome them.

...

On Thursday the House rose early but I didn't get away till 11.30 as I was dining with Hannon & discussing party affairs. The company consisted of Hannon, Leslie Wilson "Worthy" Evans[105] "Bertie" Horne, "Willie" Sutherland[106] & myself. We agreed that active propaganda was necessary on behalf of the Govt both as regards finance and anti-waste and also as regards the legislative record of the session. We also agreed that a committee of active & keen young Unionist M.P.'s should be formed to speak in the country and also to meet together & advise about the points that require attending to. Hannon was very anxious that I should be chairman of this comee. He urged that none of the others had the gifts for the place, but that they would all look up to me & he would be ready to do all the hard work. Also he said there was a great cabal going on with a view to getting rid of Austen & putting F.E. in his stead as leader of the party & he thought it wd do good if I took the job. However I firmly declined saying it was not my line & I was not well fitted for it; that they wanted a younger man and that several of the others would do it excellently. The fact is I have no inclination for it and dont feel disposed to spend my holiday in sweating for the party for which I care very little, though between ourselves I have no doubt that Hannon is right in saying that I could do it better than the other men. But there are a thousand reasons against. I dont want to be drawn off my Birmingham & Midland organisations which are quite enough to look after. As for helping Austen it might have just the opposite effect. I cant imagine anyone voting that he should be leader because he liked me, but it is conceivable either that friends might imagine that he stood in my way or that enemies might say, "the family is everywhere; lets get rid of the lot". So tho' H. returned to the charge after the others had gone I was immovable. He again said I ought to be Chairman of the party but he quite sees the difficulty with my brother as leader. And anyhow I don't want the chairmanship which would take me out of the House & immerse me in the details of party organisation – a soulless job.

---

[105] Laming Worthington-Evans (1868–1931). Conservative MP for Colchester 1910–29, Westminster St George's 1929–31. Minister of Blockade 1918–19; Minister of Pensions 1919–20; Minister without Portfolio 1920–21; Secretary for War 1921–22, 1924–29; Postmaster-General 1923–24. Created Bart 1916.

[106] William Sutherland (1880–1949). Assisted with Pensions and National Insurance Acts and Lloyd George's land policy before Great War. Private Secretary to Lloyd George 1915–18. Liberal MP for Argyll, 1918–24. PPS to Lloyd George 1919–20; Junior Lord of Treasury 1920–22; Chancellor, Duchy of Lancaster 1922. Knighted 1919.

I have accepted membership of the Royal Commission on London of which Ullswater[107] is to be chairman and declined membership of Macnamara's[108] Trade Boards Committee. "So that's that"!

...

6 September 1921
Loubcroy Lodge, Oykell, By Lairg

My dear Ida,

...

We are having the wettest fortnight I ever remember here ... The salmon fishing in particular has on several days been utter midgery & I have to fling down the rod & line to cool down the burning and smarting of my hands & face.

I have had my usual want of luck with salmon fishing! ... Yesterday I was out grouse shooting. It rained absolutely the whole day out on the moor & most of the time we were enveloped in mist. The birds were so wild that 9 times out of ten they got up out of shot ...

Well you'd suppose I was having a beastly time wouldn't you? But of course except for a few midgerable moments by the river I enjoy every bit of it.

13 September 1921
Westbourne

My dear Hilda,

...

I forget if I told you that I had arranged to break my homeward journey at Carlisle, in order to see the [Central] Control Board's work there. Anyway I did so arriving at 2 a.m. on Sunday, spending most of the morning in bed & devoting the afternoon & Monday morning to the inspection of pubs, breweries, bottling factories & spirit stores with the General Manager. I am very glad to have been and have got some ideas. The Board's publics are much less different from those of the trade than I had expected though when one thinks of it this is quite natural seeing that they are old ones taken over & altered & not new ones built for the purpose. The chief attractions are the removal of "snugs" & the conversion of the "bar" with a sitting rather than a standing place, and in a certain number of cases, the provision of food. It was clear that in Carlisle where practically nothing of the kind existed before there was room for a certain amount of

---

[107] James William Lowther, the Speaker from 1905–21, was created Viscount Ullswater in 1921 upon retirement.

[108] Thomas James Macnamara (1861–1931). Liberal MP for Camberwell North 1900–1918 and Coalition Liberal for Camberwell NW 1918–24. Parliamentary Secretary, LGB 1907–8; Parliamentary and Financial Secretary, Admiralty, 1908–20; Minister of Labour 1920–22.

catering of this kind. But it can't be forced and Eagles the Gen. Man. admitted that he was fairly sick of trying to induce people to take "snacks" who only wanted to drink.

I conclude generally that the Carlisle experiment must pass into the hands of a local Public Trust and that facilities for similar Trusts and perhaps in selected cases for local authorities to be formed & take over the distribution of liquor is the best way of advance. In Carlisle they bought up 4 breweries and now do all the work in one thus making great economies but the one (which only employed 30 men) did not look to me at all efficient and I am inclined to think that it would simplify the problem and make for safety if the manufacture of beer as well as spirits were left to private enterprise.

After all it is only the distribution which constitutes the danger to the public and if the possibility of profit making is cut down by the exclusion of the manufacture that is really rather a good thing. I would like to see what profits did ensue devoted to the provision of recreation for the people! Intelligently applied much good work could be done with such money as was available.

...

18 September 1921
Westbourne

My dear Ida,

...

... I suppose if I took my politics more seriously I should be in a terrific "feeze" about going away at such a moment. But at my time of life I conclude that it is of no use to fuss. My belief (which may turn out quite wrong) is that a settlement will be arrived at. It is very possible that the security of Great Britain may be sacrificed in the process; but I hope for the best. If a settlement is arrived at and legislation becomes necessary, it is unlikely that they will have anything ready for Parliament before I get back. On the other hand it is clear that De Valera[109] hasn't conceded anything even in his latest letter, that he *means*, if he can, to secede, and that any other interpretation of his words and thoughts is merely a deliberate ostrich movement on the part of the Times and others who take a similar line. They want peace at any price. They are not prepared to fight under any circumstances, but as that is not a heroic attitude they pretend that when De V. says "black" he means "white" or at least "grey". Now Ll.G. and the Cabinet hitherto have appeared to grasp this obvious fact. If they maintain their present attitude and deadlock ensues the only alternative is to treat the case as

---

[109] Eamon de Valera (1882–1975). Sinn Fein MP for Clare East 1917–21; member of Dáil for Co. Clare 1921–59; President of Dáil 1919–22; President Sinn Fein 1917–26; President Fianna Fail 1926–59. Minister for External Affairs 1932–48; Taoiseach 1937–48, 1951–54, 1957–59; President of the Republic 1959–73.

one of war and reconquer the country. Before adopting so drastic a course it certainly does seem conceivable that Ll.G. might go to the country and if an immediate General Election were announced while I was abroad I suppose I should have to come straight home. In that case I should cuss but it hardly seems certain enough to justify me in postponing my departure. So subject to any new condition arising between now and Tuesday we spend that evening at the Grosvenor Hotel and next morning we start by the 8.20 arriving in Rome on Friday morning at 10.20 ...

I am gratified to find that the establishment of a municipal orchestra though very far as yet from being all I wanted has already achieved one end that I prophesied. It has given the town the premier place of the country, in the musical world, eclipsing even Manchester and noted players in the London Symphony orchestra have expressed a desire to come and settle here on the ground that Birmingham appeared likely to become the musical centre of the country. There is a certain amount of exaggeration in this, but all the same it shows the prestige of association with the municipality on which I have always insisted. I have promised if I am not summoned to London for Parliament in November, to take the matter up seriously again and see if I cant get the scheme carried a stage further. What is involved is the definite engagement of first rate players of various instruments and their appointment in the School of Music. Bantock[110] is Principal of the School & they tell me he is a hopeless obstructive but that I might be able to move him. We shall see. I should like to get my three Ld Mayoral ideas carried through, Bank, orchestra & civic recreation. If only I live, I fancy I shall do it.

On Thursday ... evening [Annie] and I once more went into the constituency to open formally the new club we have started for juniors. It has begun very well with a large membership & much enthusiasm and my agent assures me that he already has a list of 50 youths & girls who are willing to come & run messages lick envelopes or whatever else may be necessary at election time. But he gloomily added that he could hear very little of my opponent and evidently fears that he may not come up to the scratch.

On Friday morning I went to Hoskins for the annual meeting of shareholders. You will have received your 15% dividend making 65% for the year – the highest we ever paid. But between ourselves, instead of 15 we could have paid 100% and never turned a hair! Only I dont know how things will go next year and moreover if you pay too much in one year the Govt get such a slice of it that there seems hardly anything left. And finally I am planning a new building which might cost £25000 quite easily. Still its a comfort that the business goes so well.

...

---

[110] Granville Bantock (1868–1946). Conductor, composer and Professor of Music at Birmingham University 1908–34. Knighted 1930.

The Chamberlains spent the rest of September and October on a visit to Italy. This much needed rest was something of a mixed blessing. Despite a 'comfortable and uneventful journey' to Rome, their luggage was unexpectedly delayed for six days in France and nearly lost altogether both on the journey from Naples to Palermo and then back again. Moreover, although they enjoyed the architecture, art and scenery, they were less enchanted by their accommodation. Forced to change location in Rome by excessive noise, in Sicily they were appalled by the squalid hotels with dirty plates, bad food and stained bedding, while their maid was 'devoured by bugs' and forced to share her room with a large rat. Blazing Sicilian heat, gout and a general strike in Syracuse only completed the picture.

7 November 1921
[No address – London]

My dear Hilda,

...

I suppose you saw the results of the Munic. Elections in Birm. We lost 6 seats to Labour and though we had only 12 to attack and 25 to defend, and though unemployment has caused great bitterness in the town, and though less than 50% of the electorate voted which always counts against us, the fact remains that we had expected to do much better and we have had a nasty knock. I was to hold 4 meetings between now & Xmas but my people want me to cancel them as they say they wd do more harm than good. I have definitely cancelled one and am going to discuss the question of the others with my officers. ...

...

Things look very nasty here. I lunched with A. on Friday and heard the latest news which was not discouraging, but there is a baddish temper among the Ulstermen today. I refer more particularly however to the general state of mind among Unionists which is distinctly mutinous. I don't suppose it goes very wide but it seems pretty deep and there is a really ugly vicious tone at question time that is unanswered by any general disapproval by the bulk of the party. The objects are 2 liberals [sic], Hamar Greenwood and Shortt[111] the first of whom deserves all he gets by his lies and the second by his bad manners but one doesn't like to see it especially when one considers the kind of people who are making themselves prominent in it.

---

[111] Edward Shortt (1862–1935). Liberal MP for Newcastle 1910–22. Chairman, Select Committee on Medical Re-examination; Chief Secretary for Ireland 1918–19; Home Secretary 1919–22; President, British Board of Film Censors 1929–35.

12 November 1921
Westbourne

My dear Ida,

…

The fag end of the session was rather boring and we had interminable speeches without any compensating "moments of emotion". I made my speech on Monday but as I had already had a note from Austen to say that at his request the Cabinet had reconsidered the question and decided that they could not alter their decision it naturally produced no effect. The temper among a section of the party which I spoke of in my last became more marked and it was evident that much intriguing and colloguing was going on as small groups of Ulster men and die-hards were to be seen in the smokeroom and lobbies at all hours. I had vaguely got a notion that there was some talk of Bonar Law's taking up the Ulster cause but there was nothing about it in the Times and I had assumed that it was only the usual journalistic stunt. However on Wednesday I was dining with Horne and Hannon and I then learned that it was true and that Bonar was "on the warpath". It was evident that Horne took a very serious view of the situation and I determined to see Austen before the session ended. So I arranged to dine with him the next night and sat up with him till nearly 12 discussing the situation. I came away feeling rather more cheerful but he expected that the Cabinets proposals would have resulted in a further conference which I see today has been turned down. I still hope, however, that things will not come to an abrupt end though there is no doubt that Bonar's incursion has stiffened the necks of the Ulstermen. It is easy to see that if the break came it would split our Party & who can tell what would happen in such a case. The Labour party might indeed slip in and their advent to power might bring about a financial disaster of the first magnitude. Of one thing I feel certain and I understand that my views are widely shared, particularly by the party organisation. The country would not respond to an appeal involving resort to coercive measures which might mean 100,000 men and one or two hundred millions of money. So that if Bonar insists on leading a crusade he may split the party and ruin the country but he will not achieve his object. If however I am correctly informed that he has a personal grievance and thinks he has been badly treated he is likely to lose sight of considerations of that kind.

…

19 November 1921
Westbourne

My dear Hilda,

Many thanks for your letter which came this morning. I didn't go to Liverpool[112] myself as I had various engagements down here which it would have

---

[112] Annual conference of the National Union, 17–18 November 1921. A concerted Diehard

been very inconvenient to have put off and because I hadn't made my arrangements beforehand to go. But I got an S.O.S. from Austen at the beginning of the week indicating that he was nervous about what might happen and asking me to do something to help. So I hustled round and actually sent in addition to those who were already going a body of 22 stalwarts prepared to vote down the Diehards. It looks as if they were not required but Hewins[113] writes me that things looked quite ugly on Thursday morning and Hannon says that the change only became apparent when Derby spoke. I always regard that man as an impostor but he is evidently a very successful one and I think it must be admitted that he understands how to appeal to the man in the street. I went in to see Malcolm Fraser on Tuesday when I had to be in London for the first meeting of my commission and I gathered from him that he had no real fear of the conference though he reported that B.L. whom he had met during the week end was in a very bellicose mood. But I should think his feet must feel cooler now and I rather doubt if he will push things any further.

Down here I called a meeting of the Unionist management committee and got them to pass a resolution of confidence in the Govt which will I think spike Steel Maitlands[114] guns if he was thinking of coming out as a Diehard.

The Washington Conference doesn't look quite as happy as it did and I expect this decision of the Govt to suspend work on the four big ships will give rise to a lot of heart burning, especially as those Yanks who started off with such a parade of anxiety to curtail their own programme have not suspended it as we have.

…

26 November 1921
Westbourne

My dear Ida,

…

I have had one or two letters from Austen in the last of which he says he has had a very satisfactory talk with B.L. so I guess he has come to see reason but I fear that negotiations are very critical and that the chances of a settlement [in Ireland] do not improve. I see that Steel-Maitland who kept away from Liverpool has written a letter to the Times to preserve the chance of coming down

---

challenge over Ireland in the home of Orange Unionism mustered fewer than seventy votes from its 1800 delegates.

[113] R.G. Hewins. Secretary, Birmingham and Midlands Liberal Unionist (from 1918 Unionist) Association until 1926. Thereafter, Secretary to Chief Agent, BUA.

[114] Arthur Herbert Drummond Ramsay Steel-Maitland (1876–1935). Conservative MP for Birmingham East 1910–18, Birmingham, Erdington 1918–29, Tamworth 1929–35. Under-Secretary, Colonies 1915–17; Joint Under-Secretary, Foreign Affairs and Parliamentary Secretary, Board of Trade (Overseas Trade Dept) 1917–19; Minister of Labour 1924–29. Created Bart 1917.

on whichever side the fence [sic] proves to be the safest. Not a very heroic attitude!

...

I have had a pretty busy week including four speeches all on different subjects but none of them political. I have also spent a good deal of time with my businesses all of which are very short of orders. BSA gives me the most worry as it is at once the biggest and the weakest. We shall make a heavy loss this year and I am not at all satisfied with the management while there isn't a single member of the Board who is really worth anything. I should be very glad to get out only that one cant run away just when things go wrong. Elliotts is probably losing money too but there at any rate we are in a strong financial position and can afford to wait till the clouds roll by.

...

I have made a start on the Memoir but it is very much in the nature of a fit as I am obliged to let it drop for days together when I have speeches on my mind. I wish I had some people's facility in talking.

...

3 December 1921
Westbourne

My dear Hilda,

...

I am sorry but not surprised to hear that Austen was worried about Ireland. My friends are all very gloomy about it and think that both sides are as impracticable as they can be but I continue to hope for the best as long as the worst does not arrive and still believe that we shall work out of our present troubles. I shall be glad if we get our mass meeting safely over. It is for Tuesday as ever is and Austen is to take the chair with F.E. as the principal speaker. Naturally at such a moment our people are very much excited at the prospect and if at the last moment they both were to say they cant come I really don't know what we shall do. F.E. is to speak at a luncheon at the local Conservative Club that day but I have been informed that if he should fail I shall be expected to take his place! Jolly for me, isn't it! I have got to speak in the evening anyhow.

...

I have managed to make some progress with my memoir having now completed 6 chapters and got up to the outbreak of war. If only I could get some continuous work at it I should soon be able to get it off my mind. Meanwhile I have been writing an article for the Popular View the Unionist Headquarters journal on Slum Areas which I think might be useful.

I am thinking of going to London on Wednesday (after the meeting on Tuesday night) by a 7.30 train in order to attend the Royal Commission [on London

Government] as Norman[115] of the L.C.C. is to give evidence that morning. I am glad to see that he is to put forward suggestions though no doubt the local authorities will firmly oppose them lest they should lose any powers or importance. But they must recognise that *something* has got to be done.

...

Today I have been out shooting with some friends near Birmingham and we had a capital day though a very cold one. I seem to have got into the knack of pheasant shooting again and generally get more than my share of the bag with the result that I much enjoy it. And Annie encourages me under the delusion that I get a lot of exercise. But even if I dont really, I do get a mental change of a very complete kind and I think thats just as good, and helps me to sleep.

...

10 December 1921
Westbourne

My dear Ida,

...

Well, in spite of all the contretemps everything went like clockwork [with the mass rally]. Up to almost the last minute I half expected that I should have to make the Ld Chancellor's speech at the club so I was greatly relieved when he appeared at the station and of course I was overjoyed to hear of the [Irish] settlement. I did have to make a speech after all for I found that they actually proposed not to thank the L.C. for coming and addressing them, but I acquitted myself to my satisfaction on the spur of the moment and of course the club was tremendously bucked at being the recipients of the first account. As a matter of fact I think the Ld Ch. ought to have reserved himself to speak on Ireland in the evening but I fancy he saw the chance of getting himself widely advertised by speaking when the press could reproduce his speech several hours before anyone else had a chance. If so he was rather paid out for he made a faux pas in his reference to James Craig[116] and a good many people were disappointed with his evening speech which was mostly padding – cleverly done of course, but not cleverly enough to disguise the paucity of matter. Austen's speech on the other hand though short was considered to have stuff in it but as usual there was general comment on his pallor and emaciated

---

[115] Ronald Collet Norman (1873–1963). Private Secretary to George Wyndham 1899 and Lord Chancellor 1900–1905. Member. LCC 1907–22 and Chairman, 1918–19. Vice-Chairman, BBC 1933–35 and Chairman 1935–39.

[116] James Craig (1871–1940). Unionist MP for East Down 1906–18 and mid-Down 1918–21. Treasurer of the Household 1916–18; Parliamentary Secretary, Ministry of Pensions 1919–20; Parliamentary and Financial Secretary, Admiralty 1920–21. Sat in Northern Ireland Parliament for Co. Down 1921–29 and North Down 1929–40. Prime Minister of Northern Ireland 1921–40. Created Bart 1918 and Viscount Craigavon 1927.

appearance. I think he always looks his worst at a public meeting but when you talk to him he seems to be in good spirits and to have plenty of vitality. He and I sat up with F.E. till 12.30 that night and I had some interesting side lights on our beloved P.M.'s little ways, – not from Austen it need hardly be said!

...

I didn't pay much attention to the Times remarks about a General Election. They are always declaring that it is imminent but obviously the effect of the Irish success will soon wear off even if it is not upset by De Valera and unemployment will remain and probably would dominate the issue. As a matter of fact I think the settlement will come and D.V. will spike his own guns. In that case and indeed anyhow it will give a fillip to trade and we at B.S.A. are sending an extra traveller to Ireland at once to try and collect some of the money which we hear is burning a hole in the pockets of the South.

I have undertaken the chairmanship of a Committee to try and organise help for the unemployed here. David Davis[117] has started a Boot & Clothing Fund but he has no gift of inspiration and it is going very badly so I am going to try and get District Committees formed to work it up and start sewing parties like those they had during the war when a great many people took part in them. Birmingham is so big nowadays that you must decentralise if you want to get any life and vigour into things, and I am sure we shall find the old hands ready to come forward again if we ask them.

...

n.d. (probably 17 December) 1921
Moreton House

[First page missing] ... they demand. No wonder they are bitter against the Home Govt and ascribe to it all their troubles. Indeed if we had had a stable policy in this country for 20 years there might never have been any need for a change in the constitution, and I think Irish loyalists may fairly say that to be deserted now is a poor reward for sticking to a connection which has brought so much unhappiness to them. I sympathise with Ulster too so suddenly finding the tables turned on her and instead of being held up for an example of loyalty courage & patriotism, suddenly pointed at as the obstacle to peace, obstinate stupid & narrow minded. And yet one must face the question which the Diehards never will face. What is the alternative? And I think I find the greatest justification & the chief consolation for a very disagreeable necessity in the chorus of approval from the Dominions & the prospects of better relations with the U.S.A. That goes very far to cancel out the "humiliation".

---

[117] David Davis (1859–1938). Birmingham Council from 1901; Alderman 1913; Lord Mayor 1921–23; Life Governor, University of Birmingham; Deputy Chairman, Birmingham Unionist Association. Knighted 1923.

The debate in the House was on the whole on a high level. Ll.G. was not very successful as he seldom is in a set speech. It was too long, too disjointed & had too many perorations. Parts of it were happy but the concluding passage painting a rosy picture of a "valiant comrade" coming in and loyally & affectionately working hand in hand with England was too much for the stomachs of most of us. "You know he did egg the pudding a bit too much" said that vulgarian Sir Newton Moore[118] to me and one felt that he had returned to his older & worser habits. Asquith was good but too solemn & pompous and too difficult to hear to move the House very much. Hugh Cecil[119] was as usual most amusing and his chaff of the P.M. was delightful but as a contribution his speech was barren & futile as ever. Winston was brilliant & convincing but I thought not absolutely at the top of his form. But B. Law was admirable and undoubtedly made one of his greatest successes. His speech just suited the House for it expressed what was in many minds and yet it gave reasons for supporting the Govt which appeared convincing. It was a pity we couldn't take a division then. One felt that what followed must be, as in fact it was, an anti-climax.

...

---

[118] Newton James Moore (1870–1936). Australian surveyor and civil engineer. Member of Western Australian Assembly 1904–11 and Premier Western Australia 1906–10; Agent-General for West Australia in London 1911–18. Conservative MP for Westminster St George's 1918 , North Islington 1918–23 and Richmond Surrey 1924–32. Chairman, Standing Orders Committee 1922–23, 1924–28. Knighted 1908.

[119] Hugh Richard Heathcote Gascoyne-Cecil (1869–1956). Conservative MP for Greenwich 1895–1906 and Oxford University 1910–37. Provost of Eton 1937–44. Styled Lord Hugh Cecil from 1869. Created Baron Quickswood 1941.

3

1922
'I Should Like to be Rid of the Goat':
Decline and Fall of the Coalition

7 January 1922
Westbourne

My dear Ida,

...

... Annie had ... a cough for 2 days ... Of course she has picked it up "slumming"[1] but she wont be able to slum any more just yet and is groaning over all the engagements she is missing. Of course the alleged imminence of a Gen. Election makes her fairly boil with energy.

What a lamentable exhibition it has been. Austen was evidently depressed by the "give away" to the Press of the secrets of the inner Cabinet but by the irony of fate it looks as if he would stand out as the only member of the Cabinet who preferred principle to party expediency. I had to write to Geo. Younger to express my gratitude for his outspoken comments.[2] This dirty little Welsh Attorney and his C.L. sycophants think they can dictate a policy to the whole Unionist party. I cant for the life of me understand why they think they would gain by an election unless it is that they are relying on the money they have received by the sale of so many "honours". But Younger's statement has evoked such a unanimous chorus of approval that the Northcliffe Press is beating a hasty retreat and I am disposed to think that not only will the Election not take place in the Spring but that after such a dust it won't come on in the autumn either. Malcolm Fraser sent me "a thousand thanks" for my letter[3] and said it would be most valuable so I trust I had some little part in the revolt. Meanwhile Ll.G. has succeeded in dealing the Coalition a rude blow, for Unionists bitterly resent the attempt to jockey them out of Second Chamber Reform and they are in no mood to accept a position in the rear of the C.L. wing.

---

[1] Chamberlain's term for his regular visits to constituents in their homes to sound opinions and consolidate support.

[2] In response to well-informed press speculation, Younger, as party Chairman, gave a series of interviews on 5–6 January denouncing the 'pure opportunism and ... narrow party spirit' behind election rumours and forcefully stated the case against it.

[3] On 29 December Chamberlain warned of severe Unionist losses in the Midlands at a January election and opposed the idea of immediate 'fusion' of the Coalition partners.

I have been "slumming" myself two evenings this week and though I cant pretend that I enjoy the prospect beforehand I feel sure that there is nothing like it for pleasing the people or for really learning something of what they are thinking. There is general agreement that unemployment was the cause of the municipal defeats in the division last November, but they seem to think that a Party election wouldn't be affected in the same way and if I am to attach any importance to what I hear from many quarters my own seat is as safe as houses. But there is considerable uneasiness about the West, where they complain that they see nothing of Austen or his wife and though they agree that he ought not to be expected to come when he occupies such an onerous and responsible position still they keep on grumbling. So although I have 15 other speeches this month I have agreed to be the principal guest at a "supper" to be held at an obscure pothouse in his division when as I have told him I shall make myself sick with boiled scrag of mutton and bad tobacco! And I have been refused the only honour I asked for! Am I a dog?

...

14 January 1922
Westbourne

My dear Hilda,

...

From the programme I sent you last week you will know that I have been pretty busy ... I have just come in from my second "slumming" round and have now paid 20 calls all of which I think have been very useful. There is no doubt that working men are very disgruntled and downcast over trade prospects but it is equally evident that the distress is not comparable with what it has sometimes been in the past. No one is starving and indeed I have had complaints from men on short time that they are worse off than if they were unemployed altogether – which naturally made them more dissatisfied still. I had my first public meeting on Wednesday. It was thought by many of my friends and supporters that it was necessary to have a ticket meeting on account of the bitterness of feeling but I finally decided that I would have an open meeting and I was justified by the result. A strong contingent of socialists arrived early with the intention of making things hot but I drew their teeth by promising to answer questions & though I was much interrupted I got a hearing all right. As soon as questions were announced there was a joyful cry as much as to say "Now we've got him", but of course the questions were perfectly futile and I was able to score handsomely. The chairman didn't want to put the resolution as he was afraid it would be lost but I said I didn't care if it was and as I expected it was carried by an overwhelming majority. I have got another next week in a rowdier quarter but though I expect a warm time I have no fears as to the result.

I had to go to London on Tuesday for the R[oyal] Commission and found time to lunch with Austen, see Malcolm Fraser and draft a resolution for the Unionist Reconstruction Committee. A. seemed rather worried I thought and indeed he has got an awkward time in front of him. George Younger writes me that he feels in his bones that Ll.G. will have his way but since then the fiasco at Cannes[4] has occurred and I fancy Ll.G. will take the line indicated in Punch's delightful cartoon of the ventriloquist. I am not going to appear at the Reconstruction Committee as I don't want it said that Austen inspired it. He told me that he wd prefer that they didn't produce a resolution at all but I think he is wrong there for now is the time to put on the screw. Anyhow, whatever line Ll.G. takes I think the mischief is done and that the Coalition wont be the same again.

I began Ld Salisbury a little while ago & found it more interesting than I expected after what you said, but I have had to put it aside for the present for I have no leisure for reading. As regards your observation on the parallel with myself there is this big difference that Salisbury had entered on politics as a career and I have come into it late and never had a very strong inclination to it. I don't think I should be likely to get another offer of office. There is the strong objection to having 2 brothers in the Cabinet also the objection to having a number of representatives from one town in the Govt which makes other towns jealous and again Ll.G.'s personal dislike to myself. But besides all that there is my own recollection of close quarters with the little Welshman and as time goes on I feel less & less inclination to sacrifice my own peace of mind for the worries of responsibility with the consciousness that one cant expect to be supported unless it is clear that no support is needed. So that although my natural caution makes me indisposed to commit myself beforehand I can hardly conceive any circumstances under which I would accept office under Ll.G. again.

Besides my public meeting I addressed last week the Midland Union and the Birm Civic Society, gave a lantern lecture on India in the constituency and yesterday went to Nottingham to see the new works on the Trent. I was received with great honour and entertained at a sumptuous luncheon by the Mayor in his chain with the Sheriff in his chain and about 30 local councillors aldermen and business men. It was a very successful day. The works are going on splendidly and I was told that my speech would do great good in encouraging the town to go on & complete its work. The only disappointment was that I found the town was not yet ready to back the idea of a Public Trust taking over the Trent & all its feeders but those to whom I talked about it agreed that they would have to come to it fairly soon so I suppose I must be patient and wait a little longer.

...

---

[4] At the Cannes Conference Lloyd George and Briand came close to agreement over reparations but an ill-fated golf match (actually only a pose for the photographers) was interpreted in France as a sign that Briand was sacrificing national interests. Briand returned to Paris next day and resigned a day later.

21 January 1922
Westbourne

My dear Ida,

...

I have not heard from Austen for some little time but from what you say of his letters to you I suppose he has been having a pretty poor time. I thought his main Glasgow speech[5] was excellent thoughtful and statesmanlike, with sufficient assertiveness in it to mark his position as leader. Evidently he had prepared it carefully and I wish he would more often take trouble with his speeches especially in Birmingham where he is very apt to be lazy and think anything will do. He has a gift for extempore speaking which I often envy but it is a very dangerous one because speeches of that kind however sonorous are apt to [sic] lacking in "bite". Evidently the conclusion come to is that the Coalition must for the present be maintained but I fear that the resentment of the Unionists will not be allayed by the kind of speeches that the C.L.'s are making at their conference with their claims to be the dominating force in politics, their insistence on full blooded free trade, their refusal to deal with the Second Chamber and their demands for more seats. I quite foresee that they will be wanting a share of Birmingham representation directly and then we shall be having a repetition of the old rows between Conservatives and L.U.'s. And we shall resist their claims until at any rate it is certain that we are not presently going to part again. Well we shall see what Ll.G. has said today.

Yes, the Tamworth election[6] was very satisfactory more especially as I had been warned that we might be unpleasantly surprised at the smallness of the majority. I had an excellent meeting in Solihull on a vile snowy night and made I thought rather a grand speech in a rather chilly atmosphere. But on Wednesday I had a great success in my own constituency. The room was absolutely jammed with people standing up all round and even sitting on the window sills. I was told when I got there that the opposition was in force and strongly organised in bands of about 20, altogether 70 or 80 they said, but I somehow felt confident that it was all right. I spoke for 45 minutes nearly all on unemployment and didn't spare the communists and socialists. It was a noisy meeting but I never had any difficulty in getting a hearing and at the end the vote of confidence was carried by an overwhelming majority. ...

The next day we had our meeting here for the Unmarried mother and child. ... [W]e had over 200 present and raised about £50 so everyone was very delighted. Last night I spent several hours again at a "social" in the constituency and that

---

[5] At Glasgow on 19 January 1922 Austen Chamberlain attempted to rally Coalition support by praising the government's achievements and the Prime Minister.

[6] Tamworth by-election, 17 January 1922. A Coalition Conservative held the seat with 68.8 per cent of the vote.

concluded my week's engagements. Next week I have got six speeches to make all on different subjects!

...

Sunday I see the little man was conciliatory to the Unionists yesterday and pretended he had had nothing to do with the election stunt.[7] In fact he *was* the ventriloquist. What an artful little codger he is. He lets the lieutenants do all the bragging and crowing to buck up the C.L.'s and then comes in with a bucket of butter to pour over the Unionists swearing that he *does* mean to reform the Lords all right – only, he says to himself, not just yet! After all Squiff did nothing so why should there be any particular hurry for me if only I can keep those idiotic Unionists quiet.

29 January 1922
Westbourne

My dear Hilda,

...

I began on Monday by receiving a deputation from a Midland constituency who wanted my assistance in finding for them at once a candidate who should be rich, handsome, distinguished a brilliant speaker and accompanied by a charming wife. I then went on to the Chamber of Commerce where I spent two hours in discussing with a delegation various matters on which the assistance of M.P.'s was required. This meeting was the result of a suggestion I had made myself in an address I delivered to the Chamber some months ago. In the evening about 150 men came to Westbourne from the constituency. They were invited at 7.45 for 8 but the first arrived at 7.15 and the last departed about 11 o'clock. The idea was to form a body who would pledge themselves to work at election time. I think we shall succeed in getting it all right but the meeting was very trying as many, including councillors would make tub thumping speeches in which they denounced "labour" with terrifying violence and adjured us to remember this "Great Empire of Ours on which the Sun ...". etc. All very eloquent & proper in its place but totally unsuitable to an audience composed wholly of supporters & invited to discuss practical methods of organisation.

Tuesday was one of the coldest days I ever remember in this country. Everything was as hard as iron and an icy wind blew clouds of dust along the street and cut one's nose and ears like a knife. I went to one of Annie's clubs in the afternoon and talked to them for 55 minutes – far too long and a thoroughly rotten speech, though Annie says they liked it. Then I got home and almost immediately after set out for the pothouse in the West, where I graciously shook

---

[7] Addressing a Coalition Liberal meeting at Central Hall, Westminster on 21 January Lloyd George denied starting election rumours, declaring 'It is my business not to do so until the last moment'.

hands with A's Executive Committee. I found they had a terrific meeting – the best of the kind they told me since Father's day; about 200 sat down to dinner and afterwards a lot more including women came in for the speeches. What an evening. First, soup, cold & very nasty. Then an enormous piece of frozen beef red, ragged, and calculated to blunt the sharpest knife. It was accompanied by a mass of very watery potato and very strong smelling cabbage. The third course was the celebrated scrag of boiled mutton which the chairman devoured without winking like the Indians in The Dog Crusoe but I fainted completely away and was only revived when they thrust beneath my nose a powerful mass of mouse-trap cheese with a good wholesome crust of bread. Well, it was got over and I delivered (without notes) a "magnificent address" which was received with great applause & satisfaction. I really thought it quite good myself. On Wednesday I delivered a short address to the Y.M.C.A. after lunch, attended a meeting of the Highbury Trustees and finished up about 7 o'clock with the Ld Mayor's Boot & Clothing Fund. On Thursday I dined with the Business Club & proposed the first toast & on Friday I went to the initiation of the Lord Mayor & others into the Royal Antidiluvian [sic] order of Buffaloes where I had to say "a few words". Owing to the railway accident to the train in which the Bishop & Steel-Maitland were travelling everything was delayed and I didn't get my dinner till 10.30 that night. Rumours went round that Annie & I had been in the accident and our telephone was kept busy but really our vicarious suffering was almost as great as if we had. There! Thank goodness I've no more speeches at present.

4 February 1922
Westbourne

My dear Ida,

...

Just think; the deposits in the Mun. Bank last month were over £111000 & withdrawals £58000 so that the net gain was £63000. The only thing I know of to compare with it is Hoskins which has £25000 lent to the Corpn & £30000 in the Bank after paying about £11000 in taxes! ... Hall says they are short of orders but he has just pulled off one of about £8000.

I find its going to cost me a little over £100 to rebuild the Vinery but on the strength of Hoskins & in order to provide work for the unemployed I think I shall venture on it.

I read your account of A's conversation with expectation but without finding myself much wiser. Generally speaking the country appears to be going to the dogs with great rapidity and in about two years we may find ourselves shorn of Ireland, Egypt and India one after another. A strange sequel to a victorious war!

Ireland appears to be returning to her normal condition. Of course Ll.G. is notorious for his habit of persuading both parties to a dispute that he has given them all they asked for when in truth he has done neither. But I myself heard him say that the boundary commission only meant a slight readjustment which wd be to the advantage of North & South by making them more homogeneous and for Michael Collins[8] who allowed that to pass without protest to pretend now that he thought it meant the possession of Tyrone Fermanagh & Derry is too audacious even for an Irishman.

...

12 February 1922
Westbourne

My dear Hilda,

We were disappointed at not having a letter this morning but perhaps you thought we were seeing too much of each other to be worth writing! Anyway I will send you a short note just to keep up the continuity.

I find there is a good deal of dissatisfaction in the Party more or less connected with the Coalition. The fact is that they miss anything in the nature of a constructive policy among the Unionist leaders and though the latter are on safe ground when they say that they can't break with Ll.G. unless there is something to break about, there is a sort of feeling, hardly definite enough to be expressed, that if only they had a few ideas of their own there soon would be something to break about, or alternatively that we should then be leading the Coalition instead of trailing after the Libs. It is certainly is curious [sic] that if you take our people Austen, the Ld Chancellor, Horne, and Worthy Evans not one of them has any original ideas and that is where both Ll.G. & Winston have the pull. I cant help thinking that if only we could get our necks out of this double harness our people would be compelled to find a policy and they might then perhaps be inclined to advocate a rearrangement of taxation which would give further opportunities of Colonial Preference.

We have had a very dull week. Austen in his speech on the Address "undid" as a junior member of the Govt said to me "some of the harm the Goat had done". The member in question is rather disgruntled just now and I dont agree with him that the Goat did do harm on this occasion. So far as I could judge his speech was well received except of course by the diehards. Austen's chaff of R. Cecil[9]

---

[8] Michael Collins (1890–1922). Sinn Fein MP for South Cork 1918 but did not take seat. Member of Northern Ireland Parliament for Amagh 1921–22. Member of Dáil for South Cork until 1922 as a pro-Treaty Member. Finance Minister in Provisional Government 1921–22 and Chairman from January 1922. C-in-C of Army July 1922. Ambushed and killed by Irish Irregulars at Bealnabla, Co. Cork August 1922.

[9] (Edward Algernon) Robert Gascoyne-Cecil (1864–1958). Conservative MP for Marylebone East 1906–10 and Hitchin 1911–23. Under-Secretary, Foreign Affairs 1915–18; Minister of Blockade 1916–18; Lord Privy Seal 1923–24; Chancellor, Duchy of Lancaster (responsible for League of Nations) 1924–27. President, League of Nations Union 1923–45. Nobel Peace Prize 1937. Called Lord Robert Cecil 1868–1923 when created Viscount Cecil of Chelwood.

& Thomas was excellent and his delivery was freeer [sic] than usual but I thought his speech suffered from lack of preparation which caused it to be rather loose and rambling and certainly at one time he lost the attention of the House.

We had a meeting of the Reconstruction Committee on Tuesday & appointed a Sub to submit names for the officers posts during this session. They were very anxious that I should take the chairmanship but in view of my relationship to the Leader of the House I felt bound to decline and they all felt the force of my objection. Finally I agreed to remain a vice chairman and Shirley Benn[10] (a nonentity) will be put up as chairman.

I was fossicking round a lot trying to get a place in the ballot for my Children of Unmarried Parents Bill. I was just arranging for it to be introduced in the Lords by Buckmaster[11] when I got a hint that the Home Office was considering it. I went at once to Shortt and to my great delight found that the Govt are actually going to bring in my Bill themselves. Provided we don't have a General Election we ought now to see it pass into law and I think I may fairly claim a considerable share of the credit.

You will be interested to hear that I have joined the Carlton Club at last. I have been in there several times already and can quite see that one ought to belong if one is going on with the H. of C. Of course I always felt that perhaps I shouldn't, but I suppose now I shall unless I am kicked out. By the way Oliver L.L.[12] told me that he had heard from a good many people that Austen's seat was in danger. People said they never saw him and they debited him with the E.P.D. & C.P.T. I think myself that the danger is exaggerated but no doubt if he or even Ivy would show themselves a little more it would help a lot.

...

25 February 1922
Westbourne

My dear Hilda,

...

I am glad you heard Austen's Irish speech in the House. It made a great impression and if it didn't actually turn votes it certainly prevented some from voting against the Govt. His speech to the Nat. Un. Conference was not so

---

[10] Arthur Shirley Benn (1858–1937). Conservative MP for Plymouth 1910–18, Plymouth Drake 1918–29 and Sheffield, Park Division 1931–35. Chairman, National Unionist Association 1921. President, Association of British Chambers of Commerce 1921–23 and Federation of Chambers of Commerce 1931–34. Created Bart 1926 and Baron Glenravel 1936.

[11] Stanley Owen Buckmaster (1861–1934). Liberal MP for Cambridge 1906–10 and Keighley 1911–15. Solicitor-General 1913–15; Lord Chancellor 1915–16; member Inter-Allied Commission on Finance and Supplies. Knighted 1913. Created Baron 1915 and Viscount 1933.

[12] Oliver Stillingfleet Locker-Lampson (1880–1954). Conservative MP for Huntingdonshire 1910–22 and Birmingham Handsworth 1922–45. PPS to Austen Chamberlain 1919–22 and a close friend.

happy.[13] I thought the atmosphere was distinctly chilly and though one got different opinions expressed I came to the conclusion that it had done nothing to consolidate the party. Nor will the Ld Chancellor's allusions to the "cabin boy" have helped matters.[14] Indeed there is so much grousing going on that I begin to wonder whether we shant be driven into an election after all though I haven't changed my opinion that we should do well to postpone it as long as we can. My own speech on Ireland (only briefly reported in the Times) was very well received and I had quite a lot of compliments about it including one which I particularly appreciated from Hugh O'Neill[15] the Speaker of the Northern Parlt – a very nice fellow who is free from the bitterness which some of the Ulster members display.

The latest news is certainly very disquieting. O'Neill said he was afraid the Treaty was done for and though I feel that his view is almost necessarily coloured by the views expressed by his friends it is difficult to preserve one's optimism in face of such a weakness on the part of Griffith[16] & Collins. I suppose we shall know more about it next week.

I had to come down here yesterday for a B.S.A. board and go back to London without getting home for the Speakers levee. I told him I had come back on purpose and he was evidently very gratified. He is determined to keep up the customs & traditions of the House and told me he had refused to allow a Cabinet minister to come in evening dress. Certainly last night there was a gorgeous display of uniforms. I ran into old Squiff and had a pleasant talk with the old ruffian about pictures.

Last Friday I was speaking for Sir Herbert Austin[17] in Selly Oak and I don't think I ever saw a member of parliament make a more pitiable exhibition of

---

[13] On 21 February Austen Chamberlain told the Council of the National Unionist Association that at the next election there would be no joint Coalition manifesto but that there would be an understanding similar to that of Balfour and Joseph Chamberlain in which each wing enjoyed some freedom although agreed on the main issues.

[14] Younger's declarations about a possible 'bill of divorcement' between Coalition partners prompted Birkenhead to accuse him of being like a 'cabin boy' who decided to take over the ship in a storm.

[15] (Robert William) Hugh O'Neill (1883–1982). Ulster Unionist MP for mid-Antrim 1915–18, Co. Antrim 1922–50 and North Antrim 1950–52. Chairman, 1922 Committee 1935–39. Under Secretary for India and Burma 1939–40. Member and first Speaker of Northern Ireland Parliament 1921–29. Created Bart 1929 and Baron Rathcavan 1953.

[16] Arthur Griffith (1872–1922). Journalist and a leader of Sinn Fein. Interned three times up to 1920. Sinn Fein MP for Cavan East June 1918 but in December 1918 did not take his seat. Member of Northern Ireland Parliament for Fermanagh and Tyrone 1921–22. Member of Dáil for Cavan East to 1921 and Cavan 1921–22 as a pro-Treaty member. Secretary for Foreign Affairs 1921–22. President of Dáil Eireann 1922.

[17] Herbert Austin (1866–1941). Assisted in founding Wolseley Tool & Motor Car Co; founder Austin Motor Company 1905. Conservative MP for Birmingham King's Norton 1918–24. Knighted 1917. Created Baron Austin 1936.

himself. He was unable to get out a coherent sentence and his ignorance of current topics was comic if it hadn't been so serious. I wouldn't give two pins for his chances and I must say he deserves to lose his seat. He pleads business troubles as an excuse for not doing his duty as an M.P. but a man ought to resign if he is in that position. Next week I have to speak for Oliver Locker Lampson and the following Monday for Sir Robert Bird[18] at Wolverhampton. I wish I didn't loathe speaking so much but anyway its good practice for the Election.

One good thing is that I haven't got any committees this session so I am getting some mornings to myself. ... I went alone to Agnew's private view and being alone I naturally got into trouble. There is the usual wealth of old masters ... &c but I fell to an interior of Seville Cathedral by David Roberts.[19] ... The price was awful but Hoskins must pay for it unless I put it down to the letting of our house the money for which we have already spent so often!

...

My secretary has finished typing the Memoir at last and it only remains to correct the sheets and put them together when I shall hand it over to Lilian. Annie has had hardly any criticisms to make and on the whole I am not dissatisfied with it myself considering the difficulties, but it remains to be seen how Lilian will like it.

...

P.S. Did you read the Ld Chancellors most amusing speech to the Civil Service on Friday? I thought the malicious impudence of attributing a *classical* epigram to the P.M. was priceless!

4 March 1922
Westbourne

My dear Ida,

The political situation as you say is terribly confused and uncertain and the London Press is enough to drive anyone distracted. Of course the Times is utterly untrustworthy. It is really very clever in suggesting the false and suppressing the true; it never repeats the categorical statements of the Mail but it manages to convey the same idea by an assumption of infallible authority and of course it keeps steadily to the front its aim of upsetting the Govt. The Telegraph produced a great sensation by its statement about the P.M.'s letter and as usual the leakage proceeded from Downing Street and was the more mischievous because it was inaccurate. I found an opportunity of seeing Austen on Wednesday and Thursday to get the correct version as I had to speak last night but I was

---

[18] Robert Bland Bird (1876–1960). Birmingham businessman and Conservative MP for Wolverhampton West 1922–29 and 1931–45. Succeeded as Bart 1922.

[19] David Roberts (1796–1864). Scene painter at Drury Lane and Scottish artist notable for paintings of Rouen and Amiens Cathedrals.

hardly surprised to find that the deadly secrets which he revealed were this morning fully detailed in both his and Worthy's speech!

I confess that I should like to be rid of the Goat but I fear it is impossible and I have little doubt that as you say the effect of the efforts of the Diehards will be to tie us up to him more completely than ever. The Diehards themselves are more & more settling into an attitude of general hostility which must I think resolve itself ultimately into secession but they are only a small section of the party and I have been rather surprised to find that the supporters of the coalition are more numerous and determined than I had imagined. I had a meeting of the Midland Union Executive yesterday and they all with one accord expressed their conviction that the separation of the Unionist party would mean disaster while in Scotland and Wales I understand that the same view is very strongly held. I dont know what Bonar is up to just now as I haven't heard anything about him lately but *Sir* Arthur Balfour[20] (ye gods!) is going to make a strong coalition speech on Tuesday and I understand that Younger is very much ashamed of himself and has promised to be more discreet in future. He was quite right to stop the election but unfortunately he went on to interpret Austen's views according to his own ideas and consequently to appear to be taking his place as leader. He did not mean to do anything disloyal but he sees that he has gone too far. When I last saw Austen on Thursday night he said everything had been arranged quite satisfactorily and appeared to be happier in his mind but changes come so quickly that one never knows what the day will bring forth.

We have had a very busy week. I went on Monday to the British Industries Fair here and made an impromptu speech at a luncheon which seemed to please the people there. It is a rotten time for a trade exhibition but the tone appears more hopeful and though I don't fancy many orders are being placed the exhibitors feel that they are getting a good advertisement and that the numbers of foreign buyers are sufficiently encouraging to give them a prospect of business whenever revival of trade begins.

...

... I got down here yesterday and spent most of the day in town presiding at political meetings or committees finishing up with a public meeting in Handsworth for O. L Lampson. He made an excellent impression speaking very easily and fluently though as he had had no time for preparation there wasn't much stuff in his speech. We had a good audience of nearly 800 with a very fair sprinkling of opposition but not enough to do more than enliven the occasion. ...

...

---

[20] Arthur James Balfour (1848–1930). Conservative MP for Hertford 1874–85, Manchester East 1885–1906 and City of London 1906–22. President, LGB 1885–86; Scottish Secretary 1886–87; Chief Secretary, Ireland 1887–91; First Lord of Treasury 1891–92, 1895–1905; Prime Minister 1902–5; First Lord of Admiralty 1915–16; Foreign Secretary 1916–19; Lord President 1919–22, 1925–29. Conservative Leader in Commons 1891–1902; Conservative Leader 1902–11. Knighted 1922. Created Earl of Balfour later in same year.

11 March 1922
Westbourne

My dear Hilda,

Thank you for your congratulations which I feel I can accept without any pricking of conscience. I was indeed immensely gratified at the result in Wolverhampton.[21] Of course when one goes down on the eve of the poll one can hardly claim to be responsible for the result unless it is very close indeed but it is a tremendous triumph for the Midland Union and taken with the Tamworth result and compared with Clayton Camberwell and Bodmin I agree with you in thinking that it must do much to sustain our Midlands reputation. Indeed I do find that many people speak as though we had the Midlands completely in our pocket. I had a wonderful meeting there, one of the biggest I have addressed for a number of years. I was rather low about my speech which I had to spin out while waiting for Bird to come on from another meeting but I received so many compliments about it afterwards (including a secondhand one from J.H. Thomas who is reported to have observed in the coffee room of the hotel that "he had heard that Chamberlain spoke rather decently") that I now begin to think it must have been a great success.

The Montagu[22] incident provided quite first class sensation.[23] We could see that he wasn't in his place but when Austen began his reply to Aubrey Herbert[24] not half a dozen men had any idea that a resignation was involved. I have heard many explanations of his extraordinary conduct. St-nl-y B-ldw-n had three alternatives, entre nous including one that the Goat had contrived the whole thing in order to get rid of him but, as he said, "without suggesting anything offensive to Ll.G.", he did not think that explanation was probable because he did not see how the Goat could do it without being found out! The most probable theory appears to be that Montagu being an emotional person subject to fits of hysteria when he cries and throws dust on his head and being moreover thrown off his balance by Winston's remarks about Kenya[25] suddenly saw red and sanctioned the publication in a fit of desperation.

---

[21] Wolverhampton West by-election, 7 March 1922. The Conservatives held the seat from Labour with 54.9 per cent of the vote, only marginally less than in 1918. Labour made sensational gains at Manchester Clayton and Camberwell North on 18 and 20 February. The Liberals also achieved a large swing to win Bodmin on 24 February.

[22] Edwin Samuel Montagu (1879–1924). Liberal MP for Cambridgeshire 1906–22. Under-Secretary for India 1910–14; Financial Secretary to Treasury 1914–15 and 1915–16; Chancellor, Duchy of Lancaster 1915 and 1916; Minister of Munitions 1916; Secretary for India 1917–22.

[23] On 9 March Montagu resigned from the India Office over his unauthorised publication of a sensitive telegram from the Viceroy pressing the Indian desire for the evacuation of Constantinople and the restoration of the Sultan's suzerainty over the Holy Places.

[24] Aubrey Nigel Henry Molyneux Herbert (1880–1923). Diplomatic service in Tokyo 1902 and Constantinople 1904. Conservative MP for South Somerset 1911–18 and Yeovil 1918–23. Private Secretary to Irish Secretary, 1916–18.

[25] On 27 January 1922, as Colonial Secretary, Churchill acknowledged the need for stricter controls on Indian immigration into Kenya and repeated assurances to the white settlers that

Anyhow, he has materially added to the political complications of the moment. If only a merciful Providence would remove the Goat in a chariot of fire, how wonderfully things would be straightened out!

...

I got down here yesterday and spent the afternoon at the annual meeting of the Midland Union of which I have now become chairman vice Dartmouth[26] resigned. We had a most successful and enthusiastic gathering the largest, one of the agents told me, that he ever remembered and Wolverhampton gave us a capital fillip. This morning I had to meet a deputation of fierce teachers who seemed very pleased at the end of a 2 hour discussion though they didn't get much out of me and the other members I had with me. I was kept so late that I didn't get my lunch till 2.30 but I spent a happy afternoon in doing up my rock garden and putting in some new plants.

...

18 March 1922
Westbourne

My dear Ida,

...

How very annoying for the Times & D.M[ail] that we should have won Cambridge![27] They *are* a spiteful pair, and the diabolical skill with which they twist everything to suit their aims is almost uncanny. The meeting of Unionist M.P.'s however was an awful fiasco.[28] It was engineered by "Paddy" Hannon, who sits for Moseley in the room of Hallewell Rogers.[29] He is a good fellow but he is inexperienced in the ways of the House & doesn't realise how much the House dislikes to see a new member trying to run things on his own. He had no men of standing to advise him (he didn't consult me!) and he made a series of blunders. If he had wanted to get only supporters of the Coalition he could have taken his resolutions round and got plenty of signatures but of course when every one was invited to a meeting all the Die-hards came and a good many

---

Indians would not be allowed to purchase land in the Highlands. This infuriated Indian opinion and Montagu's challenged it successfully in Cabinet.

[26] William Heneage Legge (1851–1936). Conservative MP for West Kent 1875–85 and Lewisham 1885–91. Conservative whip in Commons. Vice-Chamberlain of Household, 1885–86, 1886–92. Chairman, Midland Union of Conservative and Unionist Associations 1914–22. Succeeded as 6th Earl of Dartmouth 1891.

[27] Cambridge by-election, 16 March 1922. The intervention of a Liberal halved the Conservative majority over Labour but the party still achieved a majority of 3943.

[28] On 14 March a meeting of over 200 Conservative MPs failed to adopt a motion defending Coalition policy and nearly repudiated Chamberlain's leadership.

[29] Hallewell Rogers (1864–1931). Chairman, Birmingham Small Arms Co. Lord Mayor, Birmingham 1902–4. Coalition Unionist MP for Birmingham, Moseley 1918–21. Knighted 1904.

others who strongly objected to a proceeding which marked off the sheep from the goats & was rather calculated to emphasise divisions than to conceal them. So though the great majority of those present were anxious to support the Coalition and their own leaders they declined to have the question put and as the whole business had been well advertised beforehand of course it made a big réclame. Everyone is asking what the P.M. will do. It is generally supposed that he wants to get rid of the Irish Bill and the Genoa Conference before taking any steps towards resignation but his reputation as the head of a great majority is already badly shaken and I dont believe any spectacular result can come from Genoa. I am inclined to think that he will go but the interesting question is what will the other Liberals in the Govt do if he does. I should like to see a reconstruction with Austen as P.M. and a sufficient number of Liberals in the Cabinet to correspond to their numbers in the House. They would then be hostages for the good behaviour of the P.M. & the excluded ones and we might struggle on for another 8 or 9 months. But I am told that although Winston & Munro[30] would like to stop it is improbable that they would feel able to do so and if A. had to form an exclusively Unionist Govt it seems to me he would be bound to go to the country first. Probably we should then come back with an insufficient majority to carry on and I suppose that would mean another Coalition with Ll.G. again in power if not at the head of the Govt. It is an interesting situation full of all sorts of possibilities.

I managed to get seats in the Speakers gallery for Annie & Helen to hear Montagu and they had quite a thrilling evening with him and Austen and Asquith on Wednesday. Montagu was not interrupted or insulted but the only cheers came from the Labour benches while he made his statement. He was very emotional but singularly unconvincing in his defence and if he did himself no further harm he did not improve his position. Why on earth everyone is allowed to know that the office is being hawked round with no bidders[31] I cant imagine but I suppose the garden suburb is responsible as usual. One cant help feeling that Nemesis is overtaking the little Welshman at last and I cant be sorry.

By the way Montagu's explanation of his apparent misrepresentation of Curzon's letter was the one point which the House accepted. Apparently what he meant to say was "Curzon wrote that in future I was to bring such matters (not to the Cabinet as I should have expected but) to him". But Curzon did say "to me *in* the Cabinet" which is really the same thing.

   ...

---

[30] Robert Munro (1868–1955). Liberal MP for Wick Burghs 1910–18 and Roxburgh & Selkirk 1918–22. Lord Advocate of Scotland 1913–16; Secretary for Scotland 1916–22; Lord Justice Clerk with judicial title of Lord Alness 1922–33. Lord-in-Waiting and Lord's spokesman on Scottish Affairs 1940–45. Created Baron Alness 1934.

[31] Derby, Devonshire and Crawford refused the India Office before Peel was appointed on 19 March.

26 March 1922
Westbourne

My dear Hilda,

My back feeling rather middling last Sunday I got Barling[32] to come in on Monday ... and as a result have spent the whole week down here. ...

I have really found the week go by very quickly. I had a Board meeting at Elliotts on Monday and on Tuesday Friday & Saturday have been taken up with B.S.A. matters while in the intervals I have had a grand clean up of papers and letters which had been long accumulating here.

I wish I could give a cheerful account of business prospects but they seem to go from bad to worse. I should think we are just doing a little more than make both ends meet at Elliotts, but we have had to reduce our staff and discharge many of our workpeople – a disheartening process when we had done so much to build up a good feeling in the works. I believe we are equipped now to produce on a scale and with an economy we have never before approached and probably we are a long way ahead of our competitors, but until there is some trade to be got we can only sit on our hunkers and wait. B.S.A. of course is much worse. There we are certainly losing in all our factories and we have had to make the most drastic cuts. There too I believe we shall ultimately regain our prosperity but I fancy it will take much longer than at Elliotts and there are a good many holes to be filled up before the business is really in a sound condition.

My great excitement here has been the repeated visits of a Greater Spotted Woodpecker to our cocoanut which is just outside the dining room window. This is a bird which I was never able to record even at Highbury tho' once I saw a bird high in an ash tree that I thought might be one. Some weeks ago while at lunch, I saw 2 birds on a garden bench that were strange to me. I ran out but having no glasses could not identify them tho' I thought they looked something like woodpeckers. But on Monday Miss Leamon reported that a bird with a red head and a grey back had come to the cocoanut before breakfast and next morning he actually came while Annie and I were sitting at the breakfast table. I have written to the Birm. Mail about it as it really seems to me a very remarkable occurrence. The G.S. Woodpecker is not a common bird anywhere and his haunts are generally forests not gardens.

...

I have been surveying politics from a distance this week and have felt how utterly misleading the Times must be to an outsider. True anyone who thought for themselves must have seen how they have changed round indicating first that

<hr />

[32] (Harry) Gilbert Barling (1855–1940). Assistant (later full) Surgeon, Birmingham General Hospital 1881–1915. Demonstrator of Anatomy, Masons College (later Birmingham University) and later Professor of Pathology 1886–93; Professor of Surgery, Birmingham University 1893–1912. Vice-Chancellor, Birmingham University 1913–33.

the Coalition might break to pieces at any moment and next that it is going on quite happily but all the time pointing out to each wing how it is being sold and dished by the other. And as you say after all no resignation is in sight. All the same I feel as if it might come presently. If Ireland could be got into a more settled condition & if Genoa could be made to make a noise like "Peace with honour" Ll.G. might be disposed to think that the moment had arrived when he could say "I have finished my particular jobs and now I must insist on taking a holiday. You carry on as long as you can and after a Gen. Election we can consider again what we will do". He would tell his Lib. friends to stop in and keep the place warm and then he could go to the S. of France and watch the mess at home. And very soon people wd begin to say ["]Ll.G. would never have allowed things to get into this parlous condition Why shouldn't he come back & put them straight." They talked like that even about Bonar! And he wd come back nice & fresh for a whirlwind election campaign and he wd have good chances of being P.M. again afterwards. On the other hand I doubt very much if Ireland is going to quiet down or if anything can be made of Genoa and in that case probably Ll.G. will hang on and we shall all go to blazes together.

L. Amery[33] came down & spent Friday night here as I was speaking for him in Sparkbrook that night. And by the same token we had a very rowdy meeting as I should think nearly ⅓ of the audience were Socialists and by continuous & irrelevant interruptions they made it very difficult to preserve a thread & retain the attention of the audience. I must organise some Black & Tans to deal with this sort of thing which is getting beyond a joke. Afterwards we (Leo & I) had a long talk over the situation. We wondered whether anyone was thinking over a programme for the election and didn't believe they were and we discussed a lot of items which I suggested for one. I always find Leo one of the few men who has constructive ideas and if only he were half as big again he would before now have reached a much higher place. I should very much like to see him given full scope to work out his ideas as the responsible head of a department, but Austen says he has no judgement. I think he does him less than justice though I confess I was rather horrified to find that he was responsible for the Admiralty memo on the Geddes Rept. It wasn't that they didn't agree but the tone of their reply was so unfortunate.

Anyway we found ourselves very much in agreement, and if I find Austen, who is coming here next Thursday & Friday, has as I suspect got no ideas about a new programme possibly we may form a committee to discuss suggestions. To go to the country purely on economy and anti-Socialism seems bad tactics to me and I cant imagine that Father would have done it.

...

---

[33] Leopold Charles Maurice Stennett Amery (1873–1955). Conservative MP for Birmingham South (later Sparkbrook) 1911–45. Under-Secretary, Colonies 1919–21; Parliamentary and Financial Secretary to Admiralty 1921–22; First Lord of Admiralty 1922–24; Colonial Secretary 1924–29 and Dominion Secretary 1925–29; Secretary of State for India 1940–45.

1 April 1922
Westbourne

My dear Ida,

...

I spoke on the Unemployment Insurance Bill on Wednesday and next day left early to go to Stafford in order to address a "mass meeting" of women in connection with Annie's West Midlands Womens Party Area Committee. They had a conference in the morning with delegates from 43 constituencies, at which she presided. ...

I had to hurry away from the meeting to get back here for an evening gathering. It came to my knowledge some time ago that some local Unionists were planning to get the Chairmen and secretaries of all the divisions to a supper at which they were to be induced to "show our members that we are fed up with this coalition and that it is time a new centre party was formed". So I arranged to invite them all myself to a private gathering of an informal kind to meet the Leader of the party & discuss the position of Unionists with him. Of course they all jumped at it. I had light refreshments and Austen made them a speech after which they asked him questions for 2½ hours and went away in high good humour. All but the plotters, who had a suspicion that I had countermined them but didn't dare to say so. I had an awful headache next morning but it was worth it!

Next morning I had to go to the B.S.A. and spent the day there till about 5 when I went to my club for a cup of tea and then motored to Sutton where I addressed a meeting on the Importance of women's work in local government. So today I felt that in spite of 40 letters by 1st post and a deputation of teachers I was having a real holiday!

Austen had a meeting in his constituency last night and after he came home I had a good talk about the situation and the history of the last few weeks. I gather that the little Welshman has been up to his tricks but they hope to have wired him in safely and provided he doesn't break out through some new hole his speech on Genoa and the Bolshies ought to be satisfactory. If so I fear there is no chance of his resigning! I took the oppty to ask A. whether he had thought of any programme if an election did come and made some suggestions. I don't know whether they were very helpful but he said they were the first he had had and he took a note of them all and I think he will try and start some committees to work something out. He admitted that if we went to the country on a purely negative programme we should be handicapped and though of course we can't outbid the Socialists I do think we could formulate something constructive without involving ourselves in heavy expenditure. My programme included Agriculture (I couldn't suggest anything very definite but thought something might be done about rating) Women's legislation (e.g. Children of Unmarried Parents & legalisation of adoption) Poor Law reform, Trade Union legislation (secret ballot and political levy) slums & house purchase. Its a nucleus anyway and if other people set their minds to it we ought to be able to evolve something. Oh there was one more thing – unemployment insurance by industries instead of by Labour exchanges.

I dont really know much about the lock out.[34] I don't think employers want to close their works but no doubt they do feel that management has been slipping out of their hands and that they wont get again such an opportunity of recovering it. I see there is some hope of further negotiation still. It affects us at Elliotts and more at B.S.A. but we can carry on for a short time.

...

8 April 1922
Westbourne

My dear Hilda,

...

Austen had another remarkable success in the House on Wednesday over the Die-hard motion,[35] when even the Times remarked on the "brilliance" of his wit. Its the first time I have ever heard that word applied to him but he really deserved it and his mockery of "Jinks"[36] [sic] was quite excellent. The fact is that the House has never credited him either with a sense of humour or a capacity for rapier play in debate and the P.M. was right in his remark that he was more like Father on this occasion than ever before, an observation that was also made to me by several others. I confess that I had not credited him with such a power of development in debating quality as he has been showing and among M.P.'s he has enormously increased his reputation and influence this week. The effect of his Monday speech was obvious in the prolonged cheers he got when he rose to speak, cheers such as he has never had before.

I was rather vexed to see in the Times yesterday that Steel-Maitland had thrown off the mask and made a downright mutinous speech in Birmingham the night before. He has been working up to it for some time but had so persistently avoided plain speaking that I hoped he might not start a division. To my annoyance he turned up at the committee of which he is joint chairman with me. I said nothing but quietly took the chair to which he made no objection. After we had finished however I called a sub-committee to which he doesn't belong and

---

[34] An engineering lock-out from 11 March until 13 June 1922 ended in defeat for the union.

[35] On 5 April 1922 Austen Chamberlain launched an uncharacteristically savage attack upon Joynson-Hicks and the Diehards who had tabled a no-confidence motion in the government and its 'lack of definite and coherent principle'.

[36] William Joynson-Hicks (1865–1932). Conservative MP for Manchester NW 1908–10, Brentford 1911–18, Twickenham 1918–29. Parliamentary Secretary, Overseas Trade Department 1922–23; Postmaster- and Paymaster-General 1923; Financial Secretary to Treasury (with seat in Cabinet) 1923; Minister of Health 1923–24; Home Secretary 1924–29. Created Bart 1919 and Viscount Brentford 1929.

pointed out to them that on the 5th May the officers had to be re-elected by the annual meeting. I didn't mind his remaining a Vice-President but his speech had made it impossible for me to share the chairmanship with him any longer. The "sub" agreed and finally a member was deputed to him and suggest that he should decline the nomination. If he agrees, well and good; if not, we shall have to fight it out.

The Labour party kept us up till after 12 on Thursday night over Unempl Insurance and as I had been asked that evening to second a motion for 2nd reading of a Local Govt Officers Superannuation Bill on Friday morning, a very involved and technical measure which I had not read, I had to sit up till 2 to "mug it up". However, I felt pretty fresh next morning and was able to make what Mond called an "interesting" speech. Whether as a result of my speech or of the intrinsic merits of the Bill or of Banbury's absence we got it through without a division.

...

30 April 1922
Westbourne

My dear Ida,
...

Our B.S.A. annual meeting passed off without any unpleasant incident much to Rogers' relief for he had got himself into a regular stew about it. I dont know what will happen next year though for it is difficult to see how we can make any profit.

I had a good meeting of the Commission on Wednesday when we had a discussion among ourselves and made some progress with ideas but I was sorry to miss Amery's speech on the Empire Settlement Bill on which he was very eloquent after his fashion. I think it is one of the best things this Govt has done. I managed however to get in to the R.H.S. & bought one or two Auriculas encouraged there by Catt's great success with the few we have. They really are lovely things ...

I went one morning to the Cotman[37] exhibition at the Tate Gallery where I ran into Whitworth Wallis.[38] He introduced me to Aitken the Director who walked round with us and I enjoyed the drawings and pictures. Some of Cotman's colouring is rather weird especially in his water colours but he was a great artist.
...

---

[37] John Sell Cotman (1782–1842). English landscape water colourist and leading member of the 'Norwich School' 1806–34. Drawing master, King's College, London from 1834.

[38] Whitworth Wallis (1855–1927). Curator, Bethnal Green Museum 1879–81 and Indian collections of Royal Family at Kensington Museum 1881–84; Director, Birmingham Art Gallery from 1885. Knighted.

I came down on Friday evening. ... Last night I had the annual meeting of my Divisl Assn and they listened to speeches for 3 hours with apparent satisfaction and interest. I spoke without notes for 55 minutes rather to my horror for I hadn't intended to speak so long but Annie assures me that the audience was enthralled all the time. It is very satisfactory to have a wife who always finds your speeches so interesting! I am trying to train myself to speak without relying so much on notes as I had got into the way of doing for I think my delivery is better if I am not all the time trying to find my place and distracting my own attention from what I am going to say next. One of the men present said he heard my opponent was likely to withdraw but I don't think he is correct and I believe my people would be very disappointed if they didn't have a fight.

...

I have been a long walk [sic] this afternoon with Platten and we have discussed Elliotts in and out as usual. They are having rather a struggle to get orders but they are doing all right all the same and whenever trade does revive I believe they will bound forward and show all the advantages of our various amalgamations. I am scheming for the absorption of a fifth company now and believe I shall get it sooner or later.

Tomorrow for 1/- off the income tax!

7 May 1922
Westbourne

My dear Hilda,

...

I am very gratified to have such a good account of [the children] from you and to know that you do really enjoy having them. On their side they certainly delighted in their visit and it gives them an intimacy with you which will make you live people to them when they hear about you. Oliver Locker-Lampson was lunching here yesterday and was immensely taken with Dorothy. What so astounded him was the contrast between her and her cousins Diane & Joe and evidently he thought the comparison was in D's favour. I rather hypocritically suggested that it was a matter of health but he evidently considered that it involved the matter of – well, *brains*, and I may admit to you that we *are* rather proud of our bright child! But after all why should there be any resemblance between the cousins seeing how different all their parents are.

...

The garden is heavenly today. All the migrants have arrived with a rush and the air is full of the songs and calls of cuckoos, willow wrens, chiff-chaffs, greenfinches, chaffinches & turtle doves besides the common thrushes, tits, robins, hedge sparrows & wrens. Overhead the swifts are circling and I saw a kestrel pass over this morning. The daffodils are still very brilliant and the saxifrages are just opening. The early rhododendron is a blaze of scarlet and in 10 days the cherries should be at their best. ...

Genoa seems to be breaking up. If only Ll.G. would give half the attention to the Empire that he bestows on international politics he would achieve something, but there is more interest doubtless in cajoling these foreigners than in trying to enthuse the rather stolid Anglo-Saxon.

13 May 1922
Westbourne

My dear Ida,

...

The event of our week has been the dinner to Austen on Thursday. It was a great success. The Grosvenor Room at the Grand was packed with about 400 people and for once I was able to attend a public dinner without having to make a speech myself. Amery was excellent with a light touch & yet bringing out all the points which wanted emphasising. Steel Maitland was not so good but managed to come through a rather difficult ordeal without saying anything to jar. As for Austen I never cease to marvel at his capacity for weaving an impressive speech without any apparent preparation. He spoke for 40 minutes without a note and having slept most of the way down in the train on the pretext that he had left behind the piece of paper on which he had intended to make his notes. On reading the speech over it certainly did not contain anything very new or very striking. Nevertheless it did express in very good language his general ideas about the situation and his delivery is so much freer and more natural than it used to be that he does full justice to all he has to say. I am sure that the company was very pleased and that the meeting will have done him good, but I am sorry to say that the reports I get about his seat are very unsatisfactory & give me some anxiety about the next election. I can't help thinking that his position will carry him through but of course with a Labour opponent one never knows what may happen and I have got to get his people to consider seriously whether something cannot be done to make him more secure. Neither he nor Ivy have done much to help themselves.

I had rather a rowdy meeting on Monday but not so rowdy as had been expected, and I had no difficulty in getting a hearing though much interrupted. The fact that most men in the neighbourhood were locked out did not conduce to a reasonable frame of mind but now that the enquiry has gone so much in favour of the employers I hope the engineering dispute will soon come to an end.

I had intended to speak on Wednesday on the Leeds & Bradford Extension Bill but the Diehards secured the adjournment for a debate on Ireland and the Leeds & Bradford was postponed till the next night when of course I could not be present. The Bill was lost by a huge majority – so I don't suppose I could have saved it but it was very annoying to be cut out. There is a regular fight going on now between the Co. Councils and the boroughs and the Counties have won the first round. They were very artful in choosing L. & B. (whose case was anything but strong) for the battlefield, and they brought in the economy stunt with some success. I don't know whether the result will affect the London Commission but it is becoming clear to me that the L.C.C. scheme of extension has no chance of being carried and that we shall have to look elsewhere for a solution of that problem.

… Annie has a friend from Ireland, a Miss de Burgh, staying for the week end. She says that things at any rate are not as bad as before the truce, for the Republicans & Free Staters are so busy quarrelling among themselves that they have no time to bother about English people or their friends. Her stories of the Irish methods are very amusing. … Always you seem to get this mixture of make-believe or play with the seriousness and callousness of the Irish character. Coralis [?] says that the outrages we read of now are mostly committed by people belonging to no party but who take advantage of the state of lawlessness to acquire booty.

…

27 May 1922
Westbourne

My dear Ida,

…

I went to the R.H.S. on Wednesday. I couldn't get there before as I had to stay in Birmingham over Monday in order to preside at a dinner to the Australian & Dominion M.P. visitors who came down that day. They were not a big party but I think the affair was quite successful and that they were very pleased with their visit. I am convinced that the British Empire makes a strong appeal to the electorate and that the more we can do to develop some policy in that direction the more likely we are to get support at an election. But it goes without saying that I advocate it for itself and because I am firmly convinced that it leads to salvation for this country and not for vote catching purposes.

…

I see those miserable engineers have not learned wisdom yet, and I am very sorry to say that Val Bird has been out with them all the time and is one of two of those employed at Elliotts who has not returned. The reason is that he is near the time when he will be qualified for superannuation & of course he dare not do anything to jeopardise it. I hear he has lost about £50 in wages and I was wondering whether you could ascertain from Kate[39] what their position is &

---

[39] Kate Bird. Kitchen maid to Joseph Chamberlain and nurse to his children with whom Chamberlain remained in contact until his death.

whether they are in need of any help in which case I would gladly assist them. I don't quite like to write to her myself and I am not sure that she would tell me. I dont think the A.E.U. can last out much longer; Allan Smith[40] tells me they have lost 100,000 members already.

I was in the House on Thursday to hear Ll.G. He was so "restrained" not to say soporific that many members (including myself) slept peacefully during a good part of his speech but Bob Cecil gave him a chance later on and he had an easy task in demolishing him. Bob lost his temper completely several times which only made the House laugh and was so Cecilian that he failed to make anything like a case. But it is very difficult to put clearly what the Genoa Conference has achieved and I doubt if any of those who cheered the P.M. could stand cross examination on the subject. One can only say that our people came away feeling that the atmosphere was more favourable at the end than at the beginning and that has a "solid rally" though it is not easy to measure or define it.

I agree about Ireland. It is really heartbreaking and I can neither see a way out myself nor find anyone who can. And yet the country isn't in the least excited about it and goes about its business as though civil war were not staring us in the face. Anyhow I don't regret what we have done for surely the whole world must see what a hopeless people we have to deal with and that our troubles in Ireland are due to the Irish themselves and not to us.

Apparently the House will rise on Tuesday or Wednesday. Annie and I are preparing to idle in London till the end of the week when we go down to Dame Alice Godman[41] ... for the week end. After that we shall come back here and enjoy our garden and clear up chores of which there are many. ... The garden is a thing of beauty. The Japanese cherry "Buna-Fugen" has been a perfect picture ... The azaleas have never been so brilliant and full of flower ... I don't think we have ever had quite such masses of German Iris as Annie has got this time in her south border ...

...

I just asked Annie this morning what she would think if I proposed that we should go to Canada this autumn and she has already got all her clothes mapped out, arranged who is to come stay here while we are away, what is to be done with the constituency who opens my letters etc etc etc. My more ponderous mind cant bustle along at that pace.

---

[40] Allan Macgregor Smith (1870–1941). Conservative MP for Croydon South 1919–23. Chairman, Engineering Employers Federation and of Employers section of Joint Committee of Industrial Conference. Knighted 1918.

[41] Alice Mary Godman (1870–1944). Deputy President, Red Cross Society. Created Dame 1918.

4 June 1922
South Lodge, Horsham

My dear Hilda,

...

... It is sad how I have dropped out of music again; I haven't heard a concert for 12 months I should think and have ceased to read the musical critiques. Life is really not long enough to follow up more than 5 or 6 "interests" properly.

We have had quite an interesting week. First there was Winston's speech on Ireland which will I think rank with his best. I had anticipated it with some considerable anxiety lest the Goat should be giving away the position but on the vital points the speech left nothing to be desired and the peroration was so finely worded and delivered that one permitted oneself to hope that all might yet be well. But thinking it over since it seems almost impossible. W. was so guarded about the constitution that one could not express an opinion on it, yet he somehow gave the impression that there was something wrong. And now we learn that it was all wrong and dead against the Treaty. True Griffith (not Collins) is said to have returned a soft answer to the ultimatum, but what are we to think of the prospects of the Treaty being honestly worked in the future when the Provl Govt who continually profess their sincere desire to uphold it, come "trying it on" with a constitution which would mean complete independence. Moreover the speeches of M. Collins to his own people are disloyal to the last degree and I find it difficult to understand how he has the face to come to London & maintain that he "really was a good young man". "Qui trompet-on içi"? He and Griffith were in the gallery together with the German minister on Wednesday – a precious pack of scoundrels – and I watched his face while Winston was speaking. I thought it a typically Irish face, weak, merry and unreliable. Griffith was quite different and made a much more favourable impression.

After the speech I had quite a pleasant little lunch party at the House – just Mary[42] & Willie[43] [Carnegie] & ourselves and Halford Mackinder[44] with whom I am by way of being rather friendly. He is one of the few people who have original ideas and I always find him interesting though he is not the showy sort.

...

This place is an absolute dream of beauty. You wouldn't suppose there could be such colour in this country. ... Besides our hostess & her two very intelligent

---

[42] Mary Crownishield Endicott (1863–1957). See Appendix I: The Chamberlain household and family.

[43] William Hartley Carnegie (1860–1936). See Appendix I: The Chamberlain household and family.

[44] Halford John Mackinder (1861–1947). Reader in Geography, Oxford University 1887–1905. Principal, University College Reading 1892–1903; Director, LSE 1903–8; Reader in Geography, University of London 1900–1923 and Professor 1923–25. British High Commissioner to South Russia 1919. Unionist MP for Glasgow Camlachie 1910–22. Chairman, Imperial Economic Conference 1926 and Imperial Shipping Committee 1920–45. Knighted 1920.

but alas extremely plain daughters, there are three sailors … Ld & Lady Eustace Percy[45] (he is in the House & promises rather well being intellectual – & rather priggish in manner but more sensible than his brother the Duke)[46] and a very nice pretty Miss Walter of the Times family. I have brought my tennis things down & had some good sets last night, and altogether I think we shall enjoy our week end very much.

Annie declares that you have not yet appreciated the fact that we are seriously contemplating Canada, starting about Sept 19 & being away abt 10 weeks. I believe it will be *very* interesting but it sounds as if I might have to do an awful lot of speech making. A. already pictures our driving through cheering crowds to state banquets and says she *enjoys* the prospect. But *I* dont!

11 June 1922
Westbourne

My dear Ida,

This has been an uneventful week for us as well as for you. We finished up a very pleasant weekend with Dame Alice on Tuesday …A.& I came to the conclusion that we should like to see more of Lady Eustace Percy. She is immensely tall – over 6ft I should think – and has the appearance of having quite outgrown her strength. Her figure is awkward and her movements rather ungraceful but she has an extraordinarily nice face & when she has overcome her natural shyness she is very pleasant. I didn't take very much to Ld Eustace. He also has rather a nice face, decidedly intellectual in cast, but he is academic and dogmatic at once and I felt there was little in common between us. …

… I imagine the Engineers will be in very soon now. They have had a thorough beating and I should hope will keep quiet for a bit. Meanwhile they have driven a lot of trade away and injured a great many besides themselves. I am glad to say that Elliotts are at last beginning to feel the warmth and our order books show better the last few weeks than they have for many months. But B.S.A. is still in the slough and what trade we could have had we have lost owing to these beastly engineers.

…

I have finished the Memoir & am in communication with Murrays about printing so I hope to get things all settled if not absolutely finished before we go

---

[45] Eustace Sutherland Campbell Percy (1887–1958). Conservative MP for Hastings 1921–37. Parliamentary Secretary, Education 1923 and Health 1923–24; President, Board of Education 1924–29; member, Joint Select Committee on India 1933–34; Minister without Portfolio 1935–36. Known as Lord Eustace Percy from 1899. Created Baron Percy of Newcastle 1953.

[46] Alan Ian Percy (1880–1930). Succeeded as 8th Duke of Northumberland 1918. Leading figure in Diehard revolt 1921–22; Chairman, *Morning Post* 1924–30.

to Canada. If we dont go it will be all owing to those beastly Irish. I dont trust them for a minute.

I have not after all had a lot of time on my hands as of course there are always committees & business affairs to attend to. But I have been trying to devise means of making Austen's seat more secure and have produced some ideas which I hope may prove successful. We are to have another vacancy in Birm. as Dennis[47] wont stand again at the Gen. Election.

18 June 1922
Westbourne

My dear Hilda,

...

Ouf! We have had two *very* exhausting days and both of us feel rather "raggy" in consequence. We had to come down by the 9.10 a.m. train on Friday and then began a series of committees which lasted almost without intermission till ten o'clock. This comes of being Chairman both of Birm. & the Midland Un. Assn and A. is a member of both too. In both cases we had meetings of a large representative body which has very little work to do but which I want to keep interested because it is far more representative than the comparatively small management committee. To do this means that I have beforehand to grind out something that sounds exciting in the report and then at the meeting to make one fairly lengthy & a number of shorter speeches which are designed to make the audience feel that their opinion is wanted and that they are important people. It is work that takes a lot out of one but I had the reward of feeling that it had been successful. Both meetings were well attended. ... and indeed everyone seemed interested and pleased. I believe if we had an Election now even we should retain nearly all the seats we hold in the Midlands and things are improving all the time.

Yesterday we had our garden party to the constituency workers and though it was cold & for the most part dull the affair was voted a huge success. Indeed when I heard of the many gallons of cider cup that had been consumed I felt it was a mercy it was not a warm day or the 18 galls cask & the 100 bottles of mineral water together with the oceans of tea provided would have gone no-where. We had an excellent string band and heaps of games with competitions under stewards. The stewards love the importance and the prizes are an enor-mous stimulus though of course of only trifling value. I delivered a short address and Annie replied to the vote of thanks. Needless to say that she was in her element all afternoon making every one happy with smiles and graciousness and

---

[47] John William Dennis (1865–1949). Civil Servant 1883–91. Member, Tariff Reform Commis-sion 1904–21; Mayor of Westminster 1907–8; Potato Controller, Ministry of Food 1917. Coalition Unionist MP for Birmingham Deritend 1918–22.

when they had all departed at 8 o'clock she kept two back and discussed the arrangements for the next demonstration with them till 9.15. Poor weak mortal me whose tummy was gradually distending with emptiness could think of nothing but dinner that dinner which ought to have been inside me by that time but people of A's temperament literally become unconscious of such wants & weaknesses when they are excited. Its a great gift.

Next week thank goodness I have only got a board meeting at B.S.A. a luncheon and speech to the Association of Midland Unionist Agents and a party from Hoskins on Saturday afternoon!

Alas! our projected Canadian trip seems to be fading into the background as there is every probability that an autumn session will be required to deal with the Irish Constitution. I went to see Austen about it one day this week and was not sorry to have an opportunity of clearing up the situation with him so far as possible. He was evidently anxious to make the best of a bad job and to hope that things would turn out all right but when faced with a definite question he did not proclaim his faith in M. Collins 'bona fides' with the same confidence as before and I think he feels it difficult to conceive that even Irishmen could go and draft a constitution contrary to the treaty they had signed – just by accident! He doesn't know what De V. will do about issuing the declaration of adherence to the Treaty but Griffith says "Oh, they'll have to sign it." Of course its not impossible – indeed one feels inclined to say, remembering the time taken over the Treaty, it is probable that the Daill [sic] will not get the Constitution ratified in time for an autumn session & in that case we might still get away but I feel that if Parliament is called for the middle of October it would be difficult to explain my position to people in Canada if I were there instead of at Westminster.

...

24 June 1922
Westbourne

My dear Ida,

Yes, we came down here on Thursday morning for the Balfour ceremony and only heard the first rumours of the murder[48] while we were having tea with him in the Bot. Gdns. It is enough to make any one despair of Ireland and curse the Irish as a hopeless and impossible race. What is the precise significance we have yet to learn but I imagine that it was planned by people who seek to make peace between this country and Ireland impossible and they may well have succeeded. The statements issued by the "Publicity Dept" in Dublin and by De Valera are calculated further to exasperate British opinion and even Griffith's pronouncement

---

[48] On 22 June 1922 Field Marshall Sir Henry Wilson, then an Ulster MP, was assassinated by two IRA gunmen on the steps of his home in Eaton Place in full dress uniform.

sounds singularly cold and inadequate. One would not be surprised to read of desperate reprisals any morning and there needs little more to drive us all into advocating forcible suppression of the Republicans. It is a sickening tragedy and to declare that it is hypocrisy to make more fuss over the assassination of the most distinguished soldier of his generation than over a peasant is in itself the worst kind of hypocrisy and cant. I feel the gloomiest anticipations of what may follow.

I dont suppose you have seen any full report of Balfour's speech, but I wonder if you would have felt as I did while listening to it. It was nearly all in praise of Father "my great friend" "with whom I worked so long and loyally". From an impersonal point of view I felt that he had missed an opportunity of making an important and interesting pronouncement based on the Washington Conference showing what it meant to us and leading up to a statement of future Imperial policy. I had the impression that as usual Balfour had not thought of what he was going to say and that he was covering up his own laziness by dwelling at somewhat excessive length on a subject which he thought would be acceptable to his audience. From a personal point of view I could not help thinking that if he had shown a greater appreciation of his friend in his lifetime and proved his loyalty by action it would have been worth much eulogy after his death. An odious frame of mind no doubt but thats how I do feel. I have always believed that behind his courtesy and affability A.B. is profoundly indifferent to the rest of the world. He expressed himself as "deeply moved" but I saw no trace of emotion and both Annie and I were struck with his behaviour when the news of the murder came. There was a word or two of conventional horror and then with a smile he passed on to talk of how he had had to carry a revolver in Ireland but it was doubtful whether, if it had been necessary to use it, he would not have done more harm to himself than to anyone else.

I introduced Uncle Arthur to him to his (Uncle Arthur's) great delight and Frank & Dorothy were also taken up to shake hands and they too had tea with him, which they may be pleased to remember some day. But I did not tell them what I thought of him!

I haven't given up the idea of Canada yet as I think it just possible we may be able to go even if we don't cross the Rockies, but of course one cannot make definite plans with so many possibilities in view. I shouldn't wonder if this murder were to precipitate a General Election …

    …

… It is really a fearful tax, this Commission, as it means 10 or 11 a.m. till 5 p.m. two days a week and when in addition I have to go on deputations to Ministers (I had two last week) it leaves little time for the House. I think I have only spoken once this session but that is largely the reason why.

Last year I took up tennis again until I got a "tennis elbow" about halfway through the summer. I hadn't felt it since and started this year in hopes that it had healed. However a very few afternoon's play has reproduced it much worse than before and I have had to give up all idea of playing again this year, if ever

… It *is* annoying as tennis is the only form of exercise that I could enjoy, and got fairly regularly all the year round, and I was just considering the making of a hard court here.

…

1 July 1922
Westbourne

My dear Hilda,

…

I had to hurry off to the House on Thursday because I had made an appointment with the Surveyor of the M/Health who wanted to see me about slums. I saw a good deal of him when I was working at the Unhealthy Areas Committee and formed a high opinion of his knowledge and judgment [sic]. He has now worked out the plan of a new method which strikes me as very promising and particularly as avoiding certain difficulties which have arisen in connection with my own proposals. The latter involve purchase of the areas by the L.A. and not only have they no funds to spare (which might be got over as we suggested payment by bonds) but public opinion has set very much against municipalisation as well as nationalisation.

Put briefly his proposal is to serve notices on the owners that they must prepare a scheme for the area transferring all the properties to an Official Receiver who will issue bonds in proportion to the value of the several interests. He will then carry out necessary alterations and repairs for which he will borrow the money from public funds and after deducting the cost of management & interest on the loan he will distribute the balance as a dividend on the bonds. He (the Surveyor, Baxendale) says in some areas this would enable a 5% div. to be paid and he doesn't think there should be a loss anywhere. I rather doubt this but I think it would be easy to find a basis for a Govt subsidy which would very much help without being extravagant. £200,000 per ann. is allotted now but it is wasted in clearance schemes, which only pile up more trouble. The plan wants a lot of discussion and working out in detail but I think I see light in it.

…

9 July 1922
Westbourne

My dear Ida,

…

I went one day – I think it was Tuesday to see Austen but he was in such pain that I could only stop a few moments. … I am afraid that his illness has not had the compensating advantage of some complaints in giving him a rest. Constant pain is very wearing but apparently the operation gave him relief from that and

Ivy said she was going to "take him" (like a child!) into the country on Tuesday. Isn't it a sort of fate that pursues him in connection with Birmingham. This was to have been his opportunity to make a great impression and improve his position in the constituency about which I continue to hear the most gloomy accounts. I spent some time in the early part of the week trying to get another Cabinet minister to take his place at the demonstration but all in vain and finally we decided to manage by ourselves, Amery making the principal speech. We had the most awful weather. A great gale blew and poured all morning and a good part of the afternoon which kept away the crowd. Still we got between 2000 and 3000 and it cleared in time for the speeches, so that the occasion was voted a success in spite of all discouragements. ... Annie was called for a speech at the end of the programme which she made very happily and many compliments were showered upon her. ... If I were to be run over & killed I am sure she would at once be invited to stand for Parlt in my place.

Apparently it is really intended that Parlt shall rise about the end of this month & the autumn session is not likely to begin before the end of October. So we have advanced our plans very rapidly this week. It occurred to me that I might get in a cure before going to Scotland so A. telephoned to Maxwell Simpson and he examined me and pronounced me in need of liver treatment recommending Harrogate where he said even 2 weeks would be very useful. You will be glad to hear that he found my blood pressure "perfect", confirming what he said last time he took it. Accordingly we are trying to get rooms (hitherto without success) about the 25th and I have managed to get my time at Loubcroy changed to the first fortnight beginning about the 12th. On my return I should have about a week to turn round and then we think of sailing for Canada about the 7th Sept. returning at the end of October. ...

...

On Tuesday we dined with Helen & Arthur but I had to hurry back to the House for the division on the Palestine mandate & was rewarded by hearing Churchill's speech which was quite a masterpiece. You would suppose from the Times that it was all silly jokes but really there was plenty of good commonsense argument most adroitly lightened with excellent fooling at the expense of "Jinks" [sic] and the Diehards.

...

15 July 1922
Westbourne

My dear Hilda,

...

I too have heard nothing direct from Austen but Leslie Wilson told me on Tuesday that he was going on very well and hoped to be all right by next Monday in time for the Honours Debate. ...

Apparently the Govt think they are going to settle the Honours business without a scuffle. I spoke seriously about it to L. Wilson some time ago and he then said he was fed up with it – the Cabinet kept discussing and discussing without coming to any decision and he wasn't at all disposed to make any further move himself. But apparently he thought better of it as he came to me afterwards and said he had now got the P.M. into a more reasonable frame of mind. When I last saw Sam Hoare he wasn't satisfied with the proposal that proposed honours should be "vetted" by a Committee; he wanted a Comee set up to enquire and recommend how they should be "vetted". Only in that way, he said, would people be satisfied that the Govt were not appointing a Comee to conceal their misdeeds. At the same time he was very clear that enquiry into the past must be avoided. But that is just what the Govt is afraid of & why they dont want an investigating Comee. I had thought of saying a few words but the Royal Commission is to sit that afternoon to discuss policy and I shall consequently miss all the first part of the debate. I did manage to get in one speech last week on Unempl. and having broken the ice intervened again in the small hours on the Finance Bill. Unfortunately the Insurance Bill Comee came on 2 nights after while I was at dinner and having hurried up to vote with Johnnie Baird & Leo Amery, none of us having any idea what the division was about I found afterwards that I had voted against the very proposition I had supported in my speech! Accidents will happen sometimes, but it is so rare for me to vote without knowing what I am voting on that I was peculiarly unlucky this time.

...

I don't think I told you that after a number of interviews &c we have succeeded in getting assistance from the unemployed grants comee for the remainder of the work on the Trent. The Corporn has passed the necessary resolutions & the river as improved will probably be open for traffic by the end of 1924. Thus the first step forward will be completed and before I die I may possibly see the first Trust formed and working. Yesterday I saw in the Times that the Lee Navigation was to be improved to the 100 Ton standard. It does not form part of any important group of waterways and lies outside any of the 7 groups that I have suggested, still one likes to see progress on any waterway.

Alas, the time is drawing nearer when our happy home will have to be broken up by Frank's departure for school. ... Dorothy hasn't yet realised what it means and Frank himself openly rejoices at the prospect! I remember how I wanted to go and Ida's grief. But she had got her sisters to play with & poor Dorothy has none.

21 July 1922
35 Egerton Crescent, SW3

My dear Ida,

...

The House has been very dull this week. Ll.G. made a very bad speech in the Honours debate giving the impression that he was trying to evade the issue so that Austen had to explain that he "might have misunderstood" the arguments that were to have been used. There is no doubt that he has lost much of his power over the House and from what I hear he is growing more and more unpopular in the country because people dont trust him. Newdigate[49] was telling me that the Warwickshire miners say he has brought unemployment upon them by his attacks on the propertied classes and if the working man has found him out he is in a bad way.

...

I am beginning to get that restless feeling that comes when one is going away & having any number of unravelled threads. In particular I regret that I shant be able to vote on the Safeguarding of Industries Order. Did you see that the Unionist Party Committee had passed a resolution supporting Baldwin quoted by the Times to show that Unionist opinion was hardening. *I* did that, and Baldwin was very gratified for the help.

...

29 July 1922
Stray Hotel, Harrogate

My dear Hilda,

...

Our Dr made a very thorough examination of us and on the whole gave us a very good report. Annie is to have the same treatment that did her so much good before, but he does not think at present that there is much wrong with her. My heart, lungs and arteries are pronounced "splendid" and my gout is due not to uric acid but to inability to dissolve my phosphates. The practical effect of which I take to be that I need not bother about diet and there is the additional consolation that all my previous treatment must have been wrong! Of course they always begin like that, but I approve of Dr Morris because he says it would be a great mistake to get up before breakfast and that filthy sulphur water would do me more harm than good. So we breakfast at 9. saunter down to drink a glass of saline water (Annie does have some sulphur in hers but only the mild kind) at 11. with another at 3 and a bath every other day. Mine is electrical, that is, an intermittent current is passed through it which makes me dither all over for ¼ hr. I don't like it, but it doesn't hurt. Only it seems very exhausting.

We spend much of our time in writing. What the hotel will think of us I don't know for we send off 20 or 30 letters a day and their paper & envelopes keep giving out. But I expect when the House rises things will slack off a bit. I feel rather guilty at missing the Fabric Gloves debate next Monday but as you

---

[49] Francis Alexander Newdigate-Newdegate (1862–1936). Unionist MP for Nuneaton 1892–1906 and Tamworth 1909–17. Governor of Tasmania 1917–20 and Western Australia 1920–24. Knighted 1917. Assumed the additional name Newdegate 1902.

observed I put off my departure from London to take part in the debate and the division on Canadian cattle.[50] I don't imagine Austen had any very strong convictions on the subject but he probably had promised "Bosky" to support him. I spoke with the more confidence because I had been lunching with two Canadians but I was very dissatisfied with my speech from which I left out several things I had meant to say. Anyway I am glad the division went as it did.

...

We are getting together many letters of introduction and as the House is not to meet until Nov 14 we shant feel quite so rushed as I feared we might. Mr Bennett[51] a former Minister of Justice said to me that anyone of the name of Chamberlain going to Canada would have a pretty strenuous time & when I said I thought it required some courage on my part he replied uncompromisingly "Well, I think it does", and proceeded to invite me to address the luncheon club of Calgary. But I would prefer that of Medicine Hat or Moose Jaw; they sound so Dog-Crusoey!

14 August 1922
Loubcroy Lodge, Oykell, by Lairg

My dear Hilda,

...

Poor Austen! He has my deep sympathy for I have forgotten politics!

3 September 1922
Westbourne

My dear Hilda,

...

Frank's whole soul is wrapped up in his moths and caterpillars. Aunt Ida's supposed Fox turned out to be an oak eggar as I suspected when I heard it was spinning a cocoon but genuine foxes were found subsequently and after my arrival various other most exciting caterpillars & moths made every day a joy to him. They really are, after making all allowances for parental feeling, a very fascinating couple and I felt very badly at parting from them!

...

I am looking forward to our trip with immense interest & feel sure it will give us lots to think about for years to come.

---

[50] On 24 July the Commons voted to remove the embargo on the importation of Canadian cattle introduced in 1896 on health grounds. Unionists were divided 114 for retention to 104 for removal.

[51] Richard Bedford Bennett (1870–1947). Canadian barrister, businessman and Conservative politician. MP Federal Parliament 1911–17, 1925–38. Minister of Justice 1921 and 1926; Leader, Conservative Party 1927–38; Prime Minister 1930–35. Created Viscount Bennett 1941.

After a visit to Harrogate for the therapeutic waters and then fishing in Scotland, Chamberlain sailed for Canada on 7 September. After leaving Quebec with 'deep regret', they travelled to Montreal and Toronto before crossing the vast prairies to British Columbia and Vancouver Island. Writing to his sisters from a Canadian Pacific train somewhere between Moose Jaw and Medicine Hat, Chamberlain noted that the people were 'so hospitable in this country that I never get a moment to write in the towns'. The result was a series of largely pencil written scrawls describing the grandeur of the scenery and the warmth of the welcome for an 'old country man'.

4 October 1922
Empress Hotel, Victoria, BC

My dear Ida,

Your letter of 14th Sept. has just reached us one of the first batch of letters we have received since we left home ... We were much mystified by a telegram for [sic] Austen saying "Arthur better hopes to start earliest possible date" but soon after a letter arrived which cleared up the situation explaining that "Arthur better" was code for a dissolution. We had a hectic time for half an hour wondering if we should have to abandon our tour when another telegram came saying that Arthur had given up all idea of his trip! So once more we can proceed with equanimity.

...

We continue to have the most thrilling time. I wrote last just as we had arrived at Banff. We had a glorious day there and another at Lake Louise which is a little gem over 5000 ft up of the most marvellous emerald colour with great rocky peaks rising up on all sides and with a huge snowy glacier on the face of an 11,000 ft mountain at the end. We made the most of our time driving round in motors in the wonderful mountain scenery & left with sincere regret that we could not give a few more days to the Rockies. The train journey down Kicking Horse pass to Ducks quite came up to our expectation and the Selkirks which run parallel to the Rockies were almost more spectacular though the weather was not so kind & many of the peaks were hidden in the clouds. ... Vancouver is one of the coming cities of Canada, with a perfect harbour & a mild climate ...

Victoria is more like England than anything we have seen. ... The people are intensely British and I have rejoiced their hearts by the interviews I have given the papers. ...

Everyone continues to be so hospitable that our only difficulty is to get a minute to ourselves. I am writing this after midnight. ...

Both of us continue very well and we are enjoying ourselves right erling [?]

8 October 1922
Canadian Pacific Railway, Near Indian Head

My dear Hilda,

...

... Much water has flowed under the bridge since you wrote & the political barometer has moved up and down with bewildering rapidity. It is most difficult to judge the situation out here with the meagre information we get but so far I have been justified in the opinions I have expressed in public & private and it is rather pleasing to hear as I have frequently done that my words have spread comfort and encouragement over the land. People here accept views of an "old country man" ... with almost pathetic confidence and fortunately it has happened more than once that an afternoon telegram has confirmed me in the prophesy that the morning news would prove exaggerated or premature. But though I found in British Columbia much anxiety there was never any doubt that if there was a row [over Chanak] Canada would and must be in it.

...

22 October 1922
On board SS *Homeric*

My dear Ida,

What made me antedate my departure by a week was a telegram from Austen to say that wretched Arthur was better again and meant to start at once. And now has come this sudden dramatic turn which has indeed postponed the election for a brief period but has made it more necessary than ever for me to be at home. I am going to put my reflections on politics into a separate sheet so as not to mix them up with the accounts which I have been sending you of our journey ...

...

My last letter was posted ... from Winnipeg on October 8th. Early the next morning we reached the head of Lake of Superior and we travelled along its shores during the whole of that day in glorious weather. The colours were lovely especially those of the sumach & dogwood bright crimson and the yellow birch with sometimes a gorgeous maple showing all shades of yellow orange and red. ... All this country belongs to the Laurentian formation with great rounded flat slabs of rock looking like elephants lying on their sides and the soil in between is barren and shallow & often broken by "muskegs" or mossy swamps. Really this is the one physical feature of Canada that is new to me. Between Montreal and Winnipeg there is a vast tract of land 1500 miles long which seems incapable of producing anything unless hereafter minerals should be discovered in it. But perhaps some day the shores of the upper Lakes, Superior & Huron with Georgian Bay will be covered with summer residences for it looks ideal for such a purpose and if the game could be preserved there are forests and lakes rivers & swamps hills and valleys capable of providing sport of every kind.

On Tuesday, we left the main line to Montreal and turned off by Georgian Bay to Toronto. ...

Toronto is an ultra-loyal place as many of the United Empire loyalists settled here and have handed down their traditions. Father also spoke here in 1889 and so I found myself booked for 3 speeches. One to the Canadian Club on Wednesday another to the Empire Club on Thursday and the third to the Daughters of the Empire Club on the following Monday. I was very glad that I had come at the end instead of the beginning of my journey as I felt confident that I knew what they would like to hear and what I could safely tell them. All three speeches were different and all immensely successful. I had very large audiences, 500 to 600, and everywhere I heard that they had been greatly impressed and delighted. It was amusing to observe that any sly dig at America was instantly taken up and enthusiastically applauded and when I observed that "when we were accused of having profited by the war it should not be forgotten that not every nation had been willing to accept the mandate ..." the whole audience cheered so that I could not go on.

We spent the first three days at the hotel and the last at Government House with the Lt Governor, Mr Cockshutt.[52] We liked his wife better than we did him but were very glad to get a little rest there for while we were in the town our telephone bell rang every moment and we never had two minutes to ourselves. On the Friday we made our expedition to Niagara ... and I think we saw as much as it is possible to see in a day ...

...

Among the people we met in Toronto were the Meighens[53] whom we saw again afterwards in Ottawa. He is rather a dry cold person with little personal charm while she is a very pleasant unpretending woman with no great polish! He was extremely civil and very anxious to talk as in particular he was indignant at Mackenzie King's[54] behaviour over the Turkish incident & believed that he had given the country a false impression of the way the British Govt had handled the situation. Meighen wanted to get information as to the real facts which he believed were that the British Govt had kept M. King fully informed of the situation but owing to the indifference of Ministers who were all away in different parts of the country & had left no one to attend to the correspondence the telegrams were left unopened. However I have reason to believe from a

---

[52] Henry Cockshutt (1868–1944). Canadian industrialist. Lieutenant-Governor, Ontario 1921–27.

[53] Arthur Meighen (1874–1960). Canadian teacher, barrister, businessman. Liberal-Conservative MP 1908–32. Solicitor-General 1913; Secretary of State 1915–17; Minister of Interior 1917–20; Prime Minister 1920–21, 1926. Senator 1932–41. Represented Canada at Imperial Conference, 1921.

[54] William Lyon Mackenzie King (1874–1950). Canadian economist and politician. Liberal MP 1908–11, 1921–49. Deputy Minister of Labour, 1900–1908; Minister of Labour 1909–11; Liberal Leader 1919–48; Prime Minister 1921–30, 1935–48.

subsequent conversation with the P.M. that there was no foundation for this supposition and that in fact the Govt at home allowed the press to publish a statement that they had called on the Dominions for troops before their first despatch on the subject had been received.

...

The principal event of our stay [at Government House] so far as we were concerned was the Canadian Club luncheon. It was quite an important affair, in a very large room at the Chateau Laurier. The P.M. was present as well as Meighen Sir Charles Fitzpatrick[55] and a number of other influential people and I had laid myself out to do justice to the occasion & the subject which was "Britain's need & Canada's opportunity," a plea for British settlement. It proved to be the climax of my speech making efforts and had an immense success. In fact I had so many compliments about it that I got quite a swelled head. ... And indeed I do feel satisfied that, as I was told after every speech, I hit the right note and did a lot of good in stimulating the Imperial spirit.

Mackenzie King was so much impressed that he came up to Govt House in the afternoon specially to see me and I had a long and interesting private talk with him. Personally I found him much more attractive than Meighen and I am satisfied that he is a good & loyal Imperialist. But he is in a difficult position being dependent on the Quebec Liberals and the farmers party and not being a very strong man he has not been able so far to assert his independence or to follow his own inclinations. The same conditions have held him back in the matter of naval defence and immigration but if he can consolidate his position he may perhaps show a little more initiative than he has done yet. The C.O. [Colonial Office] has not hitherto appreciated his difficulties and they have very much added to his embarrassment by the manner in which they have allowed their decisions to become public before advising him of them. He seemed very glad to have an opportunity of talking frankly to one who he thought was inside things and when we parted he begged me to write to him fully and confidentially on any point that might make such communication valuable. All which im-pressed me with the value of such visits as mine by public men who may have to deal with Imperial affairs, or who can in any way influence them.

We left Ottawa on Thursday morning with many regrets that we could not stay longer and got to Montreal about the middle of the day. We were to leave again at 6 o'clock that evening so we had rather a scramble to get through our chores especially as there was a heavy fall of snow that afternoon ...

So ended our first, but I expect not our last, visit to Canada ...

---

[55] Charles Fitzpatrick (1851–1942). Member, Canadian Parliament from 1890. Solicitor-General, Canada 1896; Minister of Justice 1901–6; Chief Justice of Canada and Deputy Governor-General 1906–18; Lieutenant-Governor of Quebec 1918–23. Knighted.

24 October 1922
On board SS *Homeric*

My dear Hilda,

In writing to Ida I said I would put my reflections on the political situation into a separate letter. Already I begin to wonder whether it is worth while, as events seem to be developing in a way which may have solved my puzzles before we get in. However it may still interest you to hear the impressions produced on a traveller who has to depend on meagre telegrams for his information.

I have mentioned that at Toronto I had a wire from Austen to say that a general election was to take place at once and I spent some feverish hours in altering my arrangements so as to catch this steamer. By the time we got to Ottawa news had come that there was to be a meeting at the Carlton summoned by Austen to endorse his policy which I took to be the same as before viz. that the two wings should go to the election as separate parties under separate leaders but with the understanding that they wd co-operate afterwards. I told the reporters that there was no likelihood of this meeting doing anything but accept this policy as the Die-hards were not numerous & the Unionists could not expect to come back with a clear majority but I pointed out that this did not necessarily mean that Ll.G. would again be P.M. in the new Govt especially if the proportion of C.U.s to C.L.'s should be increased.

You can therefore understand my astonishment at the result of the meeting which showed that the Die-hards must have been joined by many other Unionists and this astonishment was further increased when I read the terms of the resolution which contained the words "While willing to co-operate with the C.L.s" How did this differ from what I understood was the policy agreed upon by the Govt and what had Austen asked the party to accept instead?

This question still remains unanswered as I have never seen any report of Austen's speech …

The next surprise was the announcement of the resignation of such ministers as Amery, Leslie Wilson, P. Lloyd-Greame and "Bosky" showing that they too differed from A. in his view of the proper policy. And then came the last surprise namely that Bonar Law had agreed to accept office.

These events opened up a painful vista for the future, especially in Birmingham. Did Austen mean to follow Ll.G. and form a new party, and if so what was to be my position? To tie myself up to the Goat and to take opposite sides to Austen seemed equally disagreeable. A split in Birmingham appeared inevitable. For a moment I thought of going out altogether, but that did not seem fair to my constituency or to my friends. However the more I thought of it the more it became clear to me that with no fundamental difference of policy but only of personalities I could not see myself following Ll.G. and that if Austen were out of the question I should have no hesitation in remaining with the Unionists & even, if I were asked, joining the new Govt. I told Amery last session that if ever he became Colonial Sec. I would like to serve under him and I should like it still more now that I have been to Canada. However I am not expecting to be asked knowing the claims there will be. But to return to the problem, what is Austen going to do?

I dont know at all, but thinking it over, I fancy he will remain outside the Govt as an independent Unionist, in which case I should hope we might keep the party united. But then again the question arises whether he will be able to retain his seat. I have been counting on his great position to counteract his lack of personal popularity in the division but for the moment his star is clouded and this may have a disastrous effect on his fortunes in the West. If the worst should happen however he might later on obtain a seat in or near London that would suit him better than Birmingham, that is if he did not retire altogether and I don't think he would do that.

The next question is what is Ll.G. going to do? His observations on the way to Leeds seemed to indicate a belligerent mood but I have seen no report of what he said at Leeds itself. If however he should decide to stand as a Liberal and head a party of Lloyd Georgians or dissentient Liberals he might easily attain a commanding position in the next Parliament, on the supposition that the Unionists do not get a clear majority. For in that case they would depend on his support for their existence and he might throw them out when he pleased.

To throw them out at once would not necessarily bring him back and he would appear likely therefore to keep them on the string for a time. If that were to be his policy one may be sure he would not spare them criticism and I picture Liberal and Labour men cheering his jibes with gradually increasing enjoyment until presently, Asquith dozing and Maclean[56] always ready to subordinate himself someone would begin to say "Why sterilise the Liberal party by division? Why not unite under the leader who can bring us back to office?" And so by degrees the Liberals would come together again and Ll.G. might have his revenge.

Well, it would be a sell [?] for the Labour party who would once more see themselves out of court and it would consolidate our people. And in time Austen might find his place again.

I see B.L. has stated that he will invite the co-operation of A's followers. I suppose this means that he will try and secure one or two ministers from among them but it is difficult to see how A. could accept.

Oct 27 Friday I resume. We have had the list of the Cabinet with the exception of about 3 ministers. It contains many peers and is not particularly brilliant but it does not contain any of A's associates. I have also seen a cable received by

---

[56] Donald Maclean (1864–1932). Liberal MP for Bath 1906–10, Selkirk & Peebles 1910–18, Peebles & Midlothian South 1918–22, Cornwall North 1929–32. Chairman, Parliamentary Liberal Party 1919–22 and Acting Leader in Commons 1919–20. President, Board of Education 1931–32. Knighted 1917.

Strauss which indicates that as I thought A. will stand as an independent Unionist & that Ll.G. will give a conditional support to the new Govt. I have had a message from A. himself to say he will be in Birmingham. I also wired to Amery but have not had a reply. I would like to see him & if he is in London I think I shall stop there Sunday night for the purpose; otherwise I hope to arrive in London in time to get home that night. What a turmoil to come home into!

A bulletin today quotes B.L. as saying in his manifesto that he is going to call an Imperial Economic Conference if the Dominions are willing. Hurrah! Thats the stuff to give 'em. Already I feel that this is going to be a much more satisfactory Govt than the last and I offer my profound thanks to Providence for delivering us from the Goat. If only A. is not too much tied up with him.

Oct 29 What rotten luck! Here we are off Cherbourg with a howling gale blowing right in our teeth & instead of arriving at Southampton at 2 we are told that we shall be lucky if we get in by six.

We have had to give up all idea of getting to Birmingham tonight and just now these few hours of quiet would have been so valuable.

However its no use to kick against the pricks. I close this now as the vessel is at the moment quiet & probably wont be again!

I see A. has declared that he has no quarrel with B.L. I hope this is quite genuine. I was afraid he might be feeling that this was the second time Bonar had snatched the leadership out of his hands.

31 October 1922
Westbourne

My dear Hilda,

...

You will probably read in tomorrow's paper that I have accepted office under B.L. as P.M.G. and what you will want to know is how A. has taken it.

Well I went to him as soon as I had the offer & he took the idea very badly evidently feeling that if I accepted it would be the last drop of bitterness in the cup.

In the evening he came to dinner and we had a very long talk. I told him that in my view my acceptance would not be regarded as putting us in opposite camps but rather as a link between him and the new Govt, making relations easier & facilitating his acceptance as one of the leaders if not the leader in the event of B.L.'s being unable to carry on. I pointed out that if he were definitely associated with Lloyd George the latter would be unable to restrain his attacks on Unionists & the breach might be irreparable. Whereas if he (A.) kept quiet he might be welcomed back by Unionists as the possible head of a new Coalition.

I failed to convince him of the truth of this view & I then said I should refuse as I cared more for our personal relations than for politics. But I felt bound to tell him that I should consider my political career as ended for one cannot go on refusing office when one does not differ on principles & my people have long been asking why I dont make a bigger figure. I said this in justice to myself but not as an argument. However it proved too strong for him and he said he could not carry such a responsibility. He declared that nothing should or could alter our personal relations and he begged me to accept. This morning he rang up to say he was still of the same mind and I feel assured now that he will feel no grievance against me in his mind.

For myself I dont regard B.L.'s chances of lasting as very brilliant though I think he may carry on for a time. But I feel convinced that the course I have taken is in Austen's interest though he doesn't yet see it & though I rather dread the result of his appearance on Ll.G's platform on Nov 10 and Birkenhead's appearance on his on Nov 11 I earnestly trust that he will induce them to curb their natural pugnacity on these occasions and that they may pass without further offence to Unionists.

A. is very sore and bitter agst B.L. I think it only natural but I hate the idea of his retiring under a cloud and I can see no prospect for him in conjunction with Ll.G. & Birkenhead unless as members of a new Coalition unlikely as that may seem.

I am very anxious about his seat but hope he may squeeze through. My agent thinks I am certain to win but with a reduced majority.

I am overwhelmed with work interviews & letters and my correspondence is in utter disorder!

11 November 1922
Westbourne

My dear Ida,

... You will perhaps be surprised at hearing from me, but I don't feel inclined to do any work this evening so I may as well send you a line.

Of course we are having a very strenuous time here and unfortunately I am much more paralysed by the sense of impending speeches than most people, so that I find it difficult to keep pace with the work. My sec. tells me she has written about 80 letters of thanks for congratulations, and by every post there pour in sheaves of questionnaires from every conceivable organisation – from Undertakers to Poultry fanciers. The absurd thing is that in many cases the vote is not affected by your answer but it may be if you dont answer.

You can imagine however that my deficiencies are more than made up for by Annie. She really is marvellous. She has got a hat with a large orange panache and every day and all day she perambulates the constituency wet or fine on her bicycle, talking encouraging scolding cajoling charming and converting the multitude. In the last few days she has paid 112 calls beside innumerable street corner talks and she comes to all the meetings & makes little speeches at the end which often make the hit of the evening. Indeed she is worth an army, and all the work she has done before is bearing fruit for her women are taking their full share. We have been able to cover the whole constituency with our own workers entirely all are brimful of enthusiasm and if the canvass cards I have seen are any guide I ought to win by a comfortable majority. I shall be a little disappointed if I dont get 5000 though really a thousand here or there doesn't much matter.

My people are frightfully bucked over my being a P.C. & in the Govt and I am absolutely confirmed in my feeling that I could not have refused office and continued in politics with any satisfaction to myself. They could hardly understand why I wasn't in before but here is a curious coincidence. From the time Father entered the Council till he was Mayor was 4 years 1 month. My corresponding period was exactly 4 years. From the time he entered Parlt till he became a member of the Govt was 3 years 10 months and my corresponding period was exactly the same. Of course there are plenty of differences but it is curious that the periods of time should coincide so exactly.

With regard to Austen I am feeling much easier and I now think he will get in all right though his majority may not be among the biggest. But his people have their tails up and his opponents have theirs down. I went & spoke for him one night to show there was no ill feeling.

In one of his speeches you may have noticed that he suggested the amalgamation of the M/Transport with the P.O. The next day I had a telephone message asking me to go and see the P.M. Annie at once said "he wants to adopt the suggestion", and I thought myself that must be it. I had quite made up my mind to refuse but when I got to Downing St I found all he wanted was to ask what line he should take in replying to Austen's speech in London. At any rate that was all he said he wanted and he apologised very much for calling me up for such a trifle! He is a funny person but as a matter of fact I wasn't sorry to have a long talk with him as we hadn't met since my appointment. He told me inter alia that the Central Office estimated we should win 320 seats in England alone and if the reports I get from the Midlands are at all typical I believe myself we shall have a pretty sweeping victory. Of course Labour has gone and "done it" with its mad programme. It is curious that they should have so misunderstood the psychology of the country as to think they could bribe the electors with such a transparent fake.

Today was to have been an "off" day so far as meetings are concerned but yesterday afternoon the Central Office telephoned that the P.M. was ill and wanted me to take his meeting at the Free Trade Hall in Manchester. I had two meetings of my own last night so it didn't leave much time for preparation but I prepared a few witticisms after I got back and finished them off in the train this morning. We had a great meeting – between 3 & 4000 – at 2 o'clock and the thing went off with a bang. I got a wire from Bonar soon after I got home congratulating me which was nice of him and I am wondering whether my speech will attract any attention as it contained some items of an unauthorised programme on housing and unemployment. Anyhow it pleased the M.P.'s who were there as they said it had furnished them with new ammunition and they had been running out.

Sunday A. is here to lunch & has shown me his canvass return on which he ought to be safer than I! ...

19 November 1922
Westbourne.

My dear Hilda,

Thanks for your letter and your interesting comments on the election. I had an awful shock for right up to the last moment I had expected a big majority when my agent discovered that a big pile of papers that he had thought were mine were Dunstans.[57] I confess I felt pretty downhearted for a bit and it is hard luck after all we have done to have come out with the lowest majority but one when others like Smedley Crooke[58] sail in with over 4000. But further reflection brought some consolation and a wonderful meeting of our own supporters on Thursday night restored our equanimity. We have to recognise that Dunstan was the strongest candidate the Socialists produced and as my seat was supposed to be absolutely safe the forces were concentrated on West and other supposedly weak places. Of course Ladywood is a desperately poor part; there is no counterbalancing district of good class and the Socialists had exploited to the uttermost the poverty and ignorance of the electors. Many were told and believed that the "dole" came from the Labour organisation confusing it with the Labour exchange. It seems incredible but I am assured that it was so. My own peoples view is that with a weaker candidate we should have lost the seat and I now think that is so except that in that case help would have poured in. Well, the main thing is that I *am* in but we shall have to work hard and try to win over the bad spots which we can do if unemployment decreases.

Yes I felt the same about Austen. His striking success which he owed largely to his own efforts has put him in countenance again and taken the edge off the bitterness which he felt. And it is very gratifying to me that we kept all 12 seats because I have put in a lot of work here and I feel the results are due largely to the efforts we have made to build up the Unionist organisation. Annie was of course very disappointed about Ladywood but she too has got over it and is full of plans for strengthening our hold on the constituency. I had an invitation to

---

[57] Dr Robert Dunstan. Liberal candidate for Totnes 1910; Labour candidate for Birmingham Moseley 1918 and Manchester Rusholme 1919 before standing against Neville Chamberlain in Ladywood in 1922 and 1923. In 1924 Dunstan stood as a Communist in West Birmingham against Austen Chamberlain.

[58] (John) Smedley Crooke (1861–1951). Conservative MP for Birmingham Deritend 1922–1929 and 1931–45. Knighted 1938.

address the unemployed last Tuesday. It came from Socialists who hoped I should refuse but I accepted. I had 1¾ hours pretty rough time of it but I believe it did me more good than harm as a good many of the more decent ones present were disgusted at the insolence of my opponents some of whom were certainly not unemployed at all and the same thing occurred after several of my meetings when we heard of various people whose sympathies were with labour but who could not stomach their rudeness and misbehaviour.

The general result is quite satisfactory. We shall have an adequate but not excessive majority and a strong opposition and I hope the party will work together much better than in the last Parlt. B.L. told me that if he had a majority of over 100 he *would* be afraid of the reactionaries but we shall be able to keep them in order & I hope he will be able to do something both for trade & housing which are the danger points. Anyhow he is not hampered by any foolish promises.

It has been a big strain and I cant do like Austen – sleep peacefully for an hour every afternoon! Lucky dog! But we are already recovering.

We have decided not to go up till tomorrow as Parlt doesn't open till Thursday. I hope in the meantime to get to my office and begin my work there.

I too was sorry for Churchill tho' I fancy the story that he was in tears is apocryphal. I don't know what Jack Hills[59] will do but it is hard lines that he should have been knocked out. Another surprise was Jack Wilson[60] who certainly didn't expect defeat. I am sorry for him too but I always felt that he was hollow and that a really strong candidate might be successful. We have done very well through the Midlands having won 4 seats and only lost one.

25 November 1922
Westbourne

My dear Hilda or Ida, (for I cant remember whose turn it is) …

We got up on Sunday evening and I began Monday with a long talk with my Permanent Secretary Sir Evelyn Murray.[61] He is a very able man and I believe we shall get on very well together although I dont think he has a particularly attractive personality. The P.M. warned me that he is said not to be very easy to work with being rather disposed to claim his own way but so far he has not shown any cloven hoof even when I have not taken the course he suggested, but we shall see. I went to the House for the election of Speaker and on the three

---

[59] John Waller Hills (1867–1938). Conservative MP for Durham 1906–22, Ripon 1925–38. Financial Secretary to Treasury 1922–March 1923 when defeated at Edge Hill by-election.

[60] John William Wilson (1858–1932). Liberal Unionist (Liberal from 1903) MP for North Worcestershire 1895–1918 and Liberal MP for Stourbridge 1918–22.

[61] (George) Evelyn Pemberton Murray (1880–1947). Entered Civil Service 1903; Private Secretary, President of Board of Trade 1905–9; Commissioner of Customs and Excise, 1909–14; Secretary to Post Office 1914–34; Chairman, Board of Customs and Excise 1934–40. Knighted 1916.

following days put in a good deal of time at St Martins seeing the staff & discussing various questions. It will take me some little time to get hold of things but I have got an excellent & valuable secretary Col. Banks[62] whom I like and who combines an agreeable manner with tact & good judgement. It *is* different from Nat. Service and I am sure I shall enjoy it if they will let me alone and not try and push me into some other office. That firebrand Nancy Astor is already tearing about shouting that I am in the wrong place & that I am the one person who ought to be Minister of Health. It is true that I have some knowledge & experience of Health affairs but I would much rather find my feet on the Treasury Bench in my present job & if possible make good there than enter at once upon one of the most difficult & controversial offices in the Govt.

Secret I was early sent for to Downing St to discuss the P.M.'s attitude to the "unemployed" marchers. He had already refused to see them once & they had sent a threatening letter reiterating their demand for an interview. To my astonishment & consternation Mr Barlow[63] urged that the P.M. should give way as otherwise public opinion would be against him. However I am glad to say that the rest of us were all unanimous that such a course would be a fatal act of weakness which would not conciliate the unemployed, or rather their Communist leaders, but would alienate the confidence of the country and finally the Ld Chancellor,[64] Douglas Hogg[65] and I were deputed to draft the P.M.'s reply. The result I thought read extremely well because it was perfectly firm but neither unsympathetic nor offensive and so far the P.M. has undoubtedly won the first round. I see they are now calling for reinforcements but I doubt if they will get them and I suspect they are looking for an excuse to say they would have succeeded only that they didn't get the support they had a right to expect. My belief is that the country is rejoicing over the change of method and will back the constitutional course we have followed.

---

[62] Donald Banks (1891–1975). Exchequer and Audit Dept 1909; Private Secretary to Postmaster-General 1920–23; Deputy-Controller, Post Office Savings 1924 and Controller 1931; first Director-General of Post Office 1934–36; Permanent Secretary, Air Ministry 1936–38; first Permanent Under-Secretary of State for Air 1938–39; Member, National Savings Committee 1931–39 and Import Duties Advisory Committee 1939; Director-General, Petroleum Warfare Dept 1940–45; Deputy-Chairman, Air Transport Advisory Committee 1947–51.

[63] (Clement) Anderson Montague-Barlow (1868–1951). Conservative MP for Salford South 1910–23. Parliamentary Secretary, Ministry of Labour 1920–22; Minister of Labour 1922–24. Knighted 1918. Created Bart 1924. Chairman, Royal Commission on Location of Industry, 1937–40. Changed name by deed poll from Barlow to Montague-Barlow in 1946.

[64] George Cave (1856–1928). Conservative MP for Kingston (Surrey) 1906–18. Solicitor General 1915–16; Home Secretary 1916–19; Lord Chancellor 1922–24, 1924–28. Knighted 1915. Created Viscount 1919.

[65] Douglas McGarel Hogg (1872–1950). Conservative MP for St Marylebone 1922–28. Attorney-General 1922–24, 1924–28; Lord Chancellor 1928–29, 1935–38; Secretary for War 1931–35; Lord President 1938; Conservative Leader in the Lords 1931–35. Knighted 1922. Created Baron Hailsham 1928 and Viscount 1929.

Poor Annie has had a most awful cold all the week brought on or rather aggravated by exposure to wind & weather in bicycling about the constituency. I got the Dr in in London and he persuaded her to spend a day in bed but I fear the Duchess of Sutherland's party did her no good ...

The party was a fearful crush and babel as usual, but we met an enormous number of friends there and many people who wished to be introduced to the P.M.G. I got such a lot of compliments about Manchester that I am seriously alarmed as these stories grow and the next thing you know is that half the country wants you to go and make another "brilliant" speech. And I haven't got a stock of them and hate the labour & worry of making them. Next week I shall have to begin the ordeal of answering questions but the sooner the better as I am always nervous in the House for want of practice.

I came down here last night just in time to rush into evening clothes and attend a public dinner at which Austen & I were the star turns. I took the opportunity of mildly chaffing him as I consider it well to keep on demonstrating what friendly terms we are on. His speech came before mine & he didn't make any allusion to me as his toast was on other lines but he displayed such high spirits that some one said he reminded him of a schoolboy home for the holidays and indeed I am sure that his success in the election has cleared away his depression.

I have spent nearly the whole of today discussing my election & constituency. Indeed I talked for 6 consecutive hours about it and haven't been inside my orchid houses yet! But the more I go into it the more satisfied I am that the small majority was not due to any inferiority of enthusiasm or organisation as compared with other divisions but rather to the unexpected strength of my opponent. I think we shall have to work pretty hard to keep the seat intact but I believe we shall do it & that the shock will make my people more determined than ever to keep the Labour candidate out.

...

2 December 1922
Westbourne

My dear Hilda,

...

I have spent most of my time this week at the P.O. where I feel I am beginning to get hold. I only had to answer questions one day when I got through the supplementaries very comfortably, but on Thursday after dining with Mary & getting back to the House I was informed that Wedgwood Benn[66] was going to

---

[66] William Wedgwood Benn (1877–1960). Liberal MP for Tower Hamlets 1906–18 and Leith 1918–27; Labour MP for Aberdeen North 1928–31 and Manchester Gorton 1937–41. Liberal Whip 1910–15; Secretary of State for India 1929–31; Secretary for Air 1945–46. Created Viscount Stansgate 1942.

raise the question of Kellaway's taking a directorship of the Marconi Company. There is nothing Godfrey Isaacs[67] touches that does not stink and personally I consider K's behaviour bad form but I believe W. Benn has a personal grudge against him & anyway I wasn't going to give away anything. I don't think we shall hear much more of it but in my opinion the Marconi Company is more likely to suffer by the incident than the P.O.

I have got two jobs next week. One is to wind up the debate for the Govt on Monday on the Safeguarding of Industries Act. This is rather a formidable undertaking but I would not shirk it as I feel we cannot leave B.L. to do everything. He says our people are rather shaky & he may have to take the job on himself but I have to be ready. The other is a minor affair – to defend an agreement with the West India & Panama Cable Co. but it will all serve to familiarise me with debate & though I dont look forward to it with pleasure I recognise I have got to face it.

We stopped in town on Friday to dine with the Peels[68] – quite a pleasant party tho' I don't like this society plan of introducing no one to no one ... Annie seems to have spent most of her time listening to the Duke of Atholl's[69] tale of woe. He was the Lord Chamberlain and one day read in the Daily Mail that he had been superseded by the Earl of Clarendon.[70] He said the appointment was made by Curzon[71] (why should the F.O. appoint the Kings Household?) who had seen a false statement in the press that he (the duke) had appeared on Lloyd George's platform. It sounds rather like Curzon I must say and it seems outrageous to make the change without informing either the King or the Duke. The latter

---

[67] Godfrey Isaacs (?-1925). Managing Director, Marconi Wireless Telegraph Company 1910–24. At the centre of the Marconi Scandal involving his brother Rufus (later Lord Reading) and Lloyd George in 1913 and a second scandal in 1914–15.

[68] William Robert Wellesley Peel (1867–1937). Conservative MP for Manchester South 1900–1906 and Taunton 1909–12. Joint-Parliamentary Secretary, Ministry of National Service 1918; Under-Secretary for War and Air 1919–21; Chancellor, Duchy of Lancaster 1921–22; Minister of Transport 1921–22; Secretary for India 1922–24 and 1928–29; First Commissioner of Works 1924–28; Lord Privy Seal 1931. Succeeded as 2nd Viscount Peel in 1912 and created Earl Peel 1929.

[69] John George Stewart-Murray (1871–1942). Unionist MP for West Perthsire 1910–17. Lord High Commissioner, Church of Scotland 1918–20; Lord Chamberlain 1921–22. Succeeded as 8th Duke of Atholl 1917.

[70] George Herbert Hyde Villiers (1877–1955). ADC to Lord-Lieutenant of Ireland 1902–5; Captain of Gentleman-at-Arms 1922–25; Chief Government Whip in Lords 1922–25; Under-Secretary, Dominion Office and Chairman, Overseas Settlement Committee 1925–27; Chairman, BBC 1927–30; Governor-General and C-in-C, Union of South Africa 1931–37, Lord Chamberlain to H.M. Household 1938–52; Permanent Lord-in-Waiting 1952–55. Succeeded as 6th Earl of Clarendon 1914.

[71] George Nathaniel Curzon (1859–1925). Conservative MP for Southport 1886–98. Viceroy of India 1898–1905; Lord Privy Seal 1915–16; Lord President 1916–19 and 1924–25; Foreign Secretary 1919–24; Conservative Leader in Lords 1916–24. Created Baron 1898, Earl 1911 and Marquess 1921.

plaintively observed "I always do get the sack and I suppose I always shall". For a duke there is something irresistibly comic about that remark.[72]

...

Sunday Last night we had a dinner party of constituents to discuss motor car arrangements while the circumstances of the election were still fresh. I think it was quite a useful function for hitherto the organisation has been a bit haphazard but now we are going to lay it out on more scientific lines so that we may have more & our opponent less benefit from the cars in future. I think there is no doubt that some of my enthusiastic supporters carried a lot of Dunstan's voters to the poll. We hear now that a good many voted for him because he had done so much for the blind soldiers! Others again because he said that if returned I should cut down their old age pensions!

9 December 1922
Westbourne

My dear Ida,

...

I had rather a hectic day last Monday. I arose soon after 7 a.m. to catch the early train to London, went to the P.O. and then on to the House, sat on the front bench from 4 till 10.40 with an hour out to dine and put together my notes, spoke till 11 and then sat on till 5 a.m. getting to bed at 5.30 and rising again at 8.30. And the following night I didn't get to bed till 1.30 a.m. after a headache that lasted nearly all day!

It was rather a formidable ordeal winding up with less than 20 minutes and in a noisy excited House but I managed to get through – if not entirely to my satisfaction yet with credit. Our people were very pleased and I had any amount of congratulations from Bonar downwards. I saw the Evening Standard was reminded of father by the "perfect coolness" with which I faced angry interruptions. If only they knew! However evidently they didn't for Simon[73] too in apologising next day for the rudeness of his supporters said "But of course you didn't mind it a bit" and as a matter of fact once I was up I wasn't as nervous as I expected. Yesterday I had to speak again on an agreement with a West India Cable Company. Unluckily it came just after the Asquith incident while the Labour party were still very raw after their humiliation and one after another got up and denounced the agreement as one to vote away the nations' money & to put money

---

[72] Atholl was actually replaced by the Earl of Cromer (1877–1953). Ironically, Clarendon did become Lord Chamberlain in 1938.

[73] John Allsebrook Simon (1873–1954). Liberal MP for Walthamstow 1906–18 and Spen Valley 1922–40 (Liberal National from 1931). Solicitor-General 1910–13; Attorney-General 1913–15; Home Secretary 1915–16 and 1935–37; Foreign Secretary 1931–35; Chancellor of Exchequer 1937–40; Lord Chancellor 1940–45. Knighted 1910. Created Viscount Simon 1940.

into the pockets of "your friends". Our people got very nervous and frightened lest they should be unable to keep a house but I refused either to adjourn or to apply the closure and finally had my reward by carrying my motion without a division. If I get a bit more practice I believe I shall be able to manage the H. of C. all right.

The week had been rather amusing in the House on account of the fierce hostility between the Wee Frees & the Labour party which has repeatedly burst out in angry passages. The L.P. particularly detest Kenworthy & Pringle[74] and we alternately applaud one side or the other and egg them on to further attacks on one another. On the whole I must say Ramsay McDonald[75] [sic] is doing very well and several times he has shown his displeasure at the want of manners of his extreme followers much to their discomfiture and our joy.

Yesterday I attended the first meeting of the Housing Committee of the Cabinet and I feel rather cheerful as it shows a disposition to follow out the ideas which I put forward. I met Mond one day and he was extraordinarily complimentary first about my speech on the Safeguarding of Industries Act & then saying how much he wished I were Minister of Health and how I ought to be in the Cabinet & finally expressing his entire approval of my ideas about Canals. I don't know what makes him so friendly but in the circumstances I was rather glad I had not had time to make the sarcastic remarks I had intended on Monday about his change of attitude!

Ll.G.'s speech on agriculture certainly held the House which was more inclined to be sympathetic because the Labour members were very rude to him, but the chief comment I heard was in the nature of speculation as to what his "game" was. I think myself that he picked out agriculture as the best vantage ground from which to preserve a position on the flank of the Govt. It is open to him now either to say "I was the first to suggest the policy which the Govt have carried out" or "I begged & implored you to do something for my country not caring how much criticism it might draw on me and you have done nothing. Now there is no other course open to me than to smite you hip and thigh". There wasn't a single constructive idea in the speech and much of the statement of facts was incorrect. Some said it was thoroughly insincere. I wouldn't go as far as that but I cannot believe that he hadn't got the idea of strategic position in his mind all the time.

This Gounaris[76] incident has made a small sensation. I understand that the F.O. has got evidence that Austen saw the letter but of course no one suggests

[74] William Mather Rutherford Pringle (1874–1928). Liberal MP for N.W. Lanarkshire 1910–18 and Penistone 1922–24. Chairman, Liberal and Radical Candidates Association 1924–28.

[75] James Ramsay MacDonald (1866–1937). Labour MP Leicester 1906–18, Aberavon 1922–29, Seaham 1929–31; National Labour MP for Seaham 1931–35 and Scottish Universities 1936–37. Labour Party Secretary 1900–1912; Chairman 1912–14 and Leader 1922–31. Prime Minister and Foreign Secretary 1924; Prime Minister 1929–35; Lord President 1935–37.

[76] Demetrios Gounaris (1867–1922). Greek Statesman. Minister of Finance 1908; Prime Minister, 1915, 1920–22. Executed in Athens 28 November 1922 as a scapegoat for Greek collapse in Asia Minor.

that either he or even Ll.G. are lying about it. People say there is such a mass of papers that it is no wonder if Ministers do not read them all carefully or fail to remember what they have read only then they ought not like Birkenhead to try to throw discredit on Curzon for what certainly is not his fault.[77] I havent seen A. to speak to for quite a long time so I dont know what attitude he takes up on this particular matter. But I overheard him and Bonar exchanging some chaff the other day in what seemed a friendly enough manner and although I dont attach much importance to that I think there was a time when A. could not have trusted himself to say a word.

I have heard very little about the Near East but so far as I can make out Curzon has done very well in that he seems to have succeeded in creating a good "atmosphere" for settlement.[78] Even the Turks seem far less truculent than they were and the longer they can be kept quiet the less likely they are to get out of control. Whether we are going to secure the freedom of the Straits seems to me doubtful; that is I doubt whether it is possible to secure it absolutely against violence by a State determined on seizing it. The nearest thing to security as it seems to me is that the responsibility for freedom should be shared by a number of nations and that appears to be what Curzon is working for. Of course the late Govt did not propose to keep the Turk out of Constantinople but I think he might have been kept out of Thrace if our affairs had been more happily managed.

You never made any comment on the P.M.'s refusal to see the "hunger marchers" but I think time has demonstrated the wisdom of his action. There can be no possible doubt that the whole thing was a plant & a fraud in which a large number of ignorant and foolish but quite honest men were made the dupes of a set of rascals. But the P.M.'s firmness has broken up & discredited the whole affair.

17 December 1922
35 Egerton Crescent, SW3

My dear Hilda,

Your letter and political comments are very interesting to me but they make me feel glad you are coming to Westbourne where we shall be able to discuss the situation at length. As this will be happening so soon I wont now argue the points on which you touch except to say as regards European debts that the policy of the late Government was expressed in the Balfour Note. In that note it

[77] On 3 December 1922 Beaverbrook's *Sunday Express* published extracts from a letter from Gounaris to Curzon appealing for aid to resist Turkey in Anatolia. Birkenhead initially declared that other Coalition leaders had never seen the exchange and that Curzon was solely responsible for Gounaris' execution. On 11 December he was compelled to retract in the Lords after evidence to the contrary was produced.

[78] Lausanne Conference, 20 November 1922 to 4 February 1923. Intended to reach a new peace with Turkey to replace the shattered Treaty of Sèvres.

was laid down that we should only cancel so much of the debts to us as was equivalent to what U.S.A. would cancel of our debt to her. The note irritated every one all round and carried us no farther towards a settlement with France or Germany. The present Govt, so far from refusing to cancel European debts, has said that it does not consider itself bound by the Balfour note, that is, that it is prepared to consider the European situation independently of what the U.S.A. may or may not do, and the P.M. with the approval of all parties in the House declared that if we could see a prospect of a final settlement we would be willing to reduce our claims on both Germany & France even if that involved our still having to pay the U.S.A. more than we received from our Allies. You see therefore that you are mistaken in supposing that B.L. has refused to cancel European debts. On the other hand I did not know that Austen did not agree with Ll.G.'s policy in this respect.

Ll.G. came in for the debate on reparations and I fancied he was hoping for an opportunity of sticking a knife into the Govt. But he found "Nothin' doin' " in that respect and on the contrary got himself involved in a personal controversy with the Labour Party. So he took the other line and said he was in complete agreement with the P.M.

I confess to being very glad that the short Session is over, for the pace has been very hot and we have all been feeling it. I went on Monday to a dinner to the Lewisham Unionist Assocn. by their member, Sir P. Dawson.[79] ... and if I didn't enjoy it myself I apparently provided good sport for the rest. ... At any rate it got me home at a fairly reasonable hour for I paired for the night with "Willie" Graham[80] the Edinburgh Labour member and so had one satisfactory nights sleep.

I wanted it, for the next night we sat up till 7 o'clock in the morning. The Labour Party arranged this under the direction of Josh Wedgwood who wanted to give them some practice in the arts of obstruction. It is amusing to recall that only a few nights before they had been virtuously dissociating themselves from Pringle & Kenworthy, who were obstructing, on the grounds that *they* were there simply to help the workers and would have nothing to do with a policy of make-believe!

On this occasion Ramsay Macdonald went home about 11 & so did Clynes[81] so Josh had the field to himself & enjoyed himself mightily till somewhere in

---

[79] Philip Dawson (1866–1938). Conservative MP for West Lewisham 1921–38. Chairman, Anglo-Italian Parliamentary Committee. Knighted 1920.

[80] William Graham (1887–1932). Journalist 1905–18. Labour MP for Edinburgh Central 1918–31. Financial Secretary, Treasury 1924; Chairman, Public Accounts Committee 1924–29; President, Board of Trade 1929–31.

[81] John Robert Clynes (1869–1949). President, National Union of General and Municipal Workers. Labour MP for N.E. Manchester 1906–18, Manchester Platting 1918–31 and 1935–45. Vice-Chairman, PLP 1910–11, 1918–21 and Chairman 1921–22; Deputy Leader 1923–31. Parliamentary Secretary, Ministry of Food 1917–18; Food Controller 1918–19; Lord Privy Seal 1924; Home Secretary 1929–31.

the small hours, when it occurred to him to be sarcastic & funny about the absence of the P.M. "Where are *your* leaders?" asked a voice and then the tale was taken up all round the House "Where are *your* leaders?" I never saw a man so taken aback. The fact was that he had been regarding himself as the leader but he couldn't say so and he couldn't think of any retort. We all laughed consumedly.

I have had nothing to do in the House myself this week for the new members have so many questions to ask and so many supplementaries to put that mine are never reached even on Tuesday when they are supposed to come early. I daresay you saw that one day we had a fearful uproar at question time half a dozen Labour members standing up & shouting and refusing to give way to the Speaker. A good many members were horrified but Winterton[82] tells me that they had many worse times in Irish Nationalist days. One noticeable point was that the Labour men all declared that they did not mean disrespect to the Speaker but of course they were just like children in failing to realise that what they were doing constituted a disrespectful act.

For myself I dont regard the incident as at all serious; it is merely part of the education which they will have to undergo and as I remarked at (another) dinner last night, the House of Commons like the Church of Rome is an "anvil that has broken a good many hammers".

...

30 December 1922
Westbourne

My dear Hilda,

We thought your visit to us was particularly nice so it is good to hear that that was your opinion too. For one thing we had never had any opportunity of talking politics since the change of Government and it is very satisfactory to feel that having discussed it thoroughly we still think alike on all essentials.

...

On Thursday we went to a childrens party in the constituency and paid a visit to the General Post Office where the P[ost] M[aster] arranged for the children to telegraph to each other across the big telegraph room to their great delight. Yesterday we had another constituency party and a long meeting of the B.U.A. management comee at which I successfully got Brooks[83] appointed vice Chair-

---

[82] Edward Turnour Winterton (1883–1962). Conservative MP for Horsham 1904–51. PPS to Financial Secretary, Admiralty 1903–5; Under-Secretary, India 1922–24 and 1924–29; Chancellor, Duchy of Lancaster 1937–39 (member of Cabinet from March 1938); Paymaster-General 1939; Father of the House 1945–51. Styled Viscount Winterton until succeeded father to Irish peerage as 6th Earl of Winterton 1907; created Baron Turnour 1952.

[83] (Arthur) David Brooks (1864–?). Solicitor. Member, Birmingham Council from 1901; Alderman 1911; Lord Mayor 1917–19. Honorary Secretary, (later Vice-Chairman and Chairman) Birmingham Conservative and Unionist Association. Knighted 1918.

man. I hope he will be the Salvidge[84] of Birmingham and relieve me of much of my responsibility for the party organisation.

...

Sunday ...

I had just made up my mind [to] stop down here for the childrens party tomorrow when I got summoned to a Housing Committee so I must take the first train tomorrow morning. I daresay you have seen the communiqués which indicate that a State assisted scheme *is* in contemplation.

---

[84] Archibald Tutton James Salvidge (1863–1928). Managing Director, Bent's Brewery and Liverpool party 'boss' until his death. Chairman, Liverpool Conservative Working Men's Association from 1892; President, Liverpool Constitutional Association. Alderman, Liverpool City Council from 1898 but declined Mayoralty 1910. Knighted 1916.

4

1923

'Things Change so Quickly in Politics': Postmaster-General, Health, the Treasury and Defeat

6 January 1923
Westbourne

My dear Ida,

...

I had hoped that by some miracle the Peace Conference[1] would produce an agreed policy but as the difference is so fundamental there is some satisfaction in the fact that we have not proclaimed complete agreement and parted (as in Ll.G.'s day) with mutual dislike and distrust.

Of course the trouble with the French is that they have budgeted on the assumption of immediate payments by Germany and they darent now tell their people that these cannot be had yet and that the hole must be filled in some other way.

Moreover they are, not unnaturally, obsessed by the fear that Germany will become strong again and use her strength to embark on a revanche. Therefore although France wants the money which can only be got out of a strong Germany she always shrinks from any course which would help Germany to pay. I can't imagine what will happen now.

I came down on Thursday for a party in the constituency and did not return on Friday as I had two more parties that day. Altogether I have got rather a hectic month in front of me with a number of speeches including one at the "bye" in Newcastle to which I dont look forward.

...

13 January 1923
Westbourne

My dear Hilda,

...

I found that the P.M. *did* want to see me about Housing. He had just got the Interim Report from Bosky but he had *not* seen him for as he said "I thought I

---

[1] Inter-Allied Conference on Reparations, Paris, 2–4 January 1923. A British compromise scheme fixing German reparations at £2,500 million with a four-year moratorium to restore its credit, was rejected by the French who then used German default in payments to occupy the Ruhr on 11 January.

should like to see you first". I explained to him that B. had gone back to rate exemption and set forth my objections. He turned it down at once and asked what my plan was. So I discoursed on that & told him my ideas which I think he approved on the whole, but he wants something which will to use an expressive Americanism "make a noise like" private enterprise. So he sent word by his p.s. to Bosky at once that he was to give up rate exemption and when he came to Cabinet next day he was told to get on with a scheme on the lines I had suggested plus the private enterprise. The committee is to meet again next Monday week.

It rather seemed to me that he wasn't putting much faith in B. but I understand the latter has got a seat all right. Its the unhappy Jack Hills who cant find one as Darlington has refused to have him.

When we had finished housing I rose to go but the P.M. said Dont hurry away so I sat down and we had quite an interesting talk on foreign affairs. He wasn't worrying much about the French. He thinks the franc will go to the devil after the mark and that the French will soon realise that the prospect of substantial Reparations is vanishing. But Poincaré[2] told him the first time they met that they must have the Ruhr and B.L. thinks they mean to sit there indefinitely by which means they will at any rate keep Germany down. Incidentally these events may throw a certain amount of trade our way.

B.L. was much more worried about Lausanne which is going very badly and he repeated what he has said before that if the Allies wouldn't play he was not prepared to fight the Turks in order to act policeman for Europe. He pointed out that there was no interest in the Straits or in Constantinople that was exclusively or even especially British. In fact in some ways the French who are intimately associated with the Little Entente have more to lose than we and we simply couldn't afford to pull the chestnuts out of the fire for other people. But he realised the danger of loss of prestige reacting on our Eastern possessions and he was anxious lest Curzon should find himself in a position from which he could not with dignity withdraw.

After I had finished I went on to see Warren Fisher[3] and found that all debates & discussions on directorships had ranged round *public* companies. No one has yet suggested any obligation in regard to private companies to which the public are not invited to subscribe so I think there will be no need for me to budge from Hoskins. Mr Hall sends me a somewhat gloomy account of the lack of orders but we can afford to wait and I hope in time the business will return.

---

[2] Raymond Poincaré (1860–1934). French Premier 1911–13; President of Republic 1913–20; Premier and Foreign Minister 1922–24; Premier 1926–29. Obstinate defender of extreme French claims.

[3] (Norman Fenwick) Warren Fisher (1879–1948). Deputy Chairman, Board of Inland Revenue 1914–18 and Chairman, 1918–19; Permanent Secretary at Treasury and Head of Civil Service 1919–39. Knighted 1919.

...

We are making preparations for a gigantic party to our supporters in the constituency to celebrate the victory. There are so many of them now that it means asking about 700 and we shall have to take the Edgbaston Assembly Rooms for the purpose. It's lucky a General Election doesn't come every year!

I am going to post this evening 8.30 [sic] and would like to know when it arrives and how that compares with what happens when I post on Sundays.

20 January 1923
Westbourne

My dear Ida,

In view of the scandalous inefficiency of our postal service I am writing this after posting hours for it is evident that "punctuality is the thief of time".

To answer your question about the children, Annie brought them both up to London on Tuesday evening. It was unfortunate that we should have a fog next day but to them it was just one of the sights and the flaring torches at Hyde Park corner were a great thrill ...

I made a great effort to get ahead of my work on Wednesday and so was able on Thursday to pay the long promised visit to the Zoo. It was most satisfactory. The lions and tigers about which they had felt a little nervous turned out rather smaller than they expected and abstained entirely from roaring – everything else was thrilling and delightful to the last degree. The bears sat up like "darlings", the elephants were immense but very quiet, the chimpanzee danced round and round and made the most humorous grimaces and the keeper took them inside the rails to feed the giraffe and the hippopotami. They came away declaring that it was all "topping" & with a comfortable feeling that there was still much more to see another time. We came home on Friday but I had an hour in which to take Frank into the Natural History Museum and his intelligent interest was most gratifying to his father!

...

I went up to Newcastle last Monday and addressed two meetings for Capt Gee.[4] They were quiet enough in spite of the presence of a few Socialists but I came away convinced that he hadn't an "earthly" and was not surprised at the result. The Labour party appeared to have unlimited resources both in money and speakers. I hear "Bosky" has got a safe seat at last but I rather feel Jack Hills is in peril and as he says this is his last chance.

I fear the French are getting in pretty deep. Apparently we are getting some orders here in consequence of the dislocation of French & German industry but I

---

[4] Robert Gee (1876–1960). Soldier. Served in ranks from 1892 until commissioned in 1915. Victoria Cross 1918. National Democratic Party MP for Woolwich East 1921–22; Conservative MP for Bishop Auckland 1923–24 and Bosworth 1924–27.

doubt if we shall ever see any reparations. As for the Turk I share all your feelings. He is flourishing like a green bay tree.

I spent a long day yesterday first with the Midland Union & then with the Birm. organisation. We won 43 seats out of 62 in our area in the Midlands and are rather pleased with ourselves there, but we are short of money and have got to raise the wind somehow this spring. As for Birm. we have begun to get our reorganisation scheme into shape and I am hopeful that we shall presently get something worked out that will prove a satisfactory solution of our difficulty.

...

The P.M. has put me on another committee on Trade Boards but as the first meeting was held yesterday at less than 24 hrs notice I was unable to attend it. We have another Housing Committee on Monday and a Cabinet Committee on Home Affairs – which wont leave much time for the P.O. I see that rascal Godfrey Isaacs is carrying on quite an intensive campaign with the object of getting the wireless station in this country but I think I shall defeat him.

27 January 1923
Westbourne

My dear Hilda,

...

I have had a busy week with committees on Housing, Home Affairs, Trade Boards & Empire Wireless but quite a satisfactory one. We finally agreed on our Housing Scheme which excludes Rate exemption but includes my Baxendale scheme for slums and Bonar asked me to come to the Cabinet which met on Friday & passed it. He said to me during the week that he wished he could have me in the Cabinet but couldn't manage it at present and after the meeting he sent for me again & said Bosky was once more in trouble over his seat & might not be able to get one. What would I think if he asked "Worthy" to take the M/ Health, adding that it would be rough on me as I ought to have it. I suppose I am something of a phenomenon because I dont want a seat in the Cabinet & £5000 a year, but I replied that "Worthy" was my own selection for the post. He seemed pleased but said as I went away "if he doesn't take it you will have to have it". I sincerely hope he will for I am just getting into the P.O. and dont want to leave it before I have had a chance of doing anything there.

The only other thing I have time to tell you is that Peel asked me to go and see him. He said that he was going to set up a Royal Commission to enquire into the Indian services and both he and Reading[5] were very anxious that Austen should

---

[5] Rufus Daniel Isaacs (1860–1935). Liberal MP for Reading 1903–13. Solicitor-General 1910; Attorney-General 1910–13; Lord Chief Justice 1913–21; Ambassador to Washington 1918–19; Viceroy of India 1921–26; Foreign Secretary 1931. Knighted 1910. Created Baron Reading 1914, Viscount 1916, Earl 1917 and Marquess of Reading 1926.

be Chairman. What did I think A. would say. I said I shouldn't be surprised if he accepted & Peel then asked me to sound him. So I got A to come & lunch with me and told him what was in the wind.

A. said if he stood alone he thought he should refuse but he must consult Ivy who, he thought, would want him to accept. He thought the Govt was not friendly to him. I told him I had no reason to suppose they were unfriendly but they didn't know what his attitude was and didn't want to get a snub and he appeared to think that not improbable. So he is considering & is to let me know tomorrow.

I think he will accept. It means a visit to India next autumn and I think it would be a good thing for him as well as a public service.

18 February 1923
Westbourne

My dear Ida,

...

I dont think it is true that Bosky has gone back on the Baxendale scheme. What has happened is that when they came to draft a bill quite a number of highly technical difficulties were encountered and a meeting was held to consider them on Friday which I was unable to attend as I had to be here. However from the minutes I see that the Committee came to provisional conclusions on all the points and that (for the first time) Baxendale himself was allowed to be present. Up to now it seemed to me that everyone was boycotting him and of course I know that the other officials dont like his scheme. The thing goes to the Home Affairs Committee on Wednesday and I must try and prepare for the occasion as I expect that will be the testing time.

With regard to Rent Restrictions of course the Govt *have* gone back on the original intention of simply carrying out the Committee's recommendations. I think it was obvious however that they could not have carried out immediate decontrol and I very much doubt if they (the committee) have gone the right way about the matter. What *I* had in mind was no distinction between different classes of house but a gradually increasing relaxation of restrictions lasting over a longer period which I should probably have fixed myself at 5 years but should have been ready to extend to 10. My principle would have been (1) to give *certainty* as to what the future had in store (2) to make the restrictions so slight at the time of final release that no one would have felt it worth while to fight for their retention. Of course not being in the Cabinet I could not put these views forward. I only indicated the above principles in a sketchy way to Bonar one day and his sole comment was that he was afraid I was too sanguine!

Anyway I don't feel that in bowing himself in the House of Mitcham Bosky is giving away anything of real value. I believe the houses in question only form 10% of the whole affected by the Act.

Of course there *is* no temptation to A to join the Govt even if there were any idea of asking him. But I fancy his sympathy with Ll.G. consists chiefly in a common resentment of the way they were treated and a common desire to see Bonar come a cropper over something. This sounds vindictive and perhaps it is but of course the natural desire of the late Govt is to be justified and to demonstrate that faced with similar difficulties their successors make a worse mess than they.

Unfortunately I dont believe things will work out so. I do think Ll.G. left us a bad legacy of suspicion and dislike in France and he is trying to make it worse since he has been out of office, but, not sharing Bonar's temperament, I continue to believe that presently we shall find some amendment. France had got to try this plan; her people would never have been satisfied without. And perhaps when she has tried it out it may be possible to reason with her. Its true that Germany meanwhile will be further off reparations than ever. Still we must adapt ourselves to new conditions of trade and I believe we shall do it successfully. I wonder whether the same reflection has occurred to you as has to me on reading the Times' recurring eulogies of S. Baldwin. I think they are preparing the party and the country for an alternative P.M. *within our present ranks* should Bonar break down. Its rather an astute plan too it seems to me.

I have been and took possession of my office as Paymaster General. I find I have an excellent "Aussichtpunkt" for any ceremonies on the Horse Guards Parade and a capital window facing Whitehall for processions. Having cleared my mind on these important points I then proceeded to get some hazy ideas of the duties and functions of the office. It appears that we are the bankers of the spending Departments. A department paying a bill draws a cheque on the P.M.G. which is paid in to his a/c with his bank by the payer. The Joint Stock Banks present these cheques not to the clearing house but to the P.M.G.'s office which then meets them by drawing on the Bank of England. In its turn the Bank of England is fed by the Treasury. The P.M.G. also has the payment of all rank & file service pensions except those in respect of service in the Great War, all officers pensions of all kinds and (lately) all R.I.C. pensions. The result has been to swell its staff from about 50 to about 330 and of course most of it has to be housed in odd places whenever a corner can be found. A number of them are working in a cellar with a vaulted roof which at one time was used as a hayloft by the Horse Guards! If I do anything for the office it will be in the direction of better equipment and accommodation.

Nothing very exciting has happened lately at the P.O. I saw the newspaper proprietors the day after we dined with you and I had the pleasure of rapping old Riddell[6] over the skull. Rascally old humbug! He's one of Ll.G.'s chief toadies! and illustrates his incorrigible taste for low company.

. . .

---

[6] George Riddell (1865–1934). Chairman, *News of the World* 1903–34. Created Baron 1920.

24 February 1923
Westbourne

My dear Hilda,

...

I have had a full week but in some ways haven't got on as fast as I hoped. The decision about the Wireless Chain is postponed as the Cabinet had not time to consider it but I expect it really will come up next week. Meanwhile I am amused to see that "angry criticisms" are being made in Australia on the terms of their "agreement" with Marconi. That old windbag Sir J. Cook[7] made another outrageous speech on Monday attacking the P.O. but fortunately he was not reported. I hear that the Australian Govt sends telegrams to the C.O. which if they came from a Foreign Govt would give rise to diplomatic incidents. It is all in connection with Empire Settlement which doesn't concern me but it shows what Kittle Cattle [?] they are.

I had Baxendale into my room one day to discuss various difficulties in connection with his scheme before it went to the Home Affairs Committee. However when it was brought up the Committee decided very properly that they had not had time to study it and it has been referred back to the Housing Committee for further discussion. I can see that it has some pretty rough water ahead of it but I hope it may remain in the Bill if only to provoke attention. But it is a very technical and difficult subject to understand except by those familiar with the subject and at present there is hardly anyone who could stand cross examination on it.

On Thursday I came down here to lunch with the Duke of York[8] who was visiting the Birm. section of the Brit. Industries Fair and I went round the Fair with him and travelled back with him in his private saloon. He is a nice youth but almost painfully shy and it is very difficult to carry on an intelligent conversation with him because he cant keep his end up. And he has a horrible stammer when he makes a speech which keeps him silent for long & distressing pauses. A curious incident happened at the Fair. The Manager came to me and asked me if I would help to give them an advert by going up in an aeroplane which was giving short passenger flights. So I thought as Annie wasn't there it was a good chance and went up in a top hat! It was quite comfortable the fuselage being enclosed with 6 wicker chairs in. We couldn't go very high because it was very foggy but I should judge we ranged about 300 or 400 ft. I had no sensation of giddiness but the strange part was the total unconsciousness of a change of position when we

---

[7] Joseph Cook (1860–1947). Australian politician. Prime Minister and Home Affairs Minister 1913–14; Minister for Navy 1917–20. Represented Australia at Paris Peace Conference 1919 and Genoa Conference 1922; Australian Treasurer 1920–21; Australian High Commissioner in UK 1921–27. Knighted 1918.

[8] Albert Frederick Arthur George (1895–1952). Created Duke of York, 1920. Became King George VI in 1936 on the abdication of his elder brother Edward VIII.

"banked". All one saw was that the earth seemed to rise up steeply on one side and down on the other, but afterwards the pilot told me that at one time the wings were nearly vertical so that I must have been sitting at right angles to the normal!

The Govt has had some more very bad divisions and one bad one on old age pensions on which a good many new candidates had unwisely pledged themselves but I fear we are making rather a mess of Rent Restrictions. This perpetual wobbling according as the tide flows on bye-elections looks weak and I fear we are not at the end yet as I understand they want the P.M. to say that he will not decontrol anything until there are sufficient houses to make it certain that there will be no increase of rent. That is an impossible proposition because if it were accepted we should never get decontrol. We have got to break out of the vicious circle somehow but I think we are on the wrong tack & that we ought to have proceeded by admitting further increases of rent. However its not my job and not being in the Cabinet I dont get any chance of putting my views. But I shouldn't wonder if Bosky lost the seat after all and if so he is done. I trust Worthy will not fail in that case.

...

France goes on her wicked way & now I hear Poincaré is flirting with the Soviet Govt. He is making things more & more difficult for us and I doubt if we can keep friends much longer. The marriage of the Ruhr coke with the Lorraine ore if the French can get the Ruhr properly organised bodes ill for our steel industry and I am told here that already there is a set back in trade owing to the disturbance of confidence. Lord! what a troubled world it is.

...

3 March 1923
Westbourne

My dear Ida,

...

I saw Austen on Tuesday and he told me of his letter and his conversation with you. As a matter of fact I did more than write to you; I went on Monday to Bonar and asked him if it was too late to consider a change of policy, pointing out that there was this alternative. But he said it *was* too late; the Cabinet had decided on Saturday to go on with it. He remarked that he wished I had mentioned it before but I said it wasn't my job and I had only come because he had asked me to do so if I ever had any suggestions to make. Of course when I heard what A. was about I went again & explained that it wasn't my suggestion & that he had probably got the idea from Talbot[9] & B. said that he would not anyway have

---

[9] Edmund Bernard Talbot (1855–1947). Unionist MP for Chichester 1894–1921. Junior Lord of Treasury 1905; Unionist Whip from 1905 and Chief Whip from 1913. Joint Parliamentary Secre-

supposed that I had anything to do with it. But he could hardly have helped thinking of it after my conversation with him so recently. I think B. himself has no faith in the present policy and I shouldn't be surprised if it has presently to be changed especially if Bosky misses fire. Unhappy Bosky! I saw he was addressing ten meetings yesterday! But the latest reports seem more hopeful of success.

...

I went to a Cabinet on Wednesday at which Leo and I put up our ideas on wireless. I had as I mentioned seen Bonar the day before and he was evidently not very favourably impressed with them. But I put some arguments which seemed to shake him and at the Cabinet I enlarged upon them at greater length. Baldwin said he had an open mind and that he had been rather struck by what I had said. Then Bonar asked some questions which seemed to indicate that he was still not convinced when Curzon suddenly woke up and remarked that he would sum up the position like this, "Capital cost small, commercial prospects good, objects excellent, decision immediate and affirmative". Whereupon our proposals were unanimously agreed to and Bonar is to make a statement on Monday. Godfrey Isaacs will *not* be pleased.

...

Sunday I expect to get my proposals for changes in postal charges under consideration this week and perhaps come to a decision subject to Treasury approval. My own feeling is not to attempt anything "bold and courageous" but to make a number of minor improvements. I am quite satisfied that penny post for instance would cost us between 5 and 6 millions a year and I cannot believe that trade would benefit appreciably. On the other hand the parcels post does cry out for relief and I should like to get down telephone charges a bit more, possibly by reducing the rental so as to increase the inducement to new subscribers to come on. I shall be interested to see how I get on with Stanley Baldwin but I fancy he will be all right. After all he is a business man himself.

8 March 1923
35 Egerton Crescent, SW3

My dear Ida & Hilda,
    You have both written me such encouraging and delightful letters that I must send you a line at once though it is out of turn and the hour is late.
    It has all come with a tremendous rush. Bonar told me on Monday that he was going to offer the M/Health to Horne and that if he wouldn't have it I should "have to" have it. He saw Horne that evening and contrary to my expectations he appeared pleased with the idea and said he would consider it. However on

---

tary to Treasury 1915–21; Lord Lieutenant of Ireland 1921–22. Created Viscount Fitzalan of Derwent 1921.

Tuesday night Bonar told me he had declined on the ground that he was not free (I am not sure whether out of regard to Austen or for business reasons) and I must consider it settled. So then I made the stipulation that Bonar very handsomely put in the Times. Ll.G. would never have done that!

Well I was very distressed at leaving the P.O. but I felt I could not refuse as it would not be playing the game. Having made up my mind I have put all regrets aside and though no one realises better than I the difficulties before me I am encouraged (and surprised) at the way in which the appointment has been welcomed. Indeed, many people have said to me that it restored confidence in the Govt and though I am puzzled at my reputation I accept the good start with gratitude.

I am being given no time to prepare myself for I had to wind up for the Govt tonight & have to speak again Monday Tuesday and Wednesday. I have just got home and am thankful to say that I got through my first ordeal successfully. I had a wonderful reception from all parts of the House and I am told that our fellows were delighted with my speech. I got off on good terms with the Labour members at once and scored off Jack Jones so I feel for the moment at peace with the world.

But oh Lord What is before me!

11 March 1923
Westbourne

My dear Hilda,

... Next week we have our party on Friday ... & the following week is the annual meeting of the Midland Union. I have however informed the latter than I can no longer officiate as Chairman and as Lord Plymouth[10] the president has just died they have an opportunity of putting me in his place. But they will be very depressed at the prospect.

I confess I am rather appalled at the amount of work before me. There seem to be so many odd jobs to be done as well as the really important ones and of course I shall now have to be constantly in the House taking an active part there. That was one of the reasons why I liked the P.O: there was a sort of comfortable obscurity about it. But it seems my fate to be given the most dangerous and responsible position in the front line and probably the fate of the Govt will now depend upon poor me. I must say however that the public has taken my appointment in a very encouraging way. Several people have said that it has to some extent restored confidence and everyone seems prepared to wait & give me a fair chance. And my first speech has given me a new sort of position among mem-

---

[10] Robert George Windsor-Clive (1857–1923). Paymaster-General 1891–92; First Commissioner of Works 1902–5. Succeeded as 14th Baron Windsor 1869; created Earl of Plymouth 1905.

bers. It's very curious how one reacts to an atmosphere but I felt I had a friendly audience and for the first time discovered that I had command of myself & of the House. No doubt I shall have plenty of times when it wont be so but to have done it once is reassuring. I have had dozens of letters of congratulations & good wishes but none which I liked better than that of which I enclose a copy. The writer is a Labour member of the Birm. Council. When I was Ld Mayor & trouble was threatening in the Gas Dept I sent for him privately and succeeded in effecting a satisfactory settlement through him and evidently he had not forgotten it.

Now I must attend to the huge bundle of papers that has come down in my pouch preparatory to speeches next week. Oh Lord! The children are very excited. They don't quite know what it means but they realise that their papa has been promoted and are anxious lest it should mean that their parents are kept more in London.

17 March 1923
Westbourne

My dear Ida,

 …

Thank you both for your birthday wishes. I still can't get over my wonder at all the "miration" about "Cabinet rank" on which I continue every day to receive congratulations. Evidently it means much to you and Hilda and I suppose in that respect you represent the man in the street and it is I who fail to realise the situation. I believe that I measure my position by the influence I believe myself to possess in the Govt and that has not changed so far as my personality is concerned though of course my office puts me in a position which necessitates my taking a far more active part in its deliberation than when I was P.M.G. I attended my first meeting on Wednesday and had a pretty easy passage as there was no opposition to either of my proposals though my people anticipated a tough fight. The fact is that at the moment I hold the key position and they are bound to give me a pretty free hand.

I should very much doubt if my subsidy will attract the small builder in rural districts. In fact I am not sure how far it will have that effect in the large ones and I shall watch with some interest to see. If it were made to include a somewhat larger house I think it might and if I had started from the beginning I think I should have made the limit higher. But I came to the conclusion that it was best now to keep that in hand and make a concession in the House if opinion in its favour manifests itself.

I had a difficult decision to make on Thursday. We had offered the municipalities £4 & they were asking £6. The obvious thing was to compromise on £5 and I think it conceivable that if I had stood firm on that figure it would have been accepted by a good many. But there would have been a wrangle and a delay and

I concluded that it was better policy to get a prompt settlement with good will than to haggle over a £1 with the prospect of their coming back later and saying "You beat us down; now we simply shant build unless you raise your figure". That would have been disastrous. The Govt would have been discredited again and probably would have had to give way. As it is I told the deputation that I considered the figure too high but that in order to secure their whole hearted co-operation I was not going to bargain with them and they went away saying "Now it is up to us".

Of course I dont think it will do much more than help us to prevent the situation getting worse but after all that is something and we can perhaps find fresh ways of stimulating enterprise in the meantime. The present arrangement only lasts for 2 years but I dont believe we can stop there. We shall have to have a new scheme when this is done though I hope we may cut down the figure.

...

I am floundering about in Rent Decontrol and haven't found a way out yet. But I am eliminating some suggestions and have just a possible glimmer of light in front of me.

We had an awful week in the House. I was up till 2.30 on Monday night 4.30 Tuesday and 12.30 on Wednesday & Thursday while last night we had our party and I went to bed at 1.30 this morning! I spoke on Tuesday on the Warrington Water Bill and safely conveyed it through 2nd Reading in spite of Ll.G.'s irrel-evant eloquence. The other two motions I managed to square the movers of. A deputation came to see me about milk and I heard afterwards that they were very pleased with me and amazed at my knowledge of the subject ... which they reckoned was almost too complicated to be intelligible except to an expert. But as you say its not so new as all that. Did I not serve on the Health Committee & did not my sister have a dairy farm.

Our party was a great success last night. We had nearly 600 guests in the Edgbaston Assembly rooms and with unlimited food & drink a whist drive downstairs and a wireless concert and a ball upstairs they all thoroughly enjoyed themselves ...

...

We were both dog tired when it was over (it began at 7!) and had breakfast in bed at 10, a thing which I dont believe has ever happened to us before. After that I was able to attend the opening of a branch of the Municipal Bank and make a speech & then go on to open a flower show in the constituency and make another. Lord what a life!

...

24 March 1923
Westbourne

My dear Hilda,

...

I agree that its not much use speculating about A's political future. Some busy bodies down here are passing resolutions urging that he should be taken into the Cabinet but obviously he wouldn't look at it if it were offered and there is nothing to do but wait and see. As for Liberal Reunion it has suffered from a similar attempt to force it before it is ready but I remain of the same opinion that it will, barring accidents, come of itself with Ll.G. on top. Asquith is gradually fading out of the picture and Simon hasn't got the gifts of a leader so Ll.G. has only to bide this time if he has sufficient patience.

I suppose you are right about the Cabinet and no doubt I can and shall exercise more influence now than I should have done as P.M.G. but so far I haven't felt that I am much more enlightened about foreign policy than I was before. The Germans have been to us in a tentative sort of way but they haven't yet made up their minds to put forward any practical scheme which could lead to a settlement and there is still no visible prospect of a release from the complications either in the Ruhr or the Near East.

I have had a very busy week with interviews questions and Housing Bill. I suppose the joke you saw was my reply to Clynes which shut him up in the most comical way. My people at the Ministry were fearfully pleased and think it a great feat to have scored off Jack Jones and Clynes already!

I am feeling round for a solution of rent decontrol and the most hopeful idea I have got is to set up Rent Tribunals to protect the tenant from the extortionate landlord when control goes. But it is full of difficulties. On the whole I think the landlords would be inclined to accept it but what the tenants really want is security of tenure and in their simple way they think this should be accompanied by a reduction of rent! It is interesting to hear that since I began to work at the idea of Rent Courts Mussolini[11] has announced it as his plan, and he has got the same idea of constituting the courts out of a panel containing representatives of both landlord and tenant with certain neutrals.

I have had to drop the Baxendale scheme for the present. It raises so many difficult points about mortgages and chief rents that it will clearly require much more time to work it out so I have decided to postpone it till I can get it into more practical shape. More and more I see that the whole problem of housing is one that can only gradually be solved taking one step at a time. Its not a bad thing that the terms agreed with the Local Authorities have been announced in advance as it gives a chance to them to discuss ways & means and to see what

---

[11] Benito Mussolini (1883–1945). Founder of Italian Fascist Party 1919; President, Council of Minister 1922–26; Prime Minister 1926–43; Foreign Minister 1924–29, 1932–36. Head of German puppet Social Republic in Northern Italy 1943–45. Captured and shot April 1945.

private enterprise is prepared for. Already I have heard that Tudor Walters[12] who had got a programme of 10,000 houses to be built for large collieries & other industrial concerns is prepared to increase it to 20,000 and that is not a bad beginning.

...

I lunched this week with Johnnie Baird to meet Lord Weir.[13] He has got an idea of building houses by "mass production" at a greatly reduced cost and if he can bring it off that too may help along. I have asked him to get out a demonstration house so that we may see what he is able to offer.

...

It has been a lovely spring day and we have much enjoyed the garden this afternoon. The crocuses are wonderful and already there are many daffodils out. ... And in the Od. House there are 6 huge spikes of Cymbidium and quite a lot of Odonts & Masdevallias coming on. Why does one pursue this giddy game of politics?

7 April 1923
Sherfield Hall, Basingstoke

My dear Hilda,

I returned from Scotland on Wednesday night so as to get in two full days at the office before coming down here. We did not have good weather for Easter. ... Curiously enough I repeated exactly my experience of last year when the only fine day was that on which I left and I repeated also my sporting record, killing 5 fish of which I got 3 on the last day.

You mustn't suppose however that my holiday was a failure. I enjoyed the open air and the sport when it came and I gained more experience in the art of salmon fishing. ...

The statements you see in the press are all unauthorised & mostly incorrect. My proposals do not specify any number of rooms or any arrangement of them. They provide only for a minimum & maximum superficies and I have decided to put them in the bill instead of in regulations, a change which will I am sure commend itself to the House. The second reading is fixed for the 24th so I shall

---

[12] John Tudor Walters (1866–1933). Liberal MP for Sheffield Brightside 1906–22 and Penryn and Falmouth 1929–31. Paymaster-General, 1919–22 and 1931. Chairman, Committee on Postwar Housing 1918. President, Housing and Town Planning Trust; Chairman, London Housing Board; founder, Industrial Housing Association; author, *The Building of 12,000 Houses* (1927). Knighted 1912.

[13] William Douglas Weir (1877–1959). Shipping contractor and pioneer manufacturer of steel houses and motor cars. Scottish Director of Munitions 1915–17; Member of Air Board 1917; Director-General of Aircraft Production 1917–19; Secretary for Air 1918; Air Ministry Advisor 1935–39; Director-General of Explosives 1939; Chairman, Tank Board 1942. Knighted 1917. Created Baron Weir 1918, Viscount 1938.

have to get it printed next week. As for R.R. I have still to get my ideas accepted by the Cabinet committee which doesn't like them at all so far. But it hasn't succeeded in evolving anything better and my own people are I think now convinced that they offer the only way out. I will tell you more about them when we meet.

...

21 April 1923
Westbourne

My dear Hilda,

... I confess that my second reading does weigh rather heavy on my chest but I have at any rate got through my two weekend meetings very successfully. Yesterday we had our M.U.A. luncheon. We got nearly 100 birds in the cage all agog to see the new Party chiefs Jackson[14] & Hall[15] both of whom came down for the purpose & we raised over £2000 on the spot. I have no doubt we shall get more and I am very well satisfied with the result.

Tonight I have been attending my annual Divisional meeting and they were very pleased with my speech. I didn't go through my Housing Bill but I did explain about parlour houses and quite convinced my audience. I am pleased with the general reception of the bill and I think from the tactical point of view it is well to keep criticism focused on the parlour controversy. I can always cut that away if necessary by yielding a little on a matter which is not in any way vital and then there will be nothing of substance left whereas if I gave way now our opponents would just concentrate on something else. Hall told me he had been at some party meeting lately and they were all "quite happy about the Bill".

You may be interested to know that I had my people up till 11.30 one night at the Ministry while I went personally through the circular which is to go out to local authorities on the day of second reading. I find it pays to do that sort of work myself for not only did I correct many errors and omissions but I discovered two "howlers" in the Bill itself which nobody else has yet found out though probably they would have done later!

I had a little triumph on Thursday. I got the Cabinet to toe the line on Wednesday and let me introduce a Rent Act Continuance Bill on Thursday under the ten minutes rule. They and the Whips had regular cold feet about it

---

[14] Francis Stanley Jackson (1870–1947). Played cricket for Yorkshire 1894–1905. Conservative MP for Howdenshire, 1915–26. Financial Secretary, War Office 1922–23. Chairman of Conservative Party 1923–26. Governor of Bengal 1927–32.

[15] (William) Reginald Hall (1870–1943). Naval career 1883–1919. Director of Naval Intelligence 1914–19. Conservative MP for Liverpool West Derby 1919–23, Eastbourne 1925–29. 'Blinker' Hall had been a Diehard during the Coalition. Principal Agent of Unionist Party 1923–24. Created Rear-Admiral 1917; Vice-Admiral 1922; Admiral 1926. Knighted 1915.

though I assured them I could see no reason for alarm. When the moment came the Labour Party passed the word round to vote with us and so after Master Pringle had challenged a division he saw he was going to be in a ridiculous minority & backed out. So we got the first reading unopposed amid derisive cheers and laughter from our people.

Meanwhile I am getting the new bill into shape. I have no doubt now of carrying the Cabinet with me and though its too early to prophecy I begin to think that the threatened storm may not be as bad as at first appeared likely. Really the proposal is not an unreasonable one and though there will be things that neither tenant nor landlord will like there are substantial advantages for both of them. Moreover it carries the critical moment over the General Election & therefore the Party managers will like it too.

Have you seen Kellaways letter in the Times about the B.B.C. Its about as dishonest as anything I have known because although my signature is appended to the agreement it was his agreement which I never altered but only signed. I think there is plenty to be said for it but I fancy K. is trying to countermine a possible suggestion that in making it he was giving a good bargain to the Marconi Co. which he joined immediately after his resignation. He is a "dirty dog".

...

I saw Austen the other night when he gave me some rather solemn warnings against neglecting the middle class. Hubbard (of the Post) came to see me and told me in confidence that O. Locker Lampson came down to Birmingham and tried to get the Post to publish the false news about Bonar's impending retirement. I fear Austen is very badly served by Oliver who does underhand things in his name without his authority. He didn't say that he came from A. but if the Post had fallen into the trap it would have been ascribed to him.

The joke is that Rothermere[16] having had the same tip from F.E. came to a Unionist for confirmation & having learned how nearly he had been duped was furious and is going to support us for 6 weeks in revenge!!!

...

28 April 1923
Westbourne

My dear Ida,

...

I am much gratified at your commendation of my speech as you are a competent critic. At the time I didn't feel quite sure how far it had been a success but I

---

[16] Harold Sidney Harmsworth (1868–1940). Northcliffe's brother. Proprietor, *Daily Mirror* 1914–31; *Daily Mail, Evening News* and Associated Newspapers Ltd. 1922–40; Secretary for Air 1917–18. Created Baron Rothermere 1914 and Viscount 1919.

have no doubt of it now after the many expressions of warm approval that I have received from members of our own party. Indeed the whole affair has given the Govt a leg up. The debate as I expected kept revolving round the parlour house and when the concession was announced there was nothing serious left to fight for. Indeed I am not sure that the Labour Party meant to divide at the last but of course Kirkwood's[17] interruptions raised the temperature so violently that a division became inevitable and in the end it really helped us as we came out with such a huge majority. The funny part was that Ll.G. voted against the closure and wanted to vote agst the Bill but his own people wouldn't let him. So he abstained while his two secretaries and chief whip came into our Lobby. He succeeded however in detaining Mond in conversation so long that when he finally burst away and rushed back to vote he found the door locked. I am going to pull his leg (What?) when I see him, as he remarked as he passed me on the way to the lobby "I'm going to vote for your Bill now". I wonder whether the little man was vexed at my bare recital of a few "fax" about the Peoples Budget, but anyway he was very affable when I met him in the Abbey on Thursday and said he heard on all sides that my speech was first rate.

You will have seen ... that B.L. is going for a sea voyage. He announced his intention to the Cabinet on Thursday and we were all very glad to hear it, as he was doing no good stewing in his room at Downing St. Of course if his voice doesn't come back he will have to resign but I think it certainly will as he is better than I have seen him for some time "in himself" and a sea voyage is just what is wanted to enable him to throw off the local ailment.

Here I must interrupt to tell you the latest Curzon story which is believed to have been invented by Horne but which has such lifelike features about it as to be indistinguishable from the real thing. It has convulsed Govt circles this week.

Curzon is well known at the Post Office as a constant complainant. I had a letter from him (in his own hand) almost as soon as I got there and was only spared more because he was at Lausanne. Anyway the story is that when "Jix" succeeded me he found waiting for him a letter with a C in the corner in these words.

"The Secretary of State presents his compliments to the Postmaster General and begs to inform him that Marchioness Curzon has a telephone at her bedside. The Secretary of State believes that the Postmaster General will be astonished and concerned to learn that last night Marchioness Curzon was rung up no fewer than *three* times and asked if she was the Hippodrome".

There's an exquisite flavour about the word Hippodrome in that connection.

I have had quite a lot of nice letters about the Memoir; in particular one from Aunt Lina in which she admitted that she had not realised before how much Norman had actually done or how clear and consistent had been his purpose. It

---

[17] David Kirkwood (1872–1955). Labour MP for Dumbarton Burghs 1922–50 and Dumbartonshire East 1950–51 (sat as an ILP MP 1931–33). Created Baron Kirkwood 1951.

was just to bring that out & put it on record that I did the work and so it is satisfactory to know that my efforts have been successful.

Byng[18] has just been in and says the same thing. He really knew little of Norman but as he is now Chairman of the Education Comee he has been enormously interested in his views & in reading of his pioneer work.

I forget whether I told you that I wrote a memorandum to Bonar in which I pointed out that I had more work in the H. of C. than any other Minister and yet was the only one who had no Under Secretary to help him. Unhappily the Act which constituted the Ministry expressly confined him to one Secretary who at present is in the Lords (Onslow). It would therefore require legislation to have another but I pressed that I should be given one all the same. Bonar consulted Leslie Wilson who jibbed at the prospect of a Bill and thought it would never pass the Commons. I believe he is wrong as he was about my Rent Restriction Continuance Bill and that I could make out so good a case for one Sec. in the Lords and one in the Commons that it would go through quite easily, especially as I voluntarily surrendered my Assistant P.M.G. However as a compromise they have lent me Eustace Percy who has nothing to do as Under Sec. to the Bd of Education and I am starting to break him in with questions and private members bills. I think he will be quite good for he has brains and energy. His worst fault is a somewhat priggish manner.

…

… I have got some fine orchids out but alas I never get a minute now to go to the shows and I havent seen a picture this year.

…

5 May 1923
Westbourne

My dear Hilda,

…

I have had a pretty stiff week. On Monday I had the money resolution of my Housing Bill in Committee all day and on Wednesday I had 2nd reading of the Rent R. Continuance Bill and then report of the money resolution till 12 o'clock. Its a tiring business sitting so many hours on the bench with your attention strained all the while but we came through very successfully and I only had to move the closure once. The wild men became quite tame and merely poured out "sob stuff" instead of yelling that they were being insulted and our people seem all very happy about the Bill. In the intervals I attended Cabinets & Cabinet Committees, received two deputations attended two dinners opened a salvage plant in Westminster and addressed the annual meeting of the B.U.A. When I

---

[18] (Wilfred) Byng Kenrick (1872–?). See Appendix I: The Chamberlain Household and Family.

add that our next door neighbour Lady Tyrrell took the opportunity of having two dances at her house during the week each lasting till about 2.30 you will not be surprised to hear that I felt rather a rag yesterday and had to go and lie down for an hour before going to my evening meeting. But I had a good sleep last night and feel all right today.

I have got an appalling programme before [me] and even with Eustace Percy to help it is rather difficult to see how I am going to manage it. The Housing Bill goes into committee next week and before I introduce the Rent Restriction Bill I have to take the Agricultural rating Bill as rating is another subject of mine. I only hope there wont be many all night sittings!

...

12 May 1923
35 Egerton Crescent, SW3

My dear Ida,

...

I have had a pretty hot week. Three days Committee on the Housing Bill, two Cabinets, an evening reception at an Agent General's, another at Lady Astors, a speech in the House on Rating of machinery a luncheon at which I was chief guest in place of Philip Lloyd-Greame who is ill, a huge dinner of 300 people at which I had to speak and finally a dinner party tonight! Luckily no very late sittings so though a little tired I am feeling fairly spry.

Yesterday the Unionist women had their annual mass meeting at which Baldwin took Bonar's place. But *the* speech of the afternoon was Annie's. She seconded a vote of thanks and only spoke quite shortly. But she had the success of her life and carried the meeting off their feet. At "Nancy's" reception I was overwhelmed with compliments. Everyone came rushing up to tell me of her "brilliant" "wonderful" "splendid" performance, which had quite eclipsed Stanley and gone to the hearts of the women. So we are feeling rather above ourselves. The fact is that those women are longing to be raised to a higher moral plane. They get sick of the ordinary party talk and Annie's appeal to their higher instincts gets them every time. She says she never speaks to a big audience without thinking of Bee[19] and in fact they had just those feelings very much in common.

As for me little "Til" [?] White[20] says he was watching Wallhead[21] the Chairman of the I.L.P. who was present at the dinner of the Asscn of Municipal

---

[19] Beatrice Chamberlain (1862–1918). See Appendix I: The Chamberlain Household and Family.

[20] Thomas White (1876–1938). Chairman, Bents' Brewery. Member, Liverpool City Council. Chairman, Central Valuation Committee for England and Wales; Chairman, Mersey Tunnel Committee 1929–38. Knighted 1928.

[21] Richard Collingham Wallhead (1869–1934). Designer, journalist and lecturer. Chairman of ILP 1920–23. Labour MP for Merthyr 1922–34 (as an ILP MP 1931–33)

Corporations while I was speaking and that the tears were running down his cheeks. Quite likely! I did some "sob stuff" and that kind of labour man always laps it up!

The Housing Bill is going very well in Committee and although I could wish our progress were more rapid I cannot say that the proceedings have been at all obstructive. Of course the first two clauses are the most controversial and when I have got through them we ought to gallop along.

I am afraid we are in for more trouble over the Irish deportees.[22] If the H of Lords goes against us as it very likely will we shall have to have a Bill of Indemnity and then our programme will be made into hay. An autumn session seems to me quite inevitable in any case but I hope we may rise before August 12.

I have got my R.R. Bill in draft now and it will be published soon after Whitsuntide. It provides for the continuance of the Act with amendments for two years and then a period of 5 years during which the tenant will be protected against "harsh or oppressive" ejection while the landlord will be able to get a higher rent. But I have put in a clause to enable the tenant to get his rent reduced if the house is in bad condition which should make the bill more acceptable to the tenant and though the landlords wont like it they will find it difficult to protect the bad landlord. It is very hard to say what its reception will be but on the whole it seems to me an equitable compromise & I somehow fancy it will come through the storm.

Just to keep me busy I have got a rating bill to get through too. I shall have to take the second reading but I hope to shove off the committee on to Eustace Percy. He is already taking a good many of my questions and some private members motions & bills.

It is all very well to say I ought not to take outside engagements. I am sure I don't want to and I decline dozens of dinners but there are some I cant very well get out of and I have got quite a lot in front of me. They cost me an amount of worry and distraction quite out of proportion to their importance and I have no doubt they dont convey to my audience any idea of the trouble they give. Ullswater who sat next to me last night said I envy you your facility in speaking like that without a note. But oh Lord he didn't know how I had sweated over it!

"Autre vexation!"

Extract from a letter from a member of the City Council and a valued supporter, to whom I had written to condole with him on the loss of his wife.

"Allow me to express my heartfelt gratitude to Mrs Chamberlain and yourself for your kind letter of sympathy and good wishes. As perhaps you are aware, my

---

[22] After the arrest and deportation of alleged IRA members to the Irish Free State in March–April 1923 the Court of Appeal and House of Lords ruled this illegal. On 17 May an Indemnity Bill was introduced to protect ministers from legal action.

wife was ill for a very long time, and apart from this I have during the last six months been very anxious about my thumb, which has caused me great pain, but I am happy to say that it now somewhat better".

19 May 1923
35 Egerton Crescent, SW3

My dear Hilda,
    ...

We have just arrived back from Westbourne ... We found Dorothy quite happy. No doubt she misses Frank but she has been kept interested by having other children constantly with her.

As for Frank we waited anxiously to have his first letter with the outpourings of his homesickness. When it came it said "We are having a lovely time here. I am top of my form. Lloyd-Greame is one of my best pals". *One* of my best pals, mark you, after three days! So we feel very happy about him and we have had a letter from Norman who says that "Francis is intelligent" and settling in comfortably. ...

I have had a pretty stiff week but feel none the worse for it. The Housing bill makes terribly slow progress in Comee as the Labour Party *will* make second reading speeches on every amendment and new amendments keep pouring in faster than I can get through the old ones. We haven't yet finished the first clause, but really the most contentious part of the bill is in the beginning and up to now I have preserved an equable temperature so that there has been no deliberate obstruction. But things are piling up and it is difficult to see how I am going to get through my programme for the session.

One night I had to attend a medical dinner and found myself seated next – the Goat! He was simply boiling over with high spirits, singing laughing, cracking jokes and waving to his friends. We got along quite comfortably without touching on any awkward topics as he has been supporting the Govt over the Russian episode. But his party seem to have grown more critical on Thursday. I cant understand how they can want us to lick Chicherin's[23] boots while he continues to stir up trouble in the East & to seize our trawlers in the West. The truth is of course that the Soviet values the Trade agreement simply for its political value. We are doing very little trade under it and should continue without it to do all it suits them to put our way. They have however just placed a contract in Sweden for about £10 [?] millions although there is no agreement with them. At the same dinner was the P. of Wales[24] who spoke very well I thought, though evidently

---

[23] Georgi Chicherin (1872–1936). Russian diplomat and politician. Social Democrat, Menshavik then Bolshevik. Commissioner for Foreign Affairs 1918–30.

[24] Edward Albert Christian George Andrew Patrick David (1894–1972). Eldest son of George V; Prince of Wales 1910–36; succeeded as King Edward VIII 1936. Abdicated in December after

racked with nervousness. When I said good night to him he remarked I wish I could talk like you! I also met the Ld CJ (Hewart) who spoke very nicely as he always does. The Goat had said that Bonar wd do no good till he went away for a prolonged rest. Hewart said the same and added You are quite strong enough to allow him to do so. All that the papers say about a weak Treasury bench is rubbish. You have an excellent front bench and the country loves you. And then he went on to express his deep regret that Austen was not in the Govt saying he had a great respect and affection for him. "He has always been so kind to me".

I have no news of Bonar and up to Thursday none of the Govt had. But from what I see in the papers I judge his voice to be no better. I believe he intends to be back next week and I rather expect he will want to resign. Personally I hope he will go on at least till August, even if he takes no part, because a further continuance of the interregnum will make the matter of the succession much more easy. If it shd be Curzon it will be difficult to say that a peer cannot be P.M. when he practically has been for months without any inconvenience to anyone.

26 May 1923
Westbourne

My dear Ida,

Up to this morning I did not know what was going to be the composition of the Govt or whether Austen was likely to come into it but I did not expect that the opposition to his coming would be so strong as to prevent an offer being made to him. Baldwin told me that if it were carried so far as to involve the resignation of any member of the Cabinet he did not feel he could insist but he evidently thought at that time that it could be overcome and that his difficulty would be with Austen and Horne. Of course that may still have been the case and I shant know definitely till I get back next week. If he has been kept out by our own people I deeply regret it for the sake of the party as well as for him. It would have been rather a bitter pill for him to have come in but if he had swallowed it I think everyone would have felt his magnanimity and appreciated his self sacrifice. Of course people will not talk to me about him so that I have great difficulty in gauging the feeling where he is concerned. I suspected however that it was not particularly friendly, but this was not so much on account of the past (I am not thinking of the Morning Post & the National Review but the party in the House and in the Govt) as because while Horne has been friendly and sociable and has several times effectively supported the Govt, Austen has kept aloof and on the few occasions when he has intervened there has been a somewhat acid note about his remarks. Moreover he is believed to have been

---

opposition to proposed marriage to Wallis Simpson. Assumed title Duke of Windsor. Governor of Bahamas 1940–45.

very closely associated with Birkenhead who is positively hated and despised. You understand I am not myself criticising him because I realise what he has had to go through better than the party does, but I am analysing the source of the differentiation which is made between him and Horne. All the same although I do know of one man who is bitter about him I did not think there were many who felt like that and I thought they would not be able to withstand persuasion.

I confess I do not like McKenna[25] as a substitute but I still hope that the door is not finally shut though the outlook is rather black.[26]

Now to go back to history. We had heard nothing of Bonar till Saturday when he returned and the evening papers gave a very gloomy account of his appearance at the station. We got these just as we were starting for South Lodge. When we got there we were very indignant at finding a party by no means congenial. Not that there was anything wrong with them, but they were just young people interested in tennis and in each other but not interesting to us and we felt that Dame Alice [Godman] ought to have had someone of more importance to meet a Cabinet Minister and his wife. Moreover she herself is rather a tiring hostess after a while … So when the papers came on Monday and announced Bonar's resignation we were not sorry to have such a good reason for anticipating our departure and we made off that afternoon and got the Amerys to dine. Amery had met Bonar in Paris on his way to Grindelwald and had dined with him. He reported him as very ill having lost a lot of weight and as plunged in unalterable gloom. He had endeavoured to stave off the resignation but only got a conditional promise to hold it up for a month if the doctors reported a reasonable chance of recovery by then. Unhappily they were unable to do so and poor Bonar was burning to rid himself of the load of responsibility which was weighing him down. Baldwin has told me since that he is better already but he fears he is in a bad way and I am afraid myself that there is something serious the matter. He sent a message asking me to come round yesterday but I couldn't get it in and have just put it off till next week, if I can get a chance then.

I had rather hoped that Curzon would have been P.M. but I had not realised the extent of his unpopularity in the country which was really what undid him. Baldwin told me that he had received quantities of letters saying "Thank God its not Curzon". In fact he had not much knowledge of or interest in domestic questions but I think he would have been ready to give a pretty free hand to his ministers. I am told he was beside himself with vexation and disappointment but

---

[25] Reginald McKenna (1863–1943). Liberal MP for Monmouthshire North 1895–1918. Financial Secretary to Treasury 1905–7; President, Board of Education 1907–8; First Lord of Admiralty 1908–11; Home Secretary 1911–15; Chancellor of Exchequer 1915–16.

[26] Baldwin had offered McKenna the Treasury but the latter made his acceptance conditional on his health improving and a safe seat being found in the City. The refusal of Sir Frederick Banbury to make way for a Liberal led to McKenna's withdrawal on 13 August 1923 and Chamberlain's reluctant promotion.

I hope he has been somewhat consoled by the tributes to his qualities which have been so freely offered by the press. He certainly has behaved very well.

The new P.M. asked me to go and see him on Wednesday and I was very favourably impressed with his confidence and determination. He is the nearest man we have to Bonar in the qualities of straightforwardness and sincerity. He has not got his charm but he has a good deal more strength & go than Bonar has had since he was P.M. and he has ideas which sounded good to me. I thought he would have been feeling overwhelmed and was rather relieved to find that on the contrary he was in excellent spirits and very pleased with himself. One good thing he has done for me & that is to give me Eustace Percy in the Commons instead of Onslow in the Lords. I should never be able to get through the work in front of me if I were alone.

The Press which has been very busy Cabinet making this week has been airily spotting me for the Chancellorship. It never seemed to occur to them that in filling one hole another equally awkward to fill would be created, nor that I might have something to say to the notion on my own account. I suppose it would be considered promotion and it is therefore assumed that I should jump at it, but it is an office which I should particularly dislike, quite apart from my objection to being continually pulled up by the roots. I never could understand finance, and moreover I should hate a place whose main function was to put spokes in other people's wheels. I see the poor old P.O. is having another change for which I am sorry but I am very glad that Bd. Carpenter[27] has been evicted. He never ought to have been made Financial Secretary.

I have a perfectly awful 2 weeks in front of me. In addition to Housing Committees every day and Cabinets I have a public dinner on Tuesday a Court on Wednesday, on Thursday I am Minister in attendance on the King who is going to see the L.C.C. housing scheme, on Friday is another public dinner, on Saturday I open a childrens Convalescent Home on Sunday I address a Sunday school, on Monday I introduce the Agricultural Rates Bill and on Wednesday & Thursday is Rent Restrictions. I shall be a regular rag when it is over.

...

9 June 1923
35 Egerton Crescent, SW3

My dear Ida,

I was glad to see you and Hilda for a few minutes even though there was no opportunity for a proper talk and I was not sorry too that you should have an

---

[27] Archibald Boyd-Carpenter (1873–1937). Conservative MP for Bradford North 1918–23, Coventry 1924–29 and Chertsey 1931–37. Parliamentary Secretary, Ministry of Labour 1922–23; Financial Secretary, Treasury 1923; Paymaster-General and Financial Secretary, Admiralty 1923–24. Knighted 1926.

opportunity of seeing for yourselves the general temper and attitude of our party in the House. There is no doubt in my mind that at this moment the Govt is more firmly established both in the House and the country than at any time since Bonar came into office and I think I may add that the Minister of Health has had his share in the growth of confidence. The P.M. evidently feels very pleased for he went up specially to Sir A. Symonds and Veale[28] (my P.S.) who were sitting together under the gallery and showered compliments upon them saying that the way the Ministry had come out was wonderful. Robinson,[29] my principal Secretary also tells me that the staff generally are feeling very "bucked" and are consequently working much better than they did.

All which is comforting as a set off against the inevitable fit of discouragement which comes occasionally and especially when one is tired. Of course I am very conscious that the Rents Bill is not nearly as well thought out as the Housing Bill. I have literally not had the time to give to it and for the same reason I could not manage to talk to the party about it before second reading. Still I believe the main lines are fairly sound and I think that is demonstrated by its reception. I expect to finish Housing Bill Comees on Tuesday & start Rents Bill Comee on Wednesday! Last Thursday I was kept up till half past two in the morning. I had been wonderfully fresh up till then but I did feel tired after that and went to bed for an hour yesterday evening before going out to the play.

...

16 June 1923
Westbourne

My dear Hilda,

...

It has been a busy week again but a week of good progress. The Housing Bill was finished on Monday without my having had to use the closure once and I have received many compliments upon my success with it. Even the Westminster published a paragraph headed "Mr Chamberlain makes good" in which it quoted a Liberal as saying His patience was wonderful, his knowledge of his subject was great and his tact of the greatest assistance in managing the business and it went on to say that high hopes were entertained for the success of the

---

[28] Douglas Veale (1891–1973). Second Class Clerk, LGB 1914; Private Secretary to Permanent Secretary, Ministry of Health 1920; Private Secretary to Minister of Health 1921–28; Registrar, Oxford University and Fellow of Corpus Christi, Oxford 1930–58. Knighted 1954.

[29] (William) Arthur Robinson (1874–1950). Entered Colonial Office 1897; Assistant Secretary, Office of Works 1912–18; Permanent Secretary, Air Ministry 1917–20 and Ministry of Health 1920–35; Chairman, Supply Board of Committee of Imperial Defence 1935–39; Permanent Secretary, Ministry of Supply 1939–40. Knighted 1917.

measure if I remained at the Ministry based on what I had already done. I accept these bouquets with satisfaction tempered by thoughts of the wrath to come, for of course it wont last and presently no doubt the welkin will ring with lamentations over the short comings that further experience will reveal. Next week I have Report & Third Reading and then I shall be rid of my first heavy burden. Rent Restriction is of course another tale. I entered on the Committee stage on Wednesday with a serried phalanx of the wild men from Glasgow in front of me. I got my first clause on Thursday without amendment & without closure but I expect trouble on the second.

On Tuesday I had to accompany their Majesties to Becontree after lunching at the Palace. They were affable and talked hard for $3\frac{1}{2}$ hours as we drove through cheering crowds. The enthusiasm always surprises me. It was quite as conspicuous in Whitechapel and West Ham as in the City & the West End and the King was much amused at the woman who cried in thrilling tones as we passed *"You dear!"* His language about the Labour Party and "these filthy rags of newspapers" was as violent as ever.

...

Things look rather more hopeful abroad. Baldwin is very determined to "get a move on" and indeed it is most necessary for the situation in Germany and France is reacting on employment here and in the last few weeks trade has had a considerable set back which means more trouble next winter unless we can get some sort of a European settlement. Fortunately Curzon seem to be working very well and has got over his disappointment. I think he is very pleased with his success over the Russian affair which indeed he thoroughly deserved for he managed it with great skill. R. McNeill[30] the undersecretary is quite enthusiastic over his knowledge and ability and declares that the more he sees of him the greater he thinks him to be.

I got down here last night and have had a busy day. A deputation this morning on Rents then to Hollymoor to open a new research laboratory, then back to Rotten Park to open a new branch bank. There are 26 branches now besides the head office and over £3 million of deposits! 1628 people have bought their own houses. I shall be able to say si monumentum requaeris, circumspire![31]

---

[30] Ronald McNeill (1861–1934). Conservative MP for St Augustine's, Kent 1911–18 and Canterbury 1918–27. Under-Secretary, Foreign Office 1922–24 and 1924–25; Financial Secretary, Treasury 1925–27; Chancellor, Duchy of Lancaster 1927–29. Created Baron Cushendun 1927.

[31] Inscription on Christopher Wren's tomb in St Paul's: 'If you seek [his] monument, look round you'.

24 June 1923
35 Egerton Crescent, SW3

My dear Ida,

...

We are certainly living at a pretty hot pace and when I look at my engagement book and see what I have undertaken to do outside my ordinary work my blood runs cold. But I find the best way is *not* to look but just to follow the maxim, Sufficient for the day &c. In this way you avoid much needless worry and when the time comes you get through better than you expect. This last week we dined out twice once with R. McNeill who had Gwynne[32] of the Morning Post and one or two ladies whom you would not know. We discussed Curzon for whom G. had no use at all, therein differing hotly from R. McNeill who has a great admiration for him. I find myself agreeing with both sides in that I have the highest opinion of Curzon's intellectual gifts and believe his mannerisms are absurdly exaggerated. But I dont call him a great Foreign Sec. for I have never grasped what his line of policy is and I do seem to feel that he is tempted into literary and debating "scores" which cause him to lose sight for the moment of the really important end at which we are or ought to be aiming. I expect it would be impossible to find anyone more difficult than Poincaré; all the same Curzon has not succeeded in making him reasonable. The Times correspondent persistently writes optimistic messages from Paris but I am bound to say I can get no confirmation or encouragement from official papers, and to my mind the only hopeful factor is that I believe Baldwin is determined on a settlement. Lausanne[33] is equally disappointing. There I feel sure we could and should have come to an agreement long ago if we had not had to take the French along with us. As it is, we shall either fail to agree or we shall have an agreement to obtain which we shall have given everything away [sic]. Force is really the only way of obtaining justice and the Turk knows perfectly well that whatever happens we are not going to war. On the other hand his army has become utterly demoralised so that his bluff can safely be called if the worst comes to the worst. It all makes one feel that it is very difficult to see that the Great War has had any beneficial effect whatever on the attitude of nations towards one another.

On Friday night we dined with Lilian[34] at her new (temporary) house in Cadogan Square. She had a biggish dinner (of very dull people) and I will recount the only gleam of humour in a story of Sir G. Murray's.[35]

---

[32] Howell Arthur Gwynne (1865–1950). Journalist. Reuters' correspondent in Roumania, Sudan, Greece and South Africa; Foreign Director, Reuters Agency 1904; Editor, *Standard* 1904–11 and *Morning Post* 1911–37.

[33] Second Lausanne Conference, 24 April – 24 July 1923. By securing the demilitarization of the Straits and restoration of Anglo-Turkish unity it was hailed a great triumph for Curzon.

[34] Lilian Cole. See Appendix I: The Chamberlain Household and Family.

[35] (Charles) Gideon Murray (1877–1951). Colonial Civil Service 1898–1917; Food Commis-

Two men were discussing whether Stanley Baldwin was a strong man or not and one said "I think he is because the other day when he was visiting his constituency a strong supporter, a sort of breezy bounder, came up and said "Well Stanley when are you going to bring Austen in?" and Baldwin turned to him & said "what the hell is that to you!"

Talking of which, A. came up the other night and said he had had it out with L. Amery & had discovered that he had been misinformed as to his being one of the objectors.[36] So they had shaken hands and were once more friends. I am very glad. It seemed very difficult to believe that Leo was one of the three but I didn't care to ask him because it would have made our relations so embarrassing if he had said yes. And, as you know we have long been rather particular friends and I have always found him not only perfectly straight but most helpful and suggestive of ideas. He has a constructive mind and there are few enough, as Father always said, who have.

...

Not only have I got Rent Bill Committee every day this week but tomorrow I finish up Housing and as a last straw my estimates are to be taken on Thursday. I shall have to leave Eustace in charge of Rents while I am in the House which will be very good for him though I am always a little nervous of what may happen while I am away. So long as I am there however I keep the temperature down and make steady progress. D. Kirkwood is very violent & yells away at me personally but some time ago I decided that the way to treat him was to appear absolutely unconscious of his presence. This has had its effect as he came to Elliott [sic] a few days ago to say he was disturbed at my attitude and wanted E. to explain that he had nothing personal against me but thought he was only following the example of Disraeli & Gladstone!

30 June 1923
Westbourne

My dear Hilda,

Annie and I are both yawning nineteen to the dozen tonight after our strenuous week ... But it has been successful times for us and so we haven't worried in spite of hard work.

I put E. Percy in charge of rents on Monday and he did quite well but made very little progress. Apparently the Chairman fell on some of the members very heavily at an early stage with the result that they obstructed all the rest of the afternoon. Meanwhile I was wearily dragging through the hours on Report of Housing Bill. There was never any steam behind the opposition and finally, as I

---

sioner for West of Scotland 1917–18. Unionist MP for Glasgow, St Rollox 1918–22. Member, Speaker's Conference on Federal Devolution 1919–20. Succeeded as 2nd Viscount Elibank 1927.

[36] Objectors to Austen's political rehabilitation and return to Cabinet in May 1923.

daresay you saw, they decided not to divide against the third reading at which our people were mightily triumphant. On Tuesday I took up rents again and having started off with what seemed like a concession though it was really little more than a change of words I made excellent progress. I got three clauses that day. Next morning we didn't sit as I had Cabinet but in the afternoon we disposed of 5 more clauses in an atmosphere of peace since the Scottish members were all down-stairs on estimates. In the evening the row took place which resulted in the expulsion of four members.[37] There can be no doubt I think that they deliberately engineered the trouble. That morning the Communists had been refused affiliation to the Labour party and the extremists wanted to show that they were just as fine fellows as any Communist. I wasn't in when the trouble began but arrived in time for the first division. Poor Ramsay & others on the front bench tried in vain to keep their men under control. They were just told to mind their own business and not interfere and on this occasion our men behaved with admirable restraint not even cheering when the figures were read out after each division. Unhappily when the third recalcitrant had been disposed of George Hamilton[38] made a fool of himself. Shinwell[39] had resumed the debate and in his cool ironical way which always exasperates our people to fury he tried to make out that intolerable provocation had been offered by Banbury (which I believe was quite untrue). Shinwell said several times that it was all "due" to him, but he pronounced the word "djue". Now Shinwell is a Polish Jew whose real name is Shinsky and G. Hamilton shouted "Jew" after him in a mocking manner. In a moment 4 or 5 were on their feet together yelling at the tops of their voices "Swine" "Dirty dogs" "White livered cowards" "Murderers" and other choice epithets. When the Chairman called on them to sit down they turned on him shouting that he was taking sides and that he was a disgrace to the House and so forth. It was a perfectly scandalous scene and for my part though I never shout at Labour members or insult them I cannot understand the psychology of some of our men who walked across to their benches and endeavoured to reason with them nor of Elliott [sic] who said in his next speech that Maxton[40] was one of the most sympathetic & finest characters in the House. I think this sloppy sentimentality is quite as bad as Hamilton's rudeness and I shall take an opportunity of telling Baldwin so when I get the chance.

---

[37] On 27 June Maxton branded the Conservatives as 'murderers' for plans to withdraw infant milk schemes leading to his suspension with Wheatley, Buchanan and Campbell Stephen.

[38] George Collingwood Hamilton (1877–1947). Conservative MP for Altrincham 1913–23 and Ilford 1928–37. PPS to Minister of Pensions 1919–20. Created Bart 1937.

[39] Emanuel Shinwell (1884–1986). Labour MP for Linlithgow 1922–24, 1928–31, Seaham 1935–50 and Easington 1950–70. Parliamentary Secretary for Mines 1924, 1930–31; Financial Secretary, War Office 1929–30; Minister of Fuel and Power 1945–47; War Secretary 1947–50; Minister of Defence 1950–51. Chairman, PLP 1964–67. Created Baron Shinwell 1970.

[40] James Maxton (1885–1946). Teacher and Labour MP for Glasgow Bridgeton 1922–46. Chairman of ILP 1931, 1934–39.

On Thursday I decided to go on with my Rent Bill and got clause 12 a very troublesome one out of the way so I thought it unnecessary to sit that afternoon. I expect to finish Rents by Wednesday at the latest and really it has gone much more easily than I anticipated. In fact except on that one afternoon when I was away there has been no temper displayed at all.

As for the estimates I really dont know why they were put down. No motion was made for reduction and no division was taken and once again our people were astounded at the way my votes slip through. I suppose its my affable ways!

...

Lord Lord. But each week is worse than the last. ...

...

8 July 1923
Westbourne

My dear Ida,

...

The Rents Bill is for tomorrow & Tuesday. The only thing that is likely to give me any trouble is the Reference Committees. It is all due to Kingsley Wood[41] who is out for self advertisement and is also disgruntled because he hasn't got office. Of course he and his friends ought to have come to me privately instead of which he gets them to sign a paper & then puts down an amendment and broadcasts it to all the newspapers. It has now become a challenge to the Govt which means embarrassment for both sides and I guess some of his supporters will be pretty vexed. I hope to squash them in the Commons but I expect I shall have further trouble with the Lords.

I went into the Lords on the Housing Bill and sat on the steps of the throne during the second reading but it was a very futile affair as nobody understood the Bill. I dont anticipate any trouble there during committee stage.

I hear that my speech on the estimates gave much satisfaction as no Minister had talked about Health since the Ministry began!

...

I was very sorry that Austen thought it necessary to make that speech on Land Valuation as it played directly into the hands of his enemies. You cant say anything to him about it because he says he did it deliberately to put a stop to the idea that he is a candidate for office which he doesn't want. The fact is he doesn't know what he does want and though I sympathise with his soreness and see the extraor-

---

[41] Howard Kingsley Wood (1881–1943). Conservative MP for Woolwich West 1918–1943. PPS to Minister of Health 1918–22; Parliamentary Secretary, Ministry of Health 1924–29 and to Education 1931; Postmaster-General 1931–35; Minister of Health 1935–38; Air Secretary 1938–40; Lord Privy Seal 1940; Chancellor of Exchequer 1940–43 and member of War Cabinet 1940–42. Chairman, Executive Committee of NUCUA 1930–32. Knighted 1918.

dinary difficulty of his position I still cannot help regreting his conduct because though he doesn't recognise it he has a lot of friends who earnestly desire to see the breach healed and it puzzles and pains them when he kicks over like that.

...

15 July 1923
Westbourne

My dear Hilda,

It seems hotter than ever this morning and I cant be too thankful that I am through with my Bills and have no speech on my mind – at least before Tuesday

...

I have been having some trouble over organisation in Birmingham owing to my having to be away so much but I believe I begin to see a way through. What has been wrong is the system of having one agent for two constituencies and the fact that neither Hewins himself nor some of the agents were quite the right men for their jobs. The situation was complicated by the fact that even if finance were forthcoming for further agents there was no accommodation for them in Edmund Street and finally Steel-Maitland has, as usual, been playing for his own hand and behind my back intriguing for the separate and special advantage of his own constituency. This was a peck of troubles and Brooks did not appear to be doing anything. However I believe it is coming right. Through my greatest enemy on the Rent Bill, Cr Talbot,[42] who sends pamphlets against it to every member of the House!, I am getting a new and splendid building *presented* to the Association. The transaction is not actually completed but I have been over the building with Talbot and I rather hope that not only will it be given but also something contributed to the cost of equipment &c. Having got this offer I had 7 members to dine with Brooks on Saturday and the latter is ready to take up finance and to *guarantee* enough to pay adequate salaries to an adequate number of agents and to a new and improved Hewins. It was generally agreed that the latter must be treated with the utmost liberality. Finally having got complete and emphatic unanimity on the main principles of organisation I have had Steel-Maitland up and I think secured his adhesion. It is a relief to my mind for I was beginning to worry considerably about Birmingham but I believe it will go ahead now. By the way I think I mentioned that A. Henderson[43] believed we

---

[42] Samuel Thomas Talbot (?–1931). Solicitor. Member, Birmingham City Council and Alderman. Chairman, West Birmingham Unionist Association.

[43] Arthur Henderson (1863–1935). Labour MP for Barnard Castle 1903–18, Widnes 1919–22, Newcastle East 1923, Burnley 1924–31, Clay Cross 1933–35. Labour Party Treasurer, 1904–12, Chairman 1908–10, 1914–17. President, Board of Education 1915–16; Paymaster-General 1916; Member of War Cabinet 1916–17; Home Secretary 1924; Foreign Secretary 1929–31. Labour leader 1931–32. Chaired World Disarmament Conference 1932–35. Nobel Peace Prize 1934.

should be in power for 10 years. I hear Buckmaster privately puts it at 15. I dont attach very much weight to either because things change so quickly in politics but it is significant of how things look to our opponents *now* and incidentally it must be borne in mind in judging the attitude of our party towards ex-Ministers.

I dont in the least object to your getting hot about Austen's position. On the contrary I think what you say is justified *but* it leaves out of account one thing which is highly important and that is human nature. I am not thinking of the R. McNeill's who openly rejoice when anything is done or said by A. to make Union more difficult. They believe him to be tied up to Ll.G. & Birkenhead whom they fear & hate and they dread lest A's return should in any way facilitate their return. But these people are in a very small minority. The majority consists partly of old members who have a great respect for A. & as much affection as he will allow them and partly of new ones who know very little of him but have a general idea that they want a united party and that his name would give weight to the Govt. All these would resent very much your accusation of ingratitude. They would say they are not in the least ungrateful and that is demonstrated by their desire for reunion. They have not the least desire to humiliate anyone; they wish to blot out the past so far as that is possible and recognising that for the leader to serve under the follower can be no easy task they will abstain from saying anything that would show that they are conscious of this change of relationship. "Be friendly with us, they would say, as we certainly feel friendly towards you. It will perhaps be a little awkward at first but every day it will grow less so". And they thought that was just what was happening and the rank and file had already made up their minds that A. would be back in the autumn when Bang! he suddenly hits them a sounding blow in the eye. *That's* why they are pained and puzzled, and its no use fighting against human psychology. People will always try to forget what is unpleasant and to believe what is pleasant and one may as well recognise it.

As for McKenna you may easily be misled about the party attitude. Either he has changed his views or there will be considerable trouble about his presence in the Govt. I don't know which is the truth though I have been told on very good authority that he is now quite sound or at least quite innocuous on vital fiscal questions. But I have found no enthusiasm over him anywhere and if after all he were to find that the difficulties of obtaining a seat were insuperable I dont believe we should suffer.

You will have seen that I got through the third reading of the Rent Bill on Friday without any difficulty. The House was much amused at "Do you really wonder Jane" and shrieked with joy when it brought Pringle to his feet. I trust the name of Jane will stick to him. Anyway I had the satisfaction of really stinging some of those insufferably conceited Liberals. One of them spent a lot of time criticising the draughtsmanship of the Bill on Report in a very superior way. Then we came to an amendment he had drafted himself and I was able to point out to the House

1. that he had said "Clause" when he meant "paragraph" thereby wiping out 4 paragraphs from the Bill which he had never meant to touch

2. he had put in a superfluous "unless" so that his clause would read "unless unless"

3. He had badly split an infinitive!

This has desperately injured his amour propre and he keeps returning to his grievance to my great delight.

...

21 July 1923
Westbourne

My dear Ida,

Exciting, you call it! I should rather call it exhausting – getting into a new house.[44] Annie started out I believe with the idea that it was going to be great fun but she has already learned better. ... I tried to get an afternoon this week to spend on settling electric lights and sundry decorations but I had my secretary on to me directly and I had to cut it short. It is astonishing how busy I am even now that my big bills are out of the Commons. Half a dozen other matters keep cropping up – smallpox, cancer, panel doctors, approved societies Boards of Guardians, necessitous areas, strikes and a succession of Cabinets are only a few of them.

...

We got here yesterday Annie in the morning and I in time for dinner. The garden is a joy, though at every point I see something neglected or forgotten that would not have been if we had been here ... We still see further improvements to make in the apple garden and someday I think it will really be very nice – only we shant be there to enjoy it.

Today 200 women came from 2 clubs. They arrived about 3 and stayed till 7.30 and they did thoroughly enjoy themselves with a hearty tea and a band next door. We didn't do much else for them but continually walked round and talked with them. ...

...

I am getting more hopeful about France and the Ruhr. There seem to be indications that even Poincaré begins to realise the dangers of isolation and the Belgians are desperately anxious to get out & put an end to a state of things which they realise is becoming more and more intolerable. The Germans too have had quite enough and will jump at any opportunity of stopping passive resistance if they can be sure that the French wont take advantage of it to kick them still harder.

---

[44] To be more conveniently located they had moved into 37 Eaton Square, SW1 after much alteration and refurbishment.

We have spent a lot of time over our note and I think its pretty good now – firm but not needlessly offensive to anyone. Someone asked what sort of impression it would create in France. "Why", said the "All Highest". "The French will be delighted. They will receive this with a gasp of delirious surprise"!

The stories of the All Highest are legion. Here is one which has the merit of being true. A certain Conservative Association telephoned to the Central Office to say they were holding a great out door demonstration and would it be possible to get Lord Curzon to come and speak. The C.O. remembering that there was a Viscount Curzon[45] in the H. of C. asked "Which Lord Curzon do you mean?" And the answer was "Oh, either will do. We dont mind which it is"!

Here is another. Curzon always pronounces his "A's" short as in "pal". He says Fránce, álternative, bránch. One of his idiosyncrasies is that he *will* answer the telephone himself and pretend that it is his secretary. A little while ago Ld Revelstoke[46] rang up the house and said "I want to speak to Lord Curzon." "Yes, who is that speaking?" "I say, I want to speak to Lord Curzon. Is that his secretary?" "Yes who is that speaking?" "Lord Revelstoke. *Is* Lord Curzon in." "I will ásk". I had this from the P.M.

Our information about Germany is that there is not likely to be a Communist revolution as the Monarchists are in most parts fairly well organised and have sufficient arms to put down a rising. But if a financial collapse occurs you might easily get a break up with a Socialist or Communist Govt in Saxony & Silesia and a monarchist Govt in Bavaria & Prussia. But of course that would be goodbye to reparations.

As for the Turk he has once more played on our disunion and upon our determination not to fight and he has whittled & whittled away our advantages till there is practically nothing left. But if it is any consolation to you the best opinion is that he is rushing to disaster and financial chaos and that before long he will be coming whining to us for assistance – which I trust we shall make him jolly well pay for.

I fear my smallpox epidemic is dying away but I am getting out fresh circulars to Bds of Guardians in a few days to stiffen up the administration of the Vaccination Acts & I am going to have a new form issued which will make it less easy to get exemption. But although I shall probably get some legislation in draft I fear it will take a more virulent outbreak (which may possibly come in the spring) before public opinion will be sufficiently roused to pass it.

...

---

[45] Francis Richard Henry Penn Curzon (1884–1964). Conservative MP for Battersea South 1918–1929. Junior Lord of Treasury and London Whip 1924–29. Chairman, British Racing Drivers' Club 1928–64. Styled Viscount Curzon from 1900; succeeded as Earl Howe 1929.

[46] John Baring (1863–1929). Partner, Baring Brothers and Director, Bank of England; member, Committee of Experts for Settlement of Reparations 1929. Succeeded as 2nd Baron Revelstoke 1897.

28 July 1923
Westbourne

My dear Hilda,

...

A whole week without appearing in the House except for questions seems almost incredible but such was my fortune. And with the Lords amendments to the Rent Bill and possibly something on the Appropriation Bill I shall finish up the Session and can go for a holiday with a good conscience. The Rent Bill went through the Lords like a knife through butter and when I reflect on the state of affairs at the time I took office it is amazing that it should be nearing its final stop without a murmur in the country. Touch wood! I shall have to suffer for this.

The incident of the week has been the "Worthy" puff. If it had been anyone else everybody would have commiserated him [sic] on the way he had been let down. As it is everyone believes that somehow or other he *was* responsible for it though no one knows how. But I expect to hear as "Jix" tells me one of his p.s.' is dining with his "opposite" at the P.O. and is looking forward to extracting the real truth.

We have dined out a lot this week but have not succeeded in meeting anyone of special interest. We went to the Royal Garden party on Thursday. We didn't happen on his Majesty[47] but the Queen[48] spotted us and sailed up looking very imposing as she always does much to A's gratification as her mother was close by and likes to see her daughter distinguished! It really was a lovely day and everybody seemed to be enjoying themselves including the newly knighted Lord Mayor of Birmingham.

We managed to get a good deal of time at the house and were able to make considerable progress with it. The decoration is going to cost me the eyes of my head but I suppose one may as well be comfortable while one is about it. At any rate we shall be all right while I am in office and as I see we have kept Leeds I suppose we are not going out just yet.

We have been over to Stoke today to open a hospital. They made a tremendous fuss over us. We were met by the Mayor and given a terrific luncheon. Then inspected a housing estate and finished up with the hospital feeling very much like Royalty! I am getting such an accumulation of gold keys that I shall have to have a special rack for them soon. I wish they would give me something more worth keeping, such as a new carpet or a dinner service!

...

---

[47] George Frederick Ernest (1865–1936). Created Prince of Wales 1901; succeeded as King George V 1910.

[48] Mary of Teck (1867–1953). Engaged to elder son of the future Edward VII but when he died in 1892 she married his younger brother Prince George in 1893. Became Queen Mary 1910.

20 August 1923
Loubcroy Lodge, Oykell, by Lairg

My dear Ida,

...

I have now been here just over a week and on the whole I think it has been the wettest week I ever remember here. But the beauty of this place is that it really doesn't matter what the weather is. If it is fine & warm it [sic] excellent for grouse shooting. If on the other hand it rains perpetually the moor is impossible but the river becomes fishable. And this year as the grouse are very scarce we were not sorry to get extra fishing and we finished our first week with no less than 10 salmon. I had 3 of them and should have had 4 but that the largest & best (a monster of phenomenal size!) got off just as he was ready for the gaff.

Our party consists of Ned & Ernest G.H.K. & self. Not a very lively lot you will say. But it doesn't much matter. You always spend most of your time practically by yourself – whether fishing or walking after grouse ...

On Thursday I received a letter (I need not emphasise the confidential nature of this) from the P.M. saying he wanted me to go to the Exchequer! It was in very complimentary terms saying how reluctant he was to move me but the Treasury was of vital importance & I was the "one man" to whom he felt he could entrust it safely.

I suppose he considers that to give it to Jix would be such rapid promotion that other & senior members wouldn't like it. On the other hand I imagine that for some reason he doesn't want to give it to Amery. Worthy has lost caste and who else is there? I have written to decline but can see that he may return to the charge and press so hard as to make it very difficult to hold out. And yet I believe it would be a mistake to accept. I should be a fish out of water. I know nothing of finance; I like spending money much better than saving it; I hate blocking other people's schemes and – I only thought of this after I had written – I should have to live in Downing St instead of Eaton Square!

26 August 1923
Stray Hotel, Harrogate

My dear Hilda,

We arrived here this afternoon and found your letter. Probably by the time this reaches you you will have seen the public announcement of my appointment.

I am not surprised at what you say and you have indeed put the case on public grounds as I put it to Baldwin though I need hardly say that I did not suggest that the safety of the Govt depended on my remaining at the Ministry. But I did point out that I had neither gifts nor inclination for the Treasury while I did know something about Health, whereas Jix was in the opposite case. The public would say that P.M.'s were incorrigible in their determination not to allow any man to remain in any job for which he had special qualifications and that I felt that I could help him & the Govt best by stopping where I was.

It was curious how the process I had gone through with Bonar was repeated. In both cases I had been thinking over the possible alternatives and B. and I discussed them with considerable frankness. Amery had no judgement, Lloyd Greame insufficient experience, "Worthy" was not acceptable in the city Woods[49] father was 85 and at any moment he might have to go to the Lords. So we came down to Jix and it was at this point that B. brought forward the consideration which finally broke down my resistance.

He said he had felt the need of a colleague at hand with whom he could discuss affairs as he had formerly discussed them with Bonar. It was an immense help to have some one at hand in whose judgement he could have confidence and hitherto it had been as though he were deprived of one of his hands. From this point of view, he said, there was no satisfactory alternative to myself. He liked me personally & he thought my judgement good & he had not the same feeling about Jix. Moreover there was the H. of C. In the absence of the P.M. the Chancellor was the leader on the Govt Bench & it was essential that he should carry weight with the House. I had brought this upon myself by my own success there. Everyone respected me and if he had to be away there was no one he could have in charge with the same feeling of comfort as myself.

Of course I have summarised the conversation very much but the result was that while remaining unimpressed by his arguments about my fitness for the office departmentally I could not consistently with ordinary (not Austens standard of) loyalty to my chief refuse to stand by him when he appealed in that way. I went back and after consultation with Annie I returned in the afternoon & told the P.M. that I was very miserable but that I was going to accede to his wishes. And he said I had taken a load off his mind.

Now I must go back to give you the previous history. I received, as I think I told you, B.'s letter in Scotland and replied by return declining. After a day or two a telegram arrived pressing strongly for acceptance and asking for a pize [?]. I didn't feel that I could just wire a negative so I gave up (very sadly) the last two days of my holiday and returned to London on Friday when I had the interviews I have described.

I cant tell you how I hate the change. I went to the Ministry on Saturday with my tail between my legs. Robinson is on holiday but I saw Symonds with whom I have done all the Parliamentary work & we both had difficulty in controlling ourselves. He is heartbroken about it for we had been planning a two years

---

[49] Edward Frederick Lindley Wood (1881–1959). Conservative MP for Ripon 1910–25. Under-Secretary, Colonies 1921–22; President, Board of Education 1922–24 and 1932–35; Minister of Agriculture 1924–25; Viceroy of India 1926–31; Secretary for War 1935; Lord Privy Seal 1935–37; Lord President 1937–38; Foreign Secretary 1938–40; Ambassador to Washington 1941–46. Created Baron Irwin 1925; succeeded as 3rd Viscount Halifax 1934. Created Earl of Halifax 1944.

programme of reforms which must now I suppose go on the scrap heap. I have had the nicest letter from him since, every word of which I know comes from his heart and I doubt if I shall ever come across a man with whom I can work with greater pleasure and community of thought. Perhaps after all I may still go back to the Ministry some day but it will be difficult as Austen knows to get away from that beastly Treasury.

However it is always my rule when the decision is taken not to spend time in useless regrets & I am endeavouring to put these thoughts out of my mind.

One thing will probably have occurred to you already, namely that this situation does reveal a certain weakness in the Govt since the P.M. feels there is no choice open to him.

Two other curious facts emerged. B. said both the King and Curzon had approved. I asked what Curzon had said as I fancied he had not formed a very high opinion of me. It appeared however that he had been struck by my contributions in Cabinet which he thought were always to the point and he had come to the conclusion that I was very sensible. The other thing was that McKenna when telling B. of his decision to stand out said "Well you needn't worry. You have got a man ready to your hand". And when B. enquired who, he named me.

So there it is, my dear Hilda. I have missed the opportunity I should have prized more than anything, but you must try and console yourselves with the thought that I cannot fail to have a very interesting life at the very hub of things and that such powers as I have will be exercised on the most important problems in a field which has hitherto been terra incognita to me. And perhaps it would have pleased Father to think that one or other of his sons should be continually found useful by successive P.M.'s to help them carry the burden of state.

You will have understood that we have got to go to Downing St. I would like to sell Eaton Sq. but Annie wont hear of it so we shall have *four* houses on our hands at any rate for a time.

...

2 September 1923
35 Egerton Crescent, SW3

My dear Ida,

Hilda's and your letters which came earlier in the week comforted me by showing that you felt, as I did, that I had no choice in the matter and that I could not refuse the P.M.'s appeal. I confess I have been altogether taken by surprise at the way it has been received. I told Annie that as so many people were away on holiday I did not expect to have more than about a dozen letters of congratulation. In one day over 70 came and every day since letters and telegrams have been pouring in not only offering good wishes but expressing confidence and support in a way that I fairly cannot understand.

...

I notice one or two paragraphs in the Press of an admonitory nature pointing out my lack of experience and remarking that I have really done very little and have evinced no sign which would indicate any knowledge of finance, and such criticism is fully justified. In fact it is what I say myself and I have very little doubt that in due course the brickbats will begin to fly. Meanwhile I take my tribute without exultation and shall endeavour to practice similar philosophy when the tide turns. It is something to start in a good atmosphere as I said when I went to the Ministry.

I had a very nice letter from Austen too but I could see that he felt some bitterness in his soul and I cant wonder. I have a sort of uncomfortable feeling for him all the time and it is extraordinarily difficult to see how he is to come back into active participation in administration. The only place I can think of for him is the F.O. and at present, if it were vacant, I dont think he could take it. It is a case of patience and waiting for an opportunity.

   …

I see there is more trouble in the Near East and that as usual the French are prepared to leave us to pull the chestnuts out of the fire for them. Mussolini is behaving like a bully and though I haven't any sympathy for the Greeks I cannot approve of his dictatorial methods.[50] The situation otherwise appears to me to be slightly less tense and as Baldwin is going to meet Poincaré I hope that the personal contact may do something to establish relations on a more satisfactory footing.

The feeling in this country is so strongly anti German that it is very difficult to protect British interests without appearing to favour ones enemies but I hope our autumn speaking campaign may do something to educate our friends and make them see that we should be foolish to saddle ourselves with further heavy burdens in order to avoid being called pro-Germans.

I am not looking forward to my work at the Exchequer with pleasure. I believe it is going to be *beastly* and that many times I shall wish myself back at the Ministry, but I suppose I shall have to go through with it as best I can.

   …

9 September 1923
35 Egerton Crescent, SW3

My dear Hilda,

It was very nice to have your letter and read your confidence in the possibilities of the Treasury. The tide of congratulatory letters has now ebbed and only a few stragglers continue to arrive but I have had over 200 and Annie more than 50

---

[50] The assassination of the three Italian members of a League commission on the Albanian–Greek frontier dispute on 27 August 1923 prompted Mussolini to demand an immediate Greek apology and a large cash indemnity. Greek refusal led to Italian occupation of Corfu on 31 August.

personal letters in addition to the formal resolutions &c which were dealt with direct at the Treasury. ...

...

There is one letter I have not sent on and that is another one from Austen written after he had received mine. It is very affectionately worded but it has distressed me because it shows that he is brooding over our difference and representing to himself, incorrectly as I think or at any rate with exaggeration, that my position in the Govt is making his impossible, that he could, if not destroy it at any rate exert a powerful influence on it and on public opinion, were he not hampered by his fear of hurting me, and that in short he is deliberately sacrificing his own career in order not to interfere with mine. He does not put it in those words of course, nor does any shade of reproach appear in his letter. Indeed I dont for a moment think that he feels that I have done anything that I might or ought to have avoided. He puts it down to fate but when he talks of not standing again owing to the difficulty of our both representing Birmingham I fear lest the impression should become established in his mind and that of his family that he gave up the career to which he had devoted himself on account of the difference with me.

To my thinking his position would be freer but not much more promising if I were out of the way and I don't see how he could even then resume a leading place unless there were some changes of attitude on his part. I dont mean "repentance" but a disposition to see with instead of against the Government as Horne is doing. I feel rather unhappy about it all.

...

15 September 1923
Westbourne

My dear Ida,

...

As to A. I can only say that I take very much the same view as you do on all the points you mention. But I know he is thinking of a Directorship now though I am not sure whether it will come to anything.

...

I see Mussolini has come down some and named his date for evacuation, so alls well that ends well. At Harrogate the Times doesn't come till noon so I was reduced to reading the Daily Mail. But really it is dangerous to do so. It warps your judgement. It has been perfectly and recklessly disloyal, onesided, and mischievous. I dont care what it says about domestic affairs but when it comes to a delicate foreign situation it is positively a danger to the country and one can only conjecture what must be its effect on excitable Italians. Mussolini has played up to it & given interviews to its correspondent of the most offensive character, all of course held up to its readers as the honest indignation of a misunderstood patriot, until I should be tempted to forget his services and his qualities altogether, were it not that Owen Seaman[51] in Punch is almost equally offensive in the opposite sense. As for the League of Nations I see it coming in for a deal of criticism but to my mind it has done infinitely better than might have been expected. After all its real purpose is to prevent war by giving public opinion time to declare itself and that is precisely what has happened in this case. Whatever Mussolini & the Daily Mail may say I cannot doubt that if there had been no League Corfu would never have been evacuated and I feel pretty sure that another Balkan war would have ensued. The French too would have backed Italy in order to secure Italian support in the Ruhr if it had not been made clear through the League that if France did so she would lose her position with the Little Entente. And though I have not had any private information I *hope* that we may have gained in prestige with the small nations, the Little Entente and Scandinavia for instance, sufficient to counterbalance the ill feeling which has been aroused so unjustly in Italy. I fancy that our attitude will have commended itself pretty strongly to the Dominions and to such elements in the U.S.A. as take an interest in the question.

Our garden is most attractive and we are rejoicing in it. I dont think we have ever had a better lot of antirrhinums or Nicotiana the latter, mingled with stocks & sweet geraniums in the border in front of the peach house. There are all sorts of things I should like to do to improve the garden still more but it is a little disheartening to spend money here in view of our largely increased expenses in London and the smaller amount of time we shall be able to give to Westbourne.

22 September 1923
Westbourne

My dear Hilda,

We feel inclined to envy you your very quiet week for we have had a very busy one and that which is before us is worse. Annie especially is having a rackety time as the engagement of 3 housemaids, kitchen maid, scullery maid, butler, footman & oddman devolves upon her, and she is also interviewing secretaries as she doesn't find the one we have had lately in London is competent to do her work. She wants to get into Downing Street on Monday Oct 1 …

I went down to the University last Saturday and addressed the students of my Trade Union classes which are still being carried on though under great difficulties as the Unions are not in a position to afford the compensation for loss of working time. I had a small audience but achieved the object I had in view viz. advertisement as my remarks were widely reported and obtained a leader in the Times. …

---

[51] Owen Seaman (1861–1936). Poet and satirist. Professor of Literature, Newcastle 1890. Wrote for *Punch* from 1897; Assistant Editor 1902–6; Editor, 1906–32. Knighted 1914.

The new valuation & rating reform bill has been drafted in consultation with Assessment Committees &c & has already been approved by most of the L.A. associations. I dont think you need worry about Sir T. Eve's[52] criticisms which were obviously merely obstructive and prejudiced. I see that already he has been pulled up in the Times and I fancy he must be rather sorry he spoke so hastily. I was not myself responsible for the draft but I passed it and authorised its issue and I think the general verdict will be that whatever faults it may have the Ministry have done a very wise thing in circulating it for criticism before introducing it in Parlt.

As for the "Industrial Group"[53] its pronouncements are all drawn up by Sir Allan Smith who is a cantankerous person and who does not carry much weight in the House. Many of the things proposed have already been done. Some, like the proposal in regard to electrification of railways, are for the industry itself to do and not the Govt. Others again are impracticable. One way and another they are not helpful, but it is interesting to see how trades are turning to the much abused Safeguarding of Industries Act and asking for protection under it.[54] I have had no opportunity of seeing the P.M. yet and until I have discussed matters with him I dont know what will be feasible. I dont think I shall attend the Economic conference regularly though of course I must have much to say on any fiscal questions which may come up but I imagine I shall be wanted at the Imperial conference all the time.

As for foreign politics again I shant know much till I have seen Baldwin but I fear from what I have heard that the public is being misled as to the interview between him and Poincaré. Still I always felt that if an interview could be arranged it might do much to help towards a better atmosphere and it seems to have had that effect.

I have begun to make the acquaintance of my new staff and I confess I don't like them or their methods so far as I have seen them. I have already turned down two draft letters they have submitted to me and I fear that if their ideal Chancellor is the one who will write the most vicious letters to other Depts they wont like me. However I didn't think I was going to like the staff at the Ministry so perhaps we may find ourselves more in agreement than seems probable at first sight.

…

We looked in at Eaton Square this morning and found it nearly finished. It has come out more than equal to our anticipations and for a London house I don't

---

[52] (Herbert) Trustram Eve (1865–1936). Auctioneer, land reformer and a leader of the Farmers' Club. Member, Unionist Agricultural Consultative Committee 1914 and adviser to Milner on land. Knighted 1918.

[53] An informal group of generally right-wing Conservative backbenchers with industrial interests, sometimes known as the 'Forty Thieves' because of their dubious reputation.

[54] The previously free trade Bradford Chamber of Commerce had just applied for protection under the 1921 Safeguarding of Industries Act.

think you could very well have anything nicer. We have got 2 nibbles at it and are hoping that we may get a tenant in presently without having to buy a lot more furniture. I think there must be a lot of people who would be glad to have a partly furnished home having some of their own which they would otherwise have to store.

I have been informed by the Lord Mayor that the citizens of Birmingham are going to give me a banquet, in recognition of my services to the city and to express their congrats & good wishes on my appointment as Chancellor. First of all I deprecated it on the ground that I had not yet justified my promotion but as he stressed the civic side I felt I could no longer without being ungracious decline such a unique and gratifying compliment. It is to take place on Oct 13 ...

29 September 1923
Westbourne

My dear Ida,

I feel so agreeably tired and sleepy tonight that I have sat in an easy chair (and allowed Annie to sit up) till 11 o'clock. Consequently I have an irresistible desire to do anything but write a letter and if nevertheless I write one it is a remarkable tribute to my fraternal affection and my strength of WILL. All this comes of my having left the house at 8.50 this morning with Barling to shoot partridges in the most heavenly country near Bridgenorth. All day long the crack of the rifle has resounded through the turnips and it was half past seven before I was restored to the bosom of my sorrowing wife, who cheered up wonderfully when she observed over my shoulder that I was accompanied by 2 brace of the little brown birds.

Well I deserved them and have been bragging about my shooting all evening. Whether Harrogate is responsible or not I dont know but certainly my aim was very deadly for I shot 12½ brace myself and all but one through the head, which I may inform you is the object of the true sportsman though he seldom achieves it.

This rare holiday was the jam after the powder of last night when I was entertained at dinner by my divisional chairman at the White Horse in Congreve Street for the delectation of my executive committee and a "few friends", composing an audience of between 60 & 70 to whom Annie and I addressed terrific orations. You would be astonished to learn the number of people who years ago when I was still buried in obscurity prophesied my future greatness and who have now recollected & embellished their predictions to the stupefaction of their friends. But truly after a day of bloodshed the world does appear less haughty than usual.

Now I must address myself more seriously to the weighty matters set forth in your letter. The scheme of the Housing Act was based upon the local authority. The Ministry deliberately divested itself of all the authority it could; not with the idea that no control was necessary, but on the principle that the local authority ought to know its own conditions best and ought to know best what conditions should be imposed in order to make the building of houses in its locality conform to these conditions. Therefore if your people argue that because the Ministry has refrained from imposing conditions no conditions should be imposed they are not fulfilling their proper functions. If 3 bedrooms are required more than two you ought to say so and frame your scheme accordingly.

It is cheering to hear what you say about Crumplin and the Hook Society. I believe from what I hear that the same thing is going on elsewhere and that the Act is building up private enterprise as it was meant to and if so it will in time solve the housing problem and the problem of rent control at the same time. And moreover it will solve the labour problem because it is just the little people like Crumplin who can get fresh labour in and train it to become skilled labour whereas training schemes by public bodies attract attention and bring down the hostility of the Unions at once.

I agree entirely with your comments on the Mussolini business. The decision of the Ambassadors Conference was a monstrous injustice[55] and has I should think shocked everyone except the Daily Mail and the National Review et hoc genus omne. All you can say for it is (1) it got the Italians out of Corfu (2) the Greeks would probably have had to pay anyhow and have got off cheaply if they preserve their territory intact and (3) Greeks are a low lot and on general principles deserve to be kicked. But what annoys me is that *we* have incurred all the odium at Rome without having achieved our object and between ourselves I think that Crewe and the Marquess between them have made a mess of it.

I have had a week of hard work and long hours trying inter alia to clear my own ideas on foreign politics. Already they are as clear as mud but I was rather pleased, when I had Sir William Tyrell[56] [sic] in to "vet" what I proposed to say last night, to find that such as they were they were very similar to his and I had a long talk with the P.M. on Friday when I urged him to strike while the iron was hot. In other words to communicate with Poincaré before the effect of his interview had worn off and try and get him to enter into conversations about the next step. The fact is that when you ask P. what he proposes to do when passive resistance comes to an end he always says "It will be time enough to talk about that when it does come to an end", and our people believe that he doesn't know himself what he *is* going to do. But my theory is that he will do something silly, or nothing at all, which is more silly, and any way we *must* be able to justify

---

[55] The Conference of Ambassadors essentially repeated Mussolini's ultimatum to Greece in somewhat softer language.

[56] William George Tyrrell (1866–1947). Entered Diplomatic Service 1889; Principal Private Secretary to Foreign Secretary 1907–15; Assistant Under-Secretary 1918–25; Permanent Under-Secretary 1925–28; Ambassador in Paris 1928–34; President, Board of Film Censors 1935–47. Knighted 1913. Created Baron Tyrrell 1929.

ourselves to this country by showing that we have tried to work with him and that we know what we want to do anyway. Generally I want us to be more active and to be in what is going on because if we sit outside & look on we cannot expect to exert any influence and I think the P.M. strongly holds the same view.

I am going to have Walter Guinness[57] as Fin. Sec. It has taken me a long time to decide as there is no one who stands out as the right man. But on the whole I conclude he is the best available having a good head & being well liked in the House.

Next week the [Imperial] conferences begin and I shall be tied up pretty closely. I am dining with Waldorf Astor[58] on the 9th to meet the Dominion P.M.'s ...

I am muddling about to see how agriculture can be helped without duties on corn. What should you say to a subsidy per acre of *arable land* over a certain minimum.

6 October 1923
11 Downing Street

My dear Hilda,

...

I have had a pretty full week with committees on Imp. Defence and Unemployment as well as Econ. Confce in addition to the routine work of the office. Now I have got a Financial Secretary I hope to shove a great deal on to him and to be free to discuss larger matters. We are all suffering as every Cabinet seems to do from the difficulty of finding time to think.

I went down to Chequers last night and spent this morning roaming over the Chilterns with Stanley. It *is* a glorious place. I knew it was a beautiful house but I had no idea there were so many beautiful pictures in it in addition to china, glass, plate, panelling, furniture &c. And the situation and views are magnificent, the downs fissured with great ravines – "Warrens" they call them – grown over with masses of box. Many of the latter have fallen over but still go on growing so that the effect is of curtains & festoons of greenery reminding one of a tropical forest.

---

[57] Walter Edward Guinness (1880–1944). Conservative MP for Bury St Edmunds 1907–31. Under-Secretary, War Office 1922–23; Financial Secretary, Treasury 1923–24, 1924–25; Minister of Agriculture 1925–29; Chairman, Royal Commission on University of Durham 1934, Committee on Cinematograph Films 1936 and Royal Commission on West Indies 1938–39; Parliamentary Secretary, Ministry of Agriculture 1940–41; Colonial Secretary and Leader in the Lords 1941–42; Deputy Minister Resident, Middle East 1942–44 and Minister Resident 1944 until assassinated by the Israeli 'Stern Gang' in Cairo. Created Baron Moyne 1932.

[58] Waldorf Astor (1879–1952). Proprietor, *Observer* 1911–52. Conservative MP for Plymouth 1910–19. Parliamentary Secretary to Prime Minister 1917; to Ministry of Food 1918–19; to LGB 1919; to Ministry of Health 1919–21. Lord Mayor of Plymouth 1939–44. Succeeded as 2nd Viscount Astor 1919.

I had a lot of interesting talks and came away much encouraged. I find the P.M. very seriously considering the party policy and disposed to go a long way in the direction of new duties with preference designed to help the Dominions and to develop Empire sugar cotton & tobacco, all of which we now have to buy from U.S.A. I need hardly say that I warmly welcome this disposition & believe it will be the salvation of the country & incidentally of the party. We are to some extent hampered by the "pledge" which in my view debars us from food taxes but not from the extension of the McKenna duties.[59] Look out for B.'s speech to the party conference on Oct 25.

21 October 1923
Chequers

My dear Hilda,

This has been a strenuous week, but I suppose not an exceptional one for a Cabinet Minister whose social or semi-social duties are an even greater burden than his department. Indeed now I have got a Financial Secretary I have had a good deal of relief, for he has been taking my place at the Economic Conference and so has left me free for other things.

We had our first dinner party at No 11 on Monday, when we invited some of the Dominions people, the Prime Ministers dining at Admiralty House. ... We had the Burtons[60] (South African Finance Minister) the Lomer Gouins[61] (French Canadian Minister of Justice) Mrs Bruce, Mrs Warren, the Guinnesses, Monty Barlow & Sir H. Mackinder and they seemed to enjoy their evening. ...

On Tuesday I had H[allewell] Rogers & Goodenough[62] to dine. The latter is chairman of Barclay's Bank of which Rogers is a director. On Wednesday I dined with the Debenhams[63] to meet the Governor of the Bank and a few other bankers, on Thursday I attended the dinner of the Canada Club where I had to speak. It was a terrible function with the Duke of Connaught,[64] 3 Ambassa-

---

[59] During the 1922 election campaign, Bonar Law excluded 'any fundamental change in the fiscal system of the country' during the next Parliament.

[60] Henry Burton (1866–1935). South African lawyer and politician. Member, Legislative Assembly 1902–24. Attorney-General 1908–10; Minister of Native Affairs 1910–12; Minister of Railways and Harbours 1912–20; Finance Minister 1916–17 and 1920–24. Attended Imperial War Conference 1918 and Imperial Economic Conference 1923.

[61] Jean-Lomer Gouin (1861–1929). Quebec politician and educational reformer. Member, Provincial Cabinet 1900; Premier of Quebec 1905; Member of Federal Parliament and Minister of Justice 1921–24; Lieutenant-Governor, Quebec 1929. Knighted 1908.

[62] Frederick Craufurd Goodenough (1866–1934). Director, Barclays Bank 1913 and Chairman 1917–34. Member, India Council 1918–30 and Council of Foreign Bondholders. Pioneer of Empire banking.

[63] Ernest Ridley Debenham (1865–1952). Married to Cecily (died 1950), daughter of William Kenrick of Birmingham. Created Bart 1931.

[64] Prince Arthur, Duke of Connaught (1850–1942). Third son of Queen Victoria. C-in-C, Ireland

dors, half the Cabinet & hosts of ex-Cabinet Ministers, dukes, marquesses, earls, and lords, together with an enormous company of Anglo-Canadians and we rose at 11.30! On Friday I was the principal guest of the Whitefriars Club, which consists mostly of journalists with artists travellers & others. They meet in Fleet Street and the principal guest is supposed to address them for 20 minutes on some topic chosen by himself after which there is a general discussion to which he replies at the end. I chose "the problem of education" and suggested that we should spend our money more wisely if we carried out a process of selection & spent more on the bright individuals and less on the undistinguished mass. It made an excellent subject of controversy & I illuminated it with sundry quips which pleased my audience & diverted them from awkward questions of finance! Cecil Harmsworth[65] was in the chair and related that the first time he met me was when I brought a deputation to McKenna who was Chancellor at the time & who after we had left had remarked "That's a devilish clever fellow!" Altogether I felt the evening had been a success, which was comforting, for it had given me a good deal of trouble to think what to talk about.

We have not yet discussed our policy in Cabinet. That will be for tomorrow but there has been a good deal of conversation going on behind the scenes. The result has been to water down the proposals considerably. Stanley has come to the conclusion that it would be premature to embark on food taxes with which I agree although I think he is convinced that they have got to come. But we both feel that a good deal of education is necessary before we could safely appeal to the country upon them. He has also come round to my view that it would not do to rush an election next month. He would be accused of slimness in evading the issue of unemployment by drawing a red herring across the trail. He then thought of going for a general tariff & having the election in January. But I have been suggesting to him that if he is not going to announce the acceptance of the colonial idea of securing to them the British market for their foodstuffs there is no need to say anything about an election at all. I dont see why we shouldn't take a dozen or 20 industries and say we are going to protect them against collapsed exchange by an extension of the principle of the Safeguarding of Industries Act, all of which I think might fairly be considered within the pledge. We havent yet finished the Economic Conference but we could point to what we had done in the way of encouraging Imperial development already and say that further extensions were not excluded. Then after the effect of our additional duties had become manifest we could make them the object lesson to say "Now

1900–1904 and Mediterranean 1907–9; Governor-General, Canada 1911–16. Created Duke of Connaught 1874.

[65] Cecil Bisshopp Harmsworth (1869–1948). Liberal MP for Droitwich 1906–10 and Luton 1911–22. Under-Secretary, Home Office 1915; PPS to Runciman and McKenna; member of PM's Secretariat 1917–19; Under-Secretary, Foreign Office 1919–22. Created Baron Harmsworth 1939.

if you want more you can get it but only by going the whole hog" and so lead up to an election in a year or 18 months.

He is actually constructing his speech now and I dont know how it will come out but it looks to me as if he might settle down on some such lines as these, and though one would rather have gone faster I am disposed to think that they offer the best prospects of carrying our own people and the country generally with us. I am not sure whether we shall avoid any resignations even so but I rather think we may.

I had an interesting talk & walk with Mackenzie King this morning. When we made our preference proposals to the Ec. Conf. Graham[66] who spoke first adopted the attitude that it was not for Canada to criticise or even to comment on what we chose to do in our own interests and therefore he would only say how nice it was of us to offer these concessions to the Dominions. I was much annoyed at this & spoke to Philip Lloyd Greame about it and he, quite agreeing, asked me to wind up the discussion. Accordingly I pointed out that we had made these proposals not because they directly affected our own interests but as our contribution to the encouragement of inter Imperial trade. We therefore wanted them criticised because if they weren't helpful we should have failed to accomplish our object. I asked the delegates accordingly to consider them and to tell us how they would be affected and to make any suggestions that occurred to them as to how we could help more. We did not commit ourselves to accepting anything beforehand but the object of the conference was to exchange information and if it was to be achieved we must know each other's wants.

M. King tells me that upon this they saw that there was more in the thing than they had supposed and they were therefore constructing a schedule to put before us so that we might see where they would like a preference and what was the order of importance which they attached to the articles scheduled. Its [sic] seems quaint that they should have so misunderstood our attitude but the fact is they are desperately afraid of asking for anything lest we should claim a reciprocity which their manufacturers would resent. However King agrees that anything we can do for them will greatly strengthen his hands in proposing an increase in their preference to us.

I have been dabbling to some extent in foreign politics, having repeated interviews with Eyre Crowe[67] and even drafting despatches myself! The Ruhr affair is getting into a more and more desperate condition & Poincaré remains as obstinate as ever but I begin to see a glimmer of hope that we may get America

---

[66] George P. Graham. Canadian politician. Minister of Railways and Canals; attended Imperial Economic Conference 1923.

[67] Eyre Alexander Crowe (1864–1925). Clerk in Foreign Office 1885; Senior Clerk 1906; Counsellor of Embassy 1907; Assistant Under-Secretary at Foreign Office 1912–19; Minister Plenipotentiary to Paris Peace Conference 1919; Permanent Under-Secretary at Foreign Office 1920–25. Knighted 1911.

to take some sort of a hand and as the prospect of having to support a starving population comes nearer and the chance of obtaining reparations recedes I think it just possible that even the French mind may become less rigid.

Well, I have written a long and very indiscreet screed. Next week I expect I shall write a short one as my ordeal of speech making will be at hand. I have got as it is to address an overflow at Plymouth.

26 October 1923
11 Downing Street

My dear Ida,

I gather from your letter that you are satisfied with S.B.'s declaration[68] yesterday and in fact I think it has produced just the effect we aimed at, i.e. it was sufficiently definite to please our people but it was vague enough to leave the country undisturbed at the thought of an election in the very near future.

The Chronicle declares that it points to some difference of opinion in the Cabinet. Where ever can it have got such an idea from! As a matter of fact when you consider that it was never mentioned at any Cabinet before Tuesday & that some members knew not that it was to be raised then it is surprising that they took it so calmly as they did. I dont know whether we shall keep them all but the attitude is rather "Give me time to *grow* my winter coat, instead of making me appear in it full grown, when only yesterday everyone knows I was saying how much better it was to get hardened to the season by retaining one's summer coat all the year round."

But it has been a very strenuous week & one full of worries and anxieties both in home & foreign affairs. I had to give up my journey to Plymouth on Wednesday but after dining quietly with the P.M. that night I accompanied him down on Thursday. He was pretty worried and I worked myself up into such a state of nerves that I felt positively sick at dinner with the Astors & could hardly touch a thing. Indeed I have by no means recovered yet so that Annie is convinced that I must have caught a chill or eaten something that disagreed with me. I hope so for it is disconcerting to find oneself so little under control.

But S.B. says I am a tower of strength to him. My judgement is so good & I am always so calm and unworried! I remember my people used to say the same thing at Nat. Service and I can only say Thank goodness they dont know what is going on inside me.

I have had an interesting correspondence with A. He was very depressed on hearing that food taxes were off & says he must "fink". But I have written again to explain that although they are out of sight they are not out of mind & S.B.

---

[68] At the Party Conference at Plymouth on 25 October Baldwin declared that although 'not a man to play with a pledge', he had come to the conclusion that the only way to fight unemployment was to protect the home market.

even thinks it conceivable that they may figure in the programme when we go to the country. If A. would declare himself delighted with the steps taken & suggest that we ought to go still further I believe he would strengthen his own position and I know S.B. would jump at any opportunity of getting him in.

If only the Marquess, full of years and honours, would seek retirement in a dukedom! It would be cheap at the price and perhaps we should have – yes, we should have a policy today.

I am interested to hear Mr Thomas' views on a subsidy and they are those which have led a good many people to think of putting it on the land rather than on the product. Up to the present the Farmer's Union have been unable to agree among themselves what they do want, & meantime S.B. has deliberately abstained from committing himself to a subsidy so as to keep the door open for a duty.

There are a good many interesting things going on. For instance there is a project for getting an agreement with the Portuguese about East Africa. They are fearfully suspicious of Smuts[69] who they think wants some of the territory (as he does) but if we can allay their fears by coming in ourselves it is possible that we may get a great development of cotton tobacco & sugar in S.E. Africa all based on Beira & this would lift a big weight off the American exchange as these three articles are the principal imports from U.S.A. I rather think I told you last week of my talk with Mackenzie King & the apples. I think that will probably come off.

We have pushed Poincaré into accepting the American proposal. He is really getting scared at the results of his policy but I rather fear we shant do much good until he is got rid of. Our pundits think the franc will begin to crumble about Christmas & if that process once starts the French will get into a panic. But it is a job keeping our end up with the Rothermere Beaver[brook] press yelling & screaming nous sommes trahis all the time.

We go to Birm. for tomorrow night only. Next week I speak at Cardiff on Friday & the following week at Leeds, Clitheroe, & Preston. So dont complain if I cant find time for a letter.

11 November 1923
11 Downing Street

My dear Ida,

I had hoped to be able to send at any rate a short letter in reply to Hilda's last week but I found it was literally impossible. ...

---

[69] Jan Christian Smuts (1870–1950). South African advocate, general and politician. Fought against British in South Africa War 1899–1902. Commanded British forces in German East Africa; Minister of Finance and Defence 1910–19; represented South Africa at Imperial War Conference; appointed to War Cabinet 1917–19. Prime Minister of South Africa 1919–24 and 1939–48; Deputy Prime Minister 1932–39.

Perhaps I had better first give you a brief account of my little "campaign" and then go on to a few remarks on the situation. If I dont comment on your local news it is not that I am not interested, but I still have only a limited time at my disposal and I think I shall be telling you what you most want to hear.

To begin then with Cardiff of which I sent you a local report. The meeting was in every way successful. My hostess (who had also been at Swansea) said there was no comparison between the two in enthusiasm, and the local managers were deeply regretting that they hadn't been courageous enough to take the drill hall which holds 5000 as they felt sure they could have filled it. And tho' at the time I was doubtful, I think since seeing the feeling in the north that they could. I need only add that this time though much happier after the meeting than before I was not more nervous than usual and was able to eat quite a good dinner!

At Leeds I spoke in the Town Hall which holds 2500 people. The local agent said they had turned enormous numbers away & could have distributed "5 times" as many tickets. The audience seemed to me rather better class than I am accustomed to. There were plenty of working men but for the most part they were of the artisan type. They were very easy to speak to, responding at once to all the points and my speech was immensely appreciated. It was fairly closely reasoned but had a good many amusing passages in it and I had so many compliments that I feel satisfied that it did what was wanted. People in those parts are inclined to be a little dubious about Protection in their habits of thought but I could see that they were prepared to consider it favourably in present circumstances and above all were intensely interested.

Great Harwood is a small Lancashire town of about 14000 inhabitants almost entirely devoted to cotton. I should not of course have gone there but to fulfil my promise to my P.P.S. Willie Brass[70] who is the member & who stood as a Free Trader! He, like others in a similar predicament, hardly knows what to say but falls back on Derby's phrase that he is not a *bigoted* Free Trader and that he is prepared to consider very carefully the new policy in the light of the new conditions. In order to make things easier for him, and also in order to make a change I devoted the major part of my speech to Imperial Developt and only said enough about Protection to suggest the main points in its favour from the side of the cotton industry. Here again the hall which holds about 1400 was packed as tight as it could hold and I was informed that 10/6 had been freely offered for a seat.

Preston where father spoke in the same hall in 1905 turned out the biggest show of the lot. The place was absolutely jammed – about 4800 I was told and the audience intensely interested. Before the meeting my host & hostess (both free traders) gave a dinner at a hotel their house being 10 miles out of the town.

---

[70] William Brass (1886–1945). Conservative MP for Clitheroe 1922–45. PPS to Chamberlain 1922–24 and 1924–27; to Amery 1927–28; to Moore-Brabazon 1940–42. Knighted 1929. Created Baron Chattisham 1945.

At this dinner there were about 10 local cotton magnates, most of them, as far as I could tell, free traders. One of them to whom I was first introduced began with this encouraging remark "Well, ye've dished the party so far as this district's concerned"! and the general tone of the conversation was enough to put anyone in the dumps! I had taken a good deal of trouble with my speech, again with special reference to cotton, and I brought in rather an effective quotation from the one Father had made there in which he said that from the first his principal object, so far as domestic affairs were concerned, was to secure better wages & more steady employment for the working man.

Well, it was a great success. The meeting gave me a tremendous ovation when I sat down & when I went out I was seized & borne shoulder high (a most dangerous proceeding) to the car. My dismal friend said "Well ye've made the very best case you could have done" and he told someone else that he would have to reconsider his views. My hostess said she was nearly converted and that I had put it far more clearly & convincingly than the P.M. at Manchester. And finally at the station next morning two railway men told my host (independently) that it was "a fair treat" and the finest speech they had heard for many years.

Now I tell you all that because of course the London press gives no idea whatever of the impression created at such meetings & very little of what the speeches contained. I think I am rather critical of my own speeches myself, but having heard a good many from various people and been present at a good number of meetings I am satisfied that this series was thoroughly successful and that the majority of those present were delighted with the speeches[.] We have all seen much advertised & long anticipated addresses a lot of which appeared at the time to go past or over the heads of the audience, but I could see that my people were not "going off" for a bit but that their attention was arrested & held to the end.

So much for that. Now let me warn you not to underrate the P.M. Its quite true he doesn't enthuse a crowded meeting, but you know after all meetings are by no means everything and his very dulness is part of the character which appeals to the country. He doesn't make up his mind very swiftly and he has his times of indecision like other people, but he thinks a lot & he has thought a good deal more about his policy than some people imagine. He is not so simple as he makes out; in fact I am getting to think that he has a good deal of astuteness and if you consider what has happened I think you must admit that.

Here he has sprung a protectionist policy on the country almost at a moments notice with a Cabinet a substantial portion of which consists of Free Traders. Not one of them has resigned and the time when they could effectively have done so has already passed. The diehards and Austen vie with one another in urging him to be more extreme in the opposite sense. Yet they all say that they will support him. At the same time he has anchored the thing on to unemployment & given every doubting Thomas a chance of saying This is not the old policy. It is something quite new, designed to meet new circumstances. He has offered the discontented worker & the unemployed an alternative to Socialism which will not merely keep our own followers within our ranks but will seriously disorganise labour. He has definitely separated Ll.G. from the ex Cabinet Ministers, and Liberal reunion won't hurt us much. At the moment of writing he has not yet exhausted his armoury and I feel pretty confident that we shall come back from the election stronger than we went in. (Though the prospect of one makes me *sick*).

Finally, I think you realise, what Austen doesn't, that to go the whole hog now means almost certain defeat. My tour would have convinced me of this if I had thought otherwise before. We aren't going to the country on lobsters & currants but on protection of the home market to fight unempt. He wants to fight the old tariff reform exactly on the old lines. He doesn't seem to see that that is playing into the hands of the enemy. Imp. preference on food products *must* come if you get it on manufactures but we must be content to go one step at a time & demonstrate by actual experience that protection helps the working man.

I am off in a few minutes to a Cabinet Committee where we shall discuss various interesting things including the date of the General Election.

17 November 1923
Westbourne

My dear Hilda,

I expect this is the last letter I shall write for some time as I shall have no time for these frivolities whilst this beastly election campaign is on. I cant tell you how I loathe it. I get so utterly sick of myself and my speechifying as I go on repeating the same thing night after night & I get none of the joy of battle that inspires some people when they get on the platform. However it has to be endured with all the indignities & humiliations which it involves and one must hope that the result will not be the greatest indignity of all!

I hardly know how to comment upon your outburst. It is very natural and yet it is very one sided because you only see part of what has happened. S.B. made an attempt to reunite the party and failed and you say if he was going to fail he ought not to have made the attempt. Yet surely if he had not tried you would have cried out that he had missed the one opportunity of doing so.

If I had had the job I should probably have gone about it differently, but I don't think I should have succeeded either. I have had grave doubts all along whether F.E. would be more of an asset or a liability to our party and for that reason I think I should have sounded the depth more carefully than he. But you have no conception of the life the P.M. leads under modern conditions. He never has a moment to think. His day is one succession of worrying problems each of which must be met instantaneously and every day there is a speech to be made often of a critical nature which alone requires hours of consideration. Really it is a hell. He was told that there was not a moment to lose & that F.E. must be seen at once before he was irrevocably committed to hostility. I asked what about Austen and he said he had wanted to see him before but couldn't get a chance. *He* did not tie up those two. They were tied already and A. told Annie that under no circumstances would he come in without him. I am not blaming him. I think I should have done the same but there's the whole root of the trouble. No one would have made any difficulty if A. had been alone. But few people seem to realise, and I dont think you do, how profoundly F.E. has shocked the moral sense of the country. It is not the things he has said about his former colleagues. That has provoked much bitterness and irritation but that would have been got over. It is his reputation as a drunkard and loose liver, on which his rectorial address has set the climax, that has roused intense feelings of abhorrence and contempt and which has made it impossible to take him in now without splitting the party again.

The under-secretaries didn't do it. It was reports from the country that convinced S.B. that he couldn't carry out his intention and though it is easy to say he ought to have known beforehand I doubt if anyone did know beforehand the strength of the hostility. A lady wrote to Annie from Dorsetshire that she hadn't met one woman who didn't resent the idea & some had said they wd vote against the party if he came into the Govt.

Even if we win I am not sure that reconciliation will be possible – at any rate until F.E. has to some extent purged himself.

F.E. himself has behaved well and has taken his fate with good temper. As for Austen he too realises where the difficulty lies and though he feels his bitterness revived I think it eases the position for him a little to know that he would be welcomed for himself.

Now to turn from this painful subject we have had a very difficult time with our Free Trade colleagues whose hair-trigger consciences and subtle minds attach more importance to words than things. Of course the apparent vaguenesses of S.B.'s pronouncements have been the result. We have to pretend that our tariff is a revenue tariff with special duties for special cases instead of a protection tariff and there has been much interchange of formulae and correspondence of the most absurd character. Derby has as usual been in many minds but in the end we have pulled the lot along with us and though a certain number of members including I am sorry to say my quondam P.P.S. Capt Brass are standing as Free Traders it is generally understood that they dont mean business and that once securely seated again they are not going to make themselves generally disagreeable. The cold feet brigade are warming up and though I dont consider that we shone particularly in the debate I think we didn't obviously lose caste. The result of the election is in doubt but my personal belief is that we shall come through as a party with a sufficient majority to enable us to carry on.

On the night of the vote of censure after Ramsay Macdonald [sic] & S.B. had spoken we had a dinner in the H. of C. to Leslie Wilson who is off to Bombay. I sat between Ramsay & Arthur Henderson and we had a very pleasant evening with excellent speeches, all the party leaders chaffing one another in a very amusing way which would certainly have shocked some of their enthusiastic followers. Squiff was particularly good declaring that it was an age of simplicity as well as tranquillity but it was too great a tax on our credulity to ask us to believe that R.M. & S.B. had sat next each other all evening without something having passed between them. This was an allusion to his own protest when we did a "deal" with the Labour M.P.'s over the Workmens Compensation Bill the other day.

The "Honourable" Mrs Ponsonby has backed out of her agreement to buy 35 E[gerton] C[rescent] at the last moment, leaving me with rent rates & taxes to pay ... I am furious ... as I wanted the cash badly. I see I am going to be ruined like all the rest of the family when they go into politics!

24 November 1923
Westbourne

My dear Ida,

I find I have a few minutes to spare this Saturday afternoon so I will use them to reply to your letter. For the moment it is difficult to talk or think of anything but the beastly election so you must excuse me if my gossip is all o' one side.

It is of course dangerous to prophesy and in any case it is too early but such indications as I can get appear to point to an improvement in my position in Ladywood. My people are better organised (*his* may be too!) and we are hoping a good deal from a little brochure which we are going to issue half way through and which will get into the homes of the people. There is an unknown number of electors who are unfamiliar with T.R. and who are frightened at the tales of dearer goods and I am glad that we haven't lingered over the election or I fancy we might have done worse. The Liberals are doing as they did in 1906, trusting to the power of lies brazenly repeated. Thus they give big lists of foods, such as rice, sago, lard margarine and fruits such as bananas, apples and oranges and baldly state that they will all go up by 3d in the 1/- or 4/- in the £. It is extraordinarily difficult to persuade ignorant people that there is not something in these statements and even if you convert them for the moment they go back again when they see the posters next day. As you would expect the L.G. papers like the Chronicle are the worst.

Still in spite of them I feel fairly confident that we shall come through all right. The shakiest seat here is Sir Herbert Austin's. It is entirely his own fault, but fortunately he has *two* women against him Mrs George Cadbury[71]

---

[71] Elizabeth Mary Cadbury. Member, Birmingham Council 1919–24. President, National Council of Women, Midland Division of YWCA and National Council of Evangelical Free Churches 1925.

and Mrs Barton[72] (Co-op). They may split the opposition vote sufficiently to let him in.

I dont think the Central Office has managed my meetings very well. I am only doing one in the neighbourhood viz Smethwick but I have one in the City one at Bath on Saturday (which means getting up early to return next Sunday) and one at Islington which is supposed to cover North London. All other nights I have double meetings in my own constituency. A week and a half of active torture, I call it.

I had an excellent meeting of women & gave them some good reasoning as well as a bit of fun.

2 December 1923
Westbourne

My dear Hilda,

I am positively so hébété by over speaking that my mind refuses to worry any more and I sit down calmly to write you my usual letter. Austen has been lunching here, Ivy being away and we had a pleasant talk and stroll round the garden. He feels quite confident and happy about his prospects, I am not quite so sanguine about mine but I have no doubt that I shall win and I shall be disappointed if I dont increase my majority. The canvass has not gone far enough to derive any information from it; I am rather going on the sort of feeling I find expressed in various quarters that I have gone up and Dunstan has gone down. I know that a big lot will vote for the Labour man just because they are feeling bitter & dissatisfied. One man told Annie he had voted for me last time but this time he was going to vote Labour and being asked why said "Well I have worked at my place 50 years and now my boss has given me a week's notice". That is typical of a certain section. Then there is the hopelessly ignorant or unintelligent voter like the one who told Annie he should vote for Dunstan because he didn't see why these foreign goods should be dumped in here! But I think on the other hand some will see that without prejudice to their political faith they had better secure Tariff Reform while there is an opportunity. My opponent says nothing about it. He concentrates upon the class war & the Rent Act and his myrmidons go round & fill up the women with the most extravagant lies about me. So far as meetings go I haven't had much to complain of. I began with a pretty rowdy one and at several others a band of roughs came with the intention of making things hot. But several times I have got them amused or interested at the start & held

---

[72] Eleanor Barton (1872–1960). Pacifist, Co-operator and Labour Party worker. Member, Central Committee of Women's Co-operative Society 1912–14, 1920; National Treasurer 1913; President 1914; Assistant Secretary 1921 and Secretary 1925–37. Labour and Co-operative Member, Sheffield City Council 1919–22. Unsuccessful Labour and Co-operative candidate for Kings Norton 1922–23 and Nottingham Central 1929. Member, Royal Commission on Licensing 1929.

them quite quiet until the end & that not only heartens up one's own people but helps to bring over the waverers.

I have addressed ten meetings during the week three of them outside the constituency! The one in the City was of course of special character but everyone seemed very pleased with my speech and I was much assisted by a disgruntled Free Trader who got up to ask questions. The Chairman wanted to rule him out of order but I magnanimously declared that I would give him an answer & as his questions were quite futile I had no difficulty in rolling him up to the satisfaction of the audience.

I really think my best speech was the one I delivered in Bath last night. I rather expect that a visit from a Cabinet Minister is a great rarity in that place. Consequently the news of my coming had caused a mild sensation and I may say they were not disappointed. I spoke for just over an hour & made fun of the Labour & Liberal manifestoes [sic]; then we had a turn at the foreigner & finished up by a stirring Imperial appeal. They *were* delighted. Quite a number came up and said they had never heard such a speech before so I had some compensation for my seven o'clock breakfast and four hour railway journey this morning.

What is going to be the result of it all? I am afraid we are not going to win West Bromwich and Walsall is very doubtful but I hope for Wednesbury & Smethwick & Worcester. Lancashire will do better than is expected. London is rather doubtful and we are supposed to be going to lose a few seats there. But I still dont see why we shouldn't have a 60 to 70 majority and that would be quite enough. Indeed the bigger the majority the smaller the hold we shall have over our own free-traders. I don't at all like some of the things the Times has said about previous enquiry and even S.B. has gone further than is quite prudent in promising universal consultation. However it will all be made clear at the postmortem!

I have got 2 speeches here tomorrow one in Islington on Tuesday two here on Wednesday and then – I love to think of next week end and feel I could put up with being defeated if only it didn't mean another election afterwards.

P.S. Annie is working like 40 beavers. Every day she is out on her bicycle whatever the weather bustling round & calling on the voters. She does 40–50 calls a day!

Polling on 6 December shattered Chamberlain's cautious optimism about a majority of sixty to seventy in the new Parliament when the Conservatives suffered a net loss of eighty-six seats and his own majority at Ladywood fell from 2443 to 1554 on a slightly increased turnout. Although the Conservatives remained the largest party in the Commons, they had been denied both an overall majority and the mandate they sought for radical reform of the fiscal system. Like Baldwin, Chamberlain initially favoured immediate resignation but both were persuaded that the safest tactical course was to meet Parliament in late January and force the opposition parties to shoulder the responsibility of turning them out and deciding who should succeed them.

23 December 1923
Westbourne

My dear Ida,

...

People seem to be rather coming round to my idea that a dissolution is not inevitable in the near future. No doubt Asquith's speech has tended to shape opinion in this direction. He seemed to think he would come in pretty soon; it may be so, but I rather fancy that Ramsay will try and hold on to office as long as he can. He and his friends must be evolving some sort of plan for dealing with unemployment and foreign affairs. They will very soon be in love with their own plan & then they will be unwilling to go till they have carried it far enough to be sure of the result one way or the other.

Meanwhile there seems to be plenty of intrigue at work. Some want a coalition, but they are a very small minority and it is difficult for them to press their view in face of Squiff's decided refusal to entertain the idea. Others still play with the notion that the Liberals might somehow be persuaded to keep us in power to keep the Labour party out. They too are finding it increasingly difficult to keep up the make believe. Then there are a number of men who say "somebody ought to be made to suffer for the blunder which has put us out" and of course they fasten on Baldwin. But they cant find anyone to put in his place and so after a certain amount of grousing I expect we shall all settle down again.

There will be a meeting of the M.P.'s of our party after we have been thrown out, at which I expect S.B. will declare his continued belief in Protection and his readiness to make way for someone else if the party does not agree. I think they [sic] can be only one reply. There *is* no one else whom the party would take as leader in any other policy.

I had to come down on Friday because I was told that my management committee – I mean the central body – was very agitated about the situation and wanted to meet the M.P.'s and pass a resolution calling on the Govt to arrange with the Liberals to keep the Socialists out. Our train was late and the meeting had progressed a good way by the time we arrived but I allowed one or two to put their views and then explained the situation to them. Thereupon they decided to pass no resolution & expressed their full confidence in the Ch. of the E. So that was all right and after dinner A. & I turned out in the snow to attend the annual dinner of a boys club in Ladywood and "say a few words". Since then we have been fairly peaceful for nearly 2 days!

...

30 December 1923
Westbourne

My dear Ida,

...

We have had quite a social week ...

In addition to these social gaieties I have found time for some other forms of amusement. I have had a long interview for instance with Hewins and hope to get a move on at the Unionist Assocn which since I have been in the Govt and unable to attend to it has been steadily going down hill. I did hope that Sir David Brooks would take up his vice-chairmanship vigorously but he has not only done nothing himself but has prevented others from doing anything and I fear he will have to be pushed out and someone else placed in his stead.[73] This morning I had Hubbard of the Post up for an interview in the course of which he told me that F.E. had broken out again & that a friend of his recently saw him drunk at a night club. It is a lamentable business. Hubbard is still hankering after an understanding with the Liberals to keep out Labour but that seems to me not only impossible, since the Libs have said they wont have anything to do with it but also undesirable, as likely to lead to a real Labour domination.

We go up tomorrow morning and as there is to be a Cabinet in the next few days I suppose we shall soon know what the Kings Speech is to contain.

---

[73] This comment is curiously disingenuous. As a free trader, Brooks had wished to resign and publish the correspondence when the election was announced, but in deference to Chamberlain's concern that it would damage the party he let it stand over until after the election.

5

1924
'Lord! Lord! What a Funny World':
Opposition and the 'New Conservatism'

5 January 1924
Westbourne

My dear Hilda,

...

I am here alone, that is without Annie. All the strain of the election has simply tired her out ...

I found Jackson very worried when I got back last Monday; he had spent too much time at the Carlton I think! But I got through to the P.M. at Stourport and he promised to come up and comfort him next morning. He, the P.M., and Willie Bridgeman came and lunched with me that day, Wednesday, and we had a good talk in the course of which I induced him to call a Cabinet for Thursday. We did none of the things the papers say we did but we had a useful talk which not only helped to clear the situation but pleased our colleagues who dont like to be separated too long – not unnaturally.

Oh dear what a lot of nonsense people do talk. I think on the whole the Times has been very sensible. Its fault is a certain want of colour nowadays but it has refused to get into a panic and has been almost alone among the London press in doing so. I dont suppose you see many papers but it has amused me to watch the Daily Mail screaming for an alliance with the Liberals while the Daily Express shrieks that alliance would mean death & disaster.

I still remain of the same opinion that Asquith has gone much too far to draw back now and that if he did it would be extremely embarrassing and damaging to us. I expect therefore to go out in the course of the next fortnight and to be replaced by a Labour Chancellor. How long a Labour Govt can remain in it would be rash to prophecy – probably longer than most people think possible. But when they go, if it be within the next 12 months, it seems to me that their game is not to ask for a dissolution but to let one of us and, to them preferably the Unionists, come in and carry our unpopularity to the polls, while the Labour party continue to say what they *would* have done if they had remained in. I contemplate therefore a reasonable possibility of our coming back before an-other election – which would be very strange.

I have one accomplishment to my credit – besides moving the table in the Treasury Board room from the window to the centre of the room[.] I have succeeded in getting Godfrey Isaacs to accept arbitration on all his multitudinous War claims on my terms. When I took the matter up I was told he was impossible and advised to let him go to law which might have meant about 70 lawsuits! But I determined to try a different method; – I wrote all the letters myself and had one interview with him and he has finally come in much to the glee of the Treasury. I believe they began by thinking I was rather "soft" but they have changed their minds now, if that were so, and from what Warren Fisher says they will be very sorry to part with me, apart from their fear of the new regime. The most difficult of my colleagues (departmentally) is Amery. The Admiralty has a very bad name at the Treasury for always adopting an attitude of infallibility and for pertinacity not to say obstinacy I think they can seldom have had anyone to beat their present chief. But though we remain perfectly friendly I will not give way to him and I very soon took to writing to "My dear First Lord" instead of "My dear Leo" in order to mark my official attitude. Only this week I composed three polite letters firmly refusing to agree to his proposals on three different subjects and I shall certainly checkmate or rather stalemate him because we shall be out before the controversy can be settled.

I haven't decided what to do about business and indeed I think I must wait a little to see how things go. But I am in touch with Elliotts and unofficially giving the individual directors advice on some rather important negotiations on which they are engaged. And they have intimated their desire to have me back, if and when, as Asquith says, I can come.

...

12 January 1924
Westbourne

My dear Ida,

...

Whatever you do about your cottages don't put in people who drink or are of bad character, however pitiable their circumstances. It is bad for the people who keep themselves decent & who are so apt to say that they would have done better to let themselves go & be looked after by others. And it is very bad for the cottages for such people will make them into pigstyes. After all if you have made this great gift I think you are entitled to insist that it shant be abused and it should be a reward for the good rather than a refuge for the bad. But I expect you are quite of the same opinion and will veto the neer-do-weels [sic].

Much wire pulling has been going on this week in both the Liberal camp and ours with the object of bringing about an arrangement of some sort. But Asquith has had a most convenient illness and my access to the P.M. is occasionally very useful. I can understand the Liberals being anxious to avoid the odium of installing a Socialist Govt but that Unionists should think it wise or feasible for us to go on without a policy and suffering daily humiliation (for it is not always remembered that in present circumstances no party can use the closure) does seem to me very extraordinary. At the bottom of some of the most active minds in this intrigue I feel sure there is still a hankering after coalition in which alone they see a fair prospect of regaining a position they have lost and I am amused to observe that it is always birds of this feather who put forward the loftiest considerations of country before party.

The question you raise about the future of Protection is one that is difficult to answer. I have succeeded this week in getting the P.M. to say definitely that he will have first a meeting of members of the Party in both houses. This will decide the question of leadership doubtless as you say in his favour. After that there will be a general party meeting at which I hope the policy which will have been announced at the first meeting will be confirmed. Much will depend on what the P.M. says at the first meeting. I hope he will say that Protection remains the principal plank of his programme but I think he would be bound to add that the moment for advocating its full & complete adoption must be left to be decided by the leaders according to circumstances. It would for example be useless to put it forward if another election came within a few months. Education must now precede resurrection but I hope we may secure that education shall go forward. I am however disposed to think that education will be best assisted by the formation of a non party organisation similar to the old Tariff Reform League which can be supported by people who dont wish definitely to associate themselves with a political party. And our best assistant would of course be a fierce continental competition. Anyway I am sure the right thing is to have these meetings at which we can see what our strength is. From what Jackson says I rather gather that the majority dont want to drop Protection but they dont want to feel that whenever and however another election comes they will be tied up to putting it in the foreground having got a bad scare at the last election.

Annie has been spending a good lot of time in bed and I hope she has made some progress. ... Perhaps when the turmoil of the next two weeks is over and we are out she may get some more rest but what we both really want is what we shant get and that is a trip to the Riviera like you. Physically I have been very well but I am conscious of being a bit "nervy" and irritable and sometimes I feel desperately depressed & wish I were out of politics.

We came down here last night as I wanted to attend a meeting of the Birm. Unionist Assoc. Committee of Management. We had an excellent meeting though it was purely for business. About 25 attended and we made real progress in a number of directions; in fact more progress than we have done since I ceased to preside at such meetings. ...

...

24 January 1924
11 Downing Street

My dear Hilda,

We are off tomorrow and I know you would like a few lines before we go to tell you the latest news. First of all I must tell you again how deeply Annie and I appreciate your generous and loving thought of us. It is a fact that I should not have felt able to consider a holiday abroad (the only kind that is any good) if I had had to find the money for it. Nor could we have accepted such a gift from anyone but you and Ida. But you have put it in such a way as to make us feel happy as well as grateful in owing our holiday to you and your cheque will enable us to get our change of surroundings in comfort and even luxury.

...

Now to give you a brief account of political matters. I think it was generally agreed that we came well through the Address. After all our trouble over the Kings Speech it was in the end a considerable success and the opposition found it extremely difficult to criticise it effectively. The last day's debate was decidedly in our favour. Simon made a poor and ineffective speech and Macdonalds [sic] was very noisy [?] but did not contain anything new. On the other hand the speeches of Austen S.B. and Hogg made a great impression and heartened up our party immensely. I was very glad Austen did so well. He had a very good reception when he got up and loud & long cheers when he sat down and I am sure the psychological effect on himself must have been excellent. He came to my room afterwards and we had a long talk in the course of which I asked him whether he was coming on to the front bench with us "No", he said "I hadn't thought of doing that. I proposed to sit behind." I asked why, & observed that it was a serious decision. He said "If that were the case it wouldn't mean merely being asked to sit on the front bench. It would mean being taken into the party councils." I said "But of course that is what it would mean". "Ah", said he, "but that raises the question of Horne and F.E." Well, that did raise a complication which I had hoped might be avoided and I felt I would not at the moment carry matters further. Today however we had a meeting of H.of C. ex-Ministers after we had given up our seals at the Palace and I brought up the question again insisting that it was one which must be considered and settled in good time. Because if A & Horne were to be brought in they must appear on the front bench at once and not go through all the press discussion which would arise if they were to be negotiated with afterwards. Our conversation was finally adjourned till tomorrow but there was a general feeling that if it were necessary it was better to have F.E. in than Austen & Horne out. The difficulty with F.E. is still the moral character and the fact that he publicly and shamelessly exhibits his weaknesses to the world. But all that he & the others can ask, it seems to me, is that they should be treated as though they had been members of the late Cabinet and there is all the difference in the world between that and appointing F.E. to a public office in which his conduct might bring discredit on the administration of the country.

What I have striven for is to get a united party with a definite attitude on the question of protection and to do that it is necessary to overcome S.B.'s disinclination to take a decision. But it looks more hopeful at this moment than it has been hitherto and I believe it may prove possible (thanks to Asquith) to achieve it. It would be a curious tit-for-tat if, as a result of S.B.'s uniting the Liberal Party, Squiff were in turn to reunite us!

As for Protection I have had a number of conversations with members of our Party and I confess that I am not much encouraged by what I have heard. I use the word in the widest sense but to most people it appears to be synonymous with a "General Tariff". Now so many candidates went down on that issue and so many others lost most of their majority that they have had a bad scare and there is a general protest against being tied up to it in the event of another election at an early date. So far as I can make out there is unanimous support for Imperial Preference general support of the principle that individual industries should not be allowed to perish owing to foreign competition but a widespread unwillingness to face the big change. I can see that Austen is fully aware of this state of things & that his experience has warned him of the difficulty of carrying out a policy about which the party is lukewarm. It seems therefore to point to a declaration that the country having rejected a General Tariff we shall not put it forward again until we are satisfied that it has changed its mind but that we hold ourselves free to take whatever measures may be necessary to protect individual industries from unfair competition.

Probably some such formula would satisfy everyone sufficiently to keep the party together. It is naturally very far from what I should like but I am bound to say that as a matter of practical politics I don't see how it is possible to get further at present, and it may after all land us at our goal quicker than any other.

His Maj. was very affable when I went to say goodbye and detained me quite a long time in conversation. He had evidently been favourably impressed by R. Macdonald [sic] and at the same time relieved by his assurances. R.M. had told him that he would not think of introducing a capital levy without going to the country first. That seems hardly to need stating but the City is very frightened about it. Among other Palace gossip I learned that Derek Keppel[1] has laid in a stock of frock coats which can be hastily donned by any right honourable gentleman who forgetfully arrives in a reach-me-down. Also that Thomas was very voluble in speaking of Bromley[2] calling him, "That 'ound".

---

[1] Derek Keppel (1863–1944). Equerry-in-Ordinary to George, Duke of York and Prince of Wales 1893–1910 and to King George V 1910–12; Master of HM Household and Extra Equerry to George V, 1912–36, to Edward VIII 1936 and George VI 1936–44. Knighted 1916.

[2] John Bromley (1876–1945). General Secretary, ASLEF 1914–36; member, General Council of TUC 1921–36 and President, TUC 1932. Labour MP for Barrow 1924–31.

I gave a farewell dinner last night to my principal staff with the Governor[3] & Walter Guinness. They all express regrets which I believe are genuine at my departure & hopes of seeing me here again. One of them said he had heard of the new Chancellor (1) that his intellectual equipment was not equal to his appearance and (2) that he was very irascible!

...

30 January 1924
Regina Hotel, Wengen, Switzerland

My dear Ida,

...

With regard to Austen I do not know what has happened since I left, but at the last meeting of Ministers (H. of C. only) which took place after our resignation I took occasion to raise the question again. Everyone wanted A. & Horne & no one wanted F.E. but when I explained that it was all or nothing they agreed they would swallow F.E. to get the others. On the Wednesday night we dined with the Londonderrys[4] & after the ladies left Salisbury came & sat by me so I sounded him on the subject & explained my views. He said he would welcome A. & would have done before but that F.E. was a drawback & a hindrance to any party. I pointed out to him that in opposition the circumstances were changed and I think I impressed him. Anyway it was arranged on Thursday that S.B. was to see him that afternoon or next morning and then write a friendly letter to Austen always supposing things had gone well. I am sure it is best to talk it over with the stickers like Salisbury or it would only be found that at the last moment they wd jib. My paper has come to an end and I must close. We constantly thank our stars for our generous sisters who sent us here and we are different people already. One feels the tension relaxed although one hardly knew it was there before.

---

[3] Montagu Collet Norman (1871–1950). Governor, Bank of England 1920–44. Created Baron Norman 1944.

[4] Charles Stewart Henry Vane-Tempest-Stewart (1878–1949). Conservative MP for Maidstone 1906–15. Under-Secretary for Air 1920–21; Leader of the N. Ireland Senate and Minister of Education 1921–26; First Commissioner of Works 1928–29, 1931; Secretary for Air 1931–35; Lord Privy Seal and Conservative Leader of Lords 1935. Styled Viscount Castlereagh 1884–1915. Succeeded as 7th Marquess of Londonderry 1915. Married to Edith Helen Vane-Tempest-Stewart (1879–1959) in 1899; founder and President, Women's Legion 1914–18; President, Women's Advisory Committee (Northern Counties) 1930–46. Known to friends and intimates as Circe.

9 February 1924
37 Eaton Square, SW1

My dear Hilda,

…

I got a message from S.B. on Monday morning asking me to go and see him. He lives almost exactly opposite to us which is very convenient and I went across at once. I found he hadn't done anything about Austen as he was afraid of making any false step but as he was ready to go on I asked him and Austen to dine here after the wedding and I carefully coached S.B. as to what he was to say. … In the evening my two guests came. A. was a bit stiff at first but gradually thawed and as soon as Annie left us I started in and called on S.B. He said what he had to say without any beating about the bush and after one moments hesitation A. frankly accepted the invitation. After that all went like clockwork and very soon it was My dear Stanley & My dear Austen as if they had ne'er been parted. They left me about midnight walking off together and as you will no doubt have seen the Shadow Cabinet met next day with Balfour Austen, F.E. & "Bal"[5] in addition to the ex-Cabinet. I got S.B. to send a note of warning to Salisbury so that he shouldn't be taken by surprise and he turned up – so that was all right. Curzon also appeared. Bob [Cecil], who may make trouble later, was on the Continent, but it wouldn't hurt us if he did break away.

So reunion has come at last, thanks, I think I may say, to me. It remains to be seen what happens on Monday but I am not apprehensive. I believe there will be some grumbling but I do not expect for a moment that there will be anything in the nature of a split and no doubt the fact that the ex-Coalition Ministers will be with us, will tend towards peace. S.B will remain leader but whether he is the next P.M. of our party will depend on how he shapes in opposition. Incidentally this development will put an end for the present to the flattering unction that Jix was beginning to lay to his soul viz that Providence had destined him for the leadership!

…

I must close as we are dining with the Murrays who want us to hear about the new P.M.G. Hartshorn. I am told the first thing he did was to ask if he could have a bottle of beer & invite Sir Evelyn Murray to share it with him!

…

---

[5] David Alexander Edward Lindsay (1871–1940). Conservative MP for Chorley 1895–1913. President, Board of Agriculture 1916; Lord Privy Seal 1916–19; Chancellor of Duchy of Lancaster 1919–21; First Commissioner of Works 1921–22; Minister of Transport 1922. Styled Lord Balcarres from 1880 until 1913 when succeeded as 27th Earl of Crawford and 10th Earl of Balcarres.

16 February 1924
Westbourne

My dear Ida,

...

The thought that Austen is also writing you about political affairs from the same standpoint rather takes the heart out of me as he can do it so much better than I. So far as I can judge, though we haven't discussed it, he has now settled down quite comfortably. He has shaken hands with R. McNeill and naturally taken his proper place as an elder statesman among us younger ones. Incidentally S.B. told me that if I had no objection he proposed to ask A. to act as deputy leader. Of course I said that nothing else was conceivable and indeed I had volunteered to S.B. when he was proposing to ask A. to join the Cabinet that he should then take this position which was obviously called for. He made a splendid speech on Thursday in the grand manner which is heard nowadays from very few and it was amusing to watch the Labour members. They began by being rather contemptuous in pursuance of their idea of his stiffness & aloofness from realities. By degrees they began to unbend then rocked with laughter at his sallies & finally listened in silence and with deep attention to the concluding appeal. The speech did not receive much comment in the press – possibly because it did not contain anything very sensational or very new – but as a debating effort it was far above the average Front Bench level. I might add that A's speech at the party meeting was generally conceded to be the best that was delivered.

There *has* been one incident which created rather a sensation & that was Asquith's statement about Poplar.[6] I believe the truth is that he was induced to make it by the strength of the feeling expressed at a party meeting and that Ll.G. was at the bottom of it. Ll.G. wants to split the Labour party & form a central group which would include the Thomases & Clyneses and he thought he saw a chance. For some time we were assured that the Liberals meant to make their motion a vote of censure and actually turn the Govt out. But neither A. nor I could bring ourselves to believe this and I think it is evident now that nothing will come of it. As a matter of fact it is the last thing we want but Jix, who fancies himself as the coming leader, is anxious to force the pace & has persuaded himself that if we got in we could win on an appeal to the country in a month or two!

I say nothing about the party meetings as no doubt you have seen the press accounts. You will have observed that no serious protest against the policy in regard to Protection has been made anywhere.

...

---

[6] On 13 February 1924 Asquith attacked Wheatley's handling of Poplar as an incitement to other Boards of Guardians to break the law and declared the Liberals would oppose the policy in the Commons.

... Dunstan & his wife are working like beavers and if an election comes soon, which Heaven forfend, it will take me all my time to hold my seat.

...

[P.S.] I forget if I ever imparted to you my design. I could not give up Ladywood for any other constity but if I were defeated I would be very pleased to step gracefully into Edgbaston next door. For this reason I desire that eminent statesman, Sir Francis Lowe, to remain there & keep the place warm until I am ready. I think that would (and nothing else *could*) earn him a peerage.

23 February 1924
Westbourne

My dear Hilda,

...

I am afraid your suggestion that I should move from Ladywood to Edgbaston is quite out of the question. I should never survive it. It would be desertion in face of the enemy. It is one thing to be honourably defeated and then to be invited to stand for another constituency but quite another to run away before the battle and I am certain that I should be condemned not only in Ladywood but all through Birmingham and that my reputation would be irretrievably ruined. Annie and I are in perfect accord on this and though she would welcome a change as much as I she fully agrees with me that it can only come through the bitter cup of defeat.

After all though defeat would be very damnable I should be in good company. Gladstone Bright Asquith Bonar Law Harcourt and many other politicians more distinguished than I went through it not once but many times and if after all I were rejected not by Birmingham but only by Ladywood I think I should not suffer very greatly. It is rather the party for which I should feel the blow of having the breach made and the fact that from Ladywood the attack on West Birmingham would be carried on with increased chance of success.

Of course I realise that I might win again with a reduced majority and in that case not only should we have to continue the present strain but the chance of moving to Edgbaston might slip by. Lowe might go and a new & vigorous member might replace him who would not be prepared to make way for a defeated ex-Minister. In that case I doubt very much whether I could bring myself to seek election elsewhere. I should more probably retire from political life and I have entered it too late and have too many other interests to break my heart over that. But I am not at present contemplating anything so serious. I am rather disposed to ride for a fall in Ladywood. I have told Annie and she agrees, that it is not good enough to kill herself in order to establish ourselves permanently in such a constituency and with this idea in mind I deliberately undertook to oppose the Rent Restrictions Bill of the Labour Party – a monstrously unfair measure avowedly designed to benefit tenants only without regard to anyone else. I had intended to move the Amendment, which I drafted myself, but owing to Kingsley Wood's dirty tricks (which it would take too long to explain here) it was decided not to put on the opposition whips and I therefore left it to private members to move and second. But I spoke and attacked the Bill and I mean to follow up that attack in Comee. If that doesn't ensure my defeat I dont know what will, and I have the satisfaction of knowing that I haven't run away from my own Act!

As a matter of fact in spite of the agitation which is being got up for purely political purposes such information as I can get leads me to suppose that the Act is working very well. If only it and the Housing Act had been left alone I believe they would together have solved the Housing problem, but evidently the Socialists are going to scrap them both and that's the sort of thing that disgusts a man like me with politics and makes me inclined to regard my severance from them with equanimity.

We have had a pretty good week in the House. The debate on the Air force brought out the differences in opinion in the Labour Party & at the same time the speeches delivered by their spokesmen were so unsatisfactory that they would certainly have been defeated if the Speaker, who always tries to protect them, had not refused to give the closure. His action was the more marked because last week when Lansbury,[7] a private member, moved the closure he gave it him at once.

The debate on the cruisers was even more amusing. The announcement that the Govt were going to proceed with part of our "anticipation" programme provoked a perfect storm of protest from the Labour back benches and Pringle, thinking he saw a chance to widen the breach, instantly moved the adjournment. Certainly the feeling in the Goat's party was bad and they all sat glum silent while Ramsay was speaking, cheered continually by our side. But his power of control is remarkable and he cowed his men into silence and into the lobby. The Liberals however got hopelessly split and there is I think no doubt that a body of them estimated at from 15 to 30 are only waiting their opportunity to come over to us.

The latest problem has arisen over the Abbey division. Winston now wants to join us and would like to stand as an Anti Socialist and be supported by us. I think that would be a great mistake. It would be said by our party, we always knew what "taking in" F.E. would mean. Here comes Winston; Lloyd George will be after him directly & we shall be back in Coalition again. And if some old Tory veteran like Pretyman,[8] who was thrown out in December, were set aside

---

[7] George Lansbury (1859–1940). Member, Poplar Council 1903–40 and Mayor 1919–20 and 1936–37. Labour MP for Bow and Bromley 1910–12 and 1922–40. Editor, *Daily Herald* 1913–22; Chairman, National Executive of Labour Party 1925–26; Leader of Labour Party and Opposition 1931–35.

[8] Ernest George Pretyman (1859–1931). Conservative MP for Woodbridge 1895–1906 and Chelms-

for Winston standing, not as a Unionist but as an anti Socialist, for an old Tory stronghold there would be the dickens of a row. Let him stand as a Liberal for a Liberal seat, or even an anti Socialist if he likes, so long as he sits with the Liberals. Then let him come over with the others later & his ratting wont be so much objected to. Though anyhow I am not personally keen to have him since he is such a pronounced Free Trader.

Stanley told me yesterday he was going to try & consult Austen this week. I wonder what he will say.

I am here without Annie for a P.S.A. address tomorrow. Leo Amery is here alas for the same purpose! A dog's life.

I have agreed to accept the invitation of Elliotts Board to rejoin and I shall attend next month. They are doing very well but Platten is very anxious to have me back for he says he wants someone with longer views than most of the Board are capable of.

                                                                1 March 1924
                                                                Westbourne

My dear Ida,

   ...

I am afraid I have little to write about this week for I have been confined to the house ever since Wednesday. ... and so Austen must be your informant as to what has been going on.

He himself was hobbling about with a stick on Tuesday but as I notice he said a few words one of the succeeding nights I suppose he is progressing favourably.

The Poplar debate was unsatisfactory in many ways and not least because the best debating speech was made by Wheatley.[9] But it split the Liberal party again and once more showed up their futility by making the majority vote against their own resolution. And the debate on Henderson's speech[10] which also rather fizzled was not thrown away as it gratified our people. Really Macdonald [sic] was rather dishonest about it because the manifesto of the Labour Party issued before the General Election & signed by him specifically says that they stand for an "immediate calling of an international conference to discuss the revision of the Treaty of Versailles".

   ...

---

ford 1908–23. Civil Lord of Admiralty 1900–3, and 1916–19; Parliamentary Secretary, Admiralty 1903–5 and to Board of Trade 1915–16. President, Land Union.

[9] John Wheatley (1869–1930). Member, Glasgow Council 1912–22. Labour MP for Glasgow Shettleston 1922–30. Minister of Health 1924.

[10] At the Burnley by-election Henderson declared revision of the Versailles Treaty was 'very much overdue', forcing MacDonald to steer evasively between repudiating Henderson and alienating the French.

9 March 1924
37 Eaton Square, SW1

My dear Hilda,

...

I wonder if Austen wrote to you about his article in the Sunday Times last week and my comments. He was so humble and contrite over his mistakes that I had to let him down gently.

Oh what a beastly week we have had over the Abbey division. Between ourselves S.B. has not been fortunate in his handling of it. To my mind there never was a doubt as to the course he should pursue, viz. to support the official candidate without hesitation or reserve. He himself recognises this but he was so anxious lest he should divide the party that he hesitated to commit himself in public. On Wednesday morning he told me he would publish a letter to Nicholson[11] that afternoon and gave me the wording which I cordially approved. But alas some one else must have got at him and so the decision was put off till the next morning and the next & though I expressed my opinion that it would be useless if it were postponed over the week end it has not appeared yet. Yesterday certain negotiations were going on with Winston but I dont believe they will come to anything. I had promised to speak for Nicholson before W.C. decided to stand but Austen passionately declared that he should speak for Winston if any ex Minister spoke for N. and now no one is to speak. I wasn't going to quarrel with A. more especially as his outburst was directed at Amery rather than at me but I think he was quite wrong. I expect now we shall have Winston in and the party will be divided once more. Undoubtedly he will be a power in the House but he is extraordinarily unpopular in the country and I doubt he will do us more harm than good [sic]. Moreover he is an anti Protection man and though he has turned round on Imperial Preference I think it would be very unsafe to count on his support for any further extension. I think I shall have to go out of politics!

...

Last night we went to "The way of the world" at Hammersmith. Really you ought to go if you can, not merely for the wittiness of the dialogue but for the wonderful acting of Edith Evans.[12] ... I havent seen any English actress to approach her for years & years. She is not exactly pretty but she is the picture of grace & charm and has a beautiful voice and a really devastating smile.

...

---

[11] Otho William Nicholson (1891–1978). Conservative MP for Abbey, Westminster 1924–32.

[12] Edith Evans (1888–1976). English actress. Created Dame 1946.

22 March 1924
37 Eaton Square, SW1

My dear Hilda,

…

We have had quite a full week. On Tuesday Annie had her first at home to wives of M.P.'s & candidates. Some 120 turned up and the affair went off most successfully. Philip Lloyd Greame made them an excellent speech on the Economic Conference which was followed by questions and quite a number expressed their gratification at the novel proceedings and their appreciation of the information they had gathered. In fact several said they would certainly like to come to the other two meetings and hear more. So Annie feels rewarded for her trouble. That night we dined with Mary to meet the American Ambassador[13] and the next night we met him again at a dinner given at the H. of C. by Sir H. Brittain.[14] But we came to the conclusion that he was a very dull dog and his wife matches him!

…

On Thursday I went down to the City to lunch with the Board of Barclay's Bank. The news of the Abbey division election came out just as I got there. Whew! What a shave.[15] But a miss is as good as a mile and for the present at any rate we have been spared the cleavage which W.C.'s return would have assuredly produced in our party.

Frankly quite apart from his behaviour in "cooperating" with us by opposing our candidate, I don't want to see a working arrangement with W.C. or any of his party. If they wish to enter our party by all means let them, but some of them including W. himself are not really in sympathy with the ideas which are most deeply rooted in the best of our people.

I had an interesting talk the other day with Edward Wood with whom I always feel more at home than almost any of our colleagues. Perhaps you saw an article by him in the Times last week on Conservative aims. He told me that one of the Labour members, who though not in the Govt is very closely associated with it, came to him and said that if our party was going to talk like that he & his friends would for the first time regard us as dangerous. And he went on to say that on those lines there was very little between us but that he did not think ideas of that kind would ever be accepted by Liberals. Therein he expressed a feeling which has gradually been growing up both in our party & among the Labour men that

---

[13] Colonel George Harvey (1864–1928). Editor and proprietor, *North American Review* 1899–1926. US Ambassador in London 1921–24.

[14] Harry Ernest Brittain (1873–1974). Journalist and Conservative MP for Acton 1918–29. Director of Intelligence, National Service Department 1917. Organiser, Imperial Press Conference 1909, 1920, 1925; President, British International Association of Journalists 1920–22. A founder member, Anti-Socialist Union and the Pilgrims' Club 1902–19. Knighted 1918.

[15] Churchill was defeated by the official Conservative by just forty-three votes.

there is a much closer community between us (that is of course the moderate sections) than between either of us & Liberals and you will recollect what I told you about Kirkwood.

Winston's arrival in the House would at once drive the Labour moderates into the arms of the extremists and though he may for electioneering purposes describe himself as a great social reformer that doesn't really represent his aims in politics. Moreover he would, as Edward Wood puts it, drive a wedge under our Protection door which would fasten it up hermetically and finally he would begin inevitably to intrigue for the leadership. So I hope he will continue to remain outside.

S.B. has gone up to Edinburgh with my notes on insurance & means I believe to stick pretty closely to my draft, which lays down four essentials for a satisfactory scheme. (1) It must be contributory (2) it must be compulsory (3) it must cover the 4 main needs for security unemployment, sickness, old age & death leaving widow & dependents (4) the provision for old age must offer sufficient to induce the old men to retire. We have now appointed a committee with myself as Chairman to go into details. We begin on Monday and I can already see that it bristles with difficulties which have never been faced by Broad.[16] But by setting out the essentials as above we shall have made the first really definite contribution to a solution & I am hopeful that Stanley's words will attract wider attention and peg out our claim to the ground before the others have had time to get in. I want presently to get a policy worked out to deal with temperance education and agriculture and then I think we shall be fairly well equipped.

I don't know if you have followed the proceedings on the Rent Restrictions Bill but they have become pretty farcical. We have not yet passed a single word of it and yesterday by raising it in the House we succeeded in bringing Clynes in to say that the Cabinet realised how unsatisfactory things were & he would make a statement early next week. What we are really trying for is to get the Government into the open. Up to now they have declined any responsibility for the Bill and have refused to say what their own policy is, thinking that they can throw odium on us for resisting a tenant's bill without disturbing landlords by taking it over themselves. It is really a low trick and in connection with such a subject it is not playing the game but I think sooner or later they will have to produce their own plan. I have had an enormous lot of letters on the bill, mostly from landlords but some from builders saying they had shut down new building in consequence of it. More & more I feel that it is most unfortunate that my work should have been upset for I am convinced that the hardships are not really greater than those which are always occurring to tenants but they are being worked up and exploited for political purposes and I fear the solution of the housing problem will once more be postponed indefinitely. The interviews which

---

[16] Thomas Tucker Broad (1863–1935). Coalition Liberal MP for Clay Cross 1918–22.

have been arranged in Ladywood have produced hardly any complaints & have disclosed no serious defects in the Act. My agent reports that they have worked a change of opinion in the constituency and that people are beginning to realise how they have been deceived by Dunstan.

... I had a long talk with Blain[17] the new Party Agent this week and on the whole he made a favourable impression on me. I shall see more of him for much depends upon him and I want to get a clear idea of what manner of man he is.

I have got a lot of speaking to do next week – in the House on Wednesday and at Walsall on Thursday & then two speeches in Birmingham. I am going to see Symonds on Monday so as to get solid ground under my feet before I begin to talk about housing.

...

30 March 1924
Westbourne

My dear Ida,

...

You are in Annies bad books because you havent even made an allusion to her [second At Home] party on Tuesday. You will probably say that you made your allusions at the time but she was hoping that you would have found some further comment after you had got home and told Hilda all about it. After we have taken a lot of trouble to make a thing like that a success we all like to have it confirmed so that there shall be no doubt about it. Anyway I feel pretty sure it *was* a success and that those who came appreciated the opportunity of acquiring information.

I didn't see any report of the Walsall proceedings in the Times but I may say that that also was successful. Representatives came from every one of the 53 constituencies concerned ranging over 6 counties & including the remotest parts of Gloucester & Hereford. When I addressed a similar meeting two years ago at Stafford there were 600 delegates. This time there were 900, which gives an idea of its vitality and enthusiasm. I believe it may fairly claim to be what one of the speakers called it, the premier womens provincial organisation of the country & the mainspring of its progress has been Annie herself. Of course there are others who do the mechanical part of the work but she has provided the inspiration. I made a long and heavy speech in the afternoon which bored me very much, but I was a little comforted at being told later on by Ruth ... that it was "clear and strong and vigorous and inspiring"! ...

I did not have to go back to London after Walsall for which I was thankful as my programme was sufficiently arduous already. I spoke in the House on Wednes-

---

[17] Herbert Edwin Blain (1870–1942). Tramways manager, West Ham 1903–13; Manager and Assistant Managing Director, London Underground & Omnibus Group 1913–24; Conservative Principal Agent 1924–27. Knighted 1925.

day on the Consold Fund Bill. Looking through the proofs of Hansard I thought it read rather well, but I was very dissatisfied with myself at the time and felt I was not doing myself justice. I suppose the gout or its remedies have got me down a bit; anyway I havent got a lot of superfluous spring just now.

I spent Friday morning at Hoskins and the afternoon at Elliotts. The former are in a pretty bad way. Orders are almost dead & what there are are scrambled for so fiercely that all profit is eliminated. Things will get better some day but meanwhile there is nothing to do but hold on and mark time. I should think we must be losing money, but I have given instruction for the payment of an interim dividend of 25% out of reserves. It is lucky we put something by for a rainy day!

Elliotts are doing very well indeed. They are full of orders which will keep them busy for a couple of months and we ought to make a good profit this year. But there are some difficult times ahead there and I am glad to be on the Board again and to be able to urge it in the right direction. It is an honest but unhappily rather weak Board which is always inclined to short views & sadly lacks imagination, but when I go out of politics I will devote some continuous attention to it.

Yesterday Annie had an awful day. She was out on her bicycle morning and afternoon and seeing constituents in the short time she spent here. And in the evening she attended a whist drive and fancy dress ball from which she returned at 11.30 p.m.! ... As for me I had a hard day too. Interviews in the morning, work at speeches in the afternoon, a Foresters dinner at *6.30* with speech and then on to join Annie at the party aforesaid. And this morning I was at an early Adult School by 9.a.m. addressing them on strikes.

When I have finished this letter I must begin to prepare for a speech at a public dinner tomorrow, my housing address to Annies Women on Tuesday, a winding up speech on Capital Levy in the House on Wednesday & a Chairmans speech at a paper before the Town Planning Institute on Thursday. *Why, why, why* are we such fools?

...

5 April 1924
37 Eaton Square, SW1

My dear Hilda,

...

I have had a busy week which has included six speeches! The ones in the House worried me the most but this time they went off most successfully and I had many congratulations and sheaves of letter of thanks from unhappy property owners. It seems almost inconceivable that the Cabinet should have allowed Wheatley to bring in such an egregious bill and I agree with you that it will do a lot of good in the country. I see that yesterday he repeated in

Glasgow what he said in the House that if this was revolutionary God help us when the Labour Party really started on their programme. I hope we shall rub that well in for it should make the quiet old ladies of both sexes realise what they are up against.

We had great fun yesterday in the House when Clynes made his statement. As usual he got rattled directly he was questioned and made a terrible muddle of it. I dont know now whether the Cabinet intended to put the liability on the local or the national purse but I put the question on purpose because I knew he would be in trouble whichever way he meant and I wasn't surprised when Kirkwood got up and denounced him as a jelly fish, to the great delight of our people. Poor little Clynes was thoroughly frightened and at once pretended he meant just the opposite of what he said, but it wouldn't work and on Monday we shall have a further mess unless Ramsay comes to the rescue. The Labour party is thoroughly disgusted. After the bill was talked out on Wednesday I heard Thomas say to a friend. "It's 'umiliating. I'd rather 'ave 'ad a defeat." And Jix overheard Margaret Bondfield[18] declare "If that's Scotch tactics Heaven defend us from Scotland".

There has been a good deal of going & coming between us and the Dissentient Liberals. They want to form a "Liberal Unionist wing" under Winston's leadership and they would like us to promise definite support to them in the constituencies. But I am glad to say we have declined to do more than say that if they like to form their group and to give us definite & continuous support in the lobby we will look benevolently upon them and endeavour to recognise their assistance with such influence as we possess. Even that will mean trouble in the constituencies and personally I would rather the thing went no further. But what we have said really amounts to no more than a recognition of facts. If they were, over a period, to support us, having first burned their own boats, we should have to recognise their services and our difficulties with the localities would be reduced just in proportion as those services were patent to the country. But I wish Winston were not with them for I foresee that where he is there will be intrigues and caves and moreover opposition to protection. I needn't say that the above information is highly secret.

...

---

[18] Margaret Grace Bondfield (1873–1953). Assistant Secretary, National Federation of Women Workers 1916–21; British Representative at Labour Convention at Washington 1919 and Geneva 1921, 1923, 1926 and 1927. Labour MP for Northampton 1923–24 and Wallsend 1926–31. Parliamentary Secretary, Ministry of Labour 1924; first woman Cabinet Minister as Minister of Labour 1929–31. Created Companion of Honour 1948.

12 April 1924
Westbourne

My dear Ida,

...

The Govt have as you say made a fine mess of the Evictions Bills and they would have done better to adopt my advice at first namely to enquire into the facts. I had rather an interesting little conversation with Ramsay after their defeat. He told me that when he saw the Bill (apparently he didn't see it till after its introduction) he was filled with consternation and told his Cabinet that it would be suicide to go on with it as it was. He had anticipated all the arguments Austen used after Wheatley spoke on Monday and declared that the case was unanswerable. He frankly admitted that the proposed amendment would not have had the slightest effect in putting the charge on the Local Authorities and finally throwing up his hands he cried "If we could only work with you!"

For the present they have dropped the case of the unemployed tenant altogether and confined themselves to a perfectly harmless amendment of the 1923 Act. R.M. told me he wanted any further legislation to be properly founded "both statistically and legally" and I think it is now fairly evident that the facts have been grossly exaggerated and distorted for political purposes. In Liverpool there have been only 73 evictions in 12 months in Birmingham 49 and in Sheffield 20 and even on the Clyde I believe such evictions as have taken place have been in connection with a rent strike engineered by the Clyde members.

I have not yet made out how Wheatley proposes to work his new housing scheme but it doesn't sound to me as if he had got anything very definite yet. I see he declares, or rather the Committee do, that houses are only being built at the rate of 40,000 a year under the 1923 Act, but that doesn't at all agree with the estimates I had previously heard which gave more than twice that number. Apparently the programme is to be administered by a Statutory Committee but up to now there has been no indication of the method of financing it on which everything depends and as Eustace Percy points out we are apparently being asked to give guarantees to obtain only what we are obtaining without them, which is rather what you would expect when the industry is allowed to draw up its own conditions. Dining with Lord Weir the other night he said he had had Wheatley to dine with him to see what sort of fellow he was and had come to the conclusion that the chances were 99 to 1 in favour of his being wrecked by his own scheme. Certainly his evictions bill doesn't give one a very high idea of his statesmanship.

I met Grigg[19] the other day in the corridor behind the Speaker's chair. He was my P.S. at the Treasury and he said Do you remember your first words to me

---

[19] Percy James Grigg (1890–1964). Civil Servant at Treasury from 1913. Private Secretary to successive Chancellors 1921–30; Chairman, Board of Customs and Excise 1930–31 and Inland Revenue 1931–33; Finance Member, Government of India 1934–39; Permanent Under-Secretary,

when this Govt came in. I said I had quite forgotten them. You said "Watch Wheatley" and we have been doing nothing else ever since.

I gave another address to ladies on Wednesday, the third in the last few weeks, this time at the Ladies Carlton. It was on widows pensions and they were much interested, at least those who were awake, for a good proportion were of the "old Cat" type and slumbered peacefully while I orated. But the livelier ones perceived that the problem wasn't so simple as it sounds and appeared to agree with my conclusion that the solution lay rather in the direction of insurance than of doles. Doles mean a lot of supervision and expense.

I had an awful day yesterday. I had a committee of the Midland Union at 2 o'clock followed by the annual meeting at which I had to deliver an address. Thence I went to a committee of the Birm. Management Comee which lasted an hour and I finished up with a public meeting in Ladywood. I had had no opportunity of proper preparation & was in an awful funk but I managed to keep going for 45 minutes and was told that it was the finest address I had ever delivered. It was far from that but it shows how one can work oneself into a feeze for nothing.

Today has been more restful and I managed to get ¾ hour in the houses where there is a fine show of orchids. ...

4 May 1924
Westbourne

My dear Ida,

...

There isn't very much to tell you of our doings since we left you. I managed to get to the leaders conference on Thursday morning and after the usual somewhat desultory discussion it was decided to take my draft "aims & principles" as a basis. We did not have time to go through it all but I daresay you will have recognised some of the passages in Baldwin's speech to the Primrose League. We are to continue our discussion early this week.

After the conference I went to the luncheon which Amery had arranged to try and make a start with the new organisation to push along the education of the country in protectionist principles. I think we may get George Lloyd[20] to take it up and give his whole time to it and as he was one of the old Tariff Reformers and has since then widened his outlook by his successful administration in

---

War Office 1939–42. National Conservative MP for Cardiff East 1942–45. Secretary for War 1942–45. British Executive Director, International Bank of Reconstruction and Development 1946–47. Knighted 1932.

[20] George Ambrose Lloyd (1879–1941). Conservative MP for Staffordshire West 1910–18 and 1924–25. Governor of Bombay 1918–23; High Commissioner for Egypt and Sudan 1925–29; Colonial Secretary and Leader of the Lords 1940–41. Knighted 1918; created Baron Lloyd 1925.

Bombay I think he ought to do it well. We got promises of guarantees of between £7000 to £8000 a year for 5 years which will not be enough but if we can increase it to £25,000 I think we shall be able to make a start. After the lunch I felt so done that I retired to Eaton Square to compose a speech for the next day and I haven't yet been back to the House.

...

There is no new development in politics but I see with pleasure that there is a good strong agitation getting up over the McKenna Duties & I shouldn't be surprised if after all we get them retained beyond August 1.

...

11 May 1924
Westbourne

My dear Ida,

...

I have done very little worth recording this week and have hardly been in the Chamber though I have been in the House attending various Committees and Conferences. Even now we havent got Aims & Principles finally settled but I did bustle my colleagues last Tuesday into the discussion of all the points that were not agreed and I think the last touches will be given this week.

Another thing I have been attending to is the formation of the Fair Trade Union for Safeguarding British Work & Wages. We have got out the draft of an appeal and it is to be settled on Wednesday after which we shall set to work to get the money. I thought it well to tell S.B. what we were doing; although Amery had done so already, for he doesnt always take in what you say to him if his mind is on other things. He declared that he hadn't known about this scheme and said he would like to talk about it but it must be after his speeches were over! I havent said anything to Austen yet nor to any other colleagues but I want it mentioned at some meeting of the Shadow Cabinet before we are much older.

I only had 3 speeches to make last week (which I mention because Austen groans at the idea of two!) On Wednesday the Town Planning Institute gave me a dinner on their tenth anniversary and as it was over at a very reasonable time I didn't "disenjoy" myself as Uncle Arthur used to say. On Friday night we had the annual meeting of the Birm Un. Ass. It used always to be held in the Town Hall when father spoke but after the War when party politics were so dead we couldn't fill as large a building and so we have during the last few years taken the temperance hall. But on Friday not only was the hall packed but hundreds were turned away seething with indignation at not getting in. Faux mieux! I think we can safely go back to the Town Hall & after all though we have no longer one supreme and dominating figure the average Birm. M.P. is much more distinguished than he was and our people are rather proud of their members.

Last night we had our Ladywood annual meeting at which there was great enthusiasm but not so large an attendance as there was last year perhaps because it is getting so late in the year.

...

Alas! I went back to a gout boot on Thursday and am still wearing it though gradually improving.

By the way, I dont know where we shall be next week as Nancy Astor is pestering me to go to Cliveden where she wants to show me a broken heart. She declares that nobody loves her & the party is going to the dogs & wants to tell me all about it. And I dont want to hear but may not be able to escape. I suspect the trouble is that the Duchess of Atholl[21] has quietly stepped into the front place & Nancy dont like a back seat.

...

18 May 1924
Westbourne

My dear Hilda,

We have not forgotten your birthday but it was impossible to write yesterday from Cliveden so we had to put off sending you our love and good wishes till today. You and Ida have been very helpful to us again this year in many ways and our weekly correspondence is one of the things that I constantly look forward to. Long may it continue!

The McKenna debate went very well for us though I think it might have gone better. Between ourselves I was disappointed in S.B.'s speech. It was perfectly clear when the day came that there were no souls to be saved on the Labour benches and nothing was to be gained by sparing the Govt, but S.B. was really incapable of a fighting speech. He strikes me as being very tired and low spirited. He grinds out speeches like I do with infinite labour and anxiety and those he has been making lately have weighed upon his mind more than usual. On this occasion he had to be told to speak up, for parts of sentences were inaudible except to those close to him and he did not seem to have any vitality left. One sees the same thing in talk. He is so overwhelmed with worry over speeches that he cant give his mind to the problems that are always coming up but I sometimes wonder whether he will last out the session.

Austen was first rate and roused our people to real enthusiasm. I see the Sunday Times which has been hunting S.B. for a long time now appoints A. as

---

[21] Catherine Marjory Stewart Murray (1874–1960). Conservative MP for Kinross 1923–38 (Conservative Whip withdrawn May-September 1935 and resigned to sit as an Independent April-November 1938). First woman member of a Conservative government as Parliamentary Secretary, Board of Education 1924–29. Chairman, British League for European Freedom 1944–60. Became Duchess of Atholl 1899.

leader on the strength of it but that is going further than is warranted. A single speech wont settle the leadership but if he were to follow it up with several other similar ones I think it might come into the range of possibility again. His knowledge of procedure stands him in good stead in opposition and contrasts again with S.B. who is always at sea when any question arises as to the proper course to take. I had an interview with Harold Begbie[22] (the "gentleman with a duster") this week. He is writing a book on The Conservative Mind and has been seeing a number of people about our "aims and principles". He mentioned this point to me but he evidently perceived that A. was not yet accepted as free from a bias towards alliance with Liberals which still remains anathema to the rank and file. Moreover I gathered that he did not think A's mind sufficiently attuned to the new spirit of Conservatism and he seemed to regard him as too much out of touch with industrial problems.

Ll.G. made a really first class speech on Friday and quite carried our people with him in his attack on the Mines Nationalisation bill. It was interesting to watch him. He was evidently in a state of great mental excitement seeing his opportunity at last and determined to make the most of it. Its the first time he has felt at home in the House since he gave up office but its a far cry from his present position to that which he occupied then. And after all four Libs. voted with the Govt and many abstained.

I had a very interesting talk with Levita[23] the chairman of the meeting of Local Authorities who came to an agreement with Wheatley on housing. It certainly is amusing to see how he has been driven back on my Act. All he is doing is to lay down that the same houses shall be let instead of sold to obtain which he has to provide a subsidy 2½ times as big. The guarantee seems to have gone unless, as is possible, there is to be a State guarantee to build houses if the local authorities wont do it. On the other hand no one seems yet to have noticed a very important change. Under the Addison Act the rents were fixed the liability of the L.A. was fixed and that of the State was unlimited. Under Wheatley's proposal the liabilities of the State & the L.A. are fixed but the tenant has to bear the unknown liability. For the rents are to be the economic return on the cost less the subsidy which is calculated to bring out a prewar rent plus 40%. But if prices go up as they surely will then the rents go up too and if they get higher than the tenant can pay the housing is to stop altogether. This certainly is not Socialism. My belief is that the L.A. will very soon jib at the £4.10.0 for 40 years = say £80 subsidy. They have none of them given more than £25 hitherto to private enter-

---

[22] Harold Begbie (1871–1929). Journalist and author of a variety of works including *The Mirrors of Downing Street* (1920) and *The Conservative Mind* (1924) under the pseudonym 'A Gentleman with a Duster'.

[23] Cecil Bingham Levita (1867–1953). Military career in South Africa. Unsuccessfully contested St Ives for the Conservatives, 1910; Member, LCC 1911–1937; Chairman, LCC 1928–29. Knighted 1929.

prise and have built very little themselves. True, they escape the unlimited liability but they have escaped that hitherto by not building themselves.

I agree that private enterprise is not now in a position to build houses to let – perhaps never will be. But I would have gone on speeding up private enterprise in building houses to sell and encouraging owner occuppiership. The constant pouring of new houses into the pool by the easiest channel would have loosened the whole position. More and more of the cream of the working class would have entered the new houses and the L.A. could have built a certain number of tenements and done something in the way of improving slums which in time would have solved the problem. As it is private enterprise will be checked the L.A. will be harassed by the finance, labour will depend on the Scheme to preserve its monopoly and the ca'canny system and though it may not be apparent all at once the houses will not be forthcoming. I understand that Wheatley is proposing to give another £1 of subsidy to rural areas but I don't see how that is going to solve the rural problem. I have dug up my letter to the Times written in Nov. 1920 and a committee is looking into it again but I doubt if they will take it up. All the same I still think it contained the germ of a plan which would have worked.

I had a go at the N.U.A. on Tuesday over their failure to issue any literature on the McKenna duties & Safeguarding of Industries Act. I suspect G. Younger as the obstacle. He is frightened to death of anything which might be construed as having a protectionist flavour and attacked me by name for my speeches at Cardiff & Plymouth last year. However I gave it him back and had the Committee with me in doing so. Some of my colleagues are very anxious that Jackson should be removed and that I should take his place, and I tease Annie by pretending to be thinking seriously of it. But I dont think its likely to be pressed upon me and I should rather regard it as an alternative than a supplement to my present work.

I recovered sufficiently to be able to attend a City dinner at the Carpenters Hall on Wednesday & afterwards to squeeze into tight shoes to attend the Court Ball ...

The Ball was a most brilliant affair and Annie enjoyed it. We saw Mr Theodore[24] there & said goodbye to him, as he was leaving next day. There is no doubt we have made a fast friend there which may be useful some day as he is said to be in

---

[24] Edward ('Red Ted') Granville Theodore (1884–1950). Founding member and Secretary, Amalgamated Workers' Association of North Queensland 1907; State President, Australian Workers' Union 1913–16. Member, Queensland Legislative Assembly 1909–25; Deputy Premier, Treasurer and Secretary for Public Works 1915–19 and Premier 1919–25; Member, Federal Parliament for NSW 1927–31; Deputy Prime Minister and Treasurer 1929–30 when resigned after being found guilty of fraud, dishonesty and abuse of ministerial position. Director-General, Allied Works Council 1942–44. In 1924 visited London to convert loans to Queensland due to mature in 1924–25.

the running for the Federal Premiership in the future. He told Annie that Mrs T. said there was no house in which she had felt so much at home as ours.

The Fair Trade Union is not, I fear, going too well. I attended a meeting last Wednesday but had to leave early for another engagement & haven't seen Leo once to ask what happened. But I thought it didn't look as if the money was coming yet. I expect it will want a lot of beating up.

After all "Nancy" fixed up her week end party and we went down yesterday. It turned out a comical affair for as I rather expected we never got to politics. ...

...

Cliveden is a most lovely place and the views over the Thames are magnificent. It was looking its best with the fresh green and the woods were full of black caps & chiffchaffs. Unluckily there was no single soul who knew one bird from another.

Alas. I have got to have some more teeth out this week. My dentist thinks one of them may have caused my gout. But I am afraid he will always say that as long as I have a tooth in my head.

Now I must go to bed or I shall get into trouble. Its half past twelve already.

23 May 1924
Westbourne

My dear Ida,

...

Poor Annie has had a fearful sell [?]. She has plagued me into going to see a gout specialist and after some hesitation Mr Simpson recommended Dr Leonard Williams. So off we went to Harley Street on Thursday morning and the only question in A's mind was which baths he would recommend for Whitsuntide. "Instead of which" this miserable specialist declares its all a question of diet and that if I will follow his advice and play fair I shall be a new man in 3 months. Now if he had merely said vaguely that I shouldn't have so much gout I should probably have declined his advice but when he confidently declares that I shall have 3 times the energy I have, I say that's worth trying and despite A's protests I *am* playing fair. Its certainly rather drastic. No butcher's meat, no sweets. Toast & butter for breakfast, fish permitted but not much approved for lunch, fish or game for dinner, no tea. Fruit & salads ad lib. A. thinks I shall fade away and longs to supplement my meagre allowance but I say its no good blaming the doctor for not curing you unless you follow his prescription and I cant die in 3 months. But of course if I don't feel a new man he will have to go on the shelf like all the others.

Its amusing to see how these doctors contradict one another. He says "diet, & baths will be unnecessary, but anyway baths are no use unless you do 6 weeks of them". Morris of Harrogate says "Diet is out of date. Live modestly & come to Harrogate as often as possible, if only for a week, it will do you good". True, I don't think he has done me any good.

I went down to Wembley on Wednesday to preside at a Conference on housing and startled my audience by declaring that the greatest benefactor would be the man who could show us how to build homes of paper. The Birm. press was a little disturbed and sent a man to know what I meant but on learning that I was only advocating a house cheap enough to be scrapped when it became out of date was comforted and said I was a courageous politician. Of course I put it that way pour épater le bourgeois, but the idea is sound. I had to spend all morning at the Conference and lunch with Miss Olga Nethersale[25] (who doesn't look very kissable now!) to get an idea of the place. I concluded that a month on the spot would not give time enough to see it properly.

The debate on unemployment was very amusing. We baited Tom Shaw[26] all afternoon and then Miss Bondfield talked out the motion at 8.15 and I tore up my notes. But the Labour men couldn't keep the private bills going beyond 1½ hours and the motion came on again. Just as I was wondering what I could say Sidney Webb[27] providentially intervened with a futile speech and I got up in a crowded and excited House at 10.40. I saw it was not an opportunity for a quiet & reasoned exposition so I just went for the Labour Party and judging by the remarks made to me in the lobby our people were delighted. I was glad for I hadn't spoken since Easter & felt I was getting out of the picture. The Liberals once more made themselves ridiculous and didn't escape the main question as we have put it down again for next week.

…

1 June 1924
Westbourne

My dear Hilda,

…

Of course I never expected any other result from the division [to reduce the Minister of Labour's salary] but I derived a certain amusement first from Macdonald's [sic] tactics & then from old Squiff's wiliness in working round gradually to the announcement of the foregone conclusion after making a speech which logically led up to exactly the opposite course. Mac. made all the persua-

---

[25] Olga Nethersale (1870–1950). Actress and manageress. Member, Women's Committee of British Empire Exhibition 1924–25.

[26] Thomas Shaw (1872–1938). Secretary, Colne Weavers' and International Textile Workers' Federation, 1911–29 and 1931–38; Secretary, Labour and Socialist International 1922–24; Director of National Service, West Midlands Region 1917–18; Labour MP for Preston 1918–31. Minister of Labour 1924; Secretary for War 1929–31.

[27] Sidney James Webb (1859–1947). Civil servant, barrister, author, Professor of Public Administration and member of various Royal Commissions. Member, LCC 1892–1910. Labour MP for Seaham 1922–29. President, Board of Trade 1924; Dominion and Colonial Secretary 1929–30; Colonial Secretary 1930–31. Created Baron Passfield 1929.

sive part of his speech to the Libs. actually turning his back on us and mellifluously arguing on the physical impossibility of working out great schemes in 4 months. But when he came to the threats of a General Election which were of course really intended for precisely the same ends he faced round and bellowed them out at us, thus attempting to save the Liberal faces. It was artfully done & no doubt helped them to arrive at the decision they had determined upon without injuring their self respect. But I think it will also help to hang them in the country. As to the resultant effect on public estimation of the Govt there is no doubt a considerable lag after the House of Commons but I cannot believe that it will be nothing. I feel that it must hearten our people and destroy the confidence of theirs even though it may not touch the apathetic mass in between. There is a certain cumulative influence of a series of blunders that works up in time though I don't think it is very perceptible yet. But as long as we can make a show of doing our best to throw the Govt out & put the odium of keeping them in on the Liberals I consider we are making in the right direction and the division was therefore satisfactory.

My speech last week was on the Finance Bill not on unemployment and it made Snowden[28] so cross that I think it must have got home. He spoke of my "superabundance of spite & spleen" and my "vitriolic rhetoric" till I felt quite above myself.

I am not sure whether Jix or I will speak on the Housing resolution which I have only had since Friday. It comes out rather different from expectation, and you will have observed that it proceeds not by way of repeal or even amendment of my Act (except to prolong it for 15 years!) but in the form of an addition to it. Wheatley proposes in fact to run two schemes side by side – a subsidy of £75 for houses to sell and one of £13.10/- p.a. (or £17 in rural areas), for houses to let, and the real question is whether it is worth while to pay an extra of £165 per house for the pleasure of transferring it from one category to the other. For, as I think I have already pointed out, the increase of productive capacity in the industry has no relation to the manner in which houses are to be disposed of. The £165 is arrived at by capitalising the £9 for 40 years = £160 plus Local authority = £80 total £240 less £75. Supposing the scheme carried, what will be the result? It is difficult to prophecy without the Bill but it seems to me that there will be a scramble for labour & materials between the subsidy builders & the local authority which will begin by forcing up the price. The builder will win the struggle because his client will pay the extra cost – up to a point, whereas the L.A. has to put the extra on to the rent if it doesn't bear it itself. When the point is reached building will stop and we shall have to abandon the scheme & begin again.

---

[28] Philip Snowden (1864–1937). Labour MP for Blackburn 1906–18 and Colne Valley 1922–31. Chancellor of Exchequer 1924, 1929–31; Lord Privy Seal 1931–32. Created Viscount 1931.

What are we to do? I haven't discussed it with anyone yet but my instinct is to let them try it & fail. If we oppose we shall be accused of blocking a plan to give everybody houses in a short time out of mere partisanship or meanness & our conduct will be contrasted with Wheatley's broad mindedness in continuing my Act & even extending his new subsidy to private enterprise, – which of course is mere wind on dressing, as it is clear that p.e. wont hold [sic] to let. I incline therefore to prophesy disaster but say you are the Govt. We are not going to stop you trying to carry out your policy but we wash our hands of the results.

… We went to the show on Tuesday morning for a short time and then again on Wednesday afternoon so that we were able to see most things rather imperfectly. One could have spent a day looking at the orchids alone. They get more and more marvellous every year and I wish I could have 3 or 4 more houses to grow them in plus the time necessary to study them. However even my two give me a lot of pleasure …

We went down to Wembley [the British Empire Exhibition] on Thursday taking Dorothy with us. … The place is so vast that you really want weeks to assimilate it, but we saw South Africa East Africa & West Africa fairly thoroughly and Canada more hastily. I do think the overseas part is very impressive. The variety of South African products for instance impressed me very much as well as the care with which they had been prepared. There must have been many thousands of people at the exhibition and they included lots of school children. I am going to try and get round again this week.

…

7 June 1924
Culmhead, Taunton

My dear Ida,

…

… Many thanks for … your congratulations. Its funny the way things work out. I had rather expected to be asked to follow Wheatley but Baldwin said Jix wanted to begin & would I mind winding up. Of course I agreed and A. was furious as a winding up speech cant be a reasoned criticism & gets no press. However later we heard that the debate was to go over to the second day & I was to wind up then. Finally some one observed that the amendts would come on the second day & if I wound up I should not be able to speak on the main question. So after all I had the opening on the second day & thereby got the bulge on Jix!

I was very anxious that our party should not be manoeuvred into a false position on the housing question and I had made up my mind that a reasoned criticism was the only way to avoid it. I remembered father's speeches on the Home Rule Bill and determined to avoid frivolity & keep debating points in the background. I had no idea till I sat down & heard the cheers that I had made such an impression but from what I heard afterwards it is evident that people were much struck with it. The fact is that it is the first speech of the kind that has been made in this Parliament; there have not been many opportunities. Hence the interest & novelty. Johnnie Baird said he had met two young men outside in a state of great excitement one said he had never heard such a speech & the other that it was the best of the session. Liberals too were very complimentary & Wheatley himself passed over a note congratulating me on my "clever analysis & generous speech".

One thing that would have amused you was the way the Socialists fell into the traps I laid for them. This was particularly so about rents. I got them to agree that what Wheatley said meant pre-war plus 40% and then proceeded to demolish that possibility, and I hope & believe that I opened their eyes to an effect of the proposals which Wheatley had carefully avoided mentioning. Oh, I must mention before leaving this subject that Veale who was my P.S. at the Ministry & now acts in a similar capacity for Wheatley was filled with admiration. He called it a magnificent performance and couldn't imagine how I had prepared it in the time without anyone to devil for me.

He said that he had remarked to Wheatley that morning that so far there had been very little in the debate and W. had answered "No but I expect we shall get it in the neck this afternoon. That's what I'm worrying about!"

I rather expect to get into hot water over what I said about passing the proposals into law in the hope of eventually convincing the Labour Party of it errors. But short of getting in ourselves with a majority, I don't see any better plan. I feel sure the Liberals wont vote against the Second reading and if they don't support us I rather fear we shall do no good by futile opposition. I think I have made it impossible for myself to oppose the Second Reading now whatever the rest of the party do and I shall be interested to see if I get hauled over the coals for it.

Preference comes on Tuesday & Wednesday but I dont expect to be called on to speak. George Tryon[29] is to have a go as he hasn't spoken this session and if any others on our front bench take part there are many who ought to be put up including S.B. Lloyd Greame and Amery.

I had a good talk with Austen on the terrace one day. I found he was resenting Amery's connection with the Fair Trade Union and he was not aware that I was in it too. I told him how I had tried to get S.B. to take it before the Shadow Cabinet before it got too far so that we might all know where we were. I said I had failed to get S.B. to move & suggested that he should try himself. He went off to do it at once but I have never been able to get him alone since to find out

---

[29] George Clement Tryon (1871–1940). Conservative MP for Brighton 1910–40. Under-Secretary for Air, 1919–20; Parliamentary Secretary, Ministry of Pensions 1920–22; Minister of Pensions 1922–24, 1924–29 and 1931–35; Postmaster-General 1935–40; Chancellor, Duchy of Lancaster 1940; First Commissioner of Works 1940; Parliamentary Secretary, Minister of Pensions 1940. Created Baron Tryon 1940.

what happened & S.B. continues to preserve his usual impenetrable silence. I see a good deal less of him than I did & he doesn't seem so much in need of council as when he was in office.

…

14 June 1924
Westbourne

My dear Hilda,

…

We have been pretty busily engaged since we got back. I took the opportunity of going into the finances of the Unionist Association which as usual the Treasurers had neglected and I found the situation so alarming that I have had to bring forward a complete new scheme under which the divisions will have to raise their own funds instead of depending on the Central [sic] as they have hitherto done. I expect there will be a lot of work before the thing is carried through but I am convinced not only that it is the sole way of carrying on our work without going into bankruptcy but that eventually it will result in greater activity and interest in the divisions themselves. Really it is the advent of the woman voter which has made it possible. Coming fresh without previous traditions they have subscribed & raised money for themselves and I believe their example has shown the men what is possible for them to do also. I started my operations on Friday by dropping a bombshell into the Finance Committee where our two Treasurers were knocked all of a heap by my figures. Then I carried their recommendations to the Management Committee who would have been quite ready to adopt them on the spot. But I said it was too serious for that and offered to bring up a detailed scheme in July for their final acceptance. From them it will have to go to the Central Council which we have now enlarged to about 500 members and it will finally come into operation next year. I must find an opportunity soon to tell the M.P.'s what I am doing! But if I had not taken the initiative we should have been in a fine mess before long.

On Friday evening A. & I went to a "social" in the constituency where we addressed a few words to the multitude & distributed prizes &c. There is no doubt that our people have got their tails up and are full of confidence for the time. They say they are having street corner meetings which draw hundreds & when Dunstan tried to hold one the other night he couldn't get an audience and sent his 3 speakers to heckle our people. Converts are being made and one of our strongest opponents recently became a member of our Workers League. The new Govt. has disappointed its friends and the repeal of the McKenna duties has roused widespread indignation. All these things I report without attaching much importance to them for I know how our people go up and down. But if there be any truth in them its very disappointing because I cant keep Edgbaston waiting after next election [sic] and if I dont get defeated then I shall have to give it over to some new man. And if, after that, I were to get defeated I should just have to retire from politics. I *wont* go and look for a constituency away from Birmingham.

Yesterday we went over to lunch with the Birds at Solihull & afterwards to open a fete held in their grounds on behalf of the Womens & Maternity Hospitals. I must say I think it is wonderful how the voluntary hospitals have kept going in these hard times. These 2 institutions whose expenditure has nearly doubled since the war are not only meeting that but adding 80 new beds with extra accommodation for nurses &c, all which will of course mean a large additional annual maintenance cost. It was a bore having to go over but I like to keep in touch with the institutions of the town and also to maintain my cordial relations with the Birds. He is a good fellow and his wife a woman of considerable organising ability and they are devoted to me because I persuaded him to stand when his father was killed and helped him to win his first election by speaking for him in Wolverhampton.

I am not to speak in the Preference debate in which we shall be represented by G. Tryon, P Lloyd Greame Austen & Stanley. I think they will be a very strong quartette but there is trouble because Amery has been excluded on the ground that he is associated with an organisation that advocates full Protection. I believe Austen is responsible for pushing Stanley into this decision which in my view is quite unjustifiable. Amery and I are demanding that the position shall be discussed by the Shadow Cabinet which is what I asked Stanley for a long time ago. It is outrageous to let us go on committing ourselves without protest and then suddenly call upon us to abandon those whom we have persuaded into the movement. But I am satisfied that if only we can get the S.C. we shall be able to arrive at an understanding.

...

[PS] ...

I forgot to mention that I finished yesterday afternoon by attending the opening of new permanent premises for the Ladywood Branch of the Municipal Bank. It seems to be getting more known that I did originate the idea of the Bank partly if not chiefly owing to Annie who drums it into the constituency, and it is becoming clear that its foundation was the most important development in the Corporation since Father's day. There are over £4,000,000 in it now & the depositors number nearly 140,000!

22 June 1924
Chevening, Sevenoaks, Kent

My dear Ida,

...

I am afraid Austen's speech was very imperfectly reported in any paper and even the comments upon it only gave an adequate account in a very few cases.

But it was the most successful speech of the Session and a tremendous personal triumph for him. Our people cheered for literally several minutes when he sat down & many said it was the best speech he had ever made. I agree so far as I have heard him in the H. of C. for of its kind I thought the speech was perfect in that it was good tempered full of easy and effective raillery, damaging to the enemy and above all persuasive. I dont know if it was possible to change votes at that hour but I think that probably it sustained some who might have been shaken by Snowdens threats & sneers and so saved votes that would not have been recorded at all. There is no doubt that it produced a very great impression on all parties but particularly in our own where there is a good deal of more or less smothered grumbling going on about the want of fire in our front bench. S.B. made one rather unfortunate observation in his speech. He had asked me to lunch in order that he might go through his notes with me. This he did and I made some suggestions, chiefly about arrangement and the way to end the speech. He adopted these suggestions as well as he could work them out in the short time then remaining but he never mentioned to me his idea of buying Dominion corn & distributing it at cost price. If he had, I should most certainly have advised him either to drop it or to elaborate it fully and very carefully. But apparently, though it seems incredible, it never occurred to him that he couldn't throw a suggestion like that across the table without assuming some responsibility for it. He apparently thought he could offer them something to "bite at" as he put it without himself being in any way committed! In some ways his innocence approaches childishness!

Apparently he had in mind some proposal made by Bruce[30] which amounted really to a system of prohibition and license, only Empire wheat being licensed until the price went up to a certain figure when foreign wheat would be allowed to enter. I always thought the proposal hopelessly impracticable but S.B. did not even mention Bruce and only gave one sentence to his scheme. It was no wonder that Ramsay & Snowden thought he meant that the Govt was to buy the wheat & store it and claimed him as a Socialist. This was what I understood myself and a cold chill went down my back as I thought of the effect on the party. As a fact I have heard since then that there is strong dissatisfaction & concern about it and I expect there will have to be a meeting & explanations.

All these things at once set men gossiping and discussing the leadership afresh, but although between ourselves I doubt S.B. being the next Conservative P.M. I dont believe in any immediate change. In the speech of Austen's successful as it was he went out of his way to pay a compliment to Lloyd George which seemed to our people not only unnecessary but undeserved. Meanwhile as you

---

[30] Stanley Melbourne Bruce (1884–1967). Australian politician and diplomat. Commonwealth Treasurer 1921–23; Prime Minister 1923–29; Minister Resident in London 1932–33; Australian High Commissioner in London 1933–45. Retired in England. Created Viscount Bruce of Melbourne 1947.

say he has accepted the chairmanship of a finance Company. The B.S.T. of which the new co is a development has been a successful concern and I have no reason to suppose that it is really in need of help or that it cannot afford to pay its Chairman substantial fees.

I got a chance of discussing further with A. the position of the F.T.U. and our relations with it. I am glad you look upon it in the same light as I do and I am sure that Austen has been prejudiced by his personal dislike of Amery. However though I told him I disagreed with his views I did not dwell on that but rather on what ought now to be done. S.B. had told him that he would prefer not to have a Shadow Cabinet but would write a personal letter to Amery. Unfortunately he omitted to do this but after the recess Amery saw him and he then said he would decide the matter himself without reference to the Shadow Cabinet. This however did not seem satisfactory to me both because I doubted S.B.'s coming to any decision at all & because even if he did there was no guarantee that our colleagues would understand what it was.

So when he had got his speech off I tackled him taking him on to the terrace where he couldnt escape and after a very strenuous attack I got a half promise to have it up to a Commons Conference this week to be followed by a Shadow Cabinet later.

But I shall have to return to the charge or my sheep will dash out of the enclosure at the last moment.

Aims & principles[31] are out. The Morning Post says it has been received with a chorus of approval throughout the country but gives no corroborative detail. The Sunday Times damns it as being without vision which is of course what you expect from the S.T. The Daily Herald thinks it has been got up by Curzon & modified by Baldwin. It is ill-tempered but obviously has been unable to find a vulnerable spot.

Tomorrow I shall enquire from the Central Office what their reports say. I have got to go there to help in drafting a new constitution.

...

28 June 1924
Westbourne

My dear Hilda,

...

This has not been a week of great excitement. I addressed a meeting of Young Conservatives at a private house on Monday on the subject of housing while the 2nd reading of the Bill was being debated in the Commons. As I had been against moving the rejection I did not want to speak again though I was prepared to do

---

[31] Published as *Looking Ahead: A Re-Statement of Unionist Principles and Aims* in June 1924.

so if Wheatley had been as outrageous as usual. But he was mild as milk and never mentioned my name except to say that my sentiments were too noble for my party. I remarked to Symonds whom I met outside the House that his Minister had not answered my speech. No, said he, "he didn't attempt to. I know he was very much impressed by it and I rather think he didn't want to get into conflict with you again". But I shall put down a few amendments though our general line is that we are not going to obstruct but try and get the Bill on the Statute book as soon as possible. The sooner it becomes an Act the sooner its failure will become manifest. Symonds made one interesting observation "The curious things is," he said, "that the applications under your Act are coming in as merrily as ever and I believe that they will continue to do so and that the Local Authorities will simply let this one become more or less a dead letter." This confirms my own view that the local authorities would seize on any reasonable pretext to avoid saddling themselves with the Wheatley liabilities. I am trying at intervals to write a brochure for the Central Office on housing.

I suppose, by the way, that you have seen Aims and Principles, which is now published. Jackson tells me that everyone is of opinion [sic] that it will be most useful. He took some to Yorkshire lately and people there were delighted with it and said it was the first political document they had ever been able to understand. Its [sic] makes me laff to see my sentences continually quoted as though they were a sort of gospel and to think that nobody knows that *I* wrote them. The Herald thinks Curzon did!

I have been turning up the Central Office on organisation too. Blain produced a new scheme to the last executive. I got up and criticised it & they referred my criticisms to a sub. of which I was a member. The sub. met last Monday and meekly accepted every one of my suggestions some of which were rather fundamental. The fact is that I have had an extraordinary useful experience in Birm. & the Midlands and the others mostly have none.

I started one very good thing this week, namely, tennis in Eaton Square. There is a court in the garden just opposite the Tryons house and I played with them & their friends 2 mornings, 5 sets each morning, without feeling either my tennis elbow or my strained heel. ...

At last, by going in desperation to Col. Storr[32] the head of the Secretariat, I have got a meeting of ex-Cab. Ministers for Monday to discuss the misdeeds of Amery & self. I have no fear but that it will go off all right and the next job will be to get a Shadow Cabinet. S.B. struggles like a broncho to avoid them.

---

[32] Lancelot Storr (1874–1944). Military career in India 1895–1914; Deputy-Assistant-Adjutant-General, War Office and on Kitchener's staff 1914–16; Assistant Secretary, Committee of Imperial Defence 1916–21, to War Cabinet 1916–18 and Imperial War Cabinet 1917–18; First Secretary, British Section, Supreme War Council 1917–18; Secretary, Conservative Shadow Cabinet 1924; Ecclesiastical Secretary to Lord Chancellor 1924–28; Personal Assistant to Chairman of Unionist Party Organisation 1929–30. Knighted 1919.

...

I have been opening the Chamberlain Gardens in Ladywood this afternoon. We had asked the Calthorpes to come to us for the ceremony & they accepted but until they arrived in time for dinner last night I had forgotten that they were *both* deaf. Our first meal was a nightmare. I bawled into her eartrumpet and Annie shrieked into his ear till we were both nearly distracted while Lewsey with that indifference to externals which is one of her charming characteristics thought it agreeable & polite to leave us 10 minutes intervals between the courses. ... We really did like both of them but two deaf people in addition to Miss Holt in the house is rather trying. I go on shouting now all the time. I have acquired the habit!

I am so pleased to think that I have already justified my re-election to Elliotts Board. I have long been anxious to break away from some of the Associations which in my view are hampering our development but there was no one on the Board with sufficient conviction and influence to act. At the second meeting I attended Arch proposed to "wait & see" but I rushed in & swept my colleagues into definite & immediate resignation. They have been rather frightened since at what they did but it has now resulted in our obtaining orders for nearly 1000 tons of the particular article and we have been enabled to reopen two mills which were standing idle. It makes one feel that if politics became impossible one might still find occupation elsewhere!

...

5 July 1924
Westbourne

My dear Ida,

... It was too bad that I couldn't squeeze in an opportunity of seeing you but it *has* been rather a strenuous week for me. I have just completed my sixth speech! ...

...

I continue to pursue my diet of a straw a day and am astonished that I never seem to feel feak and weeble. Take Friday for instance. I breakfasted on a peach and 2 crescents with butter. For lunch I had a salad with a roll and a small piece of cheese followed by a plate of strawberries. After that I had nothing more till dinner which was just 4 courses & included a little chicken. Of course that is a good deal less than I have usually had in the past but the funny thing is that I felt no hungrier. I did have rather a tender joint on Tuesday & Wednesday, but it has gone off since.

The meeting of ex-Cab. Ministers was much as I expected except that at the end S.B. said we had had a valuable discussion and he thought the best way would be for him to have a talk with Amery & me; thus leaving everyone in doubt as to what the decision was. The talk did not come till Friday & S.B.

showed the greatest readiness to talk about everything but the subject which had brought us there. Finally L.S.A. suggested that we should write him a letter setting forth our intentions. I demurred however, being of opinion that S.B. ought to commence. Two things I thought had emerged. First that our colleagues disliked our being *officially* connected with the F.T.U. which they thought was already formed, and secondly what they feared was a "raging tearing propaganda" and they would feel very differently if the work lay more in the direction of the compilation & distribution of literature or paragraphs for the press and less in the direction of meetings and speeches.

I suggested therefore that S.B. should write us a letter in which he should call attention to these two points and enquire how far we could give him assurances upon them. He took a note but as usual I was left not knowing whether he meant to adopt my suggestion or not. Meanwhile the All-Highest got wind of the meeting and was furious that the subject, of which he had already heard something, should be discussed without the presence of the peers. He was all for having Leo and myself before the Shadow Cabinet and delivering an ultimatum that we should either come out of the F.T.U. and express repentance at once or retire to the obscurity of the back benches. He wrote to this effect to S.B. who showed it to me as an example of what he had to put up with. But I bluntly said my sympathies were with the Markiss. I thought the Shadow Cabinet ought to have been called and had repeatedly told him so. Whereon he adroitly changed the subject!

There are quite a lot of underground movements going on, all of which will I expect come to nothing. A junior occupant of our front bench remarked the other day to a friend of mine that he was watching with much amusement the intrigues of his seniors; he believed that only three were absolutely out of it & probably didn't even know they were in existence. The three he named were Amery W. Bridgeman & myself and I mention it because I think you have sometimes had an idea that A. was a bit of an intriguer. I have never seen any indication of anything of the sort.

The dissentient Libs. are getting very anxious about their future as they perceive how precarious it must be unless they have an understanding with us. I know Austen takes a very similar view about our party but I believe he is almost the only man in the party to think so. The majority (I am only speaking of England & Wales) believe we have only got to sit tight and the Libs. must either come to us or go to Labour.

I hear Winston is going soon to appear on a platform with a prominent Unionist & is thinking of styling himself as "Liberal-Conservative". Can you imagine such folly? I believe at present he is off Anti Socialism and wishes to come out as the "Great Imperialist"! Oh! Lord! I trust he may remain at arm's length as long as possible. But think of the Goat's fury to have his part stolen from him – and by his own neglect to seize it.

I saved the Govt's life on Wednesday not out of love for them but because it meant £3 million at least to the tax payer to defeat a civil service ramp. They were intensely grateful & fully realised what they owed to me. Nancy Astor told me that my speech had converted a number of Liberals. If thats true, its remarkable as both Squiff & Simon spoke strongly against the clause the Govt were defending.

12 July 1924
Westbourne

My dear Hilda,

...

This has been a strenuous week in one sense for we have dined out every single night. We get a tremendous lot of dinner invitations now; sometimes they are three deep on one single evening. ...

The Faringdon dinner was a man's affair to meet London candidates. I was the principal guest and made an impassioned harangue which appeared to please them very much. I was interested in the house which is full of Burne Joneses, Watts and Albert Moore. They are certainly very decorative though not very lively! I was only able to get away for about an hour and a half as we had the Finance Bill in committee and I stuck it out till 6 in the morning. Lord! I did feel a rag that afternoon but a couple of nights good sleep revived me.

On Wednesday I went and lunched with the Times in Printing House Square and rather enjoyed myself. Moreover I wasn't sorry to have a talk with Geoffrey Dawson[33] who was more forthcoming than usual and I found myself very generally in agreement with him. He is anxious that the Govt should remain in office long enough to disillusion the country and I think he quite sees the futility of Wheatley. All the information I get confirms the view you express and I think when we get on to Comee on the Bill on Wednesday and Thursday we shall rather tear it up in argument though of course we don't mean to kill it. I had a letter from Eustace Percy this morning which was rather significant. Wheatley had sent Veale, his p.s., to him to say he would very much like to discuss our amendments with him & me to "shorten discussion". E.P. gathered that he hadn't liked to write to me for fear of a refusal and that he didn't want to meet Jicks! He himself was rather in favour of the meeting but, as at present advised, I don't quite see where we come in though I can quite understand Wheatley's idea. We don't want to join in making his bill more acceptable. Its fundamentally rotten and the sooner it fails the better and I have kept this in mind all through in drafting amendments, which I have designed chiefly with a view to showing up its deficiencies. I have been talking today to the Birmingham housing director who is much concerned with its probable effect in stopping the

---

[33] (George) Geoffrey Dawson (1874–1944). Private secretary to Milner in South Africa 1901–5. Editor, *Johannesburg Star* 1905–10; Editor, *The Times*, 1912–19, 1923–41. Known as Robinson until 1917.

selling of houses. He has sold about 560 already & is extremely anxious to sell more, but under the Bill he cant sell Wheatley houses. This is precisely the point I have been arguing with Jix. He wants to put down an amdt to make sales possible. I was against it on the ground that the more the Wheatley house was saddled with restrictions the less the local authorities would be inclined to take it on, and I pointed out to the housing director today that there was nothing to prevent his going on with my Act and quietly leaving the Wheatley plan alone. This was a new idea to him but I hope it sank in. He asked "Can we do that?" and I reminded him that Wh. had extended my Act for 15 years!

...

I spent several hours in Sub. Comee during the week amending the N.U.A. constitution and every one of my suggestions was carried unanimously. They have got to come before the Exec. next Tuesday and if they pass them I think we shall have a very decent set of rules.

Ramsay has made a fearful mess of his negotiations and although he has saved his Conference I expect it is only at the cost of losing all its inside.[34] In fact he has pretty well surrendered everything he had maintained before and I guess he will have a rough passage on Monday. I rushed round on Friday and made the unhappy Stanley hold a meeting with some of his colleagues to discuss the situation. He was very unwilling but it proved most valuable and cleared everybody's mind considerably. I tried to get him to put up Austen first but he has finally decided to speak first himself and let A. finish up. Of course A. will do a winding up speech much better than S.B. could but I wanted him to get the report because I really think we ought to show up Ramsay's folly after all his boasting and a reasoned speech early in the day might be very damaging. I believe I could do one myself but of course it isn't my pigeon. I have at last got an interim report from the Actuary on pensions but it is very incomplete and doesn't take us much further. I can see that a lot more work will be necessary before we begin to talk about it. Meanwhile I have succeeded in getting a new Comee of experts sanctioned to get out a programme of municipal reform. Arthur Collins,[35] the old Birm. Treasurer is at work on it & has got out a draft series of subjects and I have arranged with Sam Hoare to take the Chairmanship. He and I are the only Socialists in the late Govt but I think if we are agreed we should be strong enough to carry our programme. I don't think, by the way, that our colleagues know anything about it, but if we have a meeting next week I shall mention it.

We have had the new agents up here this afternoon. ... and we got a good talk with them so that I think I shall know them again. They seem a very useful lot

---

[34] Preparations for the Inter-Allied Conference in London (16 July to 16 August 1924) compelled MacDonald to make many costly compromises with the French over the Ruhr and future Reparations.

[35] Arthur Collins. Seconded from Birmingham Council to become Secretary and Accounting Officer, NSD 1917; Birmingham City Treasurer, 1918–22.

and if I can get my new financial scheme going I believe they will do very good work. In my own division we have already raised the necessary money. It is confirmed that Dunstan has joined the Communists & that the I.L.P. are looking round for another candidate. My people are very cock-a-hoop as they think it will be difficult to find any one who will command so many votes. They think also that a Liberal may put up and that if so that will not do me any harm. But what about Edgbaston?

...

19 July 1924
Westbourne

My dear Ida,

...

I have nearly worn a hole in the seat of my trousers sitting on the front bench this week, with one day on the Finance Bill & 2 on the Housing Bill, and though we did not sit up very late I dont think I have averaged 6 hours sleep the whole week through. I mean to go to bed early tonight to try & catch up. The Govt have not managed their Bill well. Neither Wheatley nor Greenwood[36] know their case and the former has not learned the elementary rule that a member of the Govt should always take an amendment seriously no matter how frivolous he thinks it. On Thursday particularly the House got into a thoroughly bad mood and wasted time till I was really ashamed of it. At last when I thought the right moment had arrived I got up and made an appeal to the Committee to resume its dignity. I was only just in time for Wheatley was actually rising to propose the closure for the second time which would certainly have had disastrous results. However my intervention was very well received, Wheatley changed his closure into a further appeal & we ran through the remainder of the clause in 20 minutes & reported progress.

Both the man who wrote to the Times & Simon were quite wrong about the extension of the 1923 Act. They had read neither the Act nor the Bill but the extraordinary things was that Wheatley didn't know the answer and I had to get up and point out the passage in his own Bill which actually provided for the extension. As Aubrey Symonds said to me "It was really pathetic"! I fancy Wheatley would not be very sorry if he could find a good excuse for saying that we had wrecked his measure for he must be aware that it is doomed to failure.

I went on Friday to see a model of a house which Lord Weir has very ingeniously designed for mass production. It is really a timber house with a steel

---

[36] Arthur Greenwood (1880–1954). Labour MP for Nelson and Colne 1922–31 and Wakefield 1932–54. Parliamentary Secretary, Ministry of Health 1924; Minister of Health 1929–31; Minister without Portfolio responsible for economic affairs 1940–42; Lord Privy Seal 1945–47; Paymaster-General 1946–47; Minister without Portfolio 1947.

plate lining on the outside and what is called "beaver board" on the inside, this being a preparation of wood pulp. No skilled labour is required and all the materials can be provided without much extra plant. The cost will apparently be about £300 for a non-parlour house but might be still further reduced if the inside fittings, grates, baths &c could be ordered in large quantities. I see no difficulty about the production and the model seemed to me to be satisfactory in appearance. I should think it would be rather more susceptible to heat & cold than a brick house but not much. The difficulty I see would be to get the local authorities to order in large quantities until they had thoroughly tried it out which I should think would take 18 months or 2 years. Weir wanted a Director of emergency housing to do the ordering but I say that wont help. He cant store the houses and must himself depend on the local authorities who haven't got their sites ready and would have to do a lot of work before they could accept delivery. But still something may come of it and I moved an amendt to provide for a reduction of contributions in case a cheap house could be produced. Wheatley refused to accept it on the ground that it wasn't necessary, which is absurd seeing that the amendt couldn't do any harm if it were not necessary to use it. I think I shall move it again on report and I have told Weir not to show the model to W. until after 3rd reading as he is so stupid. His behaviour over this Bill confirms me in the opinion that his abilities are very limited & that he is by no means quick in picking up new ideas.

I have made considerable progress with the municipal reform Committee. Sam Hoare is to be chairman and I have got S.B. to send out the invitations so as to start work before the recess. I have also got another Committee under weigh to examine Ll.G's proposals on Power. I think that as usual he has only got half the story right. He is very superficial.

My proposals came before the Exec. Comee last Tuesday. As I expected there was some opposition (from Peter Sanders) and unfortunately I had to leave when the discussion was half through to get to the House. Consequently by 7 to 6 the proposals were referred back & I have got to go into them again. Peter always was an owl [?].

Annie had her third party that afternoon but I was unable to leave the House.
Sunday morning

...

The Daily Herald announced yesterday that Oswald Mosley[37] after rejecting 40 invitations from other constituencies had decided to stand at the next election for Ladywood. I always seem to come in for the hardest fighting and it is

---

[37] Oswald Ernald Mosley (1896–1980). MP for Harrow 1918–24 as Conservative until 1920 and then Independent until joining Labour in May 1924. Labour MP for Smethwick 1926–1931 (New Party February to October 1931). Chancellor, Duchy of Lancaster 1929–30. Founder and leader, New Party 1931–32; of British Union of Fascists 1932–40 until interned 1940–44; of Union Movement 1948–66. Succeeded as 6th Bart 1928.

certainly not likely to be easier in future. But I find it difficult to believe that he could win Ladywood and if he lost I should imagine he would flit off at once. He wouldn't want to be out of the House for long.

...

3 August 1924
37 Eaton Square, SW1

My dear Ida,
  ...

Thanks for the draft of A's article.[38] I knew he had written one because he read an extract from it at one of our meetings but I had not seen it. It is well written, but I wish he hadn't done it because I feel it will tend to confirm the sort of distrustful feeling which some of our party have about him. They dont suspect him of wanting to bring about another Coalition but they say he still has a Coalition mind and that in this hankering after "co-operation" he is not in touch with the general sentiment of the party. As a matter of fact I agree with them and although I believe he and S.B. are on quite friendly terms again I think they regard the situation differently at bottom in that A. positively desires co-operation whereas S.B. reluctantly accepts it. There is a big difference between the L[iberal] U[nionist]'s of 1886 and the Churchillites of today. The former had a solid body of votes which they could bring into the field either for or against the Conservatives. The latter have no such army. W.C. himself has the greatest difficulty in finding a seat that will take him and it is questionable whether his followers will not merely keep out men who would be actual members of our party. Actually arrangements have been made in respect of about 9 seats which at present are being kept dark but I am sure that speaking generally there is no desire on the part of Unionists or Liberals to make a bargain.

So this beastly Irish problem[39] is with us again & of course Ll.G. has plunged in & is urging immediate legislation with the hope of forcing an election on an issue which he thinks would be favourable to himself. I call it downright unpatriotic because the only chance of a peaceful issue is to gain time for an accommodation. Fortunately we have been able to persuade the Govt to content themselves with the introduction of a Bill, and then to wait till the end of October. I don't think we could resist the proposal to make the Commission function but we should probably have to add an amendment which would be aired in the Lords defining the terms of reference so as to make it clear that what

---

[38] In 'Parties and Prospects' in the *Evening News* on 30 July 1924 Austen set out the case for cooperation with sympathetic Liberals in order to make Baldwin's recent less welcoming speeches on the subject appear less hostile.

[39] In August 1924 the Irish Free State insisted the British government appoint a representative from the North of Ireland to the Boundary Commission as Ulster refused to do so.

the Commission had to decide was an adjustment of boundaries & not a big transfer of territory. I have been looking up the debates on the subject in which I myself took part & it is quite clear that that was the intention of the British signatories. I stated in the House in 1922 that it was on that interpretation that the House accepted the Treaty and no one challenged it. But I fear that Ll.G. did give Michael Collins reason to think he would get Fermanagh & Tyrone and at the same time allowed Craig to believe that no such transfer could take place. Many well informed people believe now that nothing can stop the proclamation of an Irish Republic & if that did happen it is difficult to see how civil war could be averted. Still I hope that in the next 2 months some agreement will be made and that when we meet again on Oct 28 the danger will be over.

...

17 August 1924
Loubcroy Lodge, Oykell, by Lairg

My dear Hilda,

...

I am trying for the present to forget politics but every post brings in requests to speak somewhere or other. The fact is we have not got an unlimited number of speakers who can take the platform effectively & if I get off with ½ doz speeches I shall be lucky.

I never told you of a conversation I had some time ago with a junior member of the late Govt & if I do so now you must not take it as expressing my own views or ideas. I was trying to find out what was the real feeling among our rank & file about S.B. I am not sure how far he is competent to give it but he assured me that he was in touch with many of them and declared that the dissatisfaction was deep & wide. It was not that they disliked him; quite the contrary but he had not the qualities of a leader and the question was what was to be done about it. I said nothing could be done unless the party had made up its mind who it wanted instead and when it had done that I didn't think S.B. was the man to make trouble if he were not chosen. My friend then said that many of the younger men were much impressed with Austen. They greatly admired his speeches in the H. of C. they saw he could "make rings round" S.B. in the matter of debate, resourcefulness and knowledge of procedure. But the older men had not re-gained confidence in him. They said he was better in Opposition than in office, but above all he was a Coalitionist still in mind though he might have given it up in practice. He was inclined always to view things from the point of an alliance or an understanding with men who were not the men the Conservative party desired to see among their leaders (F.E. & W.C. if not Ll.G.) Consequently they were not inclined to accept Austen and if his name were to be put up there would be a bitter controversy. "Some again" went on my friend "mention Horne, but he is thought to be rather an opportunist. And others would like you but they think you wouldn't put up against Austen". "But Jix", said I "You haven't mentioned him." "Oh! No", was the reply "Not Jix. I don't think you would find ten men in favour of Jix. The fact is they want someone who is more of a gentleman!" And then he went on very diffidently to ask whether my position had been accurately gauged. I replied that I had given no thought to such an idea and I could only say that nothing would induce me to take the leadership of the party unless I were absolutely forced into it. "Ah well" he conceded "I think you had better give some thought to it. For it might come to this that others might be asked to avoid a controversy by withdrawing their claims in your favour." There the matter dropped and I have given no more thought to what I would do in such circumstances because they haven't arisen and obviously until they did one could not have the material for a decision. They are very unlikely to arise & I devoutly hope for the sake of my own peace of mind that they never will. But I do sometimes amuse myself by thinking what I should do now if I had the responsibility of leadership. And what I should not do! I know every one of my colleagues who was worth anything would have some special question assigned to him to consider during the autumn with such experts as he could command. I would not necessarily have a programme which included everything but I should try to be prepared with information which would enable me to formulate a policy about everything. In particular now I should begin to pick out particular industries & work up the case for "McKenna dutying" them. And I should get out a new policy for agriculture. In fact I've thought of it already. It was the sight of flour being put up in Chicago while we looked on helplessly that gave me the brain wave. My plan is to set up a Wheat Commission independent of govt and to let them build the number of elevators in the main ports sufficient to store a large reserve. Whenever the price went above a certain level the Commission would loose out their reserves till it came down again. And on the other hand whenever the price of wheat fell below a certain figure the Commission would buy up the *home* production at a minimum price. Thus by this scheme

1. English agriculture is given confidence in a fair price.
2. The agricultural labourer would receive a fair wage.
3. The consumer is protected against fluctuations in the price of bread.
4. National security in time of war is increased.

I have sent this scheme to Mackinder & asked him to "vet it" & give me names of wheat magnates who would advise. I have also mentioned it to S.B. who didn't seem to take it in & to Edward Wood who received it with enthusiasm.

Municipal Reform, Social Insurance, & Electrical Power I have of course got going already. This is the only constructive work that *is* going on in our Party and no one is ever invited to put forward any ideas.

Well, its a rum world!

24 August 1924
Loubcroy Lodge

My dear Ida,

...

It has rained here every day this week and most days the rain has been heavy & persistent so that shooting has been difficult ... But I have been shooting well & have enjoyed my days very much. And the river has been fishable and I have caught 3 salmon & lost several more.

Politics has receded for the time into the background except that by almost every post I get a letter to say "Could you, by any chance, spare a moment to come & make a speech – or two speeches – in this district"? but I quote the Central Office & get rid of most.

Ireland looks threatening, but I have a feeling that the crisis will blow over. Only Ll.G. & his friends want an election over it.

7 September 1924
Westbourne

My dear Hilda,

...

I enjoyed very much the short week I had at Portpatrick. ... One afternoon I went with Frank to show him how to fish for trout in one of Inskip's lochs and I found him a very keen and promising pupil. Another day we took out lunch & walked – all four of us – a round of perhaps 12 miles partly by road, partly over the moors which were as wild and lonely as one could wish even though not high, and partly by the shore. Then I got two days partridge shooting ... Finally we made a motor expedition to the Mull of Galloway ... The short grass on the top of these cliffs was decorated with small pink flowers reminding one of pink centaury only single and on short stalks, almost sessile. I know I have found the plant before, in Wales I think, but I cant recollect its name. ... If I go to Portpatrick again I shall certainly take my Bentham as it is a rich district from the botanical point of view. ...

...

So we are spending the rest of this month here and we have laid out for ourselves a programme which almost resembles a general election except that there wont be a lot of *public* speaking in it. It began last night with a visit to a club whist drive & dance and on Monday we have two more. After that practically every day there is a succession of meetings, visits, addresses to women's clubs & workers leagues and calls both by day & by night upon supporters. It is a strenuous business but it will show my people that when the House is not sitting I really do take advantage of it to come among them, while on my side it will give me confidence as to what the man in the street is thinking & saying and it will leave me free during October when I shall be touring the country. What I hear at present is that Russia is not popular, that our people are working harder & more efficiently, that a good many are dissatisfied with the choice of Mosley "a richer man than Mr Chamberlain". There is a good deal of talk, as is natural, about a General Election in November, but I am still as sceptical as ever. But I think there *is* a possibility that R.M. might find himself obliged to resign and in that case it seems to me his best game would be to advise the King to send for S.B. and let us once more be on the defensive as the outgoing Govt whenever the appeal to the country came. I certainly cant imagine the Labour wire pullers deluding themselves into the idea that they could obtain a clear majority on their record in connection with Russia, Germany and unemployment.

I shouldn't be sorry if we did come back again though I believe it would be better for our Party that we should remain out until a General Election comes. For one thing the present govt would continue to accumulate *dis*credit, and for another we could carry a constructive programme nearer to maturity. I have heard nothing more from Mackinder about wheat reserves and must remind him of his promise.

...

I have undertaken to write an article for a new Harmsworth encyclopaedia on Personality & Equipment for Success. The Editor suggested a fee of 30 guineas but observed that he knew this would not appeal to me so much as the opportunity of reaching a great circle of serious minded young people anxious for instruction. He is entirely mistaken. My forte is not in teaching but in doing things, and I only consent reluctantly to undertake so much teaching as seems necessary to induce people to let me do things. On the other hand I am very badly in need of money and I would have demanded fifty guineas if I hadn't been afraid that he would withdraw altogether! Alas! even Elliotts has failed me and has done unaccountably badly this year. Its dividend is to be reduced from 15% to 10% thereby seriously curtailing my already curtailed income. Supertax which always lags behind changes of income is quite out of proportion to present circumstances and must again be paid out of capital. I cant go on indefinitely like this, but if necessary we must let or sell our house in Eaton Square & burrow into a flat like Austen. It is tiresome, but we are not worrying ourselves about it seeing that ruin is still some way off.

...

13 September 1924
Westbourne

My dear Ida,
...
We have had a hectic week here. Annie has lived on her bicycle and has paid innumerable visits. I have addressed three women's clubs, attended a dance & visited 2 mornings and 2 nights besides presiding at a Committee of the Birm.

Association & putting one morning in at Elliotts. Mosley has I fancy been doing much the same only he has naturally done more public speaking. Up to now he has avoided any personal references and I am considering how I shall treat him at my first meeting next Wednesday. The general feeling is that he will not do as well as Dunstan. On the other hand some Labour people we met one day & with whom we entered into conversation said that "We thought Dunstan was a speaker but he can lick Dunstan into fits."

My own visits chiefly surprise me by their revelation of the comfort & even luxury in which some of the lower middle class & upper working class live. A butcher on the Dudley Road (not a very choice neighbourhood – his clientele must be almost entirely working class) casually dropped out the information that he and his friends shot 42 brace partridges [sic] last Saturday on their shoot at Marston Green, while a shopkeeper with a beer license drove me home last night in his closed covered & luxuriously upholstered car!

Today I had an invitation to go partridge shooting myself & joyfully accepted it. But it rained most of the day and birds were so scarce that at 4 o'clock our host threw it up in disgust & we came home. Looking at the blackened stooks in the stubbles I asked myself why no one had ever thought of drying corn with a fan. You would take it into a barn & pass it through a drying chamber on an endless chain. I should have thought it might have paid well in a season like this. I wrote to Mackinder, by the way, but have had no reply so I suppose he's away again.

There is no doubt that both the Russian and the German loan are thoroughly unpopular and Austen's courageous "letter to a correspondent" on the Dawes report is not welcomed by the rank & file. The more I think of it the more confident I feel that R.M. will find some way of avoiding a dissolution even if he cant avoid resignation. His own preface to "Socialism" followed by the £30,000 in McVitie & Price[40] *and* his explanation put the cap on the climax. I cannot imagine anything more hopelessly foolish from the political point of view. He can certainly give S.B. points now. Why, no Socialist will dare to make an interruption at a public meeting now lest he should have Ramsay thrust down his throat. Of course I dont suspect him of anything dishonourable. But there is no getting over the facts (1) that his practice does not square with his preaching (2) that his first explanation viz that he was only the technical proprietor of the shares was disingenuous and misleading. Incidentally he has made his dear old friend's baronetcy stink uncommonly high. Lord! Lord! what a funny world. *I hope he stays in a bit longer*!

...

---

[40] On 13 September 1924 the press carried MacDonald's confirmation of an earlier story that his old friend Alexander Grant had lent him for his lifetime a Daimler and the dividend on £30,000 in McVitie & Price shares (plus another £10,000) to relieve him of burdens while in office. In April 1924 Grant had been recommended for a Baronetcy.

20 September 1924
Westbourne

My dear Hilda,

...

You are right in supposing that we have had another strenuous week. I don't know how many visits Annie has paid but they must have passed the 100 and included some "red" strongholds. ...

My work has included 4 nights out, a tour of a Brewery, a visit to a football match, addresses to mens & womens clubs, 3 Committees of Birm & Midland Un. Assocns, a visit to the annual meeting of a football assocn, a consultation with Baldwin, James Craig, Jacker and Bobby Monsell in London and the public meeting aforesaid, which was so packed that I had to address an overflow afterwards. As I had spoken inside for over an hour against a constant stream of interruptions you can imagine that there wasn't much left of my voice. I really feel that we shall have to do something to stop this rowdyism; its discreditable, and it doesn't give a fair chance either to the speaker or to that part of the audience which wants to hear what he has to say. I told some of my people the next night that if my next meeting was interrupted in the same way they ought to do a little retaliation but I have since learned that some of Annie's women friends didn't wait for advice but went to Mosley's meeting that night and gave him a very warm time. Some say he had to sit down 3 times and he was told that they would return to future meetings & break them up if his people did not behave themselves at ours. The general conclusion I have come to so far is that O.M. is not doing as well as he expected. His speeches have not been brilliant – in fact they seem to me rather feeble in matter – and though the more snobbish Labour people like to have a rich man and a "man of birth" to represent them he is a stumbling block to the extremists. My people certainly are more confident than last year.

I asked my agent if he heard anything about the West. He said the agent there was rather despondent as there seemed to be a different spirit from that in Ladywood and he couldn't get anyone to do any work. He was so cautious in his replies that I couldn't get very definite indications from him but I cannot help feeling that there must be a good deal of comment on Austen's absence. Lowe is away as usual but most of the other members are about though I don't think any of them are doing quite as much as we are. They haven't got a candidate for the West but it is rumoured that a barrister from London is to be brought down. I daresay it will be all right on the day but I confess I wish A. were going to spend a bit of his holiday down here.

... I remain firmly of the opinion that there will be no General Election yet awhile. The Liberals are obviously preparing to run away and with the same desire animating them and the Govt. a bridge will soon be found. The Irish question looks at present insoluble. Craig is always very cautious and he very wisely did not tell me all that was in his mind. But I came away with the impression that he is fairly confident that the Commission's report would be one that he could accept. What we have to decide is what we shall do. Personally I dont think we ought to reject the Bill but we ought to amend it so as to give directions to the Commission. I don't see how we could do less in fairness to Ulster. But probably this would be out of order in the Commons. Then the Lords would do it and if their amendts on coming back to us were still out of order I think that would be the best way out. We should have done all we could & should throw the responsibility on to the Govt. The Commission would be appointed & if its Report were reasonable Ulster would accept it. I think it very possible that in that case Cosgrave[41] if he accepted it would be turned out & succeeded by a Republican Govt which perhaps might be left to stew in its own juice till it went bankrupt and asked to be taken back. On the other hand if the Lords amdt were not out of order it would then be disagreed with by the H. of C. & the question would arise What shd the Lords do then. My feeling is that they should insist & risk a General Election. I think R.M. would jump at the chance of side tracking Russia & the Daimler but I am disposed to think we should come out best though perhaps with a very narrow majority. Jacker thought if we went to the country now we should have a majority of 60 but I don't believe that unless we could get out a better programme than we have.

S.B. is going for Safeguarding of Industries at Newcastle I am glad to say. The very storm of protests & suggestions of breach of faith which this will arouse among free traders will bring the whole question into prominence again and I feel very confident that it will show a big change of feeling. Talking with Jacker & Bobby they were saying we must find an agriculture policy so I told them of mine and they were both delighted and wanted to "get on to it at once". I don't know how much they know of agriculture but they were quick to see the appeal it would make. That devil Mackinder has disappeared completely. Letters bring no acknowledgement, and I dont know where to turn to get it explored. We are to have a Shadow Cabinet (Peers included!) on Thursday so I think I shall get hold of Sam Hoare & see what he thinks of it.

Very private S.B. met the Governor at Aix and he told him that Jix had said to him. There are only two men the country cares about – myself & Baldwin. My comment was Why drag in Velasquez?

By the way, doesn't Ramsay's "explanation" remind you of

"I *dont* believe in princeuple

But oh! I du in *interest* !

...

---

[41] William Thomas Cosgrave (1880–1965). Irish politician. Sinn Fein MP for Kilkenny from 1917 but did not take seat after the 1918 election. Member of Dail for North Kilkenny to 1927 and for Cork City 1927–44. Minister of Local Government 1917–21 and 1922. President, Executive Council of Irish Free State 1922–32; Finance Minister 1922–23; Defence Minister 1924; Leader of Opposition 1932–44.

27 September 1924
Westbourne

My dear Ida,

...

I agree with you that an election could not be confined to Ireland and (partly for that reason) I am not nearly so nervous about it as some of my colleagues. But I think you may take it that the Govt will not be given the chance of trying. I was furious over the party communiqué after the meeting of the Shadow Cabinet. It did not say that we had been unable to reach a decision on account of the wide & deep division of opinion among us, but it invited that suggestion which was supplied with variation and embroideries by nearly all the press. And it was quite untrue! There may have been different shades of opinion but on the main points we were unanimous and we came to definite conclusions. I fear the communiqué must have been referred to S.B. and that he couldn't bring himself to committing us publicly. Unfortunately the natural result is that the rank & file having no lead will be committing themselves to all sorts of different lines. I was very cross.

I am rather concerned about Dunstan's move which strikes me as rather astute. The I.L.P. had not got an official candidate arranged for in the West and if they try to run one now Dunstan will say If you don't leave me alone, I shall go and upset your applecart in Ladywood. On the other hand if you will support me in the West I will help Mosley and between us we shall get both the Chamberlains out. I put this to Austen on Thursday & suggested to him that if he had Dunstan alone to fight it might be necessary to do a little more than he had been doing. Whereat he very testily replied that he *might* go down for a month, and he *might* take a house in the division, but he wasn't prepared to hold the seat on such terms and if his people thought he wasn't doing enough he was quite ready to place his resignation in their hands. I returned a soft answer & appeased him but whether on reflection he will mend his ways I know not.

Our campaign in Ladywood is nearly at an end. Annie tells me that we have between us attended 23 meetings including 3 visits to schools and she has herself paid 157 personal visits while I have done nearly 30 more. My leg still *itches* from the last one I did last night! I had been out shooting all day and had barely time to bathe, change, & swallow a couple of eggs before I was out slumming! A dog's life, but it ought to make a difference when the time comes, oughtn't it? Altogether I had four nights out this week, one of them being a public meeting. For the second time I spoke without notes for over an hour against a constant stream of disorderly, irrelevant and insulting interruptions. Quite half the audience were Communists and Socialists who had come an hour before the advertised time so as to make sure of getting in. A good many of our own people were in consequence turned away and though I said all I wanted to it must have been very difficult for anyone to follow any arguments. I was thoroughly disgusted and I think it high time we retaliated. I am urging my people to organise something, for until we stop this sort of behaviour public meetings aren't much good locally. Apparently I had a pretty good press in the country as so many of my colleagues spoke to me about the speech when I went to London next day.

... I have now agreed to write the article for St Loe[42] to appear on Dec 6th. But I fear it will take a lot of writing to make up anything substantial in the way of income.

...

5 October 1924
Westbourne

My dear Hilda,

The Liberals have shown that their deeds are as little to be relied upon as their words in estimating what they will do next. During the recess they seem to have come to the conclusion that a repetition of the Poplar affair would ruin them finally and that at all costs they must get the Socialists out before the next Budget stole their last patent medicine, viz. Land nationalisation. Of course, once they had made up their minds on that (and I imagine that Ll.G. and Mond had a good deal to do with it, although actuated by somewhat different motives) nothing could stop them and the end was bound to come and come soon. But is it not like them? They come breathing fire and slaughter on the Campbell case, Sir J. Simon actually drafts the motion of censure and the moment we put it down they get cold feet and want to try something else. I feel that in nine cases out of ten these "tactics" dont come off nowadays. The thing is to go for what you believe, whether you win or lose by it, and then at least people will believe in your sincerity. I agree entirely with you that the election will not be fought on the Hastings[43] affair whether it comes soon or late.[44] It will be fought on the Labour Govt's record, which of course includes Hastings, but only among the minor items. The major issues will be unemployment and the Russian Treaty.

Your suggestion that R.M. might avoid an election by getting the Bolshies to say they wouldn't ratify is ingenious and it certainly would be a way out. But although I believe R.M. must look forward to an election with "igstreme"

---

[42] John St Loe Strachey (1860–1927). A Liberal Unionist from 1886 and co-editor of the party's paper. Contributor to *Spectator* from 1887 and Editor and Proprietor 1898–1925. Editor, *Cornhill Magazine* 1896–97.

[43] Patrick Gardiner Hastings (1880–1952). Labour MP for Wallsend 1922–26. Attorney-General 1924. Retired from the Bar 1948; author of several plays. Knighted 1924.

[44] J.R. Campbell, acting editor of the Communist *Worker's Weekly*, was arrested under the Incitement to Mutiny Act (1797) on 5 August 1924. The case was withdrawn on 13 August. Although Sir Patrick Hastings (the Attorney-General) defended the decision in Parliament on 30 September, the Conservatives and Liberals subsequently demanded an inquiry. MacDonald made these confidence motions in the debate on 8 October and was defeated by 364 votes to 198.

disgust as well as apprehension I doubt his finding it possible to avoid it now. His own people have persuaded themselves that they are so popular that they have a chance of a clear majority and I am inclined to think that they would be very critical of anything that seemed to indicate an unwillingness for the fray.

I needn't tell you how it appeals to me. The idea of having to go through that ordeal of humiliation again is sickening – and the expense is ruinous. There certainly must be an extraordinary attraction somewhere about a career which involves such sacrifices of everything that makes life tolerable. But I have got to go through with it somehow and run the risk of being "outed" for my pains into the bargain. Not that I think the risk as great as before. A speedy election would I think be favourable both to Austen and myself, as neither of our opponents has had time to dig himself in. Labour is making a tremendous effort here. A fresh M.P. comes to speak in Ladywood every week. Today they have a grand pow-wow at the Town Hall with Wheatley as principal speaker. I fancy he will make an extreme speech but will avoid personal attacks, but I shall watch for the report tomorrow with interest.

I was so wrong last time about the result of the election that I am chary of prophecy this time. My impression however is that we shall come back much the strongest party and that we have just a chance of getting a clear working majority. What I pray for above all things is that one party will have a majority sufficient to carry it on for 5 years. I would rather the Socialists had it than that we should be condemned to a further period of such doubts and uncertainties as we have now. Our experiences should be convincing on the results of proportional representation.

Annie returned from Newcastle last night pretty well done up ... The [annual party] conference seems to have been very successful in spite of the absence of M.P.'s and Annie reports that both Jackson & Blain acquitted themselves extremely well. The most remarkable feature of the proceedings was the tremendous ovation given to Selborne[45] after his speech on agriculture. It shows how necessary it is that we should have clear ideas as to what we mean to do and I regret that we have had a wholly insufficient time to work out a general policy which would in any way satisfy me. There was apparently some criticism of S.B.'s speech both for its omissions and for its defence of the Dawes Scheme. The latter I expected and I think S.B. was right not to shirk it but to put his views forward with courage and completeness. But for a meeting of that kind I think he would have been well advised to touch on more topics and even if he had spoken for a little longer (he was well under the hour) the audience would not have minded. R.M. spoke at Derby for 1hr 47 minutes!

---

[45] William Waldegrave Palmer (1859–1942). Liberal MP for Hampshire East 1885–92 (Liberal Unionist from 1886) and Liberal Unionist MP for Edinburgh West 1892–95. Under-Secretary, Colonies 1895–1900; First Lord of Admiralty, 1900–5; High Commissioner for South Africa 1905–10; President, Board of Agriculture 1915–16. Succeeded as 2nd Earl of Selborne 1895.

...

Alas! tomorrow I have a mass meeting at Rugby – to be followed by an overflow. I wish I enjoyed these things like Jicks. He has arranged for 28 meetings!

...

11 October 1924
Westbourne

My dear Ida,

What *am* I to say to you and Hilda in return for such a gift. I can tell you that when I opened your letter this morning and saw what it contained it brought a very big lump into my throat. Indeed I felt at first that you had carried generosity too far, for although, thank goodness, you are comfortably off I know you cant give away such sums as you have done without making a very real sacrifice of something else. But on further consideration and especially when I found you were doing the same thing by Austen I came to the conclusion that I would accept your "contribution" in the spirit in which it is offered and be very proud and thankful that we brothers have such sisters. And if ever you and Hilda should find that you have gone further than you ought I depend upon you to tell me so frankly and let us share whatever sacrifices may be necessary. Hoskins is doing very badly. It has not yet got out its accounts for the year which ended on 31st July but when they do come I expect to find that it has incurred a substantial loss. Fortunately we put something by against a rainy day and I hope that before it is exhausted things may improve, but it does cause me a certain anxiety because in the past it has provided a considerable share of the family income. Meanwhile you have relieved my mind very materially and moreover have given me a real thrill of exultation at the strength of the family feeling which has prompted you to help.

We didn't know what was going to happen on Wednesday till quite late in the evening. I was against "tactics" and I believe, if it had rested with me alone I should have refused to go back on our motion of censure. I was terrified lest the Liberals should put us in the cart by voting with the Govt in the last division. But Asquith and Ll.G. gave us the most positive assurances and as the event proved they were able this time to implement them. The Attorney made the best speech of his career in the House and shook up our people a good deal at the time while the Liberals obviously had no more stomach for the fight. But old Squiff retrieved the situation in the most masterly way. He took the only line which could save us and chaffed the Govt unmercifully on their mock heroics till he got his own people once more into a comfortable frame of mind. Baldwin did very well and Hogg's summing up was a real tour-de-force. I confess to having been rattled by the special pleading on the other side and only when I heard Hogg did I realise how strong the case against the Govt still remained.

What will happen now? In any event it seems very improbable that the Socialists will come back to office. But whether we shall succeed in getting a clear majority no one can say with certainty and if we should be returned as the strongest party but without a working majority our position will be one of great embarrassment. However its no use speculating about that now. I am very glad that the election campaign is to be a short one. Its coming now is certainly to the advantage of Austen and myself. I regard Austen as safe and I think the chances are in my favour though I don't look for a big majority.

Just before the dissolution was announced Lowe wrote to me to say he should not stand again. It occurred to me at once that Edgbaston might invite me to swap but I had already determined that I could not do that unless I were first defeated in Ladywood. The same considerations however did not apply to Austen and accordingly I saw him and asked him whether he would like a change. He was rather nervous about the effect on his people in the West but finally said if things could be amicably arranged with them he would consider an invitation from Edgbaston favourably. Thereupon I wrote to Byng [Kenrick] who is now Chairman in Edgbaston, but immediately afterwards came the announcement of a General Election at once. This left no time for such delicate negotiations and so I saw Byng last night and persuaded him to write to Lowe and ask him to reconsider his decision. Meanwhile however he had taken preliminary soundings and reported that I should be readily accepted but that there was no enthusiasm about Austen. This was rather a shock as I thought they would have welcomed the opportunity but apparently he has lost touch with the younger generation in Birmingham and though I expect the thing could be arranged it would evidently require some negotiation. I don't know what Lowe will say. I expect he is jibbing at the expense but he may jump at the opportunity of putting the party under an obligation in the hope of a peerage. I shouldn't be sorry to have him there a little longer just in case of any accident!

I had a most excellent meeting at Rugby – a packed hall and a most attentive audience. Some Socialists were present but didn't make themselves objectionable. I wish I could get such meetings here. I had a long talk with my chairman on Thursday. He wanted me to have no public meeting at all but devote myself to addressing people in the courts and factories. I was much attracted by the idea but on consideration I am convinced it would not do. It would be said that I was afraid of meetings and of questions and I should eventually be driven into holding them after all. So I have arranged about 7 or 8 and shall do some speaking outside but only in the Midlands. Last night I had a private meeting of some of my own supporters and afterwards wrote my election address and composed some leaflets. Next week I shall be in full swing.

. . .

I brought up my Agricultural policy at the Shadow Cabinet this week. Austen was inclined to jump on it but Sam Hoare said he had mentioned it to one of the acutest minds in the city and so far from dismissing it with contempt he was much struck with it and thought it well worth following out. It is impossible to do anything just now but several of my colleagues are rather keen about it and guess more will be heard of it one of these days.

…

19 October 1924
Westbourne

My dear Hilda,

…

… I feel more confident this time than I did last about my own seat and Birm. generally. At the last minute yesterday a Liberal candidate appeared. He is a son of the old alderman who baked the "Two loaves of Bingley Hall" but very unlike his father. Claude who knows him tells me he is a bore and a crank obsessed with a bitter hatred of the Chamberlain family which arises I fancy from the jealousy of a weak & vain man. Last year he stood for Edgbaston and received 5000 votes. I doubt if he will save his £150 in Ladywood or make much difference to the other candidates. Some of his nomination papers are signed by men who we know voted for Dunstan last time; on the other hand I think he is bound to detach some Liberals who would have voted for me rather than a Socialist. Generally speaking cautious & friendly observers expect that I shall maintain my majority; I shall be disappointed if I dont increase it. I was very nervous about Jephcott of whom I heard bad accounts last week but I met him yesterday and found him in pretty confident mood. He had more workers than last time he said and his meetings were quieter. My only meeting so far was also quiet though in a rowdy district but it was the night Ramsay spoke here and I fancy all the toughs had gone to the rag market to see him.

I agree with all you say of Ramsay's speeches. They have been deplorable and I have been surprised at the want of matter or argument. He strikes me as having undertaken a task for which his strength was quite inadequate. He was tired to start with but his inordinate vanity drove him on and his mind has simply refused to work. Moreover he sees that the game is up, that the Bolshie Treaty excites no enthusiasm, that the unemplt figures hit him knock out blows week after week and that the Press is against him all round. He is mad with despair and vexation and in his rage he throws all dignity and self control to the winds, as when he compares his political opponents to "mangy dogs sniffing round a garbage heap"! Alas! for the highbrow who claimed to be "intellectually superior to other parties". This is only Jack Jones' "Dirty Dogs" again.

My feeling is one of considerable confidence and I confess that I am influenced by the optimism of that very astute old rascal George Younger. I have calculated that to obtain a majority of 21, which is about the least one could work with, Liberals would have to win 160 seats, Labour 125, but Unionists only 59. And of course any additional win counts 2 on a division. I think we have a fair chance of getting that, especially with the arrangements that have been made. If so, as you say, we may soon be all playing the game of Cabinet building. So amusing when you have no responsibility and so nerve wracking when you have.

I am very glad you like the article [in Encyclopaedia Britannica]. Did I tell you that I had undertaken one on Housing for St Loe? His son,[46] by the way, is "Labour" candidate for Aston against Evelyn Cecil.[47] Really these modern youths are too impossible, not because they are Socialists, but because they have no respect for their fathers. But to return to the article, it owes much to Annie's criticisms. I always say her mind works like that of the typical man in the street & as she doesn't in the least mind saying what she thinks I have to writhe under very plain comments. My agent rushed me into writing my election address in a hurry. I sent it to Annie who was coming down next day in the train and when she arrived she tore it into such tatters that I had to rewrite it entirely from beginning to end. Fortunately this time it was approved and I have learned since that in the constituency it is considered to be "lovely" and compared very favourably with Austen's which is criticised as colourless. ...

Annie isn't at all well. Her cough sticks to her like a leech in spite of every precaution. ... Fortunately Oswald Mosley has also got a throat!

26 October 1924
Westbourne

My dear Ida,

Many thanks for your letter written before the explosion of the bomb![48] My! what a bang! Never do I recollect such a sensation during an election. Much remains obscure and mysterious at present. What had R.M. to do with the publication? One cannot imagine that it could have been written sent and published without his sanction. And yet his colleagues are evidently dumbfounded and utterly taken by surprise. They dont know what to say. Ponsonby[49]

---

[46] (Evelyn) John St Loe Strachey (1901–63). Labour MP for Birmingham Aston 1929–31, Dundee (later Dundee West) 1945–63. Under-Secretary for Air 1945–46; Minister of Food 1946–50; Secretary for War 1950–51.

[47] Evelyn Cecil (1865–1941). Assistant Private Secretary to Lord Salisbury as P.M. 1891–92 and 1895–1902. Conservative MP for Hertford 1898–1900 and Aston 1900–29. Member of many Select Committees and Second Chamber Conference 1918, Royal Commission on Honours 1922 and Safety & Health in Coal Mines 1935–38. Created Baron Rockley 1934.

[48] On 25 October, four days before polling, the *Daily Mail* published the famous 'Zinoviev letter' purportedly from the President of the Communist International urging the British Communist Party to mobilise support for the Russian treaties and intensify its activity in the armed forces to wage a future class war.

[49] Arthur Augustus William Ponsonby (1871–1946). Diplomatic Service 1894–1902; Private Secretary to Campbell-Bannerman 1905–8. Liberal MP for Stirling Burghs 1908–18 and Labour

feebly murmurs that he thinks it must be a forgery. Thomas more boldly declares that either it is a forgery, or the Govt had acted courageously and patriotically. But the damage is done and they will never get the public to believe before Wednesday that the Foreign Office has made a bloomer which is so obviously disadvantageous to the Foreign Secretary or that the publication is not due to the knowledge that the Daily Mail would publish if they did not. In my opinion it has put the lid on the Labour Party and will mean sufficient seats to give us a majority.

I enclose one local cartoonists picture over which I have laughed till my sides ached. He really is first rate and just before the election I took Blain some specimens of his work to try & get him to commission some pictures for leaflets. Apparently he hasn't done so but it did seem to me that this election was pre-eminently one for pictures. I send another one of Ellison's, not so fancy but to show how quick he is to get the salient points. ...

...

What a week! I made 14 speeches myself and Annie has paid innumerable calls. The bate here is very steadily optimistic and confident and though I am still not expecting a large majority I think it should certainly be larger than before especially after the disclosure. I have been very anxious about Jephcott but I begin now to think that he will be all right. One thing I can say & that is that neither Annie nor I have felt the strain this time as much as we did last year. I have had some pretty noisy meetings but the opposition has been less confident and less pugnacious probably feeling their own weakness much more than when they had only to attack. I have been trying for some time now to train myself to rely less on notes when I am speaking. I find it enables me to free my mind more for concentration on my subject and gives me more confidence and more capacity to vary my voice. This week I spoke for a full hour at Walsall on Thursday and yesterday for 45 minutes at Stone in the afternoon and 55 minutes at Stoke in the evening and my voice is quite fresh and unstrained. I had no notes at any of the meetings except quotations & they were all packed from floor to ceiling and most successful. ... Last night I observed with much gratification how many of my audience (mostly working men and women) sat with their heads craned forward and their mouths open in rapt attention till the very end and as I came out I overheard a woman say "I could go on listening to him all night". I spoke not only about the Russian Treaty but on constructive policy. Employment food prices and housing. I am anxious, if we do come in, really to make the next Govt one that will leave behind a mark on social reforms.

MP for Sheffield Brightside 1922–30. Under-Secretary, Foreign Office 1924; to Dominion Office 1929; Parliamentary Secretary, Ministry of Transport 1929–31; Chancellor of Duchy of Lancaster 1931; Labour Leader in Lords 1931–35, resigned from Labour Party on the formation of National Government in May 1940. A founder of Union of Democratic Control 1914. Created Baron Ponsonby of Shulbrede 1930.

Between ourselves I expect to see Austen Foreign Secretary tho' what the Markis will say I can't think of without a shudder! For myself I know S.B. would like me back at the Treasury, but I have always foreseen that he might have to find room for Horne there. I shall of course leave myself entirely in his hands but I remain convinced that I might be a great Minister of Health but am not likely to be more than a second rate Chancellor. I suppose my friends would be disappointed & think I had gone downhill if I returned to Health but that would soon pass off and I should be very happy to find myself there again. You seem to suggest the possibility of my having neither. I don't think that at all likely but I would take the Colonies and believe I could be useful there too. I believe there is very good work to be done in separating Dominions from Colonies and Protectorates.

We are to have our votes counted on Wednesday night which means we shant get our results till about 3 on Thursday morning. I wanted the count on Thursday & instructed Hewins to ask for it so I don't understand how this arrangement has been made unless Austen barged in.

...

1 November 1924
Lytchett Heath, Poole

My dear Ida,

...

What an ordeal we had to go through. I had very good meetings to finish up with and when we drove round on Wednesday there was far more enthusiasm shown than I had ever seen before. The last figures I had seen of the canvass were not very encouraging as they indicated that the struggle would be very close but I had hoped that as the canvass was more thoroughly done than before I should poll a higher percentage of my promises. I was accordingly a good deal strengthened in my confidence by what I saw on Wednesday morning. In the afternoon however rain began to fall and continued to get heavier & heavier right up till 9 o'clock. Moreover the reports I got from Committee Rooms though cheerful & confident didn't seem to me to indicate that we were doing as well as I had hoped and so when we went down in the evening we prepared ourselves to face the worst with calmness. We went to the office of the Mail about 10.30 and the returns from the country were very encouraging but about midnight we adjourned to the Town Hall and Hewins told me at once that the voting papers seemed about equal and the issue entirely doubtful. What we were not prepared for was a $4\frac{1}{2}$ hours wait while they were counted & counted again. Mosley was beside himself, walking up and down the tables, hectoring & bullying the officials & once even going out to address his friends in the square to whom he announced that he was in! The first count gave me a majority of 30, then it was said to be 15 then 7, then I was out by 2 & finally at 4.30 the Lord Mayor announced that I was returned by 77. The galleries of the Town Hall were filled with Socialists who booed at us & shouted directions to the counters in the most scandalous fashion. They even invaded the floor & yelled insults which our feeble Lord Mayor pretended not to hear. Annie was splendid. She and I sat calmly by not interfering with the proceedings but waiting for whatever the decision might be. Of course we hated the thought of being beaten especially by that viper, but we consoled ourselves with the thought that we should be free of Ladywood and at times I almost persuaded myself that that would be preferable to a victory by a margin of less than 50. We got to bed somewhere about 5 and I at any rate slept till 8 quite soundly. Annie got a fit of coughing which kept her awake and you will not be surprised to hear that she is in bed. Her Dr has ordered her to remain there for a week and then to go away for a blow for another week. Her cough has been most distressing to hear & increasingly painful to herself & she is pretty well worn out with that & the nervous strain but I hope that she will soon be herself again as I think she started much stronger this year than last.

My people have nothing to reproach themselves with as my poll was actually increased by some 500 votes but the Socialists increased theirs by nearly 2000. This is the feature of the elections in Birmingham and it is difficult to account for unless it is due to their confidence that they could win if they exerted themselves and to the concentrated attention the whole party has bestowed upon us. If we were to lose a seat I am glad it should be Sir H. Austin's for he is the worst representative I have ever come across, never attending the House or doing anything in his constituency. I think we might easily win that seat back with another candidate but whether we can go on holding the inner ring where our majorities have been so much reduced seems doubtful.

Annie & I have made up our minds not to think about our future until the situation had cleared up. There may not be another election for years.

Now the question is what shall I be asked to do. I see the Evening Standard yesterday said most people thought I should go back to Health. This would be my own wish and after some hesitation Annie also agrees but I couldn't refuse the Treasury if S.B. pressed it and I am not worrying myself about it. I think many of my friends would be disappointed if I didn't return to Downing St but that would not weigh with me an iota. After all, if one is to look at it from the point of view of personal credit – which I honestly don't – I should eventually get much more if I had been able to make a success of the M/H than if I had been an ordinary C. of E. And if you look back at recent Chancellors you wont find one who stood out sufficiently to be remembered for his work there.

What alarms me now is the size of our majority which is most dangerous. We shall never keep any discipline & jealousies & intrigues will have a grand run. Unless we leave our mark as social reformers the country will take it out of us hereafter but what we do will depend on how the Cabinet is made up. Poor S.B.!

6 November 1924
37 Eaton Square, SW1

My dear Hilda,

   ...

Well I am Minister of Health again. I could have been Chancellor but told S.B. that whilst I was prepared to do what he wanted I preferred my old job. Since then he has made another of his astounding gaffes. He told me that he had offered Horne Labour but appeared to think his only difficulty would be in getting rid of his business commitments. While I was there Horne's letter of refusal came in. I didn't see it but S.B. said "Oh he wont take it." It was only afterwards that I learned how deeply he was hurt at the way he had been treated. S.B. told me he was going to take Winston into the Govt, & said "I suppose there would be a howl from the party if he were made Chancellor["]. I said I supposed there would, but there would be a howl at his coming in any way and though the idea had never entered my mind before I thought it was worth further consideration. We discussed other appts & then S.B. said he had "another visitor" & I left being carefully piloted by his Sec. so as not to meet the visitor. But I went to see Jackson upstairs & he pointed out a hat & coat which he said were Winstons! That gave the show away. S.B. must have offered him the Exchequer as soon as I left.

I am in despair and see rifts splits & resignations not immediately but in the near future.

Just when all looked so rosy.

12 November 1924
37 Eaton Square, SW1

My dear Ida,

   ...

I am *very* busy answering shoals of letters of congratulation from all parts of the country and all sorts of people. They all express thankfulness at my return to the Ministry of Health and it is a real gratification to feel that one has inspired so much confidence.

Tomorrow I start planning out a four years programme! The staff fairly fall on my neck!

   ...

15 November 1924
Westbourne

My dear Hilda,

…

I had a very pleasant time with the Stanhopes[50] last week. I like him and think there is a good deal in him in spite of that unfortunate mistake he made over Miss Douglas Pennant.[51] She has great charm (being Irish – a daughter of Lord Sligo) … She is an enthusiastic admirer of the present Minister of Health and when he bungles his pheasants finds that they really offered quite impossible shots whereas if he kills them he is a paragon of marksmanship. Fortunately she did not always sit beside me! The other guests were the Spender Clays[52] (he is in the House and she is a sister of Waldorf Astor's) Lord Cromer[53] who is very pleasant & easy though he hasn't inherited his father's brains or strength of character, Lady Younghusband a delightful old lady whose husband is governor of the Tower and the Skiffington Smyths. … We had perfect weather and capital shooting in which at any rate I didn't disgrace myself. … I see I have forgotten to mention the Tryons who were also of the party & who, though neither of them is brilliant, are really "nice" people, straightforward & honest and quite good company into the bargain.

…

Since I last wrote the political situation has cleared very considerably. The Horne incident has provoked less criticism than I feared it might and although I still think that if S.B. had known how to put his case more tactfully it would never had arisen I can see that in the public mind there is some feeling that Horne would have shown himself a bigger man if he had put his pique in his pocket. E. Wood told me that he had himself put this to Horne – he is one of the few men who can criticise others without giving offence, but in Horne's defence it may be said that he went to his interview with every expectation of being

---

[50] James Richard Stanhope (1880–1967). Parliamentary Secretary, War Office 1918–19; Civil Lord of Admiralty 1924–29; Under-Secretary, War Office 1931–34 and Foreign Office 1934–36; First Commissioner of Works 1936–37; President, Board of Education 1937–38; First Lord of Admiralty 1938–39; Leader of Lords 1938–40; Lord President of Council 1939–40. Succeeded as 7th Earl of Stanhope 1905.

[51] Violet Blanche Douglas-Pennant (?-1945). Member, LCC Education Committee; National Insurance Commissioner 1912–18; Commandant, Women's Royal Air Force 1918 until dismissed.

[52] Herbert Henry Spender-Clay (1875–1937). Conservative MP for Tonbridge 1910–37. Parliamentary Commissioner to Charity Commission 1923–24, 1924–29.

[53] Rowland Thomas Baring (1877–1953). Diplomatic Service 1900–1907; Private Secretary to Permanent Under-Secretary for Foreign Affairs 1907–11; Managing Director, Barings Bank 1913–14; ADC to Viceroy of India 1915–16 Equerry-in-Ordinary and Assistant Private Secretary to King 1916–20; Chief of Staff to Duke of Connaught India Mission 1920–21 and to Prince of Wales India visit 1921–22; Lord Chamberlain to H.M. Household 1922–38; Permanent Lord-in-Waiting to George VI 1938–52 and Queen Elizabeth II 1952–53; British Director, Suez Canal Company 1926–50. Succeeded as 2nd Earl of Cromer 1917.

invited to take the Treasury and that the shock he received when the Ministry of Labour was offered instead paralysed his mind during the rest of the conversation. I happened to meet G. Dawson the same evening. He dragged me into a corner to tell me how "splendid" he thought my behaviour but he thought that Horne's previous administration of the Treasury was sufficient reason why he should not go there again. I merely report this because I guess that it reflects S.B.'s mind; he and Dawson see a good deal of each other, I fancy.

I forget if I told you that S.B. sent me a very appreciative note. Indeed what with the Times article and private letters and public speeches I have been overwhelmed with bouquets. They ought to make me very apprehensive of the future but the fact is that I have very considerable confidence in my ability, with the help of the extremely competent staff at the Ministry, to cope with my problems and I have already started to plan out a four year programme. Of course the public thinks of nothing but Housing, but I have told my people to make no mistake. If that had been the only problem I might not have chosen to come back but I want to take the opportunity of dealing with the big questions of rating & valuation, Poor Law, Pensions & Health insurance, and the re-organisation of the medical services. It will be great fun if we dont bust up prematurely.

As to housing I have lost no time. I had a very interesting talk with Weir and have got a scheme for popularising his steel house by offering specimens to any local housing authority that likes to ask for them at a specially low price. I shall go and see them myself soon but from all I hear of them they seem likely to fill the bill even better than I thought. What do you think of a mahogany dado and copper tanks & pipes for hot water? He has got a new process for treating the steel which he believes will make repainting unnecessary.

Austen has made an excellent start and it is pleasant to see how generally his appointment has been approved abroad – particularly on account of his complete mastery of colloquial French!

...

Yesterday evening I was speaking at a meeting of the Cripples Union over which the new Labour Lord Mayor[54] presided. He was very forthcoming and showered compliments upon me but what pleased me most was to find that he had read with great attention and complete approval what I said a little while ago on City halls and that he had moved & obtained a Sub. Com. of the G.P. Com. of the Council to examine the question and if possible frame a scheme. My seed has, some of it, fallen on fruitful ground.

Today I have been "turning a sod" (with a silver trowel!) of a new garden village which is being started at Kings Heath, again in company with the Lord Mayor, and again received many compliments including one from a Liberal Councillor who stood for Kings Norton in the last election and who roundly

---

[54] Percival Bower (1880–1948). Lord Mayor of Birmingham 1924–26. Member, Central Electricity Board. Knighted 1923.

stated that though not of my party he believed I was the best man in England for my present job. On the other hand I observe that Master Mosley told an I.L.P. meeting earlier in the week that "we had got the old dud back at the Ministry of Health" a remark which called forth a vigorous letter of protest in the Post.

At the Ministry I learn that before leaving office Wheatley said that if Jicks came back they would go for him tooth and nail, but that if as they rather anticipated I returned, their attitude would be as sympathetic & helpful as party exigencies would allow.

On the other hand there aren't enough of *them* to make much trouble anyhow & probably most of my difficulties will arise among my own people.

...

23 November 1924
Moor Lane House, Briantspuddle, Dorset

My dear Ida,

...

We had a great day yesterday & with perfect weather conditions we piled up a record bag of 381 pheasants. ...

I have been harassed by the possibility that I might have to return today for a Cabinet tomorrow. But now I see the Cabinet was held yesterday and that Allenby[55] has presented our note. How thankful I am that if this wretched murder[56] had to come it should come while we have a strong Govt in power instead of Ramsay who might at the critical moment have succumbed to some "No more war" movement engineered by George Lansbury.

24 [sic] November 1924[57]
Westbourne

My dear Hilda,

...

I had a long and extremely interesting talk with the C.of E. on Wednesday. His language was so peculiar that I was left in doubt whether he had not invited me to join him in a secret plan not disclosed to any colleagues. But having taken

---

[55] Edmund Henry Hynman Allenby (1861–1936). Commander, 1st Cavalry Division and Third Army in France 1915–17; Commander, Egyptian Expeditionary Force 1917–19. Promoted to Field Marshal and High Commissioner for Egypt 1919–25. Created Viscount 1919.

[56] Sir Lee Stack, Sirdar of the Egyptian Army and Governor-General of the Sudan, was assassinated on 19 November 1924 in Cairo. Allenby immediately issued a harsh ultimatum. Zaghul, the Wafd leader, resigned as Prime Minister on 23 November after his rejection of these terms led to the seizure of the Alexandria Customs House.

[57] This letter is mis-dated. Chamberlain met Churchill on Wednesday, 26 November. This letter was thus most probably written on 30 November.

the first opportunity of seeing the P.M. I found that at any rate he had not been left out and my mind was proportionately relieved. Not that I had any objection to the plan per se which indeed seemed to me a good one, but his way of putting it was so different from what I am accustomed to that I was fairly puzzled. I suppose I shall get to know my Winston better presently. Incidentally I learned from the P.M. that he is all right about Imp. Pref. & Safeguarding of industries.

I have made four speeches this week and all without notes. I am getting confidence now in the new system and find it saves – not work for I still prepare – but no end of worry. I also had my first interview with the Building Industry Committee and got on very well with them. They were very suspicious and sticky at first but wound up as the interview proceeded till we parted on very friendly terms. I took the opportunity of putting some very searching questions to them about bricklayers labourers and heard afterwards that in subsequent discussion among themselves they agreed that they would have to find some way of bringing them in without reducing their wages. I think they are trying to make their scheme work but they have all sorts of reserves at the back of their minds and I dont think they will succeed.

Next week I am shooting down here on Saturday and go up to Glasgow that night. Sunday I am to spend inspecting Weir & Atholl's houses ... I have got the Chancellor's leave to spend £50,000 on experiment and demonstration but am still arguing about prices with Weir.

6 December 1924
Westbourne

My dear Ida,

...

I have had a busy and interesting week. I went to Oxford on Monday to address their Carlton Club – the principal Tory Club among the undergrads and very prosperous & enthusiastic. They invited ladies and crammed the meeting room so that a good many had to stand. I was therefore vexed that I did not make a better address to them. I asked John Buchan[58] whether they would like to hear about housing and he said Yes, but I concluded when I came to speak that though it might well have been included with other subjects in a general speech it was too technical to form the sole fare of an audience of that kind. I shant make that mistake again. I stayed the night with Buchan who has got a delightful house part of which dates from the 12th cent. ... But though he was very amiable, I somehow dont take to him. I think perhaps he is a snob.

---

[58] John Buchan (1875–1940). Historian, novelist and politician. Private Secretary to Milner when High Commissioner in South Africa 1901–3; Director of Information 1917–18. Conservative MP for the Scottish Universities 1927–35. Governor-General, Canada 1935–40. Created Baron Tweedsmuir 1935.

I am gradually soaking in the position of things at the Ministry. Tonight I am going to Glasgow to see Weir's and Atholl's houses, but I am afraid these Trade Unions are going to delay my demonstrations. They are determined to squeeze Weir out if they can by making him abandon piece work and pay joiner's hourly rates to his men who nail the wooden frames together as though they were skilled building industry carpenters. I rather hope to manoeuvre them into striking on brick houses which they are building for a local authority on the ground that the local authority is encouraging Weir to "blackleg" by buying his houses and not interpreting the fair wages clause to mean what they ask, viz: building Union conditions and rates. They have actually threatened to do this but I can hardly believe that they will carry it out. Anyway I hope they will hurry up because I cant make my contract with Weir till the question is settled. Meanwhile I am trying to work to a decision as to my attitude on Building prices (the Wheatley "Profiteering" Bill) Poor Law Reform, London Assessment Deductions Scale, Birth Control, the future of the Voluntary Hospitals, the Vaccination order and one or two other matters which I had better not write about just yet. In my leisure hours I make speeches at the Albert Hall and as the Press doesn't write chatty notes about functions of that kind I may tell you that I had a great succés on Thursday. I spoke for about 10 minutes *without a note* – an audacious experiment but it came off and I maintained that "indomitable composure" with which Edward Wood informs me I am credited by my colleagues – though my heart was in my throat for the Albert Hall is an alarming place to speak in. I had many congratulations from the members of the Govt who had never heard me speak on the platform before and were rather impressed.

I came down here last night. All day yesterday my footsteps were dogged by my "crack-shot guard" though I gave him the slip once. With difficulty I persuaded him not to come to Birm. but I was met on the platform by the Chief Detective Inspector and I found the house surrounded by police some of whom patrolled the grounds all night. Like old times. But I have induced them to let me go unaccompanied to Glesga.

…

6 [sic] December 1924[59]
Westbourne

My dear Hilda,

…

I had a very interesting & strenuous visit to Glasgow last week and saw all that Weir was doing as well as Atholl's house and one built by the Steel Roofing

---

[59] This letter is mis-dated. Reference to his Glasgow visit on 6–7 December suggests that it should be dated 13 December.

Co of Scotland. The two latter looked nice but I am satisfied that they are out of the picture because they are too costly & would take too much labour & too much time to be of much use. On the other hand Weir's house gives me confidence. It doesn't look bad outside and inside it is really excellent. I see that the vested interests are trying to crab it but I feel sure that, if only it can be seen by the public, public opinion will brush them aside. Unfortunately I am still held up by the fact that placing a contract with Weir brings the Govt into the dispute as a party to it and it seems to me that that would be playing into the hands of the enemy by enabling them to mobilise political pressure on their own side & I am seeing Weir again as I didn't have time to thrash things out with him.

Meanwhile the building industry Committee have taken what I said to heart and have agreed with Birmingham not only to allow the bricklayers labourers to come in but to give them their present wages to start with. If they will work on these lines it ought to give us an immediate augmentation of a substantial amount. I have also had an interview of the manufacturers of materials who object strongly to the Profiteering Bill. I had been keeping my mind open as to what course I should pursue but have come to the conclusion that I can present a good case for not going on with it. Prices of materials have not risen appreciably and there is really no evidence which would justify putting the manufacturers in the pillory and leaving out the operatives and the contractors. It will be interesting to see what line Wheatley takes on Tuesday. My people think he will not be aggressive but personally I rather doubt his ability to control himself when he once gets on his legs.

I made my first speech to the new House on Thursday. The subject was of the dullest & driest character but judging by the cheers when I sat down the House approved my exposition & the Bill went through without opposition. Tuesday will be a very different affair.

As you say, there is no end to speech making. ... Luckily this no note method does make oddment speeches easier and I have got through my various tasks without too much labour.

   ...

As a side light on Ramsay a friend told me he overheard him telling his supporters in the smokeroom that I had no business in the House as I had never been truly elected. My election had been a public scandal – wholesale corruption – gross abuse of influence – and – finally Labour men in the gallery saw my supporters go to the table & abstract papers from Mosley's packets & put them in their packets. Evidently as Lady Bonham Carter[60] said in the election What he wants is a nice lie down in a dark room with some sal volatile!

---

[60] (Helen) Violet Bonham Carter (1887–1969). Elder daughter of Asquith. Married Sir Maurice Bonham Carter 1915. President, Women's Liberal Federation 1923–25 and 1939–45; President, Liberal Party Organisation 1945–47; Governor, BBC 1941–46; Member, Royal Commission on the Press 1947–49. Created Dame 1953 and Baroness Asquith of Yarnbury 1964.

6

1925

'I Might be a Great Minister of Health': Pensions, Rating and Valuation

2 January 1925
SS *Malwa*

My dear Hilda,

...

We had a very pleasant visit to the Cunliffe Listers although the last two days were rather rough. Our fellow guests were Col & Mrs Hannay, she being Sir Philip's sister, the Margessons & Capt & Lady Evelyn Beauchamp. We liked the Hannays very much. They were simple and pleasant though she doesn't seem to have much to her brother's brains. Margesson[1] is now M.P. for Rugby where I spoke for him just before the election. I like him and her but she doesn't please everyone and neither the Hannays nor our children could abide her. As for Lady Evelyn she is a daughter of Ld Carnarvon and I thought she would be very interesting on Int-an-Khamer but she doesn't seem to have any mind. A nasty, little, common, painted, bandy legged baggage I call her, and the children evidently thought so too. Thus early are our youngsters being initiated into the world. The C-L's have 2 boys one of whom is at school with Frank and he & Dorothy enjoyed themselves mightily and won all hearts with their good looks and charming manners.

The house is a regular museum, the last Lord Masham[2] having been a great connoisseur. ... But what a place to keep up. Innumerable rooms & corridors only 3 bathrooms & electric light in only one or two rooms. Luckily the money has come to keep it up by a series of fortunate chances; for it might have been left elsewhere.

Well, they seem to be making preparations to be off so I will close. Why we should leave our happy home in order to be rocked on the bosom of the nasty deep I dont know but we shall have to go through with it now.

...

---

[1] (Henry) David Reginald Margesson (1890–1965). Conservative MP for West Ham Upton 1922–23 and Rugby 1924–42. PPS to Minister of Labour 1922–23; Assistant Whip 1924; Junior Lord of Treasury 1926–29 and 1931; Parliamentary Secretary, Treasury and Chief Government Whip 1931–40; Secretary for War 1940–42. Created Viscount Margesson 1942.

[2] John Cunliffe-Lister (1867–1924). Landowner. Succeeded as 2nd Baron Masham 1917.

18 January 1925
37 Eaton Square, SW1

My dear Ida,

...

My letter from Gibraltar gave you practically the whole account of our stay in those parts ...

Since then I have been doing nothing but read innumerable papers and haven't even touched the enormous piles of letters awaiting me here. ...

I see the wage dispute over Weir houses is going on merrily & now I am beginning to get the complaints I expected from those who are interested in other types. Of course that was inevitable but I trust the damage is done already.

Tomorrow I begin a series of deputations followed a little later by a series of speeches. I guess I am going to have a pretty strenuous time but I feel very well after my holiday.

...

I rather think Williams charged me £5.5.0 for the first consultation & £3.3.0 for the Second. But all that idea of leaving guineas on Doctor's tables has gone. They send bills now like a butcher & I never pay till they do.

23 January 1925
37 Eaton Square, SW1

My dear Hilda,

...

We had Austen & Ivy to dinner here on Wednesday and I thought Ivy whom I had not seen for some time was looking very well while A. is obviously very happy in his work. After they had gone Annie told me she had not been feeling well which she attributed to her dress being too tight. However she was unable to eat any breakfast next morning and as she was proposing to go to Birmingham to attend various Committees I got her to see Bruce Porter in the absence of Simpson who is abroad. As I expected he forbade anything of the kind. He didn't find anything organically wrong but he says she is run down and has prescribed absolute mental rest for a month. She hasn't seemed any better since; in fact she has rather gone to bits, which is I think partly psychological & partly physical. Porter doesn't want her to go away but Simpson returns on Monday and we shall hear more when they have consulted together.

It is rather disappointing that the sea voyage hasn't done more for her. Her inability to shake off her cold for so long seemed to indicate a lack of vitality and though it has pretty well disappeared now it has evidently left its mark behind. Meanwhile all engagements are cancelled which is a good thing, but the situation cannot be called satisfactory.

I have had a very busy week with deputations & interviews but nothing special to report in that connection. There is one thing however that I havent yet mentioned to you which may prove of some importance.

Some time ago I had a brain wave about the treatment of slums and just before I went away I mentioned it to Aubrey Symonds and asked him to think about it. He was very pleased with it & said he would talk it over with a friend who was knowledgeable on the subject & see how it appealed to him. I now learn from him that the friend has put him in touch with a man who is Secretary or Manager of a semi-philanthropic Company which owns some 10000 slum houses in London & for years has been managing them & making them decent & sanitary. This man at once told Symonds that he was convinced that my idea was not only sound but the *only* practical solution of the slum problem & that his experience was at my disposal.

Well you will wonder what the idea is. To explain it I must go back to my earlier ideas. You know I have long held that to solve the slum problem you must improve the tenant as well as the house and that there was no chance of doing this when the landlord owned only one or two houses & had no control over the surroundings. I therefore proposed that the local authority shd buy and manage slums doing such improvements as might seem right pending ultimate reconstruction. But I saw that the prospect of local authorities owning thousands of slum houses was not an attractive one & it opened up an awful vista of political pressure from tenants & those who would exploit tenants for political purposes. I then tried a scheme for keeping the ownership in private hands by putting the area into the hands of a sort of Receiver. But many technical difficulties particularly in relation to mortgages arose & I had not seen any way of overcoming them. Then came the "scintillation". Why not set up a statutory body consisting of persons nominated by the Council & various other interests, who would be independent of electors & to whom the slums should be handed over to manage. It would have nothing else to do and gradually you would get a standardised system of management growing up. Meanwhile you would not prejudice the future development of the town under new Town Planning legislation and the Council wd have power to take over the site for a town imp[rovemen]t. The Body wd have power to issue bonds or certificates of small amount guaranteed on the rates & this would attract working class savings. There are various other possibilities connected with the idea but it is extraordinarily interesting & encouraging to find that it has practically been carried out already with complete success in London.

It will mean a lot of education.

...

1 February 1925
37 Eaton Square, SW1

My dear Hilda,

...

I am afraid I cant give you too good an account of my invalid. She picked up wonderfully during my absence in Birmingham and has declared herself as feeling ever so much better all this week, but this morning she has gone back after a restless night and confirms my view that she is very easily upset because she has no reserves. I am glad therefore that she has no definite public engagements to fulfil and ... she is not taking on any new liabilities at present.

...

I came back on Sunday so as to have plenty of time on Monday. My secretary has certainly made good his expectation that he would be able to keep me busy till the session began and I have hardly had a moment to spare. I did however reserve one day to go down and see Welwyn Garden City which I have long wished to do and I was very much impressed with it. To take 2500 acres of bare arable and convert it into a town of 50,000 inhabitants means a prodigious effort in this country but in spite of all scepticism and discouragement it has been fairly started and success is now assured. So much building is going on that the roads are in a terrific state but the architecture and treatment of the site are admirable and they have brought off a considerable coup by inducing the Shredded Wheat Co. of America to erect a huge factory which will employ all the female labour they have got. They have raised the value of building sites now to £1000 an acre!

Politics are quiet and it is so long since I made an important speech that I am as nervous as a cat about the great Unionist meeting which I am to address in the Manchester Free Trade Hall tomorrow night. Beaverbrooks paper the Express came out with a violent attack on me this week alleging that I had wasted weeks in inaction instead of coming out with a bold scheme (not otherwise specified) for checkmating the building trade unions. They have of course no case but I have no doubt they have general instructions to knife the Government whenever they think they see a favourable opportunity. So far as I can see no other paper has taken up the cry or discovered the growing public impatience alleged by the Express so that the attack seems to have fallen flat. But no doubt it will come up again. As a matter of fact Weir is going on with his houses as if there had been no challenge so that there is no real delay and as the Unions cannot call out his men the crisis has got to come with the Local Authorities.

Meanwhile I am going to have my hands full with Valuation & Rating Reform & Old Age & Widows Pensions i.e. if Winston is able to manage the latter. At present he is engaged in a fierce struggle with the Admiralty and unless he wins he won't have enough for pensions. Investigation has convinced me that we shan't be able to increase the amount of old age pension but if we can without too large a contribution give it at an earlier age, abolish the thrift qualification and add a widows pension I think it should be sufficiently attractive.

I have suffered rather a severe blow in the loss of Sir Aubrey Symonds who is going to be permanent head of the Education Office. He is absolutely invaluable on all legislative work and during the passage of the Housing & Rent bills in 1923 he gave me more help than the rest of the office put together. Moreover he knows this horrible subject of valuation & rating in and out and last but not least his mind works so closely with mine that over & over again we have hit on the same idea independently. He will be irreplaceable but I felt that he deserved the promotion and so I did all I could to assure him the position he has now obtained. I know he is very sorry to go but of course he has jumped at the chance which might never come again.

Annie is rather vexed at Squiff's taking the title of Earl of Oxford but apparently her family is descended from the 15th earl (she being 12th in line) whereas the last (20th) earl's heirs would be the rightful claimants. I suppose there are Harley descendants too so there may be a nice muddle for the Heralds to unravel. But I expect Squiff will get his title in the end.

...

I must stop. Lord! I have got such a dull speech for Manchester. "I veesh it vos tomorrow."

8 February 1925
37 Eaton Square, SW1

My dear Ida,

...

My Manchester speech went off very well. The Free Trade Hall was full and I spoke for 65 minutes, without a note, dealing mostly with housing and the attitude of the Unions to steel houses. They are gradually coming out into the open and a day or two after I had spoken the Times came out with an admirable article. I think I have effectually answered the accusations of partiality for Weir by making similar arrangements for two other types recommended by the Moir[3] Comee. So far I have accepted and carried out every recommendation of this Comee wh. was set up by Wheatley and its not my fault if it recommended the Weir house a couple of months before any other! Between ourselves the new types are good as houses, but useless for my purpose because they are quite as costly as brick if not more so and are not likely to come down in price. They do not therefore excite the same hostility among the Unions who are not afraid of

[3] Ernest William Moir (1862–1933). Engineer and designer of harbours, docks and tunnels. Member, Admiralty Engineering Committee; member, Council of Ministry of Munitions and founded its Inventions Branch 1915–19; Chairman, Committee on New Methods of House Construction 1924–25. Created Bart 1916.

them. But they dare not give their real reasons for fearing Weir and I think they have made a mistake in tactics in threatening local authorities who have undertaken to put up demonstration houses. Anyway I returned to the charge on Thursday when I spoke in Birmingham & I shall probably rub it in again tomorrow. My purpose of course is to work up public opinion.

I am making good progress with pensions though I haven't talked to Winston yet. He is waging a desperate fight with the Admiralty carried on with wonderful fertility of illustration and vehemence of expression on his side. But he makes the mistake of fighting on technical grounds. The admirals are bound to beat him there, whereas if he would confine himself to the financial & political considerations they would never be able to get to close quarters. I think however he will end with a win on the substantial point though he may be defeated in argument, for I fancy he has got support assured from both the P.M. & the F[oreign] S[ecretary]. It seems agin our traditions to starve the navy but my feeling is that we have got to do it for the present.

The real key of the situation in my scheme is the agricultural labourer. With other workmen I could perhaps relieve the extra burden of contributory pensions by lowering the unemployment contribution. But the agricultural labourer is not insured for unempl. and as it doesn't seem administratively possible to provide for differential contributions it really comes to this. What extra can he pay per week? I should like to know whether you think he could pay 3[d] for a 10/- pension at 65 & no questions asked when he reached 70. Ditto for his wife and in addition 10/- for the wife 5/- for 1st child & 3/- for each succeeding child under 16 whenever he dies.

There is another matter on which your opinion might be helpful. I have always said agricultural housing required different treatment from urban and ideas on the subject are beginning to "womble". What would you say to a scheme of which the rough outline would be as follows. Landowners and others who either built new houses or reconstructed old ones to an approved schedule to receive a *lump sum* subsidy equivalent say to half the cost with a maximum for any one house say of £100, the subsidy to be divided between the Exchequer & the local authority on agreed proportions. In return the owner to enter into a covenant that the rent shall not be raised above present level (which must not exceed say 3/- per week) by more than -% for (twenty) years and to give the L.A. a mortgage for the amount of the subsidy to be foreclosed only if the rent condition is broken. Suggested advantages. Many impecunious landlords will put in hand long wanted repairs and improvements. Cost to State and local authority will be the minimum. Minimum interference with private enterprise or relations between landlord & tenant. Minimum demand on building industry – much work being done by estate labour – Protection of tenant against raising of rent.

I havent put these ideas up to my people yet but I fancy my Accountant General's hair will stand on end if I do. I should however like to know how they strike you.

Lord! it is interesting being in office again and everyone tells me how remarkably fit I look!

...

14 February 1925
Westbourne

My dear Hilda,

...

I went down to Plymouth last Monday to attend and speak at a dinner there. It was to please Nancy Astor that I went as I know how sore she [was] that neither she nor Waldorf got a place offered them in the Government, and though she jars upon me dreadfully I cant help a sneaking liking for her because she *is* genuine. Also I like Waldorf. But it was rather a tax – 5 hours in the train each way and *ten* speeches at the dinner. However I was rewarded first, by the local gentleman who proposed Nancy's health and declared that she was a really tiresome woman, hastily explaining in the gasping silence that followed that he had meant to say "tireless", and secondly by the fact that apparently the whole West Country was anxiously looking forward to my speech and consequently I was able to do some useful educative work. I am told that West Country audiences are very appreciative; certainly I have seldom had a greater demonstration of enthusiasm after a speech than I got at Plymouth. I talked to them about housing and trade and finished up with a peroration of Empire which fairly carried them away. It *is* satisfactory that one can always get such an immediate response to any development of Imperial sentiment. I always feel that Father is more responsible for it than any other one man and that some day it will be the salvation of this country.

It has been a thick week with the opening of Parlt. two Cabinets, questions in the House and my supplementary estimate for steel houses. The Socialists are taking exactly the line I expected about the latter. The only type they are afraid of is Weir so they concentrate on him and seek to rally all Trade Unions to the support of the Building Unions by representing my action as the first skirmish in a general engagement. "This Govt are out", they say, "to destroy Trade Unionism and the reactionary party are tumbling over one another to get a place in the ballot for the iniquitous bill which is their instrument.["] (This is how they describe the bill to allow a man to contract into the political levy instead of contracting out of it). In the same way they are all the time booming & advertising Weir. Why? Because he is out to lower the wages of the worker. ["]We love new methods of house building; we would lay down our lives to get them but we will not sell our birthright for a mess of pottage, which by the way is rotten and full of animals."

Up to the present I have succeeded, though with some difficulty in keeping the Govt out of the dispute about the Fair Wages Clause in connection with Weir contracts, but it was hard to contain myself in the debate and not say what one thought in the face of the provocation I received. My man Robinson at the Ministry is not very hopeful of Weir's success in his fight but I refuse to accept that view and I shall be desperately disappointed if we cannot get public opinion with us. But we are "up against it". The Housing & T.P. Council has condemned steel houses just as the stage coachman condemned the railways and Local Authorities are beginning to rat and cry off demonstration houses on the ground that "they dont want to get into a row with labour".

When you get my last letter you will see that I have put up a couple of problems to Ida on Rural Life. Since writing I hear that at the Bd of Agriculture they are disposed to think that for the pension benefits offered both farmer and labourer would be willing to pay an extra 4[d] a week. If this were so it would help me out considerably.

...

We are coming down again next Saturday and Hall is coming up to have a good talk about Hoskins which has been giving me a great deal of anxiety for some time past. We made a heavy loss last year and I fear that the loss is still continuing. If we had merely made no profit I could have gone on paying out substantial dividends from reserves for some time but it is another matter when you drop £13,000 in a single year and I am afraid we have got to face a very lean period for some little while. Not only is work extraordinarily scarce but we have more competitors than ever and it seems impossible to get an order which shows a profit. I am thankful to have got a salary or I should be in the soup but we shall all be hit.

21 February 1925
Westbourne

My dear Hilda,

My staff are quite convinced that no Minister is so hard worked as theirs and I believe they arent far wrong. We cover such a desperately wide field that it seems difficult for a private member to produce a Bill or a motion that does not affect us and require the Ministers presence. I did think I might get Wednesday night off but an enthusiastic Tory has decided to divert himself by attacking Poplar & West Ham so I shall have to dine early and spend my evening on the Treasury Bench instead of gossiping with you. ...

...

I dont seem to have done much of general interest this week but of course it has been a very busy one and I have had a constant succession of deputations interviews conferences lunches & dinners. Next week will be worse as I have four speeches in view besides everything else.

The Weir house controversy is getting towards a crisis and I think we shall have to risk everything on a Court of Enquiry. Weir himself is now jibbing over his contracts with L.A. as he is afraid of accepting the fair wages clause until its import has been cleared up. On the other hand until the demonstration houses have been seen & approved I am hardly in a position to fight. We have a Cabinet Comee on Tuesday & shall probably settle it then.

...

7 March 1925
Westbourne

My dear Hilda,

...

It has been a strenuous but successful week. My Metropolis Valuation Bill came off on Monday & thanks to the study I had devoted to it at Odiham I was able to give what Sidney Webb described as "really a masterpiece of exposition" and made it so clear to the House that we got the 2nd reading without a division and almost without debate. On Wednesday we had a terrific go in Cabinet at the Protocol[4] and security which lasted for two hours in the afternoon. Poor Austen had an awful bucketing as Curzon & Balfour had completely changed their minds since we last discussed the question and so many other Ministers had views, all of which differed from one another and all of which proposed something different from what he wanted that I could only admire his angelic patience. In the end he was rewarded by getting a fairly free hand but as you no doubt saw his task in the House where he had to walk very delicately was not made easier by that daft fool Kirkwood. A Foreign Minister's job was always difficult, but the difficulties are increased a thousandfold when you have to keep all the Dominions in line too.

While these complicated & troublesome questions of foreign policy were being debated in the Cabinet the party was seething with doubt and disaffection over the political levy. I dined in the House on Tuesday in order to go on to the 1900 Club afterwards and finding Bobby Monsell[5] in the depths of pessimism and worry I asked if he would like me to interview the leaders of the malcontents McQuisten[6] [sic] and George Balfour.[7] Baldwin had gone off to see his mother who is dying and I thought perhaps I could, as one who had been in favour of the Bill,[8] work on

---

[4] The Geneva Protocol for the Pacific Settlement of International Disputes. Proposed by MacDonald to strengthen the League of Nations but rejected by the Conservatives in 1925.

[5] Bolton Meredith Eyres-Monsell (1881–1969). Royal Navy 1895–1906 and 1915–16. Conservative MP for Evesham 1910–35. Unionist Whip 1911–21; Treasurer of the Household 1919–21; Civil Lord of Admiralty 1921–22; Parliamentary and Financial Secretary, Admiralty 1922–23; Parliamentary Secretary, Treasury 1923–24, 1924–29, 1931; Chief Whip 1923–31; First Lord of Admiralty 1931–36. Knighted 1929. Created Viscount Monsell 1935.

[6] Frederick Alexander MacQuisten (1870–1940). Conservative MP for Glasgow Springburn 1918–22 and Argyll 1924–40.

[7] George Balfour (1872–1941). Founder and head of Balfour, Beatty & Company. Conservative MP for Hampstead 1918–41.

their feelings. He jumped at the proposition so on Wednesday afternoon I sent for them to my room and addressed a moving appeal to them to allow the Bill to be talked out and not to force a division which would make manifest a rift in the party. They were obviously impressed but before I could get very far I had to go to a deputation and then to the adjourned Cabinet at 5.30. After the Cabinet Sam Hoare and Philip Cunliffe-Lister came to my room. Bobby had told them that the malcontents wanted a Govt amendment promising to bring in its own Bill. This was impossible but after various interruptions for divisions we concocted an amendment which we thought we could father. I was due to dine with Lilian at 8.15 and it was already 8 but the thing was too important to leave so I sent for my two ruffians again and they were finally dug out of St Stephen's Club where they had gone to dine. I read out the amendment and they both declared emphatically and at once that they would have nothing to do with it. I was in despair but I set to work again and in half an hour we had hammered out the formula which was finally adopted and which they both promised to accept. All this time my unfortunate secretary had been waiting for me to go through my Thursday questions which Kingsley was to take as I was going to Birmingham. I polished them off as soon as I could and then went down to the dining room where I found Bobby anxiously awaiting me & showed him the new formula. His relief & gratitude were comic[.] "You are always the man to get us out of our troubles" & " I can't think how you got them to take this" he said & we agreed that I should show it to Stanley next day and if he agreed telephone to London so that it could go on the paper last thing. And by 9.30 I was able to join Lilian's dinner party!

The arrangements here had given me a good deal of trouble as S.B. was unable to attend a luncheon as had been arranged. However I got Jackson to take his place and although the guests were naturally disappointed they could not complain in the circumstances. We found S.B. here when we got back in the afternoon and he had no difficulty in accepting the formula which indeed left him a free hand, so we relieved Bobby's mind and then S.B. went off to put the final touches to his speech. We had the usual awful pre-speech dinner party of 14 and then proceeded to the Town Hall for the meeting. A broadcasting arrangement had been fixed up by which the speech could be heard in the Midland Institute even more plainly than in the Town Hall, and both halls were jam full. S.B. made one of the best speeches I have ever heard from him. It might have been even better for the audience if it had had a little more light and shade, for it was certainly strong meat all through, but it evidently made a deep impression and he had a great demonstration when he sat down. I took no part in the proceedings but the family was worthily represented by Annie who delivered one of her perfect little appeals with just the right mixture of humour and sentiment. S.B. was properly impressed with the wonderful reception she got from the audience.

---

[8] MacQuisten's Private Members Bill sought to implement the pledge to replace 'contracting-out' of the political levy with 'contracting-in'.

Yesterday morning he and I travelled up to town by the 9 o'clock train and got to the House before Macquisten had proceeded very far. You will have seen from your paper that S.B. had the Parliamentary success of his career and indeed he deserved it.[9] Much of his speech was perhaps not directly relevant to the Bill, but it created the atmosphere he wanted and raised the discussion to a plane to which we do not often attain in the House of Commons. The diehards felt that their allegiance had been stretched to the utmost by the absence of any intimation that action was only postponed but they felt the force of his appeal themselves and loyally stood to their word. So thus ended in a blaze of glory for the Govt the first incident that has strained the party unity and seriously threatened its domestic peace. The only man who was left thoroughly unhappy was, I was told, Horne. But Horne made the mistake of his life when he declined the Ministry of Labour and I believe that his inclusion in the Govt now would weaken rather than strengthen it, so much has his stock declined.

I am very pleased at your approval of my slum scheme. Last night I had to speak at a dinner here and I thought I would try and make a start with the preparation of the ground. I always think its a mistake to come plumb out with a new idea because the public thinks very slowly & resents sudden shocks. So I merely rehearsed the difficulties of various other solutions and asked whether these were all that could be suggested & whether the resources of civilisation were exhausted. The passage came at the end of my speech which itself followed a 35 minute address from Amery and I felt a little discouraged because I didn't think the audience had understood or that the press would report. But behold the Post with astounding alertness put in big headlines this morning *Municipal house ownership. Mr Neville Chamberlain's question.* I had to write to Hubbard and tell him that that was what I called really intelligent journalism to seize on the first indication of a new idea. I didn't tell him what the idea was, but that was just to excite his curiosity.

This morning the Birmingham Director of Housing came to see me. He was present last night and wanted to tell me that he was already finding just those difficulties which I had touched on. So I told him my idea & asked what he thought of it. He was delighted with it, said he thought it most practical & added that it was already being done on small scale here. He then gave me an account of how a solicitor & some friends had bought some slum property, brought it up to date, and had cleared 8% on it as well as feeling very proud of the condition of their houses. He thought my plan would be self supporting.

...

---

[9] After discussing the changing industrial order in terms of a romanticised personal vision of harmony in his family ironworks, Baldwin conceded the need for limits on trade union freedom but urged his party 'not ... to fire the first shot' in an industrial war, concluding with the prayer, 'Give peace in our time, O Lord'.

14 March 1925
Westbourne

My dear Ida,

...

... I have got the draft [Pensions] Bill to look over this week. It's still not finally decided whether we have it this year, but from the way Winston talks to me I can see his mind is really made up and I don't think anything is likely to change it now.

I hope you get your chance for the Council. You will be most useful to me if you do as you can throw much light on just that part of Local Govt of which I know least. Since I saw you I have – at intervals – had some discussions with Symonds about Poor Law reform and if we follow on present lines it will be rather a gradual progress than a drastic uprooting of present arrangements. In fact I think it would mean very little alteration in the country, the change operating more in the towns.

I have had a garrulous week! Nine speeches if you please, all on different subjects. Its a wonder I survive, but somehow I have come out remarkably fresh at the end of it and every one remarks how well I look whereas a little while ago I was always being condoled with on my worn appearance to my intense annoyance. To give you 2 days as a sample. On Tuesday I began by attending the Levée and then having returned home to change I visited the Flower show with Annie and bought 2 very pretty Cymbidiums. After a hurried lunch I went to the Executive Committee of the N.U.A. in response to an S.O.S. from Jacker. It appeared that Philip Stott[10] was breathing fire & slaughter against S.B. for his behaviour over the Political Levy Bill and he actually moved a vote of censure on the Govt for its conduct. I made a reply which appeared to find favour with the Committee but I couldn't stop to see Stott executed as I had to go to the House to do what Veale calls my "stuff" and to interview a succession of members of Parlt. At 5 I went upstairs & made a speech on Housing & Rent to 100 members from our party & was afterwards heckled so long that I had barely time to get off to the dinner which was being given me by the Garden Cities Association. Annie came too & we didn't get home till 11.30 when I sat down to work on speeches and got into bed as the clock struck two. On Wednesday morning I had ½ hr at the Ministry and then went to the Cabinet which lasted till 1.45. After a snack at the House I went on to Caxton Hall at 2.30 and addressed a packed meeting of women from the Eastern area for ¾ hr when I drove back to the House in a taxi in time to move the 2nd Reading of the R.R. Bill. Afterwards I sat on the bench till 6.30 when I went out and did my "stuff" and subsequently my "stuffing" consisting of a fried sole & some cheese. Back to the House to

---

[10] Philip Sidney Stott (1858–1937). Architect, surveyor and engineer. Presented what became Philip Stott College at Overstone, near Northampton, to the Conservative Party in 1923 initially for the Unionist Labour Movement but soon used for courses for the entire party. Created Bart 1920.

hear Kinglsey Wood wind up and then to a dinner of the Institute of Metals where I was the chief guest and made a humorous speech. Sat up till one, doing Cabinet papers & trying (in vain) to compose a speech for the next night. However I concocted the speech in bits when I could next day with such success that when I delivered it at the Spectacle Makers dinner next night Bearsted[11] thought it was impromptu and A.J.B. who had never heard me speak before declared (in a speech) that he had listened to it with "especial pleasure and admiration" & proceeded to pay me quite a string of compliments which he followed up by bringing me home in his car. I must confess I was very conscious that I was speaking before him for the first time and very frightened, but I trust I did not show it and everyone appeared very delighted with the speech which not only excited much (laughter) but contained the only original contribution of the evening namely the suggestion that it would be a good thing if the House of Commons included a certain number of aldermen elected by themselves for a term of years. Of course it isn't really practicable and I finally laughed it off the stage myself but it would be a great convenience to people like the Earl of Ox and Ass and myself!

I can hear you saying But why, why, should you accept invitations to all these dinners. Well I assure you I decline 4 out of 5 of the invitations I get. But I had to accept the Garden Cities because they badly want a leg up and my department is the one they look to. And the President of the Metals Institute this year is Prof. Turner[12] who was my teacher of metallurgy at Mason College and who wont be President again or Professor much longer. And the Master of the Spectacle Makers is Sir Charles Wakefield[13] who was Ld Mayor of London when I was Ld Mayor here and who has been most kind ever since and gave Dorothy a wrist watch. So you see, what else could I do. But it was rough all coming in one week. Yesterday we only had a Unionist Management Committee in the afternoon and attended a "social" (with speech) in the evening.

Today we began with my opening a new deep therapy apparatus at the Dudley Road Infirmary where I made an "important" speech. Then we went to a flower show & said "a few words" & after that I came home and dined alone while Annie went & addressed a women's meeting. What a life! ...

...

---

[11] Marcus Samuel (1853–1927). Introduced bulk petroleum transport through Suez Canal and developed large oilfield in Far East. Alderman, City of London 1891–1902 and Lord Mayor 1902–3. Created Bart 1903, Baron 1921 and Viscount Bearsted 1925.

[12] Thomas Turner (1861–1951). Demonstrator in Chemistry, Mason's College 1883–87; Lecturer in Metallurgy 1887–94; Director, Technical Instruction at Staffordshire County Council 1894–1902; Professor of Metallurgy, University of Birmingham 1902–26.

[13] Charles Cheers Wakefield (1859–1941). Businessman and benefactor. Lord Mayor of London 1915–16. Aviator and holder of World Water Speed Record. Created Bart 1917, Baron 1930 and Viscount Wakefield of Hythe 1934.

21 March 1925
Clandon Park, Guildford

My dear Hilda,

I am delighted to hear that there are good prospects of Ida's unopposed return. The drawback to a democratic system is that you have to get elected in order to serve your country! But it is mitigated if no one else is nominated and you can dispense with the annoyances and fatigues, to say nothing of the expense of a contest.

…

You will see from the heading of this paper that we are spending the week end with the Onslows. Our idea was that we would get a rest but I dont like the look of the party much. A Miss Beaumont, hideous and brainless, Dame Helen Gwynne-Vaughan,[14] brainy but rather strident, the Duke of Argyll[15] whose letter to Sir A. Mond you may remember, an insufferable coxcomb, and now I hear "Worthy's" bass booming away in the hall. Not a very lively or congenial company I fear, but its a fine house with a good library and I shall plead letters and "work"!

There is something very pathetic about Curzon. He had such brilliant gifts and was so great in so many ways and yet one feels that he was a failure for want of a little more humanity. He wept when he was told he couldn't be Foreign Secretary again! And one doesn't know whether to laugh or cry oneself. One of his most likeable traits was his acceptance of the inevitable when it came, and so far as I could judge he was quite happy in the Cabinet after he had got over the first shock. I shall always be glad that I sat in a Cabinet with him for he was a great figure and I can imagine his acquiring posthumously a sort of legendary fame. I always felt that he belonged to another age.

I spent last night and the night before in the train and filled my day full while I was in Edinburgh. I was a good deal worried over it beforehand & found unusual difficulty in getting a line. My speech to the Conservative Club was made without reporters being present and ought therefore to have been easy but although the audience appeared to be well satisfied I did not feel that it was a successful effort. But the evening speech made to the Chamber of Commerce was certainly up to the mark, thanks really to Annie. She made some suggestions for an ending which I at once adopted and when I finished the whole audience not only cheered vociferously but rose to their feet and after toasting me a second time again sang For he's a jolly good fellow with which they had received me. And when I left to catch my train they sang "Will ye no come back again" a favourite and rather pleasing habit of theirs when they like you.

---

[14] Dame Helen Charlotte Isabella Gwynne-Vaughan (1879–1967). Professor of Botany, Birkbeck College, London 1909–44. Women's Army Auxiliary Air Force in France 1917 and Commandant 1918–19; Chief Controller, Women's Auxiliary Territorial Service 1939–41.

[15] Niall Diarmid Campbell (1872–1949). Succeeded as 10th Duke of Argyll 1914.

While I was there I took the opportunity of going through their picture gallery. It is not very large but the collection is extremely high in quality & well spread over different schools of painting. The Raeburns are I suppose the show piece but they have got one magnificent Gainsborough 2 splendid Franz Hals, a Rembrandt of fair quality and a lot of good Frenchmen ...

Of course I had to visit the housing scheme but houses are much alike – even in Scotland.

I have hardly been in the House all week, but I need hardly say that I have not been idle and I am making good progress with Pensions & Valuation[.] Legislation slips through this House at such a pace that I am trying to push forward everything I can. I got the Metropolis Valuation through Committee on Tuesday, and had good fun with Sidney Webb who came with a laudable desire to put up some opposition but as usual didn't know his case & consequently was made to look very ridiculous. The Committee enjoyed the process but poor old Nanny blushed scarlet & sucked the end of his beard in great agitation.

Invitations to public dinners roll in at a perfectly alarming rate. I found 5 awaiting me this morning at Eaton Square and I expect there are more at the Ministry.

No, I dont think Horne will get a job, but if there is a change of places I hope it will provide room for some younger men to move up. I see A.J.B. suggested in the papers. It is like the futility of our journalists who never have any imagination.

28 March 1925
Westbourne

My dear Ida,

Congratulations on your unopposed return [to Hampshire County Council]. We shall be very interested to hear of your new work and I am sure you will find plenty of fresh ideas and plans to put forward and stir up your old Council with. As my policy is to increase the activities and responsibilities of County Councils I shall expect to get a good deal of help from you as I always feel that the one gap in my own equipment is the want of personal familiarity with C.C. work.

With regard to your ideas, I dont think you could deprive a landlord entirely of rent under present circumstances of control, because you cannot in those circumstances carry out the existing law. But under Sect 5. of the 1923 Act (of which you ought to have a copy) the tenant can get a certificate from the local authority that the house is not in a reasonable state of repair and then he need not pay the 40% increase and the landlord cannot recover it from him until he has in turn got a certificate that he has carried out the repairs. The real difficulty (in towns) is that the reasonable repair is not construed and apparently cannot be construed to include repapering and painting and I have got it in mind to put a clause into my next housing bill making it incumbent on the landlord to do this internal work at least once in so many years and to obtain a certificate that this has been done. This would get over the eternal argument as to whether the condition of the house is due to the negligence of the landlord or the tenant.

As to your second point, I had not considered the case of 2 houses knocked into one. The whole scheme is dependent on the hypothesis that the rent now being obtained is not an economic rent (say not exceeding 3/- per week) and shall not be increased for 20 years save by an amount sufficient to give a fixed rate of interest (say 4%) on the money expended *by the landlord*. Presumably therefore if two houses each let at 3/- were knocked into one the new rent could be 6/- plus interest on the landlord's half of the cost of the alteration. The total cost would be limited to a maximum say £150 so the interest might amount to another 1/- or 1/3 a week. This might make the new rent too high for the class of person intended to benefit and it might be necessary therefore to limit the rent further by a special provision in the particular case you refer to.

I had a letter during the week from the Birmingham housing director warmly approving the slum scheme & making a number of suggestions in connection with it which I am having examined. I am going to send out several inspectors to visit various rural areas in the country and make enquiries to see how my rural housing scheme would be likely to work and generally to collect information. Perhaps during the autumn one might begin to draft something in the nature of a bill. Meanwhile Robinson is of opinion [sic] that with the three ideas I have mentioned, internal decoration, statutory house management committees and rural housing subsidies we can make a jolly good bill and I agree with him.

...

We dined on Tuesday with the Newdigates to meet the Premier of Western Australia who is over here and with whom Annie had a very interesting conversation. The Central Women's Unionist Comee have started a most admirable scheme of packing & selling to their organisations throughout the country "Empire boxes" of various fruits which are accompanied by a number of leaflets setting forth the advantages of buying Empire products in preference to those of foreign countries. Mr Collier[16] was delighted at this scheme and was most enthusiastic in his gratitude, saying that it was just what was wanted. His country was ten times the size of England with a population of 300,000 and they could not increase without some security of market. He struck me as an amiable man without much power and with none of the outward signs of the "Labour" demagogue.

Somehow the Newdigates managed to poison us with their dinner for neither of us could eat breakfast next morning. Annie soon recovered but I went without

---

[16] Phillip Collier (1873–1948). Labour Member, Legislative Assembly of Western Australia 1905–48. Minister of Mines and Railways 1911–14; Minister of Water Supply 1914–16; Labour Prime Minister of Western Australia and Treasurer 1924–30 and 1933–36. Visited England 1925 and reached an agreement to settle British migrants using low-interest loans.

lunch and felt very low for a couple of days. It was the more unfortunate as I had a very heavy day on Wednesday. First Cabinet then the Abbey service for Curzon, then a speech to the C.C. Association followed by a long afternoon on the bench while the R.R. Bill was being discussed. I had to wind up at 8 o'clock and then wait on for a division on a private member's motion at 11 and when I got home I found stacks of Cabinet papers which kept me up another hour and a half. However I am all right again now.

Annie had another most successful party on Tuesday. I wasn't able to get to it but everyone tells me that she is an incomparable hostess and all her guests seem to enjoy themselves. She gets them all up beforehand with little rhymes to associate them with their constituencies or wherever they come from and they are equally astounded and flattered by her accurate recollection. ...

Austen and the P.M. and I assembled at Downing St on Thursday to hear Winston expound his Budget. He will certainly arouse plenty of criticism but I think it a very good Budget and will please our people. I am working away at the Pensions Bill which is now nearly ready. It is a little difficult to keep pace with Winston who has a new idea every hour but I think it will be a good scheme. Doubtless there will be criticism from employers and perhaps from domestic servants and of course the Labour party will say they would have brought out a non-contributory scheme. But Snowden had definitely committed himself to the contributory plan and any way we shall have given the pensions while the Labour party only talked about them.

I see opposition to my Rating and Valuation Bill is heating up and I guess I shall have plenty of trouble over it. But three of my Bills have now passed second reading and I hope soon to get a couple of Consolidation Bills through. So that only leaves me about four more this session!

5 April 1925
37 Eaton Square, SW1

My dear Hilda,

...

The extraordinary thing about the incident of which Austen told you when he nearly resigned is that it has all appeared in the French Press where it was described with substantial accuracy by "Pertinax". Another incident also connected with the Foreign Office has similarly been made public by a French journalist since, although so far as I know it was supposed to be confined to the Cabinet. Somewhere we have a very leaky vessel among us and, – to change the metaphor – I believe "I knows the gun as did it". It is remarkable that the most valuable secret of all from the journalists point of view viz the Pensions scheme has remained absolutely hidden. Not a ghost of a suspicion seems to have been aroused. You will observe that in this case the only person to whom secrecy is really important is the Chancellor himself. I understand that he intends to impart all his secrets to F.E. during the Easter recess. It will be interesting to see whether the mysteries remain behind the veil until Parlt meets.

I have been lying very low this week so far as the H. of C. is concerned but I have been extremely busy behind the scenes with Pensions & Valuation Bills. Winston is rather a trying person to work with for he never sticks to anything for two minutes together and when you have had a conference in order to arrive at a final decision on doubtful points your one certainty is that the agreement arrived at will be thrown overboard a few hours afterwards. I must say I think there is something to be said for my method in contrast to his. I always postpone my decisions to the very last moment possible, but once taken I very seldom go back upon them, because I have generally been pretty well all round the subject and new considerations therefore seldom arise.

I think the bill *will* be well received on the whole. It will come as a surprise and to our party a welcome surprise as they dont now anticipate anything this session. It may disappoint a few who have been misled by Broad and Marriott[17] but public opinion will quickly adjust itself to the idea of the necessary limits. It will be a real joy and boon to all who benefit immediately or in the near future in consequence of it.

The latest thing I am considering is that while contributions shall begin at once i.e. on Jan 1. 1926 & widows pensions at once, old age pensions should not accrue until a year's contributions had been paid. This would relieve the Treasury from giving anything to those now over 70 but not in receipt of full pension, or to their wives before they reach the age of 70. Winston is so frightened of having a surplus in the earlier years that he is inclined to chuck money about with a liberal hand. No doubt this would be very popular at the moment but with industry in its present condition of depression I feel that we have no right to an exhibition of vicarious generosity for which the nation will get no return whatever. The contributory burdens are heavy enough, but one can fairly claim there that the added security given to the worker is going to make him more contented and less restless. Moreover the earlier pension will to some extent help the older ones to leave industry to the young. But presents to men who have made no contribution whatever seem to me not only unnecessary but positively immoral.

The more I see of the R. & V. Bill the more nervous I get about it. I have said goodbye to Symonds & shall have now to trust to a team who are pretty good but have not his political sense. I daresay I can supply that myself but it is rather a tall order to have R. & V. & Pensions both in Committee at once so that I shall have to keep flitting from one room to another trying to keep both coaches on their respective rails. You can't do really good work that way.

---

[17] John Arthur Ransome Marriott (1859–1945). Author and historian, Worcester College, Oxford. Conservative MP for Oxford City 1917–22 and City of York 1923–29. Chairman, Estimates Committee 1924–26.

On Monday I got my Metropolis Valuation Bill through its 3rd reading and on Tuesday I attended a very successful meeting of representatives of the C.C. of Hants together with those of the urban & rural D.C.s & the borough C's with a number of large landowners to consider a proposition that a joint committee should be appointed to prepare a regional town plan for the County. This conference was called by the Chairman of the C.C. at my request and I was quite astonished at the number of people who came & the unanimity with which they supported my proposition. I think it is very encouraging for the future. The C.C. of course is not under the present law a T.P. authority but as the main road authority it ought to be & is very vitally interested in the matter. If therefore one or two others move, and I shall poke them up too if they dont, they may induce the smaller authorities to come in and in time the whole of rural England may be controlled. Your own experience shows that even Odiham's surroundings are not safe & though Govt depts are able to get round t.p. schemes, their interference would be made more difficult for them if it spoiled the plan.

...

On Thursday I had to attend and speak at a dinner to celebrate the taking over of the Preston Hall tuberculous ex-service men's village settlement by the British legion. I made an observation which I think was of some importance but did not get much notice in the press viz that if the experiment proved successful we might attach a village settlement to every tuberculosis Sanatorium and thus get full value out of the latter. Now when men leave the San. much improved they return to their former life & promptly relapse. Mond, who was present, came up afterwards & said it was a great idea & he hoped very much I should follow it up. I intend to!

On Friday I fulfilled an old promise to Leslie Scott[18] and went to Liverpool to dine as the guest of the 1924 club & address them. This is a club of young men who must be of public school type, engaged in a profession or as partner or director in business i.e. managers are excluded. They are very keen & taking themselves very seriously roping in quite a number who would ordinarily have been disinclined to touch politics at all. I spoke to them for about ¾ hr and they were very enthusiastic and grateful.

...

I returned yesterday afternoon. I had left instructions with Annie to get seats for a play but to make sure that it was worth going to. She got such lurid accounts of the sort of plays that are going on now that she decided on St Joan. I forget if you went to see it. If not, dont. A terrible lot of piffle has been talked about it as though B.S.[19] were a great Christian thinker with a moral uplift. To

---

[18] Leslie Frederic Scott (1869–1950). Unionist MP for Liverpool Exchange 1910–29. British delegate, International Conference on Maritime Law 1909–10, 1922–23; Solicitor-General 1922; Lord Justice of Appeal 1935–48; President, National Association of British Councils. Knighted 1922.

[19] George Bernard Shaw (1856–1950). Irish dramatist, essayist, critic and socialist pamphleteer. Founding member, Fabian Society 1884–1911. Nobel Prize for Literature 1925.

my mind he has given a very skilful presentment of the sort of person Joan might have been if you could transplant a 20th century Nancy Astor into the 14th. Of course there is no pretence at Mediævalism. B.S. has even the audacity to make Duvois quote "Providence is on the Side of the big battalions". But Sybil Thorndike[20] is a clever actress. Annie shed floods of tears. I didn't because the thing was not real enough to move me, but I confess to feeling extremely uncomfortable when a woman sobs on the stage – if she does it well, and I was thankful to get away before the end.

You ask about the Weir Comee. It finishes tomorrow & the report may be expected about Wednesday. Weir tells me that the other side gave themselves away completely & evidently hopes for a favourable report. With my approval he met last week a committee of the Labour Party appointed by R.M. & including Wheatley Henderson & Greenwood. They said they had an open mind & wanted information which he supplied to them but the significant thing is that they left upon *his* mind the strong impression that what they wanted was something to make a good case to their own people for not supporting the building Unions!

Weir also told me that if he had been willing to take orders from individual visitors who have been passing through the demonstration house in Lower Regent St he could have sold 300 a day. At Newton Stewart in Ayrshire where he had a contract for 11 houses, before they were half up inhabitants of the little town came along with cheques & ordered 11 more & the provost said "You are not going to leave here until you have supplied the whole of our needs. But dont pay these unskilled men so much money they have never had so much before and they're all getting drunk in the public house every night"!

...

12 April 1925
Cairnton, Banchory

My dear Ida,

...

Well, here I am, as you see, escaped from my toils. I observed in the Scotsman that the announcement that the Minister of Health had gone to Aberdeen had given rise to facetious comment – to the effect I suppose that Aberdeen was not generally looked upon as a holiday resort, but in this lovely weather anywhere out of doors is delightful and I need hardly say that the Dee is looking its very best. In fact I have never been here under such agreeable circumstances, being more accustomed to blizzards and bitter east winds. The water is very

---

[20] Sybil Thorndike (1882–1976). English actress. Played title role in the first English performance of *St Joan* 1924. Created Dame 1931.

high – perhaps a little too high for the perfection of fishing – but there is little to complain of and though the salmon have been very "stiff" they have relaxed a little lately and I have already had 3 out and lost another – the best start I have ever made here.

I finished up all my chores on Thursday but have got a terrific density of engagements for the week beginning the 20th and about 5 hours work waiting in a box for me here. I got my Rent Restriction Bill through Committee in a single morning! but my difficulties will be considerable when I have R. & V. and Pensions on together. I do wonder how the latter will be received. I see Ramsay declaring that the Labour Party will "fight and fight" until they get pensions for widows and orphans. Humbug, of course, seeing that it is included in our programme but indicating I think that he has no idea that we shall produce anything this year. Indeed the secret has been well kept and Winston is looking eagerly forward to a *Sensation*.

I have had a brain wave about the autumn. I am going to spend a month or six weeks visiting various parts of the country where I shall inspect housing schemes hospitals and municipal schemes of one kind or another. The P.M. is delighted with the idea and so is Robinson. I believe it will be very much appreciated in the country and it will moreover be helpful to me.

...

26 April 1925
Westbourne

My dear Hilda,

...

Ida says you have written about the nursing Associations – perhaps to Eaton Sq. If so, I shall get your note this evening. Dr Lyster was to have headed a deputation of the M.O.H. to me on Thursday but he did not put in an appearance. They came to talk about propaganda on Health and in particular to suggest the formation of a Central Board on which the Ministry and *their Society* should each have 10 members & the principal local authorities Associations (including the Co. Councils Assn) one member each. I emphatically said No to such a preposterous proposal adding that whilst a Central Board was perhaps necessary they might dismiss from their minds the idea that they would have any such representation or that they would be put in a position to tell the local authorities, their employers, how to carry on their business. Whereupon they thanked me and said my answer was "extremely satisfactory"! It was exactly the old story of the miners who having enquired of their delegates how the manager had received them when they went to ask for a rise of wages and having been informed that the manager merely observed "You go to h-ll", unanimously agreed that "'e couldn't say no fairer than that".

...

I had three other deputations this week – one from West Ham Guardians who say I am "Worse than Mond" but who I believe from private information made up their minds that as I was so disagreeable they would just have to cut down their expenditure. Then I had one from Liverpool who came to try and bargain with me to be let off the consequences of their own blunders over an Addison scheme of housing. I drove a hard bargain with them. Finally the Assocn of Mun. Corpns. came to protest against the conclusions of the Comee on the rating of machinery. The conclusions are that machinery is to be rated but given a rebate of 75%. That seems to me quite illogical and I am trying to persuade the Cabinet to let me exclude machinery from rating altogether. If I succeed the A.M.C. will be very cross, and I am bound to say my office (except Robinson) are against me, but I think I am right & K. Wood is quite certain I am. (He looks solely at political expediency).

We came down here on Friday for a number of engagements including the Annual meeting of the Ladywood Assn. I took the opportunity of re-stating my position about the seat in terms which while they sounded just the same as what I had said previously were really rather different and were carefully chosen to mark that what I cared about was the *city* and not the division. I prefaced my observations with the hope that they would forgive a personal touch; – this was meant as a hint to the reporters, and I see the passage is reproduced in the Post verbatim. It may be useful to me presently!

I do wish we could show you our polyanthus border …

I wish too that you could see the orchids here. They really are very lovely …

The Daily Mail correspondent came to my p.s. on Thursday (the Cabinet was on Wednesday) and said they had information that I had put a complete scheme of widows & orphans & old age pensions before them; that they had approved the scheme and authorised the Chancellor to include the necessary arrangements in the Budget. My sec. said that much of their information was so incorrect that perhaps they would be wiser not to publish anything and they didn't. But where did they get their information and who dines with Lord Burnham![21]

---

[21] Harry Lawson Webster Lawson (1862–1933). Liberal Unionist MP for St Pancras 1885–92, Gloucestershire East 1893–95, Mile End 1905–6 and 1910–16. Chairman of Joint Committee which formulated the 'Burnham Scales' for teacher's pay 1920; Chairman, International Labour Conferences 1921, 1922, 1926; Managing proprietor, *Daily Telegraph* 1903–28; Chairman, Newspaper Proprietors Association. Succeeded as Baron Burnham 1916 and created Viscount Burnham 1919.

2 May 1925
37 Eaton Square, SW1

My dear Hilda,

...

You ask for impressions of the Budget & the Budget speech. It was a great triumph for Winston who enjoyed himself thoroughly and treated his subject with masterly skill, relating every part of the whole abounding in witticisms and overflowing with spirits & good humour. The Budget itself was regarded as very satisfactory on the whole & fully up to the expectations of its originality & boldness. The Morning Post representative told me that in 20 years experience he never remembered a Budget which had been so favourably received. But further reflection has undoubtedly produced a reaction. There was some disappointment that the income tax reduction was only 6d but I think it is recognised that expectation of a greater relief was not justified. Commendation of the boon to the black coated worker is general, but people do not like the new death duties. The McKenna duties are a cause of much rejoicing but speaking generally industry is somewhat disgruntled over silk and over the new pensions burden. I have always anticipated that this would be the most serious criticism pensions would have to face but though it means a certain amount of grousing I don't believe it will gather overwhelming force in view of the popularity of the scheme among the workers, especially if we are able to reduce the burden of unemployment dole.

As regards Winston's excursion into my preserves I perceive that things are turning out much as I foresaw. My Dept was furious but I always thought that embarrassment would fall on W. rather than on me and I observe that some of my colleagues are determined that he shant assume the whole credit for himself. His exposition was the weakest part of his speech. He did not manage it very well and the House got puzzled & a little tired until he turned to something else. But there is no doubt that the Labour Party are thoroughly sick. Their faces were the picture of gloom and we hear from various sources how thoroughly they have been disconcerted. Smillie[22] said to one Unionist "There will be no more use for Trade Unions now". Another Labour man said "We have lost our opportunity and you will be in now for 20 years". These are of course absurd exaggerations but there was more truth in what a Liberal said to Hogg. "I cannot disguise from myself that you are gaining hundreds of adherents every day and for my party I see no future at all".

The "scene" in the House on Thursday was quite unjustiable [sic] although in the light of what happened it may be said that Winston might have put what he wanted to say more judiciously.[23] But to me listening it sounded quite

---

[22] Robert Smillie (1857–1942). President, Scottish Miners' Federation 1894–1918, 1922–28; President MFGB 1912–21. Labour MP for Morpeth 1923–29. Chairman, PLP 1924.

[23] On 30 April Churchill's warning about 'a habit of qualifying for unemployment relief' and

unprovocative and the row is really a measure of the soreness of the Labour party over their own discomfiture.

Be that as it may, it seems clear that the atmosphere of the House has been changed by the Budget. Instead of that sleepy rather good tempered attitude which allowed everything to go through with a mild protest, we find an opposition thoroughly frightened and therefore determined to snap on every possible occasion. That is not a happy mood for the reception of my Bill and it is evident that I shall have all my work cut out for me to pilot my two big clumsy vessels into port. I am already collecting some of the cargo on the Rating & Valuation Bill and making it ready to be thrown overboard in the hopes of retrieving it again in the autumn.

I had a great fight to get the Second reading before Pensions as W.C. couldn't bear the thought of any interruption to the public concentration on the Budget. In order to secure this he was preparing criticisms of R. & V. suggesting the impossibility of getting it through and the desirability of avoiding controversies.

However I guessed what his attitude would be and went round to see the P.M. to make sure that he understood. The P.M. was non committal at the time but in Cabinet, just when W.C. was careering along full tilt against me, he neatly put out his foot & sent him flying head over heels. In fact W.C. got up & left the room and we saw him no more!

There seems to be a notion now that the opposn will move for the Pensions Bill to be taken on the floor of the House & that we shall not be able to resist the demand. If so, that will of course very much lengthen the procedure, but it may enable me to take R. & V. all morning & Pensions all afternoon!

...

Atholl has just been here he hasn't definitely got our house fixed but declares that he will find something. He tells me that he hopes to get a contract for 1000 of his steel houses this week. He is also supplying wards for hospitals on the same line and has just got an enquiry from the United Fruit Co of America for a shipload of houses for Florida plantations!

...

9 May 1925
Westbourne

My dear Ida,

It is just striking midnight as I start this letter, but we have been kept late at a "party" in the constituency (with speech) and I must smoke a pipe before I go to bed – where I am going to breakfast tomorrow morning.

---

refusal to withdraw the remark caused uproar from the Labour benches as 'an insult to the working classes' and he was forced to leave the Chamber unable to finish his speech.

Last night we had the annual meeting of our Association and for the first time for many years held it in the Town Hall. Lowe was in the chair and really was the limit. Fancy saying to a working class audience "I am sure we are all very glad of the reduction in income tax and supertax but I don't like this increase in the death duties. I am sure we all approve of pensions to widows but I dont like this lowering of the age for old age pensioners. I am sure we shall all sympathise with the domestic servants for having to pay so much more for insurance but whatever our anxieties and misgivings we must make the best of it. And now let us turn to a brighter subject"! That is literally what he said though it seems incredible, and the only comfort was that ¾ of the audience could not hear a word.

I confined my remarks to pensions and gave a brief outline of the main provisions. I had wondered whether after all that had appeared in the press it was worth while but I have been told already by a large number of people that after hearing or reading what I said they understood the scheme for the first time and that my account made everything clear. My agent was very delighted and said I had made a big impression and from all sides comes the view that our people are immensely bucked while the Socialists have "got the wind up."

I have noted the point you mention about the young childless widow which is being strongly run by some of the feminist societies. I am having actuarial calculations made on the assumption that the widow is only to get the pension if she has attained the age of 40 at the time of her husband's death, but I dont think the alteration is very likely to find favour. I look at the case from the point of view of the man who after all pays the contributions and who, as it seems to me, will want first & foremost to be assured that his wife will be provided for. I imagine that the pension in the event of his death might be a strong argument for the young fellow who is urging his girl to marry him at once.

The answer to your other question is that the uninsured will have none of their existing rights taken from them, only they dont get any new ones. Therefore they are still eligible for pension at 70 subject to means test.

I agree with you in disliking the death duties but as I believe I said before they would sooner or later have been raised anyhow and at any rate we have got something off the supertax in the meantime. Of course it is too late for me to insure against the extra death duties.

I have had a series of excursions & alarums about the R. & V. Bill. The whips have got in a panic about the business and have been doing all they know, short of coming direct to me, to get it dropped. Its been postponed & changed about several times but I have held my ground that it must be proceeded with and S.B. has nobly backed me up. Finally a "deal" has been arranged so far as the opposition is concerned that we shall have the 2nd reading by 8.15 on Wednesday but if, as seems certain, we dont get the Bill through all its stages by August we shall finish it in the autumn session. There still remains a danger from our own side but I hope I have squared the most active of our possible opponents and I am I think justified in believing that we shall get over the stile on Wednesday. It seems pretty certain that Pensions will go into Committee of the whole House & if that allows of my taking R. & V. upstairs myself that may be an advantage as there are parts of it which Robinson believes no one else can carry.

I daresay you saw that I got Rent Restriction through third reading without a division this week. It is significant that all efforts on the party [sic] of the Socialists to work up an agitation about it have failed already.

You may like to tell Hilda that recently I sent for a report on the Somersetshire Insurance scheme and gave instructions that the department was to consider an amendment to the law with a view to making it clear that Co. Councils may make such schemes.

I have been amusing myself with doing something for the University. Some time ago Lord Bearsted (né [sic] Sir Marcus Samuel) wrote to the Times and said he had been horrified to find that one of the youngest & most modern Universities was content to possess only German built Diesel engines of obsolete design. A couple of days after I was sitting next him at a dinner & he told me that Birmingham was the culprit. I thought his attack was not quite fair but I determined that as he had made it he should find us a new engine and after much correspondence I have brought it off. Whether the makers are giving the engine themselves or whether Bearsted is making it worth their while I dont know but anyway he negotiated the deal and we are to have a brand new engine British built. I shall try and get Bearstead [sic] an honorary degree which he wants but the Univy is rather sticky about it.

…

16 May 1925
Westbourne

My dear Hilda,

…

We have come here to get a little rest & peace after a very hard week and with another before us. But the afternoon has been made hideous by a band in the Bot. Gdns of a more than usually excruciating character …

…

The R. & V. Bill was really a triumph though not a spectacular one. After all the panic about it on the part of the Whips you see we got our 2nd Rdg quite comfortably in half a day. But it was done by sheer hard work. I slaved away at it every night till one and two in the morning so that when the time came I really felt I had mastered the beastly thing and I believe I disarmed the opposition, which had been skilfully worked up by the Poor Law people even to an intensive barrage of Members by telegrams and a tremendous display of sandwich [boards?] even outside the House, simply by convincing them that they couldn't find anything I hadn't thought of and got an answer to. I had a big meeting of our Unionist M.P.'s on Tuesday and let them heckle me for an hour and a half and then just as I was going home I had a message from Bobby Monsell that the Agricultural men were in revolt and were demanding to see me or the P.M. to get the 2nd Rdg postponed. I went in at once to see them. There were about a dozen and I must say they were extraordinarily nice to me and after I had talked to them they withdrew their objections and said they would support me through thick & thin as they believed my programme was vital to the country.

Bobby now smiles amiably upon me once more and Robinson who has always been possessed by a horrid fear that our programme was too good to come true and that somehow our Bill would slip through is now quite boisterously happy and says that "after that night" he doesn't see why we shouldn't really accomplish our objectives according to plan.

...

Now I am at work on the Pensions Bill. I had to interrupt my labours to deal with Wheatley's "Profiteering" Bill which came on in the House yesterday. W. himself didn't turn up & I had no difficulty in demolishing his basetling [?]. But I wish he had chosen some other time to introduce it. Of course I do know the P. Bill pretty well but the 2nd Rdg is an important occasion & I find it necessary to prepare very carefully. I sat up till one this morning but I don't think I shall repeat that tonight as I feel rather tired.

All the same we are both surprisingly well and I dont feel on edge as I did last year which may – or may not – be due to L. Williams diet. I have got a little plan to "dror" those Labour men into a trap over their pretence that they would have had a non-contrib. scheme.

Did you see S.B.'s remarks about me at Oxford. Very nice of him.

23 May 1925
Westbourne

My dear Ida,

I dont think I am likely to have a worse week than this last for a good long time. I had Pensions Bill on Tuesday which meant working till 2 a.m. that morning on the speech. Wednesday I had Cabinet and sat through the debate till 11 (but didn't wait on till 6) Thursday I went to the Court and today have travelled to Lancaster and back – 8 hours in the train – and addressed a mass meeting for an hour this afternoon. I had two nights during which I got practically no sleep owing to my cough and I really wonder how it is that I am alive and still comparatively fresh at the end of it. ...

Anyway things have gone very well so far and the second reading was quite a triumph with 401 in our lobby. I shouldn't pay much attention to what the Whips say. They are always wrong and though getting the R. & V. through committee will be a weary business I don't believe we have anything very serious to fear.

My chief trouble is with the Whips themselves. Their powers of passive resistance are unlimited and in spite of all my efforts it is still doubtful whether I shall get a start before Whitsuntide. I have told them that if we dont the only result will be that I shall have to ask for an earlier autumn session.

There is nothing in the opposition of the Farmers. They dont understand the Bill but they have been told by Trustram Eve that it is a plot to put them "under the heel of Whitehall" & those who are overseers dont like being abolished. But I had a deputation from the County Councils Association this week and they promised me their active support.

Your conundrum is soon answered. The uninsured woman gets her pension by virtue of her husbands and if she is older than he she must wait till he is 65. Otherwise you might have a young man get a pension for his old wife & then go out of insurance and make no more contributions. It makes no difference if the woman has been insured & has gone out. She must have been insured (to get the pension in her own right) for 5 years before attaining the age of 65 & made not less than an average of 39 contributions in each of the 3 preceding years. Have you got a copy of the "Fools guide" CMD. 2405? It is invaluable for anyone who may have to explain the Bill.

Sunday morning It is wonderful what a difference it makes to one's outlook to get a good night's sleep. Last night, for the second time this week, I took a sleeping draught (or rather tabloid) and slept from almost the moment I got to bed about 11.30 till 8 this morning. There were times last week when the world looked very black indeed but this morning as I was shaving I was thinking that though I should never be a favourite with the press like Father was or Winston is, yet, if I have 4 or 5 years of office I may leave behind as a [sic] great a reputation as Minister of Health as Father did as Colonial Secretary. Only it will probably take longer for the public to find it out and it will only be after I am dead that my administration will be talked of as the Golden Age at the Ministry!

Robinson was saying to me the other day that he & some others had been discussing what Mond would have done with a bill like R. & V. Apparently he was very lazy and would never take the trouble to learn his case. Moreover he was so irregular in his attendance that they never knew where to catch him & Robinson had to go chasing about after him when he wanted a decision. "He wouldn't have known one thing about R & V" said Robinson, "but he was so shrewd that when he was asked a question to which he didn't know the reply, he answered something else!" I can imagine though that he was a source of some anxiety to the office. "The worst of trying to brief you" said Veale "is that we never can tell you anything you dont know already".

I dont know whether the Times gave you an adequate idea of the passage in my speech in which I drew Wheatley on Snowdens scheme. The Labour men went into my trap beautifully. Veale who of course knew I had the Snowden pamphlet in reserve said he hadn't enjoyed anything so much for a long time as watching the "toils closing in upon them". And of course they did have a bad time. They knew that the Snowden scheme was contributory & they knew that we knew that it was. Worthy followed it up next morning & in the evening the Attorney fairly turned the knife round and round in the wound till they simply squirmed. I never saw even the Labour Party look so foolish. Privately, Wheatley told Robinson when he was in office that a contributory scheme was the only way of tackling pensions and this week Greenwood went up to the official gallery and remarked that "Only the General Election saved us from having a contributory scheme ourselves." Aren't they a thoroughly dishonest lot?

It's rather nice that Grigg my P.S. at the Treasury came to congratulate me particularly on my speech & my drawing of Wheatley – and by the bye I met Sir Basil Blackett[24] one evening. He is now Finance Minister in India & is home on leave but formerly he was in the Treasury and of course he had been hobnobbing with his friends there. We met almost by chance and he at once introduced himself & remarked that he heard it had been a "great time" while I was there. I said I had been there for too brief a period to do anything, but he said that wasn't at all the view of the staff and that they looked back on my term with very great satisfaction & pleasure. I was really very pleased because the staff would tell him what they thought without reserve.

We had a great meeting yesterday in a huge Winter Garden and I believe people had come from all parts of North Lancashire & even Yorkshire. From what was said afterwards I couldn't help feeling certain that it had been a complete success. One man told me on the station platform that he had been talking to a railway foreman, a rough fellow, he said, but a good Unionist. "Ba Goom", said this individual "A wouldn't have missed that for something! Yon fella knows what he's talking about and I wished he'd a goued on longer". Seeing that I was a full hour that was a compliment to a weary and jaded statesman!

I am looking out of window [sic] at my Japanese cherry. I do wish you could see it. Its the most perfect thing ever produced, a shower of pink.

I finished my speech yesterday by quoting Blake's magnificent lines but as I only thought of it in the train I didn't get the words quite right. I wonder if you can correct me from memory. This is what I said of the Govt

> We will not cease from mental strife
> Nor sheathe the sword we have in hand
> Till we have built Jerusalem
> In England's green and pleasant land

He was mad as a hatter but he got off one or two good things.

---

[24] Basil Phillott Blackett (1882–1935). Treasury official. Secretary, Indian Finance and Currency Commission 1913–14 and Capital Issues Committee 1915; Member, Anglo-French Finance Mission to USA 1915; Member, National War Savings Committee 1916; represented Treasury in USA 1917–19; Controller of Finance, Treasury 1919–22; Finance Member, Viceroy's Executive Council, India 1922–28; Director, Bank of England. Knighted 1921.

30 May 1925
37 Eaton Square, SW1

My dear Hilda,

...

Annie is accumulating a terrific lot of acquaintances in Society and was dining and attending evening parties most days this week. Twice also we lunched with friends and once attended the luncheon of the English Speaking Union to the new American Ambassador[25] who, between ourselves, is a dull poor creature unworthy to rank with the big men who have preceded him. For some reason or other I was made to support the toast of his health proposed by Birkenhead. The latter made himself exceedingly agreeable to Annie and me and gave us a lift back in his car. He was much pleased with a little joke of mine which he declared he should use himself when he spoke in the U.S.A. next.

On the whole I think you are right in your view that things are still going well with the Govt, and they are rather helped than hindered by the Opposition. See for instance the astounding blunder of the Liberals over the Speaker. The fact is that they had determined to assert themselves by keeping the House up all night over the Finance Bill. The idea of this demonstrating their importance filled them with such satisfaction as they had not experienced for a long time. They planned out all their speeches. Kenworthy had one of 1 hr & 40 minutes, Trevelyan Thompson[26] was to be nearly as long, Wedgy Benn and Runcie[27] had prepared sheaves of notes and to crown all they decided that in order to be fresh and bright they would all *go to bed* in the afternoon! And they did! And came down all bursting with importance to the consciousness of being about to enter upon a deed of derring do. And then the Speaker gave the closure and everyone went home instead of being martyred. It was *too* funny to see Wedgy Benn's frantic indignation. My belief is that Ll.G. deliberately sacrificed himself by taking part in what he knew to be a foolish demonstration in order to put W. Benn and Runcie under an obligation to him and thereby consolidate his leadership. I cant otherwise account for his behaviour. Did you see, by the way, that he called me the Mad Hatter the other day in my absence! *Ll.G.* calling *me* mad! Well!

I think Horne is an illustration of an epigram evolved by Peter Sanders in speaking of the R. & V. Bill. "A disestablished authority is an established critic".

---

[25] Alanson B. Houghton (1863–1941). American businessman and diplomat. US Ambassador to Germany 1922–25 and to London 1925–29.

[26] Walter Trevelyan Thomson (1875–1928). Liberal MP for Middlesbrough West 1918–28.

[27] Walter Runciman (1870–1949). Liberal MP for Oldham 1899–1900, Dewsbury 1902–18, Swansea West 1924–29, St Ives 1929–37 (Liberal National from 1931) Parliamentary Secretary, LGB 1905–7; Financial Secretary, Treasury 1907–8; President, Board of Education 1908–11, Board of Agriculture 1911–14, Board of Trade 1914–16 and 1931–37. Lord President of Council 1938–39. Special Envoy to Czechoslovakia 1938. Created Viscount Runciman of Doxford 1937.

As a matter of fact I didn't think he was unfriendly and he was extraordinarily complimentary to me personally (not reported) but our people were angry with him and I am sure that from the political point of view he does himself no good by speeches of that kind however justified they may be. I think Winston has now made up his mind to help out industry through the unempt insurance fund the administration of the latter being considerably tightened up and this should satisfy every one in industry except the farmers. Of course the restoration of the "gap" and the reduction of benefit will mean a tremendous howl from the Labour party but I dont myself believe it will be generally unpopular for even the working people themselves, especially the women, recognise that the dole is abused and ought to be more strictly controlled.

I like the remark about you two that Ida overheard. There aren't many of us left, but the quality keeps up! ...

...

A. & I strolled up into Hyde Park on Friday to look at the Epstein.[28] To my mind it is barbarous affected and ugly as a piece of sculpture. I am however prepared to believe that an artist may find reasons for these offences against anatomy and nature. But I find it impossible to consider such a work otherwise than as a gross piece of impertinence when it is put forward as a memorial to Hudson.[29] The Committee of course knew what they were doing when they chose Epstein and I therefore condemn them & not him. But I ought to add perhaps that Annie (who hasn't read Green Mansions) doesn't altogether agree with me.

I am finishing this at the Gathorne Hardys[30] who have got a delightful home with a clear stream running through the garden. I had my first try with the dry fly last night. The fish were not rising well but I caught two & was well satisfied.

13 June 1925
37 Eaton Square, SW1

My dear Hilda,

...

Some of the Cabinet have had a rotten time sitting up, but I retired on Monday at 1.30 and havent been later at the House than 11 since then by virtue of my

---

[28] Jacob Epstein (1880–1959). American-born sculptor living in London from 1905. His massive monumental pieces which consciously used distortion as a technique of composition aroused much protest for indecency and blasphemy. Knighted 1954.

[29] William Henry Hudson (1841–1922). British naturalist and author of studies of Argentine and British birds and a romantic novel, *Green Mansions* (1904). A bird sanctuary containing Epstein's 'Rima' sculpture was erected in Hyde Park in 1925 as a memorial.

[30] Geoffrey Malcolm Gathorne-Hardy (1878–1972). Barrister, writer and scholar. Honorary Secretary, Royal Institute of International Affairs 1920–35; Assistant Librarian, House of Lords 1923–28. Married Kathleen Goschen 1914.

general dispensation from the P.M. I felt some pricking of conscience inasmuch as my hard work has hardly begun yet, but I stifled them on the ground that I must be fresh to start with if I was to get through.

I have been working through my deputations & clearing the way for committees. I have received four this week and still have some more to get through, and I made a start with R. & V. Comee on Thursday. The Whips, being irritable after their late nights, are returning to their attack on the Bill but I dont think S.B. will pay much attention to their suggestions that I am "ruining the party"!

...

21 June 1925
37 Eaton Square, SW1

My dear Ida,

I have just got your letter on our return from the Wilfrid Ashleys[31] where we have been spending the week end at Broadlands near Romsey ... Mrs A. is I suppose very "smart", but I met her at dinner some time ago and was surprised to find that I like her. Annie also finds that she has great charm & is rather an interesting person and so when we got the invitation to Broadlands we decided to accept.

You may or may not know that "Wilfrid" is a descendant of "Pam" [Palmerston] whose home was Broadlands and the house is full of all sorts of interesting political curios. ... And to my great joy I learned that there be salmon in the Test (I only knew it as a trout river) and that a mile and a half below the house one was caught with a fly on Friday. So I spent the whole of yesterday morning and this morning flogging the water & though I didn't even get a rise I thoroughly enjoyed myself. The weather was brilliant – perhaps too brilliant – the birds sang loudly particularly the sedge warblers and lots of flowers were out or just coming out. Moreover I was all alone! It was heavenly.

But we had an amusing party as it contained such a curious mixture. The Ullswaters were the most dignified – he rather melancholy and a little embittered perhaps at feeling "out of it", she gambling away at bridge all afternoon & evening rating her unhappy partners and when not so engaged making cattish remarks about her lady friends. Then there was the Hungarian Minister, very voluble and very anxious to be agreeable, Grace, Lady Newborough, perfectly brainless & only able to discuss 2 subjects dressing and dancing, Sir Tom and Lady Bridges[32] "on leave" from their Governorship of South Australia and one

---

[31] William James Ashley (1860–1927). Economist. Professor of Political Economy, Toronto University 1888–92 and Economic History, Harvard 1892–1901 and Commerce, Birmingham University 1901–25. Vice-Principal, Birmingham University 1918–25.

[32] George Tom Molesworth Bridges (1871–1939). Lieutenant-Colonel, 1914. Head, British Military Mission, Belgian Field Army 1914–16; Major-General, 19th Division 1916–17. Head, British

or two middle aged Society men. Do you wonder what we found to do in that galère? Well, Annie listened & chuckled over the gossip advised Lady Newborough about her complexion; and asked all the men questions with such interest that they were lost in admiration of their own conversational powers and I fished, played tennis, and was conducted round the shows. Really it was a very amusing and successful week end.

...

The House has had some very late nights over the Finance Bill but I have taken advantage of my dispensation and the latest I have stopped was 1.30 on Wednesday. Tomorrow is the report stage of the Finance Bill but it is an off night for my group so I shall escape again. I havent reached the peak of my labours which will I suppose come next month with the Pensions Bill. I am rather nervous about the R. & V. when I have to leave it to others. This week I thought I must give one amendt to the Solr General to take lest he should get huffy at being asked to attend and then having nothing to do. The one I chose was very simple and I thought safe, but hey presto in a trice he had the Committee by the ears and Josh Wedgewood's [sic] protests were so lengthy that we failed to get the 3rd clause before the Comee rose. But for that I think things have gone pretty well, for though we have certainly moved slowly there has been no deliberate obstruction and no exacerbation of the malcontents on our side.

I seem to have a terrible number of deputations this time. I had another this week from the West Ham guardians who are defying me at present but want money. They threaten that if I don't give it them they will go on strike. I reply that I decline to give it them unless they reduce their extravagance in the distribution of relief. So there is a deadlock & it remains to be seen what will happen next.

Another deputation came from the British Medical Ass. who turned up about 40 strong to protest against my action in firing certain panel doctors & to demand my acceptance of 4 "principles". Robinson anticipated a "heated atmosphere" but I did not propose to give them an opportunity of developing heat, and prepared myself by thoroughly "mugging up" the case. The result was entirely satisfactory. They said afterwards to one of my people that it was the first time they had met a Minister who thoroughly understood what he was talking about, and as a matter of fact I routed them in my argument so that they had to retire, and leave their "principles" on the field. But our conversation was extremely amicable and they were quite satisfied with the result because they really had got hold of a wrong idea of what I was after and when it was made clear they approved. ...

The position about Weir is that I have at last got his new plans & sent them round to the L.A. I have up to now only heard about one viz. Bristol which has

War Mission to USA 1918 and to Allied Armies of Orient 1918–20; Governor, South Australia 1922–27. Knighted 1919.

funked the Unions. Next week I shall see better how the land lies but I dont think Weir has been very helpful lately. I fancy he has been too much absorbed in his Sugar Beet and electricity schemes to bother about housing but I am told he is now returning to it.

...

27 June 1925
Westbourne

My dear Hilda,

...

We pursued our incursions into the smart set by dining on Tuesday with Lady Henry[33] in Carlton Gardens. She is the widow of a Liberal M.P.[34] and her name was at one time rather notoriously associated with Ll.G. She is rolling in money and I fancy is pretty generous with it but she isn't exactly my taste. It was a huge party with a distinctly Liberal flavour though diluted with other parties. ...

I agree that things look rather bad industrially. The great increase in unemployment however is chiefly due to coal. Over 400 collieries have been closed since the beginning of last year and the process is still going on. Shipbuilding iron & steel & heavy engineering are also very bad & cotton seems to be going down hill. The only gleam that I can see is the fact that people are beginning to realise the situation and the miners who are at the bottom of everything are getting near a crisis. They still wont accept an increase of hours and I am told that a strike is coming, but I am hoping that the issue will have been fought out by October and that thereafter things will improve. But undoubtedly the Govt have got some very difficult months ahead and the Daily Mail & the Daily Express are making things as much worse as they can. I dont see the latter so I dont know what they are running but every day the D.M. has a leader on The Unjust Bill or The Unwanted Bill, meaning Pensions and it damns the Govt in general and the P.M. in particular with all the energy it can command. So far as I am concerned I dont much mind as it draws fire from the R. & V. which hasn't got the same drive behind it. It is not going nearly as fast as I should like in Committee but I am very well satisfied with the atmosphere which is getting much more friendly under my skilful hand! On Thursday for instance I got four clauses without a single division.

I reckon this coming week is going to be the peak. Tuesday Wednesday Thursday & Friday in Committee on Pensions and the eleven oclock rule sus-

---

[33] Julia Henry (née Lewisohn). Beautiful young American wife of Sir Charles Henry. Lloyd George's casual affair with her from 1907 until 1911 prompted a succession of embarrassing scenes.
[34] Charles Solomon Henry (1860–1919). Australian copper millionaire and Liberal MP for Wellington 1906–18 and The Wrekin 1918–19. Created Bart 1911.

pended the first three nights. I think for the time I shall abandon the R. & V. to Kingsley as it would be physically impossible to attend both Bills *and* do the necessary preparation. The amendments to the Pensions Bill are nearly all demonstrations, not real business, such as doubling the benefits and abolishing the contributions. There are however some serious ones and I am now working on a new scheme so as to have some alternative to offer as I dont want the House to get into the mood when it says What's the use of putting down suggestions when every one is rejected on this parrot cry of no money. I dont think the new scheme will be as good as the old but it will serve as a cockshy and could be worked. The idea is to increase childrens' allowances and put the age limit up to which they are payable at 16 instead of 14. To provide for this widows pension would cease 2 years after the husbands death if there are no children under 16 and otherwise 2 years after the youngest becomes 16, but the widow would come in for old age pension at 65. The actuary is making the calculations now and if there is enough saving I could either prolong the 2 years or let the o.a.p. begin before 65. I wonder how this strikes you. I call it an ingenious plan to meet the views of those who want to do more for the young widow with dependent children but of course it is hard on the elderly ones.

I didnt hear Austen's speech but was told he did very well. His pact policy seems to be working very successfully but this Chinese bother is very unfortunate & disconcerting. I suppose we have to thank the Bolshies for it and for the loss of Eastern trade involved. I am, I fear, going to have trouble on my account with the West Ham guardians. I have given them every opportunity of a compromise but they have flatly defied me and it looks as if the affair would boil up next week, just when I am in the middle of Pensions. Luckily I shall have a nice rest next week end as it happens that on Saturday Prince Arthur[35] is opening our Hall of Memory and when we have finished with that we attend our annual Unionist out door demonstration in the Botanical Gardens and harangue the multitude. And to round it off I get up early on Sunday to address an adult school in the constituency and if I can manage to avoid the H. of C. on Monday I am to open the new headquarters of the Municipal Bank. ...

    ...

5 July 1925
Westbourne

My dear Ida,

It is a perfect summer day and I am (mentally) reposing on the reflection that I have come safely through the heaviest week I am likely to have this session. It

---

[35] Prince Arthur (1883–1938). Son of Prince Arthur, Duke of Connaught, 1850–1942. Governor-General of South Africa 1920–23.

certainly has been a strenuous one. On Tuesday for instance I started on R. & V. committee at 11 and on Pensions Bill at 4 and then sat right on till 7 a.m. At 9 a.m. I got out of bed again and went to the office where I arrived soon after 10. At 11.30 we had Cabinet till 1.30. At 2.30 I addressed the International Congress of Radiologists and at 3.45 I began Pensions again & sat on till 6 a.m. on Thursday. At 11 I got out of bed having breakfasted and went to the office; I lunched at the House & answered my questions as a demonstration and then went on Pensions again till 8.15. By that time however we had made an arrangement with the Opposition as to the number of days & hours to be given to the rest of the Bill and the "kick" was out of the debate. It is true that they were unable to control their people on Friday and we are 3½ clauses behind scheduled time but they will have to make it up later.

You will see that all that was a severe test both of physical and mental endurance but I am glad to say that I came through with an ease that astonished the House. In fact it was not until I got home on Thursday & the strain relaxed that I really felt "done" & then the night's sleep made me quite fresh again. We had a pretty anxious time trying to decide whether we should use the guillotine after Wheatley's blatant obstruction on Wednesday. Many of our people – in fact I think most – thought we should never get the Bill without it. I took the view that we could do without it if our people were willing to go on sitting up and declared my own readiness to do so but the P.M. & the Chief Whip concluded, probably rightly, that it was the machine that would break down – the Chairmen of Committee, the officials, the printing & stationery & so forth. So we decided definitely against the guillotine and in default of arrangement to let the Bill go over to the autumn postponing the widows pensions till July. It was this consideration that brought the Labour Party to heel. It was hinted ever so delicately that we should have to inform the country why pensions were postponed and although they continue to declaim about the unpopularity of the Bill they werent prepared to face the postponement.

So far as concessions are concerned I have introduced them here and there just to make things go more smoothly. The reason for the increase of orphan's allowances is just what you supposed viz that so often they don't live together. As for the alternative scheme which you dont like there will be no necessity to mention it even. The "drive" against the young childless widow has completely collapsed and when Nancy moved an amendment on lines somewhat similar to mine (but not nearly so drastic) she was jumped on from all sides of the House.

I must tell you of the ludicrous incident that happened at the Radiological Conference. The "organisers" sent "notes" in the form of a speech to me and they sent the same notes to the Duke of Connaught who was to open the proceedings. Sir G. Newman[36] then told them that their notes were unsuitable

---

[36] George Newman (1870–1948). Chief Medical Officer, Board of Education 1907–35 and Ministry of Health 1919–35. Chairman, Health of Munitions Workers Committee; member of

for the Duke and sent them a new speech for him which did not mention any of the things in mine. They sent Newman's speech on but omitted to say that it was an alternative with the result that the Duke read them *both*, and opened the Congress twice once in the middle of his remarks and again at the end. You can imagine Newman's feelings, as he sat on the platform blandly smiling but sweating with anxiety as he pictured his Minister attempting hurried to construct an entirely new oration on the spur of the moment. Fortunately however the "notes" were so extraordinarily bad that the Minister had rejected them and constructed something entirely different. But someone in the Duke's entourage remarked with a puzzled air that H.R.H. had made the longest speech he had ever heard him deliver.

...

We had a tremendous gathering of Unionists here in the Botanical Gardens yesterday the numbers exceeding any previous record. Only Amery & I represented the Cabinet and we had 4 other members but perhaps it was as well that there were no more than 6 speeches! I got up this morning and duly delivered my address to the morning school & tomorrow I am to open new headquarters for the Municipal Bank. By the way Grant Robertson whom I met yesterday at the Lord Mayor's luncheon to Prince Arthur tells me the University is going to confer an honorary degree! I shall have the freedom of the City yet some day – if I dont die first.

...

11 July 1925
37 Eaton Square, SW1

My dear Hilda,

I think you are right in saying that the work this week has been nearly as heavy as the week before, and next week it will be heavier still, but about one more after that ought to see me through Pensions & the worst of R. & V.

I have had a lot of worry over R. & V. which has been making very heavy weather in Committee. This is perhaps partly due to my own absence for we had *three* Cabinets this week, but partly to the fact that the Bill has no enthusiastic friends while its enemies have been growing in consequence of the campaign organised against it.

Yesterday I got all the Unionists on the Committee to come to my room and I fought with them for 1½ hr. When I say "fought" I should rather say I "bore their attack" which was very formidable. At the end I made a speech explaining the inner meanings & purpose of the Bill and making various suggestions. Kingsley Wood was delighted & thought the meeting would do no end of good

---

Central Control Board (Liquor Trade) 1915–19 and various other committees including TB and Medical Research. Knighted 1911 but refused peerage by MacDonald.

but though the spirit was quite nice and everyone spoke with the greatest respect & even reverence, I was most impressed with the serious nature of the opposition and I resolved at once to send for the carpenter to stand by the masts with his axe!

By pitching the Revenue officer overboard and getting rid of tophamper in Railway Clauses & Ratings of Machinery I think I may yet save the ship.

But it will be a near thing and I shall be very thankful when I can feel certain about it. The Whips haven't made things easy by arranging for pensions bill to be taken 3 days running it gives one no time to prepare in between whiles.

...

19 July 1925
37 Eaton Square, SW1

My dear Ida,

Midnight is just striking so I am a bit late in beginning my letter. The fact is we haven't been to Westbourne ... but to Cliveden and we have motored back tonight starting at 10 p.m. Lord! what a party. I counted 27 just before dinner but they hadn't all turned up. They ranged from Kings & Queens, through duchesses and editors down to common or garden ministers & though I cant say it was a restful week end I must admit it was an amusing one, Nancy herself carrying on the most entertaining witty and imprudent monologue the whole time. She is a little bundle of nerves and is wearing herself out, but I believe she enjoys life. For a long time I disliked her intensely but Annie penetrated to her real self some time ago and now I have come to regard her with something like the tolerant affection one feels for a warmhearted merry and sometimes very naughty child. In return she has a great respect and liking for both of us.

I had a gruelling three days over Pensions and on Thursday afternoon I felt about done in. But a night's sleep put me right again and fit for another two days this week to finish with.

Horne is on the wrong tack about Health Insurance and is stirring up a hornets nest which will attack him pretty venomously soon. The fact which I think he has failed to appreciate is that there is no aggregate surplus. The surpluses are the individual property of the Approved Societies of which there are between 8000 & 9000. Some have surpluses running up to £10 per head others are in deficiency. And any reduction in contribution will increase the number in deficiency while leaving others with surpluses. I don't think he has made up his mind whether he wants to preserve or to abolish existing benefits.

As to R. & V. the railway clauses will form part of a new Bill next year. Rating of machinery will be left to a free vote of the House & if defeated may or may not be reintroduced in another Bill. But the sticker was the Revenue officer and now he has gone the Comee races along at such a pace that we can hardly keep up with it. Last time I was present we ran right beyond my notes so that I was quite embarrassed by not knowing what was the effect of the amdts we were discussing. I think we shall probably finish the Committee stage now.

On Monday I drove through London with Their Majesties in an open carriage with four greys & postilions amid cries of "Good old George" to open the new B.M.A. buildings. T.M. were very "gracious" & kept up a constant flow of conversation all the time they were bowing to the crowds. When we had gone round the presentations we went to the Great Hall for the addresses which went off well with two exceptions. Lutyens[37] forgot where he had put the key & was unable to produce it when suddenly called upon to present it to the King. Subsequently it was discovered in the pocket of the Archbishop of Canterbury who had put it there because Lutyens couldn't be trusted with it but had forgotten it himself! The other contretemps was that when the American Professor who was to represent his country was called for *he* couldn't be found and there was an awkward moment. At last however a red faced gentleman was seen to be struggling to get out of the middle of a row in which he had imprisoned himself. When he finally emerged he turned out to be the lost Professor. These little contretemps however were forgotten in the interest of some "specimens" which had been set out for T.M. inspection and included the ulcers which killed Napoleon! Disgusting!

The next morning I had to go and address a Congress of Opthamologists at 10 a.m. I was very vexed at its coming on a day when I had R. & V. in the morning & Pensions from 3.45 onwards. But afterwards I met some Doctor who had been there & who told me that my speech had delighted the Congress & that the American doctors in particular had been immensely impressed with my knowledge of the subject! Well! Well!

...

On Friday I got the 2nd reading of my Therapeutic Substances Bill & we finished up with a dinner party here and then went on to the Duke of York's party. What a life!

...

23 July 1925
Westbourne

My dear Hilda,

...

We have made absolutely no engagements this week end and are thankful for the rest, for both of us had about got to the end of our tether. I found again that I felt pretty fresh until I had got through my task but then I seemed to go rather to

---

[37] Edwin Landseer Lutyens (1869–1944). English architect. Works include the Cenotaph, Liverpool Roman Catholic Cathedral, the Viceroys House, New Delhi and the British Embassy in Washington. Knighted 1918.

pieces and I cursed like anything at having to go and open a nurses home in Marylebone yesterday and make two speeches. This morning we had breakfast in bed and I didn't get down till 12.

I had some anxious moments on Report of Pensions but got through safely and finished up the third reading amid showers of bouquets from the opposition as well as our own side. The only person who was thoroughly disgruntled was Horne who was evidently rattled at finding the House against him over his proposal to reduce Health contributions and displayed extraordinary bad temper while I was speaking, constantly interrupting in the most irritable way which did him no good. He has lost caste in the House which somehow suspects him of insincerity and too much devotion to shekels.

I have had so many compliments paid me that my head would be quite turned if I really were politically ambitious. I enclose a copy of a letter from the King to the P.M. which was so nice that I went and thanked him for it at the garden party on Friday. His Majesty was exceedingly affable and said that from all sides he had heard praises of my conduct of my bills. The Speaker too was very complimentary and Bryan Fell[38] who has had a very long experience of the House came up to congratulate me and said he had never seen anything like it and that it was a great Parliamentary triumph. Any way I am very glad its over and I think we have made such progress with R. & V. that we shall get that through Committee stage before we rise.

We have had a very anxious time with the Naval crisis and the coal crisis. Of course the papers describe the result of the former as a victory for the Admiralty and I suppose it is though they havent got nearly all they wanted. But the Cabinet is very sore over the way the Admirals have behaved and I don't fancy Beatty[39] will remain where he is much longer.

...

I am told now that the House is likely to rise on the 7th. ...

But all these plans may be upset by coal. Things look a little less desperate tonight but the situation is pretty serious and all along those who have been most closely in touch with the facts have been the most hopeless.

...

---

[38] Bryan Hugh Fell (1869–1955). Assistant Clerk, House of Commons 1893–1931; Principal Clerk, Public Bills Office 1931–34. Knighted 1935.

[39] David Beatty (1871–1936). Entered Navy 1884. Naval Secretary to First Lord of Admiralty 1912; commanded 1st Battle Cruiser Squadron 1913–16; C-in-C, Grand Fleet 1916–19; First Sea Lord, 1919–27. Knighted 1914. Created Earl Beatty 1919.

1 August 1925
37 Eaton Square, SW1

My dear Ida,

Before this you will have learned of the termination of the immediate crisis in the coal industry.[40] I am sure everyone's first remark will have been "Thank God", probably followed by "I always said something would happen to stop it". And it will only be after the public has got used to the comfort of taking its holiday in peace that it will begin to grouse at the Government. "What's the country coming to? Where's it going to stop. This Govts no better than any other; they all run away" and so on.

Well, we had a difficult decision to make and we were not unanimous. Everyone realised what would be said about our weakness Surrender to Communists & so forth – particularly by those who had not got our information. But I personally never had any doubts as to what we ought to do. If we had not intervened we should have had ¾ of the industries of the country crippled in a few weeks, thousands of people would have been ruined, hundreds of thousands would have suffered great & prolonged hardship, class warfare would have been stimulated to the utmost pitch and the moderates would have been thrown into the arms of the extremists. The trade of the country would have suffered a blow from which it would hardly have recovered in our lifetime, the revenue would have been diminished to an extent that might well have involved another 6d on the income tax, the pensions would probably have had to be postponed and any hope of further social reforms abandoned. *And* we might conceivably have been beaten after all, though I can hardly believe it.

There may well be moments when it is necessary to face such terrific risks, because there is no alternative but certain disaster or grave dishonour. But we are not at such a moment. The challenge is no doubt exploited by Bolshevists but it does not arise from Bolshevism. Both sides have much to put forward that is very reasonable. The public is puzzled, suspicious of the owners, sympathetic with the miners, badly informed as to what are the causes of the trouble. It would condemn us justly if we allowed the nation to drift into civil war without having probed to the bottom every possible alternative. To my mind therefore the thing to do was to play for time & to pay the lowest price that would buy that time. Having got it we should use it
1. to inform ourselves
2. to inform the public
3. To endeavour to persuade T.U.'s generally of our reasonableness & so separate them from the miners if the latter prove intractable

---

[40] 'Red Friday', 31 July 1925. After a TUC threat to embargo the movement of coal to counter a threatened mining lockout, the Government intervened at the last moment with a nine-month subsidy to avert immediate pay cuts while the Samuel Commission investigated the industry.

4.   To strengthen our defences against Communism & to build up an organisation to function in case of "direct action" by coal & transport workers

It was not the fact that I had any part in formulating the terms of the actual settlement. I think they had gradually emerged during the course of the negotiations as the only possible way of averting the general strike. But when it fell to the Cabinet to take the fateful decision on Thursday evening and it came to my turn to speak I expressed views similar to what I have written and apparently they made an impression particularly on the P.M. who asked me to come & see the owners with him & Winston. The latter remarked to the P.M. that he had never heard a case put to a Cabinet more weightily and effectively, but perhaps this observation may be coupled with the fact that he himself speaking before I did had taken a similar line & was very glad to have an ally.

We had an unpleasant time with the owners who were furious with us as we expected, but obviously although they might fume and fret they were helpless & incapable of resistance. They are *not* a prepossessing crowd & once more I am compelled to say that they are about the stupidest and most narrow minded employers I know though I must say some of the shipbuilders run them pretty hard. I believe it is not without significance that in both trades the leaders are Scotsmen or Welshmen.

I got home at 12.30 that night to find stacks of papers which took me a full hour to read and a note asking to come down early to the office next morning as some difficult points on pensions in the Lords had arisen on which it was necessary to have a speedy decision. Feeling very tired & worried already you can guess if you cannot "settingly tell, if Jacob swaw and cust"

Well, anyway its done with for the moment.

...

9 August 1925
Kindrockit, Calvine, Perthshire NB

My dear Hilda,

...

I had an awful rush in London at the last. From morning to night I was minuting papers, holding conferences, seeing deputations and interviewing M.P.'s, so that I heard hardly any of the speeches either on Thursday or any other day. But from conversation with others I gather that opinion in our party which at first was puzzled & rather unhappy about the coal arrangement has been gradually coming round to the view that we were right & you will have seen that there were only two die-hards in the division lobby on Thursday. What none of us in the Cabinet knew on the 30th (or hardly any – Steel-Maitland may have done) was that a few hours before S.B. had publicly stated that in no circumstances would the govt grant a subsidy. I can only suppose he meant a *permanent* subsidy, but certainly the words were unfortunate at such a moment because they did give the impression that we had come to a definite decision and then reversed it because we got frightened. This is very unjust because we never reversed any decision. The circumstances which required a decision were only put to us on Thursday at 6.30. But of course one cant explain in public all these things.

The gaffe about reduction of wages all round I dont blame S.B. for much. I think he was rather off his guard when he said whatever he did say but a mistake of that kind is easily made particularly when one is very tired and a little rattled. But it had a very considerable effect in consolidating the Unions & deciding them to stand together.

I am told by our Whips, who are the most persistent pessimists I know, that our party only voted with us out of loyalty and not because they agreed with us. No doubt there is some truth in that, though not much, but we are not alone in our troubles. The Parly Labour Party were not consulted at all. Neither Ramsay Thomas nor Snowden got a look in, and Thomas was so frightened that on Thursday morning he deserted to the enemy and became more Red than the Reds, greatly to the surprise & contempt of his colleagues, including Wheatley. Ramsay now characteristically blames us and declares that we have played into the hands of the Communists at his expense. But he always says it is someone else's fault.

My people are delighted with the Session which Robinson says is the best the Ministry of Health ever had. We have carried the whole of our programme except R. & V. & that we have got through Committee, contrary to almost universal expectation. Moreover the Minister is by no means dead, but already feels quite fresh again!

Certainly it has been an interesting Session. We are I think weaker than at the beginning but not much & neither Libs nor Labs can claim to be stronger. S.B. strengthened his own influence enormously at the beginning of the Session and though he hasn't quite maintained it in the House I doubt if it is seriously shaken in the country. Winston's Budget hasn't maintained its popularity but I think he has improved his own position in the House & among our party steadily. His last 3 speeches were all masterly.

Now its lunch time & I must close. TaTa.

17 August 1925
Loubcroy Lodge, Oykell, By Lairg

My dear Ida,

...

Politics haven't quite faded away and I still eagerly devour the two days old Times when it comes to see what is going on. I suppose your remarks about Austen are prompted by the article therein by a Conservative back-bencher. I thought the paragraph about him was the one mistake in an otherwise brilliant & penetrating analysis. I dont myself quite understand what prompted the suggestion of weakness as I thought his administration was generally reckoned as one of the successes of the Govt. But as I remarked to Annie almost in your own words the results of his policy will before long disprove the criticism.

The rest of the article showed the writer as a pretty shrewd judge of men. His comment on S.B.'s essential loneliness of spirit was eminently true though not generally known and I was struck with his remark about his influence on Churchill, which I believe to be true also. The little sketches of Jix and the Attorney General were particularly happy and seemed to me to attribute to them just the right niche in the party both as to views and influence. I wonder who the writer is. I have suggested Sir Henry Craik[41] as the only one I could think of.

The weather here has been remarkably fine since I came up and though very bad for fishing it has been excellent for shooting. I am glad to say that grouse this year are more plentiful than usual and we have had some very good bags. I suppose I do get a bit more tired than I used to but there is not a lot of difference and I am thankful to say I have at last found boots which dont skin my heels. ...

5 September 1925
Kindrochit

My dear Ida,
      ...

The weather since you left has remained just the same with strong winds and generally, but not always, some rain in the hills. We have had varied but always delightful days. My shoot on Tuesday was not a success ... But on Wednesday we had a great day on Firths best beat and got 51 brace of grouse. Frank came with me. He was a little nervous beforehand as was natural, but once the sport began he enjoyed himself most thoroughly and watched the shooting & marked the birds with the keenest zeal. In fact he begged to be allowed to come again and so I took him yesterday. ...

We have also had two days at the loch though we were soon blown off it. But Frank had the satisfaction of catching a half pound trout himself, the biggest we have got, and he ate it next morning with immense pride.

      ...

---

[41] Henry Craik (1846–1927). Examiner, Scottish Education Department 1870–85 and Secretary 1885–1904. Conservative MP for Glasgow and Aberdeen Universities 1906–18 and Scottish Universities 1918–27. Knighted 1897. Created Bart 1926.

23 September 1925
Westbourne

My dear Ida,

...

I really went up to London yesterday to look after my colleagues the Sec. for Scotland & the Minister of Labour who were proposing to see the Ch. of Ex. & the P.M. about a new proposition to push Weir houses in Scotland. I thought they were both vague & wild so I put down my own ideas on paper and the natural result was that having the only scheme in black and white it was unanimously adopted and I hope something may come of it. There is no doubt that Scotland presents a far more favourable battleground for the fight with the T.U.'s than England and the question is Can we screw up the local authorities there to take on the struggle. I wish I had the conduct of affairs instead of Gilmour.[42] He is thoroughly honest courageous and well meaning but he strikes me as lacking in knowledge of how to deal with his people.

While I was up I took the opportunity of making myself acquainted with the latest developments in West Ham. Matters there have now reached the critical stage, but up to now everything has gone according to plan and the impression I get is that the wind is considerably up among the Guardians. The fact that Will Thorne[43] has publicly disowned them is a nasty blow & I observe with amusement that while West Ham has the place of honour in the Times today the Daily Herald gives it only half a column on a back page. That doesn't look as if they felt very confident about the issue.

I am here till Tuesday when I go [to] London & on Wednesday I begin my provincial tour with Bath and Bristol. I shall have a somewhat strenuous but very interesting October.

27 September 1925
Westbourne

My dear Hilda,

...

Frank went back to school on Thursday – very reluctantly, but bravely. He told Miss Leamon that he wasn't distressing himself much as he "found it didn't

---

[42] John Gilmour (1876–1940). Conservative MP for Renfrewshire East 1910–18 and Glasgow Pollock 1918–40. Unionist Whip 1913–15 and 1919; Junior Lord of Treasury 1921–22 and 1923–24; Scottish Whip 1923; Scottish Secretary 1924–29; Minister of Agriculture 1931–32; Home Secretary 1932–35; Minister of Shipping 1939–40. Succeeded as Bart 1920.

[43] William James Thorne (1857–1946). Founder and General Secretary, National Union of General & Municipal Workers 1889–1934; member, TUC Parliamentary Committee 1894–1934. Labour MP for West Ham South 1906–18 and West Ham Plaistow 1918–45. Chairman, Social Democratic Federation 1930.

pay", a piece off philosophy which reminds me very strongly of myself at an age not much more advanced than himself. My mathematics master expressed some surprise at my mastery of complicated algebraical theorem and I replied that "As it was clear that I should have to learn it some time I concluded I might as well do it at once."! "I perceive that you are something of a philosopher, Chamberlain" I remember was his comment.

...

My wireless talk on Tuesday appears to have been most successful for I keep getting letters about it from all over the country. This morning I had one from Perugia from a clergyman who says he heard every word with absolute clearness. It is an uncanny affair, but one realises its power of influencing public opinion. My talk was of course "non-political", but there is little doubt that it had a very considerable political effect.

The P.M. has asked me to go to Chequers next week end as he wants to talk over various matters with me. I was engaged to shoot with Arthur but I have cancelled it as there may not be another opportunity and the moment is rather critical. There is a good deal of unrest in the party largely created I believe by the Daily Mail and S.B. will have to speak at the party Conference in Brighton on the 18th. A good deal may depend on what he says and how he says it.

Sep 28 ...

...

Tomorrow morning I go up by the early train to London and in the afternoon I am to meet these fierce West Ham Guardians again. I don't know what will come of it but I know what they will want i.e. that I shall find a way by which they may escape from the hole in which they have placed themselves without loss of face! At the moment the world seems to be in a pacific mood. They dont want to fight, nor does Cook,[44] nor, according to the Morning Post, do the Turks.

...

4 October 1925
Chequers

My dear Hilda,

...

We arrived yesterday in time for lunch, in order that I might go for a walk with S.B. before the others arrived. The country was looking very lovely and the afternoon was quite hot in bright sunshine so that it was pleasant to walk through the cool beechwoods. ...

...

---

[44] Arthur James Cook (1883–1931). Miners' Agent, Rhondda and imprisoned 1918 and 1921 for participation in strikes. Member, Executive of MFGB 1918–31 and General Secretary 1924–31; Member, Government Mines Welfare Committee and Advisory Board 1929–31.

The party consists, besides ourselves, of Douglas Hogg, Lady Curzon[45] and Marcella Duggan.[46] It seems that while the Baldwins were at Aix they saw a good deal of Lady Curzon and liked her finding her much more natural and human than they had supposed and rather pathetically anxious to help the party and somehow keep alive "George's" memory therein. Of course I havent seen anything of her to speak of yet but from such observation as has been possible and from Annie's account she seems to be another example of a fairly common type of American. She worships "George" whose name recurs every minute in her conversation, and she was well fitted to act as an ornamental head of his establishment. But she has little experience of this country and is not provided with the intellectual outfit necessary to pick it up now.

I believe some time today we are to have some discussion of S.B.'s speech at Brighton but up to the present I have only gossiped with him & have not succeeded in drawing from him any indications of how his mind is working. I wrote him a long letter while I was in Scotland in which I told him that I was reading Charnwoods "Lincoln" and how much I was struck with the truth of that resemblance which had been discovered by a "Conservative Back-bencher". This is by no means a mere compliment. Lincoln has defects very like S.B.'s – gaucheries, strange physical contortions awful clothes, a habit of saying things that made his friends gasp. And he *would* not take them really into his confidence. He was not considered a great man by his contemporaries with very few exceptions and his decisions were sharply criticised. His aim was first to preserve and afterwards to restore the unity of his country and he never allowed this ultimate object to be jeopardised by actions which sometimes seemed necessary to Northerners who looked only at the situation of the moment. Of course because there are these curious similarities in certain mental & physical characteristics and in the circumstances of the time it doesn't follow that S.B. is a Lincoln, indeed, I dont think he is or will become one. But, the comparison is interesting to follow out and in my letter I sought to find out what had been in his mind when he was forming his Cabinet. It is characteristic of him that he won't say: but first in his written reply and still more in conversation he said enough to convince me that I was right in my reconstruction of his process of thought.

Thus his offer to me [of the Treasury] was quite a genuine one and he really thought I should accept it. And in that case he had made up his mind to let Winston have the Ministry of Health. But that wasn't what he really wanted and he was sincerely grateful to me for the preference which allowed him to send Winston to the Exchequer. The two things, he said to me yesterday, which were essential if Winston were to merge successfully into the party were (1) an office

---

[45] Grace Elvina Hinds (1878–1958). American beauty. Married to Alfred Duggan until his death 1916; married Lord Curzon 1917.

[46] Marcella Duggan. Daughter of Lady Curzon by her first marriage and adored by Curzon.

which would keep him so busy as to have no time to interfere with other people and (2) one which would keep him out of contact with the working man. Obviously the Treasury was the only one which would satisfy these two conditions and Winston himself, & S.B. now congratulates himself on having effectively broken up what he regards as a dangerous alliance between Ll.G. Winston & F.E. He remarked about the latter that he thought he had quite lost his influence now & that if he were to leave us tomorrow we should in no way feel the loss. I asked him about the vice-royalty and he says that F.E. has no desire for it at all and he does not think he ever had.

Douglas Hogg is even more emphatic than others I have met as to the extraordinary unpopularity of the Govt. He says if there were an election now there would be a complete débâcle. I agree, but then there wont be an election now. And after all the people who are doing most of the grousing are the middle class who read the Daily Mail and grumble about our extravagance and our toleration of sedition, while the small manufacturer asks why we dont protect his industry and the farmer enquires when we are going to begin doing something for the "backbone of the party." But the bulk of the voters dont belong to these classes and *are* affected by the Pensions Act. Moreover there is bound to be a reaction from such a general disfavour and moreover we havent finished yet. If we avoid a disaster over coal (rather a large "if" I admit) if trade improves (and I think the tendency is to improve, bar engineering shipbuilding steel & coal) if we put on a few more import duties with results as good as those already appearing, if we do something more for urban and rural housing and finally if we give the communists a knock, I don't see why we shouldn't recover a good deal of our position before the day of battle comes round again.

Even West Ham, if it comes off according to plan, may help us. I saw the Guardians on Tuesday and after a somewhat lengthy, but very mild, discussion they caved in. I was afraid they might succeed in covering up their surrender but their own account of the proceedings was all I could wish. Of course, they havent yet got the surrender ratified but the fact that the deputation undertook to recommend it really destroys the possibility of successful resistance and I take it that the "consultation of the people outside" is merely a face saving farce. I am very pleased over the result as the decision to try the relief in kind was taken directly contrary to the advice of my department and if it produces the desired result tomorrow I shall have saved myself and the Government all the anxieties & worries of a Bill of Indemnity.

I had two very strenuous but I think very successful and useful days in Bath & Bristol. The local people were enormously delighted and although it is difficult to say exactly how I have been helped I feel that it adds a great deal to one's confidence & power of judging opinion accurately to have been on the spot and talked to the people in person. Perhaps what impressed me more than anything was the contrast between the old and new styles of building hospitals as evidenced in an extension to the Bristol fever hospital and the new Forbes [?]

Fraser hospital for paying patients at Bath. The former all gloomy red brick and stone with huge rooms, the latter one story [sic], half the floor space balcony or verandah, cheerful, clean, airy and costing only a fraction of the outlay.

I read your account of Lady Selborne's[47] doings with a foreboding of what was coming & offer you my heartfelt sympathy – what an utterly impossible woman. I always feel something antagonistic rise up in me when I hear her speak in Exec. Comee. She is the worst kind of Cecil.

...

10 October 1925
Westbourne

My dear Ida,

...

Everyone, including their own Deputy Clerk, expected the West Ham Guardians to cave in on Monday, but it seems that the Labour Majority had a meeting on Sunday behind closed doors with the "people outside" when no doubt they received their orders. At any rate all except one, including the chairman & members of the deputation who said they were going to do all they could to get my terms accepted voted against acceptance. The fact is that they are in an awful mess but daren't walk out of it. I am sitting tight waiting for something to turn up in order if possible to save my bill but I confess I haven't much hope of doing so and I have made all my preparations to take over. I have got an advisory committee of decent Guardians from other places the existence of which I haven't yet disclosed and if I have to act I shall relieve on the scale recommended by them. If, after all, the Guardians do come down they have behaved so badly that I almost think I shall have to have a bill to enable me to supersede them & others like them but of course in that case it wouldn't be retrospective and could be put off till the spring.

On the whole I think the Brighton Conference went off very well. There was less manifestation of discontent than had been expected and abundant demonstrations of loyalty to S.B. No doubt they would have liked more "punch" in his speech but I think it read extremely well – far better than Lloyd George's characteristic antics at Inverness, and after all you cant have it both ways. S.B.'s strength lies in his sympathy and thoughtfulness, not in his polemics and its of no use to try and make him talk like someone else. Anyway the Daily Mail could make nothing out of it and their leader next day was singularly ineffective ...

Meanwhile I was doing Liverpool. I had a very interesting time there, slumming first (my word, they *have* got some slums there), and then going round

---

[47] (Beatrix) Maud Cecil (1858–1950). Eldest child of 3rd Marquess of Salisbury. Married Viscount Wolmer 1883 and became Lady Selborne on death of 1st Earl 1895. Assertive, sharp-tongued and rather eccentric. Member, Hampshire County Council.

their housing estates and on the second day inspecting the fever hospital the tuberculosis sanatorium the School of Hygiene where they train Sanitary inspectors, and the main Poor Law institutions. I also visited a shop & saw it fumigated by a new process for exterminating rats! They gave me a civic banquet on Thursday evening but as it coincided with S.B.'s speech I got no report. This was rather a pity as I stated the problem without giving the solution, of the slums. The curious thing was that on the first evening the Chairman of the Housing Committee in conversation with Robinson declared that they wouldn't go on as they were, increasing indefinitely the number of municipal tenants, and that some independent body ought to be set up to which the local authority might hand over the management of its house property. His conclusion was so exactly mine that Robinson thought he must have got wind of it, but I believe he had arrived at it independently. Rather interesting is it not? I should have liked to go a bit further in the exposition of my views but I felt that I ought to put them to the Cabinet first and I want to get them crystallised a little more before I do that.

We arrived here yesterday evening in time for a late dinner and this afternoon I have been opening an extension of the maternity hospital here. At the function I met our Labour Lord Mayor [Percival Bower] who is going on for a second year and he told me that he had taken up again my suggestion that a new civic hall should be built and he thought that this time there was a good chance of its going through. The Post had supported it in a leading article and the Ld Mayor had now induced the Gen. Purposes Committee to appoint a Sub-Committee to go into it and to make an expedition to the continent to see what was being done there. I like this Lord Mayor and comparing him with those in Bristol and Liverpool I think we have decidedly got the best of the bunch.

...

17 October 1925
37 Eaton Square, SW1

My dear Hilda,

...

Austen has achieved a real triumph and he has had so many disappointments in his political life that I think it will be very sweet to him.[48] Whatever else he may do in the future he will always be able to feel that he has this great achievement to his credit and though as you say it is not of the kind which the public will appreciate yet it has received a very general acknowledgement in the press. It is evident that at Locarno everyone recognised the leading part which he has played and they showed their appreciation so unmistakably that I am sure

---

[48] The Locarno Agreements were signed on 16 October. Hailed as the greatest triumph of Austen Chamberlain's career, its Treaty of Mutual Guarantee agreed the inviolability of Germany's western frontier and the existence of a demilitarised Rhineland.

his stature must be markedly raised at home. Particularly I am glad that the House of Commons should realise what is thought of him by the foreigners, for they will perceive that they have got a bigger statesman than they thought and one who has raised this country's prestige internationally in a way very flattering to British self esteem. L. Amery was telling me today how perfectly Austen seemed to fit into his milieu at Geneva and how much at home he appeared among the foreigners. I am sure his rather old fashioned courtesy and his consideration of small trifles that appeal to sentiment attract them particularly and I expect they have conceived a real regard for him. It was a happy coincidence that his and Ivy's birthdays should fall into this week. Ll.G. never got a gold cigarette case!

Isn't West Ham priceless! The addition of that word "regretfully" was the finishing touch to their own humiliation. I am almost sorry they caved in after all for I should have liked the opportunity of demonstrating that it was possible to give relief on a reasonable scale without starving anybody. But I was conscious of "Time's winged chariots hurrying near". A bill would have taken at least 3 or 4 days of the autumn session & would have still further jeopardised my precious R. & V. Bill, so that really it is a relief to have avoided legislation. And after all they have come down from their tree with a resounding smack, and the lesson will not be lost on other "Red" Boards.

I am not surprised that you attribute the arrest of the Communists to Jix.[49] He brags so much of what he is going to do that the credit is generally given to him. But as a matter of fact he had nothing to do with it. Prosecution is the affair of the Attorney General and even the Cabinet has no power to order it as we heard in the Campbell case. Hogg has been working on this for some time and after consultation with the Public Prosecutor he believes he has sufficient evidence to convict. I believe the decision has been warmly welcomed by our people and though Clynes may snivel about it I suspect that moderate Labour men are rejoicing.

Wasn't it dreadful? I was summoned to a Privy Council on Monday and forgot all about it! Fortunately my P.S. invented a plausible tale about my having missed the box on my travels which H.M. graciously accepted and I was telephoned for to go at once, as I was, without a frock coat. H.M. was extremely forthcoming as usual and hoped I was not going to budge an inch over West Ham. I had quite a long talk with him.

I have had a pretty strenuous time this week with Dundee and Newcastle and have visited an immense number of slums hospitals and housing schemes besides addressing 3000 people at Dundee where I think we might well win a seat next time. What particularly pleases me is to see how the occupier-owner scheme

---

[49] On 14 October police raided offices of various Communist organisations and *Worker's Weekly*, arresting eight leading officials for sedition. Four more were arrested a few days later.

is going. I found them very keen about it in both places. Do you realise that whereas in all the years between the passing of the Small Dwellings Acquisition Act in 1899 and the 1923 Act less than £800,000 was advanced for purchase, since my Act the amount sanctioned is £17½ millions? We are building up a whole new class of good citizens and a representative of a Building Society told me in Newcastle that since 1923 their business had revived & grown astonishingly. Last year the Building Societies advanced £40 millions for house purchase!

It is wonderful to see how houses are springing up everywhere throughout the country as one passes through in the train. Even where there are only a few houses in a village one sees two or three new ones going up on the outskirts. In Birmingham they have averaged between 80 and 90 completed every week for the last 2 months and last week they got 131. Three an hour they describe it picturesquely. At this rate the housing problem will soon cease to be a problem.

I forgot to tell you that my host at Dundee told me that he had met the president of the local Liberal Association who had been at my meeting and asked him how he liked it. This Liberal replied that he had been delighted with it. That he had been to Inverness to hear Lloyd George but that he was "not a patch on this man".

I have followed up my Liverpool visit by getting Robinson to write to the M.O.H. to ask him to try and work out a scheme with the Medical Superintendent of the Tuberculosis Sanatorium for a sort of Papworth. I was bid to do this because the M.S. seemed to me just the man with the requisite qualities to make a success and because I could see that he had got some ideas on the subject which his Chairman wouldn't allow him to carry out. I should very much like to get something of the kind started in a place like Liverpool. If it worked well it would give the thing a fillip which is what it wants and might lead to a wide extension.

I had an interview with Winston this week on my Poor Law proposals. He knows nothing of Local Govt but his people have evidently told him that I am on the right lines and he ought to back me. Characteristically he wants to make a much bigger scheme and drag in revision of Education and Road Fund finance as well as Health services. I am confident that to do that would be to overload the ship and wreck her but I suppose he will have to splash about for a bit till he gets some water into his mouth. I observe with some amusement a considerable change in his manner to me. At first he was inclined to be a little patronising and used to walk about & orate. This time he sat quietly in a chair and listened quite a lot to what I had to say. S.B. told me that it was beginning to dawn upon him that his new colleagues were not all duds after all!

...

24 October 1925
Westbourne

My dear Ida,

I am afraid Austen's design for a family reunion on his return was frustrated as Annie and I were both away as well as Hilda. However he came and dined with me on Thursday, so I had the full story then.

I confess to being still a little puzzled at the réclame which his success has aroused – not because it is not appropriate but because foreign affairs are usually too remote to be appreciated by the general public. In fact I suppose the general public is still pretty hazy about it all but for once the press has comprehended and perhaps this too is due to Austen's careful forethought. Evidently he pleased the correspondents and they have managed to convey something of the atmosphere which prevailed at Locarno and so impressed Mussolini.

The unhappy Austen is off again on Monday to attend the League Council summoned to deal with the Greco-Bulgarian incident.[50] It is not every one who would like to have his job but he has shown to demonstration [sic] his own fitness for it and incidentally has restored to some extent the prestige of the Govt. It is extraordinary how quickly political values change.

I had an interesting and I think a very successful visit to Cardiff where I made 5 speeches in my two days and inspected innumerable works connected with my department. Once again I was impressed with the way in which the idea of house purchase is catching on. Quite a lot of houses are being sold there. Tomorrow we go to Halifax and on Tuesday to Bradford and then my travels are done.

Tonight I have been attending a public dinner here where I sat through two hours of speeches. I think they have driven everything else out of my brain for I can think of nothing to write about.

...

1 November 1925
37 Eaton Square, SW1

My dear Hilda,

...

Annie and I had another very strenuous time in Halifax and Bradford ...

Halifax ... gives one the impression of considerable comfort not to say prosperity. There are a number of very rich people who are also liberal minded and I fancy they are sometimes rather hard put to it to find anything that really needs their help. I went there originally to open a new hostel and workshop for the

---

[50] A border clash on 19 October escalated and three days later Bulgaria called on the League of Nations to intervene.

Blind but before I had done I had made speeches also at a civic luncheon given us by the Mayor and at meetings of the Junr Imps and the Exec. of the local Conservative Assocn.

Next day we motored over to Bradford which is only about 9 miles away. It is quite a different sort of place, nearly 2½ times the size and more enterprising and go-ahead. But I saw in it some of the worst slum houses I have come across yet. In one case an old couple were living in a single room with one window most of which they had blocked up with board so that the interior was like a cave. In the gloom there gradually became apparent the faces of the filthy pair who inhabited it together with another old woman who was apparently taking a meal with them. It was revolting. In one of their housing estates I went into a newly-built house with one large living room and a kitchenette. The windows were all tightly shut, the whole place reeked with a musty odour and the walls were already filthy. The bath had a board over it on which was piled a heap of dirty clothing. I learned that it was occupied by a drayman and his family of 12 – the wife was in the maternity hospital expecting the 13th. It was a sad illustration of the fact that the housing problem is not merely a problem of housing but of social education.

On Thursday I appeared before the Economy Committee of the Cabinet. Winston had circulated a note on my estimates in which he had made various suggestions for reduction of expenditure. Of course they were all impracticable and as I knew my case I had no difficulty in making hay of him. Robinson who was with me came back, as I heard from Veale, in a state of chuckling jubilation. It was the first time he had heard the Ch. of E. reduced to absolute dead silence, unable to find any reply; he hadn't enjoyed himself so much for a long time. And Sir Warren Fisher observed to me afterwards that no public entertainment could be compared to it. Unfortunately I cannot look at it entirely in that light because I am afraid there is serious trouble ahead of us. I did make my own suggestion which amounted to a 10% cut on my estimates but I made it clear that it would involve a fight in which I could hardly expect to come out victorious unless it were possible to show that comparable sacrifices were being made all round. And I am pretty certain that they are not.

Even that is not by any means the worst. I had a talk during the week with one of my old staff at the Treasury and his account filled me with very serious concern. So far as can be judged at present, the deficit in next year's Budget is far larger than can be filled by any imaginable "economies" and new taxation is therefore inevitable. And according to my informant the Chancellor is entirely responsible for this. He declares that they have all lost heart there. They never know where he will break out next with some fantastic & hopelessly impracticable idea. No warnings are effective; he only thinks they indicate a personal dislike to himself. And the final remark was "If you dont have him out he will bring you down; in fact I'm not sure that he wont bring you down anyway."

This is not a very cheerful account is it? If we had been with you today I would have told you more. But I must say that the more I get to know Winston the less I think of him. I dont mean morally; he doesn't strike me in the least as a villain though I think he is *a*moral and lacking entirely in some things that most of us think rather essential. But the fault with which he is generally credited is lack of judgement and there public opinion seems to me to be absolutely right. "We haven't got a grown man to deal with, but a careless irresponsible child" said my Treasury friend. And with his courage and strong will and power of oratory he is a very dangerous man to have in the Govt. But I dont see how he could be got out of it safely now. If only I could get my R. & V. & Poor Law Reform through before the smash!

…

7 November 1925
Westbourne

My dear Ida,

…

We have been thinking and talking a good deal about the shift to Edgbaston since we saw you and on the whole we are inclined to think you are right and that we had better begin to make a move. I tried unsuccessfully to see Austen on Thursday but I shall try again when I get an opportunity and subject to anything he may say to the contrary I shall probably put things in train. We walked over to the Grove this afternoon and I discussed the procedure with Byng who is the Edgbaston chairman. He is quite prepared to begin sounding his people whenever I give the word but I do see great difficulties if Lowe should go before the next general election. But if I were tied on first perhaps they would be less formidable, and in that case I think I should make an effort to find a stopgap and so avoid the bye election in Ladywood. I can see the whole Labour party rushing down in that event with a counter stream of our own people and if we lost the seat as I think would probably be the case I should be put in a very invidious position.

I regret to say that Byng in his old age is receding from his Protectionist views and now appears to take the line that England is so peculiarly situated in that she must always be a great importing country that a general tariff would do more harm than good! I base an exactly opposite conclusion on the same premises. My argument is that the only way to preserve our export trade is by reducing costs and the only way to reduce costs is to increase production and to spend more on labour saving machinery. But firms who are always impoverished by competition cant find the capital for new machinery nor are they prepared to instal big & costly machines when there is no prospect of keeping them fully employed. Therefore the remedy is to secure the home market and the savings from profits will be used further to reduce costs & again to increase production. I am doubtful if I convinced Byng and yet it seems so clear to me.

I had a conference with the representatives of the L.C.C. & the London boroughs on Thursday with the object of inducing them to let me cut them out of the [Rating & Valuation] Bill altogether. They have I am glad to say agreed to this and if the agreement is ratified I shall cut out a huge block of amendments & greatly facilitate the passage of the Bill. The Daily Mail keeps up its barrage but I feel fairly confident of success.

We came down here yesterday for a couple of meetings, the Midland Union in the afternoon and the Birmingham Central Council in the evening. Both were crowded and enthusiastic and Annie thinks my speeches went very well and are likely to prove helpful.

This morning I had Hall up from Hoskins. I have at last got the accounts up to the end of July and to my great relief we have turned a loss of £16,000 last year into a profit of £800. I have decided to pay a final dividend of 25% making 35% for the year. Of course we haven't earned it but we have still got considerable reserves and I think I am justified in assuming that some day we shall return to a more satisfactory state of things. The prospects are not good at present but I expect we could go on another year with perhaps a further reduction of dividend even if we don't do more than keep our heads above water.

...

14 November 1925
37 Eaton Square, SW1

My dear Hilda,

Many thanks for your letter. Please tell Ida, that Austen lunched here on Monday to discuss Edgbaston but he did not say anything about the Garter and I did not mention it to him. Of course I shall not do so & neither Annie nor I have said or will say anything to anyone else.

Austen agreed with your view about the move and so I have written to Byng to begin. I expect it will take a month or two to get things settled up.

I agree that we have never had a clear fight on the Protection issue but I am afraid we could not get one even now. It is astonishing how tightly they cling to their old fetishes in Lancs. & Yorks. and I feel sure the only way to move forward is to go extremely cautiously. My impression is that on the whole the action taken by the Govt is rather behind than in advance of the party opinion and I think it important that for the present we should preserve our relative positions. There will be a considerable difficulty I fancy over Iron & Steel.[51] Protection is pretty clearly called for but Winston (and I find Austen takes the same view) maintains that to give it to an industry affecting so many others

---

[51] On 22 June 1925 the Cabinet referred the iron and steel industry application for a duty under the Safeguarding of the Industries Act to the Committee of Civil Research. In mid-December the Cabinet rejected its recommendation to refer the application to the Safeguarding Committee.

would be going beyond the P.M.'s pledges. On the other hand the P.M. himself told me that he had been looking through them & found nothing that would inhibit him from going the whole hog with Iron & Steel. Anyway we must see what the C.C.R. reports. I am told that its proceedings consist mostly in listening to Winston's orations.

I got a very good press in Birmingham for my address in Ladywood last Sunday when I made a plea for the Locarno spirit in industry. It was interesting to find that 4 or 5 other speakers were saying the same thing about the same time quite independently of one another. I think it is a good thing to talk on these lines as it helps to form public opinion but it will be a long time I fear before industry goes to Locarno.

I tried to get out of the Cabinet on Wednesday but found it wouldn't do. But in the end I reaped all the reward of virtue without any of the drawback ...

I have had a quiet but busy week largely spent in preparing for R. & V. In spite of the fulminations of the Union of Assessment Comees I think it is generally understood that the Bill will go through and my policy in putting in a clause to exempt machinery from rating is now being justified as industry is getting busy appealing to Members to support the Bill on that ground. We have persuaded the Chief Whip that 3 days will be enough for Report & 3rd reading and the Bill is to be taken on the 23rd-25th.

Rowfant Nov 15 It does seem strange to be here again after nearly nine years. Fortunately it is a glorious day and we are soon going out for a walk to renew acquaintance with the country. The Cowdrays[52] are coming to lunch; Godfrey [Locker-Lampson] tells me that he hates Ll.G. and that all the money he gives to the Liberal party goes to Asquith. I had thought it was the opposite way so I am delighted to be put right. G. says he is worth forty millions!

...

A. & I went on Thursday to a matinée at the Old Vic. in order to see Edith Evans in "The Taming of the Shrew". Physically she is not made for the part being rather plump but she carries it off wonderfully and I am confirmed in my view that she is the best actress on our stage at present. Incidentally we discovered that the actor who played Petruchio, one Balliol [sic] Holloway,[53] was also quite above the average.

I am glad to say that the Cabinet has agreed to the proposals in regard to the Scottish subsidy which the Sec. for Scotland (prompted by me) has put up and he is now authorised, if the local authorities wont order from Weir, to order 1000 houses from him himself. I regret to say that I have very little confidence in the Scottish Office who will always make a bungle if it is possible to do so or in

---

[52] Weetman Dickinson Pearson (1856–1927). Businessman. President, Air Board 1917. Created Bart 1894, Baron Cowdray 1910, Viscount Cowdray 1917.

[53] Baliol Holloway (1883–1967). Actor and leading man, Old Vic 1925–28 before leading his own productions.

Walter Elliott [sic] who is a clever windbag. But I have told my people that this matter is too important to be allowed to go wrong and that we must therefore hold the Scotsmen firmly by the hand all through these difficult times. Fortunately Gilmour himself seems very ready to take advice from me and I think his principal secretary has a considerable respect for Robinson, so between us I hope to be able to exercise a controlling influence. It is very important that the hand should be well played and the public kept well up in line with the Govt.

I see in the Sunday Times a statement that Austen is to have a "signal mark of honour" and that as he is known to object to hereditary or titular distinctions he is to be given the O.M. From what you said to me I got the impression that he would be rather disappointed if that was all!

22 November 1925
Westbourne

My dear Ida,

I think my idea that Austen might be disappointed if he got the O.M. instead of the Garter was rather a deduction from what you said than a repetition of it. I could understand his saying that nothing would induce him to accept any honour that involved a title if that was in fact what he had said. But it wasn't. Apparently he went so far as to say that if the Garter was offered he would accept it, and went on to reflect that after all it would please the foreigners. Just as the incipient baronet observes that it will be so nice for the baby when it grows up. Of course it is quite true that the Garter will impress not merely foreigners, but the world in general and the home world in particular far more than the O.M. the existence of which is forgotten almost immediately because there is nothing to recall it. Once, therefore, a man has so far got over his own feelings against a title as to be willing to put up with it, it seems to me inevitable that he should begin to dwell on the undoubted advantages. Consequently although Austen may still believe that he prefers the O.M. I still believe that he will be disappointed if he doesn't get the Garter!

This has been *his* week – first in the Commons and then at the dinner, – and the recognition given to him and the expressions of personal esteem must have been very gratifying. I heard his first & part of his second speech in the House. I think it was the more effective of the two, as Ponsonby's rather feeble attack gave some good openings for a lively reply, whereas the expository speech was rather solid and – well a bit dull. At the dinner the most dramatic episode was when that swine Hogge[54] arose after the speech & produced an immense bouquet of cyclamen (I think but I could not quite see) picked that morning on the

---

[54] James Myles Hogge (1873–1928). Journalist, social investigator and Liberal MP for Edinburgh East 1912–24. Joint Chief Whip for Non-Coalition Liberals 1919–23. President, National Federation of Discharged and Demobilised Sailors and Soldiers 1919–20.

hills behind Locarno and despatched by aeroplane service so that it arrived an hour before the dinner. The Hogge made quite a graceful speech and handed the bouquet to Ivy who responded from her corner, but I failed to hear what she said.

I have had an awful week. I have dined out every single night and made five speeches. It meant sitting up late to prepare and about the middle of the week I began to feel rather washed out. But I have recovered and am now ready for next week which will be even more trying.

The sniping against R. & V. has continued unabated and I am told that not only the Whips but Billy Gore[55] has been attacking it in the lobbies & smoke room. What with these attacks from inside and those from the Guardians & overseers outside, Members began to get a good deal rattled again and by request I undertook to address a meeting and answer questions on Thursday evening. There was a huge gathering nearer 300 I should think than 200 and it proved a huge success. There was not a hostile note throughout. Many were genuinely seeking information and no doubt many were being made very uncomfortable with petitions from Parish Councils &c but they cheered to the echo some remarks I made to the effect that to sit still and do nothing out of fear was the most contemptible and in the long run the most fatal policy we could pursue. Kinsgley Wood tells me that they are very loyal to me personally. They think I have helped the party unlike some others (names not specified) and they have great confidence in my knowledge and judgement. At any rate I came away much encouraged and feeling sure that the Bill was quite safe. Now, if we could manage to get the 3rd Reading, without a division! I am told that the Liberals are going to obstruct as they think that if they only delay our business sufficiently the Govt may have to drop the Finance (Safeguarding of Industries) Bill.

My Poor Law proposals are I think going very well. The Assn of Munic. Corporns likes them with some reservation about non-County boroughs to which they would like to give more independence at the expense of the County Councils. On the other hand the L.C.C. seem to have difficulties in accepting although the proposals follow lines which they have repeatedly adopted by resolution in the past. But they are thoroughly frightened by Poplar and West Ham, fearing that if the responsibility for Home Assistance were given to the L.C.C. the Socialists would fight L.C.C. elections on that issue & M.R.'s[56] would lose their seats. The remedy would be to go back to the pre-1918 law and

---

[55] William Ormsby-Gore (1885–1964). Conservative MP for Stafford 1918–1938. Assistant Secretary, War Cabinet 1917–18 and with Military Intelligence Department in Egypt 1918; Under-Secretary, Colonies 1922–24 and 1924–29; Postmaster-General 1931; First Commissioner of Works 1931–36; Colonial Secretary 1936–38; High Commissioner to South Africa 1941–44. Succeeded as Baron Harlech 1938.

[56] The Conservatives fought as 'Municipal Reform' in LCC elections against Liberals labelled as 'Progressives' and Labour.

disfranchise those in receipt of relief, and if I were prepared to promise this I believe the L.C.C. would accept my proposals at once. If it were only a question of Guardians elections I wouldn't hesitate. Borough Council elections seem to me rather a tall order, but I am reflecting. What do you say?

I had some 13 press correspondents into my room on Thursday representing all the principal London & provincial dailies and I harangued them on R. & V. Housing Poor Law & Pensions. I was told afterwards that they were delighted and said it was the best show they had had. Certainly they have given us a good show since and even the Daily Mail has abated some of its venom. Of course the figures of Housing are marvellous and fully bear out the impressions I derived from my tour. Only in Scotland things are not going well and there I fancy a row is boiling up quite nicely. Its quite possible it may spread across the border when the fight comes but we must be prepared to face that. Last night I attended a complimentary dinner in a public house in Ladywood – a terrible affair – and once more flew a kite bearing my slum ideas. Again I only stated half the case but this time I took the precaution of sending a hint to the B. Post man so that although the passage came near the end of an hour's speech I dont think it will escape attention and I rather hope that as the Editor will have had Sunday morning to think over it he may see fit to write a leader on it. I felt rather guilty as I listened to the usual talk about a triumphant majority next time!

...

I imagine that Queen Alexandra's[57] death will upset all the arrangements for jollifications on the signing of the Treaty. It is most unfortunate as it was an occasion when a display would have made a powerful and useful impression on the foreigners ...

28 November 1925
37 Eaton Square, SW1

My dear Hilda,

...

I have had a note from Austen to break the news about the honour to me! I presume he will have written to you also to tell you, that he is to have the Garter and Ivy the G.B.E. I have replied admitting that I had a little shock first of all but that I had got over it and now only regretted that he hadn't taken the peerage as well! This quite honestly represents my view. I smile still over Austen's reasons for taking the Garter. "It will be so nice for the – policy"; they apply just as well to a peerage and once you have got over the shock of a title why not go the whole hog and have a good one. I cannot bring myself to regard *Sir* Austen as

---

[57] Queen Alexandra (1844–1925). Eldest daughter of King Kristian IX of Denmark and Queen-Consort of King Edward VII. Founder, Imperial (later Royal) Military Nursing Service 1902 and annual Alexandra Rose Day appeal in aid of hospitals 1912.

dignified, but Lord or Viscount Mayfield sounds quite well. Moreover Austen would make an excellent peer and Ivy an admirable peeress. They are both naturally cut out for it, and a peerage would have the great practical advantage of relieving Austen from the worry (and expense) of a constituency. I dont believe in the handicap to Joe. I believe a title would help him more than it would hamper him. – I mean to return to the subject from time to time, as I daresay the opportunity will recur.

Annie and I have been having a lazy morning, breakfast in bed and resting there till 12 o'clock. We have had rather a stiff week and both of us felt that we should be all the better for a respite. But it has been a successful week as I daresay you will have gathered from the Press and the back of my troubles is broken.

I don't think anyone who saw the amendments expected that we could really finish in 3 days. The only question was how many extra days would be wanted and what feathers should we lose in the process. Well, so far I am delighted with the proceedings and I have received many congratulations from my colleagues who are frankly astonished and declare that no one else could have accomplished such a feat. After all, we have never sat after 12.30 a.m. and we have got through 60 out of the 72 clauses and 8 schedules of which the Bill is composed. Moreover we have got our own people more solidly behind us at this moment than at any time before and yet we have somehow managed to avoid getting up the backs of either of the oppositions. The "free" vote on the rating of machinery clause was a triumph, and caused many papers to enquire whether the Govt would not do better to leave the Whips off more frequently. The Manchester Guardian speculates on this but remarks that I had made a remarkably able and adroit speech and that Governments could not always count on such speeches as mine and Runciman's. What the M.G. didn't know was that I had quietly informed my agricultural friends that I was prepared to let them have a free vote also on rating of farm buildings, pointing out how-ever that if the relief to machinery was not carried the House certainly would not pass that to farm buildings. The result was that nearly all of them went into our lobby.

There remains the task, which the Speaker does not think we shall achieve, of getting the remainder of the Report Stage & Third Reading through on Monday. So far as I know, there are only two snags. One is the clause providing that Crown Property shall be rated in future which the Committee put in against my advice and which I have got to persuade the House to strike out again, and the other is this relief to farm buildings which will require very careful handling. But if we are lucky as well as careful and if Jos. Wedgewood [sic], who is quite mad, doesn't unexpectedly go off the deep end I think we ought to manage and I believe there is a chance of avoiding a division on third reading. In any case we shouldn't require more than part of one more day and though the Whips would grumble I think they would have to give it.

I had rather a shock when in the middle of the proceedings word was brought me that the C.C. Assocn had decided, by a majority of 2, to refer the Poor Law proposals to the C.C. themselves. This means that replies will not be received until Feb 17 and makes it impossible to carry a Bill through in 1926. However further thought has brought me to the conclusion that the game is by no means up and that the delay may even be helpful in the long run. I was beginning to be nervous about the attitude of the Cabinet towards another very controversial bill after all the alarums over R. & V. and perhaps a little more time for discussion negotiation and consideration will make things easier in the long run. At any rate I have revised my programme. My new idea is to send the provisional proposals all round at once, get a bill drafted next year & introduce it fairly late in the session, announcing that it will not be proceeded with further than 2nd reading. This will keep the subject well to the front and perhaps indicate danger points. Then in 1927 I should bring in the real Bill and make it the principal measure of the session.

One advantage of this plan is that it leaves a clearer field for 1926. I have *got* to bring in a new Insurance (Health) Bill which is almost bound to be controversial and will be very much so if it includes the cut in the Exchequer grant. Then I shall want what we call in the office the Guardians Coercion Bill and I should like if possible to get in my new Housing Bill. There are two more smaller measures to which I am committed and two more to which I should like to give a place. Altogether it doesn't seem as if there would be any difficult in filling up the time.

11.30p.m. Your letter has just arrived from Birmingham and I think I have already answered all your questions about R. & V.

I agree with you about the Locarno Treaty & said as much to Austen the other day. At first he said "Well it was a difficult question and we had to decide one way or the other". But afterwards he went on to say privately that the Labour Party had stated that they would not attend any function at which Mussolini was present, and the engine drivers had threatened that they would not drive his train. This was an embarrassing situation and although it might have been overcome I rather gather that it turned the scale.

I was sorry it was such a bitter cold day for the funeral yesterday for I fear the damage to health must have been considerable. They say there were people waiting in Whitehall outside my office at four o'clock in the morning. We had excellent seats in the choir of the Abbey & so saw everything there was to be seen. I refused to be moved at the passing away so naturally of an old lady of 80 who had lost all power of enjoyment but the ceremony was very impressive as such ceremonies always must be in such a setting. I didn't like the Prince of Wales' face. It seems to me to be getting the look of a debauchee.

...

12 December 1925
Westbourne

My dear Hilda,

...

I see my friend Leonard Williams[58] has been hammering away at his old theme and endeavouring to attract attention to it by suggesting that wives overfeed their husbands in order to have them at their mercy! However that may be, I must say I think I am a remarkable demonstration of the success of his method. When I reflect on what I have done this week I do think it is a rather unusual record of physical endurance and mental alertness some part of which at any rate may be credited to "the simple life". It is interesting also from two other points of view. One is the way that with practice one can train one's mind to work. Only a few years ago mine would not have worked in this way & I should have looked with amazement on any that did. The other is a comparison. I can never remember Father's having such a week and although I should put him down as a very hard worker my impression is that even when he was in office he almost always had time to read after dinner and generally later in the night. I find it impossible to touch a book while the House is in session.

Well now just for the interest of these reflections & comparisons here is an account of my week. And though it sounds egotistical & conceited let me assure you that I am not in the least puffed up nor do I accept other peoples praises because I am always very conscious of my defects. But I do think it is interesting.

On Monday I delivered an address on the 21st anniversary of the founding of a Methodist Church in Ladywood. It was partly humorous & partly reminiscent but the main theme was the function & duty of the Churches to create the "Locarno spirit" at home. I pointed out that there were heaps of ways in which capital & labour could compose their differences with advantages to both but that none of them had a chance of success unless they met in a favourable atmosphere.

Next morning I unveiled a bust of father at the Gas Department and delivered another address pointing out some of his characteristics and then describing some of the developments in the Gas industry which he could not have foreseen and discussing their effect on health and on industry. After this function Annie and I drove up to Edgbaston Grove with John Henry Lloyd[59] the Chairman of the Gas Committee & had lunch with him. Immediately afterwards we drove to the University where I donned my robes and duly received my degree, together

---

[58] Leonard Llewelyn Bulkeley Williams (1861–1939). Physician, Metropolitan Hospital and author of works on obesity.

[59] John Henry Lloyd (1855–?). Birmingham tube manufacturer. Member, Birmingham Council from 1891; Lord Mayor and Alderman 1901; Chairman, Gas Committee 1898–1901 and from 1919; Chairman, Water Committee 1912–19.

with 3 other "eminent men". As soon as the congregation was closed I stepped forward and delivered a forty minute address on the Centenary of the Birmingham Medical School. It was a carefully prepared oration taking a general survey of health services, showing how the value of our great organisation depended on the personnel and how the personnel in turn depended on the Medical School. Barling pronounced it a remarkable tour-de-force and Sir Donald Macalister[60] who is said not to be overlavish in praise warmly repeated several times that it was "masterly".

As soon as we could get away from the University we took train to London arriving in time for dinner. I didn't go to the House as there were no divisions but sat up working till after 2 a.m.

On Wednesday I was at the Ministry by 10.30 as I had a Cabinet Committee at 11 & Cabinet at 11.30. We lunched with the Duckworths[61] at Jules but I left as soon as coffee was served for another Cabinet Comee. When that was over I received a deputation from a red and recalcitrant Board of Guardians introduced by Sidney Webb & Trevelyan.[62] Immediately afterwards I went up to a committee room to meet the Unionist Agricultural Committee & other M.P.'s (about 100) and address them on my Poor Law proposals. This was an important and rather difficult affair but it went off very well. I began with a speech and then answered questions for nearly an hour. One of those present told me next day "You made us all very happy last night". When it was through I went to see the P.M. who wished to ask my views about the iron & steel application for safeguarding, and by the time I had finished with him it was about 8 p.m. I drove home to dinner but returned to the house [sic] by 9.45 & took part in the division. When I got back to Eaton Square I found a mass of papers & was up to 1.30 working.

On Thursday morning I attended a meeting of the Economy Committee and vigorously & I think successfully defended my Dept against further "cuts". I worked all afternoon at various departmental matters and getting a pair for the evening slaved away at a speech & got to bed at 12.30.

---

[60] Donald MacAlister (1854–1934). Mathematics Master, Harrow School 1877; Lecturer in Natural Philosophy, St Bart's Hospital 1879; President, General Medical Council 1904–31; External Examiner at Birmingham University among others; Vice-Chancellor, Glasgow University 1907–29 and Chancellor from 1929. Knighted 1908. Created Bart 1924.

[61] George Herbert Duckworth (1864–1934). Secretary to Charles Booth 1892–1902; to Austen Chamberlain 1902–5; to Treasury Committee on War Risks on Shipping 1906–8; to Royal Commission on Historical Monuments 1908–33. Deputy-Director Munitions, Finance 1915–18; Controller, Labour Finance 1918; Controller, Munitions Housing Schemes 1919–20. Chairman, Irish Land Trust providing housing for ex-servicemen from 1921.

[62] Charles Philips Trevelyan (1870–1958). Liberal MP for Elland Yorkshire 1899–1918 and Labour MP for Newcastle Central 1922–31. Charity Commissioner 1906–8; Parliamentary Secretary, Board of Education 1908–14 resigning in protest at Great War; President, Board of Education 1924 and 1929–31. Succeeded as Bart 1928.

On Friday I had a deputation from the National Conference of Friendly Societies who had 8 resolutions to put to me on each of which they desired (and received) an answer. The President at the conclusion of the meeting thanked me most warmly for the great care and attention I had evidently given to their case and the ample way in which I had entered into all the details. Their coming had been postponed, he said, but it was worth postponement to have such careful & sympathetic treatment.

We got the 2.20 to Birmingham and at 8 I made a 50 minute speech in the Midland Institute to Ladywood Unionists. The audience was miserably scanty but the speech was I think an unusually good one – lively and also full of new information.

Finally yesterday A. & I attended a dinner of Hospital officers at which Sir Arthur Stanley[63] & a company of 130 were present. There I spoke about the future of the voluntary system & for the first time sketched out a definite plan of coordination of health services. According to Annie this speech evoked expressions of wonder and admiration from Sir Ch. Hyde[64] who sat next her and anyway I think I may say it showed no sign of fatigue or want of vitality.

In not one of these 5 speeches did I have a single note with me which means a considerable effort of memory for such a variety of subjects. Is not that really a rather big week?

Annie and I were frightfully disgusted with Ladywood for not turning up at our meeting on Friday. The Chairman had insisted that schools were not consistent with my dignity and indeed they are generally packed & very stuffy. Therefore we had got the Midland Institute as fortunately the Town Hall could not be secured. I was very dubious of the result but it was even worse than I expected only about 200 people in the hall. All sorts of reasons & excuses were made, change of date, womens meeting on Monday, so near to Christmas &c but there is no getting away from the bad organisation & want of enthusiasm and we feel any way that it serves to justify us in going to another constituency. Things are moving in Edgbaston but slowly at present; possibly they will begin to show towards the end of January.

---

[63] Arthur Stanley (1869–1947). Son of 16th Lord Derby. Diplomatic Service and Clerk at Foreign Office; Private Secretary to Balfour 1891–92; Diplomatic Service, Cairo 1895–98. Unionist MP for Ormskirk 1898–1918. Knighted 1916.

[64] Charles Hyde. Philanthropist and sole proprietor, *Birmingham Post*, *Birmingham Mail*, *Birmingham Weekly Post* from 1913. Chairman, War Graves Commission and Hon. Treasurer, Lord Mayor's Unemployment Fund 1920–21, 1923–24. Created Bart 1922.

7

1926
'I am an Asset ... of the Government':
West Ham, the Coal Dispute and Rural Housing

2 January 1926
Westbourne

My dear Ida,

...

We had a pleasant if not a very exciting party [in Yorkshire with the Cunliffe-Listers]. Philip's sister Mrs Hannay known to the family as "Toto" and her husband we met last year and liked. ... Jackson, now a Rt Honble, and George Bowyer who was at one time Philip's P.P.S. were the other guns in the party which was made out with local people. Bowyer is now a whip and gave a very good account of the party in the House. He confirmed my own belief that they ended up feeling quite happy over R. & V. and generally that they are in a wonderfully contented mood. Indeed it is a remarkable fact that in spite of our huge majority we are the most united party in the House.

...

17 January 1926
Westbourne

My dear Ida,

...

We came down here on Thursday too late to see anything and spent all Friday with the Baldwins leaving the house before 11 and not getting back till 7. His visit was very successful. Fifty three addresses, all different and illuminated on vellum, were presented by delegations from constituencies in the area of the West Midlands. Mrs B. is going to have the wall of a room decorated with them arranged in panels of three – rather a good idea. At the luncheon the P.M.'s speech was divided into two parts. The first, which was largely personal, was amusing & delightful, but not important. The second, which he read, was important, but it was not entertaining & the audience found it a little hard to follow. Still they regarded it as a compliment that it should be delivered on this occasion and were pleased. My own speech which lasted 20 minutes was I am assured very happy – "beautiful" S.B. called it which my speeches generally are not – but of course it wasn't well reported even in the B.P.

330

23 January 1926
37 Eaton Square, SW1

My dear Hilda,

...

I have been working pretty hard all this week at Departmental business. Your inference from what you saw in the Times was natural but unfounded. No one raised any difficulty in Cabinet about my programme though they may do so later on but some of them expressed a not unreasonable desire to know what I had in mind about Housing before it was put in the Kings Speech and a Committee was appointed to look into my proposals. I gave a brief outline of them verbally which was well received and as I thought it was time to prepare the public I gave an interview to the Times. But of course I had to warn them that they hadn't been decided on by the Cabinet and the correspondent was therefore very careful to explain that and to make it clear that no one except myself was committed. His account appears to have made a favourable impression and I have been working on the draft with my people. There are a terrible lot of difficult points involved and a lot more spadework will have to be done before we can get a Bill into shape but I think it is a good thing that people who are interested should have an idea of the main lines. I have not had any letters on the subject up to the present, but I dont think much of that. I expect they will come along later.

I have also been working at the Guardians Coercion Bill which looks like being pretty controversial. But I should think it will be popular among our people.

... We took Frank one day to see the Sargent[1] Exhibition which you must certainly have a look at. It is a wonderful collection & the technical skill is positively uncanny. I don't like all of them and I regret to say that the one of Father does not impress me any more favourably among the others than it does alone. I notice that it is never mentioned in the reviews of the Exhibition from which I conclude that other people share my opinion of it. Its an inhuman picture.

We lunched yesterday with the Churchills to meet the Italian Delegation, who are rather a long time coming to grips with the settlement because as they explain they have to educate their own people who would never believe they hadn't been sold if an agreement was come to too readily. They make rather a pleasant impression of vigour and force. I don't think we shall get anything sensational out of them but I hope it will be sufficiently substantial to help us in receiving more out of the French.

...

---

[1] John Singer Sargent (1856–1925). American artist working in London from 1885 as the most fashionable portrait painter of the age; official war artist in Great War.

7 March 1926
Westbourne

My dear Hilda,

Your letter was very welcome for as you say, it is quite a long time since we exchanged confidences and so many things happen nowadays that one very quickly gets out of touch if there is not frequent contact.

...

We came down on Friday as I was addressing the public on the Birmingham School of Architecture that afternoon and Annie & I were due at a party in the constituency in the evening. An appalling affair: – we didn't get away till after midnight. Last night I had a dinner to attend in connection with the George Dixon school but today I am free to enjoy my books and my garden. I wish you could see our crocuses under the azaleas. They are a solid eiderdown of blue and white and in the sun are glorious. ...

You ask about Weir houses, and I think you have pretty well sized up the situation. Not only the Labour party but the Building Unions recognise that public opinion is against them and they are more anxious to find a way out if only they can save their faces. We had a conference last week – the Minister of Labour, Gilmour & myself – at which at my suggestion Weir was asked to attend. I told him that I thought his weak point was – not the digging – but the building of the foundations in concrete which was no part of his original plan but which he had had to take on because the municipality in Glasgow was too timid to do anything which would identify it with the contract. You cant say that this is standardised work, it is really exactly the work that a builders labourer would do and under the fair wages clause I didn't see how you could defend paying other than building labourer's rates. Weir admitted that it would only cost about £2.10/- extra per house but at the time he made other difficulties. However I gather that his manager Richmond, has been negotiating since & is prepared to give way on this point and the negotiations only broke down because new points were raised about plumbing and wiring. On these I think we ought to stand firm and I think I shall prove correct in my anticipation that there will be no stoppage of work.

For your private information I may tell you that about a fortnight ago Winston & I had a private interview with Herbt Samuel[2] when he told us the gist of his report.[3] Of course one will have to await the Report, which is very voluminous, to get a final judgement on the details and the presentation of them (which is

---

[2] Herbert Louis Samuel (1870–1963). Liberal MP for Cleveland 1902–18 and Darwen 1929–35. Under-Secretary, Home Office 1905–9; Chancellor, Duchy of Lancaster 1909–10 and 1915–16; Postmaster-General 1910–14 and 1915–16; President, LGB 1914–15; Home Secretary 1916 and 1931–32; High Commissioner for Palestine 1920–25. Knighted 1920. Created Viscount Samuel 1937.

[3] Cmd.2600, *Report of Royal Commission on the Coal Industry*, appointed September 1925.

important). But taking the main outlines, I was very pleased. It seemed to me to face facts, to avoid the principal pitfalls and to indicate a reasonable and practicable course for the future. I think it should make for peace and Herbt Samuel himself thought it would afford no ground for a stoppage.

What a pother over Geneva.[4] Poor Austen has had a parrot of a time – all by himself too – and now I see the Briand Govt has gone. Of course the hostile press is responsible for a good deal of the trouble in this country and it has been well aided by the journals in Paris Berlin Rome & Warsaw. But looking at it from the outside I think A. has been a little over diplomatic. In his anxiety to say nothing that might arouse any foreign susceptibilities or encourage any hopes that might be disappointed or close any door that might conceivably remain unshut he managed to mystify the man in the street who really began to think that he was somehow pledged to Briand[5] to support the claims of Poland & perhaps also Spain to a permanent seat at the same time as Germany. The first suspicions grew out of the Birmingham speech to his constituents and the speech in the House failed to clear them away even from the minds of our own people. Baldwin's remarks which were plainer & less hedged about with reserves were more successful. But the cruel part of the debate for A. as it seemed to me who was sitting next him was Ll.G.'s speech. He was just as reckless and mischievous and spiteful as he could be and he left nothing unsaid that could make things more difficult. "Poisoning the cup" "bullying Germany" "destroying his own masterpiece" "breach of faith" were among his phrases every one of which is no doubt seized upon and exploited by the German Nationalists. To me such a speech was no surprise; it is in character, but it must have cut Austen deeply.

Do, by the way, get House's[6] memoirs from your library & read them & tell me what you think of them – and him! From the reviews I get a thoroughly bad impression of the man, who seems to have some of the worst American faults Pharisaism, self sufficiency and arrogance with a mean delight in depreciating the merits of other people who have been more successful than himself. Obviously he hated Page[7] and Page had a poor opinion of him and his combination of

[4] The proposed German admission to the League Council as a condition of Locarno provoked a crisis when Briand (supported by Austen Chamberlain) pressed the claims of Poland to a permanent seat on the council, provoking similar demands from Brazil, Spain and later Belgium and China and much criticism in Britain of Chamberlain's pro-French secret diplomacy.

[5] Astride Briand (1862–1932). French statesman of Third Republic. Minister of Public Instruction and Worship 1906–9; Prime Minister 1909–10, 1913, 1915–17, 1921–22, 1925–26, 1929; Minister of Justice 1912–13, 1914; Minister of Foreign Affairs, 1921–22, 1925, 1926–32. Nobel Peace Prize for his part in Locarno 1926.

[6] Edward Mandell House (1858–1938). American diplomat. Personal representative of President Wilson to European governments and conferences 1915–19.

[7] Walter Hines Page (1855–1918). American journalist, editor and publisher. US Ambassador in London 1913–18. Strongly pro-British.

self assurance and colossal ignorance of Europe. I met House once at a dinner and was not impressed with him.

This next week the Economy Bill will be made public and on the same day I have got to meet representatives of the Approved Societies and tell them what they are in for. It will need some thinking over and my people are very nervous about it. I have done my best to frighten Winston about the reception he is likely to get & think I have succeeded, but I myself have a feeling that the opposition will not be quite as bad as I am told to expect. After all I have got rather a strong card in the Minority Report of the Royal Commission which is really the official Labour view & which wants to get rid of the approved societies altogether. And I shall say to them "Adieu now, or I'll give you to this great big hugly man". Stanley wants me to wind up on the Bill which is down for second reading on the 16th. I wish I hadn't got a mass meeting in Derby on the 19th!

I think A. told you about our series of dinners and luncheons. Our second luncheon was on Thursday when we had 14 round the table and we both thought it most successful. It is very useful to get young members in touch in this way and I find I recognise their faces better after I have seen them in my own house. We ourselves lunched one day with the Salisburys. Whether it was their lunch that overcame me or what I dont know but in walking across the Mall afterwards I had a decided difference of opinion with a small motor car that was hurtling along towards the Admiralty Arch. The car didnt come off scot free for I saw loose parts lying about afterwards. As for me I was hurled to the ground but fortunately the road was clear of other vehicles so I picked myself up and collected my hat and a few minutes afterwards as I crossed the park I observed with some satisfaction that I was still smoking the cigar which I had lit on leaving the Salisburys house. In fact except for a cut & a bruise or two I wasn't hurt.

This is a long letter but I must finish by telling you of a rather interesting development here. Some time ago both the General & Queens Hospitals decided to extend on their present sites and announced that they were going to appeal for very large sums for the purpose. I believed this to be all wrong. I wanted the City to get a hospital site somewhere near the University & gradually move all the hospitals to it, and just a year ago I took the opportunity, when opening a new X-ray apparatus at the Infirmary here to appeal for "a hospital policy for Birmingham". The only visible result at the time was a letter from William Cadbury[8] warmly endorsing what I had said and saying that he had endeavoured to persuade the 2 hospitals to abandon their schemes, but all in vain. I now learn however that my speech considerably shook up the local hospital world, and when last year I followed it up with more detailed suggestions to the Hospital

---

[8] William Adlington Cadbury (1867–?). Director of Cadbury Bros. from 1899. Member, Birmingham City Council from 1911; Chairman, Public Health Committee from 1913; Lord Mayor 1919–20.

Officers Association & my address on the Medical School, things began to move. It was found that the public were not enthusiastic over the appeals. I had some talks with the Lord Mayor who was against them & Barling who began to remember that a teaching hospital near the University would have merits from his point of view. Finally a meeting of the Joint Voluntary Hospitals Committee was held to which I sent an officer from the Ministry with instructions to give a lead. And now the House Governor of the General has been to see me. He says no one else is big enough to do it but if I would give an address it might be possible to get the Queens & General to combine & go to the new site. The old Queens building could be used by the city for maternity &c: the Eye, Ear & Throat, & Skin hospitals, all of which want to extend, might occupy the General building jointly until they too moved out. Cadbury has told me that his firm will *give* the site which I have informed him should not be less than 100 acres. So it looks as if we might lead the country again!

13 March 1926
37 Eaton Square, SW1

My dear Ida,

...

Things at Geneva looked pretty black this morning but tonight's paper says they are "trying again". I expect Austen is worn to a shadow as he takes these things hardly and Briand must be utterly exhausted. But the issues are so big that I cant help feeling that somehow a way out will be found. It is maddening to see the way anonymous journalists write airily that it is all Austen's fault for keeping an open mind and things would have been "infinitely simpler" if he had gone out pledged to one course only. I was relieved to read a sensible letter in the Times pointing out that it was just the attempt to tie him down that had produced the complication, though even the writer had not fully appreciated the effect of the speeches of Ll.G. & the activities of that preposterous League of Nations Union in consolidating & petrifying German public opinion.

There has been such a plethora of important documents this week that the press has got quite distracted. I shall have to try & find time to read the Coal Commission report somehow but its going to be very difficult as everything seems to have got heaped up into next week. On Monday I have to speak to Approved Societies (a nice time to do it!) on Tuesday I speak at the Seamens Hospital and then sit through the debate on the Economy Bill. Wednesday I wind up on Economy & then take 2nd reading of a controversial Bill of my own and Friday I address a mass meeting at Derby!

I am working still at Housing & have now got the rural part pretty well into shape but I agree that the amount of legislation required for coal makes the prospects rather uncertain. Of course I might possibly run it through in the autumn if I could get 2nd reading before August.

We had a second dinner party on Wednesday with great success. ...

I had representatives of the Approved Societies up at the Ministry on Thursday in order to break to them the provisions of the Economy Bill, and although naturally they dont like the reduction of the State contributions I gather both from their behaviour at the meeting and from private remarks that have reached me since that the opposition will not be *à outrance*. Of course the official opposition in the House will exploit it for all they are worth but there is a lot of difference between that sort of worked up fury and the real bitter fight of people with a burning sense of injustice. I think all the Cabinet realise that we were wise in not going further and that our moderation will in the end prove to have secured us more than if we had gone out for bigger savings.

...

Sunday

P.S. Annie having now read the above I add a note to say that I am rather bothered about her. She has got into a condition which borders on a nervous break-down and she reacts upon herself so powerfully that she falls into the extreme of depression and actually prevents herself from getting the repose which is what she needs. She seems better & more cheerful this morning and I am driving her down to Kew this afternoon, but it is very difficult to see how one is to alter conditions of life here and yet she doesn't seem able to cope with them. However, perhaps she may presently get better. There is certainly nothing organically wrong but its the strain acting on a highly strung temperament.

20 March 1926
Westbourne

My dear Hilda,

What a speaker you are getting to be. Almost every day in the week you seem to be at it like any politician. And to think that I have never heard either you or Ida "take the platform". ... I never heard Bee speak, but she had the old fashioned objection to showing off before her family.

Please thank Ida for her birthday letter. It is nice to be remembered for the 57th time! I forgot all about it myself till I found a musical composition from my daughter upon the breakfast table.

We are spending a restful week end in retirement after one of the most exhausting weeks we have had, but I, at any rate, begin to recover as soon as the mental strain of impending speeches is over. ...

On Monday I had my lunch with the Approved Societies. The rascal who proposed my health made a most outrageous speech, which I believe he did merely to advertise himself. But I treated it as a joke and got through very comfortably. In fact I thought the audience was distinctly friendly and again I heard afterwards that some members had declared their conviction that they had got off very lightly.

On Tuesday I had to preside at the Seamen's Hospital meeting before going to the House and was unusually worried over it because I had the Economy Bill debate on my mind. ...

The Economy debate went very well. Winston made a remarkably interesting and able speech which would have been better still if he had shortened it (he spoke for just over 1½ hours.) I think he knocked out the criticism that we weren't doing enough and the speeches that followed were all pretty poor except Simon's whose facts however were incorrect and Sidney Webbs whose facts were all right but who never can command the House. On the Wednesday Lloyd George made a very amusing and very damaging speech which contained the rhetorical and foolish allusion to "plucking the feathers out of the pillow of the sick man". Then I rejoiced exceedingly because I felt sure he had forgotten the Act of 1920 which reduced the State contribution to womens benefits from ½ to ⅖. I dont know where you learnt that my speech was a success as the Times said very little about it. But it certainly produced a tremendous effect on our people. Some of them had been considerably perturbed beforehand but after it was over they one and all declared that I had absolutely washed out the case against the Bill and that now they wouldn't be afraid to defend it anywhere. The Speaker was excessively complimentary. He stopped me as I was going out to say he thought it was the best parliamentary debating speech he had ever heard. "Not a redundant word and so absolutely efficient." I wish you could have seen the Goat. I had given him a solemn rebuke for his loose talk about "breach of faith" which he took very well and he thought I had done with him. But I led up to my poisoned dart with a compliment to his captivating eloquence and then gently asked if he had forgotten the Act of 1920. His face changed and he looked the picture of apprehension. And when it finally came out and amid roars of laughter I asked what about the breach of faith. Are we to understand that we may pluck the feathers from the pillow of the sick woman but not from that of the sick man, he was as flummoxed and uncomfortable as a man could be. *That* for Geneva said I to myself. Of course he has written to the papers to try and explain but it is too late, and moreover if it were worth while to take any more notice of it he has really made matters worse for himself.

I had a terrible day at Derby yesterday. I arrived there at three, and was conducted round housing schemes till 4.45 when I went to the Council House for a cup of tea and "a few words". Then my host Dr Aiton conducted me to the station where we met Annie arriving from Birmingham and drove out to his house. Twenty minutes conversation and ten minutes unpacking brought us to the time when it was necessary to drive back to Derby for dinner and immediately afterwards we drove to the meeting. I say "we" but by an extremely humorous piece of carelessness they left me behind! I had been asked to wait as I was to go last and accordingly I was examining an old panel in the hall of the hotel when thinking I was waiting for a long time I asked the waiter whether they weren't ready. They've gone, Sir replied the waiter & so they had. Of course the car soon came rattling back again and I got to the drill hall in plenty of time and delivered a powerful oration lasting exactly an hour. I thought I was through then, but my chairman asked me just to look in at the Conservative Club, so I had to go round and make a little speech there. Even then my merciless host hadn't finished. There was just the Conservative Working Men's Club, he said, and they would appreciate a visit so much. So once more I entered a vile smoky den and once more I harangued the multitude. And then at last I was permitted to go away. But we didn't go to bed till nearly 12 and I was pretty tired by then.

...

Annie had to preside at a conference of her Midland Area on Thursday at Dudley when the Attorney General [Douglas Hogg] came down to deliver the address & spoke very warmly of both Austen and me. I don't think you know him but he is one of the best, straight & loyal and possessed of a wonderful brain. Moreover he is a first class fighting man.

I saw another friend, Edward Wood, off on Thursday. Last Saturday he and I went for a long walk round and round Hyde Park, discussing men and things. It was so interesting that when we got back to Eaton Square we kept seeing one another to our respective doors (he lives almost opposite us) and walking round the square. I think he is, without exception, the most delightful man I know, so full of sound sense, sly humour, and high principles which he never parades but which you feel are there. He told me a delicious story of Nancy Astor, who was telling him of some poor woman that she had been seeing & whom she said she *really* cared for more than anyone. And then she went on "Every night I kneel down & pray to God. Oh God teach me to love the rich. I know they are thy creatures, but, God, unless you help me I shall never, never be able to love Mrs Ronnie Greville[9] and all the people like her." I laughed till I cried. Poor Nancy. She tries so hard to be good, and she does so constantly ruin her own cause by some impetuous folly.

Sunday ...

I agree that Borah[10] is the limit. But not Borah only for he represents a considerable section of wild and woolly America. And then Hoover![11] With his squeals about the wickedness of the British rubber profiteers when he himself

---

[9] Margaret Helen Anderson (?–1942). Widow of Hon. Ronnie Greville (died 1908). Society hostess. Created Dame 1922. Extremely wealthy, close to Austen Chamberlain, but according to Boothby, 'a bit of an old bag'.

[10] William Edgar Borah (1865–1940). American politician. Republican Senator for Idaho 1907–40; Chairman, Senate Foreign Relations Committee 1925–33. Convinced isolationist and instrumental in blocking US entry to League of Nations.

[11] Herbert Clark Hoover (1874–1964). Engineer and US politician. Worked on relief of famine and distress in Europe during Great War; Secretary of Commerce 1921–28; President of USA 1929–33; Chairman, US Commission on European Economic Relief after 1945.

advised the Western farmers to restrict cultivation in order to keep up the price of wheat! I hev no *uset* [?] for America.

...

27 March 1926
Westbourne

My dear Ida,

I foresaw how it would be on Thursday because I realise that Austen is not interested in Home affairs, but it was just a rare opportunity of having Ivy to dinner and I dont want to lose touch with her altogether. Anyway, we thrashed out the Foreign affairs pretty well and I think A. feels quite happy again and is sorry he talked about a "tragedy". After you went upstairs I tackled him about the Dominions representatives. I always feel very nervous about the Dominions in these rather delicate European entanglements. They are so suspicious of being drawn into things which dont directly concern them and so touchy about recognition of their rights to separate voices that there is a constant danger of some open difference of opinion. Happily A. says (and Amery has since confirmed this) this time they were so carefully coddled and consulted and so well informed that they were able to give hearty approval and some of them at any rate learned a good deal that was very good for them. It was interesting to hear that Fitzgerald[12] the Free State representative was particularly helpful & was always the first to express approval. And I gather that Smit[13] the South African though not very brainy, also approved and understood that the game was being played straight. He was said to be very Anti-English when he came over but I am told he has modified these views considerably owing to the friendly and hospitable atmosphere in which he has found himself.

I confess to being much relieved about Annie. I was a little afraid that Leonard Williams would content himself with ordering her to give up meat and sweets. But he never mentioned diet except to say that her food had nothing to do with her stoutness. On the other hand he seemed to understand all her symptoms and to find nothing surprising or alarming in them. And finally he prescribed exactly what she and I had felt was wanted. So though I look forward to my lonely life with loathing and disgust I feel a reasonable confidence that the sacrifice will bring its reward and that I shall get rid of this uneasy shadow which has been getting gradually darker for some time. Annie herself, I think,

---

[12] Desmond Fitzgerald (1889–1947). Irish journalist and politician. Sinn Fein MP for Dublin Pembroke 1918–22; Member, Dáil Eireann 1922–37. Minister of External Affairs 1922–27; Minister of Defence 1927–32; Member, Senate 1938–47. Father of Dr Garret Fitzgerald.

[13] Jacobus Stephanus Smit (1878–1960). South African lawyer, politician and diplomat. Private Secretary to Smuts, Botha and Villiers 1906–9; Magistrate 1910–14; National Party Member, House of Assembly 1920–24. South African representative in London 1924–26 and High Commissioner 1926–27; Administrator of Transvaal 1927–34; Chairman, Diamond Board 1934–37.

has an equal confidence & rejoices in a prescription which abhors exercise but involves rest and sunshine!

...

The demand for extra time on the Electricity Bill has deprived me of one half day's Committee on the Economy Bill, but I hope to get the first 2 clauses which are what I really want to secure before the Easter break gives the Societies time to get up a ramp. Up to the present I have every reason to be satisfied as only the most superficial and conventional opposition has been put up either in the House or the country. Poor Law is also going quite comfortably. I am now engaged in "conversations" with the Associations of Local Auths. The non County Boroughs are the principal difficulty. They want to opt to come in under the County or go out as they please, which of course would be impossible and it will be difficult to get an agreed settlement with them. On the other hand the County boroughs are pretty solidly behind me and the Guardians are divided.

...

6 April 1926
Cairnton, Banchory, N.B.

My dear Hilda,

...

I daresay you saw the awful finish up I had in the House. 3.45 p.m. to 9.30 a.m. & then back at 11. However we got the wicked clause through before the Appd Societies could get up a proper ramp which, as the children say, is "snubs for them". I must say I found the sitting very trying but I endeavoured not to let the enemy see it and the Daily Mail represents me as preserving to the end my "spruce and unruffled efficiency". This last word is now my journalistic label. The little local paper here had an article yesterday by a Parliamentary correspondent, who declared that Winston could not command the admiration that was given to me for "sheer mental efficiency" & went on to declare that I was the most effective member of the Govt – much to the delight of my friends here.

I have now been here 4 days of which three were fishing days and I haven't yet succeeded in rising a salmon though I have caught 3 kelts. I feel sure it must be my fault as the others have caught a certain number ...

...

18 April 1926
Westbourne

My dear Hilda,

...

I think this has been about the worst week I have ever had in politics and I am glad its over. I suppose it was being tired that made Stockton hang over me like a nightmare all the time. And then one's heart is not in this d-d "Economy" Bill which gives one not the slightest satisfaction and has no redeeming feature from my point of view since *I* cant spend the money I shall save. In the meantime I get cursed and abused for a thief, a cad, and a bully because I resist organised obstruction and when I have broken the back of it, Winston who has been going early to bed all week comes along all smiles and his conciliatory behaviour is contrasted with the abominable manners of the Minister of Health!

Of course I know that its all sham and humbug. If only the Labour Party would make an open attack on me I have got an overwhelming case against them out of their own mouths. And I had already exhausted conciliation and toleration without the slightest response, until my own people were getting impatient. I regret nothing that I did including the closuring of Wheatley in the middle of his speech. If ex-Cabinet Ministers behave like back benchers they cannot expect to go on receiving the courtesies they abuse. And the incident in the Lobby he brought upon himself & I had nothing to do with it. Still even the least sensitive among us don't like to be treated as I was treated that night by the Labour men and though I dont believe I showed it I did feel the strain.[14]

I am glad to say that I got in two more hits on Ll.G. He made one of those rather solemn speeches when he pulls down the corners of his mouth & drawls out gloomy menaces and prophecies. On this occasion it was the financial position of the Societies that was threatened. But I remembered something he had said on Second reading and I was able to demonstrate conclusively to the House that the proposals which he had advocated as the alternative to ours would have had precisely & identically the same effect as ours. Once again he was reduced to absolute silence and I observe that he begins to treat me with considerable respect while Sir J. Simon says I am a "most accomplished debater who never misses a point". The fact is that I have ceased to have any fear of the Goat. Did I tell you how I remarked that to follow him one required to have the agility of the picturesque and hirsute animal that walks in front the Welsh regiments. At the moment I wasn't quite certain if the House had caught the allusion but from remarks that have come to me since I gather that they understood & appreciated it.

I had a tiring but quite successful expedition to Stockton, tiring really because I hadn't recovered from the all nighter when I never got to bed till 6 p.m. [sic] & then had only 2 hours before I had to get up again. I dont think my speech was one of my best, and yet the audience seemed to be straining their attention to catch what I was saying throughout the 70 minutes that I spoke. I talked a bit

---

[14] At 1.30 am on 14 April Chamberlain responded to Labour obstruction during the Committee Stage by moving the closure after Wheatley had been speaking for half an hour. This interruption provoked furious condemnation and at 5.30 am thirteen Labour MPs – including Wheatley, Lansbury and Dalton – were suspended for persistently wasting time.

about the Economy Bill but Macmillan[15] (the member) who has been holding meetings in the constituency all Easter assures me that he never had a question about it and believes the people dont understand it well enough to get excited about it! ...

I got here in time for a late lunch and last night trundled down to the Town Hall to deliver an address in connection with the Musical Festival Competition. You will say why go out of your way to take on another engagement at such a time. But of course it was made some while ago when I couldn't know that it would come into such a week and moreover I am anxious to maintain my touch with the promotion of public interest in music in Birmingham. I have done a good deal for it in the past including the establishment of the City orchestra and I want the people concerned to feel that they still have my interest & backing. And I must say that last night they were most appreciative and expressed their thanks most warmly.

...

The fact is I miss my wife! But her letters continue to show progressive improvement not so much by definite symptoms but by more subtle indications which I read between the lines & which show that her mental storms are passing off. She says however that her blood pressure is not nearly normal and it hasn't been that for a long time.

...

[Postscript] I see I have forgotten to say anything about coal! I remain hopeful. The P.M.'s conversations have been v. useful & he has actually got the miners to say they will discuss reduction of wages! (v. secret.)

25 April 1926
Westbourne

My dear Ida,

...

I continue to get satisfactory reports from Annie. She doesn't pretend that she is right yet but the relapses get less severe and less frequent and the reports on her heart lungs and inside generally seem very good. True the bacillus coli is much more abundant than he should be but I regard this rather as the result than the cause of her ill health and as she recovers strength I expect she will do the coli in. She has now been 3½ weeks away and reckons she is coming back about

---

[15] (Maurice) Harold Macmillan (1894–1986). Conservative MP for Stockton-on-Tees 1924–29 and 1931–45 and Bromley 1945–64. Parliamentary Secretary, Ministry of Supply 1940–42; Under-Secretary, Colonies 1942; Minister Resident, North-West Africa 1942–45; Air Secretary 1945; Minister of Housing and Local Government 1951–54; Defence Minister 1954–55; Foreign Secretary 1955; Chancellor of Exchequer 1955–57; Prime Minister 1957–63. Created Earl of Stockton 1984.

the middle of May, but I am still declining even to consider return until she feels she cant stand Hélianthe any longer. I fancy that will come as soon as she is really well!

Well thank Goodness we've got rid of that d-d Economy Bill. I dined pretty constantly in the House while it was on but I got let off a speech on Third Reading and the job was given to Kingsley who did it extremely well. One of the things he has learnt from his association with me is that you cant take too much trouble to learn your case and the result is that the opposition can no more trip him up than they can me. Winston finished up the debate with a rollicking "rag" which hadn't much argument about it but delighted the House including the opposition. Once again the best speech in the debate was Simon's. He has somehow managed to make a new reputation for himself on this Bill and he has done it by adopting a style in striking & deliberate contrast to Lloyd George. Avoiding all rhetoric studiously declaring that he wishes to eschew exaggeration & party prejudice he has put his arguments coolly but in the most damaging form. I don't think he has done us much damage – our case is too good but he has pleased me because he has conducted his own like a gentleman.

I got through my Leeds visit very well and didn't worry about it much until about an hour beforehand. ... The meeting was in the Town Hall which holds over 4000 when it is packed as it was when I spoke there in /23. This time the season was not so favourable and interest in politics is not so keen ... but I judged there were fully 3000 there and I made rather a good speech I thought – interesting & lively. I had to get up early next morning ... by the evening I was feeling pretty tired and headachy. But a good night's rest & breakfast in bed has set me up and I have an easy mind for I have no more political speeches for some time nor any very troublesome work in the House. I think I am probably going to drop the Guardians Coercion Bill as evidently my people are frightened of the disfranchisement proposals and if fresh difficulties arise in West Ham or elsewhere they will serve to strengthen the case for the big bill next year.

I have got on well with rural housing & see my way to a good bill to deal with it but slums are the very d-l. I believe any one else would abandon the whole thing but I am determined not to be beaten & have started my people off on a new tack which they think is hopeful.

Afternoon ...

Coal is in the balance but the T.U. Congress Council want peace so I am still hopeful. I dont envy S.B. his job these days.

2 May 1926
37 Eaton Square, SW1

My dear Hilda,

Ida will have told you of the events that took place up to lunch time yesterday. There have been many changes since then but the issue is still quite uncertain.

Of course I have not been in these negotiations from the beginning and my impressions therefore are imperfect. But there is no doubt that the situation has been extraordinarily difficult and the criticisms indulged in by Macdonald [sic] Lloyd George &c are 90% partisan.

If the Govt had barged in earlier it would have been blamed for its precipitancy nor do I think myself that it came on the scene too late. I won't say that no mistakes have been made on our side but you have no idea how difficult this [sic] Labour men are to deal with. They will never give you a straight answer to a straight question. They reply always at interminable length in sentences which have no grammatical ending and leave me in a hopeless fog.

I dont think this is to be set down entirely as a deliberate intention to deceive. Partly it is the result of their training but chiefly to their distrust of themselves and fear that they may be led into some damaging admission by men of more education & quicker minds than they have. But it makes it so difficult to understand what they are driving at. Birkenhead & I endeavoured repeatedly to ascertain what proposals they had to make to cover the period between the end of the Subsidy and the attainment of such economies as might be effected by the proposals of the R.C. proposals which would take *years* to carry out completely. To that we could get nothing but "If you are going to ask us to begin by agreeing to a reduction of wages you cant have it."

I fancy they have never clearly distinguished between the permanent re-organising of the industry and the temporary measures necessary while the permanent ones are taking shape and form. The Miners dont think of the re-organisation in precise terms of reduction of costs; they rather picture grievances, stupidities, injustices which they have personally come up against and they want to have a certainty that these things will be put right before they give up anything. They wont face up to the fact that meanwhile there is a loss and and [sic] someone has got to pay for that loss. And the more intelligent Trade Unionists like Thomas see the difficulty – on both sides but as they are mainly concerned to save their own skins they cynically declare that its all the fault of the Govt.

Last night things looked rather bad for a time. Thomas & F.E. are on rather good personal terms (they have some tastes in common!) & Thomas called to F.E. as he & I were passing through the crowd in the passage to go to the Cabinet room "This is war this time." But you cant believe what he says & we didn't! After a certain amount of manœuvring we offered to appoint a Sub. Com. of 3 if they wd do the same to discuss fundamentals & try to hammer out some way of coming to an agreement. It took them ¾ hr of hard talking (and drinking) to come to a conclusion as to who should be their representatives but finally they pitched on Pugh[16] & Thomas who both want a peace and a bad Bolshie named

---

[16] Arthur Pugh (1870–1955). Steel smelter in Wales from 1894. Assistant Secretary, British Steel-Smelters' Association 1906; General Secretary, Iron and Steel Trades Federation 1917–36. Chairman, General Congress of TUC 1925. Knighted 1935.

Swales.[17] I rejoiced in this arrangement which allowed me to get home by 11.30 and has left me free till noon today. I shall probably hear then what has happened at the Sub. and will add a line to say what are the prospects.

Later The prospects are very bad. The Sub. didn't get anything satisfactory & indeed I hope the final document agreed on will never see the light!

The threat of a General Strike has made negotiation more difficult than ever and I am afraid that the only line we could now take is one that the T.U.C. daren't accept.

The tragedy is that in their hearts they know what ought to be done.

We have another Cabinet at 5 but I see practically no hope of avoiding a fight.

8 May 1926
37 Eaton Square, SW1

My dear Ida,

I think they are managing the post remarkably well, and I got your letter yesterday so it only took 1 day to get through.

I am sure you are right to give up your foreign tour, disappointing as it is. The fact is that constitutional Govt is fighting for its life; if we failed it would be the Revolution for the nominal leaders would be whisked away in an instant. And although we all feel confident of ultimate success there are some very anxious moments and set-backs are conceivable which might make us very uncomfortable.

In such circumstances conscientious folk could not enjoy a holiday. Apart from anxiety there would be a sort of guilty feeling underlying everything mingled with constant doubts as to whether you werent losing your only chance of returning. I have cancelled all my engagements for a couple of weeks and I am sure its the only thing to do.

It turned out to be quite impossible to get away, tempting as your offer was. Not only are there constant meetings of the Cabinet (there was one at 9 p.m. last night and another at 6. tonight) but I am one of the few that S.B. likes to have always within reach and therefore I am one of the last that could leave till all this is over.

London is astonishingly quiet & good tempered. For the first two days there were streams of motors in the morning and evening only able to move slowly towards the City. But since then there has been no block and every day omnibus & underground services have improved. Taxis have disappeared completely: apparently they did a very poor business and thought it wasn't worth the risk of getting their cars damaged.

---

[17] A.B. Swales (?–1952). General Secretary, Amalgamated Engineering Union; Vice-Chairman, General Council of TUC.

All sorts of interesting things are going on which I might have told you but dont like to write. But I may say generally that the situation is improving rapidly and that as we haven't played all our cards yet it should get still better soon. The other side may also have cards but I doubt if they are equal to ours and there is no doubt that many of them would be very much relieved to find a way out now they begin to realise what they are up against.

But I dont see how there can be any settlement till matters have gone further. Until it is plain that the victory is hopeless the T.U.C. daren't show the white flag.

Evening. This has been a good day for us. One of our most serious anxieties has been the shortage of flour in certain districts owing to the action of the strikers in stopping all work in the docks & the transport for them. Matters were getting serious so a combined scheme was devised which has worked like magic. It began by a march of the Scots Guards preceded by armoured cars & headed by their own pipes playing through the East end to the selected dock. They were received with loud cheers and cries of "That's the stuff to give 'em" "These are the boys for us" &c. They proceeded to occupy the dock & put barbed wire entanglements round the area adjoining.

The next move was when at midnight a vessel left Westminster Bridge with 500 volunteers. She proceeded to the dock by the river & landed the volunteers who started at once to unload the flour ships.

Finally at 4.30 a.m. a convoy of 130 lorries left Hyde Park and rumbled down to the rendezvous where they were at once loaded up. About noon the procession left with the guards in tin hats on the lorries and the armoured cars in front & behind. I am told that not a stone was thrown but everywhere the procession was received with cheers and that an incredible amount of flour was moved. The traders were so encouraged that they begged to be allowed to move their own stuff out of another dock under protection.

Oh dear: what a lot of busy bodies there are who think they can run this business better than the Govt. That wretched old Archbishop [of Canterbury] of course is pushed on from behind. He wanted to broadcast his eirenicon suggesting that we should all cry "quits" and begin again. At least three gentlemen have independently come to various members of the Govt offering to act as mediators. And that ass Howard d'Egville[18] has just been to tell me that he is on excellent terms with the Labour Party, that he has been seeing Henderson and that he thinks he might induce the T.U.C. to withdraw their notices on a private understanding which no one need know anything about (!) that we would lend money to the coal industry to keep up wages for several years while the reorganisation was becoming operative. Can you conceive of any one being such a

---

[18] Howard d'Egville (?–1965). Barrister and lecturer on defence and foreign policy. First Secretary, Empire Parliamentary Association 1920–60; organised visits to and from Dominion Parliaments. Knighted 1918.

fool. But I think I shook him out of his complacency. And if he goes back and tells "Uncle Arthur" what I told him Uncle Arthur will get cold comfort.

...

I am just off to a Committee this morning but this afternoon Dorothy & I are going to Kew. That is, if the P.M. doesnt send for me first.

I have just heard that a second convoy of 150 went to the docks this morning & will leave today. It is considered that the dock problem is solved.

12 May 1926
37 Eaton Square, SW1

My dear Hilda,

...

Well, we have won a great victory. The collapse came more suddenly than I expected. I was up till 2. this morning waiting for the T.U.C. but they didn't succeed in arriving at a decision in time & had to put off their penance till this morning. Their friends are trying to save their faces by pretending that they got all sorts of conditions but as a matter of fact they surrendered unconditionally!

And now our troubles will begin. As A.J.B. cheerfully remarks, of course they are trying to make us say that everyone shall be taken back & no one shall suffer for having broken his contract. But we cant sell our friends for their beaux yeux.

The miners are in a nice temper and we shall have a peck of trouble with them before we have done.

However, so far so good.

P.S. What a sell for Ll.G. He was making tracks for the Labour Party as fast as he could but didn't get there in time!

25 May 1926
37 Eaton Square, SW1

My dear Ida,

...

...

Except for the fact that the Govts terms have been rejected by miners and owners practically nothing has happened since you went away. But you may be comforted to know that that is just what we expected. Our experts tell us that they are so used to long stoppages that neither side can bring itself to the proper attitude until they have been at a deadlock long enough to feel the inconvenience. At the moment we can only wait until they make another move but of course it is a lamentable thing that they pay no attention to the damage to the nation and when one sees how hopelessly they mismanage their affairs one cannot wonder that the advocates of nationalisation think that that panacea could not be worse and might be better than the present situation. Meanwhile the fur is beginning to fly. Wheatley says that the explanation of the "abject surrender" is to be found in "sheer coward-ice". Cook say Macdonald [sic] & Thomas have betrayed not only the miners but their own people. Maxton declares that Baldwin & Churchill are quite right in saying that the strike was against the Constitution & "so it ought to be". The only thing they agree about is that the Govt are a set of fools dominated by knaves; the two species being about equally represented. According to the New Statesman I am one of the knaves who threatened the peace makers (Baldwin Birkenhead & Steel-Maitland) with resignation if negotiations were not instantly broken off!

The Liberal Party is also having another internal crisis. Squiff told S.B. the other night that he had had about as much of Ll.G. as he could stand and that there was going to be the d-l of a row at the next party meeting.[19]

...

31 May 1926
37 Eaton Square, SW1

My dear Hilda,

...

... I had my agent up on Saturday. He gave an encouraging account of the constituency and thinks that Mosley has gone back. He made a fool of himself by claiming that the strike was a great "Workers victory", a statement which might go down at the moment with a mass meeting of roughs in a park but wont bear examination in the light of Labour Leader's speeches. The agent also said that rumours were constantly going round that I was not going to stand for Ladywood again but that he had faithfully contradicted them. This was embar-rassing but I had to let it pass without observation.

There is a pretty little quarrel going on in the Liberal Party isn't there. It is evident from what Grey[20] said that this is only the culmination of a long period of Ll.G.'s disloyalty and now Pringle declares openly that he made overtures to the Labour party which were rejected. No doubt there will be further develop-ments very soon.

Meanwhile the coal stoppage continues and the country is gradually freezing up. But it seems from this morning's papers that there are some indications of a break among the districts. I have just received a summons to a Cabinet at 10.15 tonight so I expect that I shall hear the latest news then.

---

[19] During the General Strike Asquith supported the Government while Lloyd George favoured negotiation. On 10 May Lloyd George declared he would not attend the Shadow Cabinet because of these differences – a move which Asquith used as a pretext for a public breach on 20 May. On 1 June twelve other Liberal leaders supported Asquith.

[20] Edward Grey (1862–1933). Liberal MP for Berwick-on-Tweed 1885–1916. Under-Secretary, Foreign Affairs 1892–95; Foreign Secretary 1905–16. Succeeded as 3rd Bart 1882. Created Vis-count Grey of Falloden 1916.

I rather think I told you a little while ago that I was thinking of having Annie's portrait painted. About 2 years since I was a good deal taken with a portrait by a man called de Glehn.[21] I have been taking notice of his pictures ever since & this year he had several portraits in the academy which seemed both to Annie and me to have more life and expression in them than any others. So at last I made up my mind to write to him and explore the ground. The result was a shock for he asked double what I expected. So I wrote politely but firmly that I couldn't afford such a charge and must reluctantly give up the idea. I thought it just possible that he would come down and in fact I got a very nice letter saying that if he was interested he didn't care about the business side.

...

6 June 1926
37 Eaton Square, SW1

My dear Ida,
...
I have very little to tell you this week for except for the Liberal squabbles it has been very uneventful. ...

We have just been spending a week end with the Ashleys at Broadlands. I am afraid I was very unsociable for I spent all the daylight hours in fishing for salmon in the Test – wholly without success. But it was very nice, all by myself with only the fishermen and the birds & I endeavoured to make up for it by sitting up till 1.30 both nights playing poker. Poker bores me and I dont want to sit up late during the week ends but Mrs Ashley demands it & we had to sacrifice ourselves as did the other guests ...

...

Rather a scoop to have downed Zaghloul[22] and got the Turks to sign the Treaty in the week!

13 June 1926
Chevening, Sevenoaks

My dear Hilda,
...
The coal stoppage seemed almost to escape notice this last week in the excitement about the Liberal split. I confess I was surprised at the amount of support Ll.G. got from the Press generally, support which cannot be accounted

---

[21] Wilfred Gabriel de Glehn (1870–1951). Portrait artist.
[22] Sa'ad Zaghlul (1860–1927). Egyptian politician and leader of nationalist Wafd party. Deported 1919, returned 1921 and deported 1921–23. Prime Minister 1924 but forced to resign after murder of Sir Lee Stack. President, Chamber of Deputies 1925–27.

for on the genial supposition put forward yesterday by Rudyard Kipling[23] that he had just bought it. To my mind it is an indication that the Goat has not lost his cunning. In a situation in which he was wholly in the wrong, when he had demonstrably been thoroughly disloyal to his chief, when he had attempted to collect a party of his own, first out of Unionists and then out of Labour, when he had held up his ill gotten gains for personal purposes and finally when for sordid pelf he – an ex-Prime Minister – had written down his country for the delectation of its enemies – in such a situation he contrived to divert attention from the real issues and to pose as a pure souled patriot despitefully [sic] treated because of his irrepressible sympathy with the suffering and the oppressed. Its a remarkable feat & for the moment he has triumphed. But he has won a barren victory by the aid of the Right with whom he has least affinity and he has not really succeeded in dissipating the universal distrust with which he is rightly regarded. I sat up till nearly one oclock this morning with Willie Tyrell [sic] & Rudyard Kipling & by the time we went to bed there wasn't enough left of Lloyd George, Woodrow Wilson & Col. House put together to find a meal for a Pekingese.

There seems no doubt that the settlement prospects rather went back last week. Cook & Smith[24] appear for some reason to have hardened and the owners are so cautious that they enable the men to say they dont want a settlement. I think the account given by a mendacious capitalist press, but never specifically denied, of the miners attitude towards the unemployed in their own industry and those engaged in other trades had been useful as showing up their obstinacy and selfishness. But I observe that they are pursuing, with the active assistance of the Labour party, a campaign designed to enlist public sympathy for their cause on the ground that they are being beaten into submission by the allied Government & owners through the starvation of their wives and babies.

So far I have had no evidence of abnormal innutrition and the infant mortality rate continues to follow the normal summer curve, going steadily down each week. But I fear that the campaign is likely to have some success among sentimental soft heads who form the majority of English people and I want to divert the issue.

If you substitute a longer working day for the wage reduction the women & children come out of the picture altogether. The whole burden then falls upon the man & he is not going to get a lot of sympathy if he is obliged to work as long as a railway man.

My suggestion to Stanley then, in the ten minutes which was all I could get with him before he went off to Chequers on Thursday, was that he should take an oppty of broadcasting a talk on the situation.

---

[23] Rudyard Kipling (1865–1936). English writer. Nobel Prize for Literature 1907.

[24] Herbert Smith (1862–1938). Miner. Vice-President, Yorkshire Miners' Association 1904 and President 1906–38; President, MFGB 1922–29; President, International Miners' Federation 1921–29.

He wd point to the failure of the parties once more to find any measure of agreement and the fact that while they were sitting idle the country was bleeding to death. This made it his duty to give his views to the country.

First he would have to make quite clear that subsidy, as such, was dead beyond possibility of revival. The situation must be faced without hopes from that quarter. No one wanted to reduce the miners standard of living least of all himself. If they could save the industry in any other way that way should be taken.

What about hours? The owners had already made an offer on 8 hours which was immensely better than that for 7 hours. He would like them to try to go further. Let them offer 1924 wages for 8 hours. If they did the men ought to take the offer at once.

In one district such an offer would shut nearly all the pits – Northd & Durham. Some *must* be shut but wholesale closing *wd* give us too great a shock and the Govt would be prepared to help. If that old three millions were spread out judiciously it would go a long way to tide things over till better times came & meanwhile owners & the Government could be working out reorganisation proposals together.

I suggested to Stanley that coming from him, a talk of this kind would so arouse public interest & sympathy that very soon afterwards he could safely call for a ballot on his proposals.

S.B. said he wd like to think over these very interesting views (which I put up as a counter to Winston's idea of legislation on 8 hours & minimum wages) but didn't I think he ought first to say all this to the H. of C. I replied "very likely". I had no objection so long as he broadcasted afterwards. We shall see what comes of it, but Lane Fox[25] & Sam Hoare to whom I confided my ideas seemed to like the plan & think it might be fruitful.

...

20 June 1926
Westbourne

My dear Ida,

What an astounding pair you are! One never knows what surprising gift will be produced without a word of warning or preparation and we are continually having our breath taken away & sit gasping at one another and trying to take it in. You fairly caught me napping with your innocent questions about de Glehn's price and I never for a moment suspected what you had in your mind.

---

[25] George Richard Lane-Fox (1870–1947). Conservative MP for Barkston Ash, 1906–31. Charity Commissioner 1921; Secretary for Mines 1922–24 and 1924–28. Member, Indian Statutory Committee 1928. Chairman, Pig Products Commission 1932 and Fatstock Reorganisation Commission 1933. Created Baron Bingley 1933.

Well, I suppose I shall have to have it done now though I do loathe it. ...

Meanwhile [Annie] continues to be very pleased with her own portrait and I am to be allowed to see it soon. I congratulate myself on having pushed it along now for she really is quite herself again and is enjoying life without public engagements.

We have got a deliciously peaceful day before us for the Railway Co have taken off our Sunday train and so we have decided to stop over until tomorrow morning. The sun is out and very soon I shall fling down this pen and rush into the garden. I had a good sleep last night and wanted it for although you might suppose I was having a pretty slack time this is not so. I have been up till nearly 1 oclock most nights and have had a great deal of work so that I dont think I have had more than about an hour to read the papers each day.

I cant remember how much I have told you about my efforts to get a post graduate school in London. It will be a big thing when it comes off and should do much to raise the standard of the panel doctor besides creating a new centre to which Dominion & Colonial M.D.'s come instead of being forced over to Germany or Switzerland. But it *is* a job getting the doctors to agree. I have about a dozen of them on a Comee of which I am chairman and they are at present divided into at least 3 groups and several independent units! Should we adapt an old hospital; – or should we build a new one; – or is it necessary to have a hospital at all. Couldn't we just group all the existing hospitals together and let our school be just an organising body with an office. The one thing that would bring them together would be a Fund and I threw a fly over Cowdray. But he immediately dived down & got under a ledge and I haven't seen him since! So I have to lead my committee along very gingerly and by a process of elimination I shall gradually arrive at a position to which no one will be able to object. That is, if I live long enough! But perhaps when I get a little further I shall find it possible to push a little harder.

This Committee has taken some of my time this week. Another whole day was occupied in coming down here to open a new salvage & town refuse treatment plant on the occasion of a visit from the Institute of Cleansing Superintendents! This was of course a familiar subject & I had no difficulty in delivering a discourse on the main principles to be observed in the treatment of refuse. It was more complicated when the next day I had to open the new laboratories of the Pharmaceutical Society and address a learned audience on the pharmacological testing of drugs by biological methods. However the gentleman who seconded the vote of thanks declared that I had given them the best exposition of their ideals that had ever been made public, so I felt my labours had not been in vain. Yesterday I was addressing an open air mass meeting at Lord Weymss'[26] place in Glostershire [sic]. So there were three speeches each of

---

[26] Hugh Richard Charteris Elcho (1857–1937). Conservative MP for Haddingtonshire 1883–85 and Ipswich 1886–95. Succeeded as 11th Earl of Wemyss 1914.

which required careful preparation of the kind that does take it out of me though some people like Amery & Austen dont seem to find much difficulty or worry in it.

West Ham is boiling up again but I am determined to stand no nonsense from them. They would really love to give way but they are desperately afraid of the "people outside" and they have so often bragged about what they would do with "the Minister" that they simply darent accept my conditions. I should myself like really to take over the relief and work it for at least 6 months. I believe I could show a saving of something like £300,000 or £400,000 a year without inflicting any hardship upon the deserving cases. The undeserving would no doubt speedily make tracks for one of the neighbouring Bolshie Paradises and it would be a glorious lesson for the country. The difficulty is to find the time for the legislation, but I have taken the precaution to arm myself with Cabinet authority. Alas! I much fear that seeing a determined front the Guardians will crawl in as they did before.

We have had a lot of discussion this week about Russia & Russian money. I am amused to read in the Sunday press of the battle in the Cabinet in which F.E. Churchill Jix & Amery are represented as holding out against Austen and Balfour. As a matter of fact Jix did raise the whole question first with fiery memoranda, but in the end he characteristically collapsed and was strongly in favour of doing nothing! Indeed F.E. & Winston, who both made impassioned speeches of inordinate length & considerable irrelevance in Cabinet, at the end found themselves, to their astonishment & indignation, in a minority of two! They live apart from the world and cannot understand how the man in the street can fail to see what seems so plain to them. But to my mind we could hardly play more completely into the hands of our opponents than by expelling the Russian Chargé d'affaires on the ground that his Government had failed to prevent the Russian workers from sending assistance to the starving (!) wives and children of the British miners.

Of course they are not within sight of starvation; – hardly of under nutrition, so well are they looked after by the Guardians. The Labour party are quite aware of this and while they send a deputation to roar very gently to the M/Health they carefully abstain from censuring or even asking him questions in the House. Therefore there is no chance of the miners being starved into submission. They are living not too uncomfortably at the expense of the ratepayer while the nation is gradually overcome by creeping paralysis.

We are importing a good deal of coal and the importation will continue to increase until we reach the point (not very far away) when the docks can handle no more. We shall still be very short of what is necessary and I am urging the Cabinet to concentrate on alternative fuels (i.e. oil) instead of trying to waste millions on attempting what is physically impossible. I am beginning to make a serious impression and personally I am convinced that the way to break the strike is to show that coal is no longer a monopoly and that if they make it too difficult to get it we can do without it. Its quite easy to do & the only reason why it hasn't been done already is that normally oil is dearer than coal. But of course it isn't now!

I read with interest about your housing plans and I see you have got wind of the possibility of a change in subsidy. You may have seen that I had a preliminary talk this week with a deputation from the A.M.C. From my point of view it was extraordinarily satisfactory & we got much further than I or my advisers had thought possible. Practically those present accepted the idea of a reduction & the only question that seemed to worry them was when it should take effect.

For your own information (and dont let anyone think you got it from me) what I am hoping for is

1. Reduction by 1/3 of subsidy on all houses completed after 1st October 1927. (Chamberlain & Wheatley)
2. Further reduction agreed on to take effect as from 1st October 1928 (I dont expect to get this)
3. Wheatley subsidy confined to houses of 850' and Ministers discretion used to permit houses below 620' and without a bathroom
4. Private enterprise subsidy to be confined to houses under £500 in value

So you had better hurry up your folks!

Weir houses *were* held up by the Strike but I understand the Building T.U. opposition has collapsed. I am taking less interest in them however. I doubt whether they will ever come in this side of the Tweed. We are getting on too well without them and they *are not cheap enough.*

I hope still to get my rural housing Bill this session. We have just been staying with Sir Philip Stott (of the Stott College) who has practically bought the village of Stanton, near Broadway, in the Cotswolds and has done just the thing that I want done elsewhere. I went into a good many reconstructed cottages and also two of those not reconstructed and was delighted with the results. He told me that he thought £150 would cover the expse per house. In several cases he had knocked 2 into 1 or 3 into 2 but he had only build 2 new ones and somehow every one seemed to have enough room. But I remember now that he had converted a barn into a house and he certainly contemplated doing the same with a chapel and other buildings. In one case he said the district nurse reported to him that although there were 4 bedrooms the whole family slept in one!

...

26 June 1926
Westbourne

My dear Hilda,

...

I see in todays paper that Mr Cook has proposed an "armistice" but as his idea of an armistice is that we should first withdraw the 8 hours Bill & then revert to the subsidy I must say I think it is like his confounded impudence and I hope the P.M. will not respond. It looks to me as if the T.U.C. and the miners were both afraid that the men would begin going back as soon as the new owners offers were open to them. Unfortunately these have been delayed in consequence of our reversing the order of our two bills & putting 8 hours second instead of first. The change was made at the last moment by the P.M. without, so far as I know, consulting any of his colleagues and according to the Times it was at the request of the Parly Labour Party who wanted to use the time to try and get the miners to make a move. We see now apparently what sort of move they contemplate viz. one by the Govt in a rearward direction!

I have made 7 speeches this week, short and long … "Too warm to last, Hardy." I keep very well but my temper gets a bit short when the speeches pile up like this and people who ask me to do something are apt to get their noses snapped off. Next week I have only got five, but some of them are very troublesome ones and they may be added to if I have to move the Guardians Default Bill.

The reports from West Ham up to the last minute were that the Guardians would give way but finally the moderates voted with the Labour people with the deliberate object of bringing me in as they saw no other solution. It will add to my anxieties but it ought to do a lot of good in the end and we shall go in and stop in now till I get some results. I expect I shall be properly abused but I am not much moved by abuse nowadays so long as it comes from the enemy.

In the Woolwich case the loss of the appeal still leaves it open to me to remit the surcharges. Surcharging impecunious guardians is not very satisfactory – what I generally do is to assume that they acted according to what they believed the law to be until it was decided against them. I therefore remit up to the date of the appeal on the understanding that thereafter the authority act in accordance with the judgement. In the Bill which I drafted earlier this year these people on losing their case would have been disqualified for five years, a much more effective penalty, but in view of the small amount of time at my disposal I have cut this clause out and reduced my Bill to the smallest possible compass.

We had an interesting but rather exhausting day yesterday. Leaving London at 9.15 we arrived at Trent about noon and were motored to Nottingham where I lunched with this business club while A. went on to the house of Sir E. Jardine[27] who was our host. He is rather a remarkable man who has built up a considerable fortune in business & is now the Chairman of the Trent Navigation Co. After lunch A. joined us again and we entered a launch in which we went down the river inspecting the new works as we passed. These comprise 4

---

[27] Ernest Jardine (1859–1947). Liberal Unionist MP for East Somerset 1910–18. Nottingham machine-builder, JP and notable. Created Bart 1919.

new locks with the necessary weirs, and they have converted a shallow rapid river into a series of deep pools so that when some further dredging has been done it will be possible for 120 ton barges to load from a ship in the Humber and pass right up to Nottingham. The work was done with the aid of a subsidy which I helped to get and in accordance with the recommendation of my Waterways Committee. It is another of my little schemes which seems in a fair way to materialise. To complete it a number of canals which now connect with the Trent would have to be improved and this would bring Leicester, Loughborough, Grantham, Chesterfield, Lincoln & Sheffield into the system. That will take a long time but meanwhile I hope to see a big increase in traffic. Jardine has got a huge sugar beet factory already at work on the bank and all the Petrol companies are preparing to use the river for transport & pipe their oil into depots near the city.

...

3 July 1926
Westbourne

My dear Ida,

...

We (A. & I) have both had a very heavy week and are rather wilted in consequence. ...

I addressed the medical school of the London Hospital on Monday afternoon

...

On Tuesday morning I addressed the R.D.C. Assocn & in the afternoon the Victoria League both in the Guildhall. I thought I had a considerable success with the Rural gentlemen who are naturally very much disposed to be critical of a "town" Minister. There was rather a rude interruption at one moment and I took full advantage of it to appeal for co-operation. I saw afterwards that some of the speakers had attacked me for "ignorance" and "soft soap". But these half educated bumpkins always take special pleasure in belabouring a bigger man than themselves *when he isnt there* and I feel confident that I impressed the audience as a whole.

...

On Wednesday we lunched with a R.C. M.P. to meet Cardinal Bourne.[28] We both took to him immensely. He has just the face you so often find among eminent R.C. ecclesiastics wise & kindly and humorous and intelligent, and in conversation he was eminently sensible and vigorous. Such a contrast to Ch. of Eng. Archbishops!

---

[28] Francis Alphonsus Bourne (1861–1935). English prelate. Ordained a priest 1884; Rector, Southwark Diocesan Seminary 1889; Bishop of Southwark 1897; domestic prelate to Pope Leo XIII 1895; Archbishop of Westminster 1903; Cardinal 1911.

Afterwards – you would never guess – we went down on the invitation of Leo Maxse[29] to Wimbledon and watched tennis matches … We both enjoyed ourselves (though we should not have wanted to go again next day) and I have read the accounts of further matches with a new interest. As far as I can remember it is the first time I have seen a match of any kind since I left school.

On the way we stopped at de Glehn's to see the portrait. Eeow! I had a sinking feeling in the pit of my stomach all afternoon after it. Leo Maxse (who knows nothing about pictures) said he wouldn't have recognised it. I thought that was absurd. There was no doubt it was *very* like but – it wasnt the expression that I hoped for. … Its very disagreeable criticising a picture to the artist, but though naturally disappointed he said he would try to alter it and yesterday I went again to see the result. It is extraordinarily difficult to know how much to attribute to his alteration and how much to the adjustment of one's own ideas when one has a second look, but certainly this time I liked it much better. I shall have to live with it to be sure, but on the whole I am inclined to think I shall be satisfied. It is a very agreeable picture and the expression is now meditative instead of aggressive. A. herself is very pleased with it and of course I am likely to be *as* critical as anyone. …

…

10 July 1926
Cliveden, Taplow

My dear Hilda,

…

I have really had an awful week. I sent Kingsley Wood to take my place at a Child Welfare Congress on Monday, but I had to lunch with the Royal Sanitary Institute and then speak to them at Guildhall before going to the House to move the 2nd Rdg of the Gdns Default Bill. I deliberately made a very long speech – over an hour – because I wanted to build up a cumulative case and I kept it pretty strictly to West Ham. The evidence was damning and I didn't spare them & the result was satisfactory. K.W. had rather alarmed me by saying that some of our people thought the Bill too drastic but we heard nothing further of that. Wheatley told K.W. that West Ham was impossible to defend and the only line was to get away from it as he did himself to generalities & denunciations of the capitalist system. But his people could not restrain themselves and kept reverting to West Ham and trying to justify it. K.W. made one of the best speeches he has ever done in winding up & we got a capital majority.

---

[29] Leopold James Maxse (1864–1932). Journalist and political writer. Owner and editor, *National Review* 1893–1932. Militant Diehard, imperialist, tariff reformer.

On Tuesday I had a big deputation to receive from which I escaped to attend Annie's party ...

On Wednesday I had to lay the foundation stone of the new School of Hygiene & Tropical Medicine & Thursday & Friday were devoted again to the Gdns Bill. In addition there was the personal attack on me.[30]

I hadn't meant to reply until the charge had developed but someone – I dont know who – had told all the papers that I was going to make a personal statement and I felt that if after that I didn't the slanders would get such a start that I shd never catch them up.

I am very glad I did as all our people are now satisfied that I have done nothing that any one could possibly criticise and they are mad at the insolence of the Socialists and the weakness of the Speaker who is so anxious to be impartial that he is very unfair to our side. Of course I did go just a little beyond the rules in saying that Johnston[31] was a "specialist in this sort of thing" – he was the one who attacked Asquith over the Sudan plantations in 1923 – and I knew it, but he would certainly have let it go if I had been a Labour member and as a matter of fact the Labour men had not protested until our people cheered. Afterwards some one on our side shouted out that Mosley was at the bottom of all this whereat Will Thorne who was on his legs bawled out "Oh you shut your mouth". There were loud protests and the Speaker rose – we thought to rebuke Thorne. Instead of that he said he hadn't heard what he said which was palpably untrue but that if he had made the remark it had been drawn from him by a provocative observation from the other side.

Our people have been getting more and more impatient with these pothouse manners and the way they are ignored by the Speaker and you may have seen the motion put down by Craik and others which though carefully worded is really a vote of censure upon him. Of course it wont be discussed but it is intended to make him aware of the dissatisfaction which is very widely felt.

As for the attacks on me they are nothing to those made on father 26 years ago and they leave me pretty cold but one does feel that they degrade politics & give justification to those who declare that politics are a dirty game with which they will not soil themselves.

---

[30] On 8 July 1926 Tom Johnston enquired whether Chamberlain was still a director of Hoskins, against a background of rumours about unspecified improprieties in using influence to obtain government contracts. Chamberlain replied that as a private concern his retention of the position was in strict accordance with the rules established in 1906. A Labour motion for a Select Committee of investigation on 12 July was defeated by 341 to 95.

[31] Thomas Johnston (1882–1965). Founder of *Forward* 1906 and Editor, 1919–46. Labour MP for Stirlingshire West 1922–24, 1929–31, 1935–45 and Dundee 1924–29. Under-Secretary for Scotland 1929–31; Lord Privy Seal 1931; Scottish Regional Commissioner, Civil Defence 1939–41; Scottish Secretary 1941–45; Chairman, Scottish Forestry Commission 1945–48; Chairman, North of Scotland Hydro-Electric Board 1946–59; Governor of BBC 1955–56.

We motored down here last night and found only Nancy & the family, Waldorf having gone to U.S.A. I must say she *is* a good hostess & most entertaining & witty herself but leaving her guests to do what they like.

I am very tired and had breakfast in bed this morning. I still feel tired this evening but shall gradually work it off. I may have to speak in the debate on Monday and have my estimates on Tuesday when I am to be attacked for starving the miners.

...

17 July 1926
Westbourne

My dear Ida,

...

You no doubt gathered from the papers that the attack on me was a fiasco. Our people were very wrought up and simply thirsting for an opportunity to use their fists on the Labour Party. But the Speaker had at length realised their condition of mind and he began by sitting heavily on Will Thorne and then administering a severe rebuke to those who had made the unseemly disturbance the week before in the Lords. Henderson was very ponderous but extremely offensive. He declined any any [sic] suggestion that he was making a charge against me but observed apropos of West Ham that those who lived in glass houses shouldn't throw stones. However after Linky's[32] brilliant chaff the thing was really dead and those who had started the insinuations Thurtle[33] and Johnston made a very poor show. But I must say Ramsay surprises me by his sensitiveness coupled with his complete inability to appreciate what is & what is not scurrilous. He suggested that I only deserved what I got for I had made charges against him in connection with the motor car which I had not the courage to make in the House. I interrupted to say I had never accused him of corruption to which he replied hotly "You accused me of something worse". Since getting here I have looked up the speech. What I said was "The Prime Minister whose moral sense is revolted by Capitalism (this was a quotation from an article) sees nothing inconsistent in accepting from a Capitalist a provision in the shape of the income on £30,000 in order that he may ride in a lordly motor car for the rest of his days". Apparently he thinks this is worse than corruption, but he himself had just before compared us to "mangy dogs sniffing round a garbage heap".

---

[32] Nickname of Lord Hugh Cecil who had moved an amendment to Henderson's motion on 12 July opposing any concession to Labour's 'organised campaign of calumny and insinuation'.

[33] Ernest Thurtle (1884–1954). Labour MP for Shoreditch 1923–31 and 1931–45. PPS to Minister of Pensions 1924 and to First Commissioner of Works 1924; Lord Commissioner of Treasury 1930–31. Parliamentary Secretary, Ministry of Information 1941–45.

I suppose what irritates him is what the Nation calls my "sharp tongue and the bitter sarcasms with which I delight to stir up the hornets nest in front of me"!

It was a curious thing that the next day when I introduced my estimates every Labour man who spoke threw me a bouquet of some sort. Perhaps they wanted to make up for their behaviour the day before. Anyway my speech though delivered to a thin house had an extraordinary success and my account of the four diseases excited general interest. The Labour Party had intended to have me "on the mat" over circular 703 but we didn't see why they should have it all their way and the debate persistently went off on to other topics of a less controversial kind.

I expect to go into West Ham on Tuesday. I see the egregious Mr Killip[34] [?] is still trying to save his face by talking of Certiorari and enquiries but I dont think we shall hear much more of that. I am preparing another circular now for panel doctors who have been getting very slack about granting certificates of "sickness" in mining areas so that miners are drawing sickness benefit instead of unemployment benefit or Poor Relief.

I have had some preliminary talks about subsidy but the municipal authorities have hardened up in consequence of the strike and now wont listen to any reduction. I think it would probably be unwise to force it on them but I may be able to do something administratively to check extravagance and I shan't guarantee them present terms after October 1927. I am sorry to say that they are also behaving badly about Poor Law Reform. We had a satisfactory talk with the Secretary of the Association of Munic. Corpns but now they have sent in a document of criticisms on the provisional proposals which, if it were accepted would pretty well cripple them. Robinson is very depressed but I am going to have a deputation in next Wednesday and talk to them like a father in the hope of inducing a more reasonable attitude. The fact is that since Sir Robert Fox[35] died they have had no one with a big mind whom they could follow.

...

We have had a giddy week of social engagements. Annie's party (which I could not attend) was more crowded and successful than ever ... We also lunched one day with Bob Cecil and dined one evening with Baron Hayaski[36] the late Ambassador to meet Baron Matsui the new one. We thought him a great improvement, highly intelligent & less impenetrable than most Japs who generally content themselves with giggling whenever they are spoken to! Finally I

---

[34] Probably James Daniel Kiley (1865–1953). Liberal MP for Whitechapel 1916–22. A supporter of the Poplar councillors.

[35] Robert Eyes Fox (1861–1924). Deputy Town Clerk, Birkenhead 1886–88; Town Clerk of Burnley 1888–92, Blackburn 1892–1904 and Leeds 1904–24. Knighted 1913.

[36] Baron Gonsuke Hayaski (1860–?). Japanese diplomat. Ambassador in Rome 1908–16; Peking 1916–18; Governor-General Kwantung Leased Territory 1919–20; Ambassador in London 1920–25. Awarded GCMG 1925.

dined one night with a group of young Tories one of whom Noel Skelton,[37] M.P. for Perthshire impressed me as being remarkably level headed as well as clever. ...

25 July 1926
Sturry Court, Sturrey

My dear Hilda,

...

I told my people to send Ida the pamphlet on the Nash house which I hope she has received. ... They speak of its "wretched appearance" but could not give me any definite criticism of cost. But Waldron Smithers[38] who was at Annie's party just before Ida came assured me that they had built about 20 and that none cost more than £250. ...

Well, you see the cat is out of the bag about Edgbaston. One cannot say as yet how it has gone and I have not so far seen the Birmingham Post. But judging by the London Sunday papers it will be received as a natural & proper proceeding. The Ladywood Executive have made things much easier for me by their letter in which they so unhesitatingly recommend me to accept the invitation.

You did have a hectic week ... Mine was somewhat less strenuous than I have been having lately; nothing in the House of Commons and only three speeches outside. But I had to receive a very important deputation from the Association of Munic. Corporns on Wednesday about Poor Law. They had prepared and sent in a memo which cut my proposals about "somethin' alarmin' " and Robinson was for throwing overboard the block grant system at once.

However I determined not to be so pessimistic and having "mugged up" the case pretty carefully I girded up my loins and went in. They began badly for themselves for both the speakers they had chosen were very long and bored their own people to tears. Moreover they were both frightened and tried to soften down what they had arranged to say so when my turn came I made a very artful reply in which I assumed that they only wanted to help and that we were all working for the same object. Also I was merry and bright and made them laugh although I was myself in a regular perspiration with anxiety. However in the end it came out all right. Lord Emmott,[39] who introduced the depn said he had never

---

[37] (Archibald) Noel Skelton (1880–1935). Conservative MP for Perth 1922–23, 1924–31 and Scottish Universities 1931–35. Under-Secretary for Scotland 1931–35.

[38] Waldron Smithers (1880–1954). Conservative MP for Chiselhurst 1924–45 and Orpington 1945–54. Knighted 1934.

[39] Alfred Emmott (1858–1926). Mayor of Oldham 1891–92; Liberal MP for Oldham 1899–1911. Deputy Speaker and Chairman, Ways and Means 1906–11; Under-Secretary, Colonial Office 1911–14; First Commissioner of Works 1914–15; Director, War Trade Department 1915–19. Created Baron Emmott 1911.

listened to a Ministerial speech on such an occasion with so much pleasure and admitted that he was pretty well converted, and on behalf of the Assn he readily agreed to my suggestion that a small comee shd be appointed to discuss "points of detail", in other words to chuck their own counter proposals overboard and see what concessions will induce them to accept mine. Robinson breathes again and thinks we may now get through.

But I lost some tissue in the process!

It has been again an active social week ...

31 July 1926
Westbourne

My dear Ida,

I expect I shall make a statement about subsidy soon but I dont think it will state the amount of the alteration as this will only appear in the order to be issued after Oct 1. *For your own information only*, I have put up a memorandum to the Cabinet (which they havent yet considered) suggesting that the present subsidies shall be paid on all houses completed by Oct 1 1927, but that after that the Wheatley subsidy shall be reduced by £1 i.e. to £8 for town & £11.10 for country for 40yrs & the Chamberlain subsidy by £2 i.e. to £4 for 20 years. The Cabinet may, of course, turn it down, but as a rule they accept my suggestions.

The text of the Rural Housing Bill is out & the 2nd Rdg will be taken on Tuesday. You will see that it is not confined to agricultural workers but to persons in substantially the same economic position. It is not intended to benefit people who are able to pay an economic rent. But if a landlord cares to borrow only and not to take a grant he will not be bound as to rent and that may help in cases where the tenant is of a better class. I understand that our agricultural members are very pleased with the Bill and what is perhaps quite as satisfactory that the Labour party and the Liberals will approve it strongly.

Edgbaston Association unanimously accepted the recommendation of their Exec. last night so that is settled. There has been very little comment but I have had some rather nice letters. I enclose a spiteful paragraph from the Nation; its nothing to the venom of its attacks on the P.M. I am now trying to find my successor.

Things are going along quietly enough at West Ham. The question about the surcharges is not decided, it is only decided that I shall come into Court and I gather that my people are not very sure how it will go. In any case it wont embarrass me.

I have been doing a lot of negotiation about Poor Law this week and am well satisfied with the progress. In the end I think it will all turn on what I can get out of the Chancellor, but as his people are on my side I am hopeful of success there.

...

10 August 1926
Station Hotel, Inverness

My dear Hilda,

...

Already last session seems far away but I must return to it for a moment or two. It has been a bad session in the House with a slack and ineffectual opposition and though after the General Strike the Govt's prestige stood at an unprecedented height I have no doubt that it has been a good deal frayed by the long drawn out coal strike.

So far as personalities are concerned Austen has been almost out of sight, but remains a great figure, gradually becoming more hazy and legendary as he is less familiar. He comes but little to the House and told me just before we adjourned that he was very weary. It is however also true that he no longer has political ambitions beyond his present office and does not feel either inclination or duty calling him thither.

S.B. has suffered most from the strike & perhaps from the fact that he was rather unduly exalted at one time. His last speech was generally considered his weakest & most ineffective and he seems rather to wilt under the blows he gets. He too is worn out & has no spirit left, but he also remains the one with the greatest influence in the country and I have no doubt he will retain his position in the autumn if the strike is over.

Winston has decidedly improved his position & is very popular I believe with our side as he is really with the whole House for the wonderful entertainment he gives them. The curious thing is that while they would go anywhere to hear him they are not convinced of his wisdom or judgement.

Ll.G. does not seem to me to have moved forward at all. He is universally distrusted and I am glad. To see him in power would be to see disaster hanging over the country.

My department is very pleased with the session. The Economy Bill is forgotten already (and of course that was unpopular though we came off all right in the debates) On the other hand West Ham is not forgotten and the opposition made a bad blunder when they asked for our estimates out of wh. we made a great deal of kudos. And in addition to a number of small but very useful bills the Rural Housing Bill has excited something like enthusiasm among the Agricultural members. The attitude of the Labour party plainly showed that they were terrified of it, but, as you say, they mean to talk about it in the town & leave the Liberals who supported it to make the running in the country. I am now quite convinced that Ll.G. means to make a working alliance with Labour at the next election in order to provide for a Coalition Govt if they can get a majority between them.

I have had a very pleasant time with Ld Weir who must I think have taken a fancy to me as I have to him. He is very simple & straightforward but a first class business man and the sort of man on whom you can always rely to help you in a difficulty.

I saw his houses which are getting on nicely and look very well. I also opened a hospital for him for wh. I received a beautiful gold cigarette case and I was really loaded with kindness by him & his wife. The weather was perfect on Saturday when we shot & fished & on Sunday we went to Loch Fyne where he has a country – castle! "Dunderave" restored & modernised so that it is very comfortable as well as picturesque.

...

15 August 1926
Loubcroy Lodge, Oykell by Lairg

My dear Ida,

...

I was sorry, but not surprised to hear that Austen was so tired for your observation confirms mine. After all he hasn't got a lot of reserve vitality and I suppose the Foreign Office work is very hard because there is no let up. But no Cabinet Minister ever thinks that his colleagues have as much to do as he has himself and to me an office which involves no legislation, very perfunctory attendance at the House, and hardly any speeches outside seems an old man's job! Not that I complain. I wd much rather have mine and except for one week end after several late nights I have not felt particularly tired and wound up quite fresh.

I agree with you in thinking that the coal strike is breaking up although I have not had any other information than what I have derived from the papers. But the number returning to work is increasing and Cooks note is changing.

I too hope the owners will be "reasonable", whatever that may mean, but unless the men realise that they have been badly led and that they have finally sustained a disastrous defeat when they might have made satisfactory terms weeks ago I dont see how we can expect them to behave more wisely another time. I have been staying with Weir, who is very shrewd, and he takes the view that the coal industry is merely bearing the brunt of a wage struggle which had got to come throughout the unsheltered trades & only came first in coal because there wages form the largest part of the cost.

He feels that Trade Unionism has outlived its usefulness, and entered upon politics to the destruction of industry. The friendly society work formerly done by T.U.'s is now performed by State Insurance Schemes and the one hope of peace & prosperity for all is individual agreements between employers & their men. This is an interesting view and there is much solid sense in it. At any rate it confirms me in the view that we must do something to amend Trade Union Law. Weir like some other employers is against the secret ballot on the ground that it will make more not less strikes and the Cabinet Comee has accepted this view. All the same I think they are wrong and I believe I shook Weir very considerably in his views.

...

18 September 1926
Beaufort Castle, Hexham

My dear Ida,

...

I was never summoned to the Cabinet thro some misunderstanding I suspect, but it would have been a great nuisance to have had to go. So far as I understand it I approve S.B.'s letter published this morning.

25 September 1926
Westbourne

My dear Ida,

...

I went up on Wednesday to see the P.M. & hear about the latest coal developments and of course attended the Cabinet yesterday. We had to take what one member described as the most difficult decision since the Evacuation of the Dardanelles i.e. whether to stand pat or come out boldly with a compulsory settlement. There was a good deal to be said for the latter course but it would have been a gamble and I fear that if we had adopted it we might well have found ourselves at the end of a month without any general return to work while having effectually checked the drift that is going on now. It is certain that the men's leaders know they are beaten and Cook is badly rattled. Perhaps after all they will accept the terms the P.M. offered before. They would I believe be wise to do so, but I confess to doubts as to whether that would ensure a satisfactory settlement. But no doubt the pinch will soon be felt and the pressure on the Govt to "do something" will be much stronger than it is now.

...

Annie has had a good holiday but I dont think she is quite as fit as I should like to see her. She shows it in a disposition to worry and to take more engagements than she ought!

...

2 October 1926
Westbourne

My dear Hilda,

...

It seems at least doubtful if the miners will accept our proposals. If they dont, it will relieve us of a peck of troubles of one kind and if once the men are convinced that nothing more is to be got out of us I believe they will go back quickly. They know they are beaten and Cook is getting more and more discredited.

I am now arguing with the Chancellor about [housing] subsidies. Of course he wants to increase the cut but I am very nervous about damping down building which would certainly follow too big a break and I think this would do us more harm politically than anything. In the long run I am sure I can carry the Cabinet against Winston on this subject, but I suppose he must put up a fight. I am glad I am M/H & not C/E!

The debate in the House was not very useful to anyone. I didn't stop for the second night as I had to attend a dinner down here … Tonight we are dining with G.H.K. & tomorrow I go to Chequers for the night as the P.M. wants to discuss some party matters. I have taken the opportunity this week of dealing with various important affairs including Ladywood. I have succeeded in raising the wind for Geoffrey Lloyd[40] and his name is now being submitted to the Selection Committee who will I hope recommend his adoption without delay. Mosley is lying very low.

I have also had a long interview with Edwards[41] our new Chief Agent & established satisfactory relations with him. He begins work on Monday. …

I am sorry to say that Hoskins has, as I expected, had a very bad year and lost £8000. Although we still have a fair sum in investments it is being gradually drained and we shall have to submit to a serious reduction of dividends. I have decided to pay out another 10% this year making 20% as against 35% last year but we shall have to pass the interim which we have generally paid in April and from what Hall tells me the outlook is still very black. The coal strike has given shipbuilding a further setback and until it revives there is no chance of making a profit.

…

10 October 1926
Westbourne

My dear Ida,

Apropos of the mining situation you enquire "How long will such forced settlements last?" But why do you call a district settlement a forced settlement. Why is it more forced than a national settlement. And can any settlement be really other than a forced settlement in the sense that a good many people accept it reluctantly. I observe your enquiry with a sort of despair because it appears to indicate that even your mind is affected by the sort of stuff that Cook and Macdonald [sic] and Bishops pour out.

---

[40] Geoffrey William Lloyd (1902–1984). Conservative MP for Birmingham Ladywood 1931–45, King's Norton 1950–55 and Sutton Coldfield 1955–74. Private Secretary to Baldwin, 1929–31 and his PPS 1931–35; Under-Secretary, Home Office 1935–39; Parliamentary Secretary for Mines 1939–40, for Petroleum 1940–42, and Fuel and Power 1942–45; Minister of Information 1945; Minister of Fuel and Power 1951–55; Minister of Education 1957–59. President, Birmingham Conservative Association 1946–75. Created Baron Geoffrey-Lloyd 1974.

[41] R.H. Edwards (1891–?). Central Office agent in Lancashire and Cheshire; Chief Agent for Bristol 1924–26; Chief Agent for Birmingham from 1926.

Now all the information that comes to me is that the men are heartily sick of being out. That except for the extreme politically minded they would be only too delighted with any settlement (district or national) which would give them a reasonable rate of earning and which they could accept without being called blacklegs. This last contains the kernel of the whole affair. Its simply a question of intimidation and the "loyalty to the Union" and "loyalty to the leaders" of which we hear so much really means fear of the consequences should they disobey.

I believe that except for the extremists aforesaid there is no bitterness among the men and that the settlements which may be arrived at will last just as long as other settlements have done in the past; – which isn't very long! The present temper is indicated by the fact that where the men have gone back the output per man is considerably more than it was before the strike.

Of course it is a thousand pities that after all this loss and damage we haven't got any prospect of a more permanent peace among the miners. But that in my view is solely the fault of the miners leaders. If Hodges had been in charge instead of Cook it would have made just the difference.

I think probably there will be a good deal of hardship as the weather gets colder in the country districts. Here they seem to be able to manage and looking into some back to back houses in the slums yesterday I saw a blazing fire in every one of them.

Annie went to the Unionist Conference at Scarbro' & reports that it went extremely well, thanks in great measure to the admirable handling of the meeting by Dame Caroline Bridgeman[42] who in addition to her invariable competence seems to be developing a certain charm! S.B. consulted me as to what he should say about T.U. legislation but he didn't take my advice, nor that of F.E. who had volunteered with a suggested passage. We had a lot of talk at Chequers about the party organisation and (in confidence) the present favourite for the Chairmanship is Sir Geoffrey Butler[43] M.P. for Cambridge University. I dont suppose you know much of him but he is a Don with a gift for enthusing young men & is said to have done wonderful work among the undergrads. But I dont know whether he will take it on.

I earned two more presentation keys this week! One was to open the new station at Welwyn Garden City where I spoke at a luncheon and afterwards made a tour of the place. They have made wonderful progress since I was there last and the population is now about 4500 & expects to reach 6000 in the course of

---

[42] Caroline Beatrix Bridgeman (1872–1961). Married William Bridgeman 1895. Prominent figure in Conservative Women's Association; Chair, National Union Women's Advisory Committee 1924–27; first woman Chair, National Union Executive 1926. Created Dame 1924.

[43] George Geoffrey Gilbert Butler (1887–1929). Fellow, Corpus Christi College, Cambridge from 1910 and President 1928–29; Foreign Office 1915–19. Conservative MP for Cambridge University 1923–29. Knighted 1919.

next year. Their houses are beautifully laid out & I should think young professional men & retired tradespeople or civil servants would find Welwyn exceedingly attractive. But what they badly need is more factories.

I came down here on Wednesday evening and spent Thursday inspecting. First I saw light treatment as practised at the Yardley Rd Sanatorium. They have (at great expense) made some marvellous cures there and no doubt there is a great future before this method of treatment. Then I went on to see the latest developments in sewage treatment by activated sludge (!). The Drainage Board now collect marsh gas from their process and use it to run an electric plant.

The whole afternoon I spent visiting housing sites. The way the houses have sprung up on the south & east sides of the town is simply bewildering. Duds Lane house has gone & there is a forest of cottages between the road & the river. All round Stirchley Kings Heath Brandwood End Billesley Common Foxhollies Yardley Wood Stechford Erdington Washwood Heath & Handsworth the country is stiff with new houses. Only here & there one sees an old landmark and recognises it – otherwise one gets completely lost. They have now completed 13000 subsidised houses & have got another 5 or 6000 contracted for. It is positively shattering! And the roads & bridges are equally astonishing the former 120 ft wide the latter all in reinforced concrete. I was specially interested in a 2 bedroom house to let at 8/6. They said they had got a similar type with 3 bedrooms at 9/6 including rates & I thought that sounded a very practical proposition. I wonder what they will say when the subsidy comes down. The Chairman volunteered the opinion that the private enterprise subsidy could come off altogether but he said nothing about the Wheatley article.

On Friday morning I inspected Monyhull where 1100 m-d [mentally deficient] men women & children are in residence. Its a splendid institution from some points of view but it leaves me very depressed after seeing all those mistakes & misfits. ....

Yesterday I visited some slum houses which have been reconditioned by Copse. They have been well done & afford a capital object lesson for the value of what I want legislation to promote.

No, I didnt reply about the milk because it is rather difficult to give a satisfactory answer especially as I never can keep the details in my own mind. Its not my Bill, but one which was passed I think in 1915, and only now has come into operation. But shortly put the difficulty has been with the farmers. We don't consider at the M/H that the bill is satisfactory but the B/Agriculture got shot at pretty heavily and we had to compromise.

...

16 October 1926
Westbourne

My dear Hilda,

...

I have had a most strenuous but very interesting and valuable week in Wilts & Devon. The distances are enormous and I often covered 100 miles in the day. I inspected 2 workhouses, 2 isolation hospitals, 3 tuberculosis sanitoria, a voluntary hospital, 2 maternity homes, a mental hospital, 2 m.d. centres, 2 m.& c.w. centres, 3 housing schemes, tuberculosis dispensaries water supplies, county offices, insanitary cottages, cowsheds, Town planning schemes, &c and interviewed innumerable mayors, chairmen, secretaries & hon. secs, County Councillors & Clerks. Everyone was delighted & "honoured" by my visit and I acquired an immense amount of information. Two things in particular emerged. One was that the Rural Housing Bill has excited immense interest and approval which is particularly gratifying because an inspector whom I had sent to enquire into this area had reported that he didn't think a great deal could be done. The other is that most of the opposition to the Poor Law proposals is bunkum and that there is real and urgent need for more central control of health services and institutions. The Guardians institutions are only ⅓ full. One I visited had 36 inmates to 24 guardians, another had 50 inmates and 44 Guardians. Too much emphasis is laid on the domiciliary relief side of their work. A third of it has been abolished already by the Widows pensions and more will go when o.a.p. at 65 begin. To say that the C.C. cannot tackle the immense amount of work that will be thrown upon them is to talk through your hat. On the other hand I found both Wilts & Devon C.C. much more active and competent than I expected and though of course they carry a big lot of deadheads that is only the ordinary experience of the County Borough.

I finished up with an amusing visit to the Crediton Union. The chairman, a well meaning old dodderer, was weighed down with a sense of the responsibility that lay upon him to demonstrate to the Minister the efficiency of Guardians in general and of his Board in particular. For this purpose he had called a special meeting of his Board and he invited me to see them at work & afterwards to listen and reply to a speech which he would make. The result was rather different from what he had hoped. There were only 4 cases to be dealt with and only one which required a decision. Forty of the Guardians did not open their mouths but the other four took a decision which was the exact opposite of that recommended by the one man who personally knew all the parties concerned!

As for the Chairman he read a speech which had evidently been carefully prepared for him out of material obtained from the Poor Law Journal. Declaring that he was expressing the views of the members of the Board he plumped for the Propert alternative proposals which set up a duplicate, directly-elected authority to deal with all the "personal" services including T.B. – V.D. – and M.& C.W. Of course it was almost too easy after that. The poor board had dimly heard his speech passing over their heads but they hadn't had the foggiest notion of what he was talking about. I spoke for 20 minutes in reply and riddled him with chaff after which I made a grand appeal to their patriotism and public spirit to carry on under the new conditions the great & noble work they had devoted themselves to in the past. You should have heard them cheer! I left them in the highest good humour with themselves & me & Robinson fairly chortling with delight. "That fairly got them between wind & water", he said & declared it made a capital & most amusing finish to a very interesting tour ...

...

22 October 1926
Westbourne

My dear Ida,

...

On Monday I went to Coventry & inspected housing parks welfare & tuberc. clinics and an infectious hospital, finishing up with the Coventry & Warw. Hospital where I made the speech which has excited the wrath of the Times – or rather of the Times Medical correspondent, Dr Wilson, who once tried to get into the Ministry & having failed has had a grievance against it ever since. I see Mond has exposed one lie today & I have sent a portentous letter to appear on Monday. It purposely omits to cross certain T's as I want to provoke discussion. This is really the third speech I have made on the same lines but the other two – in Birmingham & Glasgow – passed without much notice in the London press. I see the Med. Practitrs Union have sent a letter to the P.M. blackguarding me, but I am getting so accustomed to abuse that I dont pay much attention to it now.

I went up to town that night and next day interviewed the Press on my tour and also gave the latest figures of housing which are more amazing than ever. After that I received a deputation of Durham Labour men who came to complain of my behaviour to Guardians in their area. Apparently my behaviour to them was more satisfactory for the leader who came next day to agree a report with Veale timidly enquired whether Veale thought he had been rude to me, explaining that he had not intended to be but had been struck with the contrast between his own speech and the polished manner in which I had "hit them fairly and squarely between the eyes"! After that I went and settled the alteration in the Housing Subsidy with Winston (we compromised on *my* plan) and in the evening dined at Lancaster House. I had never seen Cosgrave before & had no opportunity of speaking to him

---

[44] Dr General James Barry Munnik Hertzog (1866–1942). South African soldier and politician. Cabinet Minister 1910–12 when resigned to establish National Party. Prime Minister 1924–39; Minister of Native Affairs 1924–29; Minister of External Affairs 1929–39.

but he is a rum 'un to look at with his mop of *yellow* hair. Hertzog[44] looks foxy and older than I expected but Coates[45] is a fine upstanding fellow though very shy and reserved.

That night I sat up till 1.30 preparing an address which I delivered next morning to the Central Valuation Committee. It was received exceedingly well and my old enemy Tom White was quite complimentary when he got up to propose a vote of thanks. I rather think I have got him nobbled now and that he wont give me any trouble over Poor Law. He has tried one fall with me and got beaten and I dont fancy he wants to repeat the experience.

In the afternoon I received a deputation from the Urban D.C. Assocn who came to protest against the P.L. proposals but there wasn't much kick in them when they came and none when they went away.

On Thursday I received a deputation from the L.C.C. who came at my request to discuss playing fields in Greater London. I asked them to make a survey to ascertain what the needs were and what land was available. The question of purchase could stand over. We argy-bargied about it for some time but finally they said they would do anything I asked. So I arranged to ask them officially. Very shortly I am going to have a conference of L.C.C. and surrounding C.C.'s & Boroughs to try and get them to start on a Greater London Regional Plan. This is a very big business.

I then had to drive at great speed to Ilford which was celebrating its incorporation as a Borough. The Duke & Duchess of York were there and I had to address the multitude and eat a dreadful lunch before I rushed back to ... Whitehall to meet the C.C. of Somerset who were trying to quarrel with me about their new assessment areas. The Clerk was G.I. Simey [?] whose fag I was at Rugby where he was head of our house and of the school. I hadn't seen him for 41 years! I told him that their proposals were impossible and though I was told they had been very fierce in expressing their intentions to disregard the Minister beforehand they went sadly away saying they would have to get their council to agree to what I wanted. After that there was just time to finish up my Departmental work & catch the train down here. *Some* week!

A friend of mine met a friend of his who is a friend of Lord Thomson[46] & lately dined with him. There he found inter alias R. Macdonald Sidney Webb & the Mosleys. R.M. wished he could deal with his followers in the H. of C. as he did with the T.U.C. Even there however he had his trials & turning to Mosley he

---

[45] Joseph Gordon Coates (1878–1943). New Zealand Reform Party politician. Minister in Massey Government 1919–25; Prime Minister 1925–38; Minister of Public Works 1931–35; Finance Minister 1933–35. Represented New Zealand at Ottawa (1932) and London Conferences (1935). Member, New Zealand War Cabinet 1940–42.

[46] Christopher Birdwood Thomson (1875–1930). Entered Royal Engineers 1894; Brigadier-General 1918; Supreme War Council 1918. Joined Labour Party 1919. Secretary for Air 1924 and 1929–30 when killed in the crash of airship R.101 at Beauvais.

observed "And you, my lad, you had much better attend to your constituency than come interfering in the T.U.C. You've got a bright young man who will work jolly hard and give you a hot time & in fact I'm not sure that you will get in".

To which M. who seemed rather low spirited meekly said he knew that & wasn't sure either. After that he seemed to spend a good deal of time in contradicting his wife who would keep bursting out with denunciations of things she alleged I had said but which Mosley hotly denied I had ever uttered!

Saturday 23rd. I am not surprised at the result of your inspection of wood houses. As you say these cheap forms of construction never materialise, but the difficulty is just to spot the nigger in the woodpile.

...

I am told that Lincoln is a particularly cold county. I cant tell you how I loathe setting out again when I might sit with my toes in the fire here and comfortably read a book. If only I could have had my week-end. But duty must be done.

Only *wont* my successors bless my memory!

...

> 31 October 1926
> Westbourne

My dear Hilda,

I read S.B.'s letter to the Yorkshire candidate this morning with great relief for I was beginning to get very worried when I saw that Winston was meeting the miners again all by his lone. I daresay you have noticed how cunningly the Goat continues to suggest that if only he were allowed to have his way Winston would be able to settle everything satisfactorily. And though W. is I believe perfectly loyal to his colleagues he is flattered by Ll.G.'s compliments which after all only confirm his own idea of his capacity. Just to show you how dangerous he is, he actually suggested to me one day that he should use the three millions "which I have still got" (though I thought they had long since vanished up the spout) to give a bonus of £5 to every man who returned by a certain date to his work! Just think how those who have already returned would rejoice to see the wicked thus rewarded and how those who would like to come back but whose employers won't have them would give thanks that others more deserving would be more fortunate than themselves! I stamped on the idea with such ferocity that I believe it died there and then, but how can you put any confidence in the judgement of a man who can suggest such a thing.

Of course what is going on now is simply and solely an attempt to save the faces of Cook and Smith and I am still afraid the T.U.C. will do it somehow, but S.B.'s letter at any rate does not encourage them.

I am in some trouble myself as although they are increasing the coal allowance they are going to regulate coke and the blockheads here interpret their instructions to mean that nothing is to be allowed for greenhouses. I am getting within a few days of the end of my stock and if I cant get some more I dont know what will happen.

I have returned from my tour remarkably fresh for it was a more tiring one than the last and I am not sorry its over. Lincolnshire contains 3 administrative counties Lindsey, Kesteven and Holland but I came to the conclusion that the two latter ought to be amalgamated as Holland seems to have none of the gentry class and in consequence is poorly administered. I wont inflict upon you another catalogue of all the places I visited, but generally the tour was intensely interesting and most valuable in giving us confidence that we are on the right lines. Everywhere there was the most gratifying appreciation of my action in making these visits and I am sure I can say that everywhere we left both councillors and officials encouraged and stimulated by the contact with G.H.Q.

...

I was very pleased with the reception of my letter to the Times especially as it was composed under difficult circumstances. Newman & Robinson prepared a draft & sent it to me. I altered & added to it & sent it back but I was unable to consult with them before publication or to find out why they had put certain things in. I observed the point which struck Ida, but on the whole decided to leave it as it shows at any rate that the policy of whole timers has not yet been carried very far. But the sentence which I put in myself about the central bodies being formed without the vol. hosps if they didn't come in was the one I counted on to make people sit up and take notice and it has had precisely that effect. I think I shall leave it to simmer a bit now as of course nothing can be done till we have got the infirmaries in under the P.L. proposals.

...

6 November 1926
37 Eaton Square, SW1

My dear Ida,

...

I have been feeling rather low this week. Partly perhaps my throat was responsible, or the condition which brought it about. But mostly I am worried about the effect on the prospects of the P.L. Reform of the municipal election disasters.[47] When things go wrong everyone tries to fix the blame in such a way as to emphasise his particular grievance and I see that Sir Reginald Blair[48] has

---

[47] In the November 1926 municipal elections Labour made a net gain of 146 with net losses of 43 to the Conservatives and 63 for 'Independents'.

[48] Reginald Blair (1881–1962). Conservative MP for Bow and Bromley 1912–22 and Hendon 1935–45. Chairman, London Municipal Society 1919–29; Chairman, Race Course Control Board and later Race Course Betting Control Board. Created Bart 1945.

been attempting to trace our troubles to the proposal to transfer out relief to Boro. Councils.

To my mind that is quite ridiculous but I fear that our people may "get the wind up" generally and be disposed to jib at any new proposal. Tomorrow I am going to work at a Cabinet memorandum. If only I can get it through the Cabinet I am not much afraid of the H. of C.

My explanation of the municipal elections is very simple. I believe its due to the fact that the Labour Party made a supreme & universal effort while we just followed our ordinary practice, leaving each place to run its own show without any special lead from headquarters. The fact that Labour had 788 candidates while we had only 489 is very significant. But if it wakes us up now it will have been worth while for I see in the Labour attack a deliberate intention to seize local power to commit local bribery in one form or other; it can be done with tramfares or house rents or even gas & electric charges quite as effectively as with out relief. And secondly, they admit frankly that a labour majority in the Councils will create a more favourable atmosphere for carrying out the acts of a Labour Govt; an ominous suggestion in view of the way they behaved in some places during the General Strike. More than ever I am disposed to think that I shall have to get powers to "West Ham" Local Authorities.

Of course I was not present at the Cabinet this morning so I dont know the latest development in coal. But it is not difficult to guess at what is taking place – trying to save Cook's face by the T.U.C. & on the part of the Govt an endeavour to avoid that very thing without laying themselves open to criticism for neglecting to take advantage of a genuine change of heart. I hope we manage to avoid legislation. If the owners wd help us by making some innocuous declaration of general principles we might perhaps get out of anything more embarrassing. But it is unlucky that the House meets next week when the Oppn including the Goat will exploit the situation for political purposes. Jix says, by the way, that Inchcape[49] says he is fed up with the Goat, and Jix is proposing him for the Carlton Club!!

...

I had a meeting of the L.A. & told them about the subsidy. They unanimously protested agst any reduction (but two of them have let me know privately that they agree with me) so I am going to let a decent interval elapse (during wh. I am "considering" their remarks) & then make an order.

...

---

[49] James Lyle MacKay (1852–1932). Shipowner. Member, Council of India in London 1897–1911; Chairman, Government's Port and Transit and other Shipping Committees 1915–19; responsible for disposal of surplus and enemy shipping 1919–21; Member, National Economy (Geddes) Committee 1921–22; Chairman, Indian Retrenchment committee 1922–23. Knighted 1894. Created Baron Inchcape 1911, Viscount 1924 and Earl Inchcape 1929.

14 November 1926
37 Eaton Square, SW1

My dear Hilda,

Thank you for your sympathetic letter. When one sees how absolutely unnoticed the Scottish [Conservative] Conference passes in England one is tempted to ask, Why *do* I agree to give up the holiday I had been so eagerly looking forward to to substitute for it a heavy mental and physical strain, to expend some £20 of my capital in travelling expenses and all for so imperceptible a result.

I suppose the answer is that it is one of the unavoidable risks of political life, just as if you are constantly motoring you must be prepared any day to find yourself in a ditch with the car on the top of you instead [of] dining comfortably in a friend's country house. Moreover one *cant* of course refuse a request of that kind from the P.M. I did try to work it off on Jix, but S.B. said "Dont tell him, – but I never thought of him"! And he refused to think of him or of Winston, while Austen had just been to Glasgow and Hogg was engaged with the electricity Bill.

Well anyway its over now as you say and as a fact it did not worry me nearly so much as other speeches have done. Perhaps the success I had so recently had in Huddersfield helped me – perhaps also the fact that I had no time to think about it prevented my getting nervous. It was pretty strenuous ... but I think it may be said to have been a complete success.

I devoted the luncheon speech party to pointing out the value of these conferences in keeping the Government informed of the opinion of the rank & file and partly to an appeal to get among the people and try and understand their conditions by personal familiarity with them. This idea of political duty I owe originally to Annie who first impressed it upon me. This time I had a hint from the Scottish Whip which made me feel that it would be appropriate and as I worked it out it was most enthusiastically received. The Scottish M.P.'s of whom a good many were present were particularly delighted and one Fanshawe[50] said it would do more good in the Scottish constituencies than anything that had been said for a long time.

The evening meeting was one of the best we have had. The hall which holds nearly 5000 was packed to the uttermost & the audience was not only enthusiastic but marvellously quick to take the points. I spoke for 50 minutes and contrived to work in a fair amount of humour with some useful information & some weighty words on Trade Union Law. You must ask Annie to give you her impressions; I will only report three opinions expressed to her or to me. Walter Elliott said it was "a triumph", Sir H. Blain in congratulating me said he was naturally of a critical turn of mind but having never heard me address a mass

---

[50] Guy Dalrymple Fanshawe (1882–1962). Joined Royal Navy 1896. Member, Inter-Allied Naval Control Commission 1919–23. Conservative MP for Stirlingshire West 1924–29. PPS to Amery, 1928–29.

meeting before he wished to say that he considered it a wonderful performance. Finally MacRobert,[51] the Scotch Solr-General declared that it was the most brilliant speech he had ever heard from that platform.

We returned yesterday – 8½ hours in the train – and were pretty weary last night. But I feel all right again this morning which is fortunate for I have an unusually heavy week before me. The Whips who never have any consideration for any one else's human weaknesses have so arranged things as to put me in charge during 4 consecutive days debates, one on my supplementary estimate for advances to Guardians one on the money resolution for the Rural Housing Bill & 2 on the Consolidated Fund. In addition I have 2 mornings in standing committee on Smoke Abatement & County Boroughs Extension respectively, a Cabinet on Wednesday a deputation from the N.F.U. a Clean Milk Conference an Arts exhibition to open and an address on Crippled Children. But I have managed to shove this last off on to Eustace!

Of course I have been very much out of the coal negotiations but they have given me a good deal of anxiety which I was glad to find was shared by a good many of my colleagues. I dont know what effect Winston produces upon Cook but I know he makes *me* tremble. He is so anxious to get a dramatic settlement and so totally unable to form a sound judgement on any terms presented to him. Fortunately he has got some very sober old gees harnessed up with him and as far as I can judge this morning they have produced a very ingenious scheme. There is all the façade of a National Tribunal Established by Statute: – only it will never come into operation because the only agreements which are not "standard", will be agreements agreed to by employers & employed in special districts, from which as they are agreed no appeal will be necessary. Cook himself has so lost his head as to condemn utterly his own leadership when he declares that the terms which the Executive recommend the men to accept "could not possibly be worse". What a confession after 6½ months.

If one may take it, as I suppose one can that the strike is practically over, I am inclined to think that we shall see a small boom in trade which will send up the Govt stock perceptibly. I fancy there is a great deal of work to be given out as soon as employers are in a position to give a firm price and a definite delivery. And then employers & many others will thank God that Ll.G. was not P.M. and that we have got a settlement in which the miners are clearly shown to be beaten.

...

---

[51] Alexander Munro MacRobert (1873–1930). Barrister and Conservative MP for East Renfrewshire 1924–30. Solicitor-General for Scotland 1925–29; Lord Advocate 1929.

21 November 1926
37 Eaton Square, SW1

My dear Ida,

...

The miners have kept up their folly to the end and I suppose one may consider now that the end has come. But whether we are out of the wood I dont quite know. I feel sure that many people will press for the Tribunal and I dont myself think it could do much harm, but I should be glad if we could be relieved of the necessity for passing the bill.

The opposition have got so flat and tame that our Chief Whip is almost in despair and thinks that he will have to organise them himself. I myself had rather an easier week than I anticipated but all the same I was pretty tired of it by Thursday night for it is an exhausting business sitting on the Treasury bench and listening to the drivel of Lansbury & Co.

We dined on Monday with the Larkins[52] to meet Mackenzie King. The Squiffs were among the guests & the old man talked a lot to A. after dinner but without saying anything very well worth recording except a significant remark that nothing good ever came out of Wales!

On Tuesday I had another meeting of my Comee on a postgraduate school. It has been very difficult but at last I do really think we are beginning to make progress for we have found a hospital which appears capable of serving our purpose and the directors of which are genuinely anxious to have us. If that comes off I shall feel that a great work has been accomplished. The same day I broadcasted an address on clean milk and in the evening wound up on my supplementary estimate. It wasn't much reported, but I believe it was considered very successful as I had a number of compliments about it afterwards.

On Wednesday I had the money resolution on Rural Housing on which I daresay you saw that Wheatley made an outrageous speech. It was so irrelevant that we decided to take no notice of it. He was very angry and slated Greenwood for allowing it to pass without reply before going on to move his first amendment but Bryan Fell (who was shooting with Ernest yesterday) says that the Labour Party were much disgusted with Wheatley.

That evening the House actually rose before 7.30 so I went home and afterwards accompanied A. to the Duke & Duchess of York's party at St James' Palace where we met all the world & his wife ... Among other people I met the Duke of Wellington[53] who is quite absurdly like his ancestor though without his force.

On Thursday night I got through my business in the House in sufficient time to dine with the Churchills where we had a very pleasant evening. Mackenzie King

---

[52] Peter Charles Larkin (1856–1930). Canadian tea magnate and diplomat. Canadian High Commissioner in London 1922–30. Friend, confidant and financial sponsor of Mackenzie King.

[53] Arthur Charles Wellesley (1849–1934). Landowner. Succeeded as 4th Duke of Wellington 1900.

& D'Abernon[54] were among the guests. The former is very pleased with the [Imperial] Conference, and he has himself been very helpful and good with Hertzog and the Irish telling them that they are where Canada was 25 years ago in their doubts & suspicions. A. who is as thick as thieves with M.K. says she has no doubt of his loyalty to the Empire & his desire to keep Canada with us and I am confident from my own talks with him that she is right. Of course I haven't been in the Conference this time but I am told that Bruce wears rather thin on further acquaintance Coates is "incredibly stupid & remote" but that M.K. has come out well and now that he has a majority seems much more confident of himself.

We began the Smoke Bill in Comee on Thursday. It was the one among this year's bills that I was rather nervous about & there were shoals of amendments on the paper. But the opposition in Committee proved feeble in the extreme and a broadside which I discharged at the beginning of the proceedings so disheartened them that for a long time they didn't dare to divide. When they did we beat them 23 to 5!

...

27 November 1926
Westbourne

My dear Hilda,

...

I had a not unsatisfactory reception at the Cabinet for my Poor Law proposals. I did not ask for any decision but was allowed to talk for about 40 minutes and Jix observed afterwards that he now knew more about the subject than he did when he was at the Ministry which is perhaps not surprising! There were some murmurings about the effect on the voters but in Walter Guinness' absence they did not go very far. Winston of course was eloquent upon his grand scheme but it seemed to me that it met a rather chilly atmosphere. On the whole I thought it was not a bad beginning.

I wonder what Ida thinks of the subsidy. It is an all round reduction equivalent to £25 in capital value. I think I could safely have knocked off the p.e. subsidy altogether but obviously the political difficulties in the way would have been very great and things will be quite warm enough without.

We had a strenuous day yesterday, breakfasting at 7 a.m. and catching an 8.30 which got us to Colwyn Bay about 1.40. There we were met and conveyed to Llandudno to a hotel where a number of local & county council people were assembled to lunch with us. ... After that we were driven to Caernarvon as they now call it and arrived at the Pavilion soon after 6. ...

---

[54] Edgar Vincent (1857–1941). Conservative MP for Exeter 1899–1906; contested Colchester for Liberals 1910. Ambassador to Germany 1920–26; Head, British Economic Mission to Argentine and Brazil 1929. Knighted 1887. Created Baron D'Abernon 1914, Viscount 1926.

... [A]ll the local people disagreed about the relative size of the meeting which they declared was much larger than the one addressed by Ll.G. Everyone seemed astonished that I was allowed to speak without interruption especially as I did not spare the Goat, but it is said that his prestige has much diminished and that his speech was criticised at the time as being all abuse and no contribution. I have never spoken to a North Welsh audience before and at the beginning I thought they were very unresponsive. But they listened with profound attention to a speech of an hour and when I sat down the applause was more enthusiastic than at any meeting I have been to lately. The people on the platform were very enthusiastic about it & Annie was well pleased so I felt my labours had not been in vain. And both the chairman & one of the subsequent speakers spoke of me as a "great Minister of Health" which, as you know, it is my ambition to be thought.

...

I suppose you have seen that there is a hitch at Smethwick. Evidently Master Mosley has been a bit too quick and has mortally offended some of the local worthies who thought they had a claim to the seat. Now the thing has been referred to the Natl. Exec. who have decided that the procedure in accepting Mosley without waiting to see whether there were other nominations was against the rules. They sent the Chairman & Secretary down to try & smoothe it over, but I gather they have been unsuccessful. I suppose Mosley will be the candidate as he has announced that he is leaving Ladywood because his job there is done, but he will have rather a bad start. I fear his defeat would be too good to be hoped for but he will anyway lose some of his prestige.

...

4 December 1926
Westbourne

My dear Ida,
...

An account of my doings must be rather a catalogue but I inflict it upon you to show how much work I have got through.

On Monday I went to open a Church Army Housing scheme at Southgate and returned in time to take the Mental Deficiency Bill 2nd Reading in the House. Sat up late preparing for Rural Housing Bill Committee which we took at 11 next morning. In the afternoon I attended two Cabinet committees and received a deputation. Waited till nearly eleven oclock to take Smoke Abatement Bill which never came on. Sat up late preparing for Cabinet and a speech for a public dinner. Wednesday – Cabinet all morning, luncheon party at Eaton Square – received and addressed a deputation of over 100 reps of Non County Boroughs on Poor Law – dinner & speech with Town Planning Institute. Sat up till 2 a.m. preparing speech on Housing Subsidy. Thursday Rural Housing in Comee all morning, lunched at House, answered questions in House, speech & on the bench till 11. Sat up late preparing speech. Friday departmental work all morning, travelled to Birm by 2.20 in order to make a presentation to Professor Turner on his retirement from the University.

Of course this diary takes no account of the consultations & interviews at the Ministry, reading of Cabinet papers &c. Every minute has been occupied but the strange thing is that I dont feel tired after it and everyone remarks how well I look. It *must* be the diet.

The Housing Subsidy debate had given me some anxiety beforehand, but it went extremely well for us. It is a remarkable thing that there has been no agitation in the Press and though local authorities have rather worried themselves especially on our side I dont fancy we shall hear much more about it. I heard indirectly through Sam Hoare that my speech which put a closely reasoned case, produced a great effect on our back benchers. It put forward grounds which apparently had not been foreseen by the Oppn. They had hoped I was going to found myself mainly on the necessity for economy and they really did not know how to meet my argument. Our people were also pleased because although I was careful to be non provocative in manner I managed to let out some plain truths about the failure of the Wheatley Act to reduce rents and the happy circumstance that Poplar showed the greatest excess of Wheatley over Chamberlain rents provoked much mirth & satisfaction. I find now that our people watch out when I am speaking and that when I make an insulting remark with an innocent face they immediately dot the I with ribald laughter & cheers. However this time the Opposition was in good temper and Wheatley came up himself afterwards to remark with a friendly smile that he hadn't said anything nasty about me this time!

The Oppn have got themselves into a nice mess about their vote of censure to which they are by no means looking forward. Our people on the other hand are simply thirsting for the fray & longing for the gloves to be off. Bobby Monsell told me that he had asked the P.M. to let me and Hogg reply but the P.M. said he couldn't avoid speaking himself & moreover he could not exclude Churchill seeing the part he had played in the later stages.

The Daily Mail (and the Express too!) had a nasty little paragraph this week saying that it was quite likely that Poor Law would be deferred owing to its unpopularity in the constituencies. Evidently some enemy hath done this thing, but who? The paragraph stated that the feeling was represented in the Cabinet which sounds ominous especially as Kingsley tells me that they get most of that sort of information from F.E. I fancy it may mean that Winston has been speaking to F.E. about it as other members of the Cabinet have told me that he has been talking to or rather at them. But I have not been idle either, and for what it is worth Balfour told someone who told someone else who told me that he thought if I stuck to it I should carry it in the Cabinet. If I didn't – well I dont like to think of such a contingency.

I have been reading the Balfourian account of Father's conversation in 1886 and was much interested to find him advocating the extension of municipal ownership of land & pointing out the dangers of too much interference with the executive in a democratic system of Govt. The observations on Poor Relief as a buffer against revolution seem opportune too at this moment. His line of thought 40 years ago was just what mine is today.

11 December 1926
37 Eaton Square, SW1

My dear Hilda,

...

Annie & I were much amused at your astuteness in drawing conclusions about the debate on Wednesday. I was so occupied that I only heard Baldwins (the last ¾ of it) & Winston's speeches. Annie heard these and also Lloyd George. Between ourselves we were absolutely consternated over Baldwins speech which struck us both & independently as absolutely lamentable. I did say that I hoped it wouldn't read as feeble as it sounded and evidently this was so. I am struck too by the indulgent way in which the back benchers talk of it saying that it was good stuff but a little disappointing in delivery, while the press has deliberately and brazenly declared it to have been a personal triumph. We thought the P.M. had simply gone to pieces; after reading the M.P. the Mail and the Express I began to ask "Do I sleep? do I dream? Is Wiscins [?] about?" I was terribly depressed at the time but I heard that some of our young men notably Capt O'Connor,[55] Capt. Eden,[56] Eddie Cadogan[57] and Capt Fairfax[58] made excellent speeches. Winstons wind-up was one of his most brilliant firework performances & some of his mots set the opposition in a roar just as much as our people. His remark that Cook had gone to Moscow "I suppose to report progress and ask leave to sit again" would not of course appeal to the outside public but to the House of Commons the use of the familiar words seemed so peculiarly apt that the whole gathering simply sat back and exhausted itself in laughter. The

---

[55] Terence James O'Connor (1891–40). Barrister and Conservative MP for Luton 1924–29 and Nottingham Central 1930–1940. Solicitor-General 1936–40. Knighted 1936.

[56] (Robert) Anthony Eden (1897–1977). Conservative MP for Warwick and Leamington 1923–57. Under-Secretary for Foreign Affairs 1931–33; Lord Privy Seal 1933–35; Minister without Portfolio for League of Nations Affairs 1935; Foreign Secretary 1935–38, 1940–45, 1951–55; Dominion Secretary 1939–40; War Secretary 1940; Prime Minister and Conservative leader 1955–57. Knighted 1954. Created Earl of Avon 1961.

[57] Edward Cecil George Cadogan (1880–1962). Secretary to Speaker of House of Commons 1911–21. Conservative MP for Reading 1922–23, Finchley 1924–35 and Bolton 1940–45. Member, Indian Statutory Commission 1927–30. Knighted 1939.

[58] James Griffyth Fairfax (1886–1976). Barrister, author, journalist and Conservative MP for Norwich 1924–29. Member, Executive of Association of Chambers of Commerce 1928–45.

speech would not I think have been particularly successful if it had been the opening statement of the case, but for the close – when there is no chance of turning anyone's vote but what is wanted is a rousing call to put one's own side in good heart & humour it was quite admirable and the general verdict after all seems to have been that we had had quite a good day.

I have had rather a terrible week and somehow the last few days I have felt distinctly below my best although I haven't really been up very late. But I have had to speak this week on 7 different subjects, including the whole discussion on Housing Bill Report stage as one subject. And when you add to that Cabinet & several Cabinet Committees two dinners and two luncheon parties the strain does become rather formidable. Last night I made a 45 minute speech to the Ladies Carlton Club to finish up the week, but today we are to "meet some people" at lunch at Reading and spend the afternoon inspecting a research (agricultural) station. Assuming, as I think I may, that I get the Mental Deficiency Bill through, I shall have passed (including the Economy Bill which was practically Ministry of Health) 9 Acts of Parliament this session. Of course they are, with the exception of the Economy, not as difficult or as long as Pensions or R.&V. but they are a very useful & creditable little bunch and I feel proud of the record. Terrible things were prophesied about the Smoke Bill but by simple force of argument we dissipated the opposition and a timely concession on Rural Workers put our people in a good temper on the only point which had excited any serious criticism i.e. the nature of the local authority.

Next week the House is supposed to rise on Wednesday. I shall have a hot time as I have for the first 2 days 2 Cabinet Committees & 2 Cabinets as well as a number of deputations and interviews & a debate in the H. of C. on necessitous areas! Poor Law is down for Tuesday and I am looking forward to it with great anxiety. I have traced the paragraph in the Mail to Jix which has relieved my mind. I was afraid it might be F.E. He would be a very formidable opponent but Jix doesn't count. I haven't canvassed any of my colleagues but certain strings have been pulled and I think I can count on support from Bob Cecil, Balfour, Sam Hoare & Eustace Percy. If opposition is serious it will probably centre round Winston & F.E. I understand that the P.M. wants to have a "heart to heart" talk with me beforehand. Well, I dont intend to threaten resignation but I should make myself very disagreeable if I didn't get my way and I am quite aware that I am an asset & not a liability of the Government.

17 December 1926
37 Eaton Square, SW1

My dear Ida,

… I did see Austen and even lunched with him at the House after his return but I forgot all about the Nobel prize. …

I am so glad to hear of the success of your insurance scheme which should encourage others to try. ... Your health services generally must be well about the average but you will have plenty more to do when Poor Law Reform comes. How do you stand with M.D.'s? I *was* vexed at losing that Bill: it was solely due to the Whips. If they had given me any backing we should have got it quite easily but they hate the M/H because we have so much legislation and they wanted to rise early.

I really did feel a bit cheap last week end and our stay at Pyrford was not exactly restful as we were inspecting dairies and institutes all the time. To tell the truth the Elvedens[59] aren't very bright people though their dulness was somewhat mitigated by the presence of Sir Walter Fletcher[60] the hon. sec. of the Medical Research Council who is always interesting. But even he has a dull wife!

I motored over to Chequers to lunch and found the Baldwins quite alone. S.B. was as usual non committal but the fact that he raised no particular objection was I thought highly significant. Discussion in Cabinet was postponed till Thursday afternoon but Eustace Percy and I arranged to have a preliminary talk with Winston that morning and by clearly settling in my mind what I wanted and judiciously playing up to Winston's little weaknesses I got all I wanted and he is now an ardent advocate. In fact he is so ardent that he has almost frightened Bob Cecil, who was a whole hearted supporter, into opposition. We talked so long on Thursday about other things that we could not finish the discussion on Poor Law & we took it up again this morning (the fifth Cabinet this week). Even now there is no definite decision but we have advanced a step and I am now pretty confident that it will go through. ...

I had a debate to take on Tuesday which was the cause of my absence. The old story of necessitous areas, but the Labour Party couldn't keep it going and it fizzled out about 8.

Today we lunched with Lady Beecham "to meet the Bernard Shaws". They were I believe invited to meet us. There was a large & ill-assorted party. I understand that Lady B. wants to show Sir Thomas that she can outdo Lady Cunard![61] I went out of curiosity to see Bernard Shaw. He looks like an elderly Satyr & is brimming over with vanity. I heard Lady B. gushing away to him about her desire to bring together all the best brains in politics literature & art in

---

[59] Rupert Edward Cecil Lee Guinness (1874–1967). Conservative MP for Shoreditch Haggerston 1908–10, South-East Essex 1912–18, Southend 1918–27. Chairman, Arthur Guinness & Company 1927–62. Styled Viscount Elveden 1919–27; succeeded as Earl of Iveagh 1927.

[60] Walter Morley Fletcher (1873–1933). Fellow, Trinity College, Cambridge; Senior Demonstrator of Physiology, Cambridge University 1903–5; Secretary, Medical Research Council and member of Health Advisory Council and other health committees. Member, Royal Commission on Oxford and Cambridge Universities 1919–22. Knighted 1918.

[61] Maud (called herself Emerald) Cunard (1872–1948). Wife of Sir Bache Cunard. One of the five great society hostesses with Mrs Ronnie Greville, Lady Astor, Colefax and Londonderry.

order to save England and his reply "The desire to do good is one of the worst & most mischievous forms of human activity that exists". Upstairs he was telling Lady Susan Townley [?] & the Duchess of Hamilton of a letter he had sent to the Times to say "Why steal dogs for vivisection when there are so many people who ought not to live?" And the Times had to his indignation sent the letter back! I believe he made up the whole story. But they took him seriously. Lady Susan got hot with wrath at his callousness while the Duchess who is mad about humane killers protested "But he is really right you know". Lord, these mortals!

...

8

1927

'Everything is Going Wrong this Session': Slums and the Frustrations of Poor Law Reform

3 January 1927
Westbourne

My dear Ida,

...

... Jackson had been very unsatisfactory as Chairman. He could not take any decision and there was much unrest in the office. Linlithgow[1] cleared out for that reason & Blain sent in his resignation. But fortunately F.E. selected Jackson as the most suitable man for Bengal and I dont think J. realises that he saved his bacon so narrowly. I thought when he went that Blain would have stopped but I think he had got thoroughly unsettled and his terms were so unreasonable that it was not possible to retain him. It remains to be seen what Davidson[2] will make of it. He has many of the qualities required but I doubt his judgement and I don't think he has much force of character. I don't know Maclachlan[3] personally but Annie has a poor opinion of him and I fear he will not show much originality or energy.

I had some useful talks with Philip [Cunliffe-Lister] about political affairs and presently I shall go over and see S.B. I feel that our Trade Union legislation will either make or mar us and I am anxious that we should not make a mistake over it. P. is not really sympathetic about Poor Law but I think my talks with him have somewhat modified his views.

...

---

[1] (Victor) Alexander John Hope (1887–1952). Civil Lord of Admiralty 1922–24; Deputy-Chairman, Conservative Party 1924–26; Chairman, Royal Commission on Indian Agriculture 1926–28; Chairman, Joint Select Committee on Indian Constitutional Reform 1933–34; Chairman, Medical Research Council 1934–36; Viceroy of India 1936–43. Styled Earl of Hopetoun from 1887; succeeded as 2nd Marquess of Linlithgow 1908.

[2] John Colin Campbell Davidson (1889–1970). Private Secretary to Lord Crewe 1910, to Harcourt 1910–15, to Bonar Law 1915–16, to Chancellor of Exchequer 1916–20. Conservative MP for Hemel Hempstead 1920–23 and 1924–37. PPS to Bonar Law 1920–21, 1922–23 and to Baldwin 1921–22; Chancellor, Duchy of Lancaster 1923–24 and 1931–37; Parliamentary and Financial Secretary, Admiralty 1924–26; Chairman, Conservative Party Organisation 1926–30. Controller of Production, Ministry of Information 1940–41. Created Viscount Davidson 1937.

[3] T.J. Leigh Maclachlan (1864–1946). Liberal Unionist District Agent, North West 1890–1905; Agent Superintendent, Liberal Unionist Council 1905–12; Visiting Agent, Central Office 1912–20; Conservative Chief Organiser 1921–26; Conservative Principal Agent 1927–28. Knighted 1927.

8 January 1927
Westbourne

My dear Hilda,

Before reading your letter I first looked at your enclosure and at once pronounced it to be poisonous stuff. "Economics" is only another name for Marxism nowadays and even as taught at the Stott College[4] I have heard that it tends to make Socialists. But I doubt if your "Eclipse study circle" is a definite offshoot of the Labour Party though I have little hesitation in believing that those responsible for it are working in that Party's interest.

Some day I suppose they will succeed in capturing rural constituencies but evidently they are a long way off it as yet. And it is difficult to be sure how the Labour Party is going to develop. Judging by a number of indications there is likely very soon to be a bitter struggle between the extremists and the moderates and perhaps that will clear the air. I put my money on the moderates but will they absorb the others or split off from them? Did you see Eustace Percy's address to the teachers? I thought it was both plucky and sensible and I was glad to read that he was very well received.

Austen must have been having an anxious time with those beastly Chinks in Hankow.[5] The Times had a disagreeable article this morning as though it were making ready to jump upon him in the event of a catastrophe but from the telegrams circular to the Cabinet I see that Miles Lampson[6] had heard of the withdrawal of the marines with consternation and indignation and in the evening paper I find a telegram that we are back again in the concession. Its a very ticklish business and we shall be lucky if we get out of it safely – no thanks to Macdonald [sic] and the Labour Party or to Lloyd George.

I am enjoying my peaceful holiday very much though the days pass much too quickly. I am doing a certain amount of work, for pouches come pretty regularly and I have just despatched some further ideas about Poor Law for my people to chew. S.B. has asked us (Annie & me) to spend tomorrow night with him at Astley Hall and I shall be glad to have the opportunity of talking over T.U. legislation with him and seeing where his mind has got to since we last met. He says he is going back to Downing Street on Wednesday and I have got a summons to a Cabinet on that day though they havent sent the agenda yet.

...

---

[4] Philip Stott College, at Overstone near Northampton, was established September 1923 to serve the Unionist Labour Movement but soon became a party college for training Conservative speakers.

[5] In October 1926 Hankow had fallen to Nationalist forces and by early January 1927 anti-British rioters compelled the abandonment of the British concession.

[6] Miles Wedderburn Lampson (1880–1964). Diplomat and Pro-Consul. Entered Foreign Office 1903. Second Secretary, Tokyo 1908–10; High Commissioner to Siberia 1920; Minister to China 1926–33; Ambassador to Egypt and High Commissioner to Sudan 1934–46; Special Commissioner to South-East Asia 1946–48. Knighted. Created Baron Killearn 1943.

16 January 1927
Westbourne

My dear Ida,

I am sorry you didn't get another look at your bird, but I expect it was a Greenshanks all right. I think you would always be likely to find snipe in that place at this time of year and it was there that for the first & only time in my life I heard one "drumming".

We had quite a pleasant visit to Astley Hall last Sunday and delightful weather. It is situated just under Abbenley Hill, not far from Witley and as you know that is lovely country. S.B. and I paid a visit to Stourport on Monday morning to see the new Super generating station there and then walked back along the river and through the fields.

As I know something of my Stanley by now I seized an opportunity before dinner on Sunday to say all I had to say about T.U. legislation and after that didn't mention politics again. Of course as usual he merely listened saying nothing himself so that I have not the slightest idea whether he was or was not impressed with what I said. But I hope for the best and in dealing with him all you can do is to put your view & hope that it has sunk in. Afterwards you find out whether it has or not. In the evening we had rather an interesting conversation when S.B. began to consider the possible alternatives to the present holders of various offices "if anything happened to them". As he says, a P.M. must continually consider such things if he is not to be taken completely by surprise. It was evident that he had contemplated the possibility of Jix's retirement but though he has evidently had rather a nasty jar I cannot imagine that he wont be well enough to go on though he may have to curtail his speech making a bit.

On Tuesday I had Hubbard, of the Post, to lunch. He is rather a maddening person in some ways having the obstinacy of the weak man about him, but I feel it necessary to keep in pretty close touch and he has *now* lost all his old shyness with me and talks quite freely. We had a happy thought & put Harvey,[7] the Editor of the Mail, into our dinner party on Thursday so we have bowled out both the press magnates this week. ...

Tomorrow I must go up for another Cabinet. ... The Chinese situation is most baffling and puzzling. No foreign nation seems the least disposed to take their share in the defence of common interests, each hoping that the whole brunt of Chinese aggression will fall upon the British. On the other hand we seem very helpless with totally inadequate forces at our disposal. I confess I feel critical of the F.O. who are always about a couple of months behind in dealing with the situation but I dont like to criticise without having an alternative & I dont know enough to produce one. I have a poor opinion of that fat Sir Victor Wellesley.[8]

---

[7] Herbert Frost Harvey (1875–1959). Staff member, *Birmingham Daily Post*, 1899–1902 and *Daily Despatch* 1902–4; Assistant Editor, *Birmingham Daily Mail* from 1904 and Editor 1907–44.

[8] Victor Alexander Augustus Henry Wellesley (1876–1954). Godson of Queen Victoria. Clerk in

It is certainly very dramatic, the way house prices have come down. The Herald is white with fury & shrieks. It cant be true, it shant be true. Chamberlain *is* a failure and here is a picture of Wheatley! But I expect it *is* true, broadly speaking, although we shall know better when we have had a few more monthly figures. I see the Sec of the Housing & T.P. Council has been writing to the Times to say that another 700,000 houses are wanted. That body has for some time been steadily going over to the Labour Party. I have no use for them at all and take a delight in giving them a bump on the nose whenever I can see an opportunity.

Did I tell you that I have at last got rid of Sir Herbert Austin. Now we can get a candidate for Kings Norton and if he is all right I see no reason why we should not win that seat back. A & I attended a management committee on Friday and saw Edwards at work. We are *very* pleased with him.

The same evening we attended an Edgbaston Unionist Ball when I delivered myself of a few appropriate words prominently reported on the front page of the Post. Thus with 1½ hrs attendance at a place 5 minutes drive from here I have kept my name before my constituency and satisfied all reasonable claims upon my attention. What a contrast to Ladywood and what we should have had to do if I had still been tied up to that place. But Lady Lowe who was at the ball said she was anxious about Sir Francis who was getting very feeble. I *do* hope she will take every possible care of him.

Still the Cymbidiums hang back ... I am sorry as I should have liked to have seen the 21 spikes that are still to come all out together. But some day when I am out of politics and if Hoskins has recovered I shall be able to indulge myself. This spring I fear H. will have to miss a dividend altogether as although it has now begun to receive enquiries they have not yet materialised into orders & it is losing money so fast in the meantime that I darent go on drawing on its reserves any longer. My annual accounts which I have just finished make rather dismal reading for last year. What they will look like next I dont know and when I go out of office & lose my salary – !!!

However sufficient unto the day.

I have finished Bismark: v. interesting & have started on Trevelyan. At present I find him dull by comparison as I cannot get very keen about the Saxons Jutes Celts Norsemen or even Normans. ...

I have nearly finished the Forsyte Saga. It is a bigger work (I mean morally & mentally) than I had supposed. I am not sure that it comes much below Thackeray at his best though somehow there is no figure that stirs one's emotions like those you find in the Newcomers & Vanity Fair.

...

Foreign Office 1899; Acting Second Secretary, Diplomatic Service 1905; Rome Embassy 1905–6; Secretary to British delegation at Berne Labour Conference 1906; Assistant Secretary, Foreign Office 1910–24; Assistant Under-Secretary 1924–25; Deputy Under-Secretary, Foreign Office 1925–36. Knighted 1919.

22 January 1927
Westbourne

My dear Hilda,

...

... I *have* had another attack of gout which has kept me in bed three days this week. ...

...

I went up on Monday for a Cabinet the result of which was a great relief to my mind. I was very uncomfortable at what I thought was the slowness and indecision of the F.O. in a situation which seemed to call for prompt & decisive action. However they have made up their minds at last to what I believe is the right line viz to stand at Shanghai and to take such measures as will enable us to make good our defence there even if other nations refuse at the last moment to do their share. But I cant help thinking that both America & Japan will find their hands forced if trouble comes and Japan in particular ought to welcome the opportunity of standing in with us in a situation where for geographical reasons she is bound to have a leading rôle. And in taking action as we have we are acting in accordance with the unanimous views of the men on the spot. I feel myself convinced that, with the Chinese, "face" counts so much that timely firmness is the best way of preventing trouble and I am hopeful, now that we are showing it, that we shall discredit the Soviet influence in China pretty effectually.

I see that Ramsay is bidding his party concentrate on seeing that the Govt does not "overdo" precautions against injury to British lives & property and advising them to keep in touch with Chen.[9] Isn't that like his dishonesty! He wants to take sides against his country but does not dare to do so openly. As for Ll.G. he knows that he blotted his copybook in making that speech about China and is anxious to shove it into the background by a great show of patriotism. He is the champion opportunist.

...

29 January 1927
The Deanery, Christ Church, Oxford

My dear Ida,

...

I have been a good deal worried over information which has come to me privately that the P.M. having been "enormously impressed" with the Poor Law case which I put to him at Chequers has now got cold feet about it again. He

---

[9] Eugene (Kung-Po) Chen (1892–1946). Chinese Koumintang politician. Held many posts in Canton Government including Foreign Minister. Collaborator with Japan 1940–45. Executed 1946.

hasn't said anything to me and I don't mean to say anything to him which would give him an opportunity of reopening the subject. But I sent for Davidson & extracted a promise that he would to the best of his ability stop & damp down all expressions of dissent or doubt in the party until the Cabinet has taken its decision and I shall go and see Winston as soon as he comes back & warn him that *his* scheme is in danger. Somehow I still think I shall get it through but I shall be happier when the struggle is over.

Another thing that bothers me is that the P.M. does not seem to have given any thought to Trade Union legislation during the session. I saw in the Morning Post a pretty good guess at the contents of the draft Bill and the Express followed it up by some bitter comments about its inadequacy. I don't consider that the comments were justified but they point to what I had rather anticipated, that if we are not going to give political levy or secret ballot we must put something constructive to take their place otherwise our people will be very disgruntled.

I am amused at your Clerk's view that it was no use to do anything about rural housing until March 31. This is exactly the way my people said the C.C.'s would behave and it was the reason why I only gave 3 months for the decision. But the circular ought to have made it plain that we did not expect them to wait but to get to work at once. So I am glad you are stirring things up. Of course I share your view that the best plan is for the C.C. to take the responsibility but to make as much use as can be done of the D.C. & its officers.

Yesterday I had to pass through the Commons Lobby & seeing the statue there I stopped & a workman took the cloth off the face for me to see. It is a tremendous way from the ground so that you dont get at all a near view but I can only say that I saw no resemblance to Father and that the figure appeared to me to be wholly lacking in distinction. In fact it is worse than I expected. For some reason Tweed[10] has cocked the head to one side; perhaps it was so in some photograph, but the result is disconcerting and unnatural. They will send you tickets for the ceremony which is to be performed by the Earl of Balfour. I would it were another!

...

P.S. I am going to "West Ham" Bedwellty in a few days!

5 February 1927
37 Eaton Square, SW1

My dear Hilda,

...

This has been a week of ups & downs and it has ended with a down. I had a feeling that the position was precarious on Wednesday for the P.M. said we

---

[10] John Tweed (?-1933). Sculptor.

should have to consider it again on Friday in the light of the Chief Whips observations and yesterday Bobby produced a time table which showed only 22 days available for legislation & 27 necessary for the short programme proposed including Poor Law. I could see at once from the joyful way in which one member of the Cabinet after another suggested that the time table was too optimistic & that this or that contingency was certain to occur & upset it, that they were only too delighted at the opportunity of shelving P.L. So when the P.M. suggested that it might be introduced in the autumn in the new session to be begun then I jumped at it as the one remaining chance. But though I am sure that he means it to come on then I confess I fear very much that all the critics & the diehards and the fainthearts will croak in chorus and I cant help the conviction that if they lift up their voices I shant get enough support to carry my way.

I have been fairly done as I had withdrawn the rest of my programme to get P.L. and now I have positively got nothing whatever. The fact is the Cabinet has got cold feet in view of the General election although we hope to put that off till 1929. I think they are all wrong, and that we shant win elections by doing nothing but by establishing a record of useful work. If I were in S.B.'s place I would call the members together and tell them that they weren't returned to Parlt to take a holiday and I believe they would respond because they are an extraordinarily loyal lot. But I suppose I cant do more and perhaps I shall turn out to be all wrong. Kingsley was told by someone (he did not say who) that if anyone else had put up P.L. to the Cabinet it would have been turned down and the P.M. himself said that he did not attach much importance to the political difficulties because he had such confidence in my judgement of what was right & my capacity of getting anything through the H. of C. And he added that others felt the same about me more than any member of the Cabinet. But though I believe myself that it was that feeling of confidence which enabled me to get so far, it could not stand up to that d-d time table. I am going through it myself presently to see if there isn't a catch somewhere!

We had a meeting earlier in the week on Trade Union legislation when once more I brought up my proposal & this time got a backing from Philip with whom I had discussed it at Swinton. Winston was very impatient saying it was too late to bring it up now and upset all the decisions at which we had arrived after sitting for seven months. (of course he counted in the months from August to Nov. when the Committee didn't sit!) I retorted that I had nothing to reproach myself with. I made my suggestion as soon as I was called in & if I repeated them now it was because I felt strongly that they would improve the Bill. Finally it was suggested that I should consult with Parly Counsel & put my ideas into clauses. So I saw the Parly Counsel & it so happened that he brought the draft some days later just when I was talking to Winston at the Treasury about Poor Law. W. asked if Counsel might bring them in. I said certainly I should like him to see them. So in came Ram[11] (the P.C.) & gave a copy to Winston who read them through and then, getting very excited, cried, "But this is very interesting. We must have a special meeting of the Committee to discuss this. And after all *there's plenty of time* for we shant have to produce the Bill for some months yet"! And then he immediately sketched out an imaginary presentation, as he called it, to the public emphasising the essential features of the Bill, one of them being my proposal! Did you *ever* come across such a brilliant erratic creature. In dealing with him you always have to bear in mind that however overwhelming the case he makes out against you, if you stand up & make the counter case he is quite likely to jump over the barricade and construct a better defence for you than you would have thought of yourself. On the other hand his defence is then so ingenious that everyone is at once convinced of its unsoundness and, as I have found to my cost before now, Winston's alliance is even more dangerous than his opposition.

It is curious that the general impression of the Press is that we have dropped political levy, which isn't true. On the other hand there has not been a whisper of my plan and if we could only keep it quiet till the Bill was produced it would I am certain prove the most interesting feature in our proposals.

As for China, it gets more and more difficult and Austen had a parroty time on Friday when he couldn't find one single member of the Cabinet to approve what he wanted to do. The fact is that we are all fed up with Chen and his impudent attempt to play off the Labour Party against us & we are entirely opposed to "giving him another chance". But we are deeply divided as to whether the 1st Brigade which is due in Hong Kong today should stop there for the present or go on to Shanghai. I am in favour of Hong Kong as I want to keep on good terms with Japan and she has expressed a strong desire that we should not land troops at Shanghai. But I would only keep the 1st Brgde at H.K. till the rest of the force arrives, say in ten days, and if nothing had happened in the meanwhile I would say that there was no more room at H.K. & therefore I must move on the mixed Brgde. But I am sure that something *would* happen in the ten days.

However that policy was not acceptable to the Diehards and finally we compromised. The first ship will go sailing round & round, not arriving anywhere, till we get a reply from Lampson to whom we have submitted alternative policies & we meet tomorrow when we hope to be able to come to a final decision. Not very dignified, nor very efficient, but inevitable with a committee of 21 or whatever we are.

...

---

[11] (Lucius Abel John) Granville Ram (1885–1952). Barrister. Third Parliamentary Counsel to Treasury 1915–29; Second Parliamentary Counsel 1929–37 and First Parliamentary Counsel 1937–47. Knighted 1931.

12 February 1927
Westbourne

My dear Hilda,

… On the whole I think the P.L. position has not worsened this week. The P.M. did not of course definitely commit the Govt to introduce it in the autumn when he spoke on Tuesday but he went pretty far and I took the opportunity yesterday of reinforcing his remarks with somewhat greater detail. And up to the present I have not seen or heard any doubts expressed about the possibility of carrying out our intentions. But there are some rather difficult stiles to get over. The Chancellor's block grant proposals have been elaborated by an Interdepartmental Committee who have produced a rather complicated formula and I have got the P.M.'s promise to set up a Cabinet Comee next week to examine them. But although Eustace rather likes them the Duchess [of Atholl] is very much against them and so is the Home Office. It comes back to this that we should have done much better to start with my original proposal dealing with Health alone. That does not involve a lot of money and when we had seen how it worked we could have added to it Education Police & Roads by successive steps. Unfortunately, Winston always wants things to be done in a spectacular way with himself in the foreground and as he holds the purse I cant get on without him. There is a long & difficult struggle before me but I haven't by any means given up hope or courage and somehow I believe I shall still get home barring accidents to the Govt as a whole.

Meanwhile I believe I shall manage to get Mental Def[icienc]y this year. We have been working the oracle and got a good many resolutions passed and forwarded to members and now I have got the Bill in a slightly amended form taken up by a private member. Leslie Scott is interesting himself in it & says he has squared Slesser[12] who was one of our chief opponents last year so if the opposition slackens I believe I may induce the Cabinet to allow the Bill to have the necessary "facilities". I feel sure Bobby Monsell has a lot of spare time up his sleeve.

You were more fortunate than I in finding one place from which you could see some likeness to Father in the statue. I am told that Mary likes it but if so she is the only person I have heard of who has a good word to say for it. I should not have so much minded its unlikeness if it had given any adequate impression of force vitality and energy. But it looks like a dreamy young parson addressing a mother's meeting. I remember that the first statue of Bright was so universally condemned that it was removed and another one made; I think that is an example that should be followed now. From something Austen said to me I thought he suspected Mary of having given too many instructions to Tweed; perhaps that is why she likes it! …

---

[12] Henry Herman Slesser (1883–1979). Barrister and lecturer on Industrial Law, University of London. Labour MP for Leeds South-East 1924–29. Solicitor-General 1924; Lord Justice of Appeal 1929–40. Adopted name Slesser in lieu of Schloesser in 1914. Knighted 1924.

While we were waiting for Balfour & wondering if he had forgotten all about the ceremony … I was talking to Ramsay Macdonald. He said he was very ill, continually losing weight and constantly plunged into the deepest depression. "In fact" he said "I think very soon I shall get out and leave you to your own devices". He has made similar remarks to other people lately and I should not be surprised if he did retire one of these days. It must be intolerable in that state of physical misery and depression to be constantly fighting with his own party who have no mercy on him and indeed despise and dislike him. But one would feel more sympathy if he were not such a moral weakling.

I was not in the House on Thursday having been "took ill" and being moreover much oppressed by the prospect of having myself to take part in the debate on Friday and make a speech at the Civil Service dinner in the evening. But I hear that Austen made one of his most effective speeches and that the debate went extremely well for us. In fact the Labour Party were so rattled that they met in the evening to decide whether to go to a division and only decided very reluctantly in the affirmative because Lansbury and his crowd declared that they would do so anyhow. As usual the extremists showed the greater determination & won and the vote should be worth much to us on the platform. S.B. said that Austen went off on Friday to Sussex, very tired but very happy and purring like a cat!

It has been rather a strenuous week for me including four speeches, 3 dinners and an evening crush! But although I shall have little to do in the H. of C. this session I foresee there will be plenty of work in other directions.

    …

19 February 1927
37 Eaton Square, SW1

My dear Hilda,

You can imagine what a dismal week this has been in London with this perpetual fog – never pea soupy, but always enough to cut off light and air. And it seems to darken counsel too for we have had a rackety time in Cabinet with China always lowering and Russia burrowing and undermining. Preserve us from a repetition of such incidents and such instruments as the well meaning old gentleman who is the brains of our Army! Seeing what a rough passage Austen was having I sent him one day a suggested draft of a despatch which I thought might help. I never thought he would pay any attention to it so I was quite flattered when he sent me a note to say it was admirable & he proposed to adopt it. The Cabinet was of the same opinion so I suppose one of these days it, or something like it, will appear in the papers.[13]

---

[13] Neville Chamberlain's draft of a stiff note warning the Russians to cease hostile action or risk a breach in diplomatic relations was eventually delivered on 23 February 1927, CP 25(27), CAB 24/184.

Annie and I are getting so popular now that we can scarcely get a meal to ourselves. I believe A. reckons we have had nearly 25 invitations to dinner since we came back to town and requests for speeches come in daily to both of us.

...

On Thursday I had promised to attend the annual dinner of the Urban D. C. Assns at 7.30 but owing to a late Cabinet I didn't get there till 9 and had to bolt my food at an alarming pace in order to make my speech. I spoke on Poor Law & had a great success the audience applauding and shouting Bravo for quite a long time after I had sat down. Unfortunately they hadn't invited reporters for which they have been very sorry since.

... This afternoon we went to hear a string quartette. They played three pieces by Stravinsky and I dont think I ever heard a more excruciating series of discords. I suppose it was a joke but I would as soon hear a quartette of Tom Cats.

This evening we have been dining with the Hoares and hearing all their adventures.[14] They had a wonderful journey but nothing would induce me to undertake a trip involving such prolonged discomfort and so many risks. I do think they are plucky and public spirited to do it but there is a lot more in Sam Hoare than people realise. Under his dry manner he has a lot of imagination and great shrewdness.

...

I have begun to work at Slums again and believe I have got some new ideas which are promising.

...

26 February 1927
37 Eaton Square, SW1

My dear Ida,

...

We are having a good deal of trouble with the C.C.'s in getting them to make a start [with the Rural Housing Act]. Of course they only meet quarterly and if they are too long in beginning to think about a scheme the building season will be over before anyone has commenced operations. We are thinking of getting the Clerks up to explain to them the necessity of getting under weigh.

...

On Monday I was interviewed by a journalist named Nicholson who, under the name of "Roberts", is writing a series of "Studies of Statesmen" in the Outlook. He has done Wheatley this week and I must say I think he has done him rather well. I believe I appear next Friday, but it is rather comical, &

---

[14] Between 26 December 1926 and 8 January 1927 Hoare and his wife had flown to India to establish popular confidence in air travel. They returned to London on 17 February to a hero's welcome.

characteristic of latter day journalism, that a man thinks himself competent to write a study after an hours talk!

We dined last night with the Master of the Rolls – a dull dinner, but enlivened by a talk with Lord Lawrence[15] of Kingsgate who told me on the authority of Riddell (and he ought to know) that Lloyd George made £150,000 for himself and £80,000 for McCurdy[16] out of the recent sale of the Daily Chronicle. I suppose, assuming it to be true or near the truth, that there was nothing he had not a right to do, but somehow one does not like the idea of a man in his position making a great sum of money for himself out of a transaction undertaken in the course of party business.

...

Annie went down to Birmingham on Thursday to preside at a womens meeting and to complete the arrangements for her area Conference at Leamington. The conference is to be addressed by the Earl of Birkenhead a circumstance which has given rise to some misgivings especially as he is going to lunch first with Sir E. Iliffe.[17] But it is hoped that as it is lunch and not dinner he will be sufficiently composed to address the ladies without giving them any such shock as Middlesex received.

I joined her yesterday in order that we might both attend the dinner given in my honour by the Midland Assocn of Local Authorities. It was quite a success but unfortunately they were provincial enough to arrange for my speech to come on at 9.45 so they got no report in the London Press. It was a pity because I was speaking on Poor Law. But I hope to make other opportunities when I can nail the P.M. down to give me the conference he has promised with the Party Chairman & the Chief Whip. I want formal leave to start propaganda but the P.M. I fancy would prefer to postpone decisions on that as on other subjects.

We have started to explore Block Grants in Committee of the Cabinet. Winston has insisted against my advice on taking the chair and we made a bad beginning because he doesn't know his case and speedily got entangled in contradictions. But I am going to have a talk with Eustace on Monday and if I can concert a line with him we may perhaps contrive to muzzle the Duchess, shepherd Jix into the

---

[15] Charles Napier Lawrence (1855–1927). Chairman, LNWR 1921–22 and LMSR 1923–24. An important figure in insurance; member, Royal Commission on Health Insurance 1924–26. Created Baron Lawrence of Kingsgate 1923.

[16] Charles Albert McCurdy (1870–1941). Liberal MP for Northampton 1910–23. Parliamentary Secretary, Ministry of Food 1919–20; Minister of Food 1920–21; Chief Coalition Liberal Whip and Joint Parliamentary Secretary to Treasury 1921–22; Chief National Liberal Whip 1922; Chairman, United Newspapers Limited 1922–27 and Managing Director 1925–27.

[17] Edward Nauger Iliffe (1877–1960). Newspaper publisher and Conservative MP for Tamworth 1923–29. Controller of Machine Tools, Ministry of Munitions 1917–18. Joint proprietor of *Daily Telegraph* 1928–37; proprietor of *Birmingham Post* and *Birmingham Mail* from 1943. Knighted 1922. Created Baron Iliffe 1933.

fold and convince Winston that he & he alone has found the solution of our difficulties.

The Soviet note has I think gone off as well as can be expected. I am satisfied that if we had not sent it the pot would have boiled over in this country and as I believe there is a substantial party in the Soviet which would be sorry to see a break I am not without hope that it may have some restraining influence at any rate for a time. Tyrrell told me the other night that he thought we should pull through in China without a row. I hope so but the people in China, as Guedalla[18] remarks, are Chinese and you never know what they will do. ...

...

Next week we have got a terribly smart dinner with the French Ambassador, the Byngs, the Stanhopes the Churchills & I dont quite know who else. I hope A. will be fresh again by then; at present she is rather exhausted after her long Conferences & Committees in Birmingham which shows that she still has to take care.

...

5 March 1927
37 Eaton Square, SW1

My dear Hilda,

Will you please tell Ida that I have had a copy made of her observations on the Housing Act & am going to take it to the Dept on Monday to discuss it with the officials who are working the Act. Before answering I should like to know whether any other difficulties are coming to light from the C.C.'s.

...

I had a talk with L. Williams but nothing special came of it as he was unable to find anything the matter with me ... So I am to go on as before & be satisfied if I only have gout once in three years. As for Annie, she is indignant at the suggestion that her tiredness last week is anything more than a sort of accident owing to a coincidental series of engagements. It is quite true that she is not like she was last year and I dont think she will go back to that but I take the warning that her strength is not unlimited. ...

...

The debate on the Note went very well for us. I didn't think A. was at his best; he was rather hoarse and I think he felt that he was skating on very thin ice in trying to put the case against a break from the point of view of European politics. But he had previously addressed a large meeting of our men upstairs

---

[18] Philip Guedalla (1889–1944). Barrister and historian. Legal Adviser, War Office and Ministry of Munitions 1915–17. Secretary, Flax Control Board 1917–20. Unsuccessful Liberal candidate 1922–31. Friend of Lloyd George and author of *Mr Churchill: A Portrait* (1941). Squadron-Leader RAF 1943.

without reporters and I hear that on that occasion he produced a great impression and convinced 80% of those present. The result was that O. Locker Lampson who delivered a sort of Albert Hall oration was received in a chilling silence and though the division was not specially good it was good enough. ...

My affairs are not going well. We have had a second meeting of the Block Grants Committee which did not pass off any better than the first and I hear Winston is very depressed about it & thinks the scheme is going to break down. Yesterday I succeeded at last in getting a conference with the P.M. the Chief Whip & the Party Chairman. The P.M. has got very cold feet again and the other two are assiduously laying ice packs to his extremities. He refuses to take any step which would definitely commit us to Poor Law reform in November and harps continually on the danger of alienating our supporters in the Rural Districts. I believe that if they were definitely told that we were going on with it they would make the best of it & set themselves to see what could be said in its favour. But so long as we are timid & vacillating & only keep asking what they think, they will play for safety and say Get the next election over & then we will see about it. I feel very depressed over the prospect but I see no advantage to any one in resignation. If Poor Law goes down it will be a nasty snub for me but I shall try and get slums through and then I think I shall have done with the Ministry of Health.

Winston has sent me a copy of his book [The World Crisis] which I am just beginning. The extracts in the Times show that it is very interesting though of course almost every page is controversial and the soldiers & sailors are all up in arms over it.

...

We are off to Cliveden for the week end: I hope no royalties this time!

12 March 1927
Westbourne

My dear Ida,

...

The letter which I showed Hilda had an instantaneous effect and next day at the Cabinet the P.M. said he proposed to cut out the Committee & have a special meeting of the Cabinet on Tuesday to consider the T.U. Bill. My proposals have been circulated and I have got another recruit in Hogg. He had been struck with the same idea as I had, namely that my proposal if adopted would come as a complete surprise to the country and would divert the attention of our party from the ballot & the political levy. But I fear the Cabinet will decide to go on with the latter, as they say the party will be so angry if they dont. This wretched seeking after popularity! It will be amusing if my suggestion turns out to be the principal feature of the Bill.

The terrifying meeting with the Agricultural Committee over P.L. came off on Wednesday. There was a huge gathering and they gave me what my P.S. describes as an ovation but what I should call a very encouraging reception when I came in. The chairman called on me almost at once and I entered upon a 20/25 minutes speech, beginning with a lurid picture of what the Labour Party might do if they came in & found we had not covered the ground. Chester le Street had appeared in time to give emphasis to this aspect which did I think make the meeting's flesh creep. I then went on to deal with Sir H. Cautley[19] whose outrageous letter in the Times had appeared that morning. Fortunately he was present & I gave him such a dressing down as must be rare on such occasions. The meeting cheered heartily & the Pig Man was so put out of countenance that he never raised his head or uttered a word throughout the proceedings. After that I put the case as strongly as I could & sat down amid much applause. Then came a volley of questions which however did not seem very bad till one member asked if he might challenge the expediency of any Bill at all. After that speaker after speaker declared that it was most dangerous to legislate and things went pretty rotten. Of course I had foreseen this and reserved my last shaft till the end. I went through the questions & answered them but finally suggested that as I had always tried in any legislation for which I was responsible to meet my friends & supporters (to which they responded with warm Hear! Hear!) so I was anxious now to get nearer to agreement. Would they appoint a Sub. Comee to discuss the proposals with me. This sounded so reasonable that they at once accepted and I believe they are appointing about ten to meet me.

Its a perilous game but I don't think I am check mated yet. My idea is to try and concentrate criticism on the administration of O.D. [outdoor] relief by C.C. Sub. Committees and then offer to substitute for them the R.D.'s & U.D.'s. Of course in the R.D.s this would mean keeping the O.D. relief in the same hands as at present though it wd be subject to conditions laid down by the C.C. as it would be a county charge. Robinson doesn't like this plan because he is very anxious to put O.D. medical relief under the C.C. but if I can get the Institutions C.C.ilised I think I shall have saved the major part of the cargo.

There still remains the difficulty of the financial proposals. I hear that Winston is so disgusted with the Block Grants Comee that he is preparing a Memorandum saying that he despairs of the general unified grant & that he wont have anything else. If that is his attitude it will give me a lot of trouble because it leaves me without a Necessitous Area policy, but I guess its not really been thought out and I may be able to move him out of it. I always knew this P.L. was going to be a difficult ship to steer into port.

A. & I dined with the Astors on Wednesday to meet the King & Queen. I sat next to Dame Caroline on one side & Lady (Herbert) Samuel on the other. The latter is a rather intelligent pleasant woman though not much to look at. Annie was next to Ramsay Macdonald [sic] & got so thick with him that he is sending

---

[19] Henry Strother Cautley (1863–1946). Barrister and Conservative MP for Leeds East 1900–6 and East Grinstead 1910–36. Created Bart 1924 and Baron Cautley 1936.

her books of poetry and music! I shall have to look after her though she swears she still doesn't trust him. ...

Last night we dined with the Dawsons (of Penn)[20] where we met the inevitable de Fleuriaus[21] and Kay Menzies[22] the M.O.H. of the London C.C. He is a very able man and agrees with me so heartily that I think he will be very useful. In particular he takes a long view of the future of hospitals and he told me that he was going to read a paper on the State & Municipality in relation to voluntary Hospitals. He had asked Eason[23] of Guys one of the most influential and able men in the voluntary hospital world to open a discussion, & Eason had replied that he would be delighted. K.M., rather surprised, asked why. E. said he had turned up an old paper of his (K.M.'s) which had much interested him and then he had seen my letter in the Times which had fairly made him jump. So he had been thinking it over & had come to the conclusion that the only thing for the Vol. Hosp. was to work in the closest cooperation with the L.A.'s.

...

19 March 1927
Westbourne

My dear Hilda,

...

We have had a busy & rather eventful week both politically & socially. I believe the social functions fall off after this month but they have been unprecedented up to now, partly I suppose because we know so many people but chiefly I fancy because Annie is so popular socially both as hostess & guest.

Thus, we lunched on Monday with Philip Sassoon[24] at his wonderful house in Park Lane. I didn't much want to go but this time it was a very pleasant party

---

[20] Bernard Dawson (1864–1945). Physician and diagnostician. Physician-in-Ordinary to King Edward VII 1906–10; to King George V 1910–36; to Prince of Wales 1929–36. Chairman, Consultative Council on Medical and Allied Services 1919; Member, Medical Research Council 1931–35, Army Medical Advisory Board 1936–45. Knighted 1911. Created Baron Dawson of Penn 1920 and Viscount 1936.

[21] Aimé Joseph de Fleuriau (1870–1938). Entered French Diplomatic Service 1892; Counsellor to London Embassy 1913–20; Minister to Peking 1921–24; Ambassador to London 1924–33.

[22] Frederick Norton Kay Menzies (1875–1949). Doctor. Medical Officer of Health for LCC 1925–40. Member of many departmental committees including on Venereal Diseases 1922–23; Midwives 1927–28; Nursing Service 1937–39. Member, General Nursing Council 1937–42; Chairman, Central Council for Maternity and Child Welfare. Knighted 1932.

[23] Herbert Lightfoot Eason (1874–1949). Ophthalmic surgeon, Guy's Hospital. Member, Departmental Committee on University of London 1924–26 and Post-Graduate Medical Education 1925–30; Vice-Chancellor, University of London 1935–37 and Principal 1937–41. Knighted 1943.

[24] Philip Albert Gustave David Sassoon (1888–1939). Private Secretary to Haig 1915–18. Conservative MP for Hythe 1912–39. PPS to Lloyd George 1920–22; Under-Secretary for Air 1924–29 and 1931–37; First Commissioner of Works 1937–39. Succeeded as Bart 1912.

and I sat next to Lady Londonderry whom I like. She is Chaplin's[25] daughter and always tells me what a high opinion he had of me and how strongly he thought I resembled Father! Sassoon had been to the R.H.S. show and knowing apparently nothing about Cymbidiums had been greatly struck by them. So he had bought about half Alexander's exhibit and there they were all through the house as though they had just come up from Lympne. Just like Monte Cristo.

The same evening we dined with the Colefaxes. Annie says we must have attained the topmost rung of the social ladder since Sybil Colefax now takes her by both hands and lays her own hand upon my arm. Be that as it may I thought the dinner dull and Arthur Colefax[26] getting very fat & prosy but A. had Sir E Lutyens beside her and made a conquest of him.

...

I have only had three speeches to make this week and only one of those required much preparation viz the unveiling of the tablet to Sir P. Manson[27] at the Albert Dock Hospital. I have always been very much interested in Tropical Medicine on the scientific side as well as because Father did so much for it and I was therefore very pleased to go and pay my tribute to old Manson who made the first discoveries of the connection between mosquitoes and tropical diseases and really inspired Ross[28] to work out the observations which demonstrated the propagation of malaria in this way. Manson's work was therefore the foundation of all the later developments in yellow fever, sleeping sickness, plague, typhus & trench fever. He is the father of the Panama Canal and working it all out there are few men to whom one can directly trace such a wide influence on men throughout the world. I was very pleased to find Ross himself amongst the audience and gratified to receive his enthusiastic & evidently genuine compliments on my speech. A Minister who get scientific facts correctly stated in a speech is a never failing wonder to scientific men!

You will, I daresay, have seen that the M[ental] D[eficiency] Bill got its second reading yesterday without a division. Crompton Wood[29] was reported to

---

[25] Henry Chaplin (1840–1923). Unionist MP for mid-Lincolnshire 1868–1906 and Wimbledon 1907–16. Chancellor, Duchy of Lancaster 1885–86; President, Board of Agriculture 1889–92; President, LGB 1895–1900. Created Viscount Chaplin 1916.

[26] (Henry) Arthur Colefax (1866–1939). Barrister. Unionist MP for South-West Manchester 1910. Served on many government committees and enquiries. Knighted 1920. Married to Sybil Colefax, one of the great Society hostesses of the period.

[27] Patrick Manson (1844–1922). Scottish physician. Known as 'Mosquito Manson' for pioneering work on malaria in Far East. Founded Hong Kong Medical School 1883; Medical adviser to Colonial Office; helped found London School of Tropical Medicine. Knighted 1903.

[28] Ronald Ross (1857–1932). British physician who discovered malaria parasite. Indian Medical Service 1881–99; Professor of Tropical Medicine, Liverpool University; Director, Ross Institute from 1926. Nobel Prize for Medicine 1902. Knighted 1911.

[29] Brooks Crompton Wood (1870–1946). Liverpool cotton merchant, Raw Cotton Adviser to War Office and Chairman, Control of Egyptian Cotton Board 1915–18. Conservative MP for Bridgwater 1924–29.

me, when he first appeared, to be an M.D. himself. But though his appearance is against him – a little frog like creature – this was an injustice. Fired with enthusiasm over a Bill of his own he entrusted himself body & soul to Mr Pinsent[30] who coached him so successfully that his speech yesterday was generally acknowledged to be one of the best heard in recent years on a Friday Bill. I have little doubt now that the Bill will go through and I shall be relieved of the shame & vexation of having lost any item of my programme.

There has been a great row over Poor Law this week which has fortunately eventuated rather in my favour. The London Municipal Reform Socy drew up a memo in which they intimated that my scheme was dead and that I should do well to consider instead a plan for West Hamming Guardians on a large scale including the Boards in Birmingham Sheffield and other important places. They handed this to the Unionist Central Office asking that it shd be published & the C.O. passed it on to the Press marked "Unofficial for guidance only please summarise tomorrow". There was no mention of the L.M.R.S. & nothing to show that it had not been written in the C.O.

Well, the D. Mail, the Morning Post & I think some provincial papers as well as the Evening Standard published the paragraph. The Times decided against publication. I hear from an inside source that "the Minister made a very great impression on the Editor at Cliveden and he has now quite changed his views about Poor Law Reform!" One of the Times staff came to see Kingsley & the result was the paragraph which appeared in the political column next day. Meanwhile I sent an indignant letter to Davidson who at once caused a searching enquiry to be made. An abject apology with promises of better behaviour in future disarmed my wrath: the young man who was responsible offered his resignation but was allowed to get off with a caution in view of his long service. The chairman of the L.M.R.S. in the meantime wrote to the Times to defend himself denying that he was opposing me and explaining away the memo quoting from an *edited* & *abridged* copy. Here he must have been let down by his people. I had a copy of the original & so had the Times. So the L.M.R.S. received an ultimatum from the Times giving them a few hours in which to withdraw the letter, failing which it wd be published with the Times own comments & quotations from the original document. Instant withdrawal and grovelling apologies followed & I think there will be no more trouble from the C.O. or the L.M.R.S.!

Robinson has been in the depths of gloom all the week because the P.M. told K. Wood last Friday that I didn't at all realise the hostility that my proposals were exciting. But I, on the other hand, am well satisfied with the way things are

---

[30] Gerald Hume Saverie Pinsent (1888–1976). Entered Treasury 1911; Assistant Secretary, Treasury 1931; Financial Adviser, British Embassy in Berlin 1932–39 and Washington 1939–41; British Food Mission, Ottawa 1942–43; Principal Assistant Secretary, Board of Trade 1943 and Treasury 1944; Comptroller-General, National Debt Office 1946–51.

going. The agricultural committee have set up their sub. and are going quite seriously into alternatives which on the whole are in the direction I want. I should chuckle if the plan came off. I did it once over R. & V. & once over Housing. It seems almost too much to expect to pull it off a third time.

We had our discussion on T.U. at a special Cabinet on Tuesday. I did not see the passage in the M[orning] P[ost] to which you refer. Did it mention my name? I have not seen any allusion anywhere even to my proposals much less to my association with them.

As a matter of fact if the M.P. says they were turned down they were quite wrong for amidst much difference of opinion the Cabinet was nearly unanimous in their favour. It is true the strongest dissentient was the M. of Labour but I have seen him since and suggested a modification which might meet his difficulty & his people are working on it now. I feel almost certain that when the Bill appears my proposals will prove the feature of chief interest!

We came down here yesterday afternoon in order that I might address the [BCUA] Central Council in the evening. There is a tremendous lot of activity going on here under Edwards and though the 2 neighbouring "byes" and the municipal elections have rather discouraged some of our people I think they will react all right when the time comes. Ladywood in particular is much more cheerful than it was and Geoffrey Lloyd is getting very well liked.

There were no reporters present last night so I was able to talk "confidentially" to a large audience of workers. I just took 8 points (1) The Labour allegation that a general election was imminent, (2) China (3) Russia (4) Imp. Confce & Preference (5) Safeguarding of Industries (6) Chester-le-Street & Poor Law (7) Rent Restriction (8) Slum improvement. Whether because it came last I dont know, but the Slum question seemed to excite the greatest interest and I think my proposals should be popular judging from the trend of the discussion that followed my speech last night.

The garden is absolutely heavenly in the sun this morning ...

26 March 1927
Westbourne

My dear Ida,

...

... We had arranged last night to go to the Ladywood Unionist Ball at the Reservoir, a very popular affair at which there were said to be 1000 present. Its an appalling function. The saxophones pound away unendingly ... The unhappy member is received with loud claps and a very feeble attempt at He's a jolly good fellow. He is then conducted to a table covered with a Union Jack in front of which gather some hundreds of the keener spirits and thence he shouts the funniest things he can think of at the utmost pitch of his voice for ten minutes. The audience are close to him but though the music (?!) stops, there is a constant shuffling of feet and noise of voices which makes it difficult to hear. The speech & the votes of thanks over, the dancing is resumed. Some of the dancers are in fancy dress and presently they are paraded and "judged" by some eminent local authority. The prizes – the vanity bag, the cruet stand and the cigarette holder – are handed out amidst cheers by the Members Wife and then He & She start on a pilgrimage round the room saying a "few kindly words" to each group. That may take ¾ hr or an hour to get through and then the Member with aching smile-muscles and swelled and weary feet begins to pluck up spirits as he approaches the door. But the relentless chairman intervenes. Just a minute or two, he explains, there are a few here you havent seen – and so there is another ¼ hr and then at last the martyrs are released. Ah! Well! We dont have to do it very often nowadays and I must say some of my friends in Ladywood did talk to me very nicely last night. They feel rather badly about our going and yet they know it is the right thing to do. I am told that Lowe is very feeble. May Heaven watch over him & preserve his life for his country a little longer!

...

I have finished Winstons book. It is a pity he did not cut out half his second volume which is loaded with padding in the shape of interminable memoranda addressed by himself to the War Cabinet or the Munitions Council or G.H.Q. I suppose he hadn't enough to fill out the second part and no time to write more. He told A. that he could have profitably spent another two years in revising it. I could revise it profitably in two hours with a pair of scissors.

Now I am undecided whether to begin on George Eliot or Webbs History of the Poor Law. I have got such a terrible week in front of me that I shant have a moment for some time to come. Last night I read Conrad's Shadow Line and escaped from the poisonous world of politics into that mysterious atmosphere of the Eastern Seas where he somehow contrives to hold you breathless for ages under the impending shadow of some unknown but steadily approaching disaster.

The fact is that everything is going wrong this session. The P.M. came to me after last Cabinet to say that he hated to disagree with me more than with any of his colleagues. I believe that to be true but the maddening thing is that if he would only set his mind to the problems & grapple with them in time we need never disagree at all. But he puts off the decision and avoids discussion for fear of disagreement until the last moment with the result that others have gone too far to stop without a painful jar.

As for Poor Law the difficulties seem to mount and multiply every day. Winston has declared his desire to drop the block grants altogether. Kingsley is as loyal as can be and is helping all he can, but Robinson tells me that privately he does not deny that he would be glad to drop the whole thing and Robinson himself more than hints his own feelings of despair and his advice to get out while the ship is still afloat. Sometimes I almost despair myself, but I cannot bring myself to give in as long as any possibility of success remains. I had a terrible conference on Thursday evening, but on Friday morning I had got some new ideas and started Robinson off to think them over during the week end while I composed a suitable letter to Winston – half cajolery and half threats. Its rather a lonely struggle but I'm very far from being dead yet.

Forber[31] is still struggling with the complexities of slum compensation. I have had a preliminary talk with him and made some more suggestions and he has promised me something like a skeleton of the scheme before Easter. I keep on wondering why no one else has thought of it; it seems so good to me.

3 April 1927
37 Eaton Square, SW1

My dear Hilda,

... I agree with your general criticisms about C.C. and only add that too often I find the officials of an inferior type. In the case of the Clerks they are often appointed because they have claims to be Clerk of the Peace. If the two offices were separated it would certainly lead to an improvement in quality. I have no doubt that the C.C. will get better as time goes on and I think I can stimulate the process by putting more responsibility upon them but vita brevis est and one has to resign oneself to the thought that the good we do lives after us.

...

Thank you for sending the cutting from the M.P. which however we had seen as it is one of the papers we take. I think it must have been written by their Lobby correspondent because R. McNeill told me he had spoken to him about the speech. He R.M. had refused to pass on to me what Emery,[32] the correspondent, said, as he wanted him to tell me himself; I did go in search of him but he wasn't about. A number of our people were very complimentary about the speech, they like to see the Opposition baited sometimes. S.B. cant do it, and they complain that Winston is so amusing that there is no bite in his chaff. So Hogg and I are left as the only ones who really annoy the Socialists and of the two I believe they hate me most. I fancy its because of my nasty sarcastic way. Very few people can stand sarcasm; the Socialists so far lose control that they have taken to hissing me. No wonder people say its like old times!

Its been a terrible week of speechmaking for me. ...I feel quite fresh this morning but I sweated blood & tears to make those speeches and I shall have to do it again this week when I have four more. Two of them come on the same day, to the Midland Union and the Edgbaston Un. Assn which is very trying as of course they have got to be different.

---

[31] Edward Rodolph Forber (1878–1960). Deputy Secretary, Ministry of Health 1925–30; Chairman, Board of Customs and Excise 1930–34; Board of Inland Revenue 1934–38. Knighted 1924.

[32] Robert George Emery (1860–1940). Lobby correspondent, *Morning Post* 1899–1932; member, Press Gallery 1932–37.

I had a splendid meeting at Darlington in a large theatre which was absolutely packed from top to bottom. The audience was most enthusiastic & they were right for I made them a very good speech over which I had taken no end of trouble. Col. Headlam[33] who is the latest recruit to the Govt having been appointed to take Davidson's place, in seconding a vote of thanks told the audience that he had often heard Father speak (he was for many years a Clerk in the House of Lords) and that there was only one man in the H. of C. today who could come up to him or even approach him. When I got up, he said, the party knew that the case would be put as well as it was possible to put it. Of course on such an occasion a man who is proposing a vote of thanks naturally lets himself go a bit; still, I confess to being pleased when comparisons so flattering can be made at all.

I have been so busy that I have made very little progress this week in Departmental work. Robinson told me of more difficulties about my new ideas for Poor Law but I think there is no doubt that we can evolve a workable scheme. The trouble is that Winston, I can see, is going to make difficulties. Like the P.M. he is unable to understand the working of the great system – he frankly says so – and he is alarmed lest we should make ourselves unpopular on the ground of excessive expenditure. I explain that what I want is not any more expenditure but some rearrangement of the present expenditure as between local and national resources and that he will have anyway to find something for this purpose. But I can't nail him down because I have not yet got a definite proposal to put before him. I am rather afraid that when I have he will be immersed in the Budget and I shant have a chance of any serious conversation.

As to slums I wont enter on an explanation of the new idea yet … My department weighed in with a long memorandum on it on Friday just as I was going away. I haven't read it yet but I looked at the conclusions and got the impression that while seeing many difficulties they thought a workable plan could be devised on the general lines I laid down. Meanwhile I have tried the idea of "reconditioning" on the public in one or two speeches & found it went down very well but I havent yet entered into details of compensation and management which are the two crucial points.

…

---

[33] Cuthbert Morley Headlam (1876–1964). Clerk of House of Lords 1897–1924. Conservative MP for Barnard Castle 1924–29, 1931–35 and Newcastle North 1940–51. Parliamentary Secretary to Admiralty 1926–29, to Pensions 1931–32 and Transport 1932–34. Chairman, NUCUA Northern Area 1937–46. Created Bart 1935.

9 April 1927
Westbourne

My dear Ida,

...

The T.U. Bill has had a very good reception from our party in the House who find it much stronger than they had expected. The Labour Party of course are raging but then they said they were going to do that before they knew what was in it and I have not yet seen any reasoned criticism from them only violent abuse. But it remains to be seen how it affects the moderate or non party trade unionist. I wish I had been allowed to put in my scheme!

So far negotiations on Poor Law are going on very satisfactorily that is to say that the Agricultural Members are being gently shepherded into the fold I have prepared for them while under the impression that *they* are shepherding *me* there. Both Kingsley & Robinson have worked the oracle very well while I have remained so far in the background. At the moment I am more afraid of trouble with Winston who has taken alarm at the Economy cry of the Daily Mail and the old grousers who take it up and echo it. But it is no use to worry over fences two fields ahead; the thing is to get over the one in front. I am not sure whether I shall see the Committee before Easter or wait till after the holidays.

...

30 April 1927
Westbourne

My dear Hilda,

...

Annie ... found you both so sympathetic in her troubles that she was a good deal comforted and full of resolutions to put her obsessions aside. But I could see that the strain was still there and she complains very much about not sleeping. As a matter of fact I cant make out that she wakes any earlier than I do & she certainly goes to sleep sooner, but that's where the psychological element comes in. When she wakes at 6 or 6.30 and doesn't go to sleep again she feels sure that she must be exhausted and accordingly she is exhausted and overstrained. I believe the visit to Cornwall will probably restore her vitality for a time but I am afraid it will only be for a time and that June and July will be a trial to her. She told me of your generous offer to you [sic] and though she refused it we do both of us appreciate very deeply your sympathy and anxiety to help. When I go back I shall enquire what I can hire a car for but I am afraid prices are very stiff.

I expect poor Frank was rather miserable last night but probably by today the holidays will already have receded into the background and I believe he will very soon find himself at home in his new surroundings [at Winchester]. I am sure public school today is very different from what it was in my time and he will have visits & holidays to look forward to so that he will not feel as cut off from his family as I used to do.

...

Nothing very exciting has happened this week but I hear that the Agr. Comees interview with the N.F.U. on Poor Law passed off very well from our point of view, the latter saying that they did not wish in any way to embarrass the Govt but only wanted to know what their proposals were as they were very much interested in them. Meanwhile we are working out the new plan in detail and Robinson now thinks that it looks like a practical scheme. I have also seen Forber about the Slum Improvement scheme and he also thinks it is getting to look more like something that will work.

I took one of the P.M.'s engagements on Wednesday ... The P.M. declares himself much better but his high spirits appear to me distinctly forced and I notice that when he is not conversing he drops again into his tired look. The poor man thought he was just going to listen to the debate on T.U. second reading next week but we all told him that it was essential that he should speak on one of the days. I was afraid I might also be selected but fortunately the choice has fallen on Worthy. Davidson tells me that the C.O. has issued over 2 million leaflets on the subject and that the Bill is having a very good reception in the country.

...

7 May 1927
Westbourne

My dear Ida,

...

We finished up the T.U. debate with an excellent speech from Tom Inskip. Far the best speech from the other side was Snowdens. It was a brilliant piece of debating except for one ungenerous gibe at the P.M. but it was not damaging because his criticism was more smart than convincing. We have started now to make our own amendments and I am impressed once more with the mistake that was made in not allotting the Bill months ago to one minister to take charge of. It was nobody's business to amend the drafting and there was no one to go to with amendments if one had made any. But the moment three or four of us sat down with Hogg we all had suggestions for improvement and every one admitted the obscurity of cl. 1 which I criticised the first time I saw it.

Nothing special has been happening in my Dept & I have had rather an easy week with only one speech. But that is over now. I have got 3 next week, one at Swansea on the T.U. Bill. I shall be interested to see what sort of reception I get there; I shouldn't wonder if we had rather a rowdy meeting!

15 May 1927
Westbourne

My dear Hilda,

...

I hope to goodness Jix isn't going to make a fool of us over his raid.[34] We have not had the slightest intimation at the Cabinet that anything of the kind was in contemplation and the Observer states today that the F.O. was never consulted. That *seems* incredible but you never know. If Austen has really been taken by surprise I imagine he must be furious at having his hand forced for I dont see how we are going to keep diplomatic relations going after this.

Annie returned distinctly better though of course not herself and still liable to be tired out by any exertion. But she is in better spirits since I have decided to get a car for her and I am setting about it at once ... If we can succeed in procuring car, chauffeur, & garage in time we may go up to Scotland in it next August.

After all I had four speeches to make last week not three as I found I had to open the new Research Labs of the M.A.B. on Monday. Of course the speech was a nuisance but I enjoyed being taken round the Lab by the Director & seeing all their marvellous and beautiful instruments. ...

...

On Tuesday I spoke for the Queens Nurses at a drawing room meeting at 10, Downing Street ... I always used to think that a meeting of that kind all composed of Society people was one of the most alarming you could have. But I dont much mind it now.

My Swansea meeting was on Friday. Fortunately my "group" was not on duty on Thursday so I did not have to sit up all night, as I had fully intended to do in spite of the railway journey & speech next day. It would have been quite a good "stunt", but rather a heavy strain. I had a capital meeting of about 2000 people in a theatre very interested and enthusiastic. I thought at the time that they were all our people but when I invited questions I perceived that there were a handful of socialists in the audience and afterwards I was told that nearly half of them were not known to be members of our party which was very satisfactory. On this occasion I took care not to be aggressive or provocative as I really wanted to persuade, and not simply to get away with some party scores. I see J. H. Thomas has been "answering" me but if he is correctly reported he has simply lied – as of course he very often does.

I think in Committee we shall improve the drafting very much but the difficulties that the Committee of the Cabinet have discussed this week have brought

---

[34] Joynson-Hicks authorised a police raid on the Soviet Trade Delegation and the All-Russian Cooperative Society (ARCOS) on 12 May 1927. Although the material seized proved disappointing, the Cabinet broke off diplomatic relations on grounds of 'anti-British espionage and propaganda'.

out clearly the weaknesses to which I drew attention from the beginning, and it is curious how often we have got back nearly to the proposition I wanted & so narrowly missed having. Winston at any rate sees I think clearly the faults of handling although at the time when I was feeling them so much he did nothing to help.

...

29 May 1927
37 Eaton Square, SW1

My dear Hilda,

...

I am writing just before dinner, having returned half an hour ago with Annie from a visit to Sir A. & Lady Weigall[35] in connection with the opening of a new Convalescent Home at Skegness. ...

... I was rather bored with my week end but the rhododendrons and azaleas in the garden were lovely and the little woods which surround the garden were full of nightingales all singing lustily day and night. My speech gave me some trouble to concoct but it was highly successful and the house party was quite enthusiastic about it. They hadn't realised before that I had a sense of humour!

...

I went to the womens Unionist Conference on Thursday morning to speak on a resolution about P.L. Reform. Four ladies spoke, all more or less representing the Guardians point of view and they got a certain amount of support but when I replied the meeting appeared entirely to appreciate my case and if I had had a counter resolution I have no doubt it would have been carried.

The vote of censure debate was not good. Austen was distinctly heavy and Jix made an ass of himself. But it doesn't matter as the papers did not give that impression.

5 June 1927
Donnington Priory, Newbury

My dear Ida,

...

So far as public engagements are concerned this has not been a very heavy week. I had clause 6 of the T.U. Bill in the House on Tuesday, but that did not give me much trouble. On Wednesday I had the Agricultural Committee which *was* rather tiring as one was kept on the stretch, parrying attacks from all sides.

---

[35] William Ernest George Archibald Weigall (1874–1952). Land Agent 1902–10. Unionist MP for Horncastle 1911–20. Governor of South Australia 1920–22. Created Bart 1938.

On Thursday I opened the new offices of the Abbey Road Building Society, partly because I wanted to pay a compliment to Building Societies in general and partly because Sir Josiah Stamp[36] is President and asked me. I do that sort of function quite well, now that I no longer feel nervous in doing it, and the Building Society people seemed to be very pleased. It was followed by a lunch. Jimmie Thomas was sitting on the other side of Stamp and he leaned across to say "Neville, the old man's done"! "What old man?" said I, thinking perhaps he meant R. Macdonald. "Why old Asquith" said Thomas & he went on to say he had been to see him and been much shocked by his condition. He has had a stroke and is partially paralysed – it sounded much like Father.

I see you have read your paper and observed how the Minister of Health has been forced to give way to the Agr.1 members who have won a great victory! It du make me laff when I read of their triumph. Yesterday I received a copy of the "Local Government Chronicle" a paper which plays up hard to the Guardians. It too was writing of what had happened as a win for the side it had espoused, though its tone was by no means unfriendly to me and I thought that was significant as showing how public opinion is likely to set. I feel pretty certain that the Guardians themselves will still be hostile & obstructionist but the public will I hope say the Minister has done everything to meet them & really they are quite unreasonable. Anyway the attitude at the moment is that P.L. Reform is certainly coming and I have managed to do a little more preparation on the financial side tho' that has not yet reached the crucial stage.

...

[Postscript] A. is writing about Orpen whom she has persuaded to paint me at 2/3 his ordinary price!

19 June 1927
Chevening, Sevenoaks, Kent

My dear Ida,

...

I entirely agree with your idea of getting the willing horses to work at the Rural Workers Housing as quickly as possible. I am much concerned at the deliberation with which the L.A.'s are going to work and I can see that some of them will only just begin to understand what can be done when the Act is about to expire. The sight of cottages actually done under its provisions would be the

---

[36] Josiah Charles Stamp (1880–1941). Economist and statistician. Entered Inland Revenue 1896 and Board of Trade 1898; resigned from Civil Service 1919. Secretary and Director, Nobel Industries 1919–26; British Representative on Reparations Committees of 1924 (Dawes) and 1929 (Young). Member, Coal Industry Dispute Enquiry 1925; Director, ICI 1927–28. Joint Secretary, Royal Statistical Society 1920–30 and President 1930–32. Knighted 1920. Created Baron Stamp 1930.

best & most effective stimulus to the others and I am most anxious to see a start made. I have now got schemes or proposals for schemes from about 50 L.A.'s but so far none has actually got to work.

...

Certainly the Opposition dont at all like the Audit Bill but there is so little kick in them that the second reading debate was a very dull & deadly affair 99% of their speeches being quite irrelevant. More and more do I feel an utter contempt for their lamentable *stupidity*, they cannot see the futility of their own arguments, and to see them wisely wagging their heads and observing that "its a funny thing that all these bills are only aimed at places where there is a Labour majority" really makes me tired. "These two, this Audit Bill and the Guardians Default Bill." remarked Mr Robert Richardson,[37] gesticulating so furiously as seriously to alarm a colleague who in an empty desert happened to be sitting just below him, "I put 'em both in the same corollary." Stanley begged me to remember that I was addressing a meeting of gentlemen. I always gave him the impression, he said, when I spoke in the H. of C. that I looked on the Labour Party as dirt. The fact is that intellectually, with a few exceptions, they *are* dirt.

Anyway the strength of their objections gives me good hope that my new bill will prove a real deterrent. Greenwood declared that as fast as one hero fell another would take his place, but I dont fink! It would be nice to disqualify whole coveys like that but they haven't got the alternatives nor do they desire to be made bankrupt. I fancy it will bust Poplar effectively.

...

27 June 1927
37 Eaton Square, SW1

My dear Hilda,

...

I am much interested to hear that you get compliments on the clearness of your exposition. That is what I am always told but I put most of it down to the fact that I take a lot of trouble and I believe that may also account for your success. I am sure you will find that doing without notes is a tremendous help; it has made a great difference to me in freeing my style and giving me more confidence.

... We have as you will have seen got ourselves committed on H. of L. Reform quite unnecessarily and indeed unexpectedly. The question arose out of Fitzlan's motion and of course we had to decide what our course was to be during the debate but I understood that while indicating the Govts views as to

---

[37] Robert Richardson (1862–1943). Durham miner 1871–1918 and member, Durham County Council 1901–25. Labour MP for Houghton-le-Spring 1918–31. Parliamentary Charity Commissioner 1924 and 1929–31.

how reform should proceed we were rather going to see what the Lords thought about it before we came to any final or definite decision ourselves. But Salisbury who was to have stated our case wasn't there (I think he wasn't well) and Cave put it more definitely than he had intended. And Birkenhead capped it by declaring positively that we were going to carry our scheme through in this Parliament. What with Jix and F.E. we never seem able to stick to what we have ourselves laid down and we are in a nice mess now with our own party in the House who don't like the proposals and are furious at being tied to them without having been consulted beforehand.

Our remarkable son reports that he is top of his form this week! … Annie has gone to bed & wont see the rest of this letter so I can say that the prospect of a car has made a wonderful change in her outlook and she has regained much of her old interest in life though not all her old vitality & power of endurance. She is much excited tonight over a chauffeur whom she has discovered & who appears to possess all the virtues possible.

I had a very interesting weekend with Monty Barlow who has many good qualities under a slightly soapy manner …

2 July 1927
Westbourne

My dear Ida,

This has been what Veale calls a "thick" week and I have been up very late most nights preparing speeches and reading papers. The Opposition are making things hot in Committee on the Audit Bill and the proceedings there have been by no means agreeable.[38] But I hope the blow up on Thursday when the pandemonium was so complete that members rushed in from the lobby to see what was going on may perhaps clear the air. I took advantage of it to make an appeal for more sportsmanlike and more dignified behaviour which was well received and it is just on the cards that we may succeed in making an arrangement. If we could do that we should come at once to an idyllic atmosphere of friendliness and reason, but of course Lansbury will try and block it. Where reason reigns he has no place; he only becomes conspicuous when it is a case of who can shout the loudest or show the most insolence. When you add to a Committee of this kind two days estimates, a couple of deputations an "address" a broadcast and a political demonstration in addition to Cabinet and departmental work things do get a bit thick.

Many thanks for your congratulations on my Estimates speech. I had many compliments on it which gratified me for I had been under the impression that it

[38] On 28–29 June 1927 Lansbury continually interrupted the Committee Stage and was particularly vociferous and abusive when a closure motion was moved.

would be dull. I am sure that what saved it from dulness was the fact that I had no notes, and as there were a good many figures in connection with housing pensions & health statistics members were rather astonished. Certainly I dont remember any occasion when criticism was so entirely absent from a discussion on health estimates. But different people are interested in different subjects. This morning I had a letter from a man, evidently well educated, full of the most violent abuse and informing me that the writer would "personally fell to the earth" anyone who presumed to enter his house for the purpose of vaccinating any member of his household!

On Thursday I lunched with Victor Cazalet[39] to meet Emil Ludwig.[40] It was a very interesting occasion. Cazalet had enquired whether I had any objection to Ramsay Macdonald [sic] being of the party and as I had none he was there, looking as yellow as a guinea. He had been thrilled by the sight of the eclipse which he had seen from the Astronomer Royal's box. It was one of the most impressive & moving sights he had ever seen he said and some one else told me that many of those present fell on their knees. Ludwig is a younger man than I had expected, about 40 perhaps, clean shaven & dark with black heavily lidded eyes and pince nez. He speaks English with some difficulty but after Ramsay left he seemed more at his ease and we had an interesting conversation about Germany & the Kaiser,[41] Hindenburg[42] who he said had greatly lost caste because he had deserted the Kaiser while the Kaiser had lost caste because he married so soon after his wife's death, and England & the English. It was fortunate Ludwig said that though there were some 20 Hohenzollerns living none of them had either courage or intelligence.

...

We have not decided to withdraw the H/L proposals but I think S.B. will have to water down F.E.'s statement so as to leave matters as indefinite as possible till the autumn when popular opinion will probably have crystallised more than it has yet done. S.B. asked me to dine alone with him on Thursday & we had a long & very interesting conversation. He is certainly much better.

---

[39] Victor Alexander Cazalet (1896–1943). Captain Household Cavalry serving later on Staff of Supreme War Council and Staff in Siberia 1919. Conservative MP for Chippenham 1924–43. Private Secretary to Cunliffe-Lister 1922–23 and his PPS 1924–27; PPS to J.H. Thomas 1931. Liason Officer with Polish Forces 1940–43. Killed in an air crash while travelling with General Sikorski.

[40] Emil Ludwig (1861–1948). German novelist, playwright and biographer of Goethe, Napoleon, Wilhelm II, Bismarck, Christ and Lincoln.

[41] Kaiser Wilhelm II (1859–1941). German Emperor and King of Prussia 1888–1918 when he abdicated and fled to settle at Doorn in the Netherlands.

[42] Field Marshal Paul von Hindenburg (1847–1934). German C-in-C, 1916–19; elected President of German Reich 1925–34.

9 July 1927
Westbourne

My dear Hilda,

...

Yes, it has been a gruelling week again though the Labour Party postponed a motion on West Ham till next week and thereby saved me from one late night. ...

...

We lunched at Guildhall and I dined at the F.O. in honour of Fuad[43] who seems to have enjoyed himself enormously in London. He is rather short and very portly but young enough to make it difficult to believe that Ismail[44] was his father. I suppose people have forgotten that rascally old spendthrift but it amuses me to see Sarwat[45] speaking of him as the Grand Khedive, as though he had been a great man instead of a selfish and worthless old scoundrel who brought his country into bankruptcy and disaster.

A.J.B. was at the dinner. He had been reading Ludwig's Napoleon and was also critical on the ground that much of it appeared to be purely imaginative. My impression in talking to Ludwig was that he did not expect a return to monarchy in Germany in any case. Of course he does not want it himself but I think he genuinely believed that therein he was with the majority.

...

Last night I addressed the College of Nursing; this afternoon I have been to a garden party (with a few words) given by the Councillor for one of the Edgbaston wards. Lady Low [sic] was there and said Sir Francis was rapidly failing adding quaintly that she must do her best to keep him going as it would be so awkward if there were a bye-election. I explained that in that case I could not stand as that would mean two bye-elections so she said she must certainly do her best to look carefully after her husband!

...

16 July 1927
Sandon Hall, Stafford

My dear Hilda,

...

I had another heavy week with so many speeches that I began to feel the strain and found my brain flagging a bit but I have got through the worst now. ...

---

[43] Ahmed Fuad (1868–1936). Youngest son of Ismail Pasha; succeeded as Khedive of Egypt 1917; assumed title of King Fuad I when British protectorate ended in 1922.

[44] Ismail Pasha (1830–95). Grandson of Mehemet Ali and Khedive of Egypt from 1867 until deposed by Sultan in 1879.

[45] Abd al Khaleh Sarwat Pasha (1873–1928). Egyptian statesman. Governor Assiat Province 1907; Minister of Justice 1915; Minister of Interior 1921; Foreign Minister 1922, 1926–27; Prime Minister 1922, 1927–28.

On Tuesday I began the day with the Audit Bill and as we had a good majority I used the closure freely [?] and got through clause 3. The Labour party who had got very sick of the Bill thereupon decided to boycott the rest of the Committee so Kingsley was able to finish it next morning.

...

That night was fixed for the debate on West Ham but the Labour Party asked to have it put off till Thursday and I was not sorry.

On Wednesday we had a big lunch party to meet the Lloyds and in the evening I dined at Trinity House. I always like their dinners because they have no speeches.

On Thursday I had a long interview with George Lloyd who was very anxious to put me wise about Egypt. He thinks another crisis is bound to arise there before long and wants to get the Cabinet to approve his policy there. I dont think he has been able to thrash it all out with Austen yet, but he evidently fears the F.O. where he says there is no one who understands Egypt or cares sufficiently about it. I must say that my sympathies are with Lloyd for it is tragic to hear of the decay of all the good work we have done there & of broken hearted officials in despair over the future of the country. But it may be that other considerations make it difficult to take a firm line and face such risks as may be involved.

The West Ham debate came on so late that it was not well reported but I believe my speech was considered successful. Four people namely Winston, Hogg, Sam Hoare & Philip Sassoon all used the same word when congratulating me upon it. They said it was "devastating". It certainly made the Socialists very angry.

... This morning I went round with Harrowby to see some of the small holdings he has established on his estate & talked with the small holders who struck me as being a very good class. Some of them began as labourers & have now fair sized farms but they all complain of low prices and foreign competition. A little safeguarding duty would make all the difference to them!

24 July 1927
37 Eaton Square, SW1

My dear Hilda,

I am beginning this letter on Sunday morning with the delicious consciousness that I have no more speeches to make before October. It seems almost incredible but so it is. ...

I really only had two last week ... I have told my Secretary that in my opinion I have rather overdone the speaking on Departmental matters this year. Of course people do appreciate having the Minister open their hospitals & sanatoria & nursing homes and laboratories, but there are so many of them that it is not worth doing unless the Institution is exceptionally large & important or you get a good report in the Press. But I think the Press has reached saturation point in this matter, and it is disappointing when you have spent time in carefully selecting phrases on matters like post graduate medical education or the place of voluntary hospitals in the health service of the future to find that they have been wasted on a few dozen well meaning elderly ladies & gentlemen. So I am going to draw in my horns a bit next year and it will be the more necessary if, as I hope, it turns out to be a busy year in the House.

...

We have had a lot of Cabinets this week and some hectic times. One of my colleagues threatened resignation three others independently besought me to intervene and find some way out.[46] Eventually I did so, – successfully – and the incident ended happily, but the next day there was more trouble & another colleague took "a grave view" of the Cabinets decision. However I believe everything will be amicably arranged on Monday.

We went to see the Amerys off on Friday & the P.M. yesterday morning. The latter seemed in good spirits and with the rest on board I think he should get through his rather heavy programme in Canada.

I shall finish up the Session I fear without any assurance as to the prospects of P.L. reform. I have squared the Agriculturists all right and have worked out an attractive scheme for housing the old folks in almshouses instead of in the Union building; but I haven't got financial provisions fixed. I have weighed in with a memorandum to Winston which he tells me he proposes to talk over before we separate, but he did not give any indication of his attitude and I fear this means that he is cherishing a mad idea of his own for changing the whole basis of rating in some way which is to benefit industry but the method of which he has only the haziest ideas about.

Slums, by dint of perpetual "push and go", continue sporadically to progress. The Department steadily brings up new snags, each more insuperable than the last, and I patiently devise a way round or over. Gradually the scheme is being ground down to something that looks like working and I hope to be able to begin private conversations with Town Clerks about it in the autumn.

...

30 July 1927
37 Eaton Square, SW1

My dear Ida,

...

After all I found I had one more speech to make late on Thursday, when the Labour Party moved to annul my order prolonging the term of office of the

---

[46] Lord Robert Cecil threatened resignation over policy towards the Three Power Naval Disarmament Conference at Geneva and finally resigned on 30 August 1927.

Chester le Street Guardians. But it was rather a halfhearted affair and I had no difficulty in demonstrating their futility amid noisy interruptions from George Lansbury and surly growls from David Kirkwood.

...

We have had a lot of Cabinet meetings over Geneva which looks now like breaking down. I trust that it will be apparent to the world that the reason for the failure is entirely due to the obstinate insistence by the Americans on conditions which would inevitably have led to increase & not decrease of armaments. But they know how to work their own Press; they are entirely devoid of scruples and I doubt if they will allow our case ever to be squarely put in the U.S.A. where they have succeeded in stirring up a bitter anti-British feeling. It is difficult to keep one's temper with them.

...

I suppose the House has risen earlier than it has done for many years; yet every one seems to be very tired. Annie is near the end of her tether but is sustained by the car. I am extremely well though a little jaded. ...

...

5 August 1927
Westbourne

My dear Hilda,

...

Somehow our visit [to Peper Harow] wasn't a success. There was a large party and it constantly changed, new faces suddenly appearing and old ones disappearing without any warning whatever. The same thing happens at Cliveden, but we generally rather like it there. I find it difficult to say what was wrong. Midleton[47] has got very deaf & rather a bore, but one doesn't see much of him. Lady M. has a good deal of charm and she certainly takes a lot of trouble. Davis[48] (the ex-American Ambassador & Coolidge's[49] opponent at the last election) I had just met before, but not to know him. I didn't like his wife but I decidedly took to him. He is a fisherman and an admirer of Conrad.

---

[47] (William) St John Brodrick (1856–1942). Conservative MP for Surrey West 1880–85 and Guildford 1885–1906. Financial Secretary, War Office 1895–98; Under-Secretary, Foreign Office 1898–1900; Secretary for War 1900–3; Secretary for India 1903–5. Succeeded as 9th Viscount Midleton 1907 and Earl 1920. Declined Irish Viceroyalty 1918.

[48] Norman Davis (1878–1944). American banker and diplomat. Financial adviser to Wilson at Paris Peace Conference 1919; Assistant Secretary to Treasury 1919–20; Under-Secretary of State 1920–21; US delegate to Geneva Economic Conference 1927; to Disarmament Conference 1932–33; to London Naval Conference 1935; to Nine Power Brussels Conference 1937. According to Vansittart, 'the most wearisome' of the 'American Amateurs'.

[49] Calvin Coolidge (1872–1933). Lawyer. Governor of Massachusetts 1919–20; Vice-President of the United States 1921–23; President, 1923–29.

Also he has a sense of humour. I dont know whether you have heard this story before (I had, but its a good one). Coolidge went to church. On his return a friend asked "What did the parson preach about this morning?". Coolidge. "Sin". Friend. "Sin, eh? And what 'dee gotta say bout sin?". Coolidge "He's against it".

By the way I read that Coolidge comes from Vermont where they speak a dialect, and in the Vermont dialect "I do not choose" is the most emphatic form of negative, meaning "I do not intend".

The most conspicuous guest at the Midletons was my Lord Reading, because he talks all the time. Moreover he talks as if he were addressing a public meeting so that it is not very easy for anyone else to talk. There is no doubt that he is a very unusual and interesting man. All the same I do not feel anything in me leaning out to him. Lady Ilchester was there … I thought I liked her before and indeed I believe I do really, but this time she seemed to be interested only in racing and bridge which she played for stakes that I thought high. You almost have to play at these parties if you are to avoid talking continuously from about 9 p.m. to 11.30 or so. Reading, who played in the day as well as at night, went off with £25! I contented myself with three guineas which I won from my esteemed colleague, the Lord Balfour. He was wonderful with his marvellous complexion and his vitality and alertness. In fact he was as witty, as cheerful, as remote from the world and as utterly heartless as ever. …

We left on Tuesday and I came on here by train leaving Annie to follow by car. I had hardly settled myself comfortably in a chair in the garden when the telephone bell rang and I was summoned to a Cabinet next morning. So I had to breakfast early & start off by the 9a.m. expecting to be back at 4. Instead of that we were kept sitting till 5 and after and I only got home to a late dinner with the knowledge that I should have to repeat the journey next morning. … When I got to the F.O. I learned that the Americans had bust the Conference and we might have spared ourselves all the discussion and all the friction of the day before. For the proceedings had been stormy and Winston had been in the worst possible mood: childishly petulant, truculent, impatient & offensive. When he is like that "team work" becomes – well – very difficult. And all for nothing!

…

I enclose a leaderette from the Birm. Post which you can destroy. The previous day it had a most complimentary paragraph from its London Corr. attributing the efficiency of my Department to the "consummate mastery" of the Minister & declaring that I had further increased my reputation in the House as a debater in the first rank. It was perhaps overcoloured but that is proper for the local paper!

13 August 1927
Cairnton, Banchory N.B.

My dear Ida,

...

You will wonder why I am writing from here. Because that particularly wicked cold that I wrote about to Hilda is Flu and it wont go away. Moreover the gout has jumped in, seeing me on the floor, and I cant get a boot on. ... If I could walk, I could fish, and I shouldn't so much mind the flue. If I could smoke I shouldn't so much mind the gout. But I am hit on all sides. What a holiday!

...

21 August 1927
Cairnton

My dear Hilda,

... Alas! Loubcroy has finally gone phut. It is easy to be wise after the event and looking back I can see that I have done every mortal thing that I shouldn't. ... I got involved in such a paroxysm of pain that I had to go straight to bed & have remained there ever since.

...

25 September 1927
Westbourne

My dear Ida,

...

I am glad to hear that you are really getting to business at last on the Rural Housing Act. At this time of year things always move desperately slowly and too often end in the excuse that its "now too late to do anything this year". But I have confidence that you will keep their noses to the grindstone in your Council, and as soon as I go back I shall start nagging again from my end. I noted that in the Times and elsewhere a good deal is being said about slums. The Times definitely divided my housing programme into three parts new houses to over-come shortage, rural houses and slums. I had done two, it said, and now it remained to do the third. And the Liberals together with some Unionists who can't see how the problem is to be tackled successfully are coming on a deputa-tion to the P.M. to ask for a Royal Commission. But, as I have a policy and know what I am aiming it [sic], I see no necessity for hanging everything up while a R.C. plods on its weary way.

...

Since we have been back here the rain has made it almost impossible to do anything. It really is spiteful of the weather to treat the harvest like this when agriculture is thoroughly depressed and it is well known that all its misfortunes are being put down to the Government. I hear (from the Times) that the farmers are turning agin us, because they say we have done nothing to help them and favouring Labour because it promises them stabilisation of prices. How is one to deal with people so stupid and ignorant.

…

I have had our Chief Agent up and received from him a satisfactory account of the Birmingham Unionist Organisation. The Socialists have rather got their tails down and we are hopeful of a successful stand against them at the municipal elections when we are defending 22 seats and attacking 8. I am glad to say that the system of divisional finance which I initiated some years ago is now really beginning to function and a number of divisions are raising £400 and £500 a year in addition to what we collect for the central fund.

…

2 October 1927
Westbourne

My dear Hilda,

I begin my reply to your letter while I am waiting for Hackney to come & see how A. is getting on. Her masseuse reports her as better in spite of some meetings this week … But it is very fortunate that by cutting the Cardiff Conference A. can get a whole week without engagements and she has, I think very wisely, decided to remain here alone even sending the car away so that she can give herself up to the cure. I am hopeful of beneficial results to her general mental condition and especially to her sleeping powers which dont seem to have been properly restored by the holiday in Scotland. She comments on your observations about her engagements that she has refused many more this year than last and I think that is true. But of course she is so much in demand that it still leaves a good many.

…

I have had quite a busy week too, though only the latter part has been concerned with public work. On Sunday I went a long walk with Platten. …

Incidentally, I got from Platten some interesting information about the negotiations between Elliotts & Imperial Chemical Industries which have been going on for some time. They seem likely to have a successful issue and if so I shall, apart from some sentimental regrets, be glad. So long as I am not myself connected with Elliotts management they seem able to hold their own but they dont seem to go ahead, and if the amalgamation takes place I shall be able readily to reduce my holding which I feel in my present circumstances to be too big.

…

I went to town on Friday to attend a Cabinet Committee on policy when we selected a number of subjects of "research" and set up Sub. Committees to investigate them. I shall be chairman of the Social Reform Sub. but what to reform, once Poor Law & Slums are done, I confess beats me! Personally, I think social reform might well take a little rest while we mend our material condition. I missed Stanley who had just gone to Chequers but met "David" (party chairman) who tells me in the strictest confidence that in about six weeks time the Liberal party will split. It will begin with a long letter from Rosebery[50] I suppose about Ll.G.'s fund & then Grey, Donald McLean [sic], Runciman, and Pringle are going to start a campaign to chuck Ll.G. out! Well! well! he *thoroughly* deserves it all, but God is not always so ready to deal out justice in this world.

...

8 October 1927
Westbourne

My dear Ida,

...

I only had two speeches last week but requests rain in ...

I had lunch with the P.M. on Wednesday and we had a long talk over possible changes among ministers, personalities and politics generally. He was in high spirits; his Canadian visit has, as I expected, restored his self-confidence and tone and he talked merrily and irreverently of our "two banditti", meaning F.E. & Winston. From another source I hear (this is very private) that in a few weeks time another Liberal campaign against Ll.G. will begin, opening with a tremendous letter on the famous fund from Rosebery. The little man is now evidently bidding hard for a Lib-Lab coalition and it looks as if the Labour fish were beginning to bite. But I guess he is going to have lots of trouble.

...

... I shall come down again next week and go from here to Manchester where I begin my official tour on the 17th. After that I have a long succession of public engagements to which I look forward with dread and loathing!

16 October 1927
Westbourne

My dear Hilda,

... I will begin by answering your question about the milk. The farmers of course all want protection but they try and get it by the backstairs, that is they pretend to great solicitude about the public health & express their anxiety lest this foreign imported milk should be dirty & tuberculous.

---

[50] Archibald Philip Primrose (1847–1929). Liberal statesman. Lord Privy Seal 1885; Foreign Secretary 1886 and 1892–94; Prime Minister 1894–95. Succeeded as 5th Earl of Rosebery 1868.

They have no evidence to produce. The samples taken over here have not disclosed anything wrong, but last summer I sent a deputation to Holland to investigate the conditions there. About 75% to 80% of imported milk comes from Holland and 20% to 15% from Denmark. The depn. consisted of one man from the M/Health, one from the Bd of Agriculture and one member of the N.F.U. I kept the thing dark so that the Dutch farmers should not have warning.

I have now got the report which is unanimous and says after describing the investigation that the Dutch regulations, though differing slightly from ours are quite as strict & that there is nothing in their methods which would justify any anxiety as the effect of their products on health. The milk is all pasteurised whether merely skimmed and condensed or dried.

This report, which is to be followed by one on Denmark, will I think knock out the health argument which is really a dishonest one. I think the farmer ought to have protection, but let it be frankly understood that it is protection against competition & not solicitude for the health of the community that he is concerned with.

…

I had to go to the B.M.A. dinner this week with a bad cold & headache but survived it. I was going out next day to dine with Elibank but I put him off and as Austen said he was alone … I invited him to come & spend the evening with me. I thought he seemed remarkably well and politically speaking he is very happy.

I suppose you will have seen my interview about hospitals. Of course there was nothing new in what I said at the B.M.A. but as I found the Press was ready to take something I thought it would be a good thing to feed it with Poor Law propaganda.

…

22 October 1927
Westbourne

My dear Ida,

…

On the whole I felt that the tour was a great success. The people were very pleased everywhere and the 8 speeches I made appeared to give general satisfaction. Moreover I acquired some useful information not so much on specific problems but in getting a general conspectus of the situation and a clearer idea of how the facts stand in the places I visited. In Manchester we stayed with the Lord Mayor … Luncheons dinners and receptions came one after another and I had plenty of opportunity of meeting and talking with the principal people. But I am sorry to say that I was confirmed in the impression that the quality of the modern Town Councillors is not improving. The Lord Mayor himself though a good fellow was quite undistinguished and incapable of guiding the policy of a big town and I did not come across a single representative who really stood out as a man of large & statesmanlike views. The explanation given me there as elsewhere was that the educated administrator and business man will not stand up to be heckled and insulted on the platform and though one may condemn that attitude as cowardly and unpatriotic the facts have to be faced. I see Lord Grey has been defending democracy in his address to the Midland Institute here but I am afraid he is too much out of touch with local government to be even aware of the modern trend. It hasn't broken down yet but it seems to me to be wilting and I cannot help attributing it to the rise of the Labour party in local politics. They have little sense of responsibility and little constructive ability and it may be that in time, though not in my time, local government by democracy will have to give way to the management of affairs by a bureaucracy.

I spent a day, but not a night, in Blackburn a typical example of a small county borough, where you find really a rather better state of things. There, there still are a few people who have been accustomed to take the lead & who command general respect. It is curious that in this town where Labour is said to be the strongest party and is only kept out of the Parliamentary representation by a coalition between the other two parties, there is only a small minority of Labour men on the Council. Probably that will change. The policy of the Socialists is definitely to capture local Government in the towns and as soon as they begin to be really aggressive I expect the better men will clear out. Meanwhile they seem to be running the town well and in several respects, though not all, they compare favourably with Manchester ...

In Ormskirk I was in a rural district. With the help of the Agricultural subsidy they have built some very nice cottages, unusually large in size, nearly 950 sq. ft. which without any cost to the rates they let out at 6/3 & 7/3 inclusive. This would be too high for your people but there the labourers seem to average about 40/- a week and I was astonished to see the style of the carpets furniture bedspreads and even mantelpiece ornaments belonging to the tenants. In one I saw a particularly fine veneered mahogany chest of drawers but I was told it was probably an heirloom.

While there I addressed a Conference of the N.W.R.D.C. Association. Of course they were all Guardians so I took the opportunity of talking about Poor Law Reform. Blundell,[51] who is the M.P. for the division & was my host at Ormskirk is also the President of this Association and he declared that in all probability they had never heard any description or justification of my proposals before, but only the criticisms of the Guardians organisations. It is difficult to be certain of the effect of my speech, but they listened with the greatest attention and apparently with approval and Blundell at any rate thought that I had con-

---

[51] Francis Nicholas Blundell (1880–1936). Landowner and Lancashire County Councillor. Conservative MP for Ormskirk 1922–29. Chairman, Catholic Education Council; Director, National Poultry Scheme 1934–36.

verted them. The Clerk, an intelligent man, observed that he thought that the latest proposals contained nothing which should give any offence.

...

30 October 1927
37 Eaton Square, SW1

My dear Hilda,

I am not altogether surprised that you and Ida have "got the wind up" about my health and I do appreciate your genuine concern though I wish you wouldn't frighten Annie with it! But, honestly, you are exaggerating, unintentionally but grossly.

Three doctors have recently examined me independently – Innes, Morris and Hackney. Each of them has declared that all my organs are exceptionally sound, my blood pressure low, my arteries soft and my joints supple. When Hackney was called in before I went to Manchester he hadn't seen me for a long time. He could hardly be expected to realise my toughness and he doesn't in the least appreciate the difficulty which a public man has in breaking his engagements without overwhelming cause ... But there is no doubt ... that he was over cautious, and the proof of this is what I have accomplished during these two weeks. ... In all I inspected some 30 institutions, besides a number of miscellaneous clinics &c, visited six slum areas and fifteen housing estates, attended two conferences, two receptions, three public luncheons and 1 dinner, and made 15 speeches averaging about half an hour, on various subjects and, though I say it, not lacking in mental vigour. A man who can go through all that and come out at the end of it feeling stronger and fitter than when he began cant have much the matter with him. So that's that!

Our second week's tour was an even greater success than the first. I had anticipated some difficulty in Sheffield where the Labour Party have used the majority which they got at the election last year to make a clean sweep of the Conservative Aldermen and so at once increase their hold on the Council and secure the Chairmenship of all the Committees. But I was told that when asked their views about a visit from the Minister they all expressed a strong wish that I should come and I must say they made rather a favourable impression upon me. I fancy the old lot were very reactionary and obstructive; the present lot are certainly not revolutionary and it did not appear to me that their programme contained anything that might not equally have figured in that of a progressive Conservative party. I have reason to suppose that they were equally pleased with me. Certainly they appreciated the interest I took in their work and the Town Clerk told Robinson that he was delighted with the visit which would make his work far easier in the future.

I really enjoyed my Sheffield visit and this was largely due to the personality of the Lord Mayor. He is a selfmade man who has built up a large business and a considerable fortune but who retains all his simplicity and modesty. His great hobby is the collecting of pictures. I have never seen a house so overcrowded with them. Every square inch of wall is covered, even in passages and bath-rooms. Most of them have been bought at Christies and other salerooms in London and though I cant say the collection is well selected it contains a great many really good pictures and few that would be set down as rubbish. The Lord Mayor is a great traveller – has visited nearly every important town in England on his bicycle and constantly explores the Continent. He is also a regular lay preacher and addresses P.S.A. meetings and, it appeared to me, any similar gathering that gives him an opportunity. In short his is a very interesting charac-ter and after Manchester it was a blessed change.

In Rotherham I came on another type of mayor, a director of some provision dealing firm who looked like a prosperous publican with an immense stomach a loud & confident voice and an almost over abundant stock of humour. Yet he turned out to be an earnest Church worker who at a moments notice is prepared to take "Matins" in the absence of the parson & who spends his spare time in visiting prisons! In Hull again the type was different. Here the Lord Mayor was a short ugly common looking little man resembling a butcher in a small way. As a matter of fact he is an undertaker. He was not prepossessing at first sight, but as I went round with him I perceived that he had a real interest in and a real understanding of the Corporation's work and in his speech at the dinner in the evening he showed not only that he knew what he was talking about but that he was very well able to express himself.

I had been rather depressed about the degradation of local Government in Manchester, but I have come to the conclusion that it is exceptionally bad there and that in all the places I have visited since, there is at present at any rate no cause for alarm. But in my speeches I have generally emphasised the need to subordinate personal considerations to the service of the public.

Two other things specially interested me. One was a scheme at Sheffield under which children suspected of being tubercular (swollen glands & contacts) are withdrawn to a ward (in an infirmary leased from the Guardians by the Corporn) for a period varying from 6 weeks to 4 or 5 months. The idea is not to withdraw them wholly from the infection to which they are already partially immune, but to build up their resisting powers and then turn them loose again. The belief is that with this early boosting they will be able to resist altogether the development of tuberculosis which often occurs about the period of adoles-cence. It has been going now some 9 years which is not long enough for a final judgement but it seems worth watching carefully in the future.

The other thing was the great interest aroused by my recent speeches on Poor Law and voluntary Hosps. The British Med. Journal says my speech at the B.M.A. dinner made a deep impression on all who heard it, which was intensi-fied by the interview in which I elaborated it. Everywhere during this visit I found that doctors and people interested in vol. hospitals were talking about it and I have evidently been unusually successful in making people think. Its all to the good, but I have had a letter from Winston about P.L. which gives me little hope that I shall have his help. As usual, he looks not at the merits but at the electioneering value of any proposal that I put up to him and he seems to want to draw me into some new mad idea which is at present simmering in that volatile and turbulent brain of his ...

5 November 1927
Westbourne

My dear Ida,

Many thanks for your letter. With regard to municipal elections in Birm. Labour gained one seat from the Liberals, one from us in Aston which is outside our central organisation and one from us in Ladywood which I cant account for as the candidate was a good one. He had not been as long before the electors as his opponent which the local people put as the cause of his defeat.

On the whole I think we came through very well as we were defending 22 seats, but I fear Labour has rather a strong hold in the lower parts of the town and Edwards thinks we shall lose two seats there next election. He also reports that the occupants of the new houses are against us, but I have hopes that they brought those views with them and will modify them in time.

...

... I see the Poor Law Officers Journal basing itself on a condensed and therefore misleading report in the Times declares that as a result of my tour I have come to the conclusion that Poor Law reform cant be carried this Parliament and made an announcement to that effect. I shall endeavour to correct that impression but I am having trouble with Winston who has got the wind up about finance. He had been deluding himself with the idea that he was going to get a big cut in estimates next year. There was never any ground for such a notion but he has only just found it out.

I had a good meeting of the London Regional Planning Committee last week. There was some rather ticklish business to get through in appointing committees and officers as they are all as jealous of one another as can be but I exhausted them with an hour's preliminary address at the end of which I ran all the business through without difficulty. An address on Smoke Abatement completed my engagements for the week ...

...

... Hoskins made a loss last year. No dividend I am afraid this time, but Hall says things look rather better.

12 November 1927
Moor Lane House, Briantspuddle, Dorset

My dear Hilda,

After so much firing I find it rather difficult to manipulate a pen – one's fingers get stiff, but I hope you will be able to read this. Up to almost the last moment I was afraid I might not get away as the 2nd Rdg of the Unemployment Insurance Bill was taken on Thursday night and I feared the opposition would fasten on its effect on Poor Law Admn. But they are so stupid that they never got on to that point & indeed they were foolish enough to let two back benchers lead off & they rambled about so that no definite point ever seemed to emerge.

...

I had another very successful meeting on Monday at Greenwich which however for some reason was not reported in the London press. The hall was packed out and there was great enthusiasm, a large crowd afterwards collecting in the street and cheering as though there were an election. I was sorry the speech got no publicity as it was on local elections and called attention to one of Snowden's which has not been noticed as much as it deserves. In effect he abandoned nationalisation in favour of municipalisation suggesting that when a Labour Govt came in it would give local authorities power to do anything that a private individual could do and pointing out the necessity for Labour to capture the local councils that they might put these powers into operation. Perhaps I may find another opportunity as I have plenty more speeches to make. Exeter put up a request for me to speak there this month or next and when I replied that I could not take any more engagements before Xmas they said they didn't want anyone else & would wait till I could come. Its very flattering no doubt but I do hate making speeches and they do add to the grind.

In coming away here I missed the special Cabinet on Friday called to consider the Egyptian Treaty but I gave the P.M. my proxy to vote for it. You have rightly guessed the principal opponent and I should think he might collect Jix and Worthy but I have no doubt Austen will have the majority well on his side.

You will have seen that I am not to lose Kingsley just yet, but I don't think I shall be able to keep him much longer. Of course I would not stand in his way if it were proposed to give him promotion but it would not be worth his while to take another Under Secretaryship and he is very happy where he is. I should like to have him with me when I do Poor Law but I have almost given up hope of getting that through in this Parliament. The worst of having a genius for a colleague is that he is always flying after some new game which diverts him from the more humdrum but more practical political paths. Winston is now off on a new idea which I believe to be utterly impossible to work out in time for the next Budget, but I am afraid that by the time he is convinced of its impossibility it will be too late to substitute my plan. But I am humouring him in the gradually diminishing hope that I may yet get my way.

The Bedwellty report is an astonishing document and full of humour. The Welshmen who complain that they cant get a decent living out of Poor Relief and have to open a garage or a butcher's shop in despair are really funny. I have been having a warm correspondence with a Labour member for the district to whom my last communication was to the effect that he would find his answer in the Report shortly to be published. I shall be interested to see if he carries it any further.

I have only got one day's work in this Parlt that I know of but that is a bad one with 3 Bills to get through, preceded by an address to a womens area Conference & followed the next day by a mass meeting at Ormskirk in Lancashire.

…

19 November 1927
Westbourne

My dear Ida,

…

I certainly have more than my share of speeches. Besides the Public Works Exhibition and the M.O.H. dinner I had an evening with the Junior Carlton Club whom I addressed for an hour and had to answer questions afterwards – an exhausting evening but I hope a useful one. With Kingsley too on the stocks I had a good many late nights but got a little relief from the adjournment of the House on Wednesday. This month I knew was a bad one, and next week was to have been the worst, but fortunately the disarmament debate is put down for Thursday when I was to have taken my three bills in the House. So now I have only got three speeches to make …

Rugeley meeting was not very large – about 600 – but it was a good one and I spoke for 70 minutes without losing the audience. But I think I shall tell the central office that they ought not to send me to such small meetings; the effort seems out of proportion to the good done, though of course the local member likes to get a Cabinet Minister down.

…

I am very disappointed at the way the R.W. Housing Bill is being dealt with and I am going to send out a circular directly to try and ginger up the authorities. The most disconcerting thing is that there are so few applications and I think the only way to stimulate them is to get the District Councils to make themselves disagreeable to the owners.

I see Davidson and the P.M. have taken the gloves off and are going for Rothermere. I am not quite happy in my mind as to their wisdom but if they have decided that he intends to work for Ll.G. it is as well that there should be no mistake about it in the public mind and he has lately been more and more hostile to the Government. In particular he is evidently trying hard to lose us Southend and it is unlucky that it has been such an awful day as that will probably tell against us.

Austen got his way about the Egyptian Treaty all right and things turned out just as I expected. I see that Bob Cecil's speech in the Lords is being quoted everywhere in the U.S.A. as clear proof that the American behaviour at Geneva was fully justified and is also affording ammunition to Ll.G. and Rothermere. He is a wrong headed creature who will never do any good in this world but with the best intentions will give material aid to those who want just the opposite of what he wants.

... The P.M. wants to avoid an autumn session and I suspect, though he wont say so, that he has already made up his mind against P.L.

We have had some discussion with the L.C.C. people about the slum scheme and they are very hostile to it at present so that is not encouraging. I see many stiles ahead which will take a lot of getting over.

...

27 November 1927
37 Eaton Square, SW1

My dear Hilda,

...

... We had a fairly successful lunch [for the Birmingham Unionist Association on Monday] that is considering the class of people who came but the amount of money collected was not very large – only about £500 in donations and about £250 in subscriptions. But we hope to get some more in and I shant have the final figures for some days yet.

On Tuesday I received the Deputation on Slums with the P.M. He only said a few genial words as I expected, but I addressed them at some length and with considerable freedom. The P.M. said he had never seen me handle a deputation before and he thought my treatment of them quite admirable. As a matter of fact they were easy to deal with. Much more difficult were two other deputations next day one from a number of independent peers who wished to have the R. Restriction Act amended & the other from a lot of grocers & provision dealers to protest against the prohibition. Those were awkward questions, but I got through them without giving way or even irritating the deputation.

We went one evening to the Mond's to hear the Lener quartette, my dear *too* Hebrew, as Topsy would say. ... We were seized on at once and carried up to the front whereupon Margot[52] solemnly marched up and said I *must* shake hands and did it & then retired again apparently overcome with shyness. So I went and asked after Squiff & she assured me that he was very well & *would* have spoken in the Lords the day before only there was no lift. All which I steadfastly

---

[52] Emma Alice Margaret Tennant (1864–1945). Known as Margot; became second wife to H.H. Asquith 1894.

disbelieved. The Lener quartette are a rum lot to look at when you get close to but they do play divinely.

On Thursday I spoke to the Middlesex women for an hour and had a great success and the meeting on Friday at Ormskirk also went off with much éclat, in spite of a drunken man in the front row who when I had been speaking for five minutes ejaculated in a loud voice Have you finished? I was afraid he was going to explode at intervals and ruin the meeting but fortunately he soon went out.

...

Southend was good – but I dont like Canterbury.

No more to say.

> 4 December 1927
> Westbourne

My dear Ida,

...

What you tell me about the R.W. Housing Act and applications under it is I suspect typical of the country generally. It will probably not wake up to the possibilities until the last year. Then it will suddenly realise that it is too late and come clamouring to the Ministry for an extension of time.

The National Housing and Town Planning Council got a proper dressing down when they came to see me and I was not surprised to see that they had worked off some of their vexation at Harrogate. But I shall pay no attention to them and I doubt if anyone else will either. They are a thoroughly ineffective and very conceited body without any real weight.

I have had a very busy week with Cabinet Committees, dinners, lunches and late nights though I did not consider it necessary to sit up to the end of the discussions on the Unemployment Insurance Bill. I addressed the Constitutional Club on Tuesday – a horrible audience of fat stock brokers and elderly die-hards. But I succeeded in drawing the Goat and I daresay you saw his letter to the Times and my reply. Eustace Percy declared that my letter was the very nastiest he had ever read, but what tickled me was that I was stopped in the Lobby by two Liberal M.P.s who exclaimed with an exulting chuckle That *was* a clever letter of yours in the Times this morning. A nice party, in which the leader is so regarded by his followers!

Austen invited me to be his guest at the Glasgow University Club dinner on Tuesday, informing me that as there were only two toasts and the speakers were already arranged for I could escape the usual penalty. But the Council as soon as they heard that I was coming requested me to respond to the guests as well as the Attorney General so I didn't get off. But it was a very pleasant affair. Austen made an excellent speech and received some very prettily worded compliments from John Buchan and I succeeded in getting out our descent from Robert the Bruce which A. declared he had been keeping for his reply to the vote of thanks.

I dined on Wednesday with the Royal Society where the P.M. made an altogether delightful speech witty and eloquent and with a wide range of literary allusion which charmed the audience. He is inimitable on such an occasion and I was glad I had gone though the other speeches were in painful contrast.

I have been rather depressed over my slum scheme which has been stamped upon by all the Town Clerks we have shown it to. But I was encouraged by a talk with that shrewd old bird Tudor Walters. I had sent him the outline for criticism & he had written a cautious and not very enthusiastic reply. But I thought he hadn't quite understood and in the course of our conversation this proved to be the case. As he gradually came to see what I was after he warmed up until finally the full possibilities began to dawn upon him and then he was evidently deeply impressed and begged me on no account to drop the scheme (I worn't a'goin to!) You have got hold of a great idea, he declared, one of national importance. Its the best thing thats been done in housing yet. It will save the Government! My people said afterwards that I had over persuaded him but I dont think he will go back on it. The funny thing is that he is the Liberal candidate for one of the Cornwall divisions, but he said half in earnest that he felt inclined to drop his candidature and come and work at this. As a matter of fact that is just what I had in mind to ask him to do for he would make an ideal chairman of a Central Board to lay down principles of management and improvement and guide & assist local Boards. He is going to ponder the scheme further and then come back for another talk and with his help I believe I shall get something workable.

The vote of censure is to come on on Wednesday. I have been very dissatisfied with the fact that the Govt has no policy for dealing with the surplus mining labour in the coal industry. To shove them on to the Poor Law in their impoverished districts is bad from every point of view but there is no one to take a superdepartmental view in a matter which requires the assistance of 3 or 4 departments. I hadn't meant to interfere but I could not sit still at the Cabinet and see the thing go by default so I up and spoke out. I said I was prepared with suggestions and so I was asked to put them before a Committee. I had a plan of my own which had long been in my head but it really required more time to work out than we have got now. Robinson with whom I had often discussed it and who is very oppressed with certain practical difficulties in administering it finally put up another alternative to me which is less complete but which would I think meet the present emergency so when the Committee met I first put my own plan which obviously much impressed them but also frightened them especially as the Ministry of Labour strongly opposed it. Then I put up the second plan which I knew beforehand the Ministry of Labour would take. They were so glad to see a way of avoiding No. 1 that they cordially welcomed No 2 which also found favour with the rest of the committee and though it is possible that further reflection may raise difficulties at present unforeseen it looks as if it would go through. In that case the rabbit will emerge from the hat on Wednesday and though it would have looked better if it had appeared earlier I believe it will be received with relief by our people and vexation by the Labour party who will once more see a promising line of criticism nipped in the bud.

I wonder if you have noticed the constant reports in the press of extravagance on the parts of various Boards of Guardians and of observations by M/H Inspectors brought to their notice. This is part of a deliberate plan of campaign designed to awaken public opinion and strengthen the hand of the good Boards. Presently I am going to start the publication of periodical figures of the cost of relief and the numbers relieved. I noticed last Thursday that it brought me a crop of questions from the Socialist benches and the threat of a discussion on the adjournment. That is all to the good. They will get no change out of debates in the House on that subject.

...

11 December 1927
Chevening, Sevenoaks

My dear Hilda,

Yes, you are right about the rabbit. It was produced so casually and even surreptitiously that no one noticed it and I observed that even the Goat went on browsing among his papers and didn't lift his head. Partly this was due to the fact that, as President of the Bd of Trade, Philip was naturally interested first & foremost in the problem of the coal industry and only secondarily in the question of what should be done with those permanently thrown out of employment. But it was also partly due to the fact that we had had a prolonged battle in the Cabinet over the proposal itself. I had to go & see Winston late on Tuesday and then discovered that he had taken exception to the plan, because it was going to cost money. By the time he got to Cabinet next morning he had worked up a terrific indictment. You would have supposed that the whole of our Poor Law system together with the Unemployment Insurance Act were being torn up by the roots and that liabilities of the most exacting and oppressive character were being laid on the Exchequer. With a wise & weighty Chancellor accustomed to consider carefully every new drain upon the national resources, spending all his spare moments in pondering how the taxes could be reduced and paring away every possible little bit of expenditure I should have felt grave difficulty in pressing my views. But knowing as I did that at that very moment Winston was planning new raids on the National funds amounting to such large sums that he talks habitually of *alternative* figures differing by *ten million* pounds, I could not regard his opposition seriously. We defeated him with great slaughter but probably Philip felt that it would be prudent rather to minimise the activities of the new [Industrial Transference] Board.

I dont really mind. What matters is not what is the immediate effect of the speech. That is what the Goat & Winston would look to. But that is only for the moment. What will signify is the actual result of the appointment. If the Board are successful in dragging 100,000–150,000 men out of these stagnant pools of labour in South Wales and Durham and distributing them in other parts of the country or the Dominions they will solve an extremely anxious and difficult problem and that will really be the best time for us to brag about them. But meanwhile there is some détente in the party, though not as much as there would have been if more attention had been directed to my plan.

I am rather seriously concerned about the possibility of a Cabinet crisis in the near future. There is the question of the naval programme in connection with which resignations have been rather too freely bandied about but I fancy we shall get through that after a somewhat stormy passage. My fears, as usual, revolve round our stormy petrel Winston, and I thought it necessary to give the P.M. a grave warning this week about what may happen if he is not checked. For some time now he has been dwelling on a plan for his next Budget, which I regard as unwise immoral and dangerous. It is dangerous because as usual it is only the idea he has got. He has nothing worked out but he gets so enamoured with his ideas that he wont listen to difficulties or wait until plans have been made to get over them. Its like Gallipoli again. Most of the Cabinet (including Austen I fancy) know nothing of these plans yet; they are to be revealed to some of them before Christmas. But I know, because I am necessary to Winston, the plans involving Local Authorities and he has endeavoured to back me into acceptance by refusing to find the money I want to carry P.L. reform unless it comes in as part of his larger plan.

I see however that he cant deliver the goods and that his plan must therefore be considered entirely on its merits. If he would have given me what I asked I would have fought to have P.L. included in next years programme. Finding him obdurate I went to the P.M. & undertook not to ask for P.L. in this Parliament on the understanding that it should be given a prominent place in the party programme at the General Election. I am satisfied with this. Once it is actually embodied in the party programme the whole party will settle down to make the most of it and it must be carried into law, probably in our first year if we come back. But by this understanding with the P.M. I have cleared myself from any entanglement with Winston and I have had to request him not in talking with me to speak of "*Our* scheme" or "*our* plan". There is no scheme yet only an idea which is his and not mine. I am quite willing to examine the practicability of making a scheme which would carry out his idea and I have allowed my people to put their heads together with the Treasury to see what would be the best lines on which to frame such a scheme. But I reserve to myself the freedom to condemn it on the ground that the best that can be done is not good enough and what I fear is that if & when that happens Winston will have gone too far to retreat and that he or I will have to go. And if he went, I suppose I should have to take the Treasury again so any way things dont look too pleasant. He *is* an uncomfortable bedfellow!

In the course of the very frank & friendly talk I had with the P.M. about the programme of next session it was evident to me that I could have slums if I wanted to and possibly a wee sma' Bill or two that I want very badly. But I am not sure that I shall be ready with slums or that it would not be better politically to hold them for an election cry. They could, as Tudor Walters said, be made extraordinarily attractive if properly handled and we should be the only party with a programme. However I shall still go on working at them though it is not made easier by the fact that all my principal officials are working overtime on Winston's d—d fantasies.

The Audit Bill comes on Monday. I have reason to know that the Labour Party wish to make a demonstration of their "flaming indignation" in order to impress the people outside, but that they are anxious not to do anything which would prevent their getting away on the 21st and moreover they do not want to sit up all night. I am therefore putting it about that I propose to sit up all Monday and all Tuesday night (which I am quite prepared to do) and I rather suspect that in the small hours on Tuesday morning we shall be offered an undertaking to finish the Bill by a certain time if we agree to break off then & go to bed. Meanwhile I have after a tremendous lot of spadework succeeded in reconciling all the opposing elements in connection with the Mental Deficiency and Nursing Homes Registration Bill so that I hope to secure both of them. It looked up to the last moment as if it would be impossible to get an accommodation on the Nursing Homes Bill, the County Councils & District Councils being up against one another & both sides declaring they would wreck the Bill than give way.

I am afraid that as you dont see the Daily Herald you will have missed Jix's glorious address "to the President and People of the United States", no other paper having given the speech the prominence it deserved. It began "I do not complain of the Presidents words; *I adopt them as my own*" and went on to say how "*I*, in common with the other members of the Govt" am not to [sic] frightened by bluster but with superb calm and self confidence will proceed untroubled upon the path I have marked out. I paraphrase slightly but that was the jixt of it. In view of the paralysing effect which this pronouncement is likely to have, not only upon the unhappy Calvin but also upon Big Bill Thompson, I am planning a new work intituled [sic] "If Jix came to Chicago".

Your account of Lady Selborne's proceedings is shattering. Really these Cecils are *too* incredible, my dear, perfectly *medieval*. ...

...

17 December 1927
Westbourne

My dear Ida,

Of course I should not lend myself to anything that was unwise, immoral, and dangerous. But if I had refused to look into the possibilities of Winston's scheme I should have appeared to him to be merely obstinate and unfriendly. My purpose was to convince him by specific reasoning that his plan would not work or alternatively to find some other scheme which would not be open to the objections I saw in the original one.

Since I wrote I have had a private conversation with a certain Treasury official which has somewhat relieved my mind because he sees very serious financial difficulties about the proposals and will certainly advise against them in their present form and my people have now sent me a paper which I have not yet read but which I believe does sketch out something more possible. I understand that Winston means to circulate an "outline" to the Cabinet which I expect I shall have to criticise and I think I shall ask for a small Committee to examine it.

As things are going, I believe that if we came back at the Gen. Election I should have to return to the Ministry of Health to carry P.L. in which case of course I should do slums too, but I should rather hope that I might move on to something else later on. Anyhow it is too early yet to speculate on the future with any certainty.

I am hoping that the Industrial Transference Board will be set up next week. We have got a very good man as Chairman who will I think attack the problem in the proper spirit, as a sort of crusade.

This has been a hard week but a very successful one. I didn't get to bed on Monday till 3.30 a.m. and last night was the first on which I was in bed before one but I got all my three bills. The debate on the Audit Bill was a very mild affair but I had rather an agitating experience. Miss Lawrence[53] had pointed out an alleged error in a statement of mine whereat I merely asked her to look at a certain subsection. She was completely bowled over, every one laughed at her discomfiture & she could only say well sometimes I find out the Minister and sometimes he finds me. I was rather pleased with myself when my officials sent me down a note to point out that I was wrong and she was right. I don't think I have ever made such a mistake about a Bill of my own before, but so long a time had elapsed since it was in Committee that I had really forgotten it. I expected every moment that Susan would discover my lapse & that I should be pulverised but the opposition is so incredibly futile that neither she nor anyone else ever found me out & I got off without an exposure!

On the Mental Deficiency Bill we managed by pegging away to square Josh Wedgewood [sic] – no easy task – but I thought we were going to be done over the Nursing Homes Bill when an obstinate opposition arose over a proposal to exempt Christian Science Homes from its operation. However I made a very persuasive speech which earned high encomiums from Jimmy Thomas and we finally got it through without a division. So I haven't yet lost a Bill in my Ministerial career.

---

[53] (Arabella) Susan Lawrence (1871–1947). Member of Poplar Borough Council 1919–24 and the LCC for Poplar 1913–27. Organiser, National Federation of Women Workers 1912–21. Labour MP for East Ham North 1923–24 and 1926–31. Member, Labour Party NEC and Chair 1929–30. Parliamentary Secretary, Ministry of Health 1929–31.

Of course the great excitement of the week has been the Prayer Book measure. I was so busy that I was unable to listen to any of the speeches except the end of the P.M.'s, the Solicitor General's and Wolmers.[54] But everything went wrong from the point of view of the supporters. Willie Bridgeman's speech was a complete failure, so was Linkie's. The P.M.'s was good, but it came at the wrong moment and its effect was destroyed by Tom Inskip while Wolmer only succeeded in exasperating the House and strengthening the Opposition. I understand that Jix's speech on "No Popery" lines was the most effective of his life and probably moved the House more than any other. Austen & I both voted for the measure on the ground that as Nonconformists it was not for us to refuse what the Church through constitutional & democratic means had asked for. I never saw the House more excited over a division. Members stood up waving handkerchiefs & cheering but I was sorry for the Archbishop who saw the fruits of all his labours snatched from him so unexpectedly at the close of his career. I wonder what will happen now.

…

I am much interested in what you tell me about the Rural W. Housing Act, which looks as if it was gradually gaining way in your parts. I shall send out my new circular early next month and meanwhile the S.P.R.E. is getting to work on admirable lines. They have got in the Architects, the Landowners and the builders. The architects have agreed to give their services free of charge and they say they are going to search out the cottages that might be dealt with, find who the owners are and then worry them till they put in an application. If they carry out their intentions they will really do valuable service and fully justify their existence.

…

---

[54] Roundell Cecil Palmer (1887–1971). Conservative MP for Newton 1910–18 and Aldershot 1918–40. Parliamentary Secretary, Board of Trade 1922–24; Assistant Postmaster-General 1924–29; Minister of Economic Warfare 1942–45. Styled Viscount Wolmer 1895–1941 when became Baron Selborne. Succeeded as 3rd Earl of Selborne 1942.

Appendix I:
The Chamberlain Household and Family

Although full biographical details accompany the first reference of all characters mentioned in the letters, a number of members of the Chamberlain household and extended family merit further detail.

Bee or B   Beatrice Chamberlain (1862–1918). Eldest child of Joseph Chamberlain. A compelling character who rather dominated Austen as a child but who selflessly took over the running of Highbury after the death of her father's second wife in childbirth. Utterly devoted to her father and of all his children she is generally agreed to have most resembled him in personality, intellectual capacity and fertile imagination. She also possessed a 'beautiful nature' which was 'simple warm … guileless and incapable of ill-thinking'.[1] Regarded by Neville and his sisters as 'our guide, philosopher and friend'. In later life, she developed many 'funny little ways' which amused the family – not least a complete disregard for dress.[2] Died soon after the Armistice in the influenza epidemic. *The Times* obituary noted she had 'the mind of a great man with the heart of a great woman'.

Byng   (Wilfred) Byng Kenrick (1872–?). Cousin and close friend of Neville and his younger sisters from childhood, accompanying him on his Asian tour in 1904–5. Active member of Birmingham Council from 1914; Chairman, Education Committee 1922–28, 1931–43; Lord Mayor 1928; Alderman 1929; Freeman 1938. Also active in Birmingham Unionist Association and as chairman of the Edgbaston constituency association invited Neville to become their MP in 1926.

Catt   P.G. Catt. Gardener at Westbourne from Chamberlain's arrival

---

[1] Beatrice Webb Diary, 28 May and 30 August 1886, Norman and Jeane Mackenzie (eds), *The Diary of Beatrice Webb* (4 vols, London, 1982–85), I, pp. 170, 175.

[2] 'Recollections of their own father's childhood written for Dorothy and Frank by their Aunt Ida Chamberlain, January 1941', BC5/11/1.

in 1911 until his death in 1940. His slow speech and odd phrases were much imitated. Lived in the lodge at the entrance to the property.

Diane　(Beatrice) Diane Chamberlain (born 1912). Second child and only daughter of Austen and Ivy. Married Terence Maxwell in 1935. Two sons and one daughter.

Dorothy　Neville Chamberlain's first child (born Christmas Day 1911). Married Stephen Lloyd. One son and three daughters.

Frank　Neville Chamberlain's second child (1914–1965). After Winchester and Trinity College, Cambridge, travelled in France, Spain and Germany during the late 1930s. Joined 6th Royal Warwickshire Regiment (Territorial Army) in 1937. Active service in the Second World War. After the war, director of Hoskins & Company before poor health compelled retirement to the country where he took up farming. Active interest in social and welfare work – particularly for the disabled. Vice-President, Birmingham Federation of Boys' Clubs and Chairman, Birmingham Fellowship for the Handicapped. Life Governor, Birmingham University. Married Roma Parrott. One son and one daughter.

Uncle George　George Hamilton Kenrick (1850–?). Bachelor living in Edgbaston.
or G.H.K.　Member, Birmingham School Board from 1880 and the council from 1902. Long-standing Chairman, Education Committee from 1902; Lord Mayor 1908; Alderman 1909. Knighted 1909. Major benefactor to City and to Neville, his favourite nephew, whom he resembled in character and appearance and whom he taught to fish and shoot.[3] Visited Loubcroy Lodge in Scotland together every September. Left Neville a substantial legacy on his death.

Hilda　(Caroline) Hilda Chamberlain (1871–1966). Fifth child of Joseph Chamberlain. Cared for her father after his stroke in 1906 at the cost of her own social life and prospect of marriage. Moved with Ida to Odiham in Hampshire in December 1914 after the death of her father and the disposal of Highbury. The more

---

[3] E. Sandford, 'Neville Chamberlain', *The [Birmingham] Central Library Magazine*, January 1948, 286.

sociable and outgoing of the two sisters with the 'more feminine side'.[4] Stalwart of the local Women's Institute and National Treasurer, Federation of Women's Institutes. With her
sister built and donated seven houses to the Rural District Council
in 1923 and established a recreation ground for the village in
memory of Beatrice. Governor of Odiham Grammar School,
1923–47.

Ida   (Florence) Ida Chamberlain (1870–1943). Fourth child of Joseph.
Although the shy and sensitive one of the two sisters, 'she was
the man of the partnership in the sense that she did all the things
that the man would do'.[5] Active in local government. Member
of Hartley Wintney RDC from 1918 and on Hampshire County
Council from 1925 until her death. Chairman of Public Health,
Housing and School Medical Services Committees. First female Alderman on county council.

Ivy   Ivy Muriel Chamberlain (née Dundas). Married Austen in 1906.
Three children.

Joe   Joseph Chamberlain, eldest child of Austen (born 1907). Married Gina Macdonald. Two sons.

Lawrence   Second son and third child of Austen and Ivy (born 1917).
Married Anne Eastwood. Three sons.

Leamie   Miss Evelyn Leamon (1884–1976). Nanny to Neville Chamberlain's children for nine years until 1928 when Dorothy left for
Paris. Recalled as wise, tactful, affectionate and sensible. Often
acting *in loco parentis*, she was liked and respected by Neville
although the sparks flew with Annie over their different ideas
about child rearing.[6]

Lilian   Lilian Cole (née Williams). Canadian. Mother of Norman and
first wife of Herbert Chamberlain, Joseph Chamberlain's brother
who died in 1904. Second marriage to Alfred Clayton Cole of
West Woodhay, Berkshire. Aunt through marriage to Anne Vere
Cole and introduced Neville to his future wife. President, Birmingham Women's Liberal Unionist Association.

---

[4] Dilks transcript, NC20/1, fol. 30.
[5] Ibid.
[6] Ibid., fol. 23.

Mary   Mary Crownishield Endicott (1863–1957). American. Daughter of Secretary for War in Grover Cleveland first administration. Married Joseph Chamberlain 1888. Married Canon Carnegie in August 1916.

Norman   Norman Gwynne Chamberlain (1884–1917). Son of Herbert and Lilian Chamberlain. Member, Birmingham Council from 1911 and Chairman, Parks Committee. Joined Grenadier Guards 1914; Acting-Captain 1915; killed with all his Company 1 December 1917. Extremely close friend to Neville who deeply respected and admired his pre-war work with Birmingham Boys' Clubs, the Street Children's Union, Children's Courts, Women's Settlements. After Norman's death, Neville took up many of these causes.

Willie   William Hartley Carnegie (1860–1936). Canon of Birmingham 1905–13 and Westminster from 1913; Chaplain to the Speaker of the House of Commons 1916–36. Archdeacon of Westminster 1918–19. Married Neville's step-mother in August 1916. Generally regarded as something of a bore.

Appendix II:
Primary Sources Consulted for Volume Two

Private papers and diaries

Addison MSS	Papers and diaries of Christopher Addison, 1st Viscount Addison, Bodleian Library, Oxford.
Altrincham MSS	Papers of Sir Edward Grigg, 1st Baron Altrincham, microfilm at the Bodleian Library, Oxford.
Baldwin MSS	Papers of Stanley Baldwin, 1st Earl Baldwin of Bewdley, Cambridge University Library.
Beaverbrook MSS	Papers of Sir William Maxwell Aitken, 1st Baron Beaverbrook, House of Lords Record Office, Hist. Coll. 184.
Bridgeman MSS	The Political Diaries of William Clive Bridgeman, 1st Viscount Bridgeman, courtesy of Mrs A. Stacey and the Trustees of the Bridgeman family archive.
Cecil MSS	Papers of Lord Robert Cecil, Viscount Cecil of Chelwood, British Library, Add. MSS.
Austen Chamberlain MSS	Papers of Sir Joseph Austen Chamberlain, Birmingham University Library.
Beatrice Chamberlain MSS	Papers of Beatrice Chamberlain, Birmingham University Library.
Neville Chamberlain MSS	Papers and diaries of Arthur Neville Chamberlain, Birmingham University Library.
Davidson MSS	Papers of Sir John Colin Campbell Davidson, 1st Viscount Davidson, House of Lords Record Office, Hist. Coll. 187.
Derby MSS	Papers and diaries of Edward George Villiers Stanley, 17th Earl of Derby, Liverpool City Central Library.
Gladstone MSS	Papers of Herbert John Gladstone, Viscount Gladstone, British Library, Add. MSS.
Hankey MSS	Papers and diaries of Sir Maurice Hankey, 1st Baron Hankey, Churchill College, Cambridge.
Hannon MSS	Papers of Sir Patrick Hannon, House of Lords Record Office, Hist. Coll. 189.

Headlam MSS	Papers and diaries of Sir Cuthbert Headlam, Durham Record Office.
Hewins MSS	Papers and diaries of William Albert Samuel Hewins, Sheffield University Library.
Irwin MSS	Papers of Edward Frederick Lindley Wood, Baron Irwin (later Earl of Halifax), as Viceroy of India, Oriental and India Office Collections, British Library.
Law MSS	Papers of Andrew Bonar Law, House of Lords Record Office, Hist. Coll. 191.
Lloyd George MSS	Papers of David Lloyd George, 1st Earl Lloyd-George of Dwyfor, House of Lords Record Office, Hist. Coll. 192.
Markham MSS	Papers of Violet Markham, British Library of Political and Economic Science.
Milner MSS	Papers and diaries of Sir Alfred Milner, 1st Viscount Milner, Bodleian Library, Oxford.
Newman MSS	Diaries of Sir George Newman, Public Record Office, MH 139/1–5.
Rey MSS	Papers of Sir Charles Rey, Rhodes House Library, Oxford.
Salisbury MSS	Papers of James Edward Hubert Gascoyne-Cecil, 4th Marquess of Salisbury, by courtesy of the 6th Marquess of Salisbury, Hatfield House.
Sanders MSS	Papers and diaries of Sir Robert Sanders, 1st Baron Bayford, first consulted at the Conservative Research Department and now held at the Bodleian Library, Oxford.
Steel-Maitland MSS	Papers of Sir Arthur Steel-Maitland, Scottish Record Office.
Strachey MSS	Papers of John St. Loe Strachey, House of Lords Record Office, Hist. Coll. 196.
Templewood MSS	Papers of Sir Samuel Hoare, 1st Viscount Templewood, Cambridge University Library.
Veale MSS	Interviews with Sir Douglas Veale by Professor Brian Harrison, British Library, National Sound Archive.
Worthington-Evans MSS	Papers of Sir Laming Worthington-Evans, Bodleian Library, Oxford.

Government Records

Cabinet Conclusions	CAB 23
Cabinet Papers	CAB 24
Ministry of Health	MH
Treasury	T

Conservative Party archives

Birmingham Conservative and Unionist Association, Minute Books, 1914–40, Birmingham Central Library.

Ladywood Division Unionist Association, Minute Books, 1914–40, Birmingham Central Library.

Ladywood Women's Unionist Association, Minute Books, 1919–33, Birmingham Central Library.

Midland Union Executive Committee, Minute Books, 1919–40, Conservative Party Archive, Bodleian Library, Oxford.

Index

Where a note reference is given in brackets, this signifies that there is a short biographical or explanatory note on the person or event concerned.